THE TIMES

Debris from the explosion of the shuttle Challenger
was scattered so widely over the Atlantic Ocean that investigators may never recover enough of it to pin down
the cause of the disaster. But suspicions quickly focused
on the craft's huge external fuel tank, a potential bomb
that carried more than 385,000 gallons of liquid hydrogen
and more than 140,000 gallons of liquid oxygen at liftoff.

The most logical explanation is that a large leak must
have occurred either in the tank itself or in the pipeline
and pumping system that carried liquid hydrogen to the
orbiter's three main engines.

Barbara Schwartz, a spokesman for the Johnson
Space Center, acknowledged that pure liquid or gaseous
hydrogen cannot burn; only if the pure hydrogen carried
in the rear section of the shuttle's tank were allowed to
come into contact with air, or with the liquid oxygen in the
tank's nose section, could it have burned or exploded.

Potential Dangers of Hydrogen Gas

But what might have started the leak, and what could

Adam Nagourney

THE TIMES

CAPE CANAVERAL, Fla., Jan. 28 — The
space shuttle Challenger exploded in a ball of fire
shortly after it left the launching pad today, and all
seven astronauts on board were lost.

The worst accident in the history of the American space program, it was witnessed by thousands
of spectators who watched in wonder, then horror,
as the ship blew apart high in the air.

Flaming debris rained down on the Atlantic
Ocean for an hour after the explosion, which occurred just after 11:39 A.M. It kept rescue teams
from reaching the area where the craft would have
fallen into the sea, about 18 miles offshore.

It seemed impossible that anyone could have
lived through the terrific explosion 10 miles in the
sky, and officials said this afternoon that there was
no evidence to indicate that the five men and two
women aboard had survived.

No Ideas Yet as to Cause

There were no clues to the cause of the accident. The space agency offered no immediate explanations, and said it was suspending all shuttle
flights indefinitely while it conducted an inquiry.
Officials discounted speculation that cold weather
at Cape Canaveral or an accident several days ago
that slightly damaged insulation on the external
fuel tank might have been a factor.

Americans who had grown used to the idea of
men and women soaring into space reacted with
shock to the disaster, the first time United States
astronauts had died in flight. President Reagan
canceled the State of the Union Message that had
been scheduled for tonight, expressing sympathy
for the families of the crew but vowing that the nation's exploration of space would continue.

Killed in the explosion were the mission com-
mander, Francis R. (Dick) Scobee; the pilot,
Comdr. Michael J. Smith of the Navy; Dr. Judith A.
Resnik; Dr. Ronald E. McNair; Lieut. Col. Ellison
S. Onizuka of the Air Force; Gregory B. Jarvis, and
Christa McAuliffe.

Mrs. McAuliffe, a high-school teacher from
Concord, N.H., was to have been the first ordinary
citizen in space.

After a Minute, Fire and Smoke

The Challenger lifted off flawlessly this morning, after three days of delays, for what was to have
been the 25th mission of the reusable shuttle fleet
that was intended to make space travel commonplace. The ship rose for about a minute on a column
of smoke and fire from its five engines.

Suddenly, without warning, it erupted in a ball
of flame.

The shuttle was about 10 miles above the earth,
in the critical seconds when the two solid-fuel
rocket boosters are firing as well as the shuttle's
main engines. There was some discrepancy about
the exact time of the blast: The National Aeronautics and Space Administration said they lost radio
contact with the craft 74 seconds into the flight, plus
or minus five seconds.

Two large white streamers raced away from
the blast, followed by a rain of debris that etched
white contrails in the cloudless sky and then slowly

HOW THE NEWSPAPER

OF RECORD SURVIVED

SCANDAL, SCORN, AND

THE TRANSFORMATION

OF JOURNALISM

CROWN

NEW YORK

Published in the United States by Crown, an imprint of
The Crown Publishing Group, a division of Penguin
Random House LLC, New York.

CROWN and the Crown colophon are registered
trademarks of Penguin Random House LLC.

LIBRARY OF CONGRESS CATALOGING-IN-PUBLICATION DATA

Names: Nagourney, Adam, author.
Title: The Times / by Adam Nagourney.
Description: First edition. | New York: Crown, 2023. |
Includes bibliographical references and index.
Identifiers: LCCN 2023012060 (print) | LCCN 2023012061 (ebook) |
ISBN 9780451499363 (hardcover) | ISBN 9780451499387 (ebook)
Subjects: LCSH: New York times—History.
Classification: LCC PN4899.N42 N3763 2023 (print) |
LCC PN4899.N42 (ebook) | DDC 071/.471—dc23/eng/20230512
LC record available at lccn.loc.gov/2023012060
LC ebook record available at lccn.loc.gov/2023012061

Printed in the United States of America on acid-free paper

crownpublishing.com

9 8 7 6 5 4 3 2 1

FIRST EDITION

Book design by Simon M. Sullivan

This book is a tribute to the memory of R. W. Apple, Jr., Francis X. Clines, Janet Elder, Richard J. Meislin, David Rosenbaum, Jeffrey Schmalz, Robin Toner, and countless other reporters and editors at *The New York Times* who did not live to see the transformation of the newspaper where they made their lives.

It is dedicated to Benjamin.

Arthur Ochs Sulzberger, Jr., was not going to be late to his own farewell, a "momentous occasion," as the invitation put it, celebrating his twenty-five years as publisher of *The New York Times*. It was the first week of June and an early hint of summer humidity hung in the air, but he intended to walk the one and a half miles from the Beaux Arts apartment house on West Seventy-first Street in Manhattan where he had lived for the past seven years to the Modern, the restaurant on the ground floor of the Museum of Modern Art, on West Fifty-third. He had curated the guest list himself, approved all 250 of the invitees, and he wanted to be there when the doors opened. He would stay until the last glasses were returned to the kitchen and the band was packing up.

Sulzberger was sixty-six years old on this late spring evening in 2018, his face fuller and his hair grayer than when he posed with his father, Arthur Ochs Sulzberger, Sr., who was known as Punch, for the portrait that appeared on the front page of *The New York Times* on January 17, 1992, announcing to the world that his father had passed the title of publisher to his son. Arthur was a picture of youth on that front page, with his full head of curls and a boyish whisper of a grin, the photograph arranged so he rose over his father. He would never look his age. And now he did not look old enough to have retired six months earlier as publisher of what was the most influential newspaper in the world. His son, Arthur Gregg Sulzberger, had taken over in an orderly succession at the age of thirty-seven, the march of family ownership reaching now into a fifth generation. The *Times* was the last remaining major family-owned newspaper in the nation, having been purchased in 1896 by Adolph

Simon Ochs, a newspaper publisher from Chattanooga, and his descendants had no intention of letting it leave the Sulzberger family. Even after stepping down as publisher, Arthur would continue coming to work, now as chairman, for four hours a day, a few days a week, settling in a tiny windowless office in the company's headquarters on Eighth Avenue, across from the Port Authority Bus Terminal. The fifty-two-story tower had been built in his second decade as publisher and stood as a testimony to his ambition, vision, and restlessness, but also, perhaps, to overreach and miscalculation, though only time would answer that question.

Sulzberger stepped out of his twelfth-floor apartment onto the elevator, glancing at his watch—it was 5:45 P.M.—as he descended slowly toward the street. He walked briskly through the lobby, waving to a doorman, and continued across a courtyard and through the wrought-iron gates onto West Seventy-first Street. Sulzberger was wearing a gray suit, a purple shirt, and a lavender print Hermès tie, a gift from his second wife, Gabrielle. He stood out, even on the Upper West Side, in this season of tank tops and shorts. Sulzberger was one of the most powerful people in journalism, and one of the better paid: his total compensation for 2017, his final year as publisher, was $5.582 million. He had guided the *Times* through the most turbulent years of its history (some of the turbulence of his own making). He had led it into an era when the time-tested business of newspapering—of assembling the events of the past twenty-four hours into a coherent package of newsprint to be deposited at newsstands and front doors—no longer made financial sense. He walked unrecognized down the street, nodding hello to a homeless man on the corner, cutting into Central Park to take a shortcut down a dirt trail.

Sulzberger arrived early for the reception. A small gathering of guests was already there, waiting for the doors to open, among them Floyd Abrams, the former counsel to *The New York Times*, who had advised Sulzberger's father through the defining chapter of his years as publisher: the publication of the Pentagon Papers, the secret government study of the Vietnam War whose publication by the *Times* won a major legal victory for the First Amendment. Sulzberger shook his hand, walked past receptionists with iPads checking names against the guest list, and pushed his way through the glass doors. The tables had been cleared from the Modern's dining room for this night. A Lucite lectern had been brought in for the speeches, and glass light globes with the *Times* logotype, replicas of the ones that had been affixed to the exterior walls of the old headquarters on West Forty-third Street, were scattered across the room. A half-dozen waiters stood ready, holding trays of drinks and platters of food. At 6:30 sharp, the doors opened, letting in a rush of people eager to be part of this celebration—of Arthur Sulzberger, Jr., but also of *The New York Times* itself: battered after these difficult decades, but still prosperous and preeminent in American journalism; a symbol of continuity that was outlasting yet another member of the Sulzberger family.

Arthur had joined the *Times* as a correspondent in the Washington bureau at the end of 1978, at twenty-seven years old, after working as a reporter for the Associated Press in London. The *Times* that young Arthur found in 1978 was a successful but hidebound and risk-averse institution, run by a generation of men (and not women), almost all of them white, who were, with few exceptions, products of the same social, economic, and educational class, confident in their abilities and the superiority of the newspaper for which they worked.

Over the next forty years, the *Times* would confront wave after wave of journalistic, societal, economic, and technological upheaval—outside its walls, but also in its newsroom—that would at times threaten its existence and its aspirations to excellence. It would struggle to come to grips with a changing business model and a changing world while attempting to protect what made it the *Times*, the reason it was read first thing each morning by a discriminating and powerful audience of world, political, business, and cultural leaders. It was a four-section newspaper then, with a daily circulation of 859,000 copies and a Sunday circulation of 1,407,000. The paper, dependent on the economy and the flow of advertising revenues, was awash in money—so much so that it was able to finance the ambitions of a newsroom that would send teams of reporters around the globe to cover not only huge moments of history but places, personalities, and conflicts that might interest only a handful of its most eclectic readers. Its sweeping ambition was one of the things that had always distinguished the *Times* in American journalism.

A. M. Rosenthal was the executive editor, awarded the title by Punch Sulzberger just under two years before Arthur joined the paper. The newspaper was influential and incredibly powerful. It was often referred to as the newspaper of record, but mainly outside the newsroom, since that was not really an accurate (or realistic) description of its mission. But it was where its readers went to learn what they should think about their presidents and mayors, to educate themselves on the foreign policy issues that might come up for discussion at cocktail parties or dinner, to be told which books to read, movies to see, plays to attend, and restaurants to patronize. Rosenthal was self-assured to the point of arrogance, and in that, he reflected the newspaper where he worked. A young man applying for a job in the sports department walked into Rosenthal's office in late summer of 1982 for his final interview; Rosenthal insisted on meeting every applicant for a job in his newsroom. Rosenthal ended their talk by asking the applicant, Michael Janofsky of the *Miami Herald,* if he had any questions. I'm curious, Janofsky responded, as he recalled the conversation. The paper has so many reporters filing stories from so many places around the world. How do you decide each day what readers are interested in reading on the front page?

Rosenthal did not pause. We *tell* them what they should be interested in, he said.

By the night of Sulzberger's farewell in 2018, there were far fewer print subscribers—487,000 on weekdays and 992,000 on Sundays. But there were 3,360,000 digital subscribers who paid to read the news or to use specialized apps, such as Cooking. The *Times* was no longer just a product to be picked up at newsstands and front stoops. It was presented to its audience on newsprint, mobile devices and computer screens, and in podcasts and video. It still told stories with words and photographs but now was buzzing with graphics and videos and interactive forms of storytelling, enabled by advances in programming and code writing, some of it pioneered in the *Times* newsroom. Advertising revenues had, to a considerable degree, fled to the Internet, and the *Times* had responded with a paywall, charging digital readers the way it had for so long charged its print readers; digital subscriptions were replacing advertising as its primary source of revenue. Audience development—a metric-based analysis of the demographics, interests, and reading habits of its audience and potential audience, designed to deepen connections with existing subscribers and to reach out to the corners of the Internet for new ones—was as integral a part of the newsroom as the desk that assembled the front page. The newspaper still published some of the dutiful stories that had helped make it indispensable for so many people. And it continued to open its pages to the kind of coverage that distinguished it from its competitors: reviews of esoteric works of classical music, long dispatches about famines and wars in faraway places, Saturday profiles of foreign figures whom many of its readers had probably not heard of before. But it also found new ways to accommodate the leisure tastes of its growing audience with an expansion of the service journalism it first presented in the late 1970s: recipes and exercise routines, lists of places to go for a hike or a long weekend, and the product-and-service rating site called Wirecutter, which helped readers choose the best high-definition television or set of kitchen knives. Dean Baquet had been the executive editor since 2014: an investigative journalist from New Orleans and the newspaper's first Black executive editor. He would talk about himself as "old-school," but he had embraced these changes, or at least did not stand in their way, which distinguished him from his predecessors. There was much at stake over these years; as the *Times* tried to reinvent itself without becoming a Facebook or *BuzzFeed.* Through it all, there was never any serious discussion about abandoning the newspaper's core identity, but the *Times* had turned into something that Rosenthal would not recognize.

It had never been certain that this transformation could happen, and it was a messy and occasionally embarrassing exercise that had sometimes seemed destined for failure. But for the most part, with some important caveats, it appeared on this night that a magnificent but flawed institution had managed to ride out the most difficult years of its existence—through seven executive editors, and newsroom scandals that shook even its most loyal readers and employees—to emerge as something that could thrive in a new century. It no longer commanded the unequivocal respect and admiration it once had, or wielded the unchallenged power in determining the narrative of a day's history— or the authority to tell readers what they should be interested in, as Rosenthal had put it. But that was as much a result of how society had changed as it was of the *Times*'s own foibles and failings. During the span of Sulzberger's years there, it had made the kind of ambitious transformation that eludes most corporations as they reach middle age. The process was, at times, excruciating for a towering institution whose prestige and place in national life had always made it a hybrid of private company and public trust. It had to balance the scrutiny of older readers (and staff members) wary of any tinkering with a revered institution and younger ones impatient with the newspaper for standing by such seemingly outdated values as objectivity. There were times when its own editors wondered whether it would survive, and if it did, at what cost; whether it would do so in a seriously diminished state.

A succession of mistakes and what-could-have-been moments accounted for an unsteady march during these years. Sulzberger was forced to dismiss two executive editors. The newspaper was roiled by a plagiarism scandal involving an ambitious young fabulist. Its credulous reporting about the threat of weapons of mass destruction in Iraq had helped to lead the country into a deadly and fruitless war. For many years, the newsroom—and particularly its senior ranks—was overwhelmingly male and overwhelmingly white; its failure to diversify its newsroom cast a cloud over the *Times* that lasted through Sulzberger's time there.

During this time, the newspaper faced hostile presidents and press critics who would chronicle its errors and question its competence and honesty. Its newsroom was quarrelsome and opinionated, filled with people whose personal contentment was determined by how they fared at the *Times*, making them the newspaper's most caustic and informed critics, ready to disparage a decision by an editor or the front-page story of a colleague. It was an organization comprised of often brilliant journalists and company executives who jostled for advantage and power, whose own struggles sometimes spilled out into public view. The *Times* was the product of fallible human beings, and understanding who they are—their flaws and frailties, as well as their talent and intelligence—is essential to understanding the transformation of the *Times* that was being celebrated with Arthur Sulzberger on this night.

Because for all its difficulties during these forty years, it remained at the pinnacle of American journalism. The guiding principles that Ochs set down after he bought the newspaper 122 years earlier—that his newspaper would operate "without fear or favor" and would offer its readers "all the news that's fit to print"—could have been recited by anyone invited to the Modern that night. It remained the place where many of the nation's most talented reporters, analysts, columnists, editorial writers, and critics came to document wars and presidential campaigns, space shots and famine, Congress and the Kremlin, restaurants and Broadway, books and Hollywood. It was still consumed every morning by a president who mocked it as "the failing *New York Times*" but who craved its recognition and approval. Its internal intrigues—what was conveyed by the placement of a story, who was elevated to the masthead or sent to London or the White House—were still a source of fascination for readers and competitors alike.

* * *

A waiter handed Sulzberger a chilled vodka martini—his drink of choice—as he came into the room; he had vowed to finish seven of them at a *Times* party celebrating the day it won seven Pulitzers in 2002. Waiters passed through the room with trays of caviar croustillant with crème fraîche, tuna tartare with summer truffles, scallop ceviche with toasted pistachio, and lobster sliders. Sulzberger took in the crowd. The editors and reporters—some still working, many retired. Members of his family, including his father's oldest sister, Marian Heiskell, who was ninety-nine years old and sat in a wheelchair, drinking a Jack Daniel's on the rocks. Senator Charles Schumer, an old friend, was there, as was Robert De Niro, who owned a house near Sulzberger in the Catskills.

Seven men and women had served as executive editor from the day Sulzberger began there as a reporter, with different strengths, interests, and management styles that shaped the way the *Times* presented the news of the world. Five of the six who still survived—Abe Rosenthal had died twelve years earlier at the age of eighty-four—were there that night. The intellectual German immigrant who did not speak English until he was ten and who edited the newspaper as the Cold War came to an end. The starchy son of a rabbi who had to deal with how the *Times* would write about a blue dress stained with a president's semen. The brilliant and opinionated Southerner who moved from hurling thunderbolts on the editorial page to curating the gray news pages, starting with the attacks of September 11, and who was fired less than two years after he was named executive editor. The investigative reporter and author from *The Wall Street Journal*, the newspaper's first woman editor, who was fired less than three years after she took over the newsroom. One editor was not there: the Pulitzer Prize–winning foreign correspondent who struggled with whether to publish a story on a secret national surveillance program. The current executive editor, Dean Baquet, was the only one of the group who would speak, in a program that Sulzberger insisted be kept brief. "One never truly leaves *The New York Times*," said Sulzberger. "My name is not Arthur Sulzberger Junior. My name is Arthur Sulzberger Junior of *The New York Times*."

This is an unfinished story. A foundation has been built: the online subscriptions and the expansion of the paper's reach across the nation and the globe, its advances in digital storytelling and audience development. But it is a prologue to this newspaper's next chapter, to the new and in some ways more complicated challenges Arthur Gregg Sulzberger faces as he settles in for what he can only hope will be his own quarter-century as the publisher of *The New York Times*.

CONTENTS

Jill Abramson, Washington bureau chief, managing editor, executive editor

R. W. Apple, Jr., chief Washington correspondent, London bureau chief, Washington bureau chief, associate editor

Dean Baquet, national editor, *Los Angeles Times* editor, Washington bureau chief, managing editor, executive editor

James Barron, reporter

Dan Barry, reporter

David Barstow, reporter

Soma Golden Behr, editorial board member, Sunday business editor, national editor

James Bennet, Jerusalem bureau chief, editor of *The Atlantic,* editorial page editor

Richard L. Berke, Washington editor, national editor, assistant managing editor

Jayson Blair, reporter

Tom Bodkin, deputy managing editor, design director

Gerald M. Boyd, special assistant to the managing editor, metropolitan editor, managing editor

Rick Bragg, reporter

Fox Butterfield, reporter

Dana Canedy, reporter, senior editor for career development

Susan Chira, foreign editor, deputy executive editor

Francis X. Clines, reporter

Adam Clymer, reporter

Roger Cohen, foreign editor

Gail Collins, columnist, editorial page editor

Anne Cronin, features editor, metropolitan desk

Paul Delaney, Washington bureau reporter, deputy national desk editor, senior editor for recruiting

Sam Dolnick, Sulzberger family member, deputy managing editor

Maureen Dowd, Washington reporter, columnist

Orvil E. Dryfoos, publisher (1961–1963); son-in-law of Arthur Hays Sulzberger

Susan W. Dryfoos, Sulzberger family member; founder and director, Times History Productions

Steve Duenes, graphic editor, assistant editor, deputy managing editor

David W. Dunlap, reporter, *Times* historian

Susan Edgerley, metropolitan editor, dining editor, assistant managing editor

Janet Elder, head of polling, deputy managing editor

Stephen Engelberg, investigations editor

Ian Fisher, deputy executive editor

Max Frankel, Washington bureau chief, editorial page editor, executive editor

Tobi Frankel, married to Max Frankel

Thomas L. Friedman, columnist

John M. Geddes, managing editor for operations

Arthur Gelb, managing editor

Jeff Gerth, reporter

Michael Golden, member of Sulzberger family, cousin of Arthur Jr., vice chairman of the New York Times Company

Jerry Gray, metropolitan political editor, head of continuous news desk

James L. Greenfield, foreign editor, Magazine editor, assistant managing editor

Gail Gregg, married to Arthur Sulzberger, Jr.

Sydney Gruson, foreign news editor, executive vice president of New York Times Company

Bernard Gwertzman, State Department reporter, editor of *Times* website

Clyde Haberman, reporter, columnist

Marian Sulzberger Heiskell, sister of Punch Sulzberger, member of Board of Directors

Bob Herbert, columnist

Warren Hoge, foreign editor, Magazine editor, assistant managing editor

David (Dave) R. Jones, national editor, assistant managing editor

Joseph Kahn, international editor, executive editor

Bill Keller, foreign editor, managing editor, executive editor

Emma Gilbey Keller, married to Bill Keller

Bill Kovach, Washington editor

Glenn Kramon, business editor, assistant managing editor

Marc Lacey, national editor, managing editor

Jonathan Landman, deputy Washington editor, metropolitan editor, culture editor, assistant managing editor, deputy managing editor

Carolyn Lee, weekend editor, director of photography, assistant managing editor

Joseph Lelyveld, foreign editor, managing editor, executive editor, 1994–2001

David Leonhardt, Washington bureau chief, managing editor of the Upshot, op-ed columnist

Meredith Kopit Levien, chief executive officer, New York Times Company

Clifford J. Levy, reporter, metropolitan editor, deputy managing editor

Russell T. Lewis, chief executive officer, New York Times Company

Eric Lichtblau, reporter

Adam Liptak, reporter

Shirley Lord, married to Abe Rosenthal

Alexandra MacCallum, assistant managing editor

Walter E. Mattson, president, New York Times Company

Robert D. McFadden, reporter

Kevin McKenna, deputy business editor, "Gang of Four" member

Richard J. Meislin, editor-in-chief of New York Times Digital, associate managing editor for Internet publishing

Judith Miller, reporter

Adam Moss, assistant managing editor for features, editor of Magazine

Martin A. Nisenholtz, head of New York Times Digital, senior vice president digital operations

Adolph S. Ochs, publisher (1896–1935); purchased the *Times* in 1896

Daniel Okrent, first public editor

Michael Oreskes, metropolitan editor, Washington bureau chief, assistant managing editor for digital news

David S. Perpich, Sulzberger family member, general manager, new digital products, senior vice president of product

Lance R. Primis, chief operating officer, New York Times Company

Todd S. Purdum, reporter

Matthew (Matt) Purdy, reporter, deputy managing editor

Joyce Purnick, metropolitan editor, columnist, married to Max Frankel

Anna Quindlen, deputy metropolitan editor, columnist

Howell Raines, Washington bureau chief, editorial page editor, executive editor

Steven Rattner, reporter

James B. Reston, columnist, executive editor

Frank Rich, theater critic, columnist

James Risen, reporter

Gene Roberts, managing editor

Jim Roberts, national editor, editor of digital news, associate managing editor, assistant managing editor

Janet L. Robinson, president, chief executive officer, New York Times Company

A. M. (Abe) Rosenthal, managing editor, executive editor

Andrew M. Rosenthal, son of Abe Rosenthal; foreign editor, assistant managing editor, editorial page editor

Jack Rosenthal (no relation to Abe or Andrew), editorial page editor, Magazine editor

Carolyn Ryan, Washington bureau chief, political editor, managing editor

Sydney H. Schanberg, reporter, metropolitan editor, columnist

Serge Schmemann, reporter

William (Bill) E. Schmidt, deputy managing editor, assistant managing editor for administration

Robert B. Semple, Jr., reporter, member of editorial board

Joe Sexton, metropolitan editor, sports editor

Allan (Al) M. Siegal, news editor, head of committee investigating Jayson Blair case, assistant managing editor

Sam Sifton, food editor, culture editor, restaurant critic, national editor, assistant managing editor

Nate Silver, editor of FiveThirtyEight blog

Alison Smale, deputy foreign editor

Fiona Spruill, editor of the Web newsroom

Robin Stone, married to Gerald Boyd

Arthur Hays Sulzberger, publisher (1935–1961); married to Iphigene Ochs

Arthur Ochs (Punch) Sulzberger, publisher (1963–1992); son of Arthur Hays and Iphigene

Arthur Ochs Sulzberger, Jr., publisher (1992–2018); son of Punch

Arthur Gregg (A.G.) Sulzberger, publisher (2018–present); son of Arthur Jr.

Carol F. Sulzberger, married to Punch Sulzberger

Iphigene Ochs Sulzberger, daughter of Adolph Ochs, mother of Arthur (Punch)

Karen A. Sulzberger, daughter of Punch, sister of Arthur Jr.

Gay Talese, reporter, writer of *The Kingdom and the Power*

Philip Taubman, Washington bureau chief, deputy editorial page editor

Mark Thompson, chief executive officer, New York Times Company

Seymour Topping, foreign editor, managing editor

Lisa Tozzi, senior digital editor, national and politics news

Patrick E. Tyler, reporter

Betsy Wade, reporter, editor, lead plaintiff in women's suit against the *Times*

Bernard Weinraub, reporter

Craig R. Whitney, Washington editor, assistant managing editor

This history of *The New York Times* begins with the appointment of A. M. Rosenthal as executive editor in 1976 and ends with the election of Donald Trump as president in 2016. It is based on official archives, collections of personal papers, memoirs, oral histories, videos, audio tapes, and over three hundred interviews conducted by the author. Quotation marks are used only when the quotes are drawn from letters, documents, interviews, oral histories, transcripts of events, and contemporaneous newspaper or magazine stories. Quotation marks are not used for conversations that are reconstructed based on the recollection of participants, which, given the passage of time and the challenges of memory, are necessarily less precise. This book is an independent work; it was not authorized by the *Times*, and the newspaper had no involvement in its preparation or publication.

PART I

KEEPING IT HONEST

1977–1986

CHAPTER 1

A Man of His Times

I t was December 17, 1976, a cool and cloudy day in New York. Jimmy Carter would be sworn in as the thirty-ninth president in just over a month. There were threats of a destabilizing oil-price war in the Middle East. The nation was emerging from a three-year economic downturn that had been particularly debilitating for New York City, which was struggling through its own financial crisis, as employees of *The New York Times* were reminded when they walked to work through Times Square, with its boarded-up stores, pornographic movie theaters, and street-corner drug dealers. A revival of *Fiddler on the Roof,* directed by Jerome Robbins and with Zero Mostel reprising his role as Tevye, was about to open at the Winter Garden Theatre. Rupert Murdoch had just purchased the *New York Post,* and the newsstands offered a morning tabloid splash of headlines about crime, sex, and the fiscal crisis, including the latest cuts in subway and bus service. This was the season of the Son of Sam shootings, and New York was on high alert.

On this day, A. M. Rosenthal wrote a note to his staff about his future, and the future of his newspaper. It was slipped into mailboxes and posted on bulletin boards in the fifteen-story building off Times Square that had been the headquarters of *The New York Times* since 1913. Abe Rosenthal, as he was known, was fifty-four years old and had joined the *Times* in 1943 as its campus correspondent at City College of New York. He had covered the United Nations, Japan, India, and Poland, where he won the Pulitzer Prize for his "perceptive and authoritative" coverage of the Communist regime. He had been a metropolitan editor, associate managing editor, assistant managing editor, and managing editor. No one defined *The*

New York Times—and by virtue of that, American journalism—as much as Rosenthal. A package of brilliance and insecurities, a remarkable foreign correspondent and editor, he paraded both his love of journalism and his contempt for reporters and editors he considered mediocre or politically suspect. His *Times* was read by presidents, cabinet secretaries, mayors, foreign leaders, members of Congress, Hollywood directors and theater producers, university presidents, scholars, publishers, business executives, television news executives, and rival editors.

You have to understand this, Rosenthal once said to a young reporter in his office, his vibrating, nasal voice resonant of his years growing up in the Bronx. When an educated, important person anywhere in America runs into another educated, important person anywhere in America, each will have assumed of the other that they have read *The New York Times.*

Rosenthal held the newspaper in the highest regard. "I do believe this would be a lesser country without *The New York Times,*" he said in an oral history in 1986. And he held himself in just as high regard. "I'm a very good editor," he once said. "I know that. And that's putting it mildly." Few would dispute either of those assertions. Rosenthal took over the newsroom in 1969, after James B. Reston, the paper's chief Washington columnist, served a brief and unsuccessful turn as executive editor. Reston would not give up his column or his home in Washington, making a weekly commute to New York, and those distractions were reflected in his performance. "A disaster," Arthur Ochs Sulzberger, Sr., the publisher, later said of Reston's time as executive editor. But Punch Sulzberger was loyal to Reston, a family friend and himself an institution in journalism of the 1950s and '60s, and, with due deference, said the appointment was always meant to be temporary as he sent Reston back to Washington. Sulzberger retired the title of executive editor and asked Rosenthal, a deputy to Reston, to settle for the lesser title of managing editor, but with all the responsibilities and authority Reston had as executive editor.

No one was surprised when Sulzberger, resurrecting the title seven years later, and broadening its responsibilities to include what had been the separate Sunday newspaper, awarded it to Rosenthal, choosing him over another former foreign correspondent and editor, Max Frankel, who had run the Sunday newspaper. Frankel would become the editorial page editor. Sulzberger left it to Rosenthal to make the announcement, and that was the purpose of the memo he distributed that December day.

> The Publisher will announce today the following promotions and additions in the top news group of the paper effective January 1. I will become executive editor.
>
> Happy holidays to all!

Even at this high point in a career filled with high points, and with more to come, Rosenthal was difficult and disconsolate, the way he had always been and would always be. "I am quite unhappy about some things I have been seeing in the paper, not seeing, or seeing too late," he wrote his editors a few weeks before his appointment, distressed that *Newsweek* had obtained the first interview with Cyrus Vance, the incoming secretary of state. Rosenthal realized the *Times* would come in second from time to time, he said, "but, believe me, I know the difference between that and a lumpish rhythm." Yet for all his unhappiness, the newspaper, after suffering through an economic downturn, was rounding a corner. Rosenthal's command over the *Times* had never been as sweeping as it was this December, and the world of journalism celebrated his promotion. WELCOME TO THE KINGDOM AND POWER OF EXECUTIVE EDITORDOM, WHATEVER IT MAY BE, Ben Bradlee, the executive editor of *The Washington Post*, wrote him in a telegraph, drawing on the title of Gay Talese's book on the *Times*, published in 1969: *The Kingdom and the Power*.

Frankel and Rosenthal were rivals, all the more so after this appointment, but that was papered over for this moment. "Abe: By any other name, you still lead a great crew," Frankel said in a hand-written note.

"Titles, schmitles!" Rosenthal responded on Christmas Eve. "It's all a lot of fun! Thank you for that sweet note." His note, addressed to "Mr. Frankel," was typed.

Sulzberger would remain loyal to Abe Rosenthal for another nine years, dazzled by his talent, their partnership, and the quality of the newspaper published day after day on his watch. Rosenthal had helped establish *The New York Times* as a prosperous business, and more importantly, as a model of daily journalism. But gradually, his eccentricities, excesses, and abuses would become impossible to ignore.

* * *

At the end of 1962, Turner Catledge, the paper's managing editor, flew to Tokyo to meet with Rosenthal, who was then the paper's correspondent there. Are you happy here, Abe? Catledge asked as they traveled around Japan. Catledge really wasn't looking for an answer; his decision was made. He wanted Rosenthal to return to New York to run the city desk. Rosenthal left reporting for editing and proceeded to reinvigorate what was probably the weakest and most neglected news desk at the *Times*. "This is the candor department?" Rosenthal responded when asked years later to describe his first impressions of the city desk, which would later be known as the metropolitan desk. "I was stunned and shocked, frankly." He described a dispirited, indolent staff producing unpublishable copy. Rosenthal seized Catledge's mandate to transform the metropolitan New York coverage, pruning the old-timers who would disappear for long lunches or drop their heads down when the editors were looking for a reporter to dispatch on a story. He had no patience for the tradition of valuing seniority over talent and energy. He had fresh ideas about what made a story for the *Times*—for instance, a long article exploring the increased visibility of homosexuals on the streets of New York, which he had noticed upon his return from overseas. The *Times* would be bolder covering its own backyard, never an easy matter for a New York–based newspaper that viewed its primary mission as chronicling Washington and the world.

Rosenthal pushed his staff hard, and he played favorites, and before long, he would glance up from his desk, which he had turned around so his back was no longer facing the rows of reporters, survey the newsroom that stretched nearly a block before him, with the coffee-stained carpets and drab metal desks under a haze of cigarette smoke, and realize that his reporters did not like him. And he would begin asking his editors a question that he would pose repeatedly over the years: Why do they hate me? It was a melancholy and no doubt manipulative query that often came after he'd had a few glasses of wine. He would try to win them over, popping by in the evenings to join reporters for drinks at Sardi's on West Forty-fourth Street. But Rosenthal could not hold his liquor. He would talk too openly about reporters and his own editors who were not at the table and awake the next morning in a cloud of regret about his indiscretions.

From his earliest days at the newspaper, Rosenthal believed that the *Times* was different from every other newspaper and that it was obliged to stand apart from, and to rise above, the world it was chronicling. He was the embodiment, however imperfect, of traditional *New York Times* aspirations to quality and objectivity, trying (and sometimes failing) to steer the institution through a period of immense social upheaval—the protests against the Vietnam War, the civil rights marches, the rise of feminism, and the beginning of the modern gay rights movement. It was a never-ending battle, he would say—protecting this institution against the onslaught of generational and political turmoil that swept the nation in the 1960s. Rosenthal had been distressed at the stories being filed by *Times* correspondents from the 1968 Democratic National Convention in Chicago. Too many of them, in his view, were biased in their recounting of the student demonstrations and the tough response of the Chicago police, and of the maneuverings inside the International Amphitheatre on Chicago's South Side as Democrats delivered their endorsement to Senator Hubert Humphrey of Minnesota, the establishment candidate. Rosenthal did not trust this new generation of reporters.

Do we become part of this movement, or do we report this movement? Rosenthal demanded of Reston, the executive editor. We make our reputation on playing it straight, and the copy is not playing it straight. Reston could override him, of course, but Rosenthal made clear what a mistake that would be. If you do, Rosenthal warned him, you will go down in history as the man who decided that the *Times* was going to become partisan in its coverage of the news.

Reston deferred to Rosenthal's strong hand.

As reporters returned to Washington and New York from Chicago, Rosenthal sent Reston a memo warning that the newspaper faced a challenge in "maintaining its character" because of these new correspondents. It is "inevitable as time goes on that the radical or militant element in the Times staff will increase in size. . . . It also strikes me as quite likely that in addition to young people who are genuinely torn or confused we will have on our staff people who quite deliberately set out to radicalize the *Times*." Rosenthal sent a similar note to Punch Sulzberger when he took over the newsroom a year later. It was his responsibility, Rosenthal told Sulzberger, to maintain "the basic impartial character of the *Times*, which strikes me as essential not only to American journalism but to American life." He made the same point in an inaugural memo to his reporters.

"The turmoil in the country is so widespread, voices and passion are at such a pitch that a newspaper that keeps cool and fair makes a positive, fundamental contribution without which the country would be infinitely poorer," he wrote. The basic responsibility, he said, lies with the reporter and not the editors: "The desk should not be cast in the role of a policeman, always on edge to catch a loaded phrase that a reporter might put in to see if he can get it by."

Rosenthal was hardly alone among members of his generation struggling to understand the world changing around them, and he had the additional burden of returning to a much different country after his tour abroad. Rosenthal had been expelled by the government from Poland as a correspondent, a formative experience which had reinforced his contempt for Communism. He did not hide his disdain for what was going on in his country: the antiwar demonstrations, the heckling of establishment politicians, the unruliness on college campuses. He later told Charlotte Curtis, the paper's op-ed editor, that his "greatest nightmare" when he was presented with the Pentagon Papers was that they would turn out to be a trap, "written by a thousand SDS kids in some loft at Harvard"—a reference to the Students for a Democratic Society, a leftist student organization. A few months before the Democratic convention in Chicago, Rosenthal had visited Columbia University as it was roiled by student demonstrations. In a departure from *Times* practice wherein the covering of events was left to reporters, he wrote a story about what he'd witnessed. It opened with a sympathetic depiction of Grayson Kirk, Columbia's president, returning to his office at four-thirty in the morning and finding it ransacked. Kirk "passed a hand over his face" as he surveyed the damage, Rosenthal wrote, and proclaimed, "My God: How could human beings do a thing like this."

Rosenthal as an editor would surely have objected to a story like the one he produced from Columbia, taking sides, assigning blame on the students. One of his reporters, Steven Roberts, wrote an essay for *The Village Voice* that presented a different perspective of the events, calling Kirk "haughty and blind to the end" and saying that "he had failed to understand for years that Columbia just could not trample on the people of Morningside Heights whenever it suited its imperial purpose." Rosenthal confronted Roberts for that, saying he "used extremely bad judgment in taking a sharp editorial position on a story which he was covering." But Rosenthal's story out of Columbia would help to color his reputation for the rest of his career. "Not to be Nixonian about it, but my life would have been pleasanter if I had not written that piece, if I had taken the easy way out," he told Sydney Gruson, a former correspondent who had become the publisher's top adviser.

Throughout his years at the *Times*, Rosenthal sent scolding notes to editors, seizing on the slightest hint of ideological bias in a reporter's copy, such as one story in which a reporter used the word "socialist" in describing Communist countries. "To call a Communist dictatorship a Socialist country is Orwellian," Rosenthal wrote to the foreign desk. He objected to a story about college activism by a young Robert D. McFadden, who would go on to become one of the *Times*'s premier correspondents. "I found McFadden's story about the campuses—particularly the first few paragraphs—editorialized in the extreme and terribly naïve," he wrote editors on the metropolitan desk. "For ten years I have been struggling against editorialization. We have succeeded in eliminating most of it. But consistently, I am sad to say, the metropolitan desk allows stories to be printed that give me nightmares." He demanded the names of the editors who had handled the story. "I intend to talk to them personally."

Rosenthal was always suspicious of the Washington bureau, a collection, in his view, of sharply dressed Ivy Leaguers who displayed the kind of ideological bias he was trying to contain. He complained to Frankel, the bureau chief, that a story on a crime bill passed by Congress allotted more space to the objections of liberal opponents than to the applause from conservatives. There is "a distinct tendency, perhaps subconscious, but troublesome nonetheless, in many stories from Washington" to "emphasize the opinion of the liberal opposition and slight the opinion of the conservative majority," he wrote Frankel. Rosenthal later promoted Bill Kovach, who had worked in Washington and New York, to run the Washington bureau, despite their history of argumentative exchanges, often fueled by drink, over Rosenthal's professed concerns about Kovach's ideology. Rosenthal celebrated Kovach's appointment with a party at his penthouse on Central Park West, at one point taking Kovach to the balcony to toast his appointment. But goddamn it, Rosenthal said, abruptly changing moods, what I'm afraid of is I probably turned the bureau over to a Communist.

"I almost quit twice over it," Kovach said years later. Their bickering became so constant that the two men made a pact not to drink when they were together.

Rosenthal would describe himself as the person who "kept the paper straight," and later, at his direction, those words would be carved into his tombstone. They were integral to how he thought of himself, to how he wanted to be remembered. Rosenthal did not always adhere to this standard, but it was a useful prism through which to view him. "It is a very goddamn difficult thing to do, Sydney," he explained to Gruson in the early 1980s. "You have to reject copy, you have to teach, you have to nag, you have to say no."

* * *

Rosenthal was not a handsome man: the messy wave of hair flopping over his head, the oversized black-rimmed glasses, the coat-shirt-tie askew. Gay Talese, who had become close to Rosenthal after he left the *Times* to write *The Kingdom and the Power,* was strolling through Central Park one afternoon and encountered Rosenthal, dressed, as Talese later put it, as if he were attending a tailgate party at a football game. You are the editor of *The New York Times,* Talese told him. You must dress like the editor of *The New York Times.* Rosenthal was five feet, nine-and-a-half inches, which he sometimes in conversation stretched to five-foot-ten, and weighed 151 pounds. He smoked a pipe, as did many professional men of his generation. He came to wear suspenders because, as Shirley Lord, his second wife, explained, he had "no bottom," and otherwise his pants would fall down.

Rosenthal was fussy in his habits and demands. Clerks and copyboys were assigned to attend to his needs, professional and personal, which included ferrying his briefcase to his penthouse at 262 Central Park West, a building known as the White House. One of those copyboys was a young Adam Moss, who had just graduated from Oberlin College. He would return to the *Times* years later to edit the Styles section and then the *Times Magazine* before becoming the editor of *New York* magazine. Rosenthal would leave the office for a waiting car; Moss would hop a West Side subway, drop off the briefcase with a housekeeper—or on occasion, Rosenthal's son, Andrew, who would grow up to become a senior editor at the *Times*. Rosenthal's secretary instructed Moss not to glance at the executive editor should he encounter him in the *Times* elevator. Another of Rosenthal's clerks, Richard J. Meislin, juggled the personal and professional needs of the editor. One day, Meislin would be calling the Brooklyn Botanic Garden to inquire about the ailing Japanese black pine tree Rosenthal had installed on his penthouse terrace. Another, he was carting bricks and dirt up to the rooftop garden. And on yet another, Meislin would scan newspapers from across the country, compiling a list of stories that had appeared in competing publications but not in the *Times*.

Rosenthal was what Anna Quindlen, who he appointed to the metropolitan desk as an editor, called "a holy-shit newspaper man," the kind of editor who would leap to his feet and shout, *You, you, you, you: get out to Astoria!* He had his rules for his empire of correspondents and editors. "Attributing information to confidential or anonymous sources is the least satisfactory form of attribution," he declared in 1974. No use of pejorative quotations from unnamed sources. "Mr. Roberts: I think that the rules against anonymous attacks should be followed by Johnny Apple as well as by anyone else. Please tell him so for me," Rosenthal said in a note to his national editor, Gene Roberts, a reference to a story R. W. Apple, Jr., one of the paper's top correspondents, had written about Raymond P. Shafer, the governor of Pennsylvania. Reporters offering a critical assessment of their subject, he said, should pause and consider how they would feel reading those same words about themselves. "We should not use a typewriter to stick our fingers in people's eyes just because we have the power to do so," he wrote. He was distressed to read a complaint from the owner of a restaurant in London, Simpson's in the Strand, because Apple, in a travel piece on London, advised his readers to "avoid it like the plague." That phrase, Rosenthal wrote his travel editors, "is ugly, overdrawn, and not in keeping with what I would hope would be the civilized level of discourse of the *Times*." And Rosenthal despaired at what he called "*aha!* journalism." It was a form of journalism he would attribute mainly to the left, particularly when it was used to criticize the *Times*.

Much of what he decreed was hardly radical. His views on newspapers were set in the context of the political environment and the rise of new journalism, with long-form, literary writing filled with lively, re-created scenes and conversations. Some of its most admired practitioners were drawing loyal readers precisely because they pushed the boundaries of traditional journalism: Talese, Tom Wolfe, Truman Capote, Pete Hamill, and Joan Didion among them. Rosenthal liked good writing, but he was resisting what he saw as journalistic excesses. He was stark, unyielding: sometimes admirable in his defense of journalistic standards but just as often pedantic and bullying. He could not understand how anyone could not share his devotion to the *Times*. When Quindlen, with one son at home and another child on the way, decided to quit, Rosenthal took her to lunch at the Four Seasons—where he ordered a bottle of wine, which he finished himself, since Quindlen was not drinking through her pregnancy—to urge her to reconsider. (He failed, though she would return later as a columnist.) As they were leaving the restaurant, where Rosenthal was such a regular that he had a usual table in a corner, Rosenthal put an arm around her shoulder. Promise me you'll never work for another newspaper, Rosenthal said. Rosenthal seemed baffled when he was once asked why he had always wanted to work at *The New York Times*. "Why the Times?" he responded. "Why do you want to be President? The Times was the greatest paper on earth, so you wanted to work for the New York Times."

For executive editors, controlling what ends up printed in the final newspaper—trying to steer what is in effect a large ocean liner with as many as a thousand employees, many of them strong-willed and by nature skeptical of authority—is a constant frustration. There is a fine line between meddling and managing, and Rosenthal had trouble straddling it. "I found the paper dull today," he wrote his editors one morning. He singled out, by name, colleagues whose work displeased him. "Our Paris bureau and our Paris Chief correspondent have virtually disappeared from the paper," he wrote the foreign desk. "I want you to call Mr. Eder *today*. Tell him the absence of his filing is embarrassing, both to him and to the paper."* Frankel, when he was running the Washington bureau, would come to dread when a clerk announced that "Mr. Rosenthal" was on the telephone. Frankel found him dismissive and belittling. "I hated getting phone calls from him," Frankel said. "I was glad to be two hundred miles away."

Newsrooms as a rule are unhappy places: roiled by self-doubt, anger, competitiveness, resentments, and vindictiveness. There may well have been no newsroom in the country as unhappy as the one Abe Rosenthal ran for those seventeen years. But few were as good. Rosenthal knew that. And so did Punch Sulzberger.

---

* Rosenthal's memo about the Paris bureau was an example of a memorandum written but not sent; a note on top said he discussed it with Craig R. Whitney, an editor on the foreign desk. Rosenthal is referring to Richard Eder, the Paris bureau chief.

CHAPTER 2

Do This for Me

The New York Times was filled with people who were at once confident in their abilities and indifferent to their faults. Abe Rosenthal fit in well. Punch Sulzberger liked that about him; he enjoyed Rosenthal's drive, brashness, creativity, and even his orneriness. "You paid your salary," the publisher wrote Rosenthal, praising his "stroke of genius" for assigning a front-page profile of John Mitchell, the former attorney general, to appear on the day he testified before the Senate Watergate Committee. (Sulzberger could not stop himself from ending his note with a needling postscript: "What are you going to do for me tomorrow?") Their relationship was competitive, cooperative, and mutually dependent, a rich collaboration that was a New York version of the alliance between Katharine Graham, the publisher of *The Washington Post*, and Ben Bradlee, its executive editor. They were partners, and they were, in their own transactional way, friends: they vacationed together, spent weekends together, and were dinner and drinking companions.

Rosenthal called Sulzberger the best male traveling companion he had known. Their travels would take them to London, Sulzberger's choice, where they stayed at Claridge's Hotel in Mayfair, or to India, the country that had captured Rosenthal's imagination from his days as a foreign correspondent. After the late-afternoon Page One conferences, where Punch Sulzberger would sit quietly to the side as the editors debated the news of the day, offering questions but not opinions, they would retire to Rosenthal's private office to share a bottle of wine and trade gossip about correspondents and salty jokes about pretty women, the kind of banter that was accepted from powerful men in that era.

For seventeen years, these two New Yorkers shaped the *Times* and thus much of American journalism. As mired in tradition and precedent as they were, Sulzberger and Rosenthal came to recognize the evolving economics of the newspaper business and the evolving tastes and demands of their readers. They discovered that the newspaper—its reporters, editors, and business executives, but also its audience and advertisers—had a greater capacity for change than they might have expected. They steered it through the standoff with the federal government over the Pentagon Papers, and a redesign born of necessity after a recession nearly bankrupted New York City and sent readers fleeing to the suburbs. The *Times*, by the end of the 1970s, was a different newspaper than it had been when Sulzberger put Rosenthal in charge of the newsroom in 1969. It had been enhanced by new sections brimming with features on the arts, home decorating, cooking, and entertainment, illustrated with lavish photographs and drawings. Newsroom editors and their corporate counterparts had collaborated, if uneasily and within limits, on designing a newspaper for a new decade. The *Times*, as Arthur Gelb, Rosenthal's deputy, put it, could be a place "to relax the reader, to give him pleasure and enjoyment, to make him smile." *The New York Times* did not have to be all spinach. That meant more readers, and it meant more advertisers. And it meant more money.

Decades later, the financial crisis that the newspaper overcame in the 1970s would seem less severe, the writing and the redesign of the newspaper less adventurous. The relationship between Sulzberger and Rosenthal would fade. But this transformation of the *Times* that occurred on their watch was a lesson: it showed that the paper, as entrenched in tradition as it was, was capable of change.

* * *

Sulzberger and Rosenthal were different in so many ways that their friendship seemed improbable. Sulzberger was fastidious and self-effacing, with a disarming sense of humor that masked an underlying intensity and focus. He was warm and engaging but controlled and a little distant, a barrier that few managed to penetrate. Sulzberger avoided confrontation until he felt backed into a corner. "If someone walks in the door and says, 'If you don't do this, I quit,' well, they quit," as he put it in 1983.

He was punctual and took notice of people who were not. In 1951, when he was a young man learning his way around the *Times*—as part of the tutorial designed by Arthur Hays Sulzberger to prepare his son to be publisher—Punch Sulzberger spent weeks shadowing Arthur Gelb on his rounds as a reporter. Gelb arrived at work at ten o'clock in the morning to find Punch waiting. The next day, Gelb arrived fifteen minutes earlier. Punch was there. "That was my first glimpse of his obsession with punctuality," Gelb wrote years later.

People liked him. He had the bearing one would expect from a publisher of *The New York Times*. He attended the Loomis School—an all-boys boarding school in Windsor, Connecticut—and Columbia University. He traveled the wealthy lanes of New York City society, with a Fifth Avenue apartment and a weekend country estate and a seat on the board of trustees of the Metropolitan Museum of Art. He enjoyed cigars, even wondering if the *Times* restaurant critic, Mimi Sheraton, should note in her reviews whether the establishment allowed a patron to indulge in a post-dinner cigar. "I would not voluntarily go to a place that did not permit cigar-smoking," he wrote Gelb. Sulzberger would shop for antiques with James L. Greenfield, a *Times* editor, on their trips to London, where he took a hand in decorating the apartment there that was used by the newspaper's correspondents. After that, it was off for a few days to a rented country house in the Cotswolds. Sulzberger prized order and organization—his desk was a model of tidiness, and he would blanch when he walked through a newsroom piled with stacks of papers, soiled coffee cups, and overflowing ashtrays. "I know we are a newspaper office, but we do not also have to be a pig pen," Sulzberger complained at one point, threatening to dispatch teams of maintenance workers into the newsroom. But he made an exception for his new executive editor, "a guy who can't even keep his shirt tucked in," as he once put it.

As the only son of Arthur Hays and Iphigene Ochs Sulzberger, there had been little doubt he would be publisher one day. He had had three sisters, but in that era, in that family, women were not contenders for the job. Punch Sulzberger found himself in charge sooner than anyone had expected, his elevation hastened by the untimely death of his brother-in-law Orvil E. Dryfoos, the husband of Punch's eldest sister, Marian. Dryfoos had been publisher for just two years when he died at the age of fifty in 1963. At thirty-seven, Punch Sulzberger was the youngest publisher in the history of the newspaper and spent the next decade trying to prove that he was up to the job.

Rosenthal, by contrast, was an unkempt product of the newsroom: irritable, combative, emotional, scolding, and judgmental. He was difficult to like. Rosenthal's childhood—in Sault Ste. Marie, Canada, where he was born, and later in the Bronx—was marked by trauma that shaped him as an adult. Before he was thirteen, his father was killed falling off scaffolding while painting a house, and four of his five sisters died while he was a child. Rosenthal was afflicted with osteomyelitis, a debilitating bone-marrow disease, that left him bedridden for months. After one unsuccessful operation, he was encased in a cast that went from his feet to his neck, and he was told he might never walk again. His family appealed for help from the Mayo Clinic in Minnesota, which took him as a charity patient. There were more operations, and he recovered, but it was a searing passage of his life. When he and Gelb would go drinking alone at Sardi's, Rosenthal would tell this story of his upbringing, and he would begin to cry, and then Gelb would begin to cry. Those who learned of Rosenthal's early life would find it easier to understand his raw emotions, his flights to anger and tears, the high standards and impatience for any reporter or editor he considered intellectually lagging or of suspect character.

Punch Sulzberger was born into New York society, but Rosenthal—who went to DeWitt Clinton High School in the Bronx and then City College—would have to push his way in with his Central Park West penthouse, his table at the Four Seasons, and his dinner parties with the likes of Beverly Sills, Barbara Walters, Henry Kissinger, and Donald Trump. Rosenthal had lunch with Trump, at the time a New York developer, at the 21 Club, and supper at Café des Artistes. Trump was a guest at a dinner party Rosenthal and his wife, Ann, hosted at their apartment. Trump apologized after Rosenthal complained he had been treated rudely when he visited Trump Tower on Fifth Avenue. When Rosenthal sent Trump condolences upon the death of his father, the developer responded with a warm note of thanks, scratching out the word "sincerely" to write in "Love" before signing it "Donald."

Rosenthal was four years older than Sulzberger, and their relationship

was weighted with all the complexities inherent in that imbalance between age and authority. Even beyond their age difference, Punch Sulzberger wrestled with the complications that face every *Times* publisher:
managing an executive editor who considers themselves intellectually
superior to the publisher. This could be a matter of frustration to Sulzberger. When a New York communications executive asked Sulzberger if
the *Times* could cover the announcement of the creation of the Weather
Channel, he pleaded with Rosenthal, "Abe, PLEASE, PLEASE staff this
news conference. I believe it is newsworthy and I want this done."*

But they were of the same generation, men of a vanishing era in New
York. They shared an unease with forces that were transforming society and advancing, if slowly, into their white, male, and straight newsroom: feminism, affirmative action, and gay rights. It was reflected in
their bawdy jokes about women, their often-grudging response to law-
suits that documented discrimination against women, Blacks, and Latinos, and their recoiling at homosexuality. Sulzberger worried when
Rosenthal told him he wanted to create sections devoted to lifestyle.
"I'm left very cold, indeed, by the thought of a section of sociological
problem-raising—the article we ran on lesbian mothers coping with
raising children inevitably comes to my mind," he wrote, referring to
objections his mother, Iphigene, had registered about a story, which
had sent her son running down to the newsroom in despair. Rosenthal
reassured him he had nothing to worry about. "It definitely would not
be a section devoted to Lesbian mothers," he said.

In their personal lives, both men engaged in marital indiscretions at a
time when such behavior did not draw public attention. When he served
as the assistant to the publisher in 1956, Sulzberger had a brief affair
with a widowed *Times* reporter, Lillian Bellison Alexanderson, who became pregnant and accused him of being the father. He denied it but
settled a paternity suit and agreed to pay child support and medical
costs. The night shift editors learned to work around Rosenthal's affairs
when he would leave the office for someplace other than his home. It
would fall to Seymour Topping, one of his senior deputies, to track him

---

* Per Sulzberger's request, a 250-word story on the Weather Channel appeared on
page C23.

down when they wanted to take a story off the front page or move a foreign correspondent to be on the ground in the morning to write about an overnight disaster or coup. Rosenthal would leave a telephone number, and on some evenings, someone would answer. At other times, the telephone rang and rang. "I would do everything I could to get in touch with Abe so I could consult with him and talk with him," Topping said years later. "I valued his judgment; if I thought that there was something he was really desperately interested in being involved with, I'd just break my ass trying to find him." In the end, as the presses prepared to roll, he would make the decision on his own.

* * *

Rosenthal understood what was elemental to being a successful executive editor: earning the trust and loyalty of the publisher. He would alert Sulzberger to a sensitive story before it was published. He took care to keep him apprised of major staff shifts. He made sure to accommodate any request from the Sulzberger family, such as publishing the wedding announcement for a friend, or an article chronicling the tenth anniversary of Mortimer's, the Upper East Side restaurant frequented by people who ran in Punch Sulzberger's circles. "As it is such a well-known place, it might be worth noting in the paper," Sulzberger wrote. (Noted it was—in two separate stories over the next two weeks.) Sulzberger passed on a handwritten "Dearest Punch" note from his mother, suggesting the book editors consider reviewing *A Snowflake in My Hand*, an account of an oncology clinic for cats. "Don't quote me," Iphigene wrote her son, "but they do review a lot of unreadable books, to my mind, but of course I am no expert." Sulzberger asked if Rosenthal might accommodate his mother. "Very few things are pleasanter than obliging your mother!" he responded, promising a review would appear "as rapidly as possible."*

Sulzberger could be a meddler. He would send notes to his editors on matters picayune and substantial. Why, he wondered, has the *Times* begun spelling the word "employee" with two *e*'s rather than one? Was this a new style? (Yes, it was.) He could be displeased with a bad headline,

---

* A succinct, if affirming, squib in the Nonfiction in Brief column of the Sunday Book Review.

a poorly chosen photograph, or even a single word in a story, which he would circle and send to Rosenthal with a sharp note. Editors would arrive to complaints from Sulzberger that often seemed trivial, like comments on a recipe: "I like to cook, but I have absolutely no idea what the expression 'stir down' means." He would protest an article that he considered politically biased, prurient, or hostile to business, complaining in one instance about a critical story on tax-free benefits for executives. "We have country club memberships for Bill Davis, executive dining rooms in which you eat, company automobiles for Jack Harrison and others, executive washrooms galore. What I object to is the feeling that permeates this article that there is something evil about these things."

Little escaped his view. He complained when a tiny hand-drawn sketch appeared, notwithstanding the *Times*'s history of not publishing comics, in the Inside box on the front page. "Now that we have put the comics on page one, can we put it in the Guinness Book of Records and leave it there?" he asked sarcastically. Rosenthal handled these diplomatically: "I have paid you the highest possible compliment: I simply re-dictated your comments and put out a memo on them under my signature."

But the rules of engagement by a publisher are murky, and Sulzberger could push too far. Senator Daniel Patrick Moynihan, the New York Democrat, complained to Sulzberger about an article that quoted Senator Jacob Javits, his Republican counterpart, but failed to quote Moynihan. Sulzberger held Moynihan in high regard. He had overruled John B. Oakes, his editorial page editor, and endorsed Moynihan over Bella Abzug, a member of Congress, for the Democratic nomination for Senate in 1976.

"Do we have any kind of a problem here?" Sulzberger asked. Rosenthal was not sympathetic. "We can't really decide on every single quote that Moynihan wants to get into the paper as to whether he was right or wrong."

At another point, Sulzberger was upset about a critical article in *The New York Times Magazine* about a friend, Armand Hammer, the billionaire industrialist and chairman of Occidental Petroleum Corporation, who pled guilty to making illegal cash contributions to Richard Nixon's reelection campaign in 1972. Hammer wrote a 7,500-word letter of rebuttal, and Sydney Gruson, Sulzberger's lieutenant, told Rosenthal that Sulzberger wanted the newspaper to publish it in its entirety. Rosenthal refused, calling Hammer's letter "a mishmosh of weak denials, misinformation and self-justification," and telling Gruson that publishing it "would destroy the magazine and the ethic of the paper."

"This is not the first time this kind of thing has happened," Rosenthal wrote in his journal. "I like Punch enormously and think on the whole he's been an excellent publisher. But time after time, under pressure from peers, he is ready to crumble." Rosenthal's private criticism of Sulzberger contrasted with his warm public praise, and it is fair to wonder if he memorialized this episode with an eye to future histories. In the end, the Hammer letter was printed but cut to 1,200 words.

Sulzberger, in turn, was aware of Rosenthal's managerial style—"He's got a bunch of bullshit inside him" was how the publisher once put it—and the tense newsroom it fostered. "Sure, he probably has moods, he has personal problems, as we all do, that affect his life, that I assume get reflected in his office," he said at one point. "But they all sit downstairs, you know, with their antennas up, waiting to see whether he's coming in smiling or whether he's coming in frowning. Thank God I don't have to watch that." Still, Sulzberger was concerned enough to talk to Rosenthal about his temperament. You don't delegate enough, Sulzberger told him. You run a very personal paper.

Gruson would say Sulzberger was unaware of how much bitterness the executive editor had engendered with his "autocratic, dictatorial methods." But, Gruson added, "Punch liked the results." Rosenthal was what he was, Sulzberger would say, and he was not going to change—and really, Sulzberger did not want him to change. "It's got enormous benefits to it in terms of the kind of a newspaper you produce, and it's got enormous deficits associated with it in terms of staff development," Sulzberger said. "And if you don't want that kind of executive editor then you get rid of Abe Rosenthal."

* * *

"There is one item that I want to give the lie to directly and flatly," the publisher said in a note to his top editors and managers. "It is the suggestion that my family may sell the *Times*."

This was the summer of 1976. A cover story in *Businessweek* had declared that the "financial health of the *Times* has seriously deteriorated," as the *Times* struggled to keep afloat during the downturn. Weekday circulation had dropped from around 940,000 in 1969, when Rosenthal took over, to 796,000 in 1976, according to figures compiled by what was known at the time as the Audit Bureau of Circulations; advertising had plummeted from seventy-seven million lines in 1970 to sixty-nine million in 1975. "Unless drastic changes are made, it seems certain that our best newspaper will slip into the red within a few years," *New York* magazine declared. Sulzberger was confident that the company's long-term strategy of buying regional newspapers, magazines, and television stations gave it the economic cushion to survive any cyclical drop in revenues. But the anxiety ran deep. The expensive labor contracts and mechanical inefficiencies that the *Times* could overlook during flusher times were becoming harder to justify. The cost of newsprint was on the rise. "For the first time, I began to worry if the paper might go the way of the *Herald Tribune*," Arthur Gelb said years later, recounting the day he walked into a meeting in the fourteenth-floor boardroom to see a row of charts depicting circulation numbers and advertising revenue with steeply sloping arrows. Gelb—a towering bundle of energy and excess—turned to a colleague: "Let's open the window and jump right now."

The difficulties reflected the downturn in New York City, and the exodus of readers to the suburbs and suburban newspapers like *Newsday* on Long Island and the Gannett newspapers in Westchester. But it was hard not to read the dropping circulation as a verdict on the *Times* itself. "The conclusion is inescapable that we have difficulty selling the daily paper because there is something lacking in the product," Walter E. Mattson, the general manager, wrote in a memorandum for his files. "This is tough for many of us to swallow because we feel—and rightfully so—that we have the finest newspaper in the world—and most people agree with us." Even Rosenthal came to acknowledge that "people liked it more than they read it." And he had noticed the success of *New York* magazine under Clay Felker, its co-founder, with features and service journalism—lists of the best places to buy roses on Valentine's Day—presented in a visually appealing and intellectually stimulating way. Clay Felker is on to something here, Rosenthal told his editors.

This was the backdrop when Sulzberger ordered newsroom executives to join business executives in devising a plan to win back readers and advertisers. It was an extraordinary request for collaboration between two departments that had always kept their distance. Rosenthal had a history of resisting anything he saw as an encroachment on the news-gathering operation—from outside or inside the *Times*. Get your ass out of here! he had shouted at an advertising executive he spotted in the newsroom. Rosenthal had protested in 1974 when business executives proposed setting aside space once a week specifically for food coverage—a scheme to lure supermarket advertising—drawing a rebuke from the publisher.

"As you well know, it is essential for the *New York Times* newspaper to remain profitable," Sulzberger told Rosenthal in response to his protest. "If we are going to do that, we have basically two approaches: 1) to reduce costs, which of course we are endeavoring to do all the time; and 2) to develop new categories of revenue." But now, two years later, Rosenthal read the publisher and realized what was at stake if Sulzberger began ordering cuts in newsroom spending. Did the *Times* really need five music critics, or sixty foreign correspondents? Rosenthal would say to his deputies, anticipating what Sulzberger might think if the budgetary situation worsened. So he joined this collaboration, considering ideas that he would have once rejected as not in keeping with the spirit of the newspaper. "This is the News Department's proposal for a five-day-a-week, four-section *Times* we think will add zest to the paper, and attract readers and advertisers," Rosenthal wrote in June 1976. "It will be new for the *Times*, but squarely within its character." This collaboration resulted in the most substantial recasting of the paper since its purchase by Adolph S. Ochs. There would be five new sections, one for each weekday, magazine-like in their eye-catching design and breezy writing, focused on the arts, culture, and lifestyle. Weekend, devoted to entertainment and weekend offerings, had already debuted on April 30, 1976. That would now be followed by sections devoted to the home and sports. It culminated on November 14, 1978, with Science Times, the final section to debut.

The turn to softer news—"The Great Dill Pickle" read the headline on a story by Mimi Sheraton that appeared in the Living section on August 3, 1977, with an illustration of a pickle curving edge to edge across the top of the page—exposed the *Times* and Rosenthal to the kind of ridicule he had feared. "Supereditor Ignores New York's Demise in Mad Scramble to Print Soufflé Recipes," proclaimed *Penthouse*. It said Rosenthal "stands in danger of being overwhelmed by a spate of special sections catering to commuters or serving up recipes for crème brulee, advice on what to wear when job hunting, and items on myriad other urgencies of The Good Life."* *Time* magazine devoted a cover story to the project with the headline "Coping with the **New** *New York Times*" in August 1977.

But *Time* also noted that it seemed to be working: the average daily circulation for the *Times* had jumped from 821,000 to 854,000 since the first appearance of Weekend. It had sold more advertising in May than in any previous month in the 126-year history of the paper. Sulzberger attributed this to the new sections. "They're super." When he saw the account in *Time*, Rosenthal did something he rarely did: praised a story written by a rival about the *Times*. "I've been an editor at the *Times* for thirteen years," he wrote Henry Grunwald, the managing editor of *Time*. "To my memory, the *Time* cover was the first full, fair and sophisticated look at the *New York Times* in all that time. And God knows, there have been lots and lots of articles about the *New York Times*."

The *Times* had taken a risk, and its rivals were taking notice; at one point, seven or eight news organizations, by Sulzberger's count, were doing stories on the "**new** *New York Times*." Rosenthal, speaking years later, said that in the end, "it was still The New York Times. My God, you pick up that paper and we may have a half a page on asparagus, but it's still The New York Times." Breaking with tradition didn't bother Sulzberger a bit. "I just wonder why we didn't do it sooner."

---

* Rosenthal had refused an interview with the writer of the *Penthouse* piece, Richard Pollak, telling him that "you have adopted in all your writing about the *Times* a consistently hostile attitude." He wrote the publisher of *Penthouse*, Bob Guccione, trying unsuccessfully to get Pollak taken off the story.

CHAPTER 3

The Tenth Floor

Max Frankel sat alone in his new office as the sun began to set on the last day of 1976, his first day as the editor of the editorial page. He had not wanted this job. When Sydney Gruson had turned up at his door to say that Punch Sulzberger wished to transfer him from his post as Sunday editor to run the editorial page, Frankel had tried to refuse. "I am not an editorial writer and I don't understand why others wish to be," he wrote the publisher. "I don't believe in group-think on weighty public issues." Frankel wanted to be the executive editor, in charge of the newly combined daily and Sunday newspapers, but Sulzberger had picked Abe Rosenthal for that, despite Frankel's warning that Rosenthal did not have the breadth or temperament for such a high-level management position. "Harsh about others as it may be, and self-serving, you are making a mistake," Frankel told Sulzberger. But Sulzberger wanted Rosenthal to run the newsroom. And Frankel was a piece on a chessboard: Sulzberger was pushing out John Oakes—the head of the editorial page, a member of the editorial board since 1949, and Sulzberger's cousin. There were too many mornings when he found the editorials too liberal, antibusiness, or just boring.*

Frankel, realizing the inevitability of his situation, set down demands to Sulzberger. He wanted the authority to force out a half-dozen editorial board members to make way for writers who could make the page lively

---

* John Oakes's father, George Oakes, was the younger brother of Punch's maternal grandfather, Adolf Ochs. During World War I, George changed his sons' last name from the Germanic "Ochs" to the Anglophonic "Oakes."

and less finger-wagging, so the *Times* editorials could become as assertive and provocative as the expressions of opinion that appeared in *The Washington Post* and *The Economist*, editorials that were to Sulzberger's liking. Out went board stalwarts like Herbert Mitgang, with his views on theater, foreign affairs, and the law, and Peter Grose, who had joined the board after a foreign correspondent's tour of the globe that took him to Saigon, Moscow, and Jerusalem. In came Roger Starr, a former New York City housing commissioner and a conservative, at least by the *Times*'s standards, and Soma Golden Behr, a business reporter and editor, and a gust of wind in any room. Frankel asked Sulzberger to find jobs elsewhere in the *Times* organization for those ousted from the editorial department, but Frankel's scythe helped earn him the nickname of Max the Axe. That was why, to a large extent, he was alone in the office of the editorial page editor as the sun set and a new year began. Gruson came to view the handling of the purge with regret. "I don't think either Punch or I did it very well, nor did we plan it very well," he said years later.

But there were few jobs in American journalism more desirable than running the single most influential opinion page in the nation. Frankel now commanded a corner suite on the tenth floor of the *Times* building, with a window overlooking West Forty-third Street. His new office was as quiet as a library. A typewriter was set on the desk, soon to be replaced by a Harris computer terminal. A salon branched off to one side of his office, with a couch, a bar for late-afternoon cocktails, and a television on which to watch an evening presidential address or candidate debate, so that he and the other editorial writers could weigh in on what had happened for the late editions of the newspaper. A line of private offices overlooked the street, one for each member of the editorial board. The *Times* library, with its book-filled shelves rising toward its soaring ceiling, arched across the center court of the floor. Visitors—governors, mayors, heads of state, civic leaders, as well as the publisher, editors, and the occasional reporter—would step off the elevator and steer around the dusty hush of the center room before either turning right to reach the editorial offices or heading straight through a hall, its walls displaying portraits of Frankel's predecessors, to the conference room. There, board members would debate, under a portrait of Henry J. Raymond, the founding editor of the *Times*, the same issues that might that day be before the White House or the British Parliament. The library—the books, the leaded windows—lent the board offices a solemnity that was fitting for this paper, and for an editor like Frankel.

It seemed miles from the newsroom, even if it was just a seven-floor elevator ride away. Frankel would soon discover how different this was from the other jobs he had held since joining the paper as a full-time reporter upon his graduation from Columbia University in 1952: Sunday editor, Washington bureau chief, chief diplomatic correspondent, Moscow correspondent. It was not just the floor where Frankel stepped off every morning that seemed unfamiliar to him. The act of writing an editorial—of publicly offering an opinion, of using the first person singular or plural—was jarring to a journalist like Frankel, as it would have been to almost anyone who had spent their lives in a newsroom. So was the power he suddenly had—to inject his views into debates in Congress or the United Nations, to tell Americans who they should vote for, to cast judgment on public figures.

Frankel was a man of unwavering confidence in his abilities, and he found himself discussing the issues of the day with men and women who knew more than him in their fields—in urban affairs, science, the Middle East, Congress, city hall, the arts. Frankel had not written an opinion piece since his days at the student newspaper at Columbia University. He was not convinced that newspapers should be in the opinion business at all. "I never fully accepted the legitimacy of editorials in the modern newspaper," Frankel wrote years later. "For who, really, do these disembodied voices speak?"

* * *

Frankel was twenty-six years old on July 26, 1956, when the SS *Andrea Doria* collided with a ship off the coast of Nantucket and went down, killing fifty-one people. The *Times* was alerted to the disaster by a distress signal that came into its radio room, a corner in the newsroom where operators would telegraph a nightly news summary to ships at sea. Frankel was working the "lobster shift": arriving at eight in the evening and staying until the start of the last pressrun, at 3:20 A.M. He called the Coast Guard, and started writing as soon as the first details of the disaster were confirmed. Frankel rewrote the story seven times during the night, proving himself fast, accurate, and unflappable. "It was just a dumb accident and nobody tried to take it away," he said years later. Disasters at sea were part of the lore of the *Times*, and as the night grew late, senior editors started streaming in from their dinners, Broadway shows, or nights around the family table.

Frankel would have to yield the next day to Meyer Berger, but who could argue with that? Berger was probably the most admired reporter of his time, a novelistic writer who turned out tales of grand tragedy and small-scale human misfortune that were eloquent and deeply moving, animated with detail, color, and sweep. Frankel studied him from a desk away and peppered him with questions. Berger told Frankel how he would take the most cursory of notes so he could focus on observing the story as it unfolded before him. He would absorb every detail, every sight and smell and sound, to create a picture that he would put down on paper as soon as he sat down before a typewriter. Frankel's performance chronicling the sinking of the *Andrea Doria* elevated his stature overnight. He would receive a twenty-five-dollar raise, bringing his salary to about eighty dollars a week.

From his earliest days at the *Times*, Frankel was admired by his colleagues. "I have run out of any way to say to you how superb your work is," Tom Wicker, the bureau chief, wrote him while Frankel was covering the White House in 1968. But he was a complicated and conflicted figure. He could be plagued by self-doubt and grievances—slighted by another's promotion, an editor's failure to consider him for a job—or resentment that he was not paid enough. He considered quitting the *Times* on several occasions and was stopped by his wife, Tobi. "Twice, entirely on her own, she tore up her husband's resignations from the *Times*, confident that she understood the institutional imperatives better than any of the men who kept prattling about them," Frankel said at her memorial service in March 1987. He did quit at least once, albeit briefly, in September 1964, to take a position as the national correspondent for *The Reporter*, a liberal magazine published by Max Ascoli, a dean at the New School for Social Research. Frankel's resignation letter to Sulzberger reflected his disquiet and ambition. "I have been suffering a deep inner restlessness and torment that cannot be satisfied at this point by anything at the *Times*, despite its unbounded generosity to me, its deserved renown, distinguished readership and exhilarating atmosphere," he wrote. "My restlessness stems from the overriding desire to be a writer of infinite dimension on national as well as international subjects, official as well as human affairs, without the tyranny of the daily deadline and without the necessary but still annoying inhibition of avoiding an ideological or philosophical commitment to cause or faction." He assured Sulzberger that his departure was not related to the announcement, two days earlier, that Wicker would succeed James Reston as the Washington bureau chief. But Frankel had second thoughts almost immediately, and with apologies, told Ascoli that he would stay at the *Times*.

Frankel again threatened to resign four years later, in 1968, when James Greenfield, an editor in New York who had worked as an airline executive before coming to the *Times*, was named to replace Wicker as the Washington bureau chief, at the urging of Rosenthal. Frankel was distressed that he was not even considered for the post and, at Reston's suggestion, called Punch Sulzberger at his home on Fifth Avenue to register his displeasure. Carol Sulzberger, who was the publisher's second wife, answered the telephone and suggested Frankel stop by that evening for a celebration of her husband's forty-second birthday. He arrived in time for dessert. Punch Sulzberger invited Frankel to a side room for a tumbler of vodka and asked him not to be distraught by the Greenfield appointment. Frankel was not appeased.

I just don't want to stay where I'm not in line for an important job like this, Frankel told him.

This was the culmination of years of tension between Washington and New York, and Reston, distressed that Wicker was being forced out, pressed Sulzberger to reverse course and rescind the Greenfield appointment. Frankel became the bureau chief.

He nearly quit yet again in 1973—this time when, as Washington bureau chief, he was appointed Sunday editor, which would require a move to New York. He drafted a letter of resignation, a portrait of a correspondent struggling to reconcile the demands of his family—of forcing Tobi to leave the comfort of life in Washington to move yet again—and the strains of commuting between Manhattan and Washington. "I am horrified to discover that I face a bitter choice between job and family, between the opportunity that you tried to give me and the serenity that Tobi and I would need to handle it properly," he wrote. That, he said, was not a choice. "Tobi resents my dragging the family to New York and the upheaval, sacrifice and genuine financial strain imposed by the move. She tried very hard to pretend to herself and to me that she was reconciled to it, but I now realize, as I should have realized sooner, that she resents it more than ever. . . . This is, therefore, my double resignation from the Sunday editorship and from the *Times*."*

But Frankel never sent the letter, and his appointment as Sunday editor was announced on September 20, 1972. That same day, Rosenthal sent a note to David R. Jones, the new national editor. "We seem to be taking a beating on the Watergate case from the *Washington Post*. Let's talk it over."

* * *

Five burglars had been arrested trying to bug the Democratic National Committee headquarters at the Watergate complex in Washington, D.C., on June 17. The morning after the break-in, Bernard Gwertzman, the paper's diplomatic correspondent, stopped by the Washington bureau and noticed a story about the burglary on the office news ticker. A former police reporter, Gwertzman suspected this was not just another break-in. The bureau was nearly empty that weekend morning, but Gwertzman pressed the duty editor to dispatch an intern to cover the arraignment. That Monday morning, a story in *The Washington Post* by Bob Woodward and Carl Bernstein reported that one of those arrested, James W. McCord, Jr., was on the payroll of Nixon's reelection committee. That was the beginning of a run of stories by Woodward and Bernstein—two reporters on the metropolitan staff—that would humble the *Times*, on what would prove to be the biggest scandal in Washington in fifty years.

A year earlier, the *Times* had published the Pentagon Papers—a secret history of the Vietnam War that had been compiled by the Defense Department. Sulzberger and Rosenthal would celebrate those days, recounting stories of journalistic stealth and defiance, of spiriting boxes

---

* Frankel later said this was triggered by "the hiring of Bill Safire as an op-ed columnist, which I had privately opposed on ideological grounds. Tobi was enraged, not only about the employment of a Nixon flack, but about my having been overlooked for an op-ed column."

stuffed with classified documents under beds, of standing up to the Nixon White House until a federal court order forced the *Times* to stop publishing excerpts from the documents while the case filed by the Justice Department made its way to the Supreme Court. The high court ultimately upheld the newspaper's right to publish the materials without prior restraint. "This was not a kid's game, it was something that would affect the history of The New York Times and the war—the latter being more important, but the first being quite important to us, too," Rosenthal said nearly twenty years later. He had decided he would leave the *Times* if Sulzberger refused to publish the documents. "If we had surrendered to Mitchell [John Mitchell, the attorney general], and had allowed the Government, without a court battle, to dictate to us," he wrote to John Hohenberg, the longtime administrator of the Pulitzer Prize, "I really do believe that the heart would have gone out of the paper and of American newspapering." Rosenthal told Neil Sheehan, the reporter who obtained the documents, that the Pentagon Papers story would prove to be "the most fruitful and important in any of our lives. . . . It was not only the best story of the century but it gave specific and tangible meaning to the free press and to free reporters."

Watergate would eclipse that. The *Times* would come close to catching up with the *Post*, throwing some of its best investigative reporters, among them Seymour Hersh, into the hunt. But Watergate would change American journalism. It would always be known as the *Post*'s story, and Rosenthal saw Watergate as the biggest failure of his years running the newsroom. At the time, Rosenthal wanted an early accounting of the front page of the *Post* every night; clerks from the Washington bureau would wait outside the *Post* headquarters to retrieve first-edition copies and rush them back to the *Times* bureau. He ordered the *Times* to match, in its final editions, any big Watergate revelation the *Post* had that the *Times* had missed. It then fell to Rosenthal to write a letter to Ben Bradlee, the executive editor of the *Post*, with copies to Woodward, Bernstein, and Katharine Graham, the publisher, congratulating his biggest rival for being awarded the Pulitzer Prize for Public Service for its Watergate coverage. "No jokes this time . . . Huge applause from Forty-third Street," he told Bradlee, a reference to their jousting, competitive relationship.

It could not have been easy. As Rosenthal once put it, "He is out to cut my throat and I am out to cut his." And he held one person responsible for the *Times*'s failure on Watergate: Max Frankel, the head of the Washington bureau. I should have fired you, Rosenthal told him.

Watergate happened on Frankel's watch, though he always resisted much of the blame (and, as would become clear in the coming years, the episode would not harm his career). Frankel had accompanied Richard Nixon to China, and his coverage of the president's diplomacy—thirty-five thousand words in all, broad, authoritative—would win him the Pulitzer Prize for International Reporting the same year that the *Post* was awarded its Pulitzer Prize for Watergate. Frankel would point to his China trip as one reason he was distracted from Watergate, along with his preparations to move his family to New York. "I had one foot out the door," he said. Watergate, as he and other *Times* editors would note for years, began as a local police story, and that put a New York newspaper at a disadvantage. "We got beat because it wasn't our home town story, basically," Frankel said years later.

But the Watergate failures spoke to a broader issue: the rules of Washington journalism were changing. The *Times* was trying to retain its magisterial distance and establishment authority as competing newspapers—led by the *Post*—turned sharply more adversarial toward the government. Watergate, coming after the disclosures in the Pentagon Papers, had undermined the assumptions that had governed the everyday working relations between journalists and the people they wrote about. Public officials lied. They covered up. They broke the law. At first, Frankel could not imagine Nixon engaging in anything like this. "Not even my most cynical view of Nixon had allowed for his stupid behavior," Frankel wrote years later. "There he sat at the peak of his power, why would he personally get involved in tapping the phone not even of his opponent but of only a Democratic party functionary?"

The *Times* could no longer assume that an event was not news until it had written about it on its front page. There was a demand for aggressive investigative reporting that stepped ahead of the FBI or the police—the kind of reporting that was being done by Woodward and Bernstein. And the standards for what kind of information was needed to back up an explosive story were changing. Rosenthal would call, riled up by the latest dispatch from Woodward and Bernstein. Frankel would assure him he shared his frustration, but he did not know what to do. So many of its rival's stories gave no hint of sources.

We got beaten on stories that I couldn't have gotten into *The New York Times*, he would say to a colleague years later.

The *Times* had long kept a dignified distance from investigative reporting. Sulzberger wanted Rosenthal to eliminate the phrase "investigative reporter" because it created two classes of reporters. "The government has investigators and The Times reporters," the publisher said. It was a cautious stance that would cloud the paper's efforts to recruit investigative reporters and constrain its reporting for another twenty years. Gene Roberts, who was the paper's national editor, would complain that the *Times* lacked an investigative mentality. He eventually left to run *The Philadelphia Inquirer*, which under Roberts would win seventeen Pulitzers over eighteen years.

* * *

Max Frankel looked the part of an editorial page editor. He was an intellectual who had been a correspondent in both Moscow and Cuba. He smoked a pipe. He had run the Washington bureau and flown on Air Force One. As bureau chief, he had regular dealings with Washington figures like Henry Kissinger (Frankel's detractors in the bureau would say the relationship between these two refugees, both of whom grew up in Washington Heights, was too close). Sulzberger would soon conclude that the difficulties that shadowed Frankel's promotion—"it was sort of a bloodbath," he said years later—were worth it. The editorials were more in keeping with Sulzberger's moderate views. Frankel took Sulzberger's instruction, and directed his board to write editorials that took a clear point of view—and if they did not do it, he would. Editorial drafts submitted to Frankel and his deputy, Jack Rosenthal, who was not related to Abe, would come back with a tangle of deletions and rewritten sentences. Writers complained about getting "Maxed and Jacked."

Frankel would come to appreciate how much running the editorial page of *The New York Times* was a perch of prestige and influence. His editorial page published in 1983 a whimsical item about acronyms that were part of the daily language of Washington, which referred to the "nine men" who sat on SCOTUS, or the Supreme Court of the United

States. That drew him a judicial reproach. "According to the information available to me, and which I had assumed was generally available, for over two years now SCOTUS has not consisted of nine men. If you have any contradictory information, I would be grateful if you would forward it as I am sure the POTUS, the SCOTUS and the undersigned (the FWOTSC) would be most interested in seeing it," wrote Sandra Day O'Connor.

More than anything, Frankel was now an established member of Sulzberger's inner circle. There were lunches in the publisher's dining room, cocktails in his office at the end of the day, chats in the hallway about issues facing the world and the *Times*. He would lead formal sessions with elected officials and dignitaries who made the pilgrimage to West Forty-third Street to meet the publisher and the editorial board. In the newsroom, this was Rosenthal's moment. But Frankel was eight years younger than Rosenthal. His time would come.

CHAPTER 4

Dead Ends

Betsy Wade grew up seventeen miles north of Times Square, in a house in Bronxville scattered with copies of the *Herald Tribune* and the *World-Telegram*, though not *The New York Times*. She graduated from Barnard College and Columbia Journalism School, where she was taught how to edit stories and write headlines by some of the most accomplished editors in the business, including journalists from the copy desk at the *Times*. She was hired after graduation as a reporter at the *Herald Tribune*, a job she lost upon disclosing she was pregnant. On October 1, 1956, Wade joined the *Times* as the first woman to edit news copy in the newspaper's history. Wade was breaking a barrier; still, she was initially assigned to the Women's section, because that is where women at the *Times* were sent in the 1950s, to work in what was known as the Four Fs section: food, fashion, family, and furnishings. Before long, she was moved into the newsroom.

It was not easy being a woman at the *Times*, adrift in a clattering sea of men who, for the most part, were not inclined to make her life at the paper any easier. Wade began her career just as the *Times* banned newsroom spittoons, where men would deposit the dank remnants of chewing tobacco—a world "as archaic as McSorley's old-time saloon," she said years later. One editor defied this new policy by coming to the office with a three-pound coffee can: his personal spittoon. At the end of his shift, he would head for the bathroom to dispel the remains of his day, and he always walked past Wade's station, swirling the spittle in the coffee can. The smell and the sound of it made Wade want to retch, but she knew she was being hazed and would do nothing that might reveal her distress.

She could not help noticing the fastidious, quirky, obsessive characters around her. The head of the national copy desk was Joseph Durso. Every afternoon, Durso, who would go on to cover the Yankees and the Mets, would come in, sharpen a fistful of pencils, and set them out so the sharp tips were all pointing the same direction. He would fold up his shirtsleeves—"exactly, so many folds"—drop his elbows on the desk, and get to work. The nicer ones would offer to write her headlines. As if she could not learn to do it herself! After six o'clock in the evening, when the secretaries had left for home, Wade would glance around and realize she was the only woman in the room.

If there had been any hesitations about planting a woman in such male territory, Wade dispatched them. She knew how to catch errors of fact and unravel the kind of clunky, convoluted sentences that often landed on her desk from the mostly male correspondents filing their stories from around the globe. She mastered, in this pre-computer era of copy paper, paste, scissors, and pencils, the art of writing headlines within the constrained space and the restrictive rules of the *Times*. Wade had a streak of irreverence, and it peeked out in headlines like the one she put on an account, by Nan Robertson, of a misstep by the Museum of Modern Art when it hung Matisse's *Le Bateau* upside down for forty-seven days. "Modern Museum Is Startled by Matisse Picture," the headline read, with the artist's name flipped upside down.*

She was an awful speller, but she knew that and checked herself diligently. Allan M. Siegal, who was the news editor, always maintained that a bad speller, if self-aware, could be a great editor, and he had Betsy Wade in mind when he said that. Before long, Wade was promoted to the foreign copy desk, and in 1972—another first—she became head of the foreign copy desk. She was firm and unflappable with a well-honed sense of self. Wade considered herself one of the best copy editors in the building, a self-assessment that, if brash, would draw no argument from those who worked with her. When Abe Rosenthal was writing a speech, he would show up at her desk, asking if she might edit it. She was recruited to help edit the stories on the Pentagon Papers. And at the request of the

---

* "OOPS!" read the caption under the photograph of the painting. "To see it as Matisse did, turn page upside down."

Sulzberger family, Wade oversaw the preparation of the advanced obituaries of Arthur Hays Sulzberger and Iphigene Ochs Sulzberger, Punch's parents—a sensitive and prestigious assignment. "I have taken pride in handling these ticklish items," she wrote Rosenthal as she provided him an update on the status of the Iphigene obituary in 1973. Still, Wade was not surprised when she hit a ceiling in the middle of her career and stopped rising in the newsroom. She had been warned: it was the price of her leadership in a newsroom movement that challenged, and ultimately began to change, a rigid male culture that dominated almost every aspect of the *Times* newsroom, starting with Abe Rosenthal and Punch Sulzberger.

* * *

On May 31, 1972, the Women's Caucus of *The New York Times*—founded the previous February over lunch at a Times Square restaurant by a small group of women, Betsy Wade among them—sent a five-page letter to Punch Sulzberger chronicling what it described as the paper's failures in hiring, promoting, and recruiting female employees. "We call your attention to the twenty-one names on the masthead—both editorial and business executives," the letter said. "Not one is a woman." Signed by fifty women, the letter demanded that the newspaper bring equity to salaries being paid to women and move more female employees into writing, editing, and management positions that were now dominated by men. "The voices of women are being heard in greater number today in this country," said the letter. "At the *Times*, we note little change in the basic situation of women." A little more than two years later, frustrated at the pace of negotiations with *Times* management and lawyers, the caucus sued the *Times* in federal district court under the Civil Rights Act of 1964, alleging disparities in the way women were paid, hired, and promoted. The case, *Elizabeth Boylan et al. v. The New York Times Co.*, would grow to be a class-action suit on behalf of approximately 550 women, a group of plaintiffs that ranged from reporters in the newsroom to clerks who answered the telephones in the classified advertisement department. Though Betsy Wade was the name she went by professionally, Wade signed Elizabeth Boylan—her married name—on the legal papers, assuring that she would appear first on the alphabetical list of the original six plaintiffs that would land on the desks of Sulzberger and the company attorneys.

Eileen Shanahan, a correspondent in Washington covering economic and tax policy, added her name as the seventh signatory to the suit after it was filed, over warnings from her husband, John V. Waits, Jr., a production manager at *The Washington Post*, that she was risking retribution from the company. Shanahan was a fiery presence in the bureau. She confronted, with equal fervor, government bureaucrats, fellow reporters, copy editors, and even her bureau chief. Shanahan had led the picket line of female reporters who protested the men-only policy of the Gridiron Club, the organization of Washington journalists whose white-tie dinners drew presidents, congressional leaders, members of the Supreme Court, and the top editors in America. She had paused one day in front of a bulletin board in the Washington bureau to inspect a list of thirty-two employee salaries posted by a guild shop steward. There were no names next to the salaries, but Shanahan knew how much she made, so she could determine where she fell on the bureau pay scale—well below men with less experience and accomplishment. "I had always assumed that I was the victim of a degree of salary discrimination, probably based on the unjust rationale that I didn't need the money because I have a husband with a good job," she told Clifton Daniel, the Washington bureau chief, as Nan Robertson recounted in *The Girls in the Balcony,* her book on the struggle by women for equity at the *Times.* "But in my darkest hour, I never imagined that my pay would place me in the lower half of the bureau's reporters."

Shanahan wanted to bring her grievance directly to Abe Rosenthal, but Daniel warned that it would infuriate the executive editor. Shanahan ignored him and sent Rosenthal a memo. She never got a response, much less a raise. But after she sent it, she stopped drawing assignments for the front-page news analyses that were a measure of a correspondent's prestige; Shanahan came to believe her husband's warning had been prescient. As the litigation dragged on, Shanahan left the *Times* to become the assistant secretary for public affairs in the Department of Health, Education, and Welfare.

The lawsuit set off a tangle of skirmishes among attorneys for the women and for the *Times.* Rosenthal and Punch Sulzberger were compelled to sit for sworn depositions, often contentious sessions, where they were confronted with a statistical indictment of the company's treatment of women employees: the absence of women in the ranks of top-line editors and corporate executives; the overwhelming number of male reporters in the newsroom; how male employees made on average $98.67 dollars more a week than their female colleagues. An out-of-court settlement was announced on October 6, 1978, the day the trial was to have begun. The *Times* agreed to pay $350,000, including $233,500 in salary compensation, to the plaintiffs, and another $100,000 to cover the plaintiffs' legal fees. It established a four-year affirmative action program to advance the placement of women in positions across the newspaper. It was not a huge settlement, and executives at the *Times* prepared a list of preemptive arguments to minimize the import of what had transpired once it was publicly announced. "Money amount is smallest of any major suit of this kind" was the first of nineteen points in the internal memo. James C. Goodale, the newspaper's executive vice president, declared that the settlement "completely vindicates The *Times* of any charge or hint of unfair employment practices." The *Times* had not admitted to discrimination or any violation of the law. It did not agree to retroactive salary increases (the payments were in the form of annuities), nor did it accelerate any promotions for the women. "Such stringent requirements have been part of most settlement[s] of other women's suits against company managements," the *Times* reported in its story on the agreement, the account placed deep inside the paper.

Rosenthal later asserted that the *Times* had settled the case because a trial would have compelled him to testify against his employees, to repeat in public the disparagements given in the privacy of the deposition. "'What do you think about this person?'" Rosenthal said to Harrison Salisbury, the retired *Times* editor, in 1979, as he previewed how his testimony might have gone. "'What do you think of Miss so-and-so. Is she guilty of inaccuracies?' Yes, I do think so." Rosenthal had never shown much reluctance in criticizing reporters he considered lacking, so there were no doubt more compelling factors at play. In settling, the *Times* avoided the spectacle of a public airing of its hiring and promotion practices, of *Times* executives like Rosenthal and Sulzberger being forced to answer questions in a public courtroom. No matter how the *Times* minimized the settlement publicly, the suit was a matter of concern for Sulzberger, who complained to Rosenthal about even the relatively brief story his newspaper wrote on its resolution. "I think our news judgments on ourselves are just way out of whack," Sulzberger wrote. "Absolutely nothing happened yesterday vis-à-vis the women's case, except the fact that the judge put his stamp on the agreed-upon and much publicized settlement."

Wade was a high-spirited presence in the newsroom, and the president of Local 3 of the Newspaper Guild. She liked being known as a troublemaker. She took pleasure in puncturing some of the *Times*'s most revered institutions. "If you want to die almost instantly, you look at an old story by Turner Catledge which meanders on and on and on and on," she said in an oral history, referring to one of the newspaper's former executive editors. Before the suit was filed, she sent Rosenthal three pages of suggestions on how the *Times* might address sexism in its pages. The *Times* should stop using the word "Mrs." in headlines about famous women, such as Indira Gandhi and Golda Meir. It should dispense with patronizing terms such as "lady" or ordinary words freighted with feminine endings, like "executrix."

But for Wade, the lawsuit was a turning point. Rosenthal decided that Wade had engaged in an act of disloyalty. He would refer to Wade as "that bitch" in front of Siegal. Fearless or not, irreverent or not, Wade found it unnerving, while the lawyers were negotiating the case, to run into Sydney Gruson in an elevator, where he delivered a not-particularly-veiled threat.

We are not in the habit of promoting people who sue us, Gruson told her. Wade would never rise higher in the newsroom than her position on the foreign copy desk. She spent her last fourteen years at the *Times* writing a tips-for-travelers column for the Travel section, Practical Traveler. It had its fans, but she always considered it a journalistic backwater. "Those of us who worked on this knew nothing was coming to us," Wade told Gail Collins, who would become the first woman to run the editorial page at the *Times* in 2001. "That's what they do when you sue them." She would often think back to the warning Gruson gave her on the elevator. "It took a while for us to get it through our charmingly delightful, agreeable minds that this was the dead end for all of us, every last one of us," she said years later.

It would be another thirty years before the *Times* appointed its first woman as executive editor. Salary disparities between men and women would persist. But the litigation would shape the sensibilities of the next publisher and the next executive editor and influence hiring, promotions, and assignment decisions for decades. Over the next ten years, Soma Golden Behr would become the paper's first female national editor. Carolyn Lee would become an assistant managing editor and the first woman to appear on the masthead. Susan Chira would be hired as a metropolitan reporter and would one day be the *Times*'s first woman foreign editor. Anna Quindlen, a twenty-four-year-old reporter for the *New York Post,* was hired by Rosenthal to work on the metropolitan desk and would rise to become a columnist on the Op-Ed page, for which she would win the Pulitzer Prize. "My whole career there is a function of the women's suit, first of all because they hired me and second of all because they pushed me along much more quickly than they would have had they not been operating in the shadow of that suit," Quindlen would say later.

The *Times* had chronicled the problems for women in the workplace on its news pages and editorialized against discrimination in its editorial pages. But it had not met those ideals within its own walls: it had taken litigation to force a change. The current plaintiffs were women employees, but the newspaper was also facing a discrimination suit that was filed later in 1974 by Black and Latino employees. The suits would ultimately force the *Times* to reconcile a fundamental belief about itself—that the newspaper was a meritocracy, with objective measures of talent and performance—with a newsroom that remained overwhelmingly male and overwhelmingly white.

* * *

The tone was set at the top. Sulzberger and Rosenthal, like many men of their generation, were bewildered by the feminist movement, as they were by much of the social turmoil of the 1960s and the 1970s. Rosenthal described himself as a feminist and asserted in 1979 that the atmosphere at the paper had improved from the days when walking into the newsroom was like "coming into a locker room." It was unfair to accuse the *Times* of bias against women, Rosenthal argued. "I am utterly confident there is no discrimination." That assertion should be viewed with skepticism. The hiring-and-salary data collected by the Women's Caucus in bringing its suit was hard to refute. The Caucus, in its initial 1972 count, found 40 women reporters, compared with 385 men. There were no women correspondents on the national staff and just three on the foreign staff. Out of the 35 reporters in Washington, just 3 were women. Rosenthal would sympathize with the complaints about sexist language that appeared in the pages of the *Times*, such as the description in one story of a woman judge being considered for a position on the Supreme Court as having a "bathing beauty figure." But he bristled when the New York chapter of the National Organization for Women pressed him to address sexist practices at the newspaper. "The people who run NOW at the present time are no longer interested in a dialogue, but in propaganda, attack and gaining publicity," he wrote the publisher.

Even after the suit was settled, men continued to dominate the newsroom and shape its culture. Male correspondents would be informed (by male superiors) they were moving to new cities or countries, and their wives were expected to pick up and follow them. Correspondents who objected, whose spouses had their own careers, or who simply did not want to uproot their families, found little sympathy from the men in charge. Women editors and reporters who became pregnant found little empathy. Quindlen was seven months pregnant, working as an editor on the metropolitan desk, when Arthur Gelb walked over to her station, as she would later recount the story.

So, this is the last one, right? he asked her.

Arthur, that's actionable, Quindlen responded. You can't just ask a woman if she's done having children.

Quindlen admired Abe Rosenthal, who would share with Quindlen the great hopes he had for her career. Someday, you will be managing editor at the *Times*, he would say. It angered her.

Managing editor is the number two job, Quindlen told Rosenthal. It's like telling a child that someday they could grow up to be vice president.

Private correspondence from Sulzberger suggests the depths of his disdain for the movement that had brought his newspaper into court. Sulzberger, who had a fondness for limericks and rhyme in his sometimes-irreverent internal communications, sent Max Frankel an unsigned bit of doggerel: "Excerpt from possible testimony at Women's Trial." A judge in this concoction directs Sulzberger to "in your own words tell the court why you hired Miss Jones. What really were the final criteria?" "Sulzberger" responds:

> *I should like to proclaim to your Honor*
> *That I followed the usual rules,*
> *And availed both myself and my office,*
> *Of the latest of management tools.*
> *I broke down and coded her answers*
> *In their logical pieces and bits.*
> *And then I discarded them fully*
> *And went out and hired her tits.*

To which the judge responds, "I'm a leg man. You're guilty."*

Rallying to his friend Rosenthal's side after he saw an unfavorable story about his editor in *Penthouse*, Sulzberger wrote, "If you insist upon reading all of the 'shit,' may I suggest that between takes you examine the girls. They are by far the best part of the magazine." He added, as a postscript, "The only thing that upset me in the article was when they said I was a lousy correspondent."

Rosenthal and Sulzberger were united in resisting what was emerging as two of the major demands of NOW: to adopt the use of "Ms." in its pages, and to end the practice of identifying women by their marital status. These were the early days of an argument that would not be resolved at the *Times* for another decade. That the newspaper still used honorifics was one of those stylistic idiosyncrasies that made the *Times* what it was, lending it an air of authority and courtliness. But its insistence on different rules for men and women, of identifying women by "Mrs." or "Miss," was galling to women and some men. Rosenthal was steadfast in his resistance to a change: the *Times*, he argued, was an arbiter of standards and norms. To endorse the use of Ms. would confer legitimacy to an honorific that, in his view, had political overtones and assure that this was not just a passing fad. "I don't think that the time has come—and I don't

---

* Frankel put a copy of Sulzberger's note into his papers at Columbia University and reprinted it in his memoir.

know now if it ever will—when we should use Ms. in the *Times*," Rosenthal wrote Sulzberger and Max Frankel, who at the time was the Sunday
editor, in 1974. The risk, he said, was that "we would lose our claim of
being the guide to the best-accepted usage, a claim which we cherish and
which is highly regarded by many readers, including teachers and other
professionals."*

Rosenthal and Sulzberger were facing a rising tide. Gloria Steinem,
the feminist and writer, had cofounded a magazine for women in 1972
and called it *Ms.* "It isn't possible to continue forcing women to disclose
marital status when men are not forced to do the same," Steinem wrote
Rosenthal. Protestors showed up at its headquarters on West Forty-third
Street, demanding the paper drop its prohibition. MISS, IF SHE CHOOSES;
MRS., IF SHE CHOOSES; MS., IF SHE CHOOSES, read one of the banners.
Sulzberger resolved the dispute that year with a sentence. "At the end of
the year, like Solomon, I cast my vote 'NO' for Ms."

---

* Thus emerged another area of dispute between Rosenthal and Frankel. "Obviously,
Abe and I are in basic disagreement—for reasons that I can respect but simply don't accept," Frankel told the publisher. The use of Miss and Mrs. "define women *entirely* in terms
of marital standard, when the standard is not applied to men."

CHAPTER 5

Winners and Sinners

here were standards that defined *The New York Times*, established from the day it was purchased by Adolph S. Ochs, and presented in a statement of principles published on August 19, 1896, in the first issue of the *Times* on Ochs's watch: "to give the news impartially, without fear or favor, regardless of party, sect, or interests involved." They evolved through the decades, but they were never forgotten. An exacting adherence to grammar and the proper usage of language. A prohibition, with the rarest of exceptions, against profanity, vulgarity, explicit sexual references, and gratuitous descriptions of violence. There should be no bias, errors of fact, clichés, or loaded language. Editors were on guard for the reporter trying to slip by an off-color insinuation or the lazy headline writer resorting to a pun. (The paper's motto, "All the News That's Fit to Print," remains on the top left corner of the front page, a relic of an increasingly unrealistic aspiration which, by the 1970s, had come to be politely ignored.)

For nearly thirty years, starting in 1977 and through his retirement in 2006, Allan Siegal was the embodiment and the enforcer of these standards. Any proposed use of a vulgarity or profanity, sexual reference, graphic description of violence—and any mention in the news columns of *The New York Times* itself—needed to be approved by the news desk, which he controlled. The responsible editor would be reprimanded if Al Siegal spotted anything that ran afoul of these standards—or any grammatical error, misuse of a word, stylebook violation, or misspelling. Siegal would be effusive in his praise of headlines and flights of writing that he thought honored the *Times*. He would circle those with his green felt-tip pen, with the phrase, "Nice, who?" and copy and staple them into a morning critique known as the Greenies, photocopies of which were circulated around the newsroom. An approving Siegal mention would lift the spirits of any reporter or editor.

But in a newsroom that began many mornings with a barrage of withering memoranda, it was the other notes from Siegal that were remembered: scorching, unequivocal, sarcastic, and vaguely menacing. "We do not use this expression," he wrote, circling in green the phrase "Pro-Abortion" in a headline. "I would like memo on how it got in. Name names pls." He complained at a meeting with editors that reporters were failing to include full and direct quotations in major stories and wrote a rebuke a few days later to Joseph Lelyveld, a deputy foreign desk editor, when he spotted a story with paraphrased quotes. "Please pay attention," Siegal wrote Lelyveld. "Once I have set the guidelines, or called for a return to practices that were being frayed or unobserved, I expect the editors to follow through, not just for one day but consistently." He was stern and imposing, a morbidly obese figure who would struggle to walk across the newsroom or squeeze into a chair. His girth, his mien, and the sheer breadth of his knowledge—on etymology, opera, history, social theory, government, literature, poetry, politics, French culture, the Bronx, and more than anything, on the *Times*—made him a figure of endless fascination in the newsroom, whose authority and influence far exceeded what was suggested by his title. He was a ferocious advocate for fresh and bright writing—willing to countenance experimentation if done well, wordplay if done perfectly. He could be tender and kind to younger reporters and would side with an underdog. But years later, he would worry that he had been a bully. He had, though it was in the cause of putting out a newspaper of the highest standards.

And he was terrified of A. M. Rosenthal.

He hated working for him. Siegal would rejoice on the days when Rosenthal was out of the office. Four months and two weeks after Rosenthal retired as executive editor, Siegal sat down with Susan W. Dryfoos, the daughter of Marian Sulzberger and Orvil Dryfoos (and niece of Punch Sulzberger), who was collecting oral histories from *Times* editors, and spoke for hours about the man who had appointed him, at the age of thirty-seven, to one of the most powerful positions in the newsroom. He set down only one condition before he began to speak. "This is Allan Siegal, it's February 28, 1987, I'm in Susan Dryfoos's office and these conversations are taking place on the understanding that they will not be heard or read by anyone except Susan so long as Abe Rosenthal and I are both employed by the Times."

There was no shortage of criticism of the executive editor of *The New York Times* as the 1980s began. Rosenthal had never been easy, but he had grown increasingly intemperate as the years passed and he confronted the retirement that presumably awaited him when he reached sixty-five.[*] That would happen on May 2, 1987, though reminders were on hand well before that date. "Is Rosenthal's Time Up at the *Times?*" read a headline in *Adweek* in early 1983. But the concerns voiced by Siegal were especially noteworthy: he was not a disaffected editor reassigned to the Sunday Real Estate section, or a foreign correspondent who had been recalled to work on the night shift. There were few other people who so personified the newspaper and its values. He had joined the *Times* in 1960 as a copyboy, two years before graduating from New York University, worked as an assistant news editor on the foreign desk, and was one of a select group of editors recruited to secretly edit the *Times*'s stories on the Pentagon Papers in 1971. He was an author, with William G. Connolly, of later editions of the official *Times* stylebook, *The New York Times Manual of Style and Usage*. Every four weeks or so, starting in 1976, he compiled *Winners & Sinners*, a two-page collection of criticism and praise for articles, headlines, first paragraphs and turns of phrase, mixed with trenchant short essays about journalistic standards and ethics.[†]

Rosenthal had turned to Siegal to prepare the newspaper's submissions for the Pulitzer Prizes, with their carefully crafted cover letters and handsome presentations. "This is an extra task for you, Al, but I mean it as a great compliment." And Rosenthal sent Siegal to Columbus, Ohio, in July 1980 to observe a presentation by CompuServe, an early online pioneer, joining representatives from eleven newspapers who witnessed a display

---

[*] The retirement date, a tradition rather than a written policy, would slip in later years to the end of the editor's sixty-fifth year.

[†] *W&S* had been created in 1951 by Theodore M. Bernstein, himself a legendary *Times* editor, and was circulated to a select readership of *Times* devotees outside the paper.

of a balky but promising new technology that permitted people to read the latest news on electronic screens at their home. Siegal returned to write a report that was prescient. There was no immediate threat to the *Times*, he said. "In the long run, however—perhaps ten or fifteen years—electronic delivery will become increasingly important in proportion to our printed output," Siegal wrote, underlining his words for emphasis.

Siegal believed deeply in the institution. And that made his concerns about Rosenthal—the way he dealt with the people who worked for him, the tenor he set in the *Times* newsroom, his ideology and journalistic standards—all worthy of attention. Siegal, as powerful and respected as he was, was afraid to discuss any of this publicly, because Rosenthal's *Times* was a hierarchical place to work, where dissenters feared banishment. As successful and admired it was as a newspaper, it was not, by later standards, a healthy newsroom. But that was the way the *Times* had operated for decades.

* * *

From the start of his tenure as news editor, Siegal was a target. Rosenthal bullied Siegal just as Siegal bullied his underlings. Rosenthal would berate and humiliate him in view of his colleagues. Election Days were a "particular kind of hell": a high-pressure race against deadlines and the need to call races so readers would have the most up-to-date election results in their morning newspaper. His wife, Gretchen Leefmans, told him he had a terror—she called it a phobia—of going into work on that day of the year. Rosenthal would sit in his office and watch as the networks projected winners, using methods that, as Siegal would remind him, did not meet the *Times*'s more rigorous standards. Siegal's first election night as the news editor was in 1977, the year Ed Koch was elected mayor of New York City, defeating Mario Cuomo, the future governor who was the secretary of state at the time. There was a tradition of editors and their guests gathering on the third floor to observe the drama, the fast-paced night of updates, deadlines, and stories rewritten mid pressrun to reflect the latest results. There was the show of editors gathered around a reporter's desk as they called a race, dictating a new first paragraph and determining the moment to order that historic front-page headline. Rosenthal was following the returns in his office, drinking wine with his friends—among them Arthur Gelb and his wife, Barbara, as Siegal described the night. Siegal was across the room, monitoring the election returns. It was not going well. Rosenthal grew agitated, complaining that his editors were taking too long to decide the outcomes of races. The *Times* was printing thousands of newspapers that would be out of date the moment they were loaded onto the trucks waiting on West Forty-third Street. Rosenthal shouted his displeasure to Siegal, in earshot of the newsroom.

"Abjectly humiliating" was how Siegal described it. Once the big races were resolved—Koch won—Gelb tried to coax an intoxicated Rosenthal to leave the newsroom. Rosenthal, unsteady on his feet, started for the elevators and paused at the warren of staff mailboxes at the entrance to the City Room. He ripped a few name tags off the boxes and flung them to the floor—including the tag bearing Siegal's name. That shit Siegal, he said. I'll fix him.

It was not an unusual outburst. Siegal had walked into the executive editor's office on an election night after Rosenthal had killed an About New York column written by Francis X. Clines because Clines had gone home for the night without waiting for the final returns.

I wonder if I could make a plea to reconsider the decision about killing Clines's column, Siegal asked.

Rosenthal refused. You have had no experience in supervising reporters or editors, he said. What the hell do you know about how Clines should be dealt with for finking out on an assignment?

The next day, Siegal returned to Rosenthal's office. If you want someone else as news editor, you should tell me, he said.

What the hell are you talking about? Rosenthal asked. When Siegal reminded him of the words of the previous evening, Rosenthal waved him away. Well, that was last night, he said.

What bothered Siegal most, though it seems he never spoke about it publicly, was how, in his view, Rosenthal was undermining the integrity of the news report. Rosenthal was under attack by critics at publications like *The Village Voice* and the *Washington Journalism Review* for using his position to promote his ideological views and to reward his friends. And Siegal agreed; he thought Rosenthal's contempt for the left during the 1960s had warped his judgment as executive editor. "Abe was able to convince himself that small expressions of dissent were the opening wedge to totalitarianism, to Nazis, to Polish communism, he had great difficulty with the gradations of gray that appeared between black and white," Siegal told Dryfoos. "If a girl stood on the Columbia University campus and shouted, up against the wall, Mother Fucker, the very next step was going to be Hitler Youth."

Rosenthal might have been prudent in his caution when he oversaw the coverage during the 1968 Democratic convention, but the world had moved on, and Rosenthal had not. Rosenthal's mindset influenced his decisions on the reporters he hired, the stories assigned, and what he ordered on to the front page—and it led him, in Siegal's words, to "twist the paper." Looking back in 1987, with Rosenthal gone from the newsroom, Siegal could think of only one threat to the impartiality of *The New York Times,* and it came not from the left but from Rosenthal: "that in the guise of keeping the paper straight he made a concerted and polluting attempt to seed the place with right of center people and that carried some penalties" was how Siegal put it.

He disapproved of Rosenthal's hiring of Shirley Christian, a *Miami Herald* reporter covering Central America. Rosenthal met her on a trip to El Salvador in the early 1980s to visit Warren Hoge, the Rio de Janeiro bureau chief for the *Times,* who was, like Christian, covering the civil war between a right-wing government and Marxist guerrillas. Rosenthal spent a week there, including one evening when he invited Christian to join him for a pig roast at a local restaurant. She had written an article in the *Washington Journalism Review* in March 1982 arguing that correspondents from *The Washington Post* and *The New York Times* had jumped on "the Sandinista bandwagon." Rosenthal presented his decision to hire her as an effort to restore balanced coverage in his own newspaper. "I've never rejected a liberal because she was a liberal—but I have looked for people who had slightly different approaches in life," he said in an oral history in 1984. "I just hired one the other day, Shirley Christian, who won the Pulitzer Prize for the Miami Herald [for her coverage of Central America] and disagrees with most of our correspondents in Latin America, thought that they were too gentle with the Sandinistas— as did I." Christian was soon startled to see her name in *The Village Voice,* offered as evidence in the ideological case against Rosenthal.

At the end of 1982, the *Times* published a 6,100-word story in the Sunday Arts and Leisure section in defense of Jerzy Kosinski, the Polish American novelist. It was a response to an article in *The Village Voice* that accused Kosinski of hiring assistants to help write his novels and reported that the CIA "apparently played a clandestine role" in the publication of his first two books. Kosinski was friends with Rosenthal and Gelb. In response to the *Times*'s Kosinski story, Charles Kaiser, a former Rosenthal clerk, made a compelling case in *Newsweek*, where he was now the magazine's media critic, that Rosenthal and Gelb used their positions at the *Times* to help Kosinski and discredit the *Voice*. "Like many powerful editors at other papers, Gelb and Rosenthal sometimes encourage pieces about their friends," Kaiser wrote. "But the Kosinski piece provided the most dramatic evidence to date of their willingness to use the power of the *Times* to reward friends and punish enemies." Rosenthal, for his part, thought John Corry, who wrote the Kosinski piece, should have been awarded a Pulitzer Prize. "We avoided writing about him because he was our friend, and it was only when we realized that we were doing him an injustice by our refusal to recognize the case, that we got into it," he wrote Corry. Gay Talese, who had left the *Times*, noticed Rosenthal's difficulties and sent him a letter of support. "They have tried to destroy you before, and they will try again, and because you are who you are I know they will always fail," he wrote.

It was easier for Rosenthal and his friends to dismiss criticism from publications like the *Voice* or *The Nation*. But concerns about how the nation's most powerful editor was steering its most powerful newspaper were moving onto more mainstream platforms. Guilty as charged, Siegal thought after he read the *Newsweek* story about Rosenthal and Kosinski. Joseph Lelyveld, who had worked as a young reporter under Rosenthal, grew disillusioned with him over the final years: the tantrums, the favorites, the questionable stories. Max Frankel, from his perch in the editorial department, came to conclude that Rosenthal was letting his ideological views sway the *Times*'s news pages.

It's ironic—Abe's politics are better known than mine, and I am the opinion writer, Frankel remarked one day to his deputy.

Rosenthal was embattled and self-pitying.

I am tired of people talking about morale in the newsroom, he complained one day to Howell Raines, at the time a reporter in the newsroom. What about my morale?

He refused an interview with two reporters from the *Washington Journalism Review*, who were writing a profile, ignoring the urgings of the newspaper's communications director, Leonard R. Harris. "If no one does speak to them, it will be a very bad piece," Harris said. Rosenthal did not, and it was. When an author, Joseph C. Goulden, sought his cooperation for a biography, Rosenthal asked Nicholas Gage, an investigative reporter who had worked for the *Times*, to look into Goulden's background and to find out what kind of material he had gathered. Ultimately, Rosenthal decided to cooperate with Goulden, a decision he came to regret when he read the outcome.

Rosenthal felt persecuted, and often by fellow journalists such as Nat Hentoff, Jack Newfield, and Pete Hamill. "I've been probably the most criticized editor in the last twenty years—attacked and criticized," he said to Sydney Gruson in 1983.

"I think you can go back longer than 20 years," Gruson countered.

"20, 30, 40!" Rosenthal responded. "I'm not your average loveable editor. And that has bothered me a great deal. Like most people, I'm at least as thin-skinned as other people, probably more. It has troubled me over the years, and all my friends know it. I spent a lot of time trying to figure out why."

So it was that Rosenthal was heartened when he came across a favorable view of his tenure in "Retreat from Radicalism," an article by Dinesh D'Souza, in *Policy Review* from the conservative Heritage Foundation. Roy Cohn, the conservative lawyer, wrote Rosenthal to tell him that the essay, "a tribute to your even-handed guidance of the *Times* to its greatness" was well-deserved. Rosenthal thanked Cohn, adding, "I expect the Left to come out in another full barrage against me any day now and, brother, that ain't paranoia."

Years later, after Rosenthal had stepped down, Al Siegal told Max Frankel that he had forced himself to go on a diet because he was convinced Rosenthal would fire him and he would need to go out on to the job market. But Siegal was never fired. And he never quit. There was always that balance when it came to Abe Rosenthal, the one that shaped Sulzberger's calculations: the trade-off between the unhappy newsroom—the humiliations and petty punishments, piques and black-balling of reporters—and the excellence that he brought to the newspaper. John Darnton, a foreign correspondent, would stop by Rosenthal's office when he made his annual trips to New York for conversations that reminded him why Rosenthal was such an extraordinary editor. Do you think Africa can feed itself? Rosenthal asked Darnton, back from Nairobi: the kind of question that sent Darnton back to Africa with a dozen new story ideas. While Siegal would savor the days that Rosenthal was out of the office—"That was like dying and going to heaven," he said—he would soon notice that the paper had begun to lose its edge. He dreaded the front page meetings, but it was Rosenthal who found the holes in the story or spotted the pattern in an array of seemingly random events. "I hated the man a lot of the time, but you stuck around and took it because he was so good. Because you learned every day."

* * *

The gay rights movement blossomed during Rosenthal's years as executive editor, part of the social and political churn he confronted from his office on Times Square: the antiwar demonstrators, the women picketing outside the *Times* building, the civil rights suits from Black and Latino employees. But Rosenthal's discomfort with gay men and women demanding political equity was deep and personal. It would shape the paper's coverage of these issues, and his treatment of gay and lesbian employees in the newsroom, throughout his tenure.

In April 1975, the Sunday Travel section published a story on its front page about an all-gay cruise through the Gulf of Mexico for 316 gay men and women, which described, in language quite unusual for the newspaper at the time, the "mating ritual called 'cruising,'" and a scene of leather men, a drag queen, nudity, G-strings, and young men doing the bump as Labelle sang, *"Voulez-vous coucher avec moi, ce soir?"* The article, "The All-Gay Cruise: Prejudice and Pride," by Cliff Jahr, distressed Iphigene Sulzberger, who had made clear her objections to stories about sexual matters—and particularly homosexuality—in the pages of her family's newspaper. She registered her displeasure with her son, Punch, and the publisher confronted Frankel, the Sunday editor, who oversaw the Travel section. Sulzberger wanted Frankel to oust the travel editor who had printed the story and to refrain from publishing more stories on this subject in sections of the newspaper under his command. Frankel refused to remove the editor, saying that he himself was responsible for its publication, but agreed to no longer publish similar stories in the future. "We will respect your wish to avoid the subject for a long time, but I think you are wrong," Frankel told Sulzberger.

Rosenthal and the publisher had similar views on the political and social turmoil of the day, and he, too, was distressed by the story. The fallout from its publication would produce a chill on gay coverage that would last for years. At the publisher's request, Rosenthal banned the use of the word "gay" in the pages of the *Times*, except when the word appeared in a quote or was the name of an official organization, an edict that would remain in place until 1987. A few months after the cruise story, Bruce Voeller, the executive director of the National Gay Task Force, complained to Rosenthal about the "lack of reportage, or the attenuated coverage" of the campaign by gay organizations to transform the way the courts, Congress, state legislatures, and the psychiatric and medical professions treated homosexuals. (The *Times* had made no mention in its pages of a decision by the American Medical Association to recommend the repeal of legal strictures on consensual homosexual acts between adults.) When Sydney H. Schanberg, the metropolitan editor, proposed a series of stories on homosexuality in New York City, Rosenthal turned him down. "As a newspaper, we have done the subject justice—and more. . . . A great amount of coverage of homosexuality at this time would simply seem naïve and déjà vu."

The muted coverage under Rosenthal would continue through some of the most historic—and traumatic—moments in the history of the gay rights movement. In November 1980, a gunman armed with an Uzi submachine gun went on a shooting rampage in Greenwich Village, the heart of New York's gay community, blasting rounds of ammunition into a crowd of men lined up outside the Ramrod, a gay leather bar. Two were killed and six were wounded. The *Times* devoted just nineteen paragraphs on the front of its Metropolitan section to the shootings. In a 1982 interview with Terry Gross of *Fresh Air* for WUHY-FM, a National Public

Radio station in Philadelphia,* Randy Shilts, an openly gay reporter for the *San Francisco Chronicle*, who would go on to write a book on the AIDS epidemic, compared the attention the *Times* paid to the Ramrod shooting to its front-page coverage of the killing of four people in the bombing of a synagogue in Paris one month earlier. That story, illustrated with a large photograph, was prominently displayed on page A1. "They're really not outraged when gay people get murdered," he said.

In the 1980s, the AIDS epidemic hit New York's gay community particularly hard, but that would have been difficult to discern from the pages of the *Times*, as gay leaders wrote Sulzberger. "The coverage of the gay community has ignored our humanity," said one letter, signed by, among others, the leaders of the National Gay Task Force and the Gay Men's Health Crisis. "While it was an irritant in general feature and political stories, it has evoked a rage during the AIDS epidemic." The *Times* had failed to take note of a benefit for the Gay Men's Health Crisis, an organization that provided assistance to people with AIDS, which had drawn 17,601 people to Madison Square Garden, including the mayor, Ed Koch. "While it may be too much to ask you to follow your tradition of leading and advocating progressive social policy and change, it is not too much to ask that you revise your current destructive policy," Mel Rosen, the executive director of the GMHC, wrote Rosenthal.† The *Times* did not run a front-page story about AIDS until May 25, 1983, when Edward N. Brandt, Jr., an assistant secretary of health and human services, described it as the number-one priority of the Public Health Service. By that point, the Federal Centers for Disease Control had logged 1,450 AIDS cases; 558 of those had already resulted in death. This was nearly two years after the first mention of the disease in the *Times*, in a relatively short story by Lawrence K. Altman, the doc-

---

* The radio network, complying with the "personal attack" rule established by the Federal Communications Commission, sent Rosenthal a transcript of Shilts's remarks to provide him an opportunity to respond. There is no record of him replying.

† Rosenthal apologized for the paper's failure to cover the benefit. "I think you are quite right that the *New York Times* should have covered the Madison Square Garden benefit to assist victims and research on AIDS. I really have no explanation for it except for one of human error," he wrote Rosen.

tor who covered medical issues, under the headline "Rare Cancer Seen in 41 Homosexuals."

The AIDS epidemic would prove particularly challenging as the paper struggled with how to report on the subterranean world of gay sex clubs and bathhouses, which were drawing the attention of city health inspectors. The inspectors' reports, recounting the sex taking place in clubs like the Mineshaft, were described in lurid accounts published in the *Post* and the *Daily News*. In the early years of the epidemic, the *Times* had largely refrained from writing on its news pages about anal intercourse, the sexual practice that was soon identified as a potent means of transmission of the virus. By contrast, Frankel made a point of writing about anal intercourse in his editorials. "We did it very deliberately because the goddamn news columns were not talking about how this was spreading," Frankel said years later.

Rosenthal's unease with homosexuality created a tense atmosphere for the gay men and women who worked under him. Two of Rosenthal's clerks—Charles Kaiser and Richard Meislin—were gay. They took care to guard their private lives, concerned their careers could be derailed if knowledge of their sexuality spread through the newsroom. Meislin would go on to become a correspondent in Albany, Miami, and Mexico City. In 1985, Rosenthal would recall Meislin from Mexico City, where he had been stationed for two and a half years, for no announced reason, though many people in the newsroom suspected it was because Rosenthal had learned that Meislin was gay. Rosenthal would deny this over the years, but, given his well-known discomfort with homosexuality and Meislin's talents as a correspondent, his denial was widely discounted.

Though Rosenthal's colleagues, among them Frankel, wondered if the executive editor shared Sulzberger's views on homosexuality or if he simply was doing the publisher's bidding, Rosenthal's antagonism toward homosexuals was deeply rooted. He wrote in his journal that while he would hire a homosexual as a critic, he would not appoint one to cover a sensitive beat like the Pentagon or city hall. And he had a dark view of their presence at the newspaper. "The real problem of hiring homosexuals," Rosenthal wrote, was they formed cliques in the newsroom.

"The homosexual clique was a problem because it was usually subterranean, which gave it a kind of conspiracy atmosphere, and because homosexuals in the clique always were convinced or tried to convince themselves that they were wiser, more acute, 'better' than the others—the old breed," he wrote.

One afternoon, he pressed Siegal, whose job included hiring copy editors, about his suspicion that there were clusters of homosexual editors on the metropolitan and national desks.

I am worried about homosexuals in the newspaper—are you hiring a lot of homosexuals? Rosenthal asked him. Siegal said he wasn't knowingly hiring them, but he wasn't shunning them, either. Rosenthal went on, as Siegal described the moment, to express "great revulsion and went on about it for quite a while about the idea of these people becoming a subversive force in the office and affecting the content of the paper subversively." A few moments later, Sulzberger walked in, and Rosenthal shared with the publisher his concerns about homosexual editors.

Punch Sulzberger nodded in agreement as Rosenthal repeated his warnings about homosexuals as a "subversive force" in the newsroom. This was the view from the most senior level of the newspaper. And it would shape the way the *Times* would cover gay and lesbian issues, and treat its gay and lesbian reporters and editors, for as long as Abe Rosenthal and Punch Sulzberger were in power.

CHAPTER 6

Upward and Onward

On January 28, 1986, the space shuttle *Challenger* lifted off Cape Canaveral carrying a crew of seven astronauts, including a high school teacher from Concord, New Hampshire, Christa McAuliffe. At 11:39 A.M., when the spacecraft was ten miles into the atmosphere, it ignited in an explosion of flame and smoke as thousands watched on the ground and millions more on television. The seven crew members perished; McAuliffe's two children and her husband, along with her students and others in classrooms across the nation, were among the spectators who watched the space craft disintegrate. This was the twenty-fifth mission for the shuttle. In New York, editors were gathered in a morning meeting at the *Times* headquarters when Howell Raines, a deputy editor, on a speakerphone from Washington, D.C., broke into the discussion.

Wait a minute—I think we better all return to our battle stations. The *Challenger* just exploded.

A. M. Rosenthal was at his desk when his secretary walked in to alert him. "Oh my God!" he exclaimed. "Was it instantaneous? I mean, did they know, any warning?" It was the worst tragedy in the history of the space program. President Reagan canceled his State of the Union address that night.

At moments like this, when the entire *New York Times* rises to report on an event of huge consequence, every aspect of the next day's newspaper is a matter of elaborate deliberation. The choice of writers, the selection of photographs, the framing of stories, the first paragraph of the main article, and the banner headline across the top of a front page that would end up framed on walls and immortalized in commemorative books. Should it be a six-column headline? Should every story on the front page be devoted to this event? How many pages should be set aside for the coverage? These were visual cues that communicated the newspaper's judgment of its historical significance to its readers. Rosenthal paused after learning of the explosion to consider whether this was simply a terrible accident or a moment that would reshape the nation. It did not take long for him to decide. The space program would never be the same. It would scar the nation's sense of confidence, and it was a shared horror; people would remember where they were when they saw the spacecraft explode. This was all clear to him as the editors gathered in his office to plan the next day's newspaper. Susan Dryfoos, the director and founder of Times History Productions, happened to be in the building that day with a camera crew, to film a documentary as part of her project. "There are one or two things that ought to be touched on somewhere," Rosenthal said, wearing red suspenders, his tie askew, a pen grasped in one hand. "Could it have been sabotage? We just can't pretend that nobody is thinking about that."

Rosenthal declared that every story on the front page would be about the tragedy, and ten pages inside would be cleared of advertisements to make way for the coverage, which was what the *Times* did at moments like this. After the stories were assigned and the reporters dispatched, Al Siegal walked into Rosenthal's office to discuss the headline that would appear on the top of the next day's newspaper.

In extraordinary events, Siegal told him, we try to keep a certain continuity across the history of the paper: a headline that evokes the spirit of a previous page of comparable gravity. What he had in mind were historic one-line headlines, such as "Nixon Resigns" or "Men Walk on Moon."

The Shuttle Explodes, Rosenthal said.

That's not newsy enough, Siegal said, listing off suggestions: Seven Die As Shuttle Explodes, Seven Die in Blast of Shuttle. Each time Siegal came back with another idea, Rosenthal had the same response.

The Shuttle Explodes, Rosenthal said. It's stately. It's dignified. It's icy cold. It's blood-curdling in its simplicity.

That was the headline.

When Rosenthal arrived at his office the next morning, desks across the newsroom were stacked with copies of the morning newspaper, with a front page ("THE SHUTTLE EXPLODES") that was at once elegant and shocking. "The space shuttle Challenger exploded in a ball of fire shortly after it left the launching pad today, and all seven astronauts on board were lost," the first paragraph, by William J. Broad, who was the science reporter, reported with the understatement the *Times* preferred in moments like this. Rosenthal did not often write notes by hand; his penmanship was crabbed. But on this morning, he sat down and wrote a note to the publisher that read almost like a valedictory.

"We put out a good paper today," it said. "It reflected the skills and creativity of the fine staff. But I simply want to tell you that our ability to do it rests on the fact that you, your parents and your sisters have honored and enriched the heritage and tradition entrusted to you.

"I wanted to say so with some formality and to express my thanks to you and your family for what you have done for us, the paper, and I believe, the country. Your friend and colleague, Abe." Sulzberger returned the sentiment. "This morning's *New York Times* was newspapering at its best," he wrote his executive editor.

On that day, Rosenthal demonstrated with his focus, drive, news judgment, and historical sensibility why he was a legendary *Times* editor, and why so many people had for so long been willing to overlook his excesses and abuses. It would be Rosenthal's final opportunity to lead his newsroom on a story of this magnitude, the kind of event that shapes an editor's legacy, though for many reasons—starting with his own refusal to accept the inevitability of his departure—he could not have realized that. Two weeks later, Harrison Salisbury, a retired senior editor, advised Sulzberger that the time had come to remove Rosenthal. The newsroom was in turmoil, and Rosenthal's life was in shambles. Sulzberger told Salisbury he had reached the same conclusion.

* * *

It could not have been easy for Sulzberger. He and Rosenthal had built the foundation of the modern *Times*. They had elevated each other's reputations even as they overlooked—and in some cases fed—each other's flaws and prejudices. But Sulzberger had been thinking about the post-Rosenthal era for at least three years. He had discussed it in an interview with Sydney Gruson on March 29, 1983, for the *Times* oral history project. There would be a new executive editor and a new publisher, he said, since the time was approaching for Sulzberger to step down from the post he had held since 1963. He had telegraphed his intentions to the public (and Rosenthal) through Gruson, who gave an interview for an article that had appeared in the *Washington Journalism Review* one year before the *Challenger* explosion, in January 1985. "Abe is under no illusions about it and Abe has accepted for some time that he's stepping down as executive editor at the age of sixty-five," Gruson said.

Rosenthal had gone to elaborate lengths to show the publisher that he was preparing for the next generation of leadership. He'd announced promotions for high-level editors (all men and all white), which he presented as try-outs for the post-Rosenthal era: Craig R. Whitney. Warren Hoge. John Vinocur. He called them in to explain what he was doing. There are rumors out there that I don't want to retire, Rosenthal said. That's not true. Rosenthal ended his talks with an admonition: Keep your mouths shut. He did not want to see lists of who was up and who was down in *New York* magazine or *The Village Voice.*

It was not convincing. Sulzberger and Rosenthal flew to London in the summer of 1984 and spent an evening with Joseph Lelyveld, who was the London bureau chief. They gathered for cocktails at Claridge's, where Rosenthal ran down the moves he was making on his chessboard. Lelyveld glanced at Sulzberger and thought, Doesn't the publisher have anything to do with this? Sulzberger listened silently, finally saying, Can we go to dinner now?

As 1985 came to a close, the reports about the *Times* and its executive editor were becoming difficult to ignore: the turmoil in the newsroom, the concerns about Rosenthal's ideology and his relationships with powerful figures in Manhattan. On August 5, 1985, the *Times* published a profile of Mort Zuckerman—the editor in chief of *U.S. News & World Report*, the owner of *The Atlantic Monthly*, and a wealthy real estate developer—on the front page of the Metropolitan Report. Zuckerman had won a bidding contest for the rights to develop the former New York Coliseum property on Columbus Circle in Manhattan. His company paid $455.1 million for the parcel, which was owned by New York City and the Metropolitan Transportation Authority. "He had just conquered

New York's real-estate world, more than five years of plotting come to fruition, but Mortimer B. Zuckerman—the flamboyant 48-year-old Canadian-born developer and magazine publisher—was not easing off a bit," read the profile, written by Jane Perlez. Zuckerman and Rosenthal moved in the same social circles. Rosenthal called him "Morty." On the morning the story appeared, Zuckerman wrote Rosenthal, listing fourteen objections to the article—from what he asserted were outright mistakes (the cost of the acquisition) to what he deemed loaded characterizations about his business dealings.

Considering the ambition and sheer size of each day's *Times,* errors inevitably crept into its pages: a wrong age, a misspelled name (including the name "Sulzberger," from time to time), an incorrect date, a quotation imprecisely rendered. These were addressed in a correction box that appeared every day on the front of the second section. But a few years earlier, Rosenthal determined the correction box could not deal with the more nuanced journalistic errors that also threatened the integrity of the *Times:* mistakes in tone, harsh language, the absence of balance, the omission of exculpatory information. He wanted the *Times* to establish a new platform, an Editors' Note to address those kinds of errors. "Under the heading 'Editors' Note' we will amplify articles or rectify what the editors consider significant lapses of fairness, balance or perspective," Rosenthal said in announcing its creation.

Rosenthal's editors did not share his enthusiasm for these notes, to his great irritation, and for a while, he wrote each one himself. "I have received virtually no cooperation," he complained to his editors. "This is not a voluntary matter and please do not underestimate my determination on this."

The Zuckerman profile struck Rosenthal as the kind of story he had in mind when he created the note.* Rosenthal thought it snide, and he called his late-shift editors shortly after the first edition appeared on

---

* Perlez had been told to "rev up" the story after she first filed it—it was too flat, John Vinocur, the metropolitan editor told her, as she recalled it—and she knew how to do that; before coming to the *Times,* Perlez had written for the *SoHo Weekly News* and the *Daily News.*

newsstands to express his objections.* A withering editors' note appeared two days after the story was published. "Through opinionated phrases and unattributed characterizations, the article established a tone that cast its subject in an unfavorable light," it read. "The pejorative phrases and anonymous criticism created an unbalanced portrait. They should not have appeared." The note was harsher about Perlez, at least implicitly, than anything Perlez had written about Zuckerman. Perlez was shocked (as, in fact, were many people in the newsroom). She was certain her career was in jeopardy.† "Gosh Abe! What's happened? Has Mortie cast a spell on you?" wrote Robert Manning, who had been the editor of *The Atlantic Monthly* until Zuckerman purchased the magazine and dismissed him in a falling-out. Murray Kempton, in his *Newsday* column, called it a "genuine rudeness to Perlez."

Rosenthal brushed away the suggestion that he was doing a favor for a friend. "The idea that Zuckerman could persuade me to do something, it's crazy," he told *The Washington Post*. "Who's Zuckerman? It's crazy. I met him two or three times at dinner." Zuckerman ribbed Rosenthal after he read that, and Rosenthal assured Zuckerman that no disrespect was intended. The words "eyes only" were scribbled at the bottom of Rosenthal's note to Zuckerman, while across the top it was marked PERSONAL & CONFIDENTIAL—SECRET. "The quote was accurate, but she didn't get the inflection," Rosenthal wrote, referring to the *Post* reporter, Eleanor Randolph, who would later join the *Times*'s editorial board. "The inflection was: 'Who's Zuckerman? Who's anybody? Who's the Pope?—to influence The Times! The main thing is I am happy I did what I did about Zuckerman, whoever he may be, and I would do it again."

But the editors' notes became one more item in the bill of particulars making the case for an editorship in decline. As news editor, Al Siegal's

---

* Rosenthal had just encountered Zuckerman at a dinner party, though he asserted, responding to questions from a *Fortune* magazine reporter, that there was no connection between that and his late-night call to his editors.

† Jane Perlez's career was in fact not finished at all; she would stay with the *Times* for more than thirty years, and she would win a Pulitzer Prize for covering the war against the Taliban and al-Qaeda in Pakistan and Afghanistan before being appointed the paper's bureau chief in Beijing.

domain included corrections, so the editors' notes fell to him. Rosenthal would walk over with a story that upset him—about Zuckerman or someone else in Rosenthal's circle. "And with all the good will in the world I would agree with him, proceed to put the editors' note in the paper and then find out after the fact that there was a personal ax being ground. And I felt more used each time," Siegal said.

A month after the editors' note on the Zuckerman story, *The Village Voice* ran a cover story, illustrated by a warlike Edward Sorel drawing that depicted Rosenthal's head as a tank turret, his nose as a blazing gun firing upon and decapitating the columnist Sydney Schanberg, whom Punch Sulzberger had removed from the Op-Ed page, in part at the urging of Rosenthal. The headline was "Fear and Favor at 'The New York Times': Pete Hamill on the Zapping of Sydney Schanberg and Other Atrocities."

"There seems to be something drastically wrong at the Times these days," Hamill wrote. "Too many of its reporters and editors are living in a state of fear; too often the news pages appear to be used for the granting or soliciting of favors. The country's greatest newspaper is shifting to the right, but nobody on the staff will talk on the record about this momentous event." Hamill was a respected figure in New York journalism, which gave his essay extra weight. Schanberg was popular among liberals in New York and had led the charge against a proposal to build Westway—a proposed landfill project along the Hudson River, with a subsurface highway and new development parcels and parkland at ground level. Schanberg had questioned the lack of scrutiny of Westway from the *Times* and other New York newspapers. In one column—it turned out to be his last at the *Times*—he contrasted the attention his own newspaper devoted to the clash between chef Paul Prudhomme and city health inspectors, who had closed his Columbus Avenue restaurant because of a fly infestation, with the attention paid to Westway.

"Our newspapers, oddly, can't seem to find space for Westway and its scandal. The lone exception in the region is the *Newark Star-Ledger*, which has lately provided first-rate coverage," Schanberg wrote.

Op-ed columnists at the *Times* are employed at the discretion of the publisher, and it was Punch Sulzberger who took Schanberg's column from him. But Rosenthal had become one of Schanberg's biggest critics and would raise his concerns at his weekly lunches with Sulzberger in the publisher's dining room.

Schanberg appealed to Sulzberger to reconsider the decision to remove him as a columnist, but the publisher refused, describing Schanberg's work as disloyal. Harrison Salisbury, who learned of the conversation, was convinced Rosenthal was behind this; that was language Rosenthal had used with the publisher in urging Schanberg's removal. "This is what obviously got under Punch's skin with his passion for neatness and order," Salisbury wrote in a note to himself after visiting Schanberg.

Schanberg and Rosenthal had not always been estranged. When Schanberg was a war correspondent in Cambodia a decade earlier and defied a request from editors in New York to evacuate Phnom Penh as Cambodia fell to the Khmer Rouge, Rosenthal cabled his respect and concern: THE ONLY THING EYE ASK AS YOUR FRIEND AND ADMIRER AND COLLEAGUE IS THAT YOU REVIEW THE SITUATION CONSTANTLY. NO RPT NO STORY IS WORTH YOUR LIFE. WITH MUCH LOVE. ROSENTHAL. But Rosenthal soured on him after Schanberg returned to New York and became metropolitan editor, where he pushed for stories about the grittier side of New York. He was "terribly dissatisfied" with how Schanberg was running the Metropolitan Report, Rosenthal told another senior editor, Seymour Topping. Schanberg was "covering New York City in a dreary manner and giving no real indication of the vitality and interest of the city."*

Schanberg's dismissal drew protests from community leaders, academics, readers, neighborhood activists, and elected officials—among them Carol Bellamy, the city council president. Gruson came to the publisher's defense. "Mr. Schanberg was not fired for opposing Westway," he wrote to one reader. "Indeed, Mr. Schanberg was not fired, period. The paper's publisher, Arthur Ochs Sulzberger, exercised his prerogative to dislike what the column had become and to end it. Mr. Sulzberger believed the tone too shrill and the focus too narrow." Schanberg's ouster

---

* At that, Rosenthal was echoing the concerns he had heard from Walter Mattson, the president of the *Times*. "I am bothered both personally and professionally by the tendency of the *New York Times* to look at every negative announcement about Manhattan as another nail in the coffin of New York City."

drew praise from some notable quarters as well. "THE NEW YORK TIMES took a great step forward with the discontinuance of Sydney Schanberg's column, 'New York,'" Donald Trump wrote Rosenthal. "Mr. Schanberg totally disregarded the true facts of a story in order to make his preconceived (and usually incorrect) point. . . . Congratulations!"

Schanberg's dismissal fed the fire of negative stories about Rosenthal, and once again he felt himself the victim. "I have been under attack now for twenty years, almost ever since I became an editor," he wrote Father Andrew M. Greeley, the priest and sociologist. "I realize that part of it must come from whatever I contribute in the way of my own personality, but I am also intelligent enough to realize that most of it is political— I am seen as a man of the right, which I am not, but I am a devout centrist as far as the paper is concerned, which is pretty much the same to the left." He went on to confide "something that is almost too painful for me to say": that he and his wife, Ann, had separated. "We were not living well together, which I know was mostly my fault." To a nephew, Harry Marten, a professor at Union College in Schenectady, Rosenthal offered ruminations that hinted at an editor at least contemplating the approaching end of a career.

"Perhaps the most important thing that aroused hostility was that I was cast—and cast myself—as the agent of change on The New York Times," he wrote, a turn of phrase that would be invoked twenty years later by another hard-driving executive editor. "We were getting quite stale as a newspaper and set in our ways. It was always a good paper, but it was losing touch with economic reality and with its readers."

There had been one name missing from the list of potential successors Rosenthal had floated. Over lunch with the publisher in his private dining room, Max Frankel broached Rosenthal's retirement. Don't respond to this, Frankel told Sulzberger, but if it came to you wanting me to be executive editor, I would gladly accept. Sulzberger thanked Frankel, and they moved to the next course.

Sydney Gruson visited London that Thanksgiving, as 1985 drew to a close. There, he sat at a manual typewriter and for two hours clacked out a letter that laid out the publisher's options for a Rosenthal succession. "The situation, I believe, has now come down to a choice that can probably be made as well now as in six or nine or 18 months," he wrote Sulzberger. "The choice is between a Frankel whose capabilities, personality and character you know and one of the other players Abe has put in motion, all of whom are admirable people but about whom not enough is known." Rosenthal would take a Frankel appointment as a harsh slap, Gruson said. But the benefits of selecting Frankel—and of "making known soon that Max will take over"—were tremendous. "Much of the unproductive tension in the newsroom will begin to dissipate with the announcement." Gruson doubted Rosenthal would graciously agree to leave. "But if it is possible to get him to accept gracefully a Frankel succession, you are the only person who can do it. . . . It is fraught with difficulties and tension. But it is worth doing."

* * *

On the day of the *Challenger* explosion, Rosenthal had another sixteen months until his sixty-fifth birthday. He did not want to retire. That was clear to the editors and reporters who worked with him every day, and who had learned to discount his talk about lists of potential successors as empty gestures intended to appease the publisher. He had balked at granting an interview to Eleanor Randolph, who was preparing a three-part series on his legacy for *The Washington Post,* until Robert G. Kaiser, the assistant managing editor of the *Post,* stepped in, invoking Ben Bradlee, the executive editor. "Ben, to the best of his recollection, has never declined to speak to a reporter from *The New York Times,*" Kaiser wrote Rosenthal. "You, of all people, ought to be able to find time to see Eleanor for these pieces, which we consider important. Please consult your conscience, again."

Rosenthal always held out the hope that Sulzberger would waive the customary retirement. Rosenthal had defined his life by where he had made his career. Why would the publisher want him to leave? They had been partners for two of the best decades in the history of the *Times.* Had he not, in his view, delivered the Sulzbergers profit and prestige, pulled the paper back from the financial precarity of the 1970s, championed the sections that were now the envy of the newspaper industry? Was his *New York Times* not the best newspaper in the country, as demonstrated yet again by the coverage of the *Challenger* explosion—for which the paper would be awarded the Pulitzer Prize for National Reporting?

Sulzberger was doing what any conscientious corporate leader would do to ensure the continuity of the organization. But his decision to push ahead, despite their history, despite Rosenthal's resistance, despite everything Rosenthal had done for the family newspaper, also reflected Sulzberger's concerns with his executive editor in these closing years.

He could have permitted Rosenthal to stay longer; Turner Catledge did not retire from the newsroom until he turned sixty-seven. But Punch Sulzberger did not want to leave the task of removing Rosenthal to his successor. This, he expected, would be his son, Arthur, Jr., who had joined the paper as a reporter in the Washington bureau, hired away from the Associated Press, at the end of 1978 and was now in New York, working his way through the building. There was a chill between the executive editor and the publisher's son. Rosenthal never thought Arthur, Jr., had the journalistic credentials to fill his father's job. When Arthur Sulzberger arrived in New York as a young editor working on the metropolitan desk, he would slip off his shoes and stroll the newsroom in socks. Don't ever come into my office again wearing your socks, Rosenthal told young Sulzberger one day. That would come, in Rosenthal's mind, to symbolize the young man's lack of respect for the institution. Arthur Sulzberger, circulating with reporters in New York and in Washington, heard of their concerns about the Rosenthal newsroom; about the atmosphere of favoritism and banishment. He would take gay employees to lunch, assuring them that the era of fear under Rosenthal (and his father) would end when a new regime took over. That got back to Rosenthal, who went to the publisher to demand that his son apologize. The publisher summoned both of them to his office and instructed Arthur, Jr., to apologize for disparaging the executive editor. It all made for a strained relationship between two generations on the hinge of a transition—between an heir apparent rising to take over the newspaper and an older editor on his way out. Years later, as he approached his own retirement, Arthur, Jr., was still grateful that Punch Sulzberger had eased Rosenthal out before he took over. It was, he said, "a blessing."

Rosenthal's personal life was spiraling out of control, and Sulzberger thought that was contributing to his erratic management. He was dating the actress Katharine Balfour, who played the mother in the movie *Love Story*, and would bring her through the newsroom—a reminder of the dalliances that had contributed to the breakup of his marriage. He was also dating one of his secretaries, which was an open and uncomfortable secret among his colleagues. He was beginning to date Shirley Lord, a magazine and newspaper editor and a novelist. The breakup of Rosenthal's marriage presented an awkward situation for Sulzberger. "I hate to raise this problem," he wrote Rosenthal. But given that he had moved out of his penthouse on Central Park West, the publisher could no longer authorize paying for a security service and a *Times* telephone line there. *Spy* magazine taunted him about his relationship with Lord, whom he had met through Beverly Sills at the Four Seasons and would go on to marry. Rosenthal would come into the newsroom and retreat to his office. "He didn't have a nervous breakdown, but he was close to it," Sulzberger told Susan E. Tifft and Alex S. Jones for *The Trust*, their 1999 book about the Sulzberger family and the *Times*. "He would get so distraught that he couldn't operate well. It was a hell of a problem."

Bill Kovach visited him in the newsroom, and Rosenthal invited him back to his office. Rosenthal seemed haunted, insecure, and isolated, pleading for Kovach's friendship and forgiveness. Kovach found himself feeling sorry for him. Harrison Salisbury raised concerns about Rosenthal's behavior over lunch with Sydney Gruson. It's turning into a Greek tragedy: he's plucking out his own eyes, Salisbury said.

As June began, Rosenthal was not acting like he was on his way out. He sent the publisher a "couple of things you might want to know about" memo on what he had in the works, including a redesign of the Metropolitan Report and the dispatching of Maureen Dowd—"one of our very best reporters"—from New York to the Washington bureau. And on June 18, Rosenthal made his final major decision as executive editor. He told Sulzberger that the time had come for the *Times* to begin using the honorific "Ms." "I think we did exactly the right thing in refusing to accept it in the beginning," Rosenthal wrote. The situation "strikes me as different now." Rosenthal wrote a memorandum to his staff announcing the new policy. "Until now, 'Ms.' has not been used because of the belief that it had not passed sufficiently into the language to be accepted as common usage," the note stated. "The *Times* believes now that 'Ms.' has become a part of the language, and is changing its policy."

The *Times*'s resistance had left it trailing other publications and much of the country. "When, oh when, will the *New York Times* move into the 20th Century with other enlightened publications, and abandon this rigid insistence on archaic titles which identify women by their marital status?" Judith Hope, the supervisor of the town of East Hampton, New York, asked Al Siegal after getting off the phone with a *Times* reporter. "*Please*. This is truly demeaning. I'm certain many other women share my view."

For *Times* reporters, the policy forced an uncomfortable reckoning in the course of interviews with women: the mutually uncomfortable moment in which they were forced to inquire about their subject's marital status. Craig Whitney, an assistant managing editor, alerted Rosenthal in early September 1985 that at a meeting with younger reporters and editors in late summer, "the issue of Ms. came up, vehemently, at the end and in the corridors afterward." A reporter told him that she just dropped second and third references to women in her stories to avoid the problem. "There's a lot of passion among the women, particularly, who have their own strong opinions about whether we should use Ms.," Whitney told him. The battle was moving to the boardroom as well. Paula Kassell, a feminist and journalist, had long ago purchased ten shares of New York Times Company stock to gain admission to the shareholders' meeting, where she would challenge the publisher about this policy, and in April 1986, she demanded that the publisher convene a panel of language experts to consider the question. Sulzberger agreed. It never got that far; Rosenthal changed the policy two months later.

Rosenthal was celebrated. Anna Quindlen ran up to him in the newsroom and threw her arms around him. If I had known it would have made all of you so happy, I would have done it sooner, he said. Betsy Wade was working as an editor on the national desk the night the announcement was made and peered over her computer screen as a delegation of women, including Gloria Steinem, arrived in the newsroom. They carried a bouquet of flowers tucked into a *Ms.* magazine tote bag and headed for Rosenthal's office, where Steinem hugged him. Wade thought of Rosenthal's resistance to the Women's Caucus, and of how long he had blocked the word "Ms." from the pages of the *Times*. "I was taken aback," she wrote years later, describing how she felt watching Rosenthal being honored by these women.

Two weeks later, on June 30, 1986, Punch Sulzberger invited Rosenthal to dinner at Alfredo's, a white-tablecloth Italian restaurant on Central Park South. It was one of the publisher's favorites, though it had seen better days.* Sulzberger went to dinner knowing that Rosenthal was not ready to step down. But if anyone could ease Rosenthal out of the newsroom, it was his partner of nearly twenty years. Sulzberger offered him a twice-a-week column on the Op-Ed page and assured him it was a distinguished new chapter in a distinguished career. Rosenthal left the dinner stricken, the distress etched across his face when he saw Shirley Lord later that night. Sulzberger wanted to celebrate the occasion with a party, but Rosenthal refused. There would be a dinner at the home of Henry Kissinger, who insisted that something be done to honor Rosenthal's career. There were the notes of congratulations from Iphigene Ochs Sulzberger, elected officials, academics, rival newspaper editors, and his colleagues at the *Times*—including Salisbury, who wrote, "You've had a great run—better I think, than even you now realize, and it is a good time to pass on the baton, as it were."

Rosenthal wrote about the dinner with Sulzberger years later, for a memoir he never completed. He called it "the Last Supper." He'd thought for a moment of trying to change Sulzberger's mind but realized it was pointless. "I knew that his duty was causing him pain." At one point in the memoir, Rosenthal engaged with a bizarre fantasy in which he leapt up, grabbed Sulzberger by the throat, and "screamed that the man he was naming as my successor would go down in journalistic history, down and down, and so would The Times, until its very name became a hissing and a stench."

On July 15, 1986, Sulzberger bid Frankel to join him for a lunch in the publisher's private dining room. Punch Sulzberger was discreet when it came to matters of family, *Times* business, and personnel, and he would glance away when anyone raised a matter with which he did not want to

---

* "Few places can match it for indifference toward guests who are not regulars," Mimi Sheraton said in her *Times* review of the restaurant several years before their dinner.

engage. But on this day, Sulzberger was direct. The time had come for Rosenthal to leave. Max Frankel would be the next executive editor. As a rule, Sulzberger did not serve alcohol at the luncheons in his private dining room—iced tea was the drink of choice—but the two drank spirits (exactly what spirits has been lost to time) to toast the new era. Frankel had a historian's appreciation of the *Times*, and of himself, and prepared a written chronology of the events around his appointment: *"EXEC ED: How it happened."* It began with the lunch and the mandate he heard that day from Sulzberger: "mission: further raise quality of product; restore calm; make place content and creative and fun. also: new plant, color?" Plant meant a printing plant, while color referred to the effort to add color to the black-and-white pages of the *Times*. Sulzberger made clear what he wanted from the next executive editor: He told him to make a great newspaper even greater, make the newsroom a happy place again—and prepare his son to be the next publisher. Frankel recounted, in shorthand, the conversation with Rosenthal the next day about when the transfer of power would take place. "AMR chooses end of yr."

That September, Rosenthal gave a heads-up to his son Andrew, who was a reporter at the Associated Press. "I want to tell you now about what is taking place in my own professional life," he said. "I will leave the post of executive editor and become a columnist for the *Times*. Max Frankel will succeed me and Artie Gelb will get the title of managing editor. There are rumors about this of course but I am not confirming them to anybody except family and a few close friends.

"I would have preferred to stay Execedit"—his portmanteau for executive editor—"if that had been possible, for a number of years," he wrote. "That would have meant cutting into column writing time but I would have preferred it. If there had been a candidacy discernibly better than Max I might have delayed it. But there wasn't. He is a decent and ethical man well known and respected and I think his selection is an obvious one.

"This means, Andy, that if you wish, you can now come to the *Times* virtually anytime, if you wish to do so."

What Rosenthal wrote to his son about Frankel was the opposite of how he felt. Sulzberger had chosen a colleague and competitor that Rosenthal thought did not deserve to succeed him.

The end of the Rosenthal era was marked by an unbylined story across three columns on the front page. "A. M. Rosenthal Leaving Executive Editor's Post at the Times, and Max Frankel Is His Successor." It appeared on October 12, 1986. "It will be upward and onward for each of us and for all of us together and for our beloved newspaper," Rosenthal wrote the staff. He was leaving behind a newsroom that was, for the most part, relieved to see him go. He would long be held up as a model of how not to run a newsroom.

Yet the *Times* Rosenthal left behind was a far better newspaper than the one he took over from James B. Reston in 1969, and it was because of his journalistic flair and sophistication and his understanding of the newspaper where he had made his life. The *Times* had confronted challenges—the Pentagon Papers, the economic downturn in New York City, the exodus of many of its readers to the suburbs—that under another executive editor might have permanently weakened it. Instead, Rosenthal was leaving his successor a newspaper that had been reimagined and positioned to continue its dominant role in American journalism. How bad could he be? "To say that I was impossible to work for and yet managed to be part of the greatest achievements within ten, fifteen years in the history of the *New York Times,* is contradictory," Rosenthal said after he stepped down. "Was I difficult to work for? I'm sure I was."

But was that trade-off worth it, or even necessary? The *Times* would always turn to its greatest journalists when it came time to select the executive editor. Yet journalists are by their nature self-reliant, secretive, insecure, competitive, sensitive, and suspicious. They have sprawling egos and high self-regard. Those are fine qualities for a correspondent, but perhaps not for someone charged with managing an organization teeming with egos, talent, daily conflicts, and drama, under such scrutiny by its readers, its employees, and by the world. There was a lesson in Rosenthal's decline and the tumult of his final years. But it was not one that the *Times* would learn for a long time to come.

PART II

THE NEWSROOM

1986–1994

CHAPTER 7

Changing Course

t had been ten years since a new executive editor had been appointed at *The New York Times.* On October 10, 1986, the evening before the *Times* would announce the change in leadership, Max Frankel marked the moment with a note to the man whose job he would assume. "It's Friday evening and our worlds are about to turn and I wish at that precise moment we could properly touch, even kiss," he wrote to A. M. Rosenthal, in flowing cursive drawn with his distinctive black felt-tip pen. "You have made us all distinguished, made a great paper greater, enlarged the mind and spirit of American journalism and made the task of succeeding you a misery, even in joy."

The note was effusive and sentimental. As a measure of the relationship between the incoming and outgoing executive editors of the *Times,* it was also somewhat disingenuous. "I had no plan except to be not-Abe," Frankel wrote years later. He did not approve of how Rosenthal had led the newsroom, the atmosphere of fear and favoritism that marked his tenure. "The trouble was that Abe displayed his angers and affections in ways that often terrorized subordinates and left him constantly wondering why he was not better loved," he said.

From the moment Frankel moved into the executive editor's office, overlooking Forty-fourth Street and Shubert Alley on the north side of the newsroom, he defined himself by who he was not—his predecessor. He was explicit about it when he talked about Rosenthal after he retired, but in those first days in the newsroom in 1986, it was not what he said but what he did as he followed Punch Sulzberger's direction to make the newsroom "a happy place again." Frankel wandered among the desks, chatting and laughing, pausing to compliment reporters for stories he had stayed up late the night before to read in a first-edition copy of the *Times* that was delivered to his home each evening in Riverdale, a verdant, hilly enclave in the Bronx. If I walk past somebody's desk and they've done a great story and I don't say something when I walk past them, I've wrecked that person for the day, Frankel said at the time.*

He accepted an invitation from Michael Oreskes, an investigative reporter on the metropolitan desk, to attend a party for reporters and editors at Oreskes's twelfth-floor penthouse apartment on West End Avenue and Ninety-ninth Street, after a staff game of touch football in Central Park. Frankel lingered well after the sun set over the Hudson River, drinking beers with his staff, who couldn't quite believe that they were socializing with the new executive editor of the *Times*. He began replacing editors from the Rosenthal regime and delegating to their successors the authority that Rosenthal had kept to himself. He considered Rosenthal's huge office ostentatious and ordered it divided, creating a separate room for the front page meetings and a more modest space for his own desk. He began permitting reporters to have two bylines in the same day's newspaper and eased the policy that prohibited more than one byline on a story, a way to address what had long been a source of resentment and rivalry. He urged reporters not to be afraid to offer perspective and insight in the authoritative voice of the *Times*, instead of falling back on the crutch of quoting an expert at a university.

And the *Times* turned its attention to stories that had been neglected during the Rosenthal years. A team of correspondents was assigned to cover the AIDS epidemic, five years after the paper first reported on its emergence. "We need more and still more articles that dramatize and explain the problem—for others to 'solve'—so that years from now we shall be seen to have done our duty," he wrote his deputies early in his tenure. He would later assign a deputy national editor, Jeffrey Schmalz, to cover gay and AIDS issues after Schmalz, who was gay, suffered a sei-

---

* Frankel said that to Joyce Purnick, a city hall bureau chief whom Frankel started dating soon after his wife, Tobi, died from a brain tumor. Purnick moved from city hall to work on the editorial board to avoid working for a man she was seeing romantically. They eventually married.

zure in the newsroom and was diagnosed with the disease.* But Frankel wanted to pick his battles during this transition, wary of what might be interpreted as a repudiation of policies that had been central to the Rosenthal-Sulzberger era.

Let's ration these, he told associates. The prohibition against using the word "gay" to describe homosexuals would not be lifted until eight months after Frankel began his tenure. And in truth, Frankel would turn out to be his own kind of bulldozer at the front page meetings, often as hectoring of his editors as Rosenthal had been.

The Frankel years would mark a new era at the *Times*, albeit a change as much in atmosphere as in journalism. Frankel would in some ways find Rosenthal an easy act to follow; it would not take much to appease a staff that was this traumatized. But the challenge was to fulfill the mission Sulzberger had given him: to bring stability to the newsroom without losing the creativity and spark that Rosenthal, for all his flaws, brought to the office every morning.

* * *

Frankel and Rosenthal were two of the most ambitious journalists of their time, and their relationship reflected that: a combustible mixture of admiration, envy, and animosity. Riding on Air Force One during his days as a White House reporter in the late 1960s, Frankel had written a letter requesting to be taken off the beat. It was anguished, undated, scrawled on official "aboard Air Force One" stationery, not addressed to any particular editor and, by Frankel's recollection a half century later, never sent. Instead, it appeared to be an opportunity for Frankel to vent about Rosenthal. "AMR and MF do not mix," the letter said. "AMR is central to the operation of the NYT as now designed. MF is peripheral." In saying he wanted to leave, Frankel likened his situation to John W. Gardner, who resigned as secretary of health, education, and welfare for President Lyndon B. Johnson in 1968. He described Gardner's departure as a "quest for relief" from an overbearing chief executive.

"Grant me relief from my duties at the earliest convenient opportunity," he wrote. "AMR needs not only to dominate, but to possess and his

---

* Schmalz would die from the disease on November 6, 1993.

great talent can flourish only by humbling others. That is, other talents may exist only through his creation or sufferance."

At this early chapter of their relationship, Rosenthal was unstinting in his admiration of Frankel's talents. "I really don't think I have ever seen a story of the quality of your appraisal produced in that short a time," he wrote after Frankel quickly turned around an appreciation of Johnson—"A Personal Politician: Johnson Pressed for Great Society and the War in a Face-to-Face Style"—when the former president dropped dead of a heart attack at his Texas ranch in 1973. Meanwhile, in a note to Clifton Daniel, another senior editor, Rosenthal described the challenges of managing a difficult personality. "I know that Max Frankel is an up and down man as far as personal moods and outlook are concerned," he wrote. "But I think that his story from Des Moines today shows us again that he is worth whatever trouble we have to take with him."

That assessment changed as Frankel became an editor and a rival. Rosenthal would never let Watergate go. One day, he was standing with Howell Raines, a fast-rising correspondent covering politics, thumbing through old papers. Someone mentioned how the *Post* had beaten the *Times* the other day on a story.

Well, you know how seriously the *Times* takes Watergate—we got beat and we all got promotions, Rosenthal said.

Their relationship worsened after Sulzberger appointed Rosenthal to run the newsroom and put Frankel in charge of the editorial page. "He didn't like my politics," Frankel said years later. "He didn't like the tone of the editorial page. He just didn't like me." Rosenthal had no authority over Frankel—he and Frankel both reported to Sulzberger—but that did not stop him from sending notes that found fault with the new editorial page. "A stylistic device has become overused almost to the point of a tic," he wrote in one. "That is the use of the word 'we.' If you look through the editorials, you'll find that virtually all of them use 'we' and many of them badly overused [it].

"The reason that I'm bringing it up, Max, is that any device can be overused and become a subject of parody," Rosenthal said. "Think upon it." Frankel responded with a note—"not a criticism," he assured the executive editor, saying he might have done the same thing—suggesting that Rosenthal consider the amount of space the news pages had devoted to the inaugural address delivered by President Jimmy Carter. "In the context in which we normally play news and texts, that full page comes on as very reverential and boosterish, almost like an inaugural committee's souvenir book," Frankel wrote.

Rosenthal often copied Sulzberger on the critical notes he sent up to the editorial page editor. In one instance, Rosenthal complained directly to Sulzberger about an editorial assailing Israel for bombing a French-built nuclear reactor near Baghdad in 1981, which Frankel's editorial page described as "an act of inexcusable and short-sighted aggression." The tone was "harsh and denunciatory," Rosenthal argued to Sulzberger. Rather than acting out of hand, Rosenthal asserted, Israel had "served a valuable notice on the world." (Frankel would later express regret for that editorial, listing it "among my major mistakes.")

Their differences were personal. Rosenthal had rebuffed a plea from Frankel's wife, Tobi, for a job after the Frankels moved from Washington to New York. Tobia Brown Frankel was a graduate of Barnard College, where she had been the campus correspondent for the *Times*. Over the course of her career, she worked as an editor, a teacher at the Georgetown Day School and the National Cathedral School for Girls, and a freelance writer. But Rosenthal rejected her bid to join the *Times*, saying he had only so many hires and preferred younger reporters. "So, Tobi, I think you can see that against this situation the chance of your coming on to the *Times* news staff now just doesn't exist," he wrote her. Tobi would, as Frankel recounted while describing his wife's struggles with depression, berate him for not getting her a position at the *Times*. Not that he didn't try. When Frankel learned there was an opening at the Week in Review in 1980, he asked Rosenthal if his wife might be considered. "If you were interested, I think you'd get a devoted and all giving editor." There is no record of a Rosenthal reply.

Frankel and Rosenthal were in some ways quite similar: Jewish men of the same generation, Pulitzer Prize–winning foreign correspondents who covered the Cold War and had never known any other newsroom. But they had different upbringings that ultimately shaped their respective terms as executive editor. Rosenthal was the son of immigrants from Byelorussia. Frankel was a refugee from Nazi Germany, who fled with his mother from Poland (his father would join them later), landing in Hoboken six weeks before he turned ten years old, speaking German, Yiddish, Polish, and some Hebrew—but not English. Frankel's life was one of striving followed by accomplishment, of appreciating the opportunity he had been granted—or the debt that he owed—because his mother had removed him from the lethal threat that Polish Jews faced in Europe in the 1940s. He mastered English and strove to erase even the slightest trace of his German accent as he grew up. He had a better command of grammar than many of the American-born editors who would work for him. Frankel was a graduate of Columbia University, a Phi Beta Kappa, the editor of the *Columbia Spectator,* and also a part-time campus correspondent for the *Times.* He glided through the foreign policy and Washington establishments; always elegantly put together, in a way that Rosenthal was not. As one of the journalists who questioned President Gerald Ford and his Democratic challenger, Jimmy Carter, at a nationally televised presidential debate in 1976, Frankel famously asked the question that prompted the president to declare that there was "no Soviet domination of Eastern Europe," to which Frankel responded, "I'm sorry, what?" Frankel believed that the job of the reporter was to inform the reader, not to ensnare a high-level elected official or candidate for office in a careless mistake. "That is why even a decade later, in the 1976 campaign, it came as second nature to me to throw a lifeline to President Ford after his catastrophic gaffe," he said years later.

* * *

Rosenthal had told Frankel he intended to stay on as executive editor through the end of the year, but left abruptly in October. Frankel had to move quickly to build up his own team of editors, as was reflected in a rapid flurry of appointments. "It's a revolution instead of an evolution—before I even knew fully which end was up," Frankel said two months into the job. He informed Al Siegal that he was now an assistant managing editor, an elevation in stature and salary that stunned and moved Siegal after his difficult voyage under Rosenthal. "I was flabbergasted, absolutely dumbfounded." Joseph Lelyveld would return from London to become foreign editor. Frankel appointed the first woman to run the national desk at the *Times*—Soma Golden Behr, who had worked for him on the editorial page and was now the editor of the Sunday business section. Golden Behr practically shouted, That's a holy-shit job—are you serious? at Frankel when he offered her the position.

Abe Rosenthal had two requests for Frankel. The first was to appoint John Vinocur, the editor he had pushed for promotion earlier that year, as managing editor. Frankel rejected that out of hand; he did not really know Vinocur and was not eager to have as his second-in-command someone who had competed for the top job. Vinocur headed to Paris to run the *International Herald Tribune*, which the *Times* jointly owned with *The Washington Post*. And Rosenthal asked that Frankel bring Andrew M. Rosenthal, his son, onto the staff. I couldn't do it before because it would be seen as nepotism, Abe Rosenthal told him. Frankel was familiar with Andrew Rosenthal. He had spent four years working for the Associated Press in Moscow—the city where Frankel had spent the early years of his own career. Frankel told Rosenthal, He's a solid journalist and I'm happy to hire him.

Andrew Rosenthal was about to turn thirty-one, and he was eager to work at the *Times.* He had written Punch Sulzberger a few weeks after his father told him of his pending departure. "I guess the *Times* has always been in my blood, and at this point in my life, when I feel it's time to move from a wire service to a newspaper, there is no other paper for which I could conceive of working," the letter said. It was a request that Sulzberger was delighted to honor. "It is something that I had been hoping to get for a considerable period of time," Sulzberger responded. With that, Frankel and Sulzberger ensured that the Rosenthal name and legacy would continue at the *Times* for one more generation.

At the urging of the publisher, Frankel appointed Arthur Gelb as his managing editor. It was not a difficult request to grant, even if it meant he was making Rosenthal's closest ally his top deputy. Gelb was three years away from retirement, and there was no other editor ready to be the managing editor, in Frankel's view. And the new executive editor did not know his way around the newsroom. I need Gelb to teach me what the hell is going on in the newsroom, he told Gruson, because I have been out of there for ten years. At Frankel's first front page meeting as executive editor, Rosenthal guided him to the seat at the head of the table, wished him good luck, and walked out the door.

Frankel had been uneasy in 1976 when he moved from the news-room, whose mission was to be free of any outward expression of opinion, to the editorial board, where he was expected to promote his opinions. And now, ten years later, as he crossed back over the line, he was wary how his new colleagues might view him. He addressed that in his first note to his staff. "From this moment on, as in my first 25 years at the *Times,* I have no editorial opinions, and I find the transition no more peculiar or difficult than that of a lawyer appointed to the bench," he wrote. "A passion for fairness dominates even our opinion pages, but partisanship and special pleading have no place in the *Times's* newsroom."

Frankel's arrival, and with it, Rosenthal's departure, was celebrated. "A sense of relief and hope" was how Peter Millones, who Rosenthal had appointed an assistant managing editor earlier that year, put it in a warm welcome to Frankel. Frankel's memorandum to the staff tipped a hat to the new era, saying "good fun" would be welcome in this newsroom. When Frankel met for the first time with his new department heads, he arrived with a message, sketched out in talking points: "my first 3 months = learn + kibitz; inspire; plan." Frankel wanted to make the *Times* less daunting for readers at a time when *USA Today* was promoting snappy stories that, for the most part, ended on the same page where they began.

Why do stories have to jump from the front page to an inside page? he asked his deputies. Frankel had studied art at the High School of Music & Art in Manhattan and was an amateur painter. He was interested in the visual presentation of the *Times:* the typefaces, the illustrations, the photographs. He would complain to Tom Bodkin, the design director, when the layout of the paper—such as when stories jumped from page to page—discouraged readers from finishing an article they had started.

He thought that stories were too long. "Yes, we want and need enterprise stories. But egads, we are drowning the reader in ink," Frankel wrote. He wanted the ages of the bride and groom included in wedding announcements. We put them in when people die, he said. Why not when they get married? The publisher's wife was not happy about that. "Carol Sulzberger was up in arms. All her friends: *Making us reveal our ages!*" Frankel said years later. He would second-guess the Page One headlines drafted by his editors before they went off to press. He drafted an organizational chart, with ordered boxes and lines of command and responsibility, that he shared with Sulzberger. "I always like to make things neat and orderly," he said later, and in that, he knew he had an appreciative audience in the ex-marine on the fourteenth floor. Gay Talese took note of his focus on process and described him at the time as an editor who possessed "a high bureaucratic mentality."

Like executive editors before him, Frankel soon learned of the frustrations attendant in trying to shape a newspaper produced out of a sea of egos and talent spread all over the world. He determined that the place to accomplish this was at the afternoon front page meetings, when editors presented memos, called "summaries," from reporters sketching out the tops of the stories they were preparing for the next day's newspaper. Since he had no time to shuttle from desk to desk inspecting stories as they were being written and edited, he seized on this opportunity in the front page meetings. His questions were stern, exacting, and often withering. He would challenge the first paragraph, the analytical "nut paragraph" that explained the significance of the story, and sometimes question whether it merited publication at all. He wanted stories to be more thoughtful and less stenographic. Editors were put on the spot to explain the in-progress work of a reporter who might be hundreds of miles away.

While the newsroom was calmer and less tense than it had been under Frankel's predecessor, the front page meeting was one stage where the differences between Rosenthal and Frankel were hardly stark at all. "I probably was more authoritarian and dictatorial in the Page One meeting than Abe," he said years later. Soma Golden Behr, the national editor, would sometimes bow out of these afternoon sessions, dispatching her deputy, Philip Taubman, to represent her. Screw it, Phil—you go, she'd say. You're nice, you're more nice than I am. Taubman dreaded these meetings. It was like going to your own execution, he thought. "There was a brutality about it that was simply unacceptable," Taubman would say years later.

It was a side of Frankel that would peek through over the years—a harsh candor; a need to say things that perhaps did not always need to be said—that seemed particularly notable given the glasnost that had been promised with his advancement. When Steven Roberts, a correspondent for twenty-five years, decided to leave the newspaper rather than become an editor, Frankel sent him a note. "You have been a loyal and friendly colleague and have served the *Times* well in many places. That you did not soar to your full potential may have more to do with your rootedness in Washington than your inherent talents. It is not a place where one should spend a lifetime—either in politics or journalism." This guy plays hardball, Howell Raines thought after seeing a copy of it.

CHAPTER 8

Two Hundred Miles

The Washington bureau had been a prestige assignment at the *Times* since Franklin Delano Roosevelt moved into the White House as the nation's thirty-second president in 1933. Its work was seen by the newspaper's most influential readers, from Washington to Wall Street, and, importantly for anyone with ambition, at the home office. Reporters and editors who made it to Washington would not want to leave. It was not easy to walk away from that kind of importance and visibility. The *Times* had long been judged by the performance of this bureau, and the pressure there could be relentless—which was, at a place like the *Times*, part of its attraction.

"When the opposition, any opposition, gets a real news beat, it's our obligation to the readers to report quickly and fully on what happened and, also, to try to take the story away from them," Rosenthal had directed Bill Kovach in the fall of 1980 after the Washington bureau, under Kovach's command, was beaten by the *Post* on a run of stories, including the unsuccessful attempt by President Jimmy Carter to appoint the first Black federal judge in Virginia. "Failure to do so has had serious consequences for this paper in the past, as you know, and I for one will not permit it to happen again," Rosenthal wrote. The allusion was obvious; the bureau was haunted by Watergate. Its editors and reporters kept a close eye on what Bob Woodward was up to at the *Post*. Hedrick Smith, who ran the bureau before Kovach, had alerted Rosenthal in the summer of 1978 after he learned that Woodward had been working on a book about the behind-the-scenes deliberations at the Supreme Court. Smith considered a preemptive strike. "Have someone get hold of Woodward's manuscript or galleys and run the best stuff first in the *Times*," he wrote. "But otherwise, we prefer to pick our own targets and make them chase us." Arthur Gelb complained a few months before Max Frankel took over as executive editor that the Washington bureau was being "consistently beaten by the *Washington Post*." Harrison Salisbury, whose roles at the paper had included directing coverage of the assassination of John F. Kennedy in 1963 when he served as the chief of correspondents, warned the new executive editor that the Washington bureau was far from the commanding force it had been back then. "We are No. 3 in something close to a tie with WSJ," he wrote, referring to *The Wall Street Journal*. "No. 3 is simply intolerable for yourself (and the *Times*)."*

Frankel took over in the midst of the biggest crisis Ronald Reagan had faced in his six years in office. Vice Admiral John Poindexter, the national security adviser, and Lieutenant Colonel Oliver North had orchestrated a scheme to facilitate the sale of arms to Iran and divert some of the proceeds to fund the Contras, a rebel force fighting a socialist regime in Nicaragua. Congress had prohibited continued funding of the Contras, and Iran was under an arms embargo. The scheme became a scandal known as Iran-Contra, and it had gripped Washington like nothing since the attempted assassination of Reagan in 1981. Salisbury told Frankel that his success as executive editor could well be determined by how the Washington bureau covered these events, framing his warning in a way sure to grab Frankel's attention. "It is ironic that, like Watergate, it comes at a moment of changing of the watch at the *Times*, but, fairly or not, it is certain to be seen as a measure of your stewardship," Salisbury wrote.

The bureau's relationship with New York had long been difficult. "Those 200 miles of distance between Washington and New York were like 1,000 miles of misunderstandings and problems," Punch Sulzberger said in an oral history in 1983. Frankel had become bureau chief in 1968 because of the messy takeover orchestrated by editors in New York, Rosenthal among them. Rosenthal had again tried to bring the bureau under his control by installing Hedrick Smith in the job at the end of

---

* Salisbury told Frankel the best coverage out of the nation's capital came from Jack Nelson at the *Los Angeles Times*, followed by *The Washington Post*.

1976, but it remained a troubled outpost. Reporters were leaving for other newspapers, and those who remained—like Adam Clymer, who covered Congress and politics—complained that Smith was more interested in appearing on the weekly news panel broadcast *Washington Week* than running the bureau. Rosenthal pushed Smith aside in 1979 to make way for Bill Kovach. This seemingly simple transfer of power came only after agonizing negotiations over titles, responsibilities, and status that offered a glimpse into the sensitivities in managing the bureau. Smith would become the chief correspondent, the *Times*'s preeminent writer in the nation's capital. The title of bureau chief would be retired, at least for a while, and Kovach would be named Washington editor, responsible for running the bureau, because, as Rosenthal explained to an aggrieved Smith, no one could do both. Rosenthal got what he wanted, or so it seemed. There would no longer be a James Reston, Tom Wicker, Arthur Krock, or Frankel—influential bureau chiefs who wrote stories, weighing in on the big events of their day. The bureau would no longer be a satellite spinning away from New York control.

Kovach was resigned to the diminished nature of his new position but was never happy about it. He was gruff and acerbic, a Southerner with a dark sense of humor and an abiding resentment at what he saw as the elite editors in New York. From his perspective, they looked down on him, the unpolished descendant of Albanians who had grown up in the mountains of east Tennessee and served in the Navy. "I didn't quite fit the New York suit of clothes," he said years later. His reporters admired his prickly manner, his journalistic instincts, and the way he stood up to New York. But if Kovach was an inspirational manager, he could be difficult to manage, often moody and morose. Kovach once returned from a vacation to offer Rosenthal a damning assessment of his own performance. "I have been forced to conclude that I have failed," he wrote. At one point, Kovach sent a note to his editors and reporters complaining about their performance. "In short, we've become a flatulent bureau," he wrote. Frankel would refer to Kovach—in a letter *to* Kovach—as "the brooding Bill." Frankel was aware of the importance of the bureau to the *Times*; he had been a player in its tangled and contentious history. And one of his first decisions upon taking over as executive editor was that Kovach would not continue in the job. He at the time described Kovach's record in

Washington as "nothing but the wrecking of a wonderful career." Kovach had hoped he would be offered the job that Frankel got; Frankel did not even offer him a position on the masthead. The disdain between the two men was mutual. "I had just had no respect for him," Kovach said. He left to become editor of *The Atlanta Journal* and *Constitution.*

* * *

Craig Whitney was an assistant managing editor for personnel and administrative matters in the fall of 1986 when Frankel recruited him to help choose the next head of the Washington bureau. Whitney had covered the war in Vietnam and the collapse of Communism in East Germany and the Soviet Union. He had logged 3,200 bylines over his forty-four years at the *Times*, from Saigon, Bonn and Berlin, Moscow, London, and Paris, and returned twice to New York to work as an editor. He spoke French, German, and Russian. A Harvard graduate, he'd begun his career at the *Times* as a clerk for James Reston. (He played Bach's Fugue in B Minor on the organ at Reston's funeral at St. Alban's Episcopal Church in Washington, D.C., in 1995.) Whitney displayed a kind of laconic ambition that set him apart from the swaggering editors of the Rosenthal generation. He was not a member of *that* line of wealthy Whitneys, which some of his colleagues assumed, as Whitney discovered from the dismissive response he drew when he asked for a raise while he and A. M. Rosenthal were returning from lunch one afternoon. Whitney did have that air about him, but he grew up in Westborough, Massachusetts, about thirty-five miles west of Boston, and his father was the chief janitor at Westborough High School.

Whitney was pleased that Frankel had turned to him with this assignment and prepared a survey of Kovach's prospective replacements. "This is for your eyes only," he wrote.

Howell Raines, an Alabamian who joined the newspaper in 1978 and was already the second-ranking editor in Washington, has "clearly been grooming himself for the job, and wants it badly," Whitney began. Raines had a command of politics and domestic policy, in Whitney's view, and he knew the reporters and editors in the bureau. But he was weak on foreign policy and, in what seemed like a particularly damning aside in a report for an editor like Frankel, had "a tendency not to think conceptually." Whitney admired R. W. (Johnny) Apple, the former national political correspondent who had just returned to Washington after serving as London bureau chief. Apple was one of the stars of his generation, but Whitney offered a harsh review of his performance in London. "I have great respect for him, because of what he used to be, and perhaps is on the way back to being again—but making him the bureau chief now, after his dismal performance up to the summer of this year, would not be a good signal to send to the Washington Bureau staff." Next on the list was Dave Jones, the national editor, who was one of the best hands in the business when it came to Washington and politics. But, Whitney warned, "he might coddle and shelter the staff instead of challenging it." Whitney did have a candidate in mind to run the Washington bureau. "Let's stop beating around the bush," he wrote. "Me."

As a former Washington bureau chief, Frankel knew the challenges of the bureau; he knew the culture and the history, the egos and the conflicts. And he agreed with Whitney about the need for someone who was diplomatic, dignified, seasoned, and self-confident, and who might finally engender the cooperation between New York and Washington that had eluded the *Times* for so many generations. This would be one of the first big decisions Frankel made. He knew the stakes—for the newspaper and for his editorship.

Howell Raines had sought to position himself for the job. "I thought your statement to the staff was graceful and wise," he wrote Frankel after he became executive editor. He asked to meet Frankel, and as Raines recalled the conversation, the new executive editor promised he would hear him out before making his decision. But in an oral history he recorded shortly after he took over, Frankel left little doubt he would not pick Raines, who he called a wonderful political correspondent who "knows almost nothing about Economics or Foreign Policy." Frankel flew to Washington and took Raines to dinner at the Mayflower Hotel, where he made his intention clear as soon as the two men ordered cocktails. The conversation was rough and abrupt.

You're not going to get this job, Frankel told him. What I want you to do is either be national editor or go abroad. If you're going to go places on this paper, you need other dimensions that Washington isn't going to give you.

The one thing you can take off the table is national editor, Raines responded. He continued: If I come to New York now, someday, someone sitting where you're sitting is going to tell me I can't be executive editor without foreign experience.

Frankel nodded. If you want to run for executive editor, then London or Paris, Frankel said. Raines never forgot those words: "run for executive editor." This guy has just won an election, Raines thought. And he's telling me this is a political campaign.

Frankel was barreling ahead because he wanted to announce his major appointments in one sweep. Raines would go to London. And Craig Whitney would move to Washington to run the sixty-five-person bureau. By passing over Raines for Whitney, Frankel was choosing someone more accomplished in the politics of the New York office than the politics of the nation's capital. It was not an unreasonable decision, but it was a risky one, and it would soon become clear what a mistake it had been.

* * *

Since Whitney had spent little time as a reporter in Washington, the selection of his two deputies took on added importance. Johnny Apple, who was now the chief Washington correspondent, the post Hedrick Smith had held, would be one of them, bringing the political and Washington knowledge that Whitney did not have. For the other, Whitney turned to a correspondent in Paris: Judith Miller, who had been hired at the *Times* in 1977; it was a job for which she was probably not qualified, as she later said, but the *Times* was under pressure to hire women in the wake of the women's discrimination suit. Her father was a Jewish Russian-born nightclub operator, her mother an Irish Catholic show dancer. She had grown up in Las Vegas, attended Barnard College, and been arrested three times—twice at demonstrations against the war in Vietnam and once in one of the student protests at Columbia University, the same ones that brought Abe Rosenthal back to his typewriter. That was one bit of personal history she had been advised not to share with Rosenthal when she went to his office for the final interview.

Miller had been a freelance writer for *The Progressive*, a liberal magazine based in Madison, Wisconsin, and from the earliest days of her career, had displayed a strong interest in national security. But when she arrived at the *Times*'s Washington bureau, she was assigned to cover the Securities and Exchange Commission. She presumed this was meant to avoid the conflict posed by her live-in relationship with Rep. Leslie Aspin, Jr., who headed the House Armed Services Committee. Miller's next assignment took her to Cairo, as the first woman to head the *Times*'s bureau there, until Rosenthal called to say he was sending her to Paris. Miller was crestfallen.

There's no news in Paris, Miller told Rosenthal. Miller had been in France for barely a year, about to turn thirty-nine years old, when Frankel, the new executive editor, asked her to become an editor in the Washington bureau. She had never been an editor before, and she was being offered one of the senior jobs in the paper's largest bureau. The idea of appointing Miller a Washington editor had come from Arthur O. Sulzberger, Jr., with whom she had struck up a friendship during her earlier days in Washington, when Sulzberger first joined the paper. He had been impressed by her intensity, drive, and competitiveness, and her name came to mind when he ran into Whitney in the office in New York in 1986, and the new head of the Washington bureau began talking about the two deputy posts he needed to fill. Why not Judy? Sulzberger said.

Whitney and Frankel liked the idea. "She's competitive," Frankel said at the time. "She's feisty. Whereas Craig Whitney is very calm and dignified, she's the very opposite." As much as anything, Frankel wanted to put a woman in that post, and he knew that appointing female editors would be a priority for Arthur should he become publisher. But it was a gamble. "Miller is a great gunslinger," Salisbury told Frankel. "I would put her on the Reagan scandal in a twinkle and she would pay off. As a No. 2 executive with her sharp tongue, high ego, inexperience in dealing with the kind of personalities the bureau possesses—I just don't know. A risk at best. Much worse if the bureau finds her abrasive."

* * *

Frankel was determined to restore morale in Washington, to put an end to "the B.S. about how brilliantly the *Post* is doing," as he put it to Gelb at the end of 1986. He wanted the Washington bureau, and not the night editors in New York, to decide which stories the late-night staff should try to match when an early edition of the next day's *Post* was delivered to the *Times* bureau close to 11 P.M. At first, it seemed that these efforts were paying off. Gelb praised Whitney, pleased with the paper's coverage of Iran-Contra and the early primary skirmishing between George H. W. Bush and Senator Bob Dole for the Republican presidential nomination. "Great report! Great staff! Great bureau!"* Gelb wrote.

But it was a short honeymoon. In May 1987, Gary Hart, a former two-term senator from Colorado, dropped out of the Democratic presidential race following reports suggesting he was engaged in an extramarital affair. Within the week, Whitney sent a letter to thirteen presidential candidates with a list of demands for biographical, professional, and personal information. The *Times* wanted military records, school transcripts, income-tax returns, net-worth statements—including information on stock and real estate transactions, marriage and driver's licenses, and medical records. The letter asked that Lawrence K. Altman, a physician who was a *Times* reporter, be allowed to interview the candidates' doctors, and demanded a roster of the candidates' friends, going back to high school, and advisers. The *Times* wanted them to waive their right to privacy and authorize its reporters to inspect any raw FBI or CIA reports on them. And it wanted the candidates to answer questions about their personal and sexual lives—their marital and, if applicable, divorce histories.

The rules of privacy and political journalism were changing. Hart's departure from the race came after the *Miami Herald* published a story asserting that the candidate, who was married, spent a weekend at a Washington townhouse with Donna Rice, a model from Miami. Shortly after that story appeared, Paul Taylor of *The Washington Post* asked Hart if he had ever committed adultery. The question—broad, intrusive by the standards of that time, and posed at a news conference—had been denounced, among other places, on the Op-Ed page of the *Times* by Anthony Lewis, who called it "the low point of the Hart story." The debate about what were appropriate lines of inquiry for a candidate for presi-

---

* The Gelb note to Whitney was dated March 17, and Gelb scribbled a note next to the date about one of his favorite correspondents in the bureau: "Is Maureen wearing her green?" He was referring to Maureen Dowd, and she almost certainly was.

dent was very much unresolved, and Whitney's questionnaire drew another round of condemnation. "This is what 'too far' looks like," Ellen
Goodman of *The Boston Globe* wrote in her column. Mike Royko, the *Chicago Tribune* columnist, prankishly telephoned the *Times*'s public relations office and asked for the marital and divorce histories of the publisher and the editors on the masthead (a rich line of inquiry, to be sure).
"And do you know what she says?" Royko wrote in his column. " 'I'm not
going to give out that information.' Click."

Even A. M. Rosenthal, now on the Op-Ed page, weighed in with a column. If the press was demanding that the candidates open their private
lives to such inspection, shouldn't reporters and editors be subject to the
same scrutiny? "Now, let's get to it. Correspondents and editors, have
you ever committed adultery? Are you now? Homosexual experiences,
any? Names, please. And surely you will not mind, Publisher, if we readers pitch in a few dollars each to put a secret cordon around your house
at night, since your reporters extend that attention to others."

Whitney was flabbergasted. He had consulted his editors and political
reporters before sending out the questionnaires, though later he admitted that "in retrospect, the idea seems naïve and brash." Frankel told
Whitney he should have been alerted beforehand and sent a note to his
staff acknowledging that the *Times* had crossed a line. "In this valid pursuit, we have put some questions to candidates that reach a bit too far,"
he wrote. Frankel's confidence was shaken; he thought that Whitney
had embarrassed the *Times*.

Frankel was hearing reports of discord in the bureau and decided to
go to Washington and talk to reporters "so that I could bathe a while in
their moods and learn how I can further help to assist the leadership
team," as he put it in a report to Whitney after his return to New York. In
Washington, Frankel heard complaints about his own management.
"The first thing I learned was the extent to which I embarrassed you in
pulling back, ever so slightly, from the inquiry to candidates," he wrote
in his report to Whitney. "I regret the embarrassment, but not the pull-
back." But most of the complaints were about the way the bureau was
being managed, the "lingering contentions between New York and
Washington editors and the dissatisfactions of some Buro reporters." He
told Whitney he found a "disturbing amount of confusion and even

some friction," and that Whitney was seen as aloof and disconnected, even "remote and hostile."

Frankel was particularly agitated about Judith Miller. She was, he told Whitney in the letter, turning out to be a difficult boss: dismissive, mistrustful, and disrespectful, often going behind her reporters to call their sources and confirm their reporting. "Judy's problem with the staff seems more difficult because, as we were duly warned from the start, of her tendency to express concern or anxiety in tense rather than soothing ways, sometimes even hostile and insulting ways. She should, frankly, know that at least several highly valued [bureau] reporters regard her periodic treatment of them as 'intolerable,' or words to that effect and that they have come to deeply resent her inability to show them respect even in questioning something they may have done."

Frankel wondered if Miller should be taken off the desk and returned to reporting. Miller was a woman in a male-dominated bureau with a difficult staff. Would anyone be talking about sharp elbows if she had been a man? In Miller's view, they would not. There was no shortage of male editors at the *Times* whose management tools included eruptive tempers, insults, and abuse; one needed to look no further than the last executive editor. But unlike Rosenthal, Miller could not argue that the bureau's work was significantly better because of her management techniques.

Less than two weeks after Frankel's visit to Washington, another embarrassment for the bureau was presented in a headline across two columns on the top of the front page. "A Correction: *Times* Was in Error on North's Secret-Fund Testimony." The *Times* had published an account of testimony by Oliver North to the congressional committees investigating the Iran-Contra affair. The story, written by Fox Butterfield, reported that North told Congress that William J. Casey, the director of Central Intelligence, wanted to create a fund to underwrite intelligence operations, and that it would be kept secret from the president and Congress. "The account of that testimony in The New York Times on Saturday went beyond Colonel North's actual words and stated incorrectly that he had testified that neither the President nor Congress were to be informed about the secret fund," read the 1,300-word correction.

Joseph Lelyveld, the foreign editor, had reviewed the Butterfield article before it was published and raised a concern: it needed an actual quote from North saying that Casey intended to keep the program secret. When he saw the story the next day, still without the quote he had requested to support its central assertion, he directed reporters in the Washington bureau to provide one; they could not. Frankel, after speaking with Lelyveld, realized that the story was incorrect, but declared that a routine correction was not sufficient for a mistake of this magnitude. The headline of the original story ran across three columns at the top of Page One. The correction, Frankel said, needed to be just as prominent. Butterfield was stunned—no one on the Hill had complained to him about the story—as was the bureau. "They felt we were publicly chastising our own reporters and our own editors," Frankel said at the time. Lelyveld thought the prominence of the correction excessive and told Frankel that. "I was not as principled as Max," he said years later. "I wouldn't have insisted on putting a correction on the top of Page One to make a point. And I was perhaps more protective of the paper." Whitney defended the correction when the *Post* called for a comment. "If that causes morale problems in my staff, it shouldn't and I hope with time I can remedy that."

* * *

Whitney had never been impressed by the reporters in Washington. "My view of this bureau before I got here was that it was fat and lazy—a few terrific seasoned reporters, a few terrific but unseasoned Washington reporters, and a whole room full of just average ones," he wrote Gelb toward the end of 1987. Whitney wanted to clear out unproductive reporters—send them to the metropolitan desk, or to an early retirement—to make way for new correspondents. And he had Frankel's support. Whitney prepared a list of correspondents who had been there too long, who rarely broke stories or demonstrated little flair for writing. Five were called to his office and told they would be reassigned to New York.

The decision roiled the bureau. Martin Tolchin, the congressional correspondent who was the Newspaper Guild shop steward, likened it to the Saturday Night Massacre. Forty-one members of the bureau—among them Andrew Rosenthal, E. J. Dionne, and Gerald M. Boyd—signed a letter to Frankel complaining "how deeply troubling we find the abrupt and brutal manner in which five of our colleagues were treated yesterday. Surely there is a more humane way to handle personnel actions that have such a profound effect on people's lives." One of the five, Irv Molotsky, who had worked at the *Times* since 1967, appealed directly to Frankel, saying his wife had given up a promising college teaching career to move to Washington from New York and she was now about to receive tenure. "Max, by imposing the transfer, you will be asking me to choose between The Times and my marriage," he said. "Please let me hear from you. I am torn apart." They spoke the next day. "I told Irv by phone Fri nite [Friday night] to becalm himself for further talks," Frankel wrote in a note to himself. "I will *not* give him a lifetime slot in DC. But if there's some temporary hardship, we'll talk about maybe some editing, if there were a slot, or pay for his commuting for a while. His failure to say 'I don't need/want lifetime commitment' suggests we do have [a] problem." Molotsky ended up staying in the Washington bureau through his retirement in 2001.

The Washington Post learned of the uproar, to the chagrin of Frankel. "Arthur—we're talking here to 5 or 6 people," Frankel wrote Gelb. "Which of them can't keep their mouths shut." Whitney called a staff meeting on Martin Luther King Day in which he offered a monologue of explanations, defenses, and irritation as he addressed a bureau that was proving far more difficult to manage than he had ever imagined. Yes, this first year "had been an unhappy one" under this team of Washington editors. But Whitney was unhappy with the work of the reporters. The failure to address the bureau's problems "leaves all of us, and you, with the prospect of more unhappiness, more insecurity, more preoccupation with ourselves than with doing a superb job covering the news." Whitney made no apologies for having moved so abruptly. (Much later, he would describe the decision to make all five staff changes at once "the biggest mistake I ever made" and a disservice to colleagues "who had worked hard and earned the right not to be exposed to such embarrassment.")

He left the meeting worried that his standing with New York had been damaged. Those concerns were confirmed when he read his annual evaluation the next month. "I realize, Craig, that Bill Kovach left you a bureau that had many problems; he'd neglected the bureau in trying to promote his own career," Gelb wrote. "We expected it would take you a little time to overcome your inexperience with Washington news, But we did not anticipate your sense of insecurity." Whitney's staff had turned against him. He had been appointed to usher in a new era in the *Times*'s most difficult bureau; already, he was in danger of joining the line of failed leaders of the Washington bureau. Why did I take this job? Whitney asked himself.

* * *

Howell Raines was enjoying England. "The longer I walk around in this London suit, the better I like the fit of it," he wrote Frankel in December 1987. "Before long, I'll be saying the entire thing was my idea." In truth, he was still disappointed that he had been passed over as head of the Washington bureau, and ambivalent about his future at the *Times*. And he had options, expressions of interest from publications who seemed eager to hire him as a senior editor: the *St. Petersburg Times*, the Raleigh *News & Observer,* and a magazine, *Southern Living.* The idea of running his own newspaper was appealing, and he flew back to the United States to meet with editors in Raleigh and St. Petersburg. Raines went to New York to press Arthur Sulzberger, Jr., who was widely presumed to be the next publisher, about his future at the *Times*.

I hate these kinds of conversations, Sulzberger began, before offering Raines the guidance he wanted. If you want to run a newspaper right now, that's one thing. But if you think you might want to run *this* newspaper one day, you should stay. Think of this as your wilderness days.

Raines's wilderness days would not last long. Punch Sulzberger kept an apartment in London and would regularly visit with his wife, Carol. The Sulzbergers would often invite the bureau chief out for dinner and drinks. Carol Sulzberger was something of an acquired taste—a strong personality who sent many *Times* editors scurrying. But she could be fun and was a source of office intelligence. Raines had been in London for twenty-one months when the Sulzbergers came to town, stopping by his apartment for cocktails before they headed out to dinner, where Carol turned to him with a question.

Are you and Susan going to be able to get your house back? she asked, referring to the Washington home Raines and his wife had rented out when they moved to London.

What do you mean? Raines responded.

Oh, maybe I'm not supposed to say that, she said.

Raines was fairly certain this was no idle slip of the tongue. His suspicions were soon confirmed.

Whitney was in New York that week. When he stepped off the elevator onto the third floor, Frankel summoned him into his office. This is a difficult thing to say, Frankel told him. I just don't think it's working out in Washington. He suggested that Whitney move to London. Frankel called Raines and asked him and Whitney to negotiate a cross-Atlantic job swap. "I had made such a mess of Washington that I brought Howell back," Frankel would later recall. He made a mistake—a big one—in his first year as editor and understood that he still had time to fix it.

CHAPTER 9

The Shoe at Home

On April 8, 1969, one year after the assassination of Martin Luther King, Jr., Punch Sulzberger assembled his top editors and managers to discuss what he considered a matter of personal and institutional embarrassment: The overwhelmingly white makeup of *The New York Times*. The newspaper had championed civil rights on its editorial pages. Its reporters were writing about the marches, protests, sit-ins, boycotts, murders, and church bombings as the tumult of the Civil Rights Movement swept the South and the nation. Yet there was not a single Black reporter in the Washington bureau, or on the foreign reporting staff, and there was not a single senior (or even not-so-senior) Black editor. Of the 5,900 men and women on the company payroll, just 500 were minorities—Blacks, mostly, but also Hispanics and Asians—and the overwhelming majority of those were service and clerical workers.

"I think it is important for us to acknowledge the failure," Sulzberger told his staff. "This just isn't good enough—not good enough for me personally; not good enough for the corporation and not even good enough to meet the legal standards set down by the government." There were reasons for Sulzberger to act, and they included a recognition that the *Times* was vulnerable to a lawsuit under the Civil Rights Act of 1964. But this was not, he said, what was motivating his speech that day. "We would want to change the situation drastically even if there was not a single legal requirement," he said.

Two months later, Paul Delaney, a thirty-six-year-old Black man who covered city hall for the *Evening Star* in the District of Columbia, returned from lunch to find a scribbled message waiting on his desk: "Call Max

Frankel." Delaney had majored in journalism at Ohio State University and, as he approached graduation, sent letters to fifty newspapers requesting a job interview. In each of those letters, he made a point of saying that he was Black; he did not want to waste time traveling for an interview that would be over the moment he passed through the door. His fifty letters drew two replies—both rejections. He eventually got hired by the *Afro-American,* a Black weekly in Baltimore, and after that, the *Atlanta Daily World,* another Black newspaper, before ending up at the *Star,* where his bylines caught the attention of Frankel, then the Washington bureau chief for the *Times.* Frankel took Delaney to lunch and asked if he wanted to work there. Frankel never mentioned race or shared Sulzberger's concern about diversity in the newsroom. But that was certainly on the mind of Frankel and other editors who wanted to to hire him.

"Mr. Delaney is a Negro," read the introductory cover letter sent out by a hiring officer to the editors who would conduct the final round of interviews of this reporter from the *Evening Star.* Delaney would be the first Black reporter hired in the history of the Washington bureau—one of the first responses by the *Times* newsroom to the "failure" Sulzberger had lamented a few months earlier. That became clear to Delaney when he walked into the Washington bureau and gazed across desks filled with white men, broken up by the occasional white woman. There were two Black employees: a secretary and an assistant in the photo lab.

Over the next decade, the *Times* would appoint a Black city hall bureau chief, Ronald Smothers, and name its first Black foreign correspondent, Thomas A. Johnson, who was sent to Lagos. Thomas Morgan III became an assistant editor on the metropolitan desk. The publisher appointed the first Black member of the editorial board, Roger Wilkins, a civil rights leader and a former assistant attorney general under Lyndon Johnson, who joined the *Times* in 1974. And Delaney advanced through the ranks. After Washington, he went to Chicago as a national correspondent; when he arrived, Black reporters from other newspapers were so heartened that the *Times* had appointed a Black national correspondent that they took him to a celebratory dinner in Kansas City, Missouri. After Chicago, Delaney went to New York to become the first Black editor on the national desk, as a deputy.

But these appointments were sporadic and isolated and did not address the growing frustration among minority employees at the *Times*. A few months after the Women's Caucus began preparing to sue the *Times* for discrimination, on October 10, 1974, a group of Black and other minority employees filed its own class-action suit, *Rosario et al. v. The New York Times Company*, asserting the *Times* had discriminated in hiring, promoting, and compensating minorities. For the next six years, the *Times* was confronted with evidence and damaging testimony about its hiring and promotion of Blacks and other minorities. A white high school graduate employed at the *Times* in 1976, to name one example cited by the plaintiffs, made $380.07 a week, or thirty-six cents more than what was paid to a Black *college graduate*. Among those testifying in support of the suit was Paul Delaney. "I believe that the door to equal employment opportunities in every area has always been and remains closed to Blacks and other minorities," he said in an affidavit. Wilkins, who had left the editorial board to become a columnist in the newsroom, expressed his frustrations as the litigation grinded along. "The employment practices of this newspaper are racist," he told *The Village Voice* in 1979. "Some of the editors here get deeply insulted when they're called racist," he said. "After all, they opposed segregation and were on the right side of the civil rights issues of the 1960s. But these are the 1970s, the issues have come north, and the shoe at home pinches."

The *Times* settled out of court in September 1980, agreeing to pay $549,000 for the training and recruitment of minority employees. As in its settlement with the female employees, the *Times* admitted no discrimination but agreed to an affirmative action plan that required a systematic accounting by editors of every potential minority recruit considered, interviewed, or hired. It made little difference. In April 1983, William Stockton, a senior administrative editor, recommended that the newspaper decline to cooperate with a minority employment survey from the American Society of Newspaper Editors, after having participated in the past—a recognition of the potential embarrassment of sharing internal hiring and promotion statistics. "This year has been a poor one in terms of minority hiring," he reported. An internal newsroom survey in

October 1983 found there were still no minorities among the twenty-nine highest-level news management jobs, and that minorities were paid 5.2 percent less than whites, whose salaries at the time ranged from $34,536 for a researcher to $55,750 for a bureau chief.

Over the next three years, senior editors began fanning out to conventions of Black, Latino, and Asian journalists, sitting at recruitment desks where they talked up the *Times* as a place to work, and circulating at *Times*-sponsored receptions with open bars and waiters passing around platters of shrimp for potential recruits. It was the kind of supplication that might have once been considered un-*Times*-like, or at least unnecessary, given that most people who worked at the *Times* assumed that everyone else wanted to work at the *Times*.

Abe Rosenthal offered a relatively upbeat report to Punch Sulzberger on a National Association of Black Journalists convention he attended in Atlanta in 1984, while he was still executive editor, recounting the *Times*'s recruiting efforts there, including how "we gave a big buffet dinner which several hundred black journalists attended . . . I have no illusions that our problems are solved or anywhere near being solved. But I do have a feeling, more than ever, that we are making some progress in coming to grips with it." Yet, speaking a few years later to the American Society of Newspaper Editors, after he stepped down as executive editor, Rosenthal conceded that there was a "failure on the part of management, which includes myself, to bring Blacks into management. I assume we could have done better than we have, but I did the best I could."

That assertion ("I did the best I could") was questionable; Delaney thought that Rosenthal was very much part of the problem: a white editor who would talk grudgingly about affirmative action programs and too often thought minority correspondents were not good enough to merit choice assignments and prestigious foreign postings. Rosenthal would come bouncing out of his office toward Delaney and cast his arm across the newsroom. Paul, look at all those Black reporters out there, Rosenthal said.

And Delaney would look across the newsroom and count five Black faces and ask Rosenthal why there were so few Black editors at the paper.

We're looking, Rosenthal told him.

* * *

When Max Frankel took over as executive editor in 1986, seventeen years after he had hired Paul Delaney to work in the Washington bureau, Blacks were as rare in the newsroom as women had been ten years before. "We have a sprinkling of minority reporters on the paper—a few on Metro, two in Washington, 3 abroad (Rule, Delaney, and Suro) and Cummings on National," Peter Millones, an editor in charge of hiring, said in a report for Frankel. "A couple in Sports and Financial, but only one in Culture and none in Style."* Of thirty-five top editors, none were Black. Minority employees made up 9 percent of the total professional staff at the *Times;* half of those were Black, according to a count by the newspaper. Frankel had brought Delaney to the *Times,* so Delaney assumed he was in line for a top position, such as national editor, now that Frankel was executive editor. But Frankel took him to lunch and said there was no place for Delaney on the national desk; he should consider going to Madrid for more seasoning. Frankel did not mention that Abe Rosenthal had told him he did not consider Delaney qualified to run the national desk, and that this was one instance where Frankel and Rosenthal were in agreement. "He was not good enough, and he knows it, to be National Editor," Frankel said in an oral history at the time. "He wasn't even a very good deputy editor. Everybody has been afraid to move him because he's Black. And, we can't engage in that kind of tokenism anymore. And, it's not fair to Paul."

Delaney's departure for Europe would leave Frankel with a circle of white editors and advisers. And while he declined to appoint Delaney national editor, Frankel instituted one of the most aggressive programs to redress the absence of Blacks in the newsroom in the paper's history. Nine months after he took office, Frankel ordered that there should be one Black professional—reporter or editor—hired for every white one. He called his editors together to explain the plan and pledge to enforce it.

"My impression is that Max will end it when he is convinced that his staff has done everything possible to recruit blacks," George Freeman, the chief First Amendment lawyer in the paper's legal office, wrote Kath-

---

* The references were to Sheila Rule, Roberto Suro, and Judith Cummings.

arine P. Darrow, the paper's general counsel. Freeman said that Frankel had told him he would be "very tough in hiring only blacks who are qualified and should succeed at the *Times*." Frankel had also leaked the news of the initiative to *The Economist* and to *Time* magazine, Freeman confided to Darrow, to "stave off any attacks on the *Times* either by blacks in the newsroom" or "by civil rights leaders such as Jesse Jackson."

Frankel hectored his editors and kept a chart that tracked each department's performance. Warren Hoge, the assistant managing editor for personnel, would send him a list of employees "already hired and matched": a list of white names, each set alongside the corresponding Black hire, set off in parentheses. But his editors would often resist, saying they were being forced to cast aside what they considered top-notch white candidates for Blacks and Latinos, although the quota did not apply to Latinos, who were also a faint presence in the newsroom. The paper remained an institutionally conservative and elite organization, filled with Ivy League graduates; devotion to tradition meant resistance to change. Carolyn Lee, an assistant managing editor, would listen to editors—white men, almost always—assert that the *Times* was a meritocracy and hold themselves out as examples of that: they were appointed to the jobs they had because of their talent.

As executive editor, Frankel was frustrated by the continued failure of the paper to address a shortcoming that had been so glaring for so long. But Frankel, too, held entrenched notions of what made a person qualified for a job: he would argue that it was a mistake to appoint Blacks or other minorities to jobs for which they were not yet ready or might never be ready; it would hurt them, and it would harm the institution. "There was a natural shortage of qualified people that you could hire," he said years later. "It's not just that you would betray your own standards. It's that you would set these people up for failure, if you hired unqualified people simply because they were Black or Latino." For the handful of Black reporters and editors in the newsroom, struggling to break into the higher ranks at this institution, the subjective standards set by their white colleagues in determining who was qualified to work and be promoted was racism—if not by intent, certainly by result.

Frankel had long been angered by newspapers that raided talented Black journalists from competitors (much like he had done with Delaney and the *Evening Star*). It did nothing to increase the number of minorities in majority-white American newsrooms. "People, suddenly interested in showing that they had minorities on the staff, would start stealing them from each other," Frankel said years later. "To the point that there was—the backroom talk was that there was a Black tax. The Blacks knew that they could extract more money by shifting from one to the other." Frankel was not the only editor complaining about this. Jack Driscoll, the executive editor of *The Boston Globe*, complained to Rosenthal when the *Times* snatched a Black editor, Fletcher Roberts, from the *Globe*. "The problem, as I see it, is a domino-like scenario in which the big papers provide exorbitant salaries and perks to minorities in order to correct a white imbalance on their staffs," he wrote Rosenthal. "Pretty soon the industry is contending with large numbers of minorities with inflated salaries and an inflated idea of their abilities." Rosenthal responded: "What you really are saying is that it is perfectly alright for the *New York Times* to be interested in a first-rate white reporter or editor on the Boston Globe, but there is a stockade around first-rate Black reporters and editors."

A year after his one-for-one policy was put in place, Frankel acknowledged to Punch Sulzberger that the results had been, as he put it, "uneven." The *Times* had hired seven Black journalists, including two reporter-trainees, compared with nine people who were not Black, "leaving us two behind our own goal." There were now ninety-six Blacks in a news department of 936. His report came as the publisher was preparing to attend a convention of the National Association of Black Journalists, where, Frankel warned him, he should expect "a fair amount of curiosity—and perhaps some criticism—about our News Department's affirmative action program."

Frankel kept Delaney, now in Madrid, apprised of what was going on in New York. "We really need to get busy now and make a brand new assault," he wrote him. But Delaney was skeptical of these kinds of promises. He wrote Frankel, telling him what he did not want to hear: that the *Times* newsroom would not change unless editors were willing to take chances on less experienced minority candidates, who had not enjoyed the same opportunities for advancement growing up, or attended the same Ivy League colleges, as their white counterparts. That criticism rankled Frankel. "We have certainly taken those risks in hiring in the first place and also moving some people to special correspondencies and editing slots," he wrote back. "What we need in return we don't always get: the right to fail without being accused of racism."

But two months later, Frankel bowed to Delaney's request and brought him back to New York as a senior editor in charge of minority recruitment. Once again, Frankel was turning to Delaney to help him redress the newspaper's struggle with diversity. It was a concession that everything he had done, starting with Delaney's hiring from the *Star*, had failed to significantly change the racial makeup of this newsroom. Delaney welcomed the assignment; it brought him back to New York and put him at Frankel's side, in a position of authority, dealing with a matter of urgency.

He would last four years. In 1992, discouraged and deflated, Delaney announced he would end his career at the *Times* to become the chairman of the journalism department at the University of Alabama.

CHAPTER 10

Palm Beach

Soma Golden Behr could not remember ever being as scared, as she put it at the time, as she was the night after she learned she would be the next national editor of *The New York Times*. She had been the chief economics writer at *Businessweek* for eleven years before the *Times* hired her to cover economics in 1973. She had written editorials under Max Frankel and edited the Sunday Business section for five years. But that was different from running a staff of correspondents covering the country every day of the week. She was staggered by the prospect, and wasn't the kind of person who would hide her feelings—which she made clear three months after she began, when she sat down to talk about her new job for an oral history project. "Jesus! I mean it's so limitless, it's got no edges, it's got no definition. Business was much more defined."

Golden Behr was forty-seven years old and had grown up in Washington, D.C. She was cerebral, contemplative, and explosive, all at once, which could make her slightly exhausting. "I'm a word salad; I explode a lot," was how she put it years later. At five feet, ten-and-a-half inches tall, her presence could fill just about any room, and she rarely had to worry about men talking over her, which gave her an advantage over many women at the *Times*. She was academic in a way reporters tended not to be. Policy excited her. She did not think the national report was particularly good when she took over in 1987. "A little nugget there, here's what's going on downtown here, here's what's going on in a shopping center there" was the way she put it at the time. Her national desk was going to cover the country differently than it had under the man she was replacing. She wanted more attention paid to social policy, the widening income gap under Ronald Reagan, the plights of United States veterans and of Blacks, Latinos, and women. She talked about capturing the "national tapestry." And she was not particularly impressed with the correspondents coming under her command. "The staff doesn't have the great writers it used to have," she said. After her first year, Arthur Gelb, the managing editor, wrote in her annual evaluation that she had "reawakened the national desk, after its long period of dormancy, and . . . done so with an infectious, warm, witty enthusiasm—an incomparable bounce."

Golden Behr never doubted that Max Frankel appointed her because she was a woman (she was most certainly qualified for the job, she knew, but she wasn't the only person qualified for the job). Frankel would assure her that was not the case, though of course it was.

Max, it's okay. I am a woman, and that is not a bad thing, she would say as he shook his head. She was the second woman to run a news desk at the *Times*.* Appointing women to senior positions was a priority for Frankel, as it was for Punch Sulzberger and his son, Arthur Sulzberger, Jr., who would soon succeed him. And while Golden Behr found herself being the *first* or *only* at many junctures in her career, she never viewed herself as a feminist—or as much of a pioneer, even if other women in the newsroom did. That made her uncomfortable. "There's kind of a feeling I have that I'm out there for the women a little bit," she said at the time. "You know, 'we're pulling for you,' and all this." That, she said, puts "a little pressure on you."

* * *

On April 3, 1991, a twenty-nine-year-old woman reported to the police that she had been raped at the Kennedy family oceanfront compound in Palm Beach, Florida. The woman had spent the night at a nightclub, Au Bar, with a group that included Senator Edward M. Kennedy, his son Patrick, and his nephew William Kennedy Smith. After a night of drinking, they left around last call, close to three-thirty in the morning, for a nightcap at the Kennedy estate, La Guerida, on North Ocean Boulevard. The

---

* Le Anne Schreiber was the first woman to run a desk at the *Times*; she was appointed sports editor in 1978, as the newspaper was settling the class-action discrimination suit brought by female employees.

woman said she was raped at about four in the morning. Smith, who was thirty years old, was staying at the compound and would be accused of the assault. The story exploded—within a few days, there were three hundred journalists camped out in Palm Beach—which was no surprise given its elements: sex, wealth, alcohol, privilege, celebrity, and of course, the Kennedys. The *Times* could not ignore that.

Smith, who was in his final term at Georgetown University School of Medicine in Washington, became the focus of attention: a scion of the hard-living, hard-drinking Kennedy family, the entitled medical school student carousing behind the hedges of the family compound, charged with forcing himself on a woman of less stature. The victim was initially not identified, in keeping with journalistic standards in the reporting of sexual assault cases, to protect the woman's privacy. The coverage in the *Times* and other news outlets described her as a habitué of the Palm Beach bars and club circuit—"an integral part of the Palm Beach night scene," a *Times* story said early on—who was from a "well-to-do family" in Jupiter, Florida.

It offended Max Frankel. Young Smith is being dragged through the mud and we don't know anything about the accuser, he thought. Now in his fifth year as executive editor of the *Times*, he had the power to correct what he saw as a journalistic imbalance. Frankel ordered the national desk to prepare an in-depth profile of the accuser. Fox Butterfield, the Boston bureau chief, a contemporary of Golden Behr at Harvard, and a part of the *Times* team that worked on the Pentagon Papers, flew to Florida. He was accompanied by a part-time news assistant in the Boston bureau, Mary B. W. Tabor. Butterfield knew the Kennedy family from his years in Boston, and that was one of the reasons Golden Behr chose to send him to Florida. He and Tabor combed through the accuser's past; they interviewed her friends and associates, they examined court and school records, they even went to her empty home in Jupiter one night and peered through windows. When it came time to write the story, Butterfield, instructed not to use her name, labored through verbal contortions that would permit him to meet the demands of his editors, and he filed the dispatch.

Frankel accepted the policy of not naming the accuser in sexual assault cases, as a way of protecting their privacy. But he had always had his doubts; a newspaper, with the rarest of exceptions, should not be withholding newsworthy information from its readers. And the question of protecting the identity of the victim—the accuser, actually, Frankel thought—was different when it was a tale that involved a celebrity, when it drew so much attention and interest as it moved from the police blotter to the front page of the tabloids and *The New York Times.* His irritation grew by the day. The accuser was the subject of gossip among the reporters covering her.

We are depriving the readers of relevant information even as we slam the hell out of Smith, he would say at the daily news meetings.

He faced some dissent. Joseph Lelyveld, who Frankel named as his managing editor at the start of 1990, admired the integrity of Frankel's argument, but thought it pointless. It was not a matter of principle for Lelyveld; he just thought it was a bad idea. Why are we asking for trouble? he asked.

The argument was resolved by *NBC Nightly News* on April 16. In a segment on the Smith case and the debate over naming accusers in rape cases, NBC identified the accuser in Palm Beach: Patricia Bowman. Frankel was watching in his office. He rose from his seat and walked out into the newsroom, which was humming with the quiet early-evening intensity of an approaching deadline, and over to Golden Behr at the national desk.

The lid's off, Frankel proclaimed. We know the name and NBC knows the name, and the world knows the name. Let's use it.

Golden Behr was not sure the Butterfield story was ready to be published. And she did not think the *Times* needed to publish the name simply because NBC had disclosed it on its nightly news. It was a television minute, she argued to Frankel. (This was well before the advent of sophisticated cellphones, which would have assured instant and widespread circulation of the report.) Frankel was not swayed.

A television network was one thing. A decision by the newspaper that set the standards for much of the news industry to break with precedent and, alone among the nation's most prestigious newspapers, identify the victim in this high-profile sexual assault would have reverberations in newsrooms across the country—and for the *Times.* Frankel was surely aware of that. He very well may have welcomed that.

The story was rewritten to incorporate Bowman's name, and it was rushed through the copyediting desk as deadline approached. Butterfield only learned that her name would be included when he made a routine call for last-minute questions from the copy editor. The story appeared across the top of page A17, under the headline "Woman in Florida Rape Inquiry Fought Adversity and Sought Acceptance." A small sidebar story explained why the *Times* was printing her name, concluding, "The *Times* has withheld Ms. Bowman's name until now, but editors said yesterday that NBC's nationwide broadcast took the matter of her privacy out of their hands." Her name had also appeared in the *Sunday Mirror* in London, a scandal tabloid, and in *Globe,* a supermarket tabloid based in Boca Raton, Florida.

The original story filed by Butterfield and Tabor was filled with anonymous quotes and details about the accuser. It quoted "a woman who knew her at the time" as saying she had "a little wild streak" in high school. It said she went to parties and skipped classes and liked driving in fast cars. The story reported that she had a poor academic record at Tallmadge High School, which she attended growing up outside of Akron, Ohio, and recounted how she withdrew from school in the tenth grade after a debilitating automobile accident in which she broke her neck. Readers were told of an affair she had that resulted in a child born out of wedlock, how she liked to drink at "expensive bars and nightclubs," and how she had received seventeen tickets—for speeding, careless driving, and being involved in an accident. And the story described how the reporters had visited the empty home in Jupiter, where all the blinds were drawn except those in her daughter's room, and they had peered inside. "There, on a shelf, are children's books, including a copy of 'Babar's Anniversary Album' and 'Two Minute Bible Stories,'" the story noted. It was voyeuristic and an ultimately questionable work of reporting, certainly by the standards of the *Times,* and it would draw considerable criticism.

There were about two hours between the moment Frankel made the decision to publish the name and when the story received its final review by an editor. That was enough time to rewrite a story, to edit it for grammar and spelling, to inspect it for inconsistences and factual mistakes. But it did not allow for the kind of contemplative editing that distinguished the *Times:* for an editor to step back and give the story one last dispassionate read for fairness and tone. Frankel called Golden Behr at her townhouse around eleven o'clock that night. The first edition of the *Times* had been delivered to his home, and he had read the story. Great job, he told her. Golden Behr was not so sure. As Frankel was about to learn, his newsroom—the editors and reporters who had grown accustomed over these years to a new atmosphere of discussion and dissent, the very atmosphere Frankel had tried to encourage after A. M. Rosenthal—was also not so sure.

The power of an executive editor at the *Times* had traditionally been a function of his relationship with the publisher. But now, after Rosenthal had moved on, it also came from the confidence and trust of the reporters and editors. And this was becoming a newly assertive newsroom, emboldened by a generation of reporters and editors with a different sensibility and by women attaining more positions of influence. The tides were turning in a way that Frankel would never quite appreciate and that his successors at the *Times*, and at other newspapers, would have to learn to navigate.

Frankel realized there was a problem as soon as he arrived at the office. The complaints began at his first meeting of the day; many women could not understand why the *Times* had published the name of a victim in a sexual assault case. The *Times* was a different place than it had been when the discrimination suit was filed, but it was still a male-dominated culture, and the sensitivity that many of the women had about the treatment of sexual abuse victims was not necessarily shared, or even understood, by some of the men in the newsroom. Frankel pulled Golden Behr aside as she arrived at work.

Let me tell you what's going on, he said. There's a revolution. I don't want an inch of daylight between you and me on this.

At that moment, Frankel felt relief that he had put Golden Behr into that job. Her "female sensibility stood guard over national news, sparing us the charge that only priggish males would have dared to explore the character of Smith's accuser," he said years later.

Two days after the article appeared, nearly three hundred people crowded into elevators after lunch and rode up to the WQXR auditorium on the ninth floor of the *Times* building for a hastily called meeting to discuss the newspaper's policies in writing about rapes and sexual assaults. Frankel, Golden Behr, and Al Siegal spent one hour and fifteen minutes fielding questions from a crowd of colleagues. Many of them were indignant: The *Times* had broken one of the great taboos of journalism. I'm confused about what the standards are here, said Todd S. Purdum, a reporter for the metropolitan desk. Are we going to have to now name every girl he ever shtooped? His Yiddishism drew a gale of laughter, but it was only a momentary relief in an uncomfortable meeting. It fell to Golden Behr to explain and defend the decision—even as she found that she agreed with some of the colleagues who were staring at her from the auditorium. "This is the most troubling time of my career," she told them. "I am shocked by the depth of the response." She was not bothered that her reporters had peeked through a window to examine Bowman's bookshelves; reporters are snoops. Small details are what bring profiles to life—the description of the children's Bible on the shelf, a book she had enjoyed as a child, being a perfect example of what Golden Behr had in mind.

"I read of a woman who had a confusing life," she said. "Not a damning portrait. It was a portrait, period." She acknowledged the piece made some readers think the woman was a "loose girl," as she later described the victim, but said that, even if she was one, it did not excuse the actions of an attacker. "I think we can trust readers to make the right judgments," she said at the session. "I can't account for every weird mind that reads the *New York Times*." That set off a rustle. "The people with the weird minds are the ones who thought that was journalism," someone in the audience responded.

Siegal explained that the editors had originally ruled against using her name but changed their minds after learning of the NBC broadcast. "The right thing became a forlorn gesture, because it would have no consequences, and we are not in the business of keeping information from our readers just for public relations," he said. But Siegal regretted leaving in the reference to a wild streak. "We edited in a hurry, and a lot of awful stuff was taken out. The next morning I would probably have done a lot of things differently." Throughout the session, the editors were met with defiance, anger, hoots, and shouts. "I read it as: here is a woman who is a slut who, speeds in a car, who deserves to be raped," one called out. Rosemary Bray, an editor on the Sunday Book Review, drew a loud round of applause when she presented herself as a "person who believes in common standards of decency. I didn't need to know about the parking tickets the woman received, or the wallpaper," she said.

The meeting did little to quell the uproar. That Sunday, a column appeared on the Op-Ed page by Anna Quindlen under the headline "A Mistake." The column took the institution on directly, and in its own pages.

"For The New York Times, a paper that has been justly proud of taking the lead on matters of journalistic moment, to announce that it was forced to follow was beneath its traditions," she wrote. "To do so in a story that contained not only the alleged victim's 'wild streak' but the past sexual history of her mother could not help but suggest that the use of the name was not informative but punitive." Frankel did not understand why Quindlen had not given him the courtesy of asking why he had done what he had done. "I don't have any problem about being criticized," he would say years later. But, he said, he appreciated it when those criticizing his decisions "ask me what my side of the story is and she never did."

Quindlen worried that she might now be in danger of losing her position; no one criticized the *Times* in the pages of the *Times*, as Sydney Schanberg had learned. When she arrived at the newsroom later that week, Arthur Sulzberger, Jr., whom she had befriended while they worked on the metropolitan desk, threw his arms around her and gave her a hug and a kiss—a conspicuous gesture of affirmation and support. Frankel observed the moment and took it as a rebuke. But Sulzberger was not trying to send a message about the merits of Frankel's decision, though he thought it was a mistake. He expected to become publisher one day, and when he did, he would choose the columnists on the Op-Ed pages. He knew the history of his father and Schanberg, and he wanted his columnists to feel they could criticize the *Times* without fear of retribution.

Abe Rosenthal had been the target of criticism within the newsroom, but it was almost always in discreet conversations around desks or whispers from reporters to news organizations like *The Village Voice* or *New York* magazine. The idea of reporters and editors publicly confronting Rosenthal would have been unthinkable. But there was a new spirit among staff members, and this was not the first time Frankel had felt their wrath. The previous year, Frankel had set off a small storm when he dismissed a survey that found the *Times* ranked last among major newspapers in quoting women on its front page. "If you are covering local teas, you've got more women than if you're *The Wall Street Journal*," he told an interviewer from *The Washington Post*. Women, among them Betsy Wade, turned up at work with tea bags affixed to their lapels. It drew the attention of Page Six, the gossip column at the *New York Post*. Frankel apologized, and the *Times* moved on. But he would not apologize over Bowman.

Frankel had exercised an act of news judgment. It was in keeping with his penchant for challenging assumptions and traditions, and it was in keeping with his certitude. Frankel could be the refreshing face in the newsroom, but he could also come across as arrogant and stubborn. He was being publicly berated by his staff, some of whom shared what took place at the *Times* auditorium with a reporter from *The Washington Post*. He was confronted with a petition signed by one hundred employees—men and women—to express "their outrage about the profile in yesterday's paper." Letters of condemnation were followed by letters of support. "You are a great journalist and a great editor, Max," Dan Rather, the anchor of the CBS Evening News, wrote. "And the *Times* is a beacon of excellence. You know all of that. But especially just now it may not hurt for you to hear others say it. Stay strong."

The *Times* published an editors' note and an article about itself in the middle of a storm—something it was institutionally loath to do—written by a media reporter, William Glaberson. Critics of the paper were let down because "the one who has always stood for a certain kind of standard altered that standard," as Joan Konner, the dean of the Columbia Journalism School told Glaberson. Frankel, in that same story, described the situation as a "crisis" because so "many people feel The Times betrayed its standards."

Two weeks after Bowman's name was published, Frankel was called to meet with Punch and Arthur Sulzberger. They were not happy with how Frankel had handled the story. He should not have let NBC trigger a decision like that by the *Times*. The story devoted too much attention to "inside affairs," and too much attention to the *Times*, as Frankel described it in a note he wrote himself after the meeting.

Frankel had, by his account, not read the entire story before it went to print. "I didn't realize then that the story had all of this smarmy stuff about her in it because they were going to run that without her name," he later said. He was uncomfortable as he reread it the day after he called Golden Behr at home to praise the article—but never quite as uncomfortable as all those critics. Frankel would come to describe this episode as a low point of his time as executive editor. But he never regretted his decision to publish the name.

CHAPTER 11

Not Punch

Arthur Ochs Sulzberger, Jr., was four years old in 1955 when his parents, Punch and Barbara Winslow Grant, separated, young enough that as an adult, he could not picture them as a married couple. At the time the family was living in France while Punch worked for the Paris bureau of the *Times.* When he discovered that his wife was having an affair, he left Paris for New York. Barbara, struggling with exhaustion and depression, moved with Arthur and his sister Karen, who was one year younger, to the South of France, where they lived for a year before returning to New York and moving into an apartment on East Seventy-fourth Street, between Lexington Avenue and Third Avenue. This was home for Arthur until he decided at the age of fifteen that he wanted to live with his father and stepmother, Carol Sulzberger, at their Fifth Avenue apartment. Punch was "always a man of some distance," Arthur would say, and he wanted to establish a relationship with his father and begin to live the life of a publisher's son—and, presumably, future publisher.

Punch's father, Arthur Hays Sulzberger, would host dinners with mayors and senators, college presidents, diplomats, artists, and luminaries like Amelia Earhart. You can listen, but you can't repeat a single thing, he would instruct his daughter Marian Heiskell.

Punch Sulzberger did not bring his work home with him in quite the same way, and Arthur Sulzberger did not take from his years on Fifth Avenue those lessons of observing the life of a powerful publisher. Still, Arthur Sulzberger's interest in the *Times* and journalism blossomed during his teenage years. He began reading the newspaper regularly. He worked for his high school newspaper. His father arranged a summer internship on Fleet Street in London, for *The Daily Telegraph*. "I had a front-page story every day," Arthur Sulzberger would say. "I did the weather." He worked, before leaving for college, as a reporter at the *Vineyard Gazette* on Martha's Vineyard, which had been purchased by James Reston, the Washington columnist for the *Times*, and his wife, Sally Fulton Reston. When Arthur graduated from Tufts University in 1974, Punch Sulzberger turned to his old friend Seymour Topping, the foreign correspondent who was now second-in-command under Abe Rosenthal, to mentor the young man who the publisher wanted to succeed him.

By now, there was little question in the newsroom that Punch Sulzberger's only son would one day become publisher—Karen was closer to her mother and had little interest in working at the family business—though that seemed difficult to imagine at the time. Arthur was bright but impetuous; in college, he had long hair, rode a motorcycle, smoked marijuana, dabbled with LSD, and had been arrested at two demonstrations against the Vietnam War—to the distress of his father, a former marine who served in World War II and Korea. Even then, Arthur was trying to prove he was different from Punch. It was the uneasy relationship a son has with a father in a broken marriage, aggravated by the political, cultural, and generational divisions that were roiling so many families in that era. Topping, who was known as Top, and his wife, Audrey, were regular visitors at Hillandale, the Sulzbergers' weekend retreat. Topping would join young Sulzberger by the pool. They had long conversations about where Sulzberger might start a reporting career, and the burdens he would face, because of his last name, trying to quietly break into the newspaper business. Topping always assumed he was speaking to the next publisher of *The New York Times* but never mentioned it; he would offer Sulzberger the same advice that any older *Times* journalist might give to any young reporter aspiring to join the *Times:* leave New York for a newspaper in a medium-sized city.

Sulzberger began as a reporter for the *Raleigh Times* in North Carolina before moving to London to join the Associated Press. He would send his clips to Topping, share his gripes—they are making me write short stories! An editor rewrote me!—and Topping would respond with suggestions and praise. Sulzberger mailed Topping a clipping of one story, with this note: "Being a small town paper, it was naturally rewritten by my overeager editor. The sad effect of having time to spare." Sulzberger's personality, irreverent and brash, and perhaps too flippant for a *Times* publisher (this would be a concern that would trail him throughout his career), was beginning to take shape. "As for their style, I am writing this letter in it. Short sentences, short graphs, short words, short everything. It's annoying as hell." Topping would study not only the clips Sulzberger sent him, which had been edited and published, but also raw copy the young man wrote; he discreetly contacted editors in Raleigh and asked them to mail him printouts of unedited versions of Sulzberger's stories. "I could not be more delighted with your clips," he wrote Arthur a year into his reporting career. "The pieces show that you are beginning to probe more deeply in your reporting. Although your material has become more complicated, you are retaining that nice easy style that was so evident in your earlier pieces." He is a good reporter, Topping told Punch. Arthur Sulzberger was concerned about what his father thought of him, as was evident in the note he attached to one packet of clips sent to Topping. "Perhaps, if the desire ever hits you, you might throw them up to the 14th floor and let the old man see them. If not, burn them—or better yet do you have a shredder."

Punch Sulzberger's short reporting career had been defined in 1955 when, as a young correspondent in the Paris bureau, he attended an automobile race in Le Mans, France. A race car tumbled out of control and careened into the stands, killing eighty-two spectators and the driver. Sulzberger, horrified, left but never thought of alerting the bureau of what he had seen. By contrast, in May 1977, Arthur, as an Associated Press reporter working out of London, hustled his way to the front lines after terrorists seized a passenger train near Assen, Holland. He was well aware of his father's failure in Le Mans, having read about it in Gay Talese's book. Sulzberger stayed at the scene after the *New York Times* reporter—Craig Whitney, who would go on to run the Washington bureau—left and returned to Bonn. He had been tipped off by military sources that Dutch commandos would stage a raid to free the hostages that night; he jerry-rigged a telephone line to a nearby home and hid behind a tree. Thus, he was there to provide a dramatic first-hand account. "I was literally on the phone when they hit," he said years later.

He wrote Topping about his adventure. "As you can well imagine, Assen has been the highlight of my experience abroad. As far as I'm concerned, it is one highlight I'd rather not repeat."

The *Times* used an Associated Press dispatch, written by a reporter at the press center, that quoted its correspondent on the scene as an eyewitness. Topping mailed Sulzberger the front page so he could see his name in print. "I was in the office on Friday night when your copy came booming in from Assen," Topping wrote Sulzberger. "To say the least, I was very proud to see you doing so well on the firing line. . . . I thought you would be interested in seeing what your copy looked like in the *New York Times*. We used it as an off-lead in the third edition." Sulzberger later called it "my greatest moment as a journalist."*

On June 1, 1978, Punch Sulzberger sent Topping a note. "Top, I would very much appreciate your making the necessary arrangements on a business-like basis with Arthur as to the date of his starting, salary, hours, etc." The next day, Topping informed Abe Rosenthal that it was time to bring Arthur, Jr., to the *Times*. "Punch says he has already spoken to you about this matter, and he would like us to deal directly with Arthur when he arrives here to arrange his employment on a business-like basis." Arthur, Jr., began his *Times* career as a general assignment reporter in the Washington bureau. His first print byline—over a story headlined "A Wage-Price Hot Line," buried in the Business section—appeared on November 6, 1978, a day worthy of note not only because it was the first *Times* story by this future publisher but because it marked a return to publication after a strike by the pressmen shut down the *Times* and the *Daily News* for eighty-eight days.

* * *

Arthur was twenty-seven years old when he arrived in Washington in 1978, aware that young reporters from the Associated Press did not typ-

---

* The future publisher had his moment because Robert B. Semple, Jr., the foreign editor, had told Whitney that the story appeared under control and he could return home. This is the kind of bad call that every editor dreads. He would remind Arthur Sulzberger of it years later, when Sulzberger became the publisher and Semple was the op-ed editor: Arthur, I put you on the map: Page One of *The New York Times*, your own newspaper, because of a fucking blunder I made.

ically begin their *Times* careers in the Washington bureau. He was determined to prove his worth. He accepted without complaint the ministerial stories that tended to go to the new reporters. He covered a hearing of the Senate Committee on Banking, Housing, and Urban Affairs, producing a story about Miami banks being complicit in financing illicit drug dealers. He wrote a profile of William E. Timmons, a lobbyist who ran Ronald Reagan's political operation at the Republican National Convention of 1980. He was assigned to ride the campaign plane of George H. W. Bush, Reagan's running mate for vice president. It was not the choicest of assignments but hardly a bad one, particularly for a reporter of Sulzberger's level of experience. Bush took notice of this correspondent and, four days after he and Reagan were elected, sent Punch Sulzberger a note. *"Your son is a class act,"* he wrote. "He won the *respect* of everyone on our plane. He is a genuine, warm human being. We Republicans are all supposed to 'assail' the *Times* from time to time. But with Arthur doing his number—fair, strong reporting—it's hard to do."

Arthur and his wife, Gail Gregg, lived at the Woodley Park Towers near Rock Creek Park, and Arthur would walk the two miles down Connecticut Avenue to the bureau near the White House, at 1000 Connecticut Avenue NW. He found himself sitting next to Steven Rattner, another young reporter in the bureau. Rattner was assigned there in 1977, after President Jimmy Carter declared that the nation was facing an energy crisis, because the *Times* didn't have anyone in Washington bureau with the expertise Rattner had to write about this complex new problem facing the nation. Sulzberger and Rattner became lifelong friends; Sulzberger would introduce Rattner to his future wife, Maureen White.* They were part of what became a close band of reporters in the office, along with Philip Taubman, Steven Weisman, and Judith Miller, who Rattner would later date. There were drinks and dinner after deadline, and a weekend house called Blue Goose in Bethany Beach on the Delaware shore, shared one summer by Arthur and Gail and Rattner and Miller. They were all of a type: ambitious, young, brainy, already in the Washington bureau, and all quite confident about their talents and futures.

---

* Rattner left the *Times* in 1982 to become a Wall Street financier and so escaped Sulzberger's eventual self-imposed stricture on being friends with his employees.

Arthur was not modest or retiring but also rarely reminded people of who he was. "Arthur bore his son-ship with unusual grace," Howell Raines, who was also beginning his *Times* career in the bureau and befriended the future publisher, would say years later. Of course, everyone in the bureau knew who Sulzberger was, not that it was openly discussed. "Everybody pretended, including him, that he was just another reporter—but everybody, including him, knew that he was a Sulzberger, and it was like finding a unicorn because most of us had never seen a Sulzberger or known a Sulzberger," Rattner said years later. Still, as far as Bill Kovach, the head of the Washington bureau, was concerned, it was a clique that revolved around a future publisher, and that was not good for office morale—or good for Arthur. Kovach summoned him to his office.

I don't want to tell you how to live your life, Kovach said to him. But I do want to tell you to think more clearly about how you behave in this bureau. Everybody in this bureau, when they look at you, they are looking at who they think is going to be the next publisher of this newspaper. You have to behave like someone who cares about everyone at this newspaper.

Kovach made a point of stopping by Sulzberger's desk, asking what he was working on, engaging him in discussion about world events: the Iranian hostage crisis, Carter's reelection campaign, the rise of Reagan. Their conversations would be "light—very light, skimming the surface of whatever you were talking about," as Kovach later described them, and it was always Kovach who would ask the questions.

The Washington editor found Sulzberger so underwhelming that when he encountered him years later in New York, now working in management, he was struck by how he had changed. Sulzberger was initiating conversations on his own, sticking to one topic instead of careening from subject to subject. He had grown, clearly, as he had moved methodically onward from Washington, under the supervision of his father, Frankel, and Walter Mattson, the company president, through a course of study in *Times* business and news management. He had gone from a reporter in city hall to an assignment editor on the metropolitan desk; he worked in the advertising department (which proved far more enjoyable than he'd ever expected) and strategic planning (which he disliked).

When he moved into night production, Sulzberger would pick up his two children at school, take them home, and arrive at the office around six, wearing jeans and a leather jacket instead of his customary dress shirt and suspenders, in time to supervise the pressrun. The presses were still located in the basement of the building on West Forty-third, and he would stay until three in the morning, when they rumbled to a halt.

* * *

The first time Punch Sulzberger went to his board of directors—in November 1986—and said he wanted to name his son assistant publisher, setting in place a succession plan for when he retired, the publisher encountered such a wave of skepticism that he pulled back. The younger Sulzberger had been waiting outside the room, where the board had assembled, for his father to emerge with the good tidings of his promotion.

It's not going to work, Punch Sulzberger told his son. They are very upset. It was a moment of awkwardness for the father and lasting embarrassment for the son.

Members of the board did not really know Arthur, and Punch had done little to prepare them for the transition. Punch, who had been publisher since June 1963 and who himself took office amid doubts over his capabilities, spent the next two months assuring the board that his son was a worthy successor. The board ratified his choice on a second vote early the following year, but it was a deeply unsettling moment for Arthur, undermining his confidence just as he was trying to forge his identity as the next publisher. He blamed his father for not preparing the board for this moment and made sure not to make the same mistakes when it was his time to retire a quarter-century later.

Arthur was thirty-five years old, but in appearance and demeanor, he seemed quite a bit younger: puckish and not quite fully formed. His quirky manner—the jauntiness, the clumsy jokes, the affected self-confidence—was off-putting, even obnoxious. If Punch Sulzberger was to the manner born, Arthur Sulzberger was a child of the 1960s, a self-described product of the "hippie-dippy" world, who rode the subway to work. Punch—charming, funny, with his sense of self and the confidence that came with age—put people at ease. He would laugh at himself. When Clyde Haberman, a *Times* reporter, sat down with Punch to interview him for an obituary that would be published upon Sulzberger's death, Haberman began with a confession. Can I just tell you how uncomfortable this makes me? Haberman said.

Punch stared at his interlocutor. *You?* he responded.

Arthur Sulzberger was slightly distant and easily distracted; he was not a warm presence in a room. He dressed like a vaguely English toff, with wide suspenders, striped double-breasted suits, and tailored blue shirts with white colors and cuffs, clipped with cuff links. He smoked a cigar. His tendency to overcompensate with the remark spoken too loudly, or to conspicuously quote Churchill and mention the latest history book on his nightstand, conveyed insecurity, a sense that he was trying too hard. And that was often true, but he was certainly intelligent and perceptive. Sydney Gruson, who with his experience on the business side and in the newsroom was the publisher's closest adviser, tried to counsel Arthur about his manner. One of your biggest dangers is the appearance of arrogance that you give, Gruson told him. Gruson found that his advice went unheeded.

Both father and son would ask blunt questions, seemingly unconcerned about coming across as naïve. I want to know something: Why are those little packages of peanuts so hard to open? Punch asked an airline executive who visited the editorial board to talk about FAA regulations. But while this trait was seen in the newsroom as endearing with Punch, it was taken as evidence of cluelessness by the son.

The reservations about young Arthur included some members of his family. Punch's oldest sister, Marian, found him cold and unapproachable; she did not think he had the qualities needed to run the family business—not that she had much to say about the decision. Carol Sulzberger, the publisher's second wife, made little attempt to hide her contempt for Punch's only son and urged her husband not to make him his successor. Warren Hoge, an assistant managing editor, was asked by other *Times* executives to nurture Arthur Sulzberger as he moved through the ranks, to "see if you can just make him act more like an adult," as he later described it.

Try not to read off a page when you are at a public event, Hoge told him. Keep the humor appropriate.

Hoge invited him to a dinner party at his home so he could introduce the future publisher to his friends in New York society. The table was humming with the city's elite media, a Punch Sulzberger crowd, among them the television news anchors Peter Jennings of ABC and Tom Brokaw of NBC, and Richard E. Snyder, the president of Simon & Schuster. The night did not go well, as Hoge learned the next day. "That whole crowd was saying how feckless Arthur Junior was," he said. A strong judgment, no doubt. But if these doubts rattled Arthur, he did not show it.

Arthur was promoted from assistant publisher to deputy publisher in April 1988; the board had grown comfortable with him, and his ascension to publisher was all but assured. He was now second-in-command, but in truth, Arthur was publisher in all but title from that day forward. His father was ready to move on. Punch had begun devoting his attention to other passions, such as the Metropolitan Museum of Art, of which he had been named chairman in 1987.

Arthur began keeping an eye on the daily operations of the newsroom. He pressed Frankel on what the *Times* could do to appeal to younger readers, suggesting the creation of a section written for a new generation of readers. "Perhaps the idea is goofy, but I have to believe that we have a role to play in meeting the needs of the young," he said. He oversaw the introduction of color to the pages of the *Times*, which meant appeasing one particularly strong skeptic: his father. "He needs to be assured that our use of color will not embarrass him or the institution, and so far I have proven unable to give him that feeling," Arthur Sulzberger wrote Frankel and Lance R. Primis, the general manager of the *Times* newspaper. It was Arthur to whom Max Frankel appealed in negotiating cuts in newsroom spending as the newspaper grappled with the economic recession that hit the nation in 1987. And there were reminders already of what his life as a publisher would be like: Arthur Sulzberger was invited to the White House by Barbara and George H. W. Bush. Upon his return to New York, he responded to concerns Mrs. Bush had raised with him about ink smudging off the *Times* onto the First Lady's hands. He sent her a stack of blank newspapers.

Arthur had kept his counsel, for the most part, as he moved up the ranks, but there were things his father did as publisher with which he disagreed, and he would now demonstrate that by his actions. Punch

Sulzberger sought the company of the vibrant stable of correspondents and editors who were in his employ, particularly those who worked in London. That was where he kept an apartment and would host dinners and cocktail parties, including an annual Thanksgiving celebration. Correspondents based there—R. W. Apple, Howell Raines, Joseph Lelyveld, Craig Whitney, William E. Schmidt—would learn to accommodate the last-minute we-are-in-town invitations to dinner at Claridge's or cocktails at the Sulzberger flat. Punch Sulzberger would travel the world with editors and executives like Abe Rosenthal, Sydney Gruson, and Seymour Topping.

Young Arthur had socialized with reporters when he first arrived in Washington and upon moving to New York, and he invited colleagues to his apartment just off Central Park West, for a Thanksgiving eve party, where guests could watch the inflating of the balloons for the Thanksgiving Day parade on the side streets off the park. But that stopped when he became an assistant publisher; unlike his father, he did not think a publisher should be friends with the people who worked for him.

Punch Sulzberger had embroidered himself into the civic fabric of New York. But young Arthur avoided those kinds of entanglements, aware of the potential for conflict when an employee of the *Times*—to say nothing of its publisher—had a relationship with a potential subject of a news story. This had come up with Punch when Walter Annenberg, the publisher and philanthropist, was deliberating where to donate his $1 billion collection of Impressionist art, and the Metropolitan Museum of Art was one of his most ardent suitors. As he came close to reaching a decision, Annenberg complained to Punch that the *Times*, whenever it wrote about him, noted that his father, Moses Annenberg, also a publisher, had gone to jail for tax evasion. Sulzberger went to Joseph Lelyveld, who was managing editor. Is it really necessary to do this? the publisher asked, as Lelyveld later recounted. (Lelyveld understood his concern: he, too, thought the mentions were often gratuitous.) After Annenberg donated his collection to the Met, Sulzberger sent Frankel a note asking "as a personal favor" to make sure the review of the Annenberg exhibition, by Michael Kimmelman, was "devoid of zingers. I have no problem with him using his critical eye to determine which of Walter's paintings are world class and which may be of a more minimal nature. But there are ways of indicating this (as our friend John Russell so wonderfully does) without cutting off the balls of the owner. This is truly important for me and for New York." Kimmelman's review, published on June 2, 1991, praised the exhibit and ran under the headline "From Strength to Strength: A Collector's Gift to the Met."*

The two men shared a passion for the *Times*, but beyond that, father and son were quite different. Punch Sulzberger would find time for a round of golf. Arthur Sulzberger could barely make it past the first tee. "What did Churchill call golf?" he remarked later, as he reminisced about his father. "A good walk, ruined."† Punch Sulzberger enjoyed gardening at Hillandale, the family weekend estate, and later at a home in Southampton. Arthur Sulzberger preferred rock climbing near his weekend home in New Paltz in the Hudson Valley. Young Arthur was molded by his years in Outward Bound, which took him and his crew on excursions into the wilderness, to learn "individual success in a team environment." Punch's personality had been forged by the training and discipline he received as a marine. When James M. Markham, the Paris bureau chief, committed suicide at the age of forty-six in August of 1989, Arthur told Frankel to organize sessions with staff members so they could discuss their grief.

What's to talk about? Frankel responded. Suicide is a tragic thing. These things happen to people.‡

Frankel thought about the contrast between father and son: Punch Sulzberger was a marine who had watched people die; he would never have responded this way to the tragedy. But for a newsroom wondering if the *Times* had become such a difficult place to work that it drove people to kill themselves, the grief-counseling sessions were welcome. Frankel reluctantly relented to "a ritual which struck me as superfluous and patronizing but for which I received much praise."

---

* Kimmelman, years later, said he never again saw evidence of the publisher interfering with his work.

† The quote on golf is more commonly ascribed to Mark Twain, though even that is a matter of dispute.

‡ Markham had been ordered to return to New York to become an editor on the foreign desk, a move he clearly was reluctant to make; as Frankel later noted, he was struggling with marital discord.

Young Arthur chafed at comparisons with his father, and particularly the nickname "Pinch" that the tabloids and other news organizations began to use to distinguish him from his father. "Prince Pinch," read the headline on a profile that appeared in August 1988 in *Manhattan, Inc.* It was a name that was not used by anyone who really knew him or counted him a friend. "Just for your records, I generally shy away from the nickname 'Pinch,'" he wrote to Edgar Cullman, Jr., the president and CEO of the General Cigar Company, who had invited him to attend a thousand-dollar-a-head cocktail party on behalf of Senator Joseph Biden, Jr. Donald Trump also addressed Sulzberger as "Pinch" in a letter soliciting him to buy a table at the thirty-second annual Superstar Dinner of the Police Athletic League. He scrawled the word "no" across the bottom of that invitation. "A man deserves his own nickname, and 'Pinch' is clearly my father's name, twisted," Arthur Sulzberger once said.

The differences between the two men were more than stylistic: the new publisher intended to take the newspaper in a new direction. Arthur thought it too stuffy, and that in its adherence to tradition, it risked losing a new generation of readers. He thought the divisions between the newsroom and business side was a relic of a passing era. He was distressed to hear business colleagues say they were wary of raising ideas with anyone in the newsroom on how to attract new readers. Punch Sulzberger would show up at the Page One meetings most days, absorbed by the discussion that led to the creation of the next day's front page. Arthur Sulzberger attended them on occasion, but before long, his visits became infrequent. Lelyveld, who worked with father and son during his years as a correspondent and later editor, liked to say that Punch Sulzberger never made a decision before he had to, while Arthur Sulzberger would make a decision before he knew what he wanted to do. Max Frankel was quoted in *The New Yorker* as making a cutting joke (and one he said he meant only as a joke) about Arthur Sulzberger's management capabilities. "I'll say this about Arthur: he'll never make the same mistake three times."

Father and son agreed about the need to transform a newsroom that was overwhelmingly white, a challenge that neither man met. But Arthur Sulzberger had grown up as civil rights protestors marched across the South. As deputy publisher, he would join the delegation of

Times editors on recruiting missions to minority journalist conventions. He hosted a luncheon for delegates at the National Association of Black Journalists in Kansas City in July 1991. "Keep pushing, keep pushing to turn your vision of diversity into our reality," he told them. Punch Sulzberger was concerned with the frustration among minorities at the newspaper, as he had made clear back in 1969, but seemed almost offended by the lawsuit they filed to force the *Times* to address their grievances. He could barely hide his annoyance when the newspaper made gestures to expand its appeal beyond its traditional base of readers, such as a story in the magazine about cooking in the Dominican Republic. The magazine's food pages, he complained to Frankel, "have become more and more ethnic in our approach. I can't imagine that last Sunday's Hispanic recipes could interest the vast majority of our readers. Can't we spin around and come back to some of the old-fashioned virtues such as that wonderful world of chocolate cake and remain there for a time until the ethnic food passes through the system?"

Arthur Sulzberger disapproved of the way gay men and lesbians had been treated in the newsroom under his father and intended to change that when he took over. As one of management's representatives to Guild negotiations, he helped negotiate a deal which provided benefits to same-sex domestic partnerships. It was a rare moment in which the *Times* led rather than followed society on a contentious issue, and his father was angered when he learned what his son had done. "My father was anti-gay," Arthur Sulzberger said in 2017. Attitudes toward homosexuality were shifting, but Punch Sulzberger's views would barely change over the years. He complained to his son, after Arthur became publisher, about a Style section feature on the decline of drag balls, a world of mostly nonwhite drag queens devastated by the AIDS epidemic. The story, "Paris Has Burned"—the headline referring to the 1990 documentary on the drag ball scene called *Paris Is Burning*—was accompanied by a photograph of Angie Xtravaganza, "a Queen among queens," who died in 1993. The story made it "look as though the *Times* endorses this kind of homosexual dress and behavior," Punch Sulzberger wrote his son. "I get a very definitive and positive feeling that we have swerved far off course and we need to replot our way. I truly do not believe that homosexual and Black fashion reflects the editorial balance of you, Max or Joe, and I do not know who it is that we are trying to please. Certainly, it does not reflect the taste or interest of the average readers of the *New York Times.*"

* * *

Arthur Ochs Sulzberger, Jr., was named publisher of *The New York Times* on January 16, 1992—the fifth member of the Ochs-Sulzberger family to lead the newspaper since his great-grandfather, Adolph Ochs, purchased it in 1896. The new publisher was forty years old, three years older than his father had been when he became publisher. When Arthur, Jr., became publisher, Punch stayed on as the chairman and chief executive. It would be another five years before Arthur would be awarded those titles and that authority, a concession to members of the board who were still nervous about the young new publisher and needed assurances that Punch would have the final word over company governance.

As would become clear, Arthur brought with him the promise of generational change, and a deliberate—if not explicitly stated—effort to demonstrate that while he may be his father's son, he was not his father's son. For the next twenty-five years, he would oversee some of the most turbulent chapters in the newspaper's history as it tried to navigate an era of business, journalistic, and political upheaval. He would have a long learning curve, and he began (like his father) with little confidence from the board of directors and many in the newsroom. Arthur would prove as devoted to the mission of the *Times* as his father, grandfather, and great-grandfather, but he was driven more by pragmatism than sentiment and was more willing to cast aside some of its traditions in the interest of change. That would be the most lasting difference between father and son.

CHAPTER 12

The Next Horizon

From his first days at *The New York Times*, Howell Raines approached the newsroom as if he were a foreign correspondent embarking on the adventure of a new posting. He was going to study it; learn its culture and rhythms, try to understand why some of his new colleagues thrived while others faded into an overnight shift or left for a lesser newspaper or a think tank. Raines was, from his early days, considering his future. Arthur Sulzberger, Jr., met Raines in the Washington bureau in 1980, when Raines was covering Ronald Reagan's presidential campaign and Sulzberger was assigned to cover Reagan's running mate, George H. W. Bush. "We hit it off immediately, not as buddies but as colleagues," Raines later wrote. "We were both true believers in the inherent superiority of the *Times*, but we were close enough in age to take a satirical, sixties view of its foibles and pretentions." Even then, Raines struck the future publisher as someone "always looking over the next horizon."

Raines thought that he might be the executive editor of the *Times* one day. Yet Raines, who by the summer of 1992 was running the Washington bureau, was caught by surprise when Sulzberger flew down to ask him to become editor of the editorial page. This was no small honor. Sulzberger had been named publisher at the beginning of the year, and this was his first major appointment. Raines reacted much the same way Max Frankel had responded fifteen years earlier when he was offered the same position by Arthur's father, Punch. It is not my first choice, Raines told the new publisher. Raines shared the reservations that anyone who worked in the newsroom might have had. It would take him away from the action of assembling each day's *Times*. He was unaccustomed to stating his opinions in a public forum. And Raines barely read the *Times*'s editorial pages; they struck him as dutiful and stolid. He told Sulzberger he would prefer to be a columnist, and he offered himself as a liberal counterweight to William Safire. But Sulzberger pressed Raines to take the job.

This will give you the chance to get to know New York hierarchically, organizationally, Sulzberger told him. You're going to really need to do this.

That statement—*You're going to really need to do this*—required no elaboration. He was being tested, and he was being groomed. Few people work as closely with the publisher as the editorial page editor. Frankel's career in the newsroom had not ended after Punch Sulzberger made him the editorial page editor—a lesson that was not lost on either Raines or the younger Sulzberger. The new publisher wanted Raines to learn how the *Times* worked, from the corporate offices to the newsroom. He wanted to get to know him better.

Raines would not require much courting. He was coming off a divorce and living as a bachelor in Georgetown. He was finishing a memoir—*Fly Fishing Through the Midlife Crisis*. He was directing the coverage of the 1992 presidential campaign, but that would end in November. I am being offered the chance to run the editorial page of the most important liberal newspaper in the country, Raines told himself. As Washington editor, Raines had no control over space in the newspaper. Editors in New York determined how many column inches would be allocated to the Washington report, and where those stories would appear. He would be in control of some of the most-read sections of the newspaper: the editorial page and the Op-Ed page. Raines would oversee a twelve-member editorial board, a roster of columnists, and the editors who choose from the flood of submissions, hundreds over the course of a week, offered for publication on the Op-Ed page and as letters to the editor.

And he would join Sulzberger's inner group of counselors and become a powerful voice in the management of the newspaper—a major selling point for Raines as he considered the offer. He would be there for the weekly Wednesday lunch, in a private dining room with the publisher and executive editor, where waiters in uniforms served three-course lunches prepared in the *Times* kitchen as they settled in to discuss the news report, personnel issues, the budget, or whatever else might be on Sulzberger's mind. It would put him next to the person who would, as it turned out, select the next five executive editors of the *Times*.

Arthur Sulzberger was ten months into the job, looking to show how he was different from his father. He wanted the editorial page to be lively and provocative, to drive the national debate. He was a believer in change—everyone has a timeline, he liked to say—and six years was long enough for Jack Rosenthal, who had run the page since Frankel became executive editor. He was convinced Raines would shake up the board the way he had shaken up the Washington bureau, infuse its editorials with the assertiveness and muscularity that had animated his political dispatches and their conversations over dinner. And Raines could write, with authority and passion. Applicants to become copy editors at the *Times* were given a test that included the typescript, without byline, of a story Raines had written as a national correspondent about dove hunting out of Cartersville, Georgia. "Joe Bishop had everything a dove hunter needs on opening day: a cane-bottom rocker, a front porch overlooking Glenn Taylor's dove fields, a small boy to fetch the birds he hit, and a sense of humor about the ones he missed." Any applicant who changed Raines's copy was unlikely to get hired. He had won the Pulitzer Prize for a feature in the *Times Magazine* recounting a childhood friendship with his family's Black housekeeper, a gripping piece of writing that described the nuances and complexities of growing up in an upper-middle-class white family in Birmingham in the slowly changing segregated South.

Raines would transform the editorial page—in some ways for the better and in some ways for the worse, but he turned it into something both men wanted. Let's be more aggressive, Arthur Sulzberger told him. "He wanted editorials with greater muzzle velocity and a sharper, more distinctive style," Raines wrote later. It would be the first mark that young Arthur put on the newspaper. And it was the first chapter in an alliance between two men that would eventually move—with the same ambitions and brashness—into the newsroom.

* * *

In February 1978, Raines stepped off the elevator and into the newsroom of *The New York Times*. He was thirty-four years old and he was there for a job interview. This was the apex of the Rosenthal era. Raines was the author of two books, published within weeks of each other—an oral history on the civil rights struggle in the South and a novel—and he had a portfolio of newspaper stories about the South. The editors who'd hired and promoted him in Alabama, Georgia, and Florida had recognized his talent and flair, not to mention his strutting self-regard. As a twenty-one-year-old new hire for the *Birmingham Post-Herald* in 1964, he'd produced three different stories from the sidelines of the Alabama-Auburn college football game. They were his first bylines. Raines drew the assignment because it was Thanksgiving weekend, and he'd agreed to work without pay. He was now the chief political reporter for the *St. Petersburg Times*. His editors in St. Petersburg nominated him for a Pulitzer for his coverage of the 1976 presidential campaign. His civil rights history, *My Soul Is Rested*, drew an enthusiastic review from Anthony Lewis in *The New York Times* Book Review. "Every so often a book is so touching, so exhilarating that one laughs and murmurs and cries out while reading, wanting to tell others about it," Lewis wrote. " 'My Soul Is Rested' is like that."

It was a heady time for Raines as he arrived in the *Times* newsroom. Two of the leading news organizations in the nation were courting him—*The New York Times* and *Time* magazine—which was why he had come to New York City and was staying with his wife, Susan, at the Algonquin Hotel on West Forty-fourth Street. Dave Jones, the *Times*'s national editor, kept an eye out for talent as he scoured papers from across the nation, and Raines had caught his attention. Raines had taken care to inform Jones that the *Times* was not the only news organization bidding for his services, which has always been one sure way to coax a job offer from the *Times*. Not that Raines needed to do that. Abe Rosenthal had been trying to stock his newsroom with flashy, analytical writers since his days as the metropolitan editor. He had read both Raines's novel, *Whiskey Man*, and *My Soul Is Rested* and was struck by the clarity and strength of the writing. Rosenthal had made his decision before Raines walked through the door. "I want this guy on the paper," as he put it in a *New Yorker* profile of Raines years later. Rosenthal was going to

make Raines understand why he wanted to work at *The New York Times*.
That was clear as soon as Raines entered Rosenthal's private office, set
behind a conference room, with a mahogany table where editors would
assemble every afternoon to present their offerings for the next day's
front page. It was a swirl of Japanese wall hangings and furnishings,
every surface flecked with splashes of red enamel. Raines felt like he had
just wandered into a Japanese imperial court.

Rosenthal praised Raines's books and his coverage of the South. I
know from reading your work you're not the type of writer that would
skewer somebody, he said. (Raines thought about the stories he had written while in Florida and wondered if Rosenthal had actually read his
work.)

People say I am a maniac, Rosenthal said. And I am a maniac for *The
New York Times*.

Raines decided at that moment that Rosenthal was his kind of editor
and the *Times* was his kind of newspaper.

Raines began in New York and was quickly struck by the solemnity
and breadth of knowledge that coursed through the *Times* newsroom. It
enchanted him. Everything he had read in Gay Talese's book (any person
considering a career in journalism in the 1970s would have read both
The Kingdom and the Power and *All the President's Men* by Bob Woodward
and Carl Bernstein) was laid out before him. There was the pageantry
and eccentricities, the culture of competition cloaked in an atmosphere
of collegiality, the rivalries, and the dedication to mission—slightly
pompous but mostly well-intentioned. The *Times* was Victorian, Raines
thought, with its courteous tradition of honorific salutations in even the
most biting memos, the feuding fiefdoms, and the slights never forgotten.
But most of all, the characters, whom Raines had admired as he worked
his way through the South, now walking by his desk. On the day he was
hired, Raines met Sydney Schanberg, the metropolitan editor, who had
returned from Southeast Asia after a harrowing reporting adventure
with Dith Pran, a Cambodian refugee and photojournalist, that would
later be the subject of a movie, *The Killing Fields*, and which won him a
Pulitzer Prize.

Raines was young enough to be wide-eyed and seasoned enough to
take it all in with some detachment. "The habit I was forming was to

study the institution you're a part of—the journalistic institution—with the same skills you would apply to covering a political story," he would say years later. "Try to look behind the appearances and understand the subtext." He considered what it took to be a successful correspondent at the *Times*—the ability to write on highly complicated subjects under the constraint of a tight deadline, and to maneuver in a ruthless environment, where colleagues were always looking to get a stick on the ball, as he put it. Raines was struck by the bounty of resources in this newsroom, of what it meant to work at a newspaper owned by the Sulzberger family. The pay was good. The expense accounts were generous. There were layers of meticulous editing, meaning that stories would have the extra depth and authority that comes from the hands of an experienced editor, who very well might once have covered the same beat as the reporter writing the article. But Raines also noted how that same cushion of support bred lethargy. Too many of his colleagues were indifferent if a competitor beat them on a big story; the idea that it was only news when it appeared in the *Times* had great currency in those days. Reporters would stand around gossiping and griping, as if this were just another newsroom in America. Why are these reporters complaining? Raines asked himself. On one of his early days in the city room, Raines watched as a reporter at the next desk slid open his top drawer and pulled out a bottle of white vermouth and a stack of plastic cups. This was at eleven o'clock in the morning. These early impressions would shape the way Raines would approach his next twenty-five years at the *Times*.

Raines wasn't like Frankel, or Rosenthal, or many of his new colleagues who had been at the *Times* from when they were young men. Reporters who came to the *Times* in the middle of their careers were different than those who began as news clerks and rose through the ranks. They knew what it was like to wait by their desk, worrying about whether a telephone call to an important source would be returned. They were hungry. Raines was humming with ambition. He knew this was where he wanted to spend the rest of his career.

Raines's rise was rapid. He had been a correspondent in the Atlanta bureau, where he had headed after New York, for only two years when he was asked to cover Reagan's campaign for president. He had written the front-page "Man in the News" profile of the former California governor, published when Reagan was nominated at the Republican convention in Detroit in July of 1980—a prestigious assignment that signaled his rising status. At the end of the year, Dave Jones told Rosenthal that Raines had done "the best of anyone covering" Reagan, and recommended that he be given a pay hike to reward his work.

Raines was covering Reagan when the president was shot walking toward his motorcade after delivering a speech to the Building and Construction Trades Department of the AFL-CIO at the Washington Hilton Hotel. There were more seasoned correspondents in the bureau on March 30, 1981, but Bill Kovach, a fellow southerner who was running the Washington bureau, told Raines that he would write the lead story. Raines swept his desk clean of papers—the stacks of notebooks, the drafts of stories, memos, a calendar—and settled in front of an IBM Selectric typewriter. Bureau reporters fed Raines information gathered from the briefings at the White House and the hospital, the interviews from witnesses, and the paragraphs of historical context that would provide the setting for the events of this monumental day. The Raines story appeared under a three-line headline across the top of the front page.

"President Reagan was shot in the chest yesterday by a gunman, apparently acting alone, as Mr. Reagan walked to his limousine after addressing a labor meeting at the Washington Hilton Hotel," Raines wrote. The account was filled with the kind of flourishes that had characterized Raines's writing from the start of his journalism career. "Mr. Reagan, apparently at first unaware that he had been wounded, was shoved forcefully by a Secret Service agent into the Presidential limousine, which sped away with the President in a sitting position in the backseat. Behind him lay a scene of turmoil. A Secret Service agent writhed in pain on the rain-slick sidewalk. Nearby a District of Columbia plainclothesman had fallen alongside [Reagan's press secretary, James] Brady. The press secretary lay face down, blood from a gushing head wound dripping into a steel grate. A pistol, apparently dropped by one of the security aides, lay near his head." The following year, Kovach told Rosenthal that he wanted Adam Clymer and Howell Raines assigned to cover the 1984 race for president. "Howell because he has a gut instinct for political reporting and a skill with words unmatched since R.W.," a reference to Johnny Apple.

Raines moved with a swagger that impressed younger reporters like Bill Keller, who had come to the *Times* from the Washington bureau of the *Dallas Times Herald* to cover the Pentagon. Raines struck Keller as a classic Timesman, to use the language of the era: the way he dressed, his confidence, the authority he brought to his stories. Abe Rosenthal, while he was still the executive editor, had the same thought when he informed Punch Sulzberger that Raines was being promoted in 1985 to the number-two Washington editor under Kovach. "I would really be quite surprised and disappointed if in the future, Howell was not one of the top leaders of the news department."

Kovach had made Raines the deputy editor because he wanted to "pick up the heartbeat of the bureau." Raines would certainly do all that, but he would also display a competitive and sometimes ruthless nature, an intolerance for sloth or correspondents too enamored with the perks and prominence of being a *Times* reporter covering Washington. Shortly after he became the Washington news editor, Leslie H. Gelb, the national security reporter and arms-control expert who was a former assistant secretary of state, filed a story on developments in arms-control negotiations. (Leslie Gelb was not related to Arthur Gelb.) It was late in the afternoon. Raines glanced at the story and told Gelb that he would not send it to New York that day. It needed rewriting, and Raines had neither the time nor the expertise to do that on deadline. The next day, Gelb came into his office, as Raines told the story, waving a cigar.

Let me tell you the mistake you made yesterday, Gelb said.

No, Les, let me tell you the mistake you made yesterday, Raines shot back. I got here from Birmingham on my gut. And yesterday you made me choose between your expertise and my gut, under time pressure. And I'm going to go with my gut every time that you make me do that.

When Raines returned from his short time as London bureau chief to run the Washington bureau in the fall of 1988, he was determined to shake up a staff that was struggling after those two years under Craig Whitney. He would reward the correspondents who were the kind of reporters he had been: aggressive, swashbuckling. He summoned the staff to a brown-bag luncheon. The A-list reporters, he announced, would draw the top assignments and would see their stories promoted for Page One.

If you want to be an A reporter in this bureau, you're not going to be on the subway at six o'clock, Raines said.

If there was an A list, that meant there was a B list. The reporters relegated to the B list came to resent being shut out of the best assignments, cast off to junior editors on the desk, and of how Raines would not even look at them as he walked through the bureau. They resented the afternoon ritual of Raines's preferred reporters gathering in his office, closing the door behind them, for late-afternoon cocktails. Raines began noticing unflattering portrayals of his style in publications like *Spy* magazine. How he instructed his clerk to move his office plants outdoors so they could be nourished by fresh rainwater. How he ordered the installation of a hotline on the clerks' desk so they knew he was calling and would jump to pick up the call.*

On one of his first days as Washington editor, Raines was settled in at his desk for an afternoon conference call with editors in New York. From beyond the door to his office, he heard the echo of the call crackling across the newsroom. Judith Miller, a deputy, had had a speaker installed by her desk while she was running the bureau in the interval between when Whitney left and Raines arrived. That would allow her to participate in the news meetings without having to get up and go inside the bureau chief's office. Any reporter within earshot could hear editors deliberating about their stories. Raines rose from his chair and walked outside.

This ends today, Raines told her. He ordered the speaker removed.

Raines had agreed to keep Miller in her deputy position after Whitney left, but he, like Whitney before him, found her a disruptive presence on the editing desk, where she clashed with her reporters and fellow editors. He flew to New York and told Frankel he wanted to move Miller out. She was brought back to New York as an editor on the media desk.

Raines was unsentimental in managing reporters and editors, rarely concerned about bruising an ego or picking a fight. If you won't do this story, I will find someone who will, he would tell any reporter who balked

---

* The teletype machines were on the other side of the newsroom, and he needed a clerk to retrieve the printouts. He would sit in the office, his frustration growing as the telephone would ring unanswered.

at an idea. He was hardly the first *New York Times* editor to bring his eccentricities to the office, but he was establishing a reputation as an autocratic boss. None of this was apparent to him at the time; he never thought he was guilty of any egregious behavior. The *Times* had always operated on a star system, rewarding correspondents like R. W. Apple or Hedrick Smith. He had little patience with reporters who treated the privilege of covering the nation's capital for the *Times* as just another punch-the-clock job. "You drive the report with the top talent," he said years later. "And if you're going to hire top talent, you've got to reward them."

Tactics and personality aside, Raines took charge of a bureau that was foundering under Whitney and set it on a new track; the *Times* would set the agenda, rather than chase what had appeared that morning in *The Washington Post*. When Maureen Dowd was a reporter in the bureau in late 1991, Raines called her in to his office and wondered aloud about how women were reacting to the all-white, all-male Senate Judiciary Committee's dismissive handling of the sexual harassment allegations by Anita Hill in the Supreme Court confirmation hearings of Clarence Thomas.

Just because all the members of the House Judiciary Committee are white men doesn't mean they're sexist, she said.

Why don't you make a few calls, Maureen? he said.

She did, and it produced a front-page story: "The Senate and Sexism: Panel's Handling of Harassment Allegation Renews Questions About an All-Male Club." The *Times* nominated her coverage for a Pulitzer Prize.

And that is what his superiors noted in New York—how he had elevated the Washington report; not the grumbling of some reporters. "It's hard to believe that it's been only six months since you inherited a shell-shocked bureau," Arthur Gelb, the managing editor, wrote in Raines's first evaluation in 1989. "In that short period wounds appear to have healed and morale is again high. It was heartening to witness the calm and wisdom with which you got the bureau back on track."

* * *

The editorial board convened at ten o'clock in the morning every Monday, Wednesday, and Thursday in the conference room of the tenth floor.

The meetings rarely began on time, as Raines discovered to his annoyance when he took over in May 1993. Board members would arrive well past ten o'clock, ambling past the old library, clutching hot cups of coffee and morning pastries. Raines would already be at the table, impatient as the minutes ticked past. The food was an irritant, the rustle of the paper and the sound of eating. This casual atmosphere lasted less than a month.

We are going to start this meeting at ten-fifteen, since that is when it clearly wants to start, Raines announced one morning. And we're not going to bring food into the meeting.

The no-food policy was just one of many changes Raines put in place. Jack Rosenthal had prohibited editorial writers from using the words "must" or "should," lest they appear to be "sending thunderbolts from the heavens down to the mere earthlings." Raines reversed that. Editorials needed to be direct, compelling, and unequivocal.

We're going to write one-sided editorials, Raines announced to the board. If people disagree, they have the burden of finding forums to explain their points of view. We don't have to make it for them on our editorial page.

He expanded on his philosophy in an essay for *Inside the New York Times,* a subscribers' newsletter. Harry Truman said he wanted one-armed economists, so they couldn't talk about on the one hand this, on the other hand that, he noted. "I've always identified with Truman's point. I believe in the one-armed style of editorial writing." Raines's not-so-subtle rebuking of the way business had been conducted before rankled his predecessors. The idea that *Times* editorials were equivocal was a myth, Frankel wrote years later, one which led Raines "to promise rashly that his page would print only 'one-handed' opinions. His fist did rattle the china for a while, but if he had read more of yesteryear's papers, he'd have recognized that mere invective is no substitute for vigor and verve. We had plenty of both."

Sulzberger and Raines wanted the board to carry a banner for environmental causes, and Robert B. Semple, Jr., who had joined the editorial board after his years on the foreign desk, was empowered to write editorials crusading against the opening of a gold mine less than three miles from Yellowstone National Park. "Congress is in a mood to abandon the preservation of America's ecological heritage," one editorial declared. The *Times* would win a Pulitzer for its editorials on the environment that year.

But it was the acidic editorials that drew attention, and those were almost always written by Raines. The *Times* branded Mario Cuomo of New York as "Governor Moonlight," for taking speaking fees. Bob Dole, the Senate Republican leader, was "the Dark Prince of Gridlock," a "churlish partisan" who was blocking legislation in Congress. Dole denounced Raines on the Senate floor, saying he had smeared him and abandoned the paper's "traditional high road for the gutter." *The New York Observer* found the new editorial page editor noteworthy enough to assign a story on him. "Times Pulpit: More Taste, Less Filling," the headline proclaimed, riffing on a famous commercial for Miller Lite. That did not chasten Raines. "One of the things I learned a long time ago in this business is you've got to get your love from your family and friends," he said at the time. "Not from the people you write about." He believed his editorial, "Mr. McNamara's War," which he woke up one morning and wrote in a "white heat," set the tone for the public's response to the penitent memoir from Robert McNamara, who served as the secretary of defense under Lyndon Johnson. The defense secretary wrote that the war in Vietnam that he had prosecuted had been a mistake, and that he had realized that at the time. "His regret cannot be huge enough to balance the books for our dead soldiers," the editorial declared. "The ghosts of those unlived lives circle close around Mr. McNamara. Surely he must in every quiet and prosperous moment hear the ceaseless whispers of those poor boys in the infantry, dying in the tall grass, platoon by platoon, for no purpose."

The attacks by the *Times* on the newly elected Democratic president, Bill Clinton, were perplexing for anyone accustomed to the Democratic voice that had usually spoken from that page. "On-the-job training is a messy process, and when you're president everyone gets to watch," the *Times* wrote, one week after Clinton had been sworn in and less than a month into Raines's tenure. It was not long until this confrontation was presented as a battle between two powerful symbols of the modern South, notably in *The New Yorker.* "The Howell Raines Question: The *Times* endorsed Bill Clinton, and Howell Raines is a liberal, so why is the paper's editorial page so hard on the White House?" read the headline.

Clinton complained to Arthur Sulzberger when the publisher visited the White House. Sulzberger told the president that he should consider the criticism in the *Times* as "tough love," according to *The New Yorker.* "Well, just don't forget the love part," Clinton responded.

The criticisms of Raines's editorial page were not only coming from outside the *Times.* "I find the current page too often shrill and yet not really wise or instructive on the big issues of our society," Frankel wrote Sulzberger as he prepared to end his time as executive editor. As for Lelyveld, even when he agreed with the arguments that Raines was making, he often found its language and tone excessive. "It was too much Howell's page," he said years later. Sulzberger stood behind Raines, telling the *Observer* he was "very happy" with the page, though he allowed that "it's lost certain things that Jack gave it." Such as? "I'm not sure I want to get into that." In fact, Sulzberger said years later, he thought Raines had gone too far in his criticism of Clinton. He descried that as his "biggest disagreement" with Raines, but not big enough to shake his confidence in Raines.

Raines was proving to be as hard-driving a boss on the editorial page as he had been in Washington. He wanted the editorial department to be on top of the news, even if that meant coming in to write an editorial on a Sunday to reflect news developments over the weekend. Raines forced the head of the Letters section, Robert A. Barzilay, out of his job because he was taking too long to publish letters from readers. He would scold writers who submitted editorials that he found meek or mushy and rewrite them himself. It would fall to Raines's deputy, Phil Boffey, to reassure editorial board members distressed by their encounters and worried about their futures.

Howell's not pissed at you, Boffey would say. His face in repose is a frown.

Soon after Raines took over the board, Sulzberger stopped by his office. I wish you were easier on people, Sulzberger told him. A year later, Raines asked Sulzberger if he recalled their conversation and if he had noticed any change. Sulzberger said he had.

Good, Raines said. I want you to remember that I was responsive to what you wanted.

CHAPTER 13

A Timex Watch

The memorandum read like a primer. "What is the Internet?" it asked. This was the fall of 1993. The Internet was still new to many people, certainly to people of an older generation, and that would include many people at the *Times*. The author was Richard Meislin, a former Mexico City correspondent who was now the editor in charge of graphics, and its recipients were three top *Times* editors: Max Frankel, the executive editor; Joseph Lelyveld, the managing editor; and Allan Siegal, an assistant managing editor. "At the most basic," Meislin wrote, answering the question he posed, "the Internet is just a network that connects computers to each other, much in the same way New York Telephone connects local subscribers." The note was instructional, but it was also a warning, an alert to a gathering hurricane that seemed capable of upending everything about the business of newspapers. "A committee has been formed to look at the issue but the going seems to be slow," he wrote.

The *Times* was capable of intermittent change, as had become clear over the previous fifteen years. But for the next twenty years, this question—what is the Internet?—would force a reconsideration of every business and journalistic assumption that had guided the paper for a century. It would test the ability of not only the *Times* but the entire media industry to adapt to a landscape that had begun to roll and lurch under its feet. It would transform the jobs of reporters, editors, graphic designers, photographers, strategic planners, the advertising sales force, circulation managers, accountants, right up to the president and the publisher. It would diffuse the power of the executive editor. It would force, in short, a reconsideration of what it meant to be a newspaper. These changes would happen with relative speed across the industry, though more slowly at the *Times*, and their sweep, and the extent to which they changed the newspaper, would only become clear many years later.

It would prove a particular challenge for the *Times*, an institution of such self-certitude and adherence to tradition. "The *New York Times* is a newspaper for people who want to read and hold a newspaper and leaf through it," A. M. Rosenthal said in August 1983, when he was still the executive editor. "I see the growing importance of electronics and tele-electronics and so on, but I do not see the *New York Times* as we know it coming out of a black box, or on a screen." Max Frankel bristled when he was urged, by a young new publisher breaking from his more tradition-bound father, to consider even small steps that might make the *Times* available on other platforms besides a sheet of newsprint. "I must apologize for what seems to be a daily gripe about some new project of the company that I deem to be counterproductive," he wrote Arthur Sulzberger, Jr., in April 1993 about a short-lived initiative called MediaFax—a six-page fax containing the entire media report in the day's Business section for distribution to one hundred business executives, under the sponsorship of MTV. "We are going to tell 100 media readers, then surely 200, then 500, that if all they want is the media poop from the NYT, they don't have to buy the paper. I think this corporation has gone mad."

And among the greatest skeptics was Punch Sulzberger. As the company chairman, he had steered the *Times* into spending $1.1 billion to purchase what he called "one of the country's great newspapers," *The Boston Globe*, in 1993. It was an affirmation of his faith in print—and his skeptical view of the Internet—as he made clear in a speech to the Midwest Research Institute, a not-for-profit science and technology research laboratory, in Kansas City in May 1994. "It is my contention that newspapers are here to stay," Punch Sulzberger said. "They are not going the way of the dinosaur—rendered extinct, in this case, by the wonders of a new technology that will speed us down an interactive information superhighway of communications. I'll go one step further. I believe that for a long time to come this information superhighway, far from resembling a modern interstate, will more likely approach a roadway in India: chaotic, crowded and swarming with cows. Or, as one might say, udder confusion."

One person in particular disagreed with the chairman. Arthur Sulzberger, Jr., liked science fiction and was intrigued by the futuristic fantasies he had seen on television shows like *Star Trek: The Next Generation.* He had been trained at a wire service, the Associated Press, where he would write a story that would be transmitted to the world when it was done, no matter the time of day. Sulzberger was never wedded to the idea that a newspaper had to be presented on newsprint. He had named Jack Rosenthal, when he was the editorial page editor, to run what was called the Futures Committee in the late 1980s, and Jack Rosenthal had come up, as Sulzberger remembered it, with the phrase "platform-agnostic." It grabbed Sulzberger's imagination, and the phrase, and everything it suggested, burrowed its way into his conversation and speeches. "Hell, if someone would be kind enough to invent the technology, I'll be pleased to beam it directly into your cortex," he said of the *Times* news report. A few months before his father spoke in Kansas City, young Arthur had unequivocally taken the other side of the argument. "If we don't pursue our digital future, it will pursue us," he said at a town hall meeting of *Times* employees in February 1994. Arthur Sulzberger had not even been publisher for three years, and there were a number of ways he was trying to define himself as a different publisher than his father, but nothing would be as lasting in significance as the difference between father and son that emerged this year on the digital future of newspapers.

* * *

Meislin was forty years old when he wrote the "what is the Internet" memo. Like the young publisher, he had been drawn to computers since he was a teenager. He'd learned to program an IBM 1620—a mainframe computer the size of a large desk, developed for small businesses and scientific applications—in his high school computer club. He enrolled in a computer programming course at the Stevens Institute of Technology in the summer between his sophomore and junior years. But after high school, Meislin's interest shifted from computers to newspapers. He ran *The Harvard Crimson* and was hired, upon graduation at the age of twenty-two, as a copyboy at the *Times.* By 1993, after serving as a copyboy, foreign correspondent, and editor of statistical news, including graphics, Meislin was among a small group of people at the *Times* frustrated by the newspaper's halting efforts to engage with this electronic frontier that had intrigued him since high school. Meislin invited Joseph Lelyveld, recently appointed as Frankel's managing editor, and his wife, Carolyn, for dinner at his home one evening, and after the meal, brought Lelyveld to his home office. Meislin had learned there were few better ways to help someone grasp the potential of the Internet than to run a search of their name, so he typed, using the precise formula needed for a search, "joseph NEAR lelyveld" into an early version of a search engine on his home computer (this was before Google). Lelyveld watched as a primitive listing of his articles, and stories about his career, scrolled across Meislin's screen. The memorandum Meislin prepared for Frankel, Lelyveld, and Siegal was offered in much the same spirit. "There are millions of people using the Internet each day," Meislin wrote. "They are sending e-mails, playing video games and reading bulletin boards which cover topics from nuclear war to foot fetishism." It was a big enough community that the *Times* could cover it as if it were a large city. He suggested a computer column in the Science section, subscriptions to the daily news summary, and creating an electronic "custom newspaper" tailored to the interests of each reader.

But the first public venture by the *Times* into this new electronic world was hardly that ambitious. It began, unsteadily and with little fanfare, in June 1994, as @times appeared on a corner of the AOL site. The idea did not come from the newsroom. It was announced by Lance Primis, who was now the president and chief operating officer of the Times Company, who promised it would be "an extension of what we give readers through the pages of The Times." There would be stories from the front page, movie reviews, and sports and business articles. They would stay on the site for twenty-four hours, because the *Times* had sold, in what would come to be remembered as a particularly cloddish deal, the rights to its electronic contents to Mead Data Central, the owner of LexisNexis, in 1983, outside of an initial twenty-four-hour window. (The *Times* was eventually able to reclaim control over its electronic library after Mead was sold in 1994, giving the newspaper an opening to undo its previous mistake.)

The *Times* corporate side, which at the time often held product quality in lower esteem than the newsroom did, was frequently of the opinion that involving reporters and editors in a project was a guarantee of slower development and higher costs. Meislin wrote to Frankel about the absence of any newsroom editors or reporters in developing @times. "Make no mistake about it: for the half-million people who subscribe to America Online, and millions more who hear about it, this will be the first face of the *New York Times* newsroom in the electronic world," Meislin wrote. "I'm being presumptuous enough to write this memo because everything I hear makes me believe that the newspaper has had frighteningly little input into this project to date." Allowing the project to be steered from outside the newsroom would mean "ceding our responsibilities as editors, no less than if we let the Marketing Department put out the national edition each night."* Frankel passed it on to Sulzberger and told the publisher that the *Times* was "being careless by leaving experienced editors out of this 'America On Line' venture."

The warnings were ignored as @times marched ahead. "It's functional, but humiliating in a relative sense—relative to what I think the newsroom believes the *New York Times* name stands for," Meislin wrote in his assessment of an early iteration of the project. "It really is the Tiffany name on a Timex watch." The arrival of the *Times* to the digital era was noted in a story in *New York* magazine under the subheading "An Online Dud." The magazine's media critic, Jon Katz, wrote: "Not only was there no hoopla to herald this previously unimaginable venture into electronic publishing but, once online, the *Times* seemed embarrassed and slightly disgusted with itself, like a Victorian lady who'd stepped in dog poop. . . . @times seems especially half-hearted, market-driven, and soulless."

Arthur Sulzberger was not discouraged. He was convinced that this technology would radically alter how the *Times* would be distributed to readers. He did not know whether advertisers would follow the *Times* online or whether the newspaper should be charging online readers to read its digital offering. His foresight didn't extend to anticipating how the

---

* Meislin ended by asking that his note be viewed as an application for the currently nonexistent post of editor of the electronic editions of *The New York Times*.

same technology would also change the way information could be presented to readers. But he was setting a direction for the company. "The *Times* must not be afraid of this new world," Sulzberger told his senior managers at the end of 1994. "On the contrary, we must stand ready to embrace it.

> We are in the newspaper business. By that I don't mean for an instant to suggest we are in a business defined by paper. On the contrary, it is a relic of our history that we print on paper. The paper in newspaper is not central to our function.
>
> My point is a simple one: I am absolutely agnostic regarding methods of distribution. One doesn't have to be a rocket scientist to recognize that ink on wood via trucks is a time consuming and expensive operation.

There were other news organizations ahead of the *Times*, who were taking more risks in beginning this transformation. There were people in the newsroom, like Meislin, who saw the situation as more urgent, who were pushing the *Times* to move aggressively to catch up with the world that was leaving it behind. But Arthur Sulzberger was atop a big and slow-moving company filled with strong-minded people—including his father—who were committed to a fixed notion of what made the *Times* the journalistic success that it was. It would take years to turn that around.

PART III

A REPORTER'S EDITOR

1994–2001

CHAPTER 14

Marching Around My Head

Max Frankel was ready to retire, and he was certain who should succeed him.

We have to decide about Joe Lelyveld, Frankel told Arthur Sulzberger, Jr., as they rode an Amtrak train from New York to Washington in early 1993. Because he's my choice. And if he's not your man, we are going to have a hell of a problem.

Frankel intended to step down in the summer of 1994, at the age of sixty-four, a year before the customary retirement age for an executive editor at the *Times*. Frankel wanted to write his memoirs. He was a little bored of the job, or at least the "executive" part of being the executive editor. How many restaurant critics could he appoint? The newsroom was about to be renovated, and the staff was moving from the third floor to a makeshift newsroom on the sixth floor while the new quarters for reporters and editors were completed. He did not have the patience to adjudicate the squabbles ahead over desks and who got to sit by the Forty-third Street windows. He did not want to spend his final year sidelined in a newsroom awash in speculation over who might succeed him, making decisions that his successor would carry out.

And he was weary. His wife, Joyce Purnick, who was on the editorial board, had been diagnosed with breast cancer, less than a decade after Frankel had lost his first wife to brain cancer. Jack Rosenthal, who met with Frankel each week to review the Sunday magazine cover, thought he looked beaten down after years of haggling over budgets and the latest marketing notions being pushed by the business side. "Do I feel overworked and overburdened?" Frankel told *The New Yorker* in June of 1993.

"Yes. I say sometimes in jest that the only time I enjoy the New York *Times* is when I'm away and reading it, because from the moment I come in the door what I hear about is what's gone wrong."

With the decision to name William Kennedy Smith's accuser, the up-heaval in the Washington bureau, and the front-page correction on the account of testimony to the congressional committees investigating the Iran-Contra affair, it had not been the easiest of eight years. As 1992 came to a close, at an editors' retreat at the Hyatt Regency Hotel in Greenwich, Connecticut, Frankel was confronted with complaints over the manner in which he ran front page meetings.* Frankel felt am-bushed, in front of an audience that included the publisher. "I think of the page-one meeting as a colloquy," Frankel said as he parried the criti-cism.

"I've been to a lot of page-one meetings, and the one thing I can tell you, Max, is that it ain't no colloquy," Sulzberger said.

That spring, as Frankel was moving into his final year, an article in *Es-quire* magazine offered a harsh judgment on his tenure, describing a news-paper that was demoralized and had come to miss the kinetic creativity of A. M. Rosenthal. Wounded, and with some justification, Frankel sent a note to his staff attesting to the successes of his newsroom. "*Esquire* of-fers an article about us that consists, believe me, of a little fact and a lot of fiction (and much of that a mere paste-up of decades-old fictions, to boot)," he wrote. Letters of sympathy began landing on Frankel's desk, as tends to happen when an executive at the *Times* is the subject of an unflattering article. Donald E. Graham, the publisher of *The Washington Post*, urged Frankel not to be distressed by the "snippy little piece on you and the *Times*" in *Esquire*. "Whenever you choose to hang 'em up, you'll be a hero," Graham said in a handwritten note. "Meantime, you have to settle for being an editor, I guess." And even with missteps, the paper under Frankel had continued to excel at what it had always done best. Pulitzer Prizes were awarded to a gallery of reporters—Alex S. Jones, Thomas L. Friedman, Natalie Angier, Bill Keller, Sheryl WuDunn and

---

* It was one of five retreats Arthur Sulzberger had organized for managers, editors, and executives as he pushed for a more cooperative and less hierarchal newsroom, imple-menting the management philosophy of W. Edwards Deming.

Nicholas Kristof, Anna Quindlen, Serge Schmemann, Howell Raines, and John Burns—that were testimony to the strength of the newspaper's chronicling of the end of the Cold War, the fall of the Berlin Wall, as well as the upheaval in the Soviet Union, the Middle East, and China. Frankel had fulfilled the mandate Punch Sulzberger gave him when he appointed him in 1986. Life in the newsroom was less unhappy than it had been under Rosenthal, no matter the complaints at the front page meeting. He had prepared Punch's son to be publisher, and in the process, he earned the gratitude of father and son.

"From a very personal perspective, no one has been better served by your leadership than have I," Arthur Sulzberger wrote Frankel on the fifth anniversary of his appointment as executive editor. "For there is one other thing you have done since you were named Executive Editor. You have helped break in a very grateful Deputy Publisher who will not forget the lessons he has learned." When it came time to mark Frankel's retirement, on April 7, 1994, as the clock on the newsroom wall read 3:39 P.M., Sulzberger—wearing wide yellow suspenders, his jacket cast off to the side, clutching a plastic glass bubbling with sparkling wine—leapt onto a desk surrounded by onlookers, including his father and Abe Rosenthal. It seemed for a moment that his voice was trembling. "I feel very awkward in speaking about Max because he is my friend and he is my mentor," he said. "He trained me for what it means to be the publisher of this newspaper, of the journalism that the New York Times has. He has saved me from more mistakes than I can care to tell. And he has done it almost always gently. And almost always with humor and grace. And I am going to be in his debt for years and years to come."

Arthur Sulzberger had inherited Frankel as executive editor from his father. Now it was his turn to put his own mark on the newsroom, a choice that he knew would be scrutinized—even more so than his selection of Howell Raines to run the editorial page.

* * *

Joseph Lelyveld was twenty-one years old as he stood on the steps of Widener Library, gazing across the courtyard at Harvard University, contemplating a career as a professor: seminars, stuffy classrooms, and quiet libraries. It was the fall of 1958, and Lelyveld, a first-year graduate student in history, had just left a seminar with Bernard Bailyn, a professor of early American history. He had a moment of clarity. I'm not going to do this for the rest of my life, he thought. Lelyveld was, even as a young man, restless, curious, and itinerant, given to moments of self-doubt and anguish, drifting along a path with no clear destination. He had considered psychiatry before he went into history, and now he would drop out of graduate school and return to New York City to attend Columbia Journalism School. He wanted to be a writer and wondered if he could make a living working for a quarterly like *Partisan Review*. His instructors at the journalism school were not encouraging. John Hohenberg, who would write one of the most widely used journalism textbooks in the nation and serve as the administrator for the Pulitzer Prizes, told Lelyveld that his writing reminded him of an overstuffed Victorian couch and advised his student to return to Harvard. Lelyveld ignored the advice, but, of course, he never forgot it. He was someone who remembered slights proudly; the trait was integral to his character.

While at Columbia, Lelyveld took a position as a temporary copyboy at the *Times*, and upon graduation, at the age of twenty-three, left New York and the newspaper with his wife of one year, Carolyn, for a trip to Southeast Asia on a Fulbright fellowship—"for which I'd applied without credentials or purpose," he recounted years later. In Burma, he wrote stories for the *Times* foreign desk, sending them to New York by mail, for which he was paid by the column inch. He had been enraptured by India when he first read about it as an undergraduate at Harvard, in dispatches written by the India correspondent for the *Times*, Abe Rosenthal; and when he and Carolyn arrived there for a month, he found it as enthralling as Rosenthal had portrayed it.

Lelyveld wanted to be a foreign correspondent, and he wanted to be sent to India. He returned to New York and eventually took a job as a full-time copyboy at the *Times;* he was promoted within six months to the broadcast desk, where he worked alongside another up-and-coming *Times* reporter, Robert McFadden, who had joined the newspaper as a copyboy in 1961. The two young men would comb through the *Times* and the wire services and churn out eight thousand words a day between them, broken into dispatches of about seventy typewritten lines and sent to the WQXR broadcast booth with the *whoosh* of a pneumatic tube. It taught them how to write quickly—Lelyveld liked to say his first thrill as a journalist was when he and McFadden rushed out a bulletin to announce the news that Khrushchev had backed down from threats that had nearly started a nuclear war, signaling the end of the thirteen-day Cuban Missile Crisis in 1962. Those grinding days on the broadcast desk produced two writers who were fast and graceful and confident. By 1964, Rosenthal had returned from overseas to run the metropolitan desk. Lelyveld, now a reporter on the business desk, wrote asking if there was a spot for him under Rosenthal.

There was a spot, and thus marked the start of a long, often tortured, and sometimes operatic relationship between two men who would both become towering figures in the *Times* newsroom over the next thirty-five years. They admired each other's talents—it is difficult to see how they could have coexisted had they not—and they despaired at each other's flaws. They were both brilliant and willful. Rosenthal found Lelyveld exasperating, with his temporizing and often cantankerous ways, and Lelyveld came to feel that his encounters with Rosenthal were as emotionally fraught as those with his own father, Arthur J. Lelyveld, a rabbi and leader of the American Jewish reform movement, with whom he always had a strained relationship.

This began almost from the moment Lelyveld came under Rosenthal's command in 1964, when he was dispatched to Maspeth, Queens, to run down a tip from Simon Wiesenthal, the Nazi hunter, that a former German death camp guard had settled into a secret life there as a homemaker, known to the tipster only as Mrs. Ryan. Lelyveld knocked on doors until he found her, guessing her identity because of her heavy accent, as he later recounted.

"Mrs. Ryan, I need to ask about your time in Poland, at the Majdanek camp, during the war," Lelyveld said.

"Oh my God, I knew this would happen," Hermine Braunsteiner Ryan responded, breaking out in sobs. "This is the end. This is the end of everything for me."

Lelyveld returned to the newsroom, filed his account about Mrs. Ryan, of how the guards had tortured and executed the prisoners—details that propelled Lelyveld's story to a spot on the front page, at the direction of Rosenthal. Lelyveld returned to his typewriter, when the telephone on his desk rang with a call from Russell Ryan, an electrician who had married Mrs. Ryan and brought her to the United States. He said he knew nothing about his wife's past and told Lelyveld he found the accusation that she had been a Nazi guard implausible.

"My wife, sir, wouldn't hurt a fly," he said, as Lelyveld later recounted the conversation. "Didn't they ever hear the expression, 'Let the dead rest?' "

Unnerved, Lelyveld went to the night editor to say he was uncomfortable publishing the most incendiary details he had uncovered without verifying that Mrs. Ryan was one of the guards guilty of the abuses. Reporters as a rule never argue that their stories do not belong on Page One, so the concerns of a novice reporter were enough to convince the night desk to pull it off the front page. The story was printed on page ten, under the headline "Former Nazi Camp Guard Is Now a Housewife in Queens" and shorn of many of its most colorful details.

Rosenthal called Lelyveld into his office the next morning. If I get a story of yours on the front page, don't you ever again go behind my back to get it taken off, Rosenthal told him.

Over the next twenty-two years, Lelyveld found himself resisting assignments from Rosenthal—prominent assignments: Beijing, Washington, Tokyo, national education correspondent—typically with long, tormented handwritten letters. "In the past six days I've drafted several long letters explaining at terrible length why I'm inclined to say no," Lelyveld wrote in response to Rosenthal's request that he go to Japan. "But I haven't been able to mail them. In part, that's because I wouldn't want you to connect me to such maudlin prose. In part, it's because Tokyo has a very powerful allure for me." Lelyveld never wanted to do what Rosenthal wanted him to do when Rosenthal wanted him to do it. "He just thought there was something wacky about how my mind worked," Lelyveld said later. "Which is probably true." Their interactions became almost comical; the stuff of a Neil Simon play: two stiff-necked men engaged in a battle of wills. For years, Lelyveld had lobbied to go to China. He studied the language and relished the challenge of telling the world about this wide and mostly, at least for Western correspondents, unexplored nation. But when the Beijing position finally opened up, Lelyveld had moved on: his eye was on South Africa, the country that had expelled him after his first tour of duty there. Lelyveld went to Rosenthal to tell him he wished to refuse the assignment he had long sought and instead put his stake in Johannesburg. Rosenthal eyed him with a combination of astonishment and disgust. Do whatever the fuck you want to do, Rosenthal said. (Lelyveld did precisely that, and his return tour in South Africa produced the book that won him a Pulitzer Prize.)

All of this made Lelyveld a difficult man to manage; clearly worth it, in Rosenthal's estimation, but nonetheless a source of aggravation. Lelyveld would be an honorary pallbearer at Rosenthal's funeral at Central Synagogue in Manhattan in 2006, but he long before came to consider their relationship unhealthy. "It was very distressing," he said many years later. "He replaced my father as a kind of oedipal figure. He was always marching around in my head arguing with me." Lelyveld's reference to his father was revealing. As an adult and as an editor, Lelyveld could be Talmudic in his deliberations and righteous in his indignation. His childhood had been one of disruption and abandonment; his mother, Toby, attempted to take her own life at least three times, and his father was involved with other women. They had long slept in separate beds. They announced their divorce on the occasion of Joe and Carolyn Lelyveld's fifth-anniversary dinner. "It was hard to know what to say," Lelyveld wrote in his memoir. " 'I'm sorry' wouldn't have been welcomed. 'I'm not surprised' would have seemed unfeeling. 'Mazel tov' would have sounded sarcastic." Whatever the correct response, the news was hardly unexpected.

Lelyveld buried his father in 1996 at a funeral in Cleveland that drew a large crowd, befitting his prominence as a religious leader in a city that the rabbi called home for thirty-eight years. As Lelyveld sat there, surrounded by his family, struggling to think in a moment of grief, an image sprang to his head. "Suddenly I imagined a little boy with curly blond hair, a projection from pictures taken when I was three or four, running up a slight slope, through high grass, on a summery day. The little boy was calling, 'Daddy, Daddy, Daddy . . .' I've no idea whether there was a trace of memory in that scene imagined by the fifty-nine-year-old executive I'd somehow become. But I knew at once, as the service ran on and the little boy kept calling, that it was a feeling I'd suppressed practically all my life."

The death of Lelyveld's father produced a revealing response from Arthur Sulzberger. "For reasons I'm not sure I want to fully explore, I've felt surprisingly uncomfortable in writing you about the death of your father," he wrote Lelyveld. "I know you had a difficult relationship with him, though I don't know why. . . . Even if my supposition is faulty I will think of your experience as a personal wake-up call."

* * *

The *Times* was overseen by editors who rewrote many of the most important dispatches, those being considered for the front page. It was a newsroom where editors, and not reporters, would determine how stories would be framed and presented. It had been this way through a cast of executive editors: Turner Catledge, A. M. Rosenthal, Max Frankel. The opening sentence, the sweeping explanatory paragraph that put the story into perspective, the choice and placement of the first quotation, would often be determined by editors gathered at the front page meeting or, as afternoon turned into evening, by the executive editor or the senior editors running the newspaper through the night. There were exceptions. Editors were wary of touching a story by, say, a Johnny Apple— a writer who did not take kindly to anything but the lightest of editing. But that was why there was a uniformity of style at the *Times* and, in theory at least, a depth and reliability in its stories. It was the way things were done, which was fine for the editors, many of whom were former correspondents with years of experience that imbued them with an understanding of what made a *Times* story. And it was a matter of annoyance to writers. Francis X. Clines, a correspondent who wrote with wit and depth, and who editors turned to when major stories were unfolding, likened his role to the kneeling tailor with pins in his mouth. Just tell me how you want the cuffs, he would say.

When Lelyveld arrived at the *Times* as a copyboy in the early 1960s, he learned the difference between an editors' newspaper and a writers' newspaper, like the *Herald Tribune*. An enterprising *Times* reporter who tried to slip in a neat turn of phrase or experimented with a different approach to telling a story would pick up the next day's newspaper and find the printed version of the article bore little resemblance to what had been filed. That had never stopped annoying Lelyveld. I would rather have a story run inside that no one fucked with than a Page One story that someone had breathed all over and ruined, Lelyveld would say.

He was not easy to edit. Why didn't you ask me to do it? Lelyveld bristled to an editor when he saw a story that had been altered. It chafed on Lelyveld, how stories would pass four different editors (one senior writer described it to him as the "editing of editing") each with their own notion of how it should be written. "What all this kibitzing bespeaks, of course, is a tremendous devotion to high standards," Lelyveld wrote in a memorandum after he became an editor himself. "But it also reflects the many layers of hierarchy in this joint and a general twitchiness about what senior editors may say in the morning." When there were disputes between correspondents and editors in New York, Lelyveld, after he became an editor, was more likely to side with the correspondent. Maureen Dowd, a White House reporter, wrote a 2,400-word front-page account of an unauthorized biography of Nancy Reagan by Kitty Kelley, under the headline "All That Glitters Is Not Real, Book on Nancy Reagan Says." The story, published on April 7, 1991, recounted some of the unsubstantiated claims in the book, including one that Nancy Reagan had engaged in an affair with Frank Sinatra. Frankel assailed the Dowd piece at a meeting of editors in New York the day after it was published; he dismissed it as "unsubstantiated gossip" that did not belong in the pages of the *Times.** The meeting was piped by telephone to Washington, where Dowd heard Frankel's remarks and left the office in dismay for her home. She had written the story that had been assigned to her; a *Times* editor had obtained a copy of the book and ordered Dowd to fly back from Los Angeles to quickly write about its contents. Her story had been reviewed by editors, who placed it prominently on the front page. Frankel had not voiced any objections until after it was published and criticism started rolling in.† Lelyveld sent Dowd a bouquet of roses without telling Frankel, who was annoyed by what he saw as Lelyveld's "stealthy disagreement with or undermining of my critique." It was a rare break between the two men.

---

* Frankel called the *Times* story on the Kelley book "a ghastly mistake" in a note to Arthur Sulzberger, Jr., eighteen months later.

† Frankel, by his later recollection, did not see the Dowd story before it was published.

* * *

Frankel's thoughts on his successor could not have been a surprise to Arthur Sulzberger. On his first week as executive editor, Frankel announced he was bringing Lelyveld back from London to be his foreign editor. Nearly two years after making Lelyveld foreign editor, Frankel informed Punch and Arthur Sulzberger that he intended to promote Lelyveld to managing editor when Arthur Gelb retired in eighteen months. "I am now satisfied that Joe Lelyveld is by far the most astute and broadgauged journalist in my sight and also the most impressive managerial talent," he wrote them. That would put Lelyveld at the top of any list to succeed him. Arthur Sulzberger, preparing to be publisher, registered some concern.

Are you leaving me with no choice? he asked Frankel.

In a certain sense I am, Frankel responded. But he's my overwhelming choice.

Sulzberger had his own candidate in mind: Dave Jones, who had become national editor during Watergate and was a respected fixture in the newsroom. He was comfortable with Jones, with his easy manner and his executive bearing. He had no quarrel with Lelyveld's qualifications. But Lelyveld was an austere and aloof figure, a man of intimidating intelligence, who could fall into long silences—his eyes wandering across the room, unsettling anyone in his presence with the suggestion he was bored with their company. "You've got to be more outgoing," his father would tell him as a young man. To Lelyveld, that was like being instructed to be more funny or more spontaneous. Lelyveld knew he could be morose and described himself, in letters to Rosenthal, as a brooder who was "excessively self-involved," as his wife liked to remind him. "I spent much of the morning in a mood of lugubrious brooding on the usual themes: how my options in my chosen way of life have dwindled, how I've painted myself into a corner on the *Times,* etc.," he wrote Rosenthal on the occasion of his thirty-ninth birthday.

A publisher and executive editor needed to have a warm working relationship, as Punch Sulzberger had had with Abe Rosenthal. But Arthur Sulzberger was uncomfortable in Lelyveld's presence; he thought of him as "a little tight." Sulzberger invited Lelyveld to join him on a trip to Berlin, to attend the general assembly of the International Press Institute, so he could get a better measure of him. They were together for three days, and every morning went for a jog on the dirt trails that crisscross the grounds of Tiergarten. "It became literally a running colloquium on the newspaper and where it was headed and we found ourselves in a sweaty and amicable disagreement as much as not," Lelyveld said years later. "I thought I was talking myself out of a job." Sulzberger filled the time by asking him questions, some on subjects that Lelyveld had never considered, and that frankly did not interest him.

What do you think, Sulzberger wondered, about distributing different editions of the newspaper tailored to specific regions of the coverage area. On the last day of the conference, Sulzberger was stepping onto an elevator when he spotted Lelyveld and called out a question.

If you're not made managing editor, will you stay at the paper anyway?

As the doors closed, Lelyveld looked at Sulzberger with a shrug and an enigmatic wave of his hand. When Lelyveld returned to New York, Frankel greeted him warmly. Your trip went very well, I hear, he said. With Sulzberger's blessing, in late spring of 1989, Frankel took Lelyveld to dinner and said he wanted to appoint him as deputy managing editor, with the understanding that he would succeed Gelb when he retired. I need a brother, Frankel said.

Sulzberger and Lelyveld owned weekend houses in the Hudson Valley near New Paltz, in the woods and mountains about eighty-five miles north of New York. Sulzberger would spend his time there rock-climbing; Lelyveld would spend his weekends reading. One afternoon around Christmas of 1993, Sulzberger invited Joe and Carolyn Lelyveld over to his home. As Lelyveld arrived, Sulzberger put a cup of coffee into his hand and invited him for a walk in the woods—the forty-two-year-old publisher with the future executive editor, fourteen years his senior. The conversation took five minutes. When Joe and Carolyn Lelyveld climbed back into the car, his wife turned to him. What was that all about? she asked.

He told her that Sulzberger had offered him the job of executive editor.

What did you say? she asked.

He said he had accepted it.

Frankel had not alerted Lelyveld he was leaving early, so Lelyveld was caught by surprise. It had not occurred to him to discuss it first with his wife. They drove home in silence.

Arthur Sulzberger had taken a chance in appointing Howell Raines the editorial page editor. But now, picking a new executive editor, and with an obvious choice before him, he was not ready to be as adventurous. Lelyveld and Frankel were different in many ways, but Lelyveld represented an extension of Frankel, in his view of journalism and of the *Times*. He was a safe choice. He was the kind of executive editor his father would have chosen.

CHAPTER 15

"Our Jackie Robinson"

Gerald Boyd was a White House correspondent for the *St. Louis Post-Dispatch* when *The New York Times* hired him for its Washington bureau. He had been a Nieman Fellow at Harvard University, and had worked at the *Post-Dispatch* since he graduated from the University of Missouri at Columbia. Boyd was a Black man, and one of two Black journalists hired in the Washington bureau in 1983.*

Boyd was a stiff and slightly formal presence who preferred to be addressed as Gerald. When President Ronald Reagan had called him "Gerry" at a White House news conference, Boyd thought he was being patronized by a white president who had talked about welfare queens and was disdainful of programs that helped the poor and minorities. Still, the moment of presidential recognition enhanced his profile in Washington. Bill Kovach, the head of the *Times* Washington bureau, asked Boyd to send over his clips in the summer of 1983. Boyd was hired that November. You have the job, Abe Rosenthal told him as soon as Boyd sat down for the interview. Boyd returned home and wrote Rosenthal, pledging "to bust my butt for a news organization that bears your imprint." Rosenthal matched his enthusiasm. "We will bust our butts for each other," he wrote him. Boyd was assigned to cover urban affairs ("a euphemism for blacks, poverty, and civil rights," as Boyd later put it; this was also Paul Delaney's first assignment in the bureau). Boyd would later be promoted to cover the Bush White House.

Max Frankel wanted to make Boyd an editor when he took over the

---

* The other was Charlise Lyles, who was hired as a news clerk for Hedrick Smith.

newsroom in 1986 but delayed his decision because of what he said he learned observing Delaney as an editor on the national desk before sending him to Madrid as a reporter. It was a mistake, Frankel said shortly after he took over, to promote younger Black journalists—he had Delaney in mind—who were "not ready to be editors. And, if we do to them what we did to Paul, they will fail on the job and that's the wrong thing to do." Two years later, anxious to move up at the *Times*, aware that he needed foreign experience if he wanted to be a senior editor, Boyd went to New York to talk to editors on the foreign desk about an assignment in the Philippines. This time, Frankel intervened and told him he did not need overseas experience; Frankel was ready to make him an editor. "A special assignment for a special person," Frankel declared in his announcement of Boyd's appointment as special assistant to the managing editor. From that moment on, Boyd was on a fast track to the top editing ranks of the paper. Frankel welcomed him into this new chapter of his career, though warned him about the scrutiny he was about to face. You are going to be our Jackie Robinson, Frankel told him.

Boyd's name first appeared on the masthead—a roster of the most senior editors at the newspaper that was published every day at the top of the editorial page—on September 6, 1993, after Frankel appointed him an assistant managing editor in his final year as executive editor, closing the circle he'd opened in 1988. Frankel had pledged from his first days as executive editor to bring more Black and Latino reporters and editors into the newsroom, and particularly into its upper ranks. But it was now seven years later, and Boyd was the first Black person in the newspaper's history to be put on the masthead, so the departing gesture by Frankel, like his attempt to impose the one-for-one hiring plans to bring more Blacks on staff, suggested the limits to the progress. Frankel promoted Boyd knowing that it would put him in contention to be the number-two editor at the newspaper once he left. This would present his successor, Joseph Lelyveld, with a difficult decision immediately upon taking over; Lelyveld did not think Boyd was qualified to be the managing editor. It would create a rift that would never heal between Lelyveld and Boyd, an editor whose career had become freighted with symbolism and expectations.

* * *

Boyd had risen quickly after Frankel plucked him from the ranks of Washington reporters. He had been deputy Washington editor, deputy national editor, and deputy metropolitan editor, and in December 1990, he was appointed metropolitan editor. Boyd had dozens of reporters under his command and edited a stand-alone section, with its own front page, that competed with the *Daily News*, the *New York Post*, and *New York Newsday*. It was like running his own newspaper. Boyd had lived in New York for barely two years and, as he put it, "did not know the A train from the Q." It would not be an easy job for anyone, but it proved particularly stressful for Boyd. He would find himself the only Black person at the front page meetings, the publisher's lunches, and the private sessions with elected officials like Mario Cuomo, the governor of New York. He would gaze around the newsroom and see few Black editors. Boyd was wary of any whiff of condescension from colleagues who might doubt his judgment or assume he had risen so fast solely because of his race. He arrived at a tense city and newsroom, aswirl in the passions over the case of Tawana Brawley, the Black teenager who claimed she had been kidnapped and raped by a gang of white men, an allegation that was later found false. "In this highly charged atmosphere, I saw that I needed to tread carefully," Boyd wrote years later. "I could be both a change agent and a lightning rod for racist views and assumptions."

Michael Oreskes, who was his deputy, would find Boyd in a stairwell off the third-floor newsroom, smoking cigarette after cigarette.* His face would be heavy with worry, the look of a man who felt he had to prove himself every day. There was an awkwardness around him; his jokes could fall flat, his stern countenance seeming harsh or patronizing. He would pause before answering a question or offering his opinion, a tentativeness that conveyed a lack of confidence to some colleagues but was more a reflection of how mistrustful he was of the people in his workplace. He had a cutting manner that he would direct at underlings: reporters, editors, clerks, and even secretaries and job applicants. There

---

* The *Times* banned smoking in the newsroom on April 28, 1987.

are no slow news days—only slow editors, Boyd would proclaim, as he tried to goad the staff into filling empty pages.

There had always been editors who treated their employees harshly. But Boyd's style drew the attention of Arthur Sulzberger, Jr., who sent him to a weeklong management training program, Leadership at the Peak, in Colorado Springs. (In the shorthand of the newsroom, he was sent to charm school.) Boyd arrived to a stack of confidential assessments of his performance from his colleagues, collected in advance to confront participants with their shortcomings. He learned, as he later said, that he "could be a bully. They saw me as guarded and selfish, and concerned primarily about rising to the top. I could not believe that people considered me to be so arrogant." He pledged to change. But Boyd would struggle to find the right tone, to juggle all those conflicting forces—his insecurities, his doubts, and most of all, the pressure of being "our Jackie Robinson"—for years to come.

If Boyd needed reassurance about his abilities as an editor, it came on February 26, 1993. A yellow Ryder rental van loaded with more than 1,200 pounds of urea nitrate exploded on the second level of a four-story underground parking garage under the north tower of the World Trade Center, killing six people and injuring more than a thousand others. It was a terrorist attack on New York City, and Boyd, as metropolitan editor, would direct the coverage, which won the *Times* the Pulitzer Prize, its first for local coverage in over two decades. The bomb went off eighteen minutes after noon on a Friday, and by the next morning, the coverage, beginning on Page One, filled three full pages of the Metropolitan section. Robert McFadden was pressed into service to write the lead story, as he often was when editors needed a writer who could assemble the feeds called in from reporters out in the field to render a searing and complicated story. ("On a day of high drama, tragedy and heroism, there were a thousand stories: rescuers digging frantically for victims in the collapsed PATH station under the towers, soot-streaked evacuees groping for hours in the city's tallest buildings, a woman in a wheelchair carried down 66 stories by two friends, a pregnant woman airlifted by helicopter from a tower roof, and the tales of many others stumbling out, gasping for air, terrified but glad to be alive.") At one point that afternoon, Lelyveld, then the managing editor, wandered over to instruct Boyd how the masthead wanted the lead story written. Boyd shooed him away.

Will you just stay over there and let us do our work? Boyd said. And Lelyveld—who had complained for years about intrusive editors; the irony did not escape him—not only walked away but quietly admired Boyd for standing up to his boss.

Boyd's appointment to the masthead* by Frankel boosted his confidence and left him almost certain he would be considered for managing editor under the next executive editor, and that he might one day be the first Black executive editor of the *Times.* But the new executive editor did not think anyone currently in the newsroom was ready to be his managing editor, and he had particular doubts about Boyd. In the spring of 1994, Lelyveld asked Gene Roberts, who had left the *Times* in 1972 to become the executive editor of *The Philadelphia Inquirer,* to fill the job. Roberts and Lelyveld went back more than twenty-five years. Roberts, as national editor, had sent Lelyveld, then a thirty-two-year-old reporter on the metropolitan desk, to Chappaquiddick in the summer of 1969, when Senator Edward M. Kennedy drove his car off a bridge after a party, killing the young woman who was with him. Lelyveld was drawn to the idea of recruiting this "wise old editor" whose newspaper had captured a gallery of Pulitzer Prizes, now a professor of journalism at the College of Journalism at the University of Maryland. Roberts would be sixty-two years old when he began, three years away from retirement age, which would give Lelyveld time to prepare a successor from the newsroom. "My old mentor and friend is finally coming home," Lelyveld said in announcing his choice. He assumed his colleagues—including Boyd—would applaud his appointment of an accomplished former *Times* editor to the position.

Lelyveld informed Boyd of his decision at the bar of the Four Seasons restaurant. It was a difficult conversation and what precisely transpired that evening is a matter of dispute. "He said that Roberts's contract

---

* Boyd was one of two assistant managing editors named that day. The other was Soma Golden Behr, who became the second woman named to the masthead. Carolyn Lee was the first, also by Frankel, in 1990.

would be up in three years and that, by then, I would be ready," Boyd wrote later. "Lelyveld's words were unambiguous, the kind of commitment I had never heard from him. He assured me that the job was mine the next time around. I could wait three years for such a prize, I responded, if I was certain it would come." Lelyveld said in an interview years later he made no such promise; that he only made clear Boyd had a promising future at the *Times,* and that he could benefit from working under Roberts. "I knew better than that," Lelyveld said. "You can't promise anything years in advance."

It seems unlikely that Lelyveld would offer a commitment to fill a job three years away, and certainly not this job.* It is more likely that Lelyveld was vaguely encouraging, in the way *Times* editors could be in navigating through sensitive conversations of this sort. Boyd might well have walked away hearing what he wanted to hear, and Lelyveld, knowingly or not, let him walk away hearing what he wanted to hear.

When Roberts reached his retirement age three years later, Lelyveld paid tribute to his old mentor at a retreat in Tarrytown, and editors rose in applause. Boyd did not applaud, and he did not stand. With Roberts gone, Lelyveld would now be choosing someone from the newsroom as managing editor. And again, it would not be Boyd.

Shortly after he took over the newsroom, Lelyveld had flown to South Africa to ask Bill Keller, who held the Johannesburg posting that Lelyveld filled twice in his career, to return to New York as an editor, and start on the road to becoming managing editor. Their conversation took place as they drove the vast expanse of the South African countryside, stopping along the way to meet with local leaders who remembered Lelyveld from his assignment there. The adventure reminded Keller why he loved being a foreign correspondent, and he turned Lelyveld down.

I'd rather stick pencils in my eyes than sit at a desk and boss other people around, Keller thought. Lelyveld pressed him again after he got back to New York, this time with a handwritten note offering him the job

---

* A pledge like that would constrain Sulzberger when it came time to choose Lelyveld's successor; it would have been difficult to say no to what would have been the newspaper's first Black executive editor.

of foreign editor. Foreign editor is one of the most prestigious positions in the newsroom, and Keller found it more difficult to turn down.

When the time came to replace Roberts, Lelyveld saw in Keller an editor like himself: a correspondent who had spent years overseas—Moscow and South Africa—and been awarded the Pulitzer Prize. An executive editor of the *Times* should have foreign experience, in Lelyveld's view, and Boyd had not spent any time reporting abroad (though not for lack of trying: Frankel had assured him it was not necessary). Lelyveld consulted other editors before making a decision about Boyd, including Dean Baquet, the national editor. Baquet and Boyd were the two highest-ranking Black editors in the newsroom and had an uneasy, competitive relationship. Baquet, who would turn forty-one later that year, was too young, at least in this newsroom, to be considered for the managing editor position himself. Baquet respected Boyd's skills as a reporter but never thought he should be managing editor, and he said as much when Lelyveld solicited his view on whether to appoint Boyd to that role.

Boyd felt betrayed when Lelyveld told him in the spring of 1997 he was getting passed over again for the managing editor job, this time for Bill Keller, rising from his seat to end the conversation. "The name felt like a dagger thrust into my gut," Boyd wrote years later, referring to Keller. "My emotions swirled together: hurt, betrayal, embarrassment, abandonment. But bitterness—bitterness reigned."

Lelyveld put a hand on his arm and pleaded with him to stay. I need you, he said.

Boyd stayed. He would go on to praise Lelyveld, expressing his admiration, for example, in a handwritten note the following year as the *Times* awaited the announcement of the Pulitzers. "There are those who spend a lot of time patting themselves on the back but not you," Boyd wrote Lelyveld. "So please let me do it for you. You are a remarkable editor, who produces remarkable results. Be proud of what you have done, your friends and colleagues are. And as both, thanks for having me along for the ride." Those warm remarks seem intended for Lelyveld's consumption, the praise from someone who understood how to manage the politics of a newsroom. By Boyd's account, he would never trust Joe Lelyveld again.

As a correspondent, Lelyveld had been an eyewitness to racial injustices and, like many of his fellow *Times* colleagues, hoped to address these injustices at home as an editor by pushing to change the racial composition of the newsroom. But once again, for all the talk of diversity—Punch Sulzberger's speech in 1969, Frankel's efforts with Delaney and Boyd, and the one-for-one-hiring plan—the paper under Lelyveld remained overwhelmingly white. Sulzberger asked Lelyveld at the end of his first year as executive editor for an overview on minority recruitment. "I can only repeat what I've said in conversation: That it's a major preoccupation but that, with the exception of Dean Baquet, we're not rich in obvious candidates for major roles in the near term," Lelyveld responded.

Years later, discussing Sulzberger's drive for diversity, Lelyveld said: "It became such a preoccupation that it, to some degree, got in the way of news."

CHAPTER 16

Newspaper Dot Com

Shortly after New Year's Day of 1996, Kevin McKenna stepped off the elevator on the fourteenth floor of the *New York Times* building and walked down a hallway, past a bank of secretaries, and into the office of Punch Sulzberger, the chairman of *The New York Times*. He had been summoned by Arthur Sulzberger, Jr., the publisher. McKenna, a native of Southern California, had come to the *Times* in 1984 as an editor on the foreign copy desk and spent four years on the news desk, a newsroom bulwark that provided the final and most exacting edit of the day's most important stories and headlines, including every article that appeared on the front page. Editors on the news desk were steeped in the traditions, history, and standards that governed the *Times*, which is why Joseph Lelyveld turned to McKenna in early 1995 to be his representative on a project commissioned by the publisher to create the first website for *The New York Times*.

McKenna joined William Stockton, a former business editor who was now an assistant to the executive editor for special projects; Daniel Donaghy, an advertising executive; and Steve Luciani, the director of the advanced technology group, who monitored new technologies emerging across the newspaper landscape. Luciani had come to think of himself as "the resident Chicken Little," warning his colleagues of the threat over the horizon, which struck him as he realized his two teenage children were getting their news not from the newspaper where he worked, but from a computer screen. By contrast, this digital world was new for the representative from the newsroom; McKenna would scribble down notes after the committee meetings in a fifth-floor hideaway office and later research terms and theories he had never encountered before. "A book to get: 'Big Dummies' Guide to the Internet,'" McKenna wrote to himself in a note after one of those sessions.

The committee had been at work for a year when he walked into Punch Sulzberger's office. Three generations of Sulzbergers awaited him, gathered around a computer monitor set on the chairman's desk: Arthur Sulzberger, Jr., the publisher; his father, Punch, the former publisher; and Arthur Sulzberger's only son, Arthur Gregg Sulzberger, who was fifteen years old and a future publisher. McKenna had been previewing prototypes of the new website around the *Times* headquarters and was now fairly certain that what he was about to present was potentially the future of the Sulzberger family business and the nation's newspaper industry. As the Sulzbergers gazed at the screen, McKenna clicked on the prototype for the home page, compact and primitive by later standards, a procession of section fronts—Op-Ed, Politics, Arts and Leisure—and a sampling of articles so the Sulzbergers could appreciate how a story printed on the page of a newspaper would translate to a computer screen. Arthur Gregg, a fan of the NBA, had one pressing question: Would the new *Times* site include the late-night scores from Seattle SuperSonics games—those West Coast results that almost always came in too late to make the deadline for the morning newspaper? It would.

The committee called itself the Gang of Four, a collaboration that recalled the cooperation between editors and business executives in the late 1970s that led to the creation of the daily feature sections. And once again, there was a sense of urgency. Other news organizations were ahead of the *Times* in exploring the potential of an Internet-based platform, including *The Washington Post* and *USA Today*. The Raleigh *News & Observer* had a website up and running, advanced enough that members of the Gang of Four flew to North Carolina to inspect the operation in person. Organizations that were not the traditional newspaper competitors of the past—AOL, Yahoo, and CNN, among them—were becoming powerful players on the field, providing a steady stream of news, updated throughout the day. The changing media landscape was once again revealing the *Times* as a muscle-bound company that held on to its dedication to tradition at the cost of being slow to change.

There was a journalistic and business imperative to respond to this emerging technology. Newspapers, particularly the *Times*, had been moneymaking machines in the early 1990s. The newspaper industry was accustomed to riding out the ups and downs of the economic cycle, cutting costs to survive recessions, but always with the confidence that the economy, and thus advertising revenues, would recover. There were signs now that something more systemic and threatening was unfolding. The Internet was shaping up as a threat to the two pillars of the *Times*'s revenue base: subscribers and advertisements—particularly classified advertisements, which would account for $300 million for the *Times* in 1996.

This was a concern Luciani heard as he and some *Times* executives watched the rapid expansion of Monster.com, with its online offering of job openings—the same kind of employment classified advertisements that had once filled a whole section of the Sunday newspaper. Monster never became the threat that he thought it might, but before long, those columns of real estate, job, and automobile classifieds were drifting to AOL and Microsoft—and by the end of the decade, and at a considerably larger magnitude, to Craigslist. And the Internet was, for the most part, free for readers. While the idea that print newspapers would become obsolete seemed implausible to older editors, younger journalists—and, importantly, Arthur Sulzberger, Jr.—found the prospect of readers moving from newsprint to computers not only credible but inevitable. To them, competing in a digital world was not an experiment or an extravagance. It was urgent.

For the next twenty years, questions that McKenna effectively raised when he walked into that room with the Sulzbergers—the seriousness of the digital threat, the future of print, and whether the *Times* needed to transform how it collected and presented the news—would consume the newspaper. McKenna's presentation went beyond the "What is the Internet?" primer Richard Meislin had offered the newspaper's top editors three years before; this was a blueprint for how the *Times* would compete in this world, for how the newspaper could be presented on the Web. If this wasn't quite a battle for its journalistic soul, it was something that would prove to be nearly as momentous: a philosophical argument, the outcome of which would help determine the newspaper's success as a business and journalistic enterprise.

It took a year from the group's first meeting for the Gang of Four to finish the proposal for a *Times* website—one that turned out to be four times longer than projected, though that should not have been a surprise. The committee was struggling with questions that would confront the *Times* for years. Should the new website be a computer-screen replication of the newsprint product? How do you protect *Times* standards on a website being produced by a new staff, and at a faster pace? Should the online version of the newspaper post articles before they appeared in the print paper, potentially eating into the paying subscriber base and handing scoops to competitors? Should the *Times* charge for online customers, the way it charged subscribers to buy the print edition? And, of course, what should it be called?

The committee drew up a list of names, among them Webbreak (an inside joke referring to newsprint tearing on the web of a running press), and brought it to Sulzberger, Lelyveld, and Russell T. Lewis, the president and general manager of the Times Company. Well, of course we're going to call it *The New York Times*, Lelyveld said, ending the discussion before it even really began.

The committee, within weeks of its first meeting, decided that the newspaper needed to be ambitious with its website, to meet the expectations and standards of a new audience. Unlike @times, the *Times*'s halting entry into the digital world on the AOL website, it needed to do more than convey a computer screen representation of the print newspaper. "We must generate a distinctive 'buzz' about our home page among those denizens of the [Internet], creating what we call the 'ooh and ahh' factor," the committee wrote in an early report. "We want them to configure their computers so that the first place they stop each time they fire up their machines will be the *New York Times* home page. We believe the best strategy to accomplish this is to establish the *Times* website as the newspaper of record in cyberspace."

* * *

In the spring of 1995, Lelyveld stopped by the office of his foreign editor, Bernard Gwertzman, to tell him it was time to move on. Gwertzman had been in the job for six years. He was not ready to retire. He was turning sixty years old and had no interest in being shuffled into one of the cubbyhole jobs where the *Times* deposited editors and reporters to pass the time between their last productive assignment and retirement. Gwertzman proposed his next assignment to Lelyveld: helping the *Times* expand its reach to this digital world.

A few years earlier, he had gone to Harvard to visit his son James, who was a computer science major. James took his father to a computer science lab, to show off a computer that could display text and pictures—in this case, an early version of the Library of Congress website. Why can't we put *The New York Times* on the screen like that? Gwertzman asked his son. (Not enough bandwidth, James explained.)*

By now, the Gang of Four was five months into its project. The *Times* was hiring "kids with no journalistic background at all," as Lelyveld put it, as it began building a digital operation. It made Lelyveld nervous. He welcomed the idea of installing Gwertzman in this new digital venture. He wanted a figure of Gwertzman's stature, experience, and institutional loyalty—a product of print who could assure that *Times* standards would be adhered to in this moment of churning experimentation. Gwertzman was relieved, though aware of Lelyveld's doubts about this venture. "I am looking forward with great enthusiasm to the challenge of the On-Line newspaper, and just hope we can stick with it long enough to see it work out," he wrote Lelyveld. He was named a senior editor, "concerned with news competitiveness of our on-line offerings," as Lelyveld put it in announcing the appointment. "Many of us will sleep better knowing he's on the case," Lelyveld told his staff. In truth, Lelyveld's primary reason for naming Gwertzman to this new job was to clear the way for Bill Keller to return from South Africa, to put Keller in line to be managing editor. The Gwertzman appointment turned out to be, as Lelyveld put it years later, "a lucky throw."

Gwertzman was the embodiment of a print reporter. He would tell people he majored in journalism at Harvard University (class of 1957), but there was no undergraduate journalism major at Harvard. What he meant was that he had majored in English but spent as much time as he could in the offices of *The Harvard Crimson,* writing and editing with colleagues who would go on to become major figures in journalism: David

---

* Lelyveld, by his account, thinks it was *his* idea to move Gwertzman to the digital job.

Halberstam, Jack Rosenthal, and J. Anthony Lukas. His first newspaper job was at *The Washington Star.* He joined the *Times* in 1968, hired by Seymour Topping at a salary of $325 a week.

Gwertzman had earned a master's degree in Soviet studies at Harvard, and the *Times* sent him to Moscow soon after his hiring. He returned to Washington as the chief diplomatic correspondent and for twenty-four years, as a reporter and an editor, he was the face of diplomatic coverage for the newspaper. No other correspondent in Washington during that era was as closely identified with matters of state, and the Department of State, as Bernie Gwertzman; his colleagues would refer to him as Ambassador Gwertzman. James Reston told Topping in 1982 that Gwertzman was "the best foreign affairs reporter that I have seen in Washington in the last 40 years."

He trailed Henry Kissinger, the secretary of state, around the world, and chronicled the Middle East peace talks under the Carter Administration. Gwertzman had a framed copy of the front page from March 27, 1979, with its three-deck banner headline over his byline, when President Anwar el-Sadat of Egypt and Prime Minister Menachem Begin of Israel signed a peace treaty as they stood before President Jimmy Carter. The Gwertzman byline was over the *Times* account about the failed raid to rescue fifty-three U.S. embassy hostages held by Iran in 1980; he called in to the newsroom in New York after midnight to dictate the story off the top of his head. "The White House announced early this morning that the United States had attempted to rescue the American hostages in Teheran but that the effort failed, and eight American crewmen died in Iran after the attempt was called off," he wrote.

Gwertzman liked to say he had the most front-page bylines of anyone in the history of the *Times,* and he was probably right. Editors knew they could turn to him on a quiet Sunday afternoon, and that Gwertzman could find a lead-of-the-paper story for Monday. At his desk, he was an air traffic controller, juggling telephone pitches from undersecretaries of state urging him to cover their diplomatic initiatives in the pages of the *Times.* The stories were like the correspondent: authoritative, though most certainly not flashy. But he was determined; like an elephant forging through the jungle and parting the vegetation before him, as Howell Raines, who worked beside him in the bureau, once put it. Gwertzman was frumpy and affable, self-assured without coming across as arrogant.

When Lelyveld was appointed foreign editor at the end of 1986, he asked Gwertzman to end his reporting career and come to New York as his deputy. Lelyveld had no doubt who should succeed him when his own tour was up as foreign editor. "It won't be my call but it seems obvious to me that you should be foreign editor when I finally am pried out of my chair," Lelyveld wrote Gwertzman in 1989. Six months later, in July 1989, when Frankel made Lelyveld deputy managing editor, the way was cleared for Gwertzman to become foreign editor.

Gwertzman would go on to run the foreign desk during, as Lelyveld would put it, "the greatest run of foreign news since World War II—huge, transforming events like the fall of Communism, the breakup of the Soviet Union, the end of the cold war, the flaring of the Gulf War, majority rule in South Africa, Arafat greeting Rabin and the return of murderous ethnic conflict to Western Europe." Gwertzman loved the job. The first edition of the *Times* would be delivered to his home by taxi every night, though that was because he lived in Riverdale—near Max Frankel, who was executive editor at the time. (Once Frankel moved to Manhattan, the extravagance of driving a copy of the *Times* up to the Bronx each night—which cost the *Times* $9,890.58 for 1990—was brought to an end.) From his desk on the third floor of the *Times* building, he could move correspondents around the globe. When the Berlin Wall fell, he was commanding reporters across Europe to fly in so the *Times* could capture this moment with the depth and authority it merited. There was, it seemed, no limit on what he could spend to cover the story, and no limit on how much space there was to tell it.

In his new website position, Gwertzman was stationed first at a desk in the wire room, once the nerve center for the receipt of all cable and wireless communication—a vestige tucked away in a corner of the newsroom. He would not stay there long. The offices of the new website would be placed outside the *Times* headquarters, in 8,400 square feet of space on the sixth floor of the Hippodrome Building, two blocks away on Sixth Avenue. There was not enough space at the *Times* headquarters for a new division that had the potential to keep expanding. And lawyers at the *Times* counseled that keeping the operation away from the headquarters would allow the newspaper to claim the new hires did not fall under the jurisdiction of the Newspaper Guild, with its salary scales and workplace rules. (It would ultimately abandon its effort to make it a non-union shop.) The *Times* would create a new subsidiary to run its electronic operations. The president of the new subsidiary, which did not even have a formal name when the appointment was announced in June 1995, would be Martin A. Nisenholtz.

There had never been a position quite like the one Nisenholtz would fill at the *Times*, and there had never been a *Times* executive quite like him. He would report to both Joe Lelyveld in the newsroom and Russ Lewis on the business side. As such, his appointment was a sign of the reconsideration of the institutional divisions between the business side and the newsroom, which was what Sulzberger wanted. Nisenholtz understood that from the start, but it made Lelyveld wary. Nisenholtz was hardly a newspaper person in the traditional sense of the term, much less a product of the *Times*. He was an early pioneer in digital and interactive media. He had worked as the director of content strategy at Ameritech Corporation, a regional telephone company based in Chicago, for just under a year. Before that, he had spent eleven years as founder and president of Ogilvy's Interactive Marketing Group, the first digital media division at a major advertising agency, which later became Ogilvy Interactive. He had received a master's degree at the Annenberg School for Communication at the University of Pennsylvania and was on the founding faculty of the Interactive Telecommunications Program at New York University.

Nisenholtz was a rapid-fire speaker and an even faster thinker, clearly intelligent and personally engaging, though he could appear at times to struggle to contain his impatience with people who did not grasp how the world was changing. He was ahead of his time, and he knew it, and he was willing to poke at the *Times*'s more hidebound assumptions. That became clear when he flew in from Chicago for his first interview with Sulzberger, Lelyveld, and Lewis. Before they could say a word, Nisenholtz challenged them with his own question.

Why do you want to do this? Nisenholtz asked. He was testing his prospective employers. Sulzberger answered vaguely, saying this was something the *Times* should be doing, before finally asking his own question.

Why don't you tell us? he said. But the publisher knew from that moment that he wanted to hire Nisenholtz; he could not recall a job candidate starting off an interview that provocatively. Sulzberger would later describe recruiting Nisenholtz as "one of the smartest things we ever did."

Nisenholtz was struck by Sulzberger's focus on the future, how he was unencumbered by sentiment, if not quite as adventurous as Nisenholtz would like. At one point, in an aside that for Nisenholtz spoke to Sulzberger's view of the future of printed newspapers, the publisher said that a $315 million printing plant being constructed in College Point, Queens, to replace the presses at the *Times* Manhattan headquarters, would be the last such facility the company would ever build. The business of the *Times* was quality journalism, Sulzberger told Nisenholtz, and he did not care how it was delivered to its readers. As Nisenholtz recounted his interview in a speech years later, Sulzberger asked Nisenholtz if he had any concerns about joining the *Times*. "I replied, probably too bluntly, that the *Times* Company was known for political infighting, which I believe is a complete waste of time, though many regard it as an entertaining extracurricular activity." But by this point in the interview, Nisenholtz was certain he wanted to work there.

Nisenholtz had just turned forty years old. He was a handsome man with wavy hair that was already streaked with gray and a lantern jaw that jutted into a room. A bit of a professor in his demeanor, he was also a disrupter. He was there, he thought, to force the *Times* to do things it had not done or considered before. He would almost immediately hit a wall—it would not be the first time this would happen over the next ten years—with his expansive view of how the *Times* should emulate Yahoo, to become a global resource to explore the vast terrain that was the Web. He realized that was not going to happen any time soon. What the *Times* wanted was to publish its journalism on the Web. That was what its readers expected and what its journalists, led by Lelyveld, were comfortable doing. It was low-risk and it was low-cost, since it would not mean spending money to create new content. He understood that, even if he did not entirely agree.

The *New York Times* website went live at 11:59 P.M. on Friday, January 19, 1996, in an off-hours flick of the switch that gave engineers the weekend to work out any glitches. Despite the late hour, a crowd of people gathered around two computer screens in the Web offices in the Hippodrome, a clock on the wall behind them. A photograph of the event, taken at six minutes after midnight, captured Kevin McKenna, wearing a white shirt, his tie askew, staring at the screen as nytimes.com was launched into cyberspace. Two other members of the Gang of Four, Dan Donaghy and Steve Luciani, crowded around the desk.* Gwertzman sat off to one side, his arm draped over a cubicle partition, with Martin Nisenholtz over his left shoulder and Richard Meislin, who had written the "What is the Internet?" memorandum three years earlier, to his right. A case of French champagne, Veuve Clicquot, had been delivered earlier in the day, a gift from Sulzberger, Lelyveld, and Lewis. Toasts were made, and Nisenholtz held back one bottle and asked everyone to sign it, a memento of the evening.

The arrival of nytimes.com was announced to the world in an understated way the following Monday morning: a seventeen-paragraph story on the bottom right corner of the seventh page of the Business section. "The *New York Times* Introduces a Web Site," read the headline over the story by Peter H. Lewis. The blurb headline accompanying the story read: "A service hopes to build readership in cyberspace."

At Nisenholtz's insistence, readers were required to register to gain access to the site, providing their names, email addresses, and some demographic information. That way, the *Times* could measure who was reading what and when, and provide advertisers data they could use to tailor their advertisements. In those first hours, a new reader was registering every second. By March 1997, 1 million people had registered, and the site was drawing 60,000 visitors a day. By way of comparison, in 1997, there were 1.1 million print subscribers on weekdays and 1.6 million on Sundays.

The new website was rudimentary in ways that would be hard to imagine even ten years later. There were generally four stories on the

---

* The fourth member of the Gang of Four, William Stockton, resigned from the *Times* after Martin Nisenholtz was hired in June 1995 for a job he had wanted. "Characteristically, Bill doesn't want me to be artfully ambiguous about the reason for his departure," Lelyveld wrote the staff. "It has to do with our decision to look outside for the leader of the new electronic group."

home page, presented with minimal adornments in the form of photographs and graphic designs. Customers who wanted to read the new website from home would have to dial in on a telephone connection so slow—1,200- and 2,400-baud modems were still fairly common at the time—that it would take from five to fifteen seconds to download a story. It was like watching an hourglass fill up with sand, and *Times* engineers, checking the Web logs, saw the price of this in the number of "connection rest by peer" error messages, which meant that a frustrated potential reader had given up and closed out the story before it finished loading. The *Times*'s online operation required the efforts of twenty-two journalists and tech engineers who worked every night to transform the print paper onto the Web, starting with the editorials and letters and ending with Page One and sports—the last pages locked down before the newspaper went to the presses. (It could be challenging. As is the case with many buildings in New York, the Hippodrome switched off the heat and air conditioning on nights and weekends, making for often-grueling working conditions for producers working off-hours.)

The new site was not as ambitious as Nisenholtz had hoped for—it was not trying to compete with Yahoo as a browser—but it was also not "newspaper-dot-com," a term Nisenholtz used with derision. It included most of the stories that appeared in that day's *Times*, along with classified ads. But there were also reader forums, hosted by the likes of journalist Marvin Kalb, diplomat Richard N. Haass, and science writer James Gleick. There was an interactive crossword puzzle. There was a "tax calculator," which would allow readers to calculate their annual payments to the federal government under a 15 percent tax cut proposed by Bob Dole, the Republican challenger to Bill Clinton, in 1996. There was an online-only section called CyberTimes, which covered technology and new media, with freelance authors writing stories tackling such subjects as the protocol of using email to send condolence notes and whether eBay should be permitted to sell guns online. There were slide shows and news updates. There were also new-frontier arguments with editors on West Forty-third Street about whether stories should contain links to articles written by competitors of the *Times*, and if the email address of the writer should be included at the end of the story.

The *Times* online would be free for any reader in the United States.

(There was a fee of thirty-five dollars a month for oversees subscribers; that only lasted for eighteen months.) This was a matter of some discussion, but it was not a huge debate. Nisenholtz argued that nytimes.com should be free because subscriptions would be a barrier to building the biggest possible audience, needed to attract the advertisers that he and others believed would eventually finance the online version of the *Times*. No objections came from Sulzberger or the newsroom, though there was concern in the circulation department that this would tempt readers to cancel their print subscriptions. Most news sites were free; *The Wall Street Journal* was nearly alone in preparing to create a paywall starting in 1996. And as far as most people in the newsroom were concerned, this was just a laboratory experiment unfolding in another building that did not really concern them. In years to come, there would be huge debates about whether to charge, but when nytimes.com went up on the Internet at the start of 1996, the stakes did not seem high.

Gwertzman had his own office in the Hippodrome. He was thirty years older than most everyone on his staff, many of whom had come right out of college or from jobs at other Internet companies. They would talk years later about how much they admired the *Times*, and how they could never quite believe they were working there. But their views of journalism were different from what had animated Gwertzman when he'd first stepped into the Washington bureau. Gwertzman was there as the guardian of *Times* standards, to make sure that whatever appeared "didn't embarrass us," as Lelyveld put it. He was a kindly shepherd for this new generation of people working for the website, many of whom were unfamiliar with the traditional rules of journalism and the ways of the *Times*.

Everyone called him Bernie; he was good-natured, warm, energetic, and enthusiastic. He liked being a mentor and the old hand; he would talk about what made the *Times* the *Times* and would make sure nothing ended up online that was not ready to be shared with the public. Gwertzman made it a practice to say yes when one of the younger staff members came up with some idea—even if he did not really understand what they were talking about. He would take his staff to lunch at the Harvard Club. They would return to the office for meetings, where Gwertzman would lean far back in his chair and promptly fall asleep as the discussions rolled on without him. Gwertzman was the bridge between West Forty-third Street and the Hippodrome, between these two worlds of "my God, the world is changing" and "holy crap, the world is changing," as Lisa Napoli, who would write for CyberTimes in the early days, put it. His presence would "calm the waters," Sulzberger would say.

Gwertzman became passionate about the Internet, with all the fervor of a new convert. He joined Nisenholtz in arguing that the website could not operate on the same clock as the newspaper. If a prominent figure died at one in the afternoon, nytimes.com could not wait until the evening to post it, even if the *Times* writer preparing the obituary was still at work. And if the *Times* had an exclusive story, it should not hold back putting it online. Gwertzman began to feel more welcome at the Hippodrome than at the *Times* headquarters. He would attend the front page meetings, as he had as a foreign editor, but none of the editors there seemed particularly interested in his new adventure. People from the newsroom rarely ventured over to the Hippodrome. We are, like, totally in Antarctica, Gwertzman thought.

Lelyveld was guarded about the website: the threat it posed to cannibalize his newsroom, to draw away money that he needed to hire reporters and editors. He read the online version of the newspaper, but only protectively, to make sure it did not do anything that would, in his view, undercut the standards of the print newspaper. He understood the interest in the project and was aware of how important it was to the publisher. But it reminded him of the hourly broadcasts he and Robert McFadden used to write for WQXR: important enough, but hardly central to the mission of the *Times*. "I never really believed that the digital *New York Times* could have the same authority and sway that the paper *New York Times* had," he said.

CHAPTER 17

No Cigar

Joe Lelyveld had barely heard of the *Drudge Report*—a three-year-old website that offered a provocative mix of reporting, gossip, innuendo, and links to other news sites—when it posted a story that *Newsweek* had refused to run an article alleging that President Bill Clinton had engaged in a sexual affair with a young intern in the Oval Office. "Newsweek Kills Story on White House Intern; Blockbuster Report: 23-Year-Old, Former White House Intern, Sex Relationship with President," read the headline that appeared on the evening of January 17, 1998.

The website, run by Matt Drudge, an independent journalist, was willing to publish stories without the verification that other news organizations required; in this case, it was disclosing that a correspondent at *Newsweek*, Michael Isikoff, had found "the story of his career" but the magazine would not publish it. The reporting in *Drudge* was often poorly sourced and not always correct, but it forced other organizations to pay attention to stories and rumors that they might otherwise have let slip by. The site would rise to national prominence with its focus on the president's involvement with a young intern, Monica Lewinsky.

Drudge's reporting about the allegations was picked up and confirmed by mainstream news outlets, including *The Washington Post*, the *Los Angeles Times*, and ABC News but not, at least at first, by Lelyveld's *Times*. These were not the kind of stories that the *Times* covered—allegations about a politician's private life, particularly ones based on questionable sources—and it was putting the newspaper in an uncomfortable position. "We were asleep, I have to admit it," Lelyveld told a private Sulzberger family gathering the following year as he reviewed twelve critical months that would force the *Times* to reconsider its standards for reporting in the Internet era—and what news was, in fact, fit to print.

For all the continuity that Lelyveld had represented when he took over from Max Frankel four years earlier, his would not be a status-quo editorship. It could not be. The *Times* did not exist independently from the world it covered. It was subject to the same political, financial, societal, and moral forces as the people and organizations it wrote about, not to mention the changing interests of its readers. This was a president for a new generation—a chief executive who talked about what kind of underwear he wore and about experimenting with marijuana, and one who shaded the truth as he grappled with questions about his sexual exploits both before and after he became president. Clinton had confounded the *Times*'s notions of what it should cover during the 1992 presidential campaign when a one-time Arkansas state worker, Gennifer Flowers, asserted in a story that appeared in the supermarket tabloid the *Star* that she'd had an affair with him while he was the governor of Arkansas. The episode drew a flurry of attention, but not in *The New York Times*. The paper tucked a modest, unbylined story about the *Star* story onto the bottom right corner of page fourteen: "Clinton Denounces New Report of Affair."

When Clinton and his wife, Hillary, went on *60 Minutes*, the CBS television news program, to deny Flowers's account a few days later, the *Times* noted the moment with another modest story, this time on the bottom left corner of page sixteen: "Clinton Attempts to Ignore Rumors." Frankel, the executive editor at the time, decided it deserved no more attention than that, given the nature of the allegation and the fact that Clinton flatly denied it.

He could barely contain his contempt for news organizations that acted differently. "I'm quite ashamed for my profession," Frankel told *The Washington Post*. "We don't want to report on the candidates' sex lives. . . . We don't want to take our news or our news tips from the likes of the Star . . . or from someone whose ultimate veracity we can't vouch for." Frankel made a similar case when responding to complaints that the *Times* had paid relatively little attention to a story in the *Los Angeles Times* that four members of Clinton's security detail, while he was governor of Arkansas, had helped cover up his extramarital activities.

"Our modest handling of that story when it first broke had nothing to do with its 'unpleasantness,'" Frankel wrote Joseph C. Goulden, director of media analysis at Accuracy in Media, a conservative media watchdog organization. "By and large, we are not interested in the sex lives or habits of public figures—except when those habits impinge on official duty or responsibility." It was a posture that guided the *Times* from the campaign and into the White House, from Frankel to Lelyveld. "We worked extremely hard to ignore Bill Clinton's sex life for six years," Lelyveld told the Sulzberger family conclave in 1999. "Gennifer Flowers got less ink in the *New York Times* than she did anywhere."

As Frankel's managing editor, and after he took over as executive editor, Lelyveld had often been a force of restraint in the newsroom. He would resist the changes sweeping American journalism in the 1990s: the expanding definition of what was news, the compromised safeguards and standards that resulted from the speed and competitiveness fueled by the Internet and websites like *Drudge*. Lelyveld thought public officials were entitled to a zone of privacy, as he put it, whether it was Clinton or, later and closer to Times Square, the mayor of New York, Rudolph Giuliani, in the midst of an affair that led to the public unraveling of his marriage. Lelyveld was bothered by an increasingly competitive media environment, where news organizations felt compelled to chase rumors that appeared on gossipy websites. It stiffened his resolve to resist the stories on celebrity and personality that, in his view, seemed more appropriate for supermarket tabloids and reality television. Michael Jackson. The Menendez brothers. Tonya Harding. Lorena Bobbitt. O. J. Simpson.

When news that Diana, the princess of Wales, had been killed in a car accident in Paris in 1997 reached New York, the *Times* nudged aside the lead story, a report on Mexican immigrants, to make way for an article about her death, with a single-line headline across three columns. A few days later, when a reporter from *Time* magazine asked Lelyveld if the *Times* would have given the story bigger display, as most other newspapers had, if it had more time that night before deadline, Lelyveld responded, "Actually, I might have given it less." He would get a "sneaking pleasure" in leading the newspaper with a story out of Bosnia, even if a headline like that would sell few newspapers off the newsstands in New York City. He did not care; he thought those kinds of stories showed readers the seriousness of purpose of the *Times*. His mindset said much about how the *Times* viewed itself. Lelyveld could not know that these were the final years of an era when the newspaper could just assume profitability and dominance, when it thought it knew better than its readers what they should be reading, when the newsroom could be dismissive of the notion that it had a responsibility to help attract new readers to assure the newspaper's financial success.

Bill Keller, in the toast he gave at his wedding, had teased Lelyveld—his best man—calling him "the house prude," and "the abstemious, puritanical, uptight morals cop of the *New York Times*." Now, it had fallen on Lelyveld to shepherd the newspaper that people still called the Gray Lady through an era in which other news organizations were casting aside old rules and standards, embracing coverage of celebrity, sex, and scandal, relying on questionable sourcing, and often skipping rigorous fact-checking before publishing. "That is not why most of us got into this business, that is not where we want to take it," Lelyveld told the Sulzberger family. "If others were doing it, let them do it. We will deal with the consequences. We can lead on other stories."

This high ground became harder to hold once it was reported in *The Washington Post* that Kenneth W. Starr, an independent counsel originally appointed to look at the Clintons' involvement in the complicated Whitewater real estate deal in Arkansas, had turned his investigation to focus on whether Clinton had a sexual liaison with an intern in the White House and encouraged her to lie about it. The import of the story was undeniable. This was not Gennifer Flowers or even Paula Jones, who had accused Clinton of recklessly propositioning her when he was governor of Arkansas—which resulted in the sitting president being compelled to submit to a six-hour deposition on his sex life, a story the *Times* had in fact put on its front page. Clinton was under investigation for misdeeds in the Oval Office, and his presidency was on the line. What once could be seen as good manners by the *Times* was beginning to seem prim, and the newspaper shifted gears. Lelyveld and Keller were not about to let the *Times* fall behind *The Washington Post* on another presidential investigation that might lead to an impeachment.

On January 22, five days after the first *Drudge* report, a headline—"Subpoenas Sent As Clinton Denies Reports of an Affair with Aide at

White House"—appeared at the top of the front page. The *Times* began throwing reporters and editors at the unfolding scandal. Lelyveld and Keller, attending a birthday celebration for Punch Sulzberger at the Metropolitan Museum of Art, spent much of the evening huddled by a catering station, sharing a cellphone as they wrestled with the desk, and a reporter, about how to cast the first paragraphs of a story that would prove to be the *Times*'s biggest scoop on the investigation. The story recounted how Clinton had called his personal secretary, Betty Currie, who was a witness in the case, into the Oval Office to discuss the investigation. Keller wanted the first paragraph to say that the president attempted to "coach" her what to tell investigators about Clinton's relationship with Lewinsky. Jeff Gerth, the lead reporter on the piece, pushed back, saying that took the story further than what his two sources had told him. The dispute grew heated as the deadline approached, and Gerth, one of the bureau's top investigative reporters, threatened to take his name off the story. Keller backed down and agreed to a more precise and less judgmental lead.* The next day Keller sent Gerth a note saying he had been right.

As the *Times* joined its competitors in covering the story, Lelyveld found himself struggling with questions about journalistic standards— how do you respond to a competitive story in a rival newspaper based on one unnamed source?—as well as questions of what was news and thus appropriate to publish. Lelyveld was standing near the news desk when Dean Baquet, the national editor, brought him a copy of an early draft of a story that reported that Lewinsky had told a friend, Linda Tripp, about a semen-stained dress she had kept as a memento of one of her sexual encounters with Clinton, and that Tripp had recorded the conversation.

I think we have to publish it, Baquet told him.

Lelyveld used one hand to hold the printout and pressed the other against the wall as he sought to steady himself. Well, he responded, I guess we do have to print this. It might have been the most challenging

---

* "WASHINGTON—President Clinton's personal secretary has told investigators that Clinton called her into his office last month and led her through an account of his relationship with Monica S. Lewinsky that differs in one critical aspect from her own recollections, according to lawyers familiar with her account."

decision of his years as executive editor, he would later say, even including the decision to jointly publish with *The Washington Post* a thirty-five-
thousand-word manifesto of a serial killer known as the Unabomber, at
the request of Attorney General Janet Reno and the FBI.*

Those early days saw a frenzy of competitive pressure, and the *Times*
just missed committing a major error. The newspaper had tips from
three sources that a Secret Service agent had stumbled across Clinton
and Lewinsky in a compromising position in the White House movie
theater and had reported the episode to Leon Panetta, who was the
White House chief of staff at the time. The story was edited and ready to
publish; Lelyveld had ordered a four-column-wide story on the front
page when Michael Oreskes, the Washington bureau chief, called to say
that his White House reporter, John M. Broder, was warning him off the
story. Panetta, who by then had left the White House and moved to Carmel Valley, California, was not answering telephone calls. Oreskes instructed Todd Purdum, the Los Angeles bureau chief, to fly to Monterey
and knock on Panetta's door. Purdum was on the way when he reached
Panetta's wife, Sylvia, who told him her husband had said flatly it was
not true. The story was killed.

"If we had published that story," Lelyveld told the Sulzberger family, "I
wouldn't be standing here now." Other newspapers failed to exercise
such restraint; variations of the story turned up in *The Dallas Morning
News*, among other news outlets.

Lelyveld had tried to apply the rules of journalism he had grown up
with to decisions about how to cover Clinton. It worked during the early
scandals, when Clinton was one of many candidates for office. But it became untenable when he was a sitting president being investigated by a
special prosecutor. Lelyveld felt lucky that the *Times* was still a print newspaper, with time to check rumors that were racing across the Internet.
But he realized, as he watched the emergence of what he would call the

---

* This was a condition set by the Unabomber for ending a seventeen-year killing spree.
It was paid for by both newspapers, but only the *Post* published it as an insert, because the
Times did not have the mechanical capacity to print stand-alone sections during the week.
The *Times* and the *Post* were criticized for bowing to the demands of a terrorist. ("Yuppie
Publishers Sulzberger and Graham Kowtow to Terrorist" read the headline over an edito-
rial in *The New York Observer*.)

newspaper's "electronic arm," that the cushion was disappearing—that the *Times* was going to be part of a world where stories were being published as they happened. It all made Lelyveld so uncomfortable that he asked Martin Baron—an associate managing editor who would go on to become the editor of the *Miami Herald, The Boston Globe,* and *The Washington Post*—to conduct an audit of the first nine days of coverage of the Lewinsky story by the *Times,* to see if "our standards were slipping." Baron brought distance to the assignment, since he was away on vacation in Mexico during that period. Lelyveld distributed Baron's report, marked confidential, to his top editors, with the admonition that it be "closely held (and not left around on desktops)."

Baron found that the *Times* "on the whole" did "reasonably well"; it did not make the kind of mistake that *The Dallas Morning News* had made on the story similar to the one that the *Times* had nearly published. But his report was most certainly critical; he said stories were filled with questionable sources and attributions that did not meet the *Times's* standards. "Major portions of our January 22 lead story were largely unsourced—omissions that were thinly disguised, often through the use of the passive tense, with phrases like, 'said to be' and 'reportedly were to be,'" he wrote. There was information that was contradictory, and "sourcing that is meaningless," such as a story "attributed to an 'associate' of Lewinsky 'who had spoken to her' as well as 'others who know Ms. Lewinsky's version of what happened.'"

Lelyveld did not deny his own fault in the lapses. "I was involved, under the gun, in working out some of the strained formulations that Marty quite properly questions," he wrote the other editors. "And even now I'm far from sure that I'd have done it differently if holding ourselves to Marty's rigorous standard would have meant holding important stories: That's my true confession. . . . At the same time—more than a little contradictorily—I'd say the rigorous standard is the one we mean to hold to now," he wrote.

* * *

It was an early September day in 1998, nine months after Drudge first reported on Lewinsky, and the newsroom had the anxious, expectant atmosphere that fell over it on days when a major story was unfolding:

the soft-double-trilling of telephones, the taut conversations of reporters and editors, the murmur from television screens perched over desks. Editors were gathered in clusters and seated at their desks, refreshing their screens, or using yellow magic markers to highlight passages in the legal documents assembled in three-ring binders by newsroom clerks. The televisions were tuned to CNN, which had a banner chyron on the bottom of the screen: "Breaking News: The Starr Report."

Lelyveld looked perturbed. He had studied the 445-page Starr report that offered the House of Representatives a case for the impeachment of Clinton, as well as the seventy-three-page response by David E. Kendall, who was Clinton's personal lawyer. The Starr report described in detail the president's sexual encounters with Lewinsky in the West Wing of the White House. It recounted the episodes of oral sex, telephone sex, the likely provenance of the semen stain on Lewinsky's blue dress, and his use of a cigar during one of their sexual encounters, at least according to the testimony from Lewinsky. It also recounted Clinton's legalistic explanation of why none of this constituted sexual relations. Lelyveld wandered the rows of desks in the newsroom, pausing at the national desk, the news desk, the foreign desk, before finally arriving at the doorway of the office of Bill Keller, who was on the telephone with Oreskes in Washington. Lelyveld walked into Keller's office, sat down, and lifted his feet on a desk. Keller sat across from Lelyveld, behind another desk. A framed headline from a South African tabloid—"I Killed Winnie's Sex Slave," a piece of memorabilia from Keller's years in Johannesburg—hung on a wall over his shoulder. Susan Dryfoos was in the room with a camera, capturing this moment as part of her *Times* history project.

"Okay, this is a quote from our nation's leader," Lelyveld said dryly, reading from the Starr report. " 'On the question of, uh, uh, uh . . .' "

"Does it cover oral sex?" Keller said, finishing the sentence.

Lelyveld continued. "Whether oral sex is sexual relations. 'If the deponent is the person who has oral sex performed on him, then the contact is with—not with anything on that list, but with the lips of another person.' "

This assertion from the president, as uncomfortably conveyed by Lelyveld, drew nervous laughter from Keller and Oreskes, listening in from Washington.

Lelyveld went on reading the president's testimony. " 'It seems to be self-evident that that's what it is. Let me remind you, sir, I read this carefully . . .' "

Keller broke in again. "That's kind of the quote of the day," he said.

Lelyveld glanced up, pained, and continued. "And then it quotes the president as saying, 'Any person, reasonable person,' would recognize that oral sex performed on the deponent falls outside the definition."

Oreskes's voice crackled over the speakerphone. "I didn't inhale, and she didn't swallow: is that what the defense is?"

"In fact, she didn't," Lelyveld responded to Oreskes. "If you read on, in the first eight encounters, he wouldn't allow her to get to the point of ejaculation because he didn't feel he knew her well enough."

The lead story was being written in the Washington bureau by John Broder and Don Van Natta, Jr., an investigative reporter, so Oreskes asked Lelyveld for guidance on how they should handle these kinds of details. Lelyveld stumbled around a bit, paused, and then gave his ruling.

"I mean I just want to keep it as 'gave details of sexual encounters.' Which consisted mainly of oral sex and—you know, what we've had in the paper. That Ms. Lewinsky testified that he touched her breasts and genital area. But I don't want to say where it happened, or the sequence. I don't want to go move by move in each sexual encounter." At that, he gave Keller a stern look. "We must report the direct quotes of the president," Lelyveld said. "But I don't think we need to report the direct quotes of Ms. Lewinsky where they relate to sexual acts."

He added, "I would leave the cigar out as long as we possibly can."

Drawing the meeting to a close, Lelyveld said the reporters should mention the "very touching business about how he told her he'd call her back and she waited home all weekend." He tipped back in the chair, holding his glasses in one hand. "Anything about the emotional quality is fine. But ejaculation, where he touched me, you know, dah-dah-dah. Let's just stay away from that."

"Okay," Keller said. "Yuck."

"Are we going to deliver this in one of those plastic bags tomorrow?" Oreskes said, referring to the way the *Times* was delivered on doorsteps.

"Maybe we can deliver it in a condom," Lelyveld said.

The *Times,* as was its practice with documents of historic significance, reprinted much of the Starr report in its pages, including those details that did not appear in the news columns. And it would mention in its stories that the president's semen had been found on Lewinsky's dress, since that was evidence that went to the heart of the special prosecutor's case. The disclosure about the semen stain did not appear until the twelfth paragraph of the lead story in the next day's newspaper, after the article had continued off the front page.

Lelyveld enjoyed the thrill of running a big story, of producing a newspaper that was chronicling a moment of the nation's history. Five of the six stories that appeared on the front page the day after Lelyveld sat down in Keller's office were devoted to Clinton, Lewinsky, and the Starr report.* The newspaper pressed its top correspondents into service: R. W. "Johnny" Apple, Jr.; James Bennet; Jill Abramson, who would become executive editor; and Linda Greenhouse, the newspaper's Supreme Court correspondent.

The publisher was happy. "Journalistically, this has been as complex and difficult a year as we've ever known," Sulzberger wrote Lelyveld in his annual evaluation in October 1998. "You've guided our news report with an almost unerring sense of propriety and aggressive reporting."

But Lelyveld's own recollection of this period would be characteristically mordant. Abe Rosenthal had the Pentagon Papers, Lelyveld would say. I got the semen-stained dress.

* * *

If the *Times*'s navigation of the Clinton intern story was a highlight of Lelyveld's tenure, its handling of another story—one also freighted with difficult journalistic questions, and one that was a reminder of how much the newspaper was being scrutinized by critics—was more of a low point. "China Stole Nuclear Secrets for Bombs, U.S. Aides Say," read the headline over a two-column story that led the newspaper on March 6, 1999. "Breach at Los Alamos: A Special Report." The story declared that China had achieved a major advance in the development of miniaturized nuclear warheads, and that it had done so using stolen secrets. It

---

* The sixth story on the front page of September 12, 1998, was a dispatch out of Moscow on a change of leadership in Russia.

reported that a scientist, who it did not name, had failed a lie-detector test administered by investigators, and quoted officials invoking some of the most notorious spy cases in the nation's history, such as those of Julius and Ethel Rosenberg and Aldrich Ames.

Three days later, the *Times* named the scientist, Wen Ho Lee, a Chinese American scientist assigned to the Los Alamos National Laboratory, reporting he had been fired by the Department of Energy for security violations after the FBI questioned him in connection with the suspected thefts. The story said that "Mr. Lee has been the prime suspect in a nearly three-year investigation of reports of Beijing's theft of nuclear technology," according to senior officials from the bureau and the Energy Department.

The coverage over the next eighteen months was an episode of overreach in a murky case filled with contradictory evidence. The newspaper published nearly three hundred stories, editorials, op-ed columns, and letters to the editor about the investigation of Lee, and about China stealing nuclear secrets. The articles detailed how federal investigators were investigating whether Lee had "improperly transferred huge amounts of secret data from a computer system at a government laboratory, compromising virtually every nuclear weapon in the United States arsenal." It reported how the FBI said Lee had tried to hide evidence from investigators. It said Lee had admitted, under questioning, to unauthorized contacts with Chinese scientists, and that at one point, he'd stopped cooperating with investigators. The *Times* columnist William Safire seized on the *Times*'s reporting, also invoking Aldrich Ames. "We are now informed by The New York Times's Pulitzer-Prize-winning investigative team that the codes—'legacy codes,' as they are known at Los Alamos— were allegedly downloaded by Wen Ho Lee in 1994," Safire wrote in another column. "Our nuclear genie is out of the bottle." Television news crews gathered outside Lee's front door; he and his wife disconnected the telephone and refused to answer the doorbell, according to reporters who were there. And in December 1999, Lee was indicted by a federal grand jury in New Mexico on fifty-nine counts of illegally moving a trove of classified information from the Los Alamos weapons lab to an unsecure computer. He was labeled a security risk and imprisoned without bail. He would spend nine months in solitary confinement, in a cell where the lights were left burning around the clock and his legs were shackled during his recreation time.

But problems soon emerged with the case. An FBI agent, appearing in federal court in Albuquerque in August 2000, recanted his testimony that Lee lied to a colleague to gain access to his computer so he could download files. A prominent weapons designer, John Richter, who had supplied information that helped launch the espionage investigation, testified that Lee should go free. "Keeping him locked up the way he is is much more injurious to the reputation of the United States," he said. Judge James A. Parker of the federal district court in Albuquerque excoriated the government for the "demeaning, unnecessarily punitive conditions" of Lee's confinement. The judge apologized to Lee in open court and chastised officials in the Clinton Administration for their mishandling of the investigation. "They have embarrassed our entire nation and each of us who is a citizen of it." The case sputtered to a close when Lee pleaded guilty to a single count of mishandling classified information and was freed on the spot.

For much of those eighteen months, the *Times* was as identified with this prosecution nearly as much as the federal government—accused by civil rights groups and press critics of rushing into print with dubious accusations from anonymous FBI agents against a Chinese American immigrant. The case had become a self-perpetuating frenzy: The disclosures in the *Times* and other newspapers about the investigation put more pressure on investigators and politicians to investigate, which in turn put pressure on news organizations to publish more stories about the investigation. The *Times* was torn between readers who accused the paper of railroading an innocent man in an episode that suggested racial profiling and the institutional imperative of sticking by its reporters. The main stories were written by James Risen, one of the *Times*'s most prominent investigative reporters; on some of the stories he worked with Jeff Gerth, the reporter who had been singled out by the Pulitzer Board when it awarded the *Times* a Pulitzer in 1999 for articles on the exportation of American technology to China.

Lelyveld and Keller grew worried and decided the newspaper had to respond to concerns about the coverage. At Lelyveld's instruction, Keller and Stephen Engelberg, an investigations editor, agreed to write an early draft of an editors' note. This was hardly a clear-cut case of journalistic misdeed. Lelyveld and Keller met skepticism from the highest levels of the paper.

We've got this in balance now—why open it up again? Sulzberger said to his executive editor, as Lelyveld described the conversation. They faced stronger resistance when Risen and Gerth went to New York to discuss the story with senior editors. They were accompanied by Jill Abramson, the Washington editor who had been an investigative reporter at *The Wall Street Journal* before the *Times* recruited her to become a reporter in its Washington bureau. The three of them argued that attaching an editors' note to the story would set a precedent that would make reporters wary of tackling high-risk investigative articles. Abramson warned that it would turn reporters into prognosticators, who not only have to dig out facts that trusted sources believed to be true but determine if they would be borne out with time. The reporters had diligently reported on what FBI investigators believed; there was, at the time they wrote the stories, no way to know that much of the case would fall apart.

The FBI screwed up—no question, Gerth said to his colleagues as they debated what to do. That's not my problem. I'm not responsible for the FBI. He pleaded guilty to one felony. What if he had pleaded guilty to more than one felony? Where do we draw the line? At one point, Risen left the meeting in anger, protesting that the editors were caving in to critics. Abramson went and found him at a Starbucks on Eighth Avenue and convinced him to return.

A final version of the note was presented to Lelyveld on a Friday afternoon. We have done what you asked—we now ask that you do not run this, Engelberg said. Lelyveld took the draft to his weekend home in Maine and worked his way through the language. He shared the concern that the earlier drafts were too tough on the *Times* and put too much of the blame on the reporters. Howell Raines, who was preparing to write an editorial addressing his own department's excesses in commenting on the case, was shown the early version of the editors' note and was struck by how self-lacerating it was. But Raines was more stunned when he saw the final version: shorn of much of the self-criticism that he saw in the first draft.

On September 26, 2000, the *Times* ran a 1,600-word editors' note that said that it was proud of much of the coverage and of its reporters but acknowledged flaws—among them a "problem of tone" that "fell short of our standards." The note was at once defensive, combative, and contrite, nodding to the criticism that "contended that our reporting had stimulated a political frenzy amounting to a witch hunt."

"We could have pushed harder to uncover weaknesses in the F.B.I. case against Dr. Lee," the editors said. The newspaper failed to take into account the possibility that Lee was only a minor player in the removal of the intelligence—or had not been involved at all. "In place of a tone of journalistic detachment from our sources, we occasionally used language that adopted the sense of alarm that was contained in official reports and was being voiced to us by investigators, members of Congress and administration officials with knowledge of the case."

It had been seventeen years since Abe Rosenthal had created the editors' note to handle stories with journalistic missteps that were grave enough to merit more than a correction. There had never been a note quite like this one, addressing such a long and substantial body of work. It drew praise from outside the paper. "I thought your editors' note on Wen Ho Lee was impressive indeed," Donald Graham, the chairman of the board of *The Washington Post*, scribbled in a handwritten note to Lelyveld. But there had also never been one that stirred such an anguished debate inside the newspaper, pitting reporters against the paper's senior editors over issues of fairness and a newspaper's obligations in reporting the findings of anonymous agents in an investigation that touched on vital issues of national security.

Risen had always thought the editors' note was a terrible idea. He had come to *The New York Times* a year earlier from the *Los Angeles Times*, and as he listened to his editors question his stories in the face of the attacks, he thought about all the criticism he had heard about the *Times* before taking the job. This is the way they treat reporters? he thought. But over time, Risen would come to believe that much of the criticism of the coverage was valid. The stories did not contain enough caveats. Most of all, they were too credulous of what federal agents were saying about Lee. Risen would learn, he would say, never to be quite so trusting of what the government told him again.

The final version of the editors' note ended with an announcement that the newspaper had dispatched a team of reporters to "go back to the beginning of these controversies and do more reporting, drawing on sources and documents that were not previously available. Our coverage of this case is not over." Four months later, the *Times* published a fifteen-thousand-word reexamination of the case, spread over two days. The findings, written by Matt Purdy, were summarized at the top of the first story.

"Investigators took fragmentary, often ambiguous evidence about Dr. Lee's behavior and Chinese atomic espionage and wove it into a grander case that eventually collapsed of its own light weight."

Lee would be awarded $1,645,000 in 2006 to settle an invasion-of-privacy suit he filed against the government, charging it had provided reporters with personal data about his finances, employment history, and polygraph test results. Five news organizations paid half of the settlement to avoid contempt citations for refusing to disclose the names of sources in their stories about Lee. ABC News, the Associated Press, the *Los Angeles Times,* and *The Washington Post* joined the *Times* in making the payment, but Lee would always hold *The New York Times* particularly accountable for his time in jail and troubles in court.

"The *New York Times* didn't bother to point out that they had no proof of any of the allegations, nor did they ever suggest I could possibly be innocent," he later wrote. "Maybe that's how they sell newspapers, but it came at the expense of my family and me."

CHAPTER 18

Please Read This Column

Punch Sulzberger would not tell his op-ed columnists what to write or share the complaints he heard about them from friends, public officials, and advertisers. We will only discuss this column when I offer it to you and, if necessary, when I ask you to step down, Sulzberger said to Anna Quindlen when he appointed her op-ed columnist in 1989. In between, you are on your own.

But he was hardly a bystander. Op-ed columnists at *The New York Times* hold some of the most coveted positions in American journalism; they served at the pleasure of the publisher who, in consultation with the editorial page editor, recruited them, appointed them, and adjudicated such ministerial matters as which days their column would appear. If Sulzberger thought a columnist was getting stale or lazy he would push them out. Sydney Schanberg was a high-profile example of the publisher's authority, but he was not the only one. "At the end of the month, I am being retired by The New York Times," C. L. Sulzberger wrote in his farewell column on December 11, 1977, after Punch Sulzberger, his cousin, removed him from the page, marking the end of his twenty-four years as foreign affairs columnist for the *Times*. He was sixty-five years old, but more than that, he was a prickly character and had a contentious relationship with his cousin. In his final years, C. L. Sulzberger had been shadowed by accusations that he had worked with the CIA; he was featured prominently in a story by Carl Bernstein for *Rolling Stone* in 1977 about the CIA co-opting key figures in the media.

The op-ed columnists occupied one of the few corners of the *Times* where the publisher had relatively unchallenged authority over editorial content, and Arthur Sulzberger, Jr., came to enjoy that as much as his father had. He had not waited until his father stepped down to begin putting his mark on the page. Anna Quindlen surmised, correctly, that Arthur, a contemporary who had worked with her on the metropolitan desk, was behind his father offering her a column on the Op-Ed page. Why else would Punch Sulzberger appoint this former *New York Post* reporter who had never spent time in Washington or abroad—a thirty-six-year-old woman, six months pregnant with her third child—as a columnist? Arthur Sulzberger had taken a chance on her with his father, and his judgment would be vindicated three years later when Quindlen (a columnist) and Arthur (the publisher) went to lunch with Jack Rosenthal, who was editor of the editorial page, on the day the Pulitzer awards were to be revealed. She followed Arthur up to his office at the hour when the awards were to be announced. He threw his arms around her, and the two of them jumped up and down in excitement; she had won the Pulitzer Prize.

When the first *Times* Op-Ed page appeared on September 21, 1970, it was a collection of opinions offered by white men: James Reston, Anthony Lewis, C. L. Sulzberger, and Tom Wicker among them. A quarter-century later, as Arthur Sulzberger took over, it had hardly changed. The lineup was older, overwhelmingly male, and still entirely white. The writing tended to be ponderous. Sulzberger and his editorial page editor, Howell Raines, wanted the page to be vibrant and more diverse, a platform for a new generation of columnists who would write with panache and who would address a wider range of topics—culture, life in American society, the arts, the economy. In a letter to Frank Rich, the paper's chief theater critic, during early discussions about Rich joining the Op-Ed page, Sulzberger telegraphed his intentions. "I joked once before that there are over 1,000 men and women in the newsroom, of whom 998 want to become columnists and two want to (become) Executive Editor," he wrote, adding: "Let me be as straightforward with you as I feel I can be, given the delicacies involved. The underlying idea is to continue the effort begun with Anna, to broaden the voice and scope and reach of Op-Ed page columnists beyond our present preoccupation with geopolitics."

Sulzberger had his goals, but Raines had the networks outside the newspaper, and knowledge of the talent in the building, and proposed writers who could replace the deader wood on the page. The new class included Maureen Dowd, who had been one of Raines's preeminent reporters in the Washington bureau. Bob Herbert, a former columnist for the *Daily News*, joined the page in early 1993—also at the suggestion of Raines, who'd noticed him at NBC where he had been a national correspondent for two years. Herbert was the first Black op-ed columnist in the paper's history, though the *Times* story announcing the appointment made no mention of that. Rich was named a columnist in 1994, writing about American society and culture. Sulzberger and Raines would move out Leslie Gelb, a fifty-seven-year-old foreign affairs columnist whose writing was dry and unappealing, and replace him with Thomas Friedman, a foreign correspondent. At forty-one, Friedman had already won two Pulitzers—for his reporting from Lebanon in 1983 and for his stories out of Israel in 1988—and had long aspired to write the foreign affairs column. It was an exciting time on the page, and a long-needed rejuvenation.

* * *

Abe Rosenthal's first column for the Op-Ed page—"Please Read This Column!" was the headline—appeared on January 6, 1987. Rosenthal had been furious when Punch Sulzberger told him over dinner in 1986 that it was time to step down as executive editor; the offer of a column was intended to ease the passage. He was seated in another part of the building, far away from the newsroom he had ruled for seventeen years. Rosenthal would spend thirteen years on the Op-Ed page, addressing subjects ranging from human rights in Tibet and Africa to the threat of anti-Semitism. Rosenthal spoke to friends of winning a second Pulitzer Prize, though that never happened. He had always assumed he would be writing his column well into his old age.* He had something to say, he was sure of it. And there was a readership eager to hear his thoughts on the world; he was sure of that as well.

---

* "I expect to be a columnist for twenty or thirty years and then I'll start worrying about a career," Rosenthal wrote a reader who inquired about his future when he was moved out as executive editor.

But turning out 860 words of fresh observation and opinion twice a week is not easy, particularly for someone trained in the detachment of assembling a daily news report. "As you cultivate the garden of controversy, burn the bridges of objectivity," William Safire, the columnist, advised him in an essay for *Times Talk*, the in-house publication, as he welcomed Rosenthal ("the Rookie") to the page. "What is required in a great editor and expected of a great reporter is death to a provocative pundit."

Rosenthal never seemed to absorb that lesson. His column was the subject of derision from the very start; that "please read this column" headline had the tone of a man straining to adjust from running a newsroom to becoming just another opinion writer competing for attention. His friends would cringe. "He was one of the worst columnists. Great reporter but terrible columnist," said Gay Talese. His column-writing was jarring—all the more so coming from a journalist who had made a career of keeping the views of reporters out of the pages of the *Times*. "Among his critics, the charitable view is that Rosenthal is simply out of practice, struggling to find his voice in full view of a select group of readers who hold him to a higher standard than the usual rookie columnist," wrote Jonathan Alter, the media critic for *Newsweek*. "One column actually began, 'The city of Washington is very interesting,' as if that would be enough to attract the reader."

Rosenthal brushed off the reviews. "Although I don't believe in the conspiracy theory of life, I am one of *Newsweek*'s greatest targets," he said at a conference of the American Society of Newspaper Editors in San Francisco in April 1987. "I expected them to have at me as soon as I started the column." And once he settled in and began writing twice a week, Rosenthal enjoyed the life of being a *Times* columnist. His personal life, which had been so tumultuous during his years as executive editor, fell into place as well. After the collapse of his marriage to Ann Rosenthal played out in the public eye, thanks to the gossipy interest Rosenthal's life held for *Spy* magazine, among other publications, he had married Shirley Lord, the author and editor he had been dating. The wedding took place in June 1987 at the home of John W. Kluge, the wealthy media executive, and the attendees included Barbara Walters,

Beverly Sills, Mayor Ed Koch, and Donald Trump.* (Punch Sulzberger and Arthur Gelb shared the duties of best man.)

* * *

By the end of 1999, Rosenthal had worked at the *Times* for fifty-five years. He had served under four publishers, spanning three generations of Sulzbergers, from Arthur Hays Sulzberger to Arthur Sulzberger, Jr. For most of his career, Rosenthal had had a friend and advocate in Punch Sulzberger. But he was now working for Arthur Sulzberger, Jr., who had never liked him and who found his column an embarrassment. (Years later, the publisher would refer to Rosenthal as "Abe I'm-writing-as-bad-as-I-can Rosenthal," lifting the epithet from *Spy* magazine.) It might have been unkind, but it was hardly out of step with the consensus. For all that, Rosenthal was stunned when Sulzberger showed up at his office in late 1999 to inform him that his next column would be his last. His career at the *Times* was over. Gail Collins, a member of the editorial board, realized what a powerful moment this was when she glanced up from her desk later that day to see a stunning assemblage of *Times* leadership moving somberly past her door toward Rosenthal's office, like the men (again, because they were all men) of a neighborhood gathering to comfort a stunned and grieving widower: Howell Raines, Andrew Rosenthal, Joseph Lelyveld, and even the young publisher who had ended his career at the *Times*. Raines spent Rosenthal's final hours with him in his office, sympathetic and observant, as if he were a writer envisioning the final scene of his novel—the aching symmetry of the last moments of the *Times* career of the executive editor who had hired him. Raines admired Rosenthal, despite all his flaws, though he also thought the time had come for Rosenthal to stop writing, and thought the departure needed to be handled with the appropriate grace.

The nature of his dismissal by Sulzberger might have made that im-

---

* Harrison Salisbury wrote Ann Rosenthal a note of support upon learning of the marriage. "Any man who puts Shirley Lord ahead of Ann Rosenthal has lost control of his judgement—to put it mildly," he wrote. Ann was grateful for the note. "I know one thing: the man who married Shirley Lord is not the man I married and lived with and loved for thirty-six years," she wrote Salisbury.

possible. Rosenthal was white-faced, trembling, and nauseous with rage when he arrived for dinner later that day at an Italian restaurant on the Upper East Side with Shirley Lord and Rose Newman, his surviving sister. He later vowed to Arthur Gelb that he would never set foot in the *Times* building again. The *Times* article marking the end of the Rosenthal era, written by Clyde Haberman, did not directly address the circumstances of his departure, though there really was no need. "I've seen happier days," Rosenthal said in the story.

In the coming weeks, Rosenthal did not disguise the fact that he had been dismissed; there was no talk of leaving to pursue other opportunities or to spend more time with his family. "The decision of one man on the *Times* to kill my column stunned me and I still do not know why," Rosenthal wrote one of his readers. "Perhaps it was decided that after a half century on the paper I had not passed my probationary period." Sulzberger had offered him no explanation, "except a mumble that it was time," Rosenthal wrote Teddy Kollek, a friend who was the former mayor of Jerusalem. The *Times* asked him to say he retired on his own, but Rosenthal refused. "You can understand that it has been a hard time for me emotionally, departing at somebody else's choice in a manner that was without manners," he told Kollek.

His last column would appear on November 5, 1999, with a familiar headline: "Please Read This Column!" "Still, who could work his entire journalistic career—so far—for one paper and not leave with sadnesses, particularly when the paper is The *Times*?" he wrote. "Our beloved, proud New York Times . . ."

Arthur Sulzberger's decision to get rid of Rosenthal—his father's partner and friend—was one more step in forging his own identity and making the *Times* his newspaper. It was part of the young publisher's campaign to remake an Op-Ed page that he thought had become stale. But it carried all the freight of Rosenthal's complicated history with the *Times* and the family that owned it. Sulzberger had delayed acting on the Rosenthal column; he knew it was the most difficult change he would make. He was nervous—as his father had been when he had to remove Rosenthal as executive editor—and thought out what he would say in advance. And he wanted cover. Sulzberger approached other columnists who were approaching retirement age; he wanted to be able to tell Rosenthal that he was one of a number of op-ed writers whom he was moving out to make room for new writers—like Paul Krugman, an economics professor at the Massachusetts Institute of Technology, who Sulzberger had just recruited to write a column devoted to economics, business, and finance.

Rosenthal's friends rallied around him. Talese suggested Rosenthal write the sequel to his book on the *Times.* "There is only one person who can write his own version of 'The Kingdom and the Power,' and that of course is you," Talese wrote. "Only you can tell us what it was like . . . so be happy, my dear Abe, you are now (as Dr. King said) free at last!" In early 2000 Mort Zuckerman, who owned the *Daily News* and was part of Rosenthal's dinner-party circle, offered him a position as a columnist at the *News.* Rosenthal sought permission from Sulzberger, noting a *Times* rule restricting its executives, who typically remained on the payroll after retirement, from working for competing organizations. "I hope that the Times would waive it so that I could express myself in the only New York newspaper other than the Times whose ethics would allow me to consider writing for it." Sulzberger agreed. It was a perplexing move by the former executive editor. The two newspapers could hardly be more different, and Rosenthal knew that as well as anyone. "The fact is that the *Daily News* simply was not a vehicle for foreign affairs and heavy national stories," he wrote a *Times* media reporter who had been working on a story about the struggles of the *News*'s afternoon edition, back when he was executive editor. Shirley Lord always thought the decision was born of bitterness at Arthur Sulzberger. Zuckerman had enticed him with a promise of an advertising campaign that would promote Rosenthal on the sides of buses rolling around New York City. New Yorkers would know that Rosenthal was still there and still part of the conversation: the man who was the symbol of *The New York Times* would spend the next five years of his career writing for a tabloid. At seventy-seven years old, Rosenthal, commanded by the insecurities of a journalist whose ego and identity had been defined by something as fleeting as a daily newspaper, was unable to let go.

CHAPTER 19

Renegades

isa Tozzi learned to read from the weather box in *The New York Times*—or at least that was what her mother told her—and watched the evening television news every night, perking up when Gabe Pressman of WNBC came on the screen. Tozzi was, by her description, a newspaper geek; there was always a newspaper, a *New York Times*, left on a table in the home where she grew up in suburban Chatham, New Jersey. She had wanted to be a journalist since she was eleven or twelve years old and studied journalism at Rutgers University.

Tozzi covered the police and courts and school boards at her first newspaper job at the *News Tribune* of Woodbridge, New Jersey, and moved to Austin, where she worked as assistant politics editor at *The Austin Chronicle*, an alternative weekly. Tozzi had just turned thirty years old when Bernard Gwertzman hired her to work at the *Times* website, as it geared up to cover the presidential election of 2000. She was a politics producer, in charge of *Political Points*, a fifteen-minute live show that streamed on the website, which the newspaper was doing in a collaboration with ABC News. The show featured Michael Oreskes, the Washington bureau chief for the *Times*, and Mark Halperin, the political director of ABC News. It was one of a number of fitful attempts by the *Times* to break into television over the years, and it was technologically amateurish, at least by later standards, relying on slow and jerky dial-up connections. No matter. This was the *Times*, and Tozzi was working alongside people she knew by the weight of their bylines; James Bennet and David Rohde and, of course, Bernie Gwertzman.

She would come to realize that the correspondents she admired from afar were quite human, with flaws and quirks and tempers, who made mistakes and disappeared on deadline. But for now, that hardly mattered. Tozzi was part of the *Times* politics team. She was sent to the Republican convention in Philadelphia and the Democratic convention in Los Angeles, and she found herself at the glamorous parties that revolve around these political gatherings. She was on the guest list for the convention party Todd Purdum, the *Times*'s Los Angeles bureau chief, and his wife, Dee Dee Myers, a former White House press secretary, held at their home. Tozzi was dazzled at the scene before her, where Barbra Streisand held court on the front lawn while Warren Beatty and Annette Bening and the cast of *The West Wing* mingled with a gallery of journalists and senior officials from the Clinton White House (Warren Christopher!) and the Al Gore presidential campaign, drinking Bombay Sapphire martinis and the house drink for the night, watermelon margaritas.

This is the best party of my life, Tozzi thought as she gawked around the yard, bathing in the celebrity on this cool summer night in Los Angeles. This is what it is like to work at the *Times*. But it was not.

Tozzi and her website colleagues never felt like they were part of *The New York Times*, no matter what it said on their paychecks. Working in their office away from the *Times* headquarters, they were regularly reminded that their print colleagues thought of them as little more than kids who needed to be monitored. While the Web version of the *Times* had gained more and more currency in the digital world, and had improved markedly over its first four years, it had not been embraced by the print newsroom. Joe Lelyveld had been wary of the website from the day it went online. Tozzi had a front-row appreciation of this from shuttling between the Hippodrome, at 1120 Sixth Avenue, and 229 West Forty-third Street to sit in at meetings where the political coverage was planned. Sometimes she ventured to offer ideas on how print stories could be presented and augmented on the Web. But Tozzi often felt she was on a reconnaissance mission, and she would share what she gleaned at headquarters with her friends at the website: the eye-rolling about the Internet and about the website, the way people shrugged it off as a passing fad, or the way their print colleagues were convinced that its try-something-different spirit—and the fact that the website was giving the newspaper's work away for free—was a threat to what people described as "the *Times* brand."

There were still some reporters and editors who were intrigued by the venture; these were journalists who were by nature curious about what was over the horizon. Some were thinking about their own futures as much as the newspaper's future, sensing that this was where the power might shift one day. These newsroom colleagues took notice of how, when an important story broke during the day and editors and reporters gathered to discuss how to cover it for the next day's print edition, Tozzi would break away and command a computer to make sure it was posted on the *Times* website *right away*. But too often, she would notice a whisper of elitism, the implied judgment that she and her website colleagues had not earned the privilege of working at the *Times*. Editors would sometimes not share with her what stories were in the works, as if they did not trust someone in their own organization.

Tozzi was unflappable and generally cheerful, but she would joke darkly about it back in the Web newsroom. Here I am: destroying the brand, Tozzi would announce to her colleagues as she threw out an idea for a slide show or a graphic presentation, and everybody would laugh. They really were in a different world, as they were reminded by a telephone call one day from the *Times* newsroom to Aimee Rinehart, a producer for the home page.

This is Joe Lelyveld: I am the executive editor of *The New York Times*, the caller announced. As if the people at the *New York Times* website did not know that Joe Lelyveld was the executive editor of the *Times*. Lelyveld presumably had no idea who might be answering the telephone and was identifying himself to someone he did not know, but the story of the call quickly became legend and loaded with meaning. It was more evidence of their second-class status. Alessandra Stanley, the Rome bureau chief, showed up at the Hippodrome one afternoon to attend a news meeting during a home visit to New York.

I feel like I'm sitting in with the cast of *Friends*, Stanley joked, referring to the television situation comedy about six buddies in their twenties living in New York.

Rinehart was crestfallen; she thought about how everyone at the website was trying so hard to be taken seriously—with daily news meetings, just like what took place at the print newsroom, and conscientious adherence to *Times* standards. They believed they, too, were working to build the future of the *Times*, even if they had different ideas about how to do that than their colleagues at headquarters. And now Stanley was comparing them to a sitcom. It was, Rinehart felt, the very kind of condescension (intentional or not) they had come to expect from the newsroom.

But a remaking of the structure and the culture of the newsroom and the company that had begun a few years earlier was underway. It was messy and divisive and there was no guarantee that the *Times* could succeed without losing what distinguished it. Tensions between old and new media were rippling across the industry in the late 1990s, but they were particularly pronounced at the *Times*, whose reporters and editors took such a proprietary pride in its reputation and its standards. Richard Meislin, who had become the editor in chief of *Times* digital after twenty-two years in the print newsroom, grew distressed at how his colleagues on West Forty-third Street dismissed the young staff at the Hippodrome as renegades who did not understand the *Times* or care about its values. Meislin thought they cherished the *Times* as much as he did. But they were part of a new generation, not as bound by history and tradition, who were invigorated rather than threatened by the changes banging at the door. A divide was emerging between those who wanted to help the *Times* prepare and thrive in this new world and those who were determined to protect tradition.

* * *

In fact, they were in many ways renegades. They were in a world of their own, a ten-minute walk from the *Times* building, and while that had been done for logistical reasons, Martin Nisenholtz, the chief executive officer of *Times* digital, and Russell Lewis, the chief executive officer of the New York Times Company, had come to view the distance as a gift. They were free of the constraints and the institutional inertia that came with working at the *Times*. They could take risks and defy tradition in a way that would never be countenanced at the *Times* headquarters. In the late 1990s Lewis and Nisenholtz were, like many people, riding the wave of technological innovation. They were drawn to the management theories advanced in *The Innovator's Dilemma*, published in 1997 by Clayton M. Christensen, a professor at the Harvard Business School. Christensen argued that established, thriving businesses that were attentive to the demands of their most loyal customers—who followed, in short, the accepted best practices of American business—were vulnerable to fast-moving, risk-taking enterprises that were hunting for new customers and new markets. Established businesses had little motivation to take risks and, as a result, often did not notice a threat off in the distance. The disruption presented to the *Times* by the digital revolution was the kind of phenomenon that Christensen had in mind. Lewis called a meeting of the Web staff in the ninth-floor auditorium of the *Times* headquarters in 1998 and, with Nisenholtz at his side, walked onto the stage holding up a copy of *The Innovator's Dilemma*. At his side were boxes filled with copies of the book, which he handed out to his audience.

You guys are our answer to this book. Go read it, Lewis said, gazing over his young audience, where there were as many pairs of blue jeans as there were ties. What it says is, old farts like us are going to be too focused on protecting what we already have, so we can't see the opportunity. We want you guys to have your own culture, your own vision, your own metabolism.

There was something free-form, chaotic, and, well, fun about the life at the Hippodrome; a let's-put-on-a-show spirit. The desks were buzzing with young people who, in theory at least, made up with passion what they lacked in *Times* experience. Fiona Spruill was hired as an intern on the website in August 1999. She was a graduate of Duke University who worked a summer on a tennis website—and that, in those early days, was enough expertise to bring her to the top of the résumé pile. "We were hiring anyone who knew what HTML was," Gwertzman told two early Web hires, as he interviewed them while researching his memoirs. Intern or not, Spruill did everything: writing code to govern the primitive system of moving stories from the newspaper word-processing program to the Web, selecting photographs for the home page, writing headlines. In less than a year, she was promoted to night editor, meaning that at the age of twenty-two, she was controlling the home page of *The New York Times*.

The cultures of the newsroom and the website clashed from the start. Six months after nytimes.com was launched, in July 1996, a security guard at the summer Olympics in Atlanta, Richard Jewell, was identified by authorities as the suspect in a bombing at Centennial Olympic Park. His name was published in *The Atlanta Journal,* and this set off a flurry of coverage in other media organizations. David Johnston, a Justice Department reporter based in the *Times*'s Washington bureau, had been warned by senior officials in the FBI that the case against Jewell seemed shaky. Johnston passed on those cautions to Lelyveld and Dean Baquet, the national editor. Taking Johnston's admonition into account, they assigned a small story focusing on the media furor around the publication of Jewell's name rather than Jewell himself. "Coverage of the investigation of the bombing at the Olympics here was dominated for hours today by a report in The Atlanta Journal naming a local security guard as the leading suspect," the *Times*'s Atlanta reporter, Kevin Sack, wrote in the first paragraph. "Federal law-enforcement officials said in interviews that the guard was among the suspects in the bombing, but that they did not have sufficient evidence to charge him with a crime. They cautioned that there were other suspects."

The warning would prove well-founded: Jewell would turn out to have had no involvement in the bombing.* But after deciding to downplay the story, Baquet returned to his desk, glanced at his computer monitor, and saw a headline on the *Times* website proclaiming that Jewell had been named as a suspect. He had not considered the website in planning the coverage by the *Times;* he would not make that mistake again.

The editors at the website were beginning to think differently than editors on the print newspaper; speed mattered, and stories that drew readers mattered. Lelyveld had been skeptical of the excesses in the coverage of the death of Diana, the princess of Wales, but it was a turning-point for the *Times* website.

We need to get that story on the home page, Gwertzman said when an editor called him late one evening to alert him that Princess Diana had been injured in a high-speed car crash. And Gwertzman was relieved—in the way that can make journalists seem cold-blooded to someone outside the business—that Diana died in time for the editor to update the

---

* Johnston would be made a senior writer after this episode, a designation reserved for the top ranks of correspondents and that carried an annual bonus of $15,000. "As far as I know the only time a reporter got named as a SW for what he kept out of the paper, not for what he wrote into it," Johnston later said.

home page before ending his shift. Until that night, the website had followed the lead of the newsroom, which closed down around three o'clock in the morning, after the late-night editor stood up at his desk and bellowed, "Good night!" That signaled to a nearly empty newsroom that the last edition had gone to press, freeing everyone to head home or for a nightcap at Gough's Chop House across the street from the *Times* headquarters. But after Diana, it became clear that this needed to be an around-the-clock operation, with an overnight editor in position to update the website. And Gwertzman began to push to have stories updated throughout the day.

We are not going to be static; if something big is going on, we're going to post it, he told Spruill.

Gwertzman went down to meet with his old colleagues in the Washington bureau over a brown-bag lunch to share how his thinking had changed about the pace of the newsroom. He was met with skepticism. Reporters did not want their names on stories that were incomplete or lacked the nuanced polishing that came with more reporting and writing. They worried that publishing a story on the website would give their competition time to write their own versions of the story, and they wanted to hold their reporting back for the next day's print paper. There were more prosaic objections as well: The website was looking to have stories updated every few hours. That could mean more work, and for no more money. If reporters did not turn over early versions of their stories, Meislin and Gwertzman would use wire stories from Reuters or the Associated Press. That assured that the website was timely, and it also played to the insecurities of reporters who might blanch at seeing a wire story on nytimes.com about a news event on their beat. Relations with the newspaper "are not bad, but not very strong either," Gwertzman reported to Kevin McKenna, who had left the digital operation to do a one-year fellowship at Stanford University at the beginning of 1998. "Reason is primarily the fact that most people on the paper really are not into the web yet. There still is a reluctance to see nytimes stories appear first on the web, as if it is some stepsister." That said, what really mattered, Gwertzman reported, was that the site had already registered three million users.

The newsroom would have to adapt to the twenty-four-hour demand for new information or risk becoming the caboose on the website. In early August 1999, Bill Keller, the managing editor and Lelyveld's deputy, called Jerry Gray, a former Associated Press foreign correspondent who had joined the *Times* sixteen years earlier and was now the political editor on the metropolitan desk, to his office. The *Times* wanted to create a round-the-clock news operation to be called the continuous news desk, staffed by *Times* reporters and editors, to work full-time for the website. Keller wanted Gray to run it. If nytimes.com was going to present itself as the website of *The New York Times*, it needed to provide its readers stories by *Times* correspondents. The newsroom's editors were under no illusions about how the newsroom would react to the creation of a continuous news desk. "This needs to be presented to the newspaper staff as a high-level priority, and explained in some detail," Lelyveld and Keller wrote Sulzberger. "Some reporters will resent the imposition on their time. It will be important to get across that this is an undertaking of importance to the newsroom, in which the full cooperation of the staff will be expected."

Keller's announcement to the staff reflected the sensitivity of the newsroom. "Your lives are about to change—a little," he wrote. "Our aim in all of this is not to turn the world's finest news organization into another wire service. . . . We intend to offer our own reports not on every story, but on stories where we believe we can add real value beyond what is available from AP or Reuters." Reporters should write about breaking events or help writers on the continuous news desk update the dispatches throughout the day. But this was a request, not a directive. "We do not want to sacrifice the standards of the daily news report for the sake of continuous news," Keller said. Gray's promotion was announced in the same spirit. Gray "is comfortable with the Internet, but he is of The Times—which means he has not yet slipped into the 'digirati' habit of referring to what we do as 'content.'" Gray had the experience of a wire service reporter and an understanding of the ebbs and flows of the *Times* newsroom. He was patient, with an easygoing sense of humor. He set a large jar of candy on the edge of his desk, and when reporters stopped by for a snack, he'd ask them what they were working on and if they might have a few moments to drop him a few words for the website. Early on, he called Dan Barry, the city hall bureau chief, and asked him if he had time to write seven hundred words about the upcoming release of the mayor's budget, as Gray recalled the exchange. The story wasn't particularly important, but it meant that when Gray next called a reporter at city hall or Albany or the Washington bureau, he could point out how the city hall bureau chief had written for the website. Gray saw the continuous news desk as temporary; with time, he told Keller, writing stories for the website would become part of the daily routine of every reporter.

* * *

Joseph Lelyveld could not resist a sly joke directed at Martin Nisenholtz when he addressed the seventy editors and managers at a retreat at the Tarrytown House Estate, atop a wooded hill in a pretty dot of a village on the Hudson River. He had devoted most of his speech to editing: granular observations about backfield editors and copy editors and copy flows and production. "I'm very conscious that I've been talking about fine-tuning, when, perhaps, the occasion called for a keynote address with millennial vision," Lelyveld said as he drew to a close. "I could have talked about twenty-four-hour newsgathering in the electronic future that is almost upon us—any week or month now—as we negotiate with various moguls or wannabe moguls of our supposed information age, an age in which everyone sells information that fewer and fewer people gather.

"But Martin Nisenholtz was too busy writing his talk for tomorrow morning to write mine for today," he continued. "So I've tried to be a provocateur in a small-bore way."

This was September 1998, and it had been nearly three years since Nisenholtz joined the *Times* as president of what would initially be called Times Company Digital. (It later was named New York Times Digital.) The *Times*'s website was drawing readers and advertisers. But storm clouds were gathering, as suggested by Lelyveld's remarks at the two-day session in Tarrytown, where small clusters of editors sat cross-legged in circles scattered across rolling green lawns. Within the year, the *Times* would announce plans to spin off New York Times Digital, with Nisenholtz at its helm, as a separate company controlled by the *Times*. This would be financed by an IPO, or initial public offering, plunging the company into the frenzy of investment and speculation that was sweeping the tech industry. The announcement set off one of the most bitter struggles in the newspaper's history, bringing to the surface rivalries between the business executives and the newsroom editors that Arthur Sulzberger, Jr., had tried to contain. And it exposed new ones over who controlled the newspaper and the website as it moved into this new era. There was a divide between these two worlds, as there was among the reporters and editors on the website and in the print newsroom, and it was deepening as the website showed signs of success. And nowhere was it more on display than in the relationship between Lelyveld and Nisenholtz.

These two men were symbols of different visions of journalism and, it is tempting to say, symbols of the newspaper's past and future. Lelyveld had supported hiring Nisenholtz in 1995 but had come to regard him as "a menace," as he would say years later. He felt that Nisenholtz was determined to run his own news operation, out of the control of Lelyveld and his editors on West Forty-third Street, much the way *The Washington Post* had set up its electronic newsroom as a separate operation across the Potomac River from the *Post*'s newsroom in downtown Washington.

Lelyveld saw Nisenholtz's operation, with its growing appetite for employees, technology, and money, as competition for the support he needed for his newsroom. He resented the salary packages the emerging *Times* digital operation was offering to lure people over, including for Nisenholtz. He recoiled at the ideas that Nisenholtz came up with to push the *Times* into new frontiers. Sulzberger tried to reassure him. "The Internet is a sexy topic right now," the publisher wrote in Lelyveld's employment review in 1999. "One result is that Martin and his operation is getting a great deal of press and overall attention. This is a moment in time, and it will pass. The driver of our Company today and in the years ahead is and will remain the *New York Times* newspaper."

But Lelyveld wanted the digital operation firmly under the control of the newsroom, to assure that what appeared on the home page met the standards of the print newspaper. "Martin is maneuvering for a kind of autonomy that's beyond his managerial capacity, let alone the best interests of the *New York Times*," Lelyveld wrote the publisher. He said Nisenholtz told him he wanted to replace Gwertzman with someone who was not from the newsroom. "That would take my approval, which he wouldn't easily get," Lelyveld wrote. "Still those were—and are—his desires. . . . Martin wants what he deems to be the dead hand of the news-room off his organization. He'll take our continuous news, be courteous and collegial in personal encounters but grant us as little stake in what is done with *Times* news on the Web as he possibly can."

Sulzberger returned in late summer of 1999 from vacation in "the deepest wilds of Italy," as he put it, and again tried to reassure his executive editor. But he sided with Nisenholtz. "For the record, I don't believe that Martin's goal has been to eliminate the role of the *Times* from our Web operations," Sulzberger wrote Lelyveld. "Such a goal is an impossibility. I do believe that he wishes to grow our web offerings beyond news, a goal I share." Sulzberger was trying to manage the conflict, but he was impatient with a newsroom that he thought was trying to cut out the website staff from any role in the news report—and in the process, driving digital talent to other news organizations.

Nisenholtz would later say he never understood Lelyveld's hostility. He had no interest in running his own newsroom. He thought he had a fine relationship with the newsroom, certainly better than the one he had with the circulation and advertising departments, which worried that the online *Times* would cut into the newspaper's subscriber and advertiser base. But Nisenholtz was frustrated with the resistance to his new ideas. In his first year, reviewing the state of the paper's electronic media division at a meeting with editors, he noted that Sulzberger had recently argued that the fact that the *Times* was printed "on paper is a relic of our history easy to give up."

Nisenholtz paused at Sulzberger's optimism. "I'm not so sure, Mr. Publisher, for if the last ten months in this job have taught me anything, it is that 'easy' it will not be."

He hated "this stupid traditional by-the-clock news cycle." He could not understand how editors at the *Times* failed to appreciate that their competition was no longer just *The Washington Post* but also websites like Yahoo and CNN that were "kicking our ass" with constant updates to reflect new developments in news stories or the late-night results of a Yankee game. Nisenholtz would say years later he had made peace with the modest digital ambitions of his new employer, but in truth this outsider—restless, inventive, a digital pioneer—could not escape his aggravation with this proscribed vision of the Internet. How hard it was, Nisenholtz felt, to arrive at a place like the *Times* at the age of forty-one from a non-newspaper background, to run a new division that held little interest to most of his colleagues. Nisenholtz asked for an office in the third-floor newsroom. He wanted to build relationships with reporters and editors and photographers. He would walk over from the Hippodrome, settle into his desk, and watch the room outside his door. No one stopped by to say hello. It was not hostility; it was indifference. Few people at the *Times* took the Internet or Nisenholtz that seriously. He felt like an oddity.

* * *

Lelyveld understood how the Web might one day rise to become a threat to the *Times*'s prosperity. But he was devoted to the tradition of the newspaper where he had worked for his entire life. And he was sensitive to any challenge to the primacy of the newsroom.

He and Nisenholtz clashed again when the New York Times Company purchased Abuzz Technologies, a small Cambridge, Massachusetts–based firm that built software for interactive question-and-answer sites, an acquisition that Nisenholtz saw as a way to extend the reach, mission, and technological prowess of the *Times.* Nisenholtz wanted to create a community of experts and readers, where a query—say, on the best restaurants in Paris or how long to cellar a 1982 Bordeaux before drinking it—could be farmed out to people who were part of the community drawn to the *Times* site, including *Times* reporters and columnists. Lelyveld was sour on the idea from the start. Why would people come to *The New York Times* for something non–*New York Times?* Lelyveld asked a boardroom filled with executives and editors. His objection was met with silence. Lelyveld felt like the old man at the table whom people were treating with polite tolerance. "I didn't really understand what he was talking about," he said later. "And I didn't really care about what he was talking about."

The debate over making the *Times* digital a stand-alone operation separated from the newsroom, was more wrenching. It would be financed by a tracking stock—a class of shares that would be linked directly to the performance of this one division. From a business perspective, it was an alluring idea. Investors were putting their money into start-ups, drawn by the excitement of this new frontier and the promise of fast profits. Other companies were spinning off their digital divisions, including Barnes & Noble and the Walt Disney Company. And the *Times* website needed money. Nisenholtz had long complained that it was suffering because of a lack of investment; by 1999, it was crashing whenever a big news story—such as the Academy Awards or the plane accident that killed John F. Kennedy, Jr.—brought in a crush of readers.

And the *Times* website was struggling to compete for talent. Personnel was being lured away by competitors with the promise of equity and the prospects of huge payouts. "So far, we've been fighting this battle with both hands and feet tied behind our backs," Nisenholtz complained in a meeting with editors. "We haven't been able to invest substantially in marketing and technology, in continuous news or multimedia, in strategic partnerships or acquisitions. We haven't been able to compensate people in ways consistent with the entrepreneurial community."

Russ Lewis proposed an IPO to raise the funds the digital operation needed. The idea was embraced by Nisenholtz and Sulzberger. "It gives us an ability to attract and retain critical talent with stock options tied to the success of this operation, in keeping with the dictates of this new industry," the publisher told a conference of senior managers in Palm Beach in June 1999.

Lelyveld was skeptical from the start. This would be, in his view, the final step in taking the website out of the newsroom and putting it under Nisenholtz's control. It would be its own company with its own executives and editors, its own offices, and its own stock. It would make its own decisions about what stories to cover, and what to promote. And Lelyveld resented the lucrative compensation offers that were being contemplated in the form of stock options for employees of the new company, and what that might do to morale in the newsroom. Lelyveld, in a note to Cynthia H. Augustine, the senior vice president for human relations, wrote that the tracking stock options being offered to Nisenholtz, by his "very rough and probably ill-formed calculation," would over two years be equal in value to four times the total combined earnings of the newspaper's fifty-two senior writers. "Nobody asked me, but I think that this is grotesque if not obscene and that some day, maybe some day very soon, we will look back on these decisions with a mixture of amazement and embarrassment."

Augustine told Lelyveld that she understood his objections, but there was little choice. "We are faced with an unhappy dilemma of paying what the market demands . . . or settl[ing] for Internet talent which is either untested or second rate," she wrote. "We've also found that our strongest pull in terms of attracting talent—the fact that we are the *Times*—does not have that magical pull in the Internet world. So our choice Joe, was to either compromise our practices of hiring the best people, or compromise our pay practices. In the land of no good alternatives, we decided to compromise our pay practices to allow us to attract and retain the best talent."

This was a genuine debate about how to finance a critical part of the *Times*, but in this era of overnight millionaires, the issue of compensation was polarizing. To deal with the resentments, Sulzberger announced that print employees would be allowed to buy limited shares of the tracking stock at a family-and-friends insider price. Lelyveld told his colleagues that the compromise—stock options for the digital staff, inside stock purchases for the print staff—might prove acceptable. "What I am asking you is to hold the envy—at least till you see Rich Meislin tooling around in his new Lamborghini, which won't be for a few years at best," he said in a briefing with newspaper editors and managers in September of 1999. At the same meeting, Keller and Lelyveld assured their editors that the newsroom would maintain full editorial control over the digital news division, though that assertion was relayed back to Nisenholtz with some skepticism by Meislin. "If anything, I thought he and Bill went too far in declaring how much control the newsroom would have over the content of the website, but that's to be expected in playing to that audience," Meislin wrote Nisenholtz.

* * *

The *Times* announced an initial public offering to raise up to $100 million for its digital arm in January 2000. Sulzberger invited editors and executives to his home in March to celebrate the launch. The plan was approved by *Times* shareholders in May, and Nisenholtz and other *Times* executives began meeting with Goldman Sachs bankers to get coached on the presentation they would make to potential investors. It all seemed so promising.

Nisenholtz was rehearsing his pitch for investors with the Goldman Sachs bankers when the quiet of the room was pierced by the *beep beep beep* of pagers going off in unison. Nisenholtz stopped short, watching as the bankers excused themselves to call their home office. The Nasdaq Composite index had crashed. The Goldman Sachs bankers left that day and never came back. In October, the *Times* withdrew its application for an IPO with the Securities and Exchange Commission. That started a spiral that took the bottom out of the digital expansion. Nisenholtz would be forced to oversee the layoffs of sixty-nine people, or 17 percent of the digital workforce, with another forty-seven layoffs following in April. Lelyveld found some vindication in the collapse of the IPO, but that did little to ease his concern that the *Times* was moving on two separate tracks. "We all accepted the argument that this company needs a corps of people who wake up every morning worrying about nothing else than its digital future," Lelyveld wrote Sulzberger. "But they're not smarter and they're not more valuable: the collapse of the equity market for their wares has shown that."

"Increasingly I feel that people at the newspaper—Janet Robinson for one and Bill Keller for another—are as nimble and alert about the future as anyone in the company," he wrote, referring to the company's future chief executive officer—the comparison with Nisenholtz left unstated. "Part of your job is to celebrate and indeed seize the future. Another part is to avoid leaving the impression that there's a revolutionary vanguard that excludes most of us."

The collapse of the IPO, the cuts that Nisenholtz was forced to impose on his growing digital operation, the deep wariness that Lelyveld and other leaders of the newsroom exhibited toward Nisenholtz's ambitions, would stall the digital evolution of the *Times* at a critical time. It sapped Nisenholtz and others' creative energy and sent a message that the *Times* was not the place to go for this younger generation of journalists who wanted to be part of this new frontier of the Internet. It was a setback, and a serious one. But it was just a setback.

PART IV

A PASSING STORM

2001–2003

CHAPTER 20

Tête d'Armée

The election between George W. Bush, the Republican, and Al Gore, the Democrat, ended on December 12, 2000, and the *Times* marked its tumultuous conclusion with two words set in sixty-point type at the top of the front page: BUSH PREVAILS. The United States Supreme Court had, by a single vote, halted a recount in Florida and "effectively handed the presidential election to George W. Bush," as Linda Greenhouse, the paper's Supreme Court correspondent, wrote. It had been a grueling month—for the nation, and also for the *Times*—since that election night on West Forty-third Street, a blur of changing headlines and stories rewritten in the space of minutes. Joseph Lelyveld twice ordered the presses to stop, and the *Times* recalled 121,000 copies of an early-morning edition that prematurely declared Bush the forty-third president of the United States, based on Gore's concession, which he withdrew at three-thirty Wednesday morning. The headline on that edition, which went to press at 2:48 A.M., read: "BUSH APPEARS TO DEFEAT GORE; HAIR-BREADTH ELECTORAL VOTE." The final headline, at 3:52 A.M., was an unsatisfying "BUSH AND GORE VIE FOR AN EDGE WITH NARROW ELECTORAL SPLIT" stripped across two lines.

Lelyveld mobilized the resources of his newspaper to cover the thirty-six-day battle that followed, dispatching reporters and editors to Tallahassee and flying Todd Purdum, one of the newspaper's most authoritative writers, from Los Angeles, where he was the bureau chief, to anchor the coverage. On all but eight mornings between the Wednesday after election night and the Supreme Court ruling, the *Times* updated readers on each chapter of this legal and political struggle with banner headlines across the top of the front page. "We treated it like World War II," Lelyveld would later say.

Arthur Sulzberger, Jr., sent his annual—and final—evaluation of Lelyveld on the day of the "BUSH PREVAILS" front page and used it as a platform to turn to the matter of another succession, the choice of the next executive editor of the *Times*. "If ever there was an occasion to focus an evaluation not on the year that was, but rather on the year ahead, this is it," Sulzberger wrote him. "With your upcoming retirement, we enter a year of leadership transition in the newsroom. So far, I believe we've been able to manage this situation well. But the pressures will inevitably build, and we both need to be acutely sensitive to the signals we send, often inadvertently. Both of us have a tendency to be seen as hip shooters. Our ability to guard against this instinct over the next year will be critical.

"I look forward to hearing your thoughts, and I promise to insure that both Bill and Howell feel they've had a fair and open hearing before making the final call," the publisher wrote, referring to Bill Keller, the managing editor, and Howell Raines, the editorial page editor. "Looking at this next year, my greatest fear isn't for them. . . . Rather, I worry about factions appearing that will make this feel like more of a tug-of-war than it need be."

Lelyveld knew who he wanted to succeed him. But Sulzberger had a different idea. He admired how Lelyveld had kept the *Times* on an even course these past seven years but had decided the newsroom needed to change, and that meant taking a chance in choosing its next leader. Sulzberger was ready to do that.

* * *

Howell Raines had never forgotten the phrase Max Frankel, who had just taken over as executive editor, used in 1986 as they discussed his future over dinner at the Mayflower Hotel in Washington: "if you want to run for executive editor." Raines held those words close as he marched steadily up the ranks at the paper. He cultivated his ties with then-publisher Punch Sulzberger and his wife, Carol Sulzberger, while he was the London bureau chief. His later years as the editorial page editor, and all those hours with Arthur Sulzberger, Jr., created an intimacy with the new publisher that Bill Keller could never hope to match.

Raines liked the fight and was invigorated by the scrum of the *Times* newsroom—jostling with ambition, editors squeezing up an ever-narrowing pyramid. He hadn't thought he had a chance of becoming executive editor when Arthur Sulzberger picked Lelyveld for the job in 1994, but he nonetheless confronted the publisher after learning the selection had been made without his knowledge. He would have appreciated the courtesy of an interview. Raines was thinking about the future, his future, and the next time Sulzberger would be making this decision.

Raines had been preparing for this moment for years. He was, at heart, a political reporter, and he was a student of the *Times*. He'd constructed a campaign for this job with all that he had learned studying the campaigns of candidates running for the White House. He had studied how A. M. Rosenthal had outmaneuvered Frankel to take control of the combined daily and Sunday newspapers in 1976, with a meticulous memorandum to Punch Sulzberger outlining the paper's vulnerabilities and offering a plan for what he would do about them. He had nurtured relationships with the older *Times* editors who were Punch Sulzberger's dinner, drinking, and travel companions. Arthur Gelb was part of that Sulzberger circle, a creature of the paper, who had joined the *Times* as a copyboy in 1944 and been appointed managing editor in the final years of his career. Gelb loved to gossip, and he loved to gossip about the *Times*, and he let Raines know that Lelyveld, as he prepared to step down, was lobbying the former publisher on behalf of Keller. It was, by Raines's account, a much-appreciated heads-up. And Raines fostered his alliance with Punch Sulzberger; he went on two fly-fishing trips with the publisher and his third wife, Allison S. Cowles, in the mid-1990s, at a lodge owned by Oscar and Annette de la Renta, the fashion designer and his philanthropist wife, along the Cascapédia River on the Gaspé Peninsula in Quebec. He would return to the office talking about his leisurely hours casting lines into the water with the *Times* chairman.

Wow, he's really good at this, thought Philip Taubman, who was Raines's deputy, as he watched his friend position himself within the *Times* hierarchy.

But while the decision on the next executive editor would be heavily influenced by the former publisher, it would be made by the current publisher, and Arthur Sulzberger, Jr., would want to display his independence from his father. Raines, as the head of the editorial board, would host dinners with members of the editorial board in a private dining room at Picholine, an upscale French restaurant near Lincoln Center, and invite Arthur and his wife, Gail Gregg. He was the charming, worldly, and urbane host, leading discussions about American politics and foreign affairs and the state of the nation. Raines brought Janet L. Robinson, the president of the *Times* newspaper, and Russell Lewis, the president and chief operating officer of the Times Company, both members of the younger Sulzberger's cabinet of advisers, to lunches where he laid out his concerns about stagnant circulation and print-advertising revenues and the long-term prospects of the *Times* in a deteriorating publishing environment. His attention to such matters would please a young publisher who viewed the division between the newsroom and the company as an impediment to the challenges the paper faced over the next decade.

Raines had assumed Sulzberger would succeed his father as publisher from their days in the Washington bureau when the two worked there together. They already had a rapport when the younger Sulzberger took Raines to dinner to talk about who would replace Lelyveld. They went to Aquavit, a Scandinavian restaurant in Midtown, settling in a small, quiet table in front of an indoor waterfall.* Sulzberger had a Grey Goose martini, his drink of choice, and Raines stuck to white wine rather than his customary martini (he wanted to keep sharp this night). He'd typed up talking points in preparation for his interview with Sulzberger. "National report—stale, reactive, has lost its old ability to paint a living portrait of America—staff has gotten lax, stays at home," read one of them.

Ultimately, the case that Raines made for himself was also a case against Lelyveld and, by extension, Bill Keller—Lelyveld's candidate to be his successor. This was a transitional time for the *Times*, and business as usual would no longer do, Raines said. The stagnant circulation figures were a warning. The *Times* was coasting, Raines told the publisher,

---

* This was one of two dinners Sulzberger and Raines had to discuss the job. The other was at an even more lavish Midtown restaurant, Le Bernardin.

its front page too often dull, in danger of losing audience and influence if it did not rise to the challenge of this new century. It needed to become more of a national newspaper; there were millions of potential *Times* readers across the country who were being left on the table.

Raines understood the power of the promise of change to this publisher, and he told Sulzberger that Lelyveld had been a stewardship editor.

I want to go in as a change agent—not as a custodial executive editor, Raines said.

The newsroom was still bogged down with the same complacency and exaggerated superiority (It's not news until the *Times* says it's news) that Raines had seen when he first walked in there in 1978. He vowed to shake that up and impose a performance culture on a workforce he compared to a tenured faculty.

The *Times* is like a canoe, Raines said. If you want an executive editor who is going to sit in that big, stable canoe and let it drift down the river, okay, you will make it through. But I want to paddle the canoe. I want to drive it down the river.

The lack of spark that Raines spoke of at his meeting with the publisher is common in the waning days of any editorship. Still, Sulzberger was receptive to these kinds of arguments, and Raines had constructed a case to appeal to the publisher's appetite for something new. Raines knew Sulzberger was concerned about the absence of high-ranking minorities at the paper. He pledged that if he were named executive editor, he would do what Lelyveld had not done: choose Gerald Boyd as his second-in-command, making him the newspaper's first Black managing editor. And he would embrace the digital challenge that Lelyveld had resisted.

You have gotten passive cooperation on the digital operation from Joe, Raines told him. Don't give me this job unless you want active cooperation. Raines, doing most of the talking, told the publisher how much he admired the way William Tecumseh Sherman, the Union Army general, described his place in battle: tête d'armée.

It's a French term, Raines continued. It means "head of the army." I intend to lead from the head of the army.

That's fine, Sulzberger responded. But you can get shot in that position.

Bill Keller would say that he considered himself a long shot against Raines, but in fact he also brought compelling credentials to the competition: he was the distinguished foreign correspondent who had chronicled the end of white rule in South Africa and the historic presidency of Nelson Mandela. He'd covered the demise of Communism and the dissolution of the Soviet Union, for which he won a Pulitzer Prize. He had been the foreign editor. He had been the managing editor. He was known and respected in the newsroom; Raines had kept his distance from the third floor, as befits the editorial page editor. And Keller was Lelyveld's choice. Lelyveld had tended to Keller's career the way Frankel had tended to Lelyveld's career. Keller may not have been as calculating or politically sophisticated as Raines, but he was no less competitive. Nonetheless, he never approached the quest for the job with the same intensity or shrewdness. If Raines set out to dazzle with his sweeping agenda of action and change, Keller's answers to Sulzberger's questions—also over dinner, also at Aquavit, also by the waterfall, the first time he ever tried Arctic char—were, by his own description, dutiful and obvious. We're going to have to deal with digital, Keller said. We should explore how to expand the *Times*'s audience into television.

Keller also wanted to reorganize the investigative unit. And when Sulzberger asked him who he would name as his managing editor, he threw out a few names.

What about Gerald? Sulzberger asked him.

I'd be open to it, but probably not, Keller responded.

If Raines was the agent of change, Keller was the candidate of continuity. He was Lelyveld's protégé. He admired the way Lelyveld had guarded the newsroom's standards through the coverage of Monica Lewinsky. Keller wanted the *Times* to keep doing what it had been doing—only better.

When he picked Lelyveld, Sulzberger had made the conventional choice. He never regretted that decision. But now he was five years older, and five years more confident, and more comfortable than ever about taking risks. Although he had assured Lelyveld that Keller and Raines would get fair hearings, there was little question in Sulzberger's mind that he wanted the job to go to Raines. Keller was the kind of editor his father might have chosen. Keller could be aloof, and he often struck Sulzberger as irreverent and dismissive, particularly in his dealings with people who worked on the business side.

Sulzberger was familiar with criticisms about Raines's tenure in Washington. He had read of them in places like *Spy* magazine, and he had heard them directly from disaffected staffers, including Janet W. Battaile, an editor in Washington. When Raines left Washington, Battaile sent the publisher a letter containing a catalogue of complaints about his leadership. "I've encountered broken promises, the worst sexism I've ever seen and an institutional bias in favor of reporters that leaves career editors like me on the outside looking in," she wrote the publisher.

"At the heart of it is the hostile treatment I've received here from Howell Raines," she wrote. She described a "head-on collision between his militaristic methods of managing and my kinder-gentler approach." She said she had numerous tense confrontations with Raines. "He said that I lacked leadership qualities. ('If you want to play with the big boys, you've got to act like the big boys.')" Raines, when later shown the letter, did not remember the specifics of the exchanges, but her observations were in keeping with the criticism that had shadowed him. Raines played favorites with reporters and editors. He gravitated to reporters and editors he saw as stars, rewarding them with his attention, promotions, and the best assignments. Battaile was low-key and amiable—not the kind of person Raines would invite to his office for late-afternoon cocktails with the bureau's most prominent reporters—such as Maureen Dowd, Michael Kelly, or Robin Toner. He would describe her as a "competent mover of copy." Sulzberger remembers seeing the letter from Battaile, but he never acted on it. By every indication, he considered it the complaint of an unhappy employee.

Now that he was considering whether to promote Raines again, Sulzberger spent weeks interviewing acquaintances of both men, seeking, ultimately, affirmation of a decision almost made. The publisher's deskmate from the Washington bureau, Steven Rattner, who had left the *Times* to become an investment banker, warned Sulzberger of the risks of picking someone like Raines.

You are going to bring in a guy who is going to shake things up—which you want—but who's also never really run anything of this scale, Rattner told Sulzberger.

But as Sulzberger talked to people around the building, the overall consensus, from Max Frankel to Janet Robinson, was that Raines was the better choice. Gerald Boyd told Sulzberger that it "really wasn't a contest" and that Raines "was a stronger leader and would bring more passion and energy to the newsroom." Even Dean Baquet, who was a close friend of Lelyveld, added his voice to the Raines choir: It's time for something new, Baquet told the publisher. Sulzberger asked Phil Taubman, who had worked with Raines in Washington and on the editorial page, if Raines had improved as manager during his years at the editorial page, as Raines had assured him he had. Was he arrogant? Sulzberger asked. Did he still play favorites? Did he take criticism well? Taubman assured the publisher that Raines had become a more gracious and judicious manager in his years on the editorial page; that he had taken criticism of his style to heart.

There was much about Raines that appealed to Sulzberger—the swagger, the energy, the drive and aggression, his romanticism about journalism and about the *Times*. When Sulzberger went to Raines in early 2001 and told him that he planned to replace Lelyveld by September, Raines urged him to move even quicker. "I thought the paper was becoming duller, slower, and more uneven in quality with every passing day," Raines wrote later. Sulzberger declined the advice, but it was what he liked about Raines: he was drawn to ambitious men and women, pushy people who, like him, would take chances. He admired what Raines had done on the editorial page; he would describe him, in announcing his pick to run the newsroom, as "our esteemed fire-breathing, take-no-prisoners editorial page editor." Raines was a gamble, and that made him even more appealing to the publisher. "If you don't fail sometimes, it means you're not trying hard enough" was a favorite Sulzberger aphorism.

Lelyveld had become a mentor and adviser to the publisher over his years as executive editor, and he sent Sulzberger a letter in the final days of his deliberations with one last plea for Keller. But the publisher had made up his mind. "I felt from the start that the time was right for Howell," he wrote Lelyveld. "I wanted to give myself the time necessary to put that gut feeling under greater intellectual scrutiny. Also, I wanted to see if I could begin to establish a greater rapport with Bill than I've had in the past.

"But that spark that I find so critical to a strong working relationship wasn't there."

Sulzberger told Lelyveld that he imagined "this is a difficult moment for you." Lelyveld assured him he was not troubled. "I do not expect to see the place run the way I ran it and I'm leaving on my own timetable. You've treated me with great consideration and I don't need any more."

Sulzberger was struggling with the spasms of a sprained back—a condition that he noticed was often triggered by stress—as he prepared to reveal his decision. He was in too much discomfort and too woozy from pain medication to take a bus down to the office. Instead, he summoned each of the contenders separately to his apartment on Central Park West. He was leaning on a cane and shuffling around the apartment in boat shoes, as Raines described the moment of his arrival. Sulzberger invited him to his narrow balcony with a view of Central Park, just big enough to hold two chairs, and lit up a cigar. I'd like you to be the next executive editor of the *Times*, he said.

Sulzberger was changing clothes when Keller came to the apartment. When the publisher told Keller of the decision, Keller asked the same question Sulzberger had asked him over dinner. I'm curious who Howell's thinking of as managing editor, Keller said.

That guy you said you wouldn't pick as your managing editor, Sulzberger responded, seemingly blanking on Boyd's name.* If Keller was crestfallen, he never showed it. Only two people thought I had a chance, Keller said years later when asked by a colleague whether he had expected to be appointed. Emma [his wife], because she believed in me, and Joe Lelyveld, who believed in Joe Lelyveld.

It was, not surprisingly, an uneasy transition of power. To Raines's frustration, Lelyveld had made three major appointments as Sulzberger deliberated on his successor—most significantly, promoting Jill

---

* It is no surprise Sulzberger blanked on Raines's choice for managing editor. Sulzberger frequently forgot people's names, even people he knew well, and particularly during uncomfortable moments, which this surely was.

Abramson to be the Washington bureau chief and Nicholas Kristof to be the associate managing editor responsible for the Sunday newspaper.* From Lelyveld's perspective, he had a newspaper to run, and he was not going to delay filling positions simply because his time was coming to an end. After Sulzberger made his announcement, Lelyveld used the three-month interregnum to leave even more of a mark on the newspaper. He oversaw a redesign of the front page and called Raines to his office to proudly display the product. Raines went to the publisher. You don't let a lame-duck editor announce a redesign of the paper, he told Sulzberger. This will be read as a vote of no confidence in me if you do. The redesign was scrapped.

At one point, Lelyveld came up to Raines's office to inform him he was about to appoint a new editor of the Travel section.

This won't do, Raines told him. I'm not prepared to give away a top job before I take office.

Just because we're going through a transition, the gears can't stop turning, Lelyveld responded, as Raines recounted the moment. But he retreated.

In his final months, Lelyveld had brought Todd Purdum back from Los Angeles, with the expectation of eventually making him the chief Washington correspondent. But Raines had his own candidate for the bureau's top writing job: Patrick E. Tyler, a friend who he had lured from *The Washington Post* when he was running the *Times*'s Washington bureau. He wanted to position him to replace Abramson as bureau chief. Raines, preparing to take over, pushed ahead with the appointment that Lelyveld had declined to make: Gerald Boyd would be his managing editor. He went ahead with that appointment against the advice of, among others, Max Frankel, who had promoted Boyd to the masthead. Frankel had admired Boyd's performance as metropolitan editor and, later, how he and Soma Golden Behr had edited a year-long examination of racial tensions in America, "How Race Is Lived in America," which won the newspaper a Pulitzer Prize for national reporting. But Frankel thought that Boyd had neither the intellectual breadth nor the depth of experience needed to be executive editor, should he be called upon to step into

---

* Lelyveld also made Carolyn Lee an assistant managing editor.

the job. That was the message he brought when Raines asked for his advice during a lunch at Café des Artistes. Frankel remembers telling Raines that he had supported his appointment as executive editor but had urged him not to make Boyd his managing editor.

What if you get hit by a truck? Frankel asked Raines. How could Sulzberger say no to the appointment of the *Times*'s first Black executive editor? (Raines has a different recollection of the meeting: that Frankel never questioned Boyd's qualifications and never warned that promoting him would compromise Sulzberger.) As far as Raines was concerned, the decision was made. There were no other strong candidates, and he did not think it was fair to have promoted Boyd up the ranks, to have offered him the prospect of being the managing editor or executive editor one day, only to yank it away at the last moment. White editors of unproven ability had been given a chance at leadership.

The assumption in the newsroom was that Raines had pushed Boyd in part to cater favor with a publisher eager to redress the newspaper's failures on promoting and hiring Black journalists. In truth, Boyd's appointment gave Sulzberger pause; he knew about the reservations that Lelyveld, Frankel, and Keller had about Boyd. And when Sulzberger met privately with Boyd, just before the announcement was made, he worried aloud whether Boyd could lead the newspaper if anything happened to Raines. Boyd was shocked and offended. "I could not believe that at this point I still needed to prove myself," he later wrote.*

Raines did not wait for Lelyveld to step down before beginning his promised shake-up of the newsroom. In August, he and Boyd flew to Atlanta, the city where Raines had served as bureau chief during his early years at the *Times*, to meet with national reporters based in the South. He asked Kevin Sack, the bureau chief, to book a private room in a local restaurant, and after the reporters settled in for dinner, he made clear how unhappy he was with their performance.

You shouldn't be filling up a chair around here unless you're giving one hundred percent of your talent, Raines said. The paper understands

---

* Boyd would ultimately have a falling out with Raines, but he treasured what Raines did for his career. "The fact of the matter is I never would have become managing editor if it were not for Howell Raines," he said years later.

you've got a personal life, family. But these are travel jobs. Don't take them if you don't want to travel.

The reporters were stunned into silence. In their view, they were already missing family dinners and school plays and Little League games to jump on planes and cover stories far from home. Boyd felt he was watching the return of the old Howell Raines. "We both wanted the paper to change, but on this occasion, and many others, he would be so hard charging and heavy-handed that his message would get lost in the force of the delivery," Boyd wrote later. Raines was sending a message with this trip to the whole newspaper.

* * *

Raines recommended Gail Collins as his successor to run the editorial page. Sulzberger and his wife, Gail Gregg, knew Collins socially, and Anna Quindlen had been talking about her to Sulzberger for years. Why is Gail Collins not writing for *The New York Times*? Quindlen would ask the publisher.

Collins had spent years working at tabloid newspapers and wire services. She'd started at a local news service in Connecticut, covering legislative news for small regional papers from an office in the attic of the statehouse. She had, over the course of fifteen years, worked at United Press International, the *Daily News,* and *New York Newsday.* She was a columnist at *Newsday* when Raines offered her a job in 1995 writing editorials at the *Times.* He needed a colorful writer, and he needed someone who knew New York. At the time, the idea of writing unsigned editorials for the *Times* struck her as boring. But it felt like a first step to being awarded her own column on the Op-Ed page, and in any event, *New York Newsday* was going to be shut down. Collins took the job on the editorial board and became a *Times* columnist four years later.

Her promotion from columnist to editorial page editor made sense to everyone but Collins. She was fifty-five years old and had been at the *Times* for six years. She was stylistically quite different from the editorial crusader she was replacing: modest in bearing, preferring pointed humor over stentorian pronouncements to make a point. "If God really wanted campaign finance reform, he would have made it easier to understand," she wrote in a column three months before her appointment.

Collins knew New York and she knew national politics, but she had only spent six months of her career writing about foreign affairs, on the international desk for United Press International at the old *Daily News* building in New York. "It taught me never to deal with international news, because I realized how much everybody else knew and I didn't," she said years later. When Collins demurred at first, suggesting that the *Times* could do better with someone versed in world affairs, Raines urged her to accept the offer. There are not going to be many chances left to be the first woman ever, he said.

Collins would be the first woman ever to run the editorial page in the history of the *Times*, and one of two women—Janet Robinson was the other—in Sulzberger's inner circle. She decided not to worry about the gap in her résumé, particularly after Sulzberger told her that Philip Taubman, the former Moscow bureau chief, would be her deputy.

I don't know anything about foreign policy, Collins said, wryly, to her husband. But you know, nothing much is going on on the foreign policy front anyway.

CHAPTER 21

A Terrible Beauty

Howell Raines was fifty-eight years old—"the cusp of sixty," as he put it—when he walked into his new office in the northeast corner of the newsroom. It was September 5, 2001, his first day as executive editor. Raines was impatient, and he was driven—determined to shake up the *Times*, just as he had told the publisher he would. He knew he did not have that much time. His three immediate predecessors, A. M. Rosenthal, Max Frankel, and Joseph Lelyveld, had stepped down before they turned sixty-five, and Raines had learned from covering politics that at any institution, a new executive had only so long before hitting the barrier of institutional resistance. He gave himself five years.

He marked the day with an exuberant memorandum to the staff that did not really convey the aggressiveness of his ambitions. "In my first communication as executive editor, I wanted to tell you how honored I am to be working with the best news staff in the world," he wrote. "Together we will share the adventure of sustaining the Times's quality, affirming its tradition of journalistic excellence, and preserving this irreplaceable institution for future generations of *Times* readers and journalists."

Raines perched a copy of *Stay Hungry*, a 1972 novel by Charles Gaines, a college classmate, on his desk. He hoped it would set the tone of the new newsroom culture for the editors and reporters stopping by to talk to the new executive editor. Raines announced a morning meeting for his masthead, at ten-thirty, so he and his deputies could weigh in early on what reporters should be covering. He was energetic, interventionist, and goading. On the weekend before he took over, he called Jill Abramson, the Washington bureau chief, while she was at her weekend home in Madison, Connecticut, to say he wanted a Washington bureau story that would land with a bang for his first Sunday front page.

Okay, she responded, do you have a sense of what you want?

He suggested a grading report on the first nine months of the George W. Bush presidency. She thought the idea trite though did not tell him so, and instead asked two of her reporters—Richard L. Berke, the national political correspondent, and David E. Sanger, a White House reporter—to look for a behind-the-scenes White House story that would please the new executive editor. Sanger and Berke produced a report that led the Sunday newspaper, detailing how prominent Republicans had warned the White House that Bush was already entering treacherous waters, and that if the president "did not take more forceful steps to resuscitate the economy, he would risk repeating the mistake that brought an early end to his father's presidency." Raines was so pleased that he called Berke at home on Saturday afternoon, when the first edition went to press, to thank him for his work.

Raines was as much a stranger to many of the people in the newsroom as they were to him. He was moving fast and did not particularly care what people thought of him—he never really had—other than that they realize that he would be more than a caretaker. Still, as he awoke and poured himself a cup of coffee on his seventh day of work, on the morning of September 11, 2001, he was certain he had some time to learn this new terrain, to determine which reporters he wanted on the front lines, to surround himself with senior editors who shared his view about the problems with the newsroom and the urgency for change.

On that same day, Robert McFadden was settling in on the first day of a two-week vacation at a home he was renting in East Hampton. He set out for an early walk on this bright and warm morning, wandering the backroads on Cedar Point off Gardiners Bay. He returned just after nine to find a neighbor waving for his attention, gesturing to the television inside her house. McFadden walked in to see the televised image of smoke and flames pouring out of the side of the South Tower of the World Trade Center. It had just been struck by United Airlines Flight 175. The North Tower was already in flames. For thirty years, McFadden had been the person the *Times* turned to for big stories like this, to produce the authoritative article that captured a moment in history. They were called lede-alls and they required a combination of command, meticulous organization, precision, speed, writerly flair, and a sense of history and *Times* style. He called in to the metropolitan desk and spoke to a deputy editor, Susan Edgerley, who told him that if he could make it in to the office, where he would be best positioned to manage the information coming in from reporters, the latest updates on television, and the requests of the editors, he would write the lede-all.

East Hampton is 105 miles by car and three hours on the Long Island Rail Road from Manhattan. The bridges into Manhattan had been shut down, so driving was not an option. McFadden called the public relations officer for the Long Island Rail Road, who told him that a single train was heading into Manhattan from Ronkonkoma, carrying firefighters to help battle the flames at what would become known as Ground Zero. By the time McFadden made it to Ronkonkoma, the third of four planes hijacked that morning had crashed into the Pentagon. McFadden boarded a car loaded with firefighters, grim and silent and in full uniform: rubber coats, hatchets, and helmets. The train stopped at what felt to McFadden like every one of the twenty-three stations between Ronkonkoma and Pennsylvania Station, arriving in New York at six in the evening. He emerged from Penn Station into a city gripped by chaos and fear: honking cars and knots of traffic and sidewalks teeming with anxious crowds. He was too late to write for the next day's newspaper, and Edgerley told him to go to his home on the Upper West Side and get some rest. You'll be doing the lede-alls from here on out, she said. It would be ten days before he made it back to East Hampton.

* * *

The *Times* newsroom rose slowly to life each morning in those days. Reporters and editors would begin drifting in around ten, carrying coffee in blue-and-white paper Anthora cups bought from a street vendor on the corner of West Forty-third Street and Seventh Avenue. On the morning of September 11, Alison Smale was there in the empty newsroom at eight-thirty, since she was the early editor on the foreign desk, and was on the telephone with James Bennet, the new Jerusalem bureau chief, who was objecting to how his story had been edited. The lines on the telephone at her desk began lighting up, and she asked Bennet if she could put him on hold for a moment. Smale picked up a phone to hear Judith Miller on the line. Miller, who lived near the World Trade Center, had gone to vote in that morning's New York City mayoral primary and had looked up to see flames and smoke billowing into the sky.

The World Trade Center blew up! she said. A few minutes later, Roger Cohen, who had become acting foreign editor effective that morning, arrived at the *Times*—he made one of the last subways out of Brooklyn Heights—to find Gerald Boyd, the new managing editor, out front nervously smoking a cigarette.

Thank God you're here—go to your desk, Boyd said, grabbing Cohen by the shoulders and pushing him through the door.

On this primary day, New Yorkers were selecting a successor to Mayor Rudolph Giuliani. It was an important election, marking the final chapters of Giuliani's rule in New York, so most metropolitan editors had been told not to show up before noon, because it would be a late night. But someone needed to cover the desk in the morning, and that assignment fell to Anne Cronin, a features editor on the metropolitan desk. She was the person Joe Sexton, a deputy, asked to fill the early-morning watch.

What if a cop gets shot? she asked Sexton the night before, since that is the kind of story she would not have handled as features editor.

If a cop gets shot, we will get you somebody, he told her.

Cronin voted early that morning and took the subway to Times Square. She emerged from the subway to see crowds glancing up at the huge screen perched over the square. It showed the World Trade Center ablaze. She hurried to the office, and found Melena Ryzik, a clerk stationed at the metropolitan desk, struggling with a barrage of telephone calls. William K. Rashbaum, a reporter who was downtown with Giuliani, had telephoned to alert his editors about what he had just witnessed.

Who's there? Rashbaum asked. Who is on the desk?

Nobody, Ryzik responded.

Rashbaum told her about the explosion at the World Trade Center. She transferred his call to the photo desk. The telephone never stopped after that—reporters and editors, but also readers who wanted to make sure the *Times* was aware of the attack on downtown Manhattan. Before long, Ryzik was answering each call with the same greeting: We know about the World Trade Center.

Cronin gazed around the newsroom and saw John M. Geddes, a deputy managing editor who had arrived at work at eight that morning, sitting at the metropolitan desk. He handed her the phone. I've got to go kill airline ads in tomorrow's newspaper, he said, referring to the industry-wide practice of removing advertisements from airlines when there was a plane crash, or at least advertisements that are on the same page as or the page facing the coverage. Cronin began calling reporters who lived or worked downtown to dispatch them to the scene. It was harrowing. For the rest of the day, whenever she heard from a reporter, she would draw a line through their name. I don't have to worry about them anymore, she thought. For two days after the collapse, she worried that one of the reporters she had sent downtown might perish.

Editors and reporters began rushing in. Jonathan Landman, the metropolitan editor, had been working out at his gym on 106th Street near Broadway that morning when, glancing out the windows from the third floor, he saw his wife, Bonnie, running toward the building to alert her husband that a plane had flown into the World Trade Center. Landman went home, changed, and headed for work. As his taxi arrived at the edge of Times Square, he heard over the radio that the first tower had fallen.

This was a catastrophic event with no shortage of eyewitnesses, in Manhattan, Brooklyn, Staten Island, and New Jersey, and it became clear from the volume of telephone calls into the newsroom that there was an archive of first-hand accounts from New Yorkers that demanded to be collected. Cronin looked up from her desk to see six typists from the classified department, who normally would be answering calls and transcribing used car and employment ads for the next day's newspaper. They asked if their skills might be of use in dealing with the crush of this breaking story. Cronin dispatched them to a conference room, equipped with six phones, and instructed clerks to send all calls from eyewitnesses there. The transcriptionists were given detailed instructions as they were pressed into duty as journalists: note the time of the call and where it came from, ask for a contact number so a reporter can call back, and inquire what the caller was doing at the time of the crash (taking kid to school, going to work, et cetera).

Reporters, photographers, and graphic artists headed for the World Trade Center—some on the instruction of editors, others on their own initiative—swimming upstream against crowds of people covered in dust trying to escape the destruction. Katherine E. Finkelstein, a reporter, grabbed her cellphone and a charger, jumped on a bicycle, and rode downtown. She locked her bicycle a block and a half from the North Tower and ran toward the building. She froze at the sound of the low rumble just before a mountainous cloud of dust came down the block as the tower collapsed. She would spend the next thirty-six hours near Ground Zero. Sarah Slobin, a graphics designer, made it as far as Cedar Street, just a few blocks from Ground Zero, where she began drawing a sketch for a map. Her notes, scribbled in the terror and chaos of the moment, captured what she saw on the sidewalk. "Glass, woman's shoe, office paper, fiberglass." She turned and fled for safety when the building collapsed in front of her.

For those staffers who lived outside of Manhattan, the struggle to get to work, or to the scene of the attack, would prove daunting.

Manhattan is closed, a police officer guarding the Queensboro Bridge told Lew Serviss, a metropolitan desk editor trying to walk from his home to work.

How would it look if they stopped *The New York Times* from publishing? he responded. Serviss walked over to another checkpoint and held his *Times* identification to another officer, who waved him through.

Jose Lopez, a photographer who lived in Brooklyn, was blocked as he tried to cross the Brooklyn Bridge. He ran into another *Times* photographer, Ruby Washington, covered head to foot in dust, who had taken photographs of the building collapsing before she was pushed with the crowd across the Brooklyn Bridge. There was little chance that either of them would make it to the office that day. Washington retrieved her rolls of film and gave them to Lopez, who brought them to a one-hour photo processing store in the neighborhood, took the prints home, and transmitted them over a telephone line to the photo desk across the river in Manhattan.

Serge Schmemann, the United Nations correspondent, left his apartment on the Upper West Side and jumped a ride with a Con Edison emergency truck heading downtown. Schmemann was a Moscow correspondent for the Associated Press when he joined the *Times* in 1980. From across Europe, he had written the lede-alls on the collapse of the Soviet Union, the fall of the Berlin Wall, and the assassination of Yitzhak Rabin, the Israeli prime minister, in November 1995. Schmemann was fifty-six years old, a thoughtful writer with a sense of history and grasp of current events. Anne Cronin realized McFadden could not get into the office in time, and she needed a reporter to handle the main story. If Schmemann can write about the fall of the Berlin Wall, he can write about this, she thought. He took a desk and stayed there for the next fourteen hours, sifting through the eyewitness transcriptions and debriefing those reporters who made it into the newsroom, notebooks in hand. (The cellphone and landline networks were overloaded, so at least initially, this was the most effective way to collect information from reporters in the field.) Schmemann was struck by the silence in the room; the "grim sense of duty," he thought, of people working to make sense of a terrifying attack in their backyard, and who were worried that the *Times* building might be the next target. "While we have no reason to believe that we are in any danger, we are taking all reasonable security precautions," the newspaper said in a note to employees that went out at 10:29 A.M. But the note cautioned the staff not to leave the building.

When the television screens around the room showed the second tower collapsing, there was just silence; no one paused, there were no gasps or cries. Cronin first thought they were just replaying the first crash from a different angle, until the telephone consoles on her desk again lit up with calls.

The day of the attack, Boyd called home repeatedly to check on his wife and son and was met by a busy signal; slightly panicked, he left the office and went to a bank to withdraw hundreds of dollars from a cash machine. He was never quite sure why he did that. Landman lost track of his daughter, Rachel, from the moment she left home for a subway that morning on the way to Stuyvesant High School, where she was a senior, which was four blocks from the World Trade Center complex. He did not know she was safe until she turned up at the office at noon. In Washington, Jill Abramson's son, Will, was jolted awake in his bed when the third hijacked plane hit the Pentagon in Arlington, blocks from their home.

* * *

Raines had woken at seven o'clock in the morning and was reading the *Times* over coffee at a long, narrow maple table at his four-story townhouse on Eleventh Street, when Arthur Sulzberger, Jr., called him.

Are you watching television?

Raines turned on the television to see one of the towers in flames. As he was getting ready to leave, Sulzberger called again to report that the second tower had been hit. The publisher and his wife, Gail, had been planning a dinner party that evening at their apartment to celebrate Raines's editorship and the promotion of Gail Collins to editorial page editor. The dinner that night would not take place. Raines walked over to Seventh Avenue, where a throng of hospital workers wearing green scrubs waited for the fleet of ambulances carrying survivors from the attack. He stopped a cab driver and offered him fifty dollars to take him to the *Times* building. From the corner where Greenwich Avenue cut on an angle into Seventh Avenue, Raines had an unencumbered view over the low-rise skyline of Greenwich Village to the towers engulfed in smoke and flame. Looking toward the southern tip of Manhattan at those early images, he thought this was a story that demanded compelling photographs. He had told Sulzberger, as they discussed the job, that the *Times* needed to publish more—and better—photographs in its pages if it wished to compete in the more visual world of television and the Internet. Joseph Lelyveld was admired among his reporters but less so among his photographers. When, in a discussion of how to package the "How Race Is Lived in America" series, photo editors requested more space, even if that meant cutting back on some stories—arguing that photographs would make the powerful words assembled by the journalists more compelling—Lelyveld refused. Better luck with the next guy, he'd said.

Raines arrived in the newsroom, his shirt soaked with sweat, and stopped by the metropolitan desk to talk to Cronin, who gave him a rundown of the initial story assignments. He inspected the pictures gathered by the *Times* and wire service photographers as they came in during the day, displayed on a screen in the photo department, pointing to the ones he wanted for the next day's newspaper. His choices included an

Associated Press photograph of a man who had jumped from the tower to escape the searing heat, plunging headfirst to his death. Some of his editors were concerned that this was too gruesome for the *Times*—an invasion of privacy for the man's family, should they be able to identify him from the photograph. But Raines likened the picture to the famous Robert Capa photograph that appeared to depict the death of a Spanish civil war soldier, falling backward after being struck by a bullet.

This is a historically violent, world-shaping event, Raines said. The *Times* would publish this picture. And that evening, as editors and photographers gathered to plan the second edition, Raines announced that he would not follow the usual practice of trimming photographs between editions to make more space for more news stories. Jim Wilson, a photo editor, was stunned; this, he would say years later, clearly marked the beginning of a new era at the top of the newspaper.

Al Siegal, the assistant managing editor who had worked with A. M. Rosenthal in writing the front-page headline for the explosion of the space shuttle, was, like many editors and reporters that day, stranded at home—in his case, in New Jersey, since ferry service between Hoboken and Manhattan had been suspended. He sent his proposal for the headline to capture this moment of attack: "Terror Rocks U.S." Paul Winfield, a news editor, who was in the newsroom, did not like Siegal's idea. It did not capture the enormity of the day, the brutality and calculation of the attack, or the nation's vulnerability: the Pentagon (and perhaps the White House) had been targets. Raines and other editors were huddled, sketching out the layout of the front page, when Winfield came over with his own idea for the words that should go across the top of the page: "U.S. Attacked."

Raines liked it immediately. It was evocative of the headlines on the front pages in the days after the bombing of Pearl Harbor by Japan on December 7, 1941. Its understatement recalled the *Times*'s "THE SHUTTLE EXPLODES" headline in Rosenthal's last year. Under the "U.S. ATTACKED" headline, a huge color photograph of the towers engulfed in flames spilled down much of the front page. There was an analysis of what this moment meant for the nation by R. W. Apple, one of Raines's friends and star writers, and a detailed story describing the scene by N. R. Kleinfield. "The horror arrived in episodic bursts of chilling disbelief, signified first by trembling floors, sharp eruptions, cracked windows," he wrote.

Schmemann spent most of the afternoon on September 11 writing and rewriting the first four paragraphs of the main story that would appear at the top of the page; those were the paragraphs that people would remember.

> Hijackers rammed jetliners into each of New York's World Trade Center towers yesterday, toppling both in a hellish storm of ash, glass, smoke and leaping victims, while a third jetliner crashed into the Pentagon in Virginia. There was no official count, but President Bush said thousands had perished, and in the immediate aftermath the calamity was already being ranked the worst and most audacious terror attack in American history.

Schmemann was sitting a few feet from James Barron, an engaging writer who had joined the *Times* as a copyboy in June 1977, after graduating from Princeton University. He was a reporter who editors turned to over the years to command big deadline stories such as the 1989 earthquake in San Francisco, a deadly airplane crash at LaGuardia Airport when a Cleveland-bound USAir jetliner tried to take off in a snowstorm in 1992, and a fire at Happy Land, a social club in the Bronx, that killed eighty-seven people in 1990. For the past three years, he'd written Boldface Names, a society column. He was one of the reporters who rushed into the office after learning of the attacks but arrived to find assignments had been handed out. Barron was at his desk, a spectator to the coverage of one of the biggest stories of his career, when Michael Oreskes walked over. The *Times* had sent out its first news alert about the attack five minutes after the plane hit, and there was a four-hundred-word story that had been rushed out by an early-morning writer and posted on the website.

We want you to write a story for the website, Oreskes told Barron.

He would be writing for the continuous news desk that had been created to feed the website with breaking news. For Barron, the assignment was a reason for both relief and despair. Yes, he would have something to do. But he was disheartened that he had been relegated to a story that would never appear in a newspaper. Who reads the website? Barron and Schmemann were writing about the same events, relying on the same feed of information from reporters and eyewitnesses, keeping an eye on the live coverage on television. But Schmemann was working on a different clock; he could wait after a third building in the complex, Seven World Trade Center, collapsed at 5:20 P.M. in a pile of fire and debris; he had time to fold this latest development in a story he was hours away from filing. Barron was updating his story every hour or so, sending a new first paragraph or a few inserts to Jerry Gray, the continuous news editor.

Schmemann didn't know anyone in the newsroom was writing a story for the website. In Washington, Jill Abramson, who had jumped off an elliptical trainer at the gym to head to the office after watching the second plane hit a building, never thought about how this story would be covered on the website as she directed the coverage of the attack on the Pentagon and the response of President Bush. Neither did Howell Raines. The lack of interest—or at least the lack of awareness—of what was going on a few steps from the metropolitan desk showed how much the *Times* was a newspaper of paper; and that the ambitions and visions of people like Martin Nisenholtz were not shared by people in the newsroom.

But if the attacks proved to be a defining moment for the new executive editor, they would turn out to be even more transformative for the website—a demonstration of the potential of the Internet to do what the print newspaper could not: provide information to a huge readership that was hungry for minute-to-minute coverage. So many readers came to the website that it almost collapsed. Editors and engineers shrank the size of the type and the photographs and stripped away design flourishes to quicken the download speed and accommodate the surge of demand. The website presented stories in ways that the newsroom had resisted before, such as slideshows, narrated by the *Times* photographers who had taken the pictures. "In some ways, it had the same effect on our business as the Gulf War had on cable news," Nisenholtz told a meeting of the *Times* board of directors the following February. "It put us on the map in a major way." Over the next three weeks, seventeen million read-

ers came to the site. The daily print circulation for the *Times* in 2001 was
1.1 million.

Barron never realized how many people were seeing his story, still
convinced that he had drawn a dead-end assignment. That changed a
few weeks later when, back to writing his Boldface Names column, he
and his wife, Jane, attended a book party at the home of Peter Jennings,
the ABC news anchor, on Central Park West. The room was filled with
television reporters, anchors, and producers—people who had been im-
mersed in the coverage of the attacks. They did not have the time to wait
for the first edition of the *Times* to hit the streets. They had all read the
Times coverage on nytimes.com—checking in all day, right before they
went on the air, and during the commercial breaks. And they had read
the stories written by James Barron.

* * *

When Abramson drove home after midnight at the end of that first day,
she could see the glow of the embers from the Pentagon as she crossed
the Fourteenth Street Bridge. Cronin returned to her apartment in
Greenwich Village to find barricades and military vehicles on Fourteenth
Street in Manhattan. She walked into her bedroom, where that morning
she had gazed at the World Trade Center. Now all she could see was bil-
lows of dust and smoke illuminated by the glow of television lights.
Raines left the office after midnight, after the newspaper had gone to
press, and checked into a hotel around the corner rather than negotiate
the police barriers that had risen across downtown Manhattan. This was
probably the peak of my career, he thought. He had been on the job for
barely a week. The next day, he sat down to write a note of gratitude to
his new staff. "Thank you one and all for a magnificent effort in putting
out, in the midst of a heartbreaking day, a paper of which we can be
proud for years to come," he wrote.

There were sixty-six stories about the attacks on the World Trade
Center and the Pentagon in the newspaper of September 12, 2001. They
filled the twenty-eight-page first section with the exception of the editorial page and the Op-Ed page, which were also devoted to the attack. Almost every paid advertisement in the first section was thrown out that

morning to make way for the coverage. Raines wanted a front page that people would collect and save for years.

With his response to the attacks on the World Trade Center and the Pentagon, Raines had shown how he intended to run the newsroom; how he would "raise the competitive metabolism" of his staff—a phrase which would become an overused if accurate description of Raines's style—and "flood the zone" to deploy all of the *Times*'s resources to cover big stories. The troops may have been assembled by Lelyveld and Keller, but Raines was the head of the army that day.

The *Times* would be awarded a record seven Pulitzer Prizes the following April—six of them for the coverage of the terrorist attacks. Almost every day for the rest of the year, Raines would go through his mail and savor the praise. "Just wanted to say how much I've admired the extraordinary *Times* coverage since Sept. 11," Pete Hamill, a columnist at the *Daily News*, wrote him. "It's been just as good as it ever can get." Raines forwarded a stack of the notes of praise to Sulzberger. "Howell: These are amazing & wonderful letters," Sulzberger wrote back later that fall. "Keep them."

Sulzberger shared one that he had received from Russell Baker, the paper's now-retired columnist who had written for the *Times* Op-Ed page for thirty-six years. "The old guys ought to leave the publisher in peace, and I've done my best, but I must tell you what I think and it's this: From the 11th of September the Times has consistently, day after day after day, done the most astonishing, amazing, extraordinary, wonderful and elegant job of covering a story that has ever been done by anyone anyplace." On the last day of 2001, from retirement, Lelyveld sent his own note to Raines and Boyd. "I can't let the year end without saying what a remarkable run it has been—the greatest team effort, I should think, in the paper's entire history," Lelyveld wrote. "You should feel great pride."

CHAPTER 22

Custer's Horse

owell Raines woke up early on September 12, 2001, and walked the three blocks from the Paramount Hotel on West Forty-sixth Street, where he had spent the night, to the office. Krystyna Anna Stacho-wiak, a Polish-born public relations consultant and former reporter whom he would marry eighteen months later, brought him a change of clothes from their Greenwich Village townhouse. Raines had spent most of September 11 focused on the next day's front page. But from the moment he arrived in the newsroom that next morning—and each morning for the next three months—he was consumed with driving every aspect of the news report. *Let's do this, let's do this, let's do this!* Raines would say, sounding like a football coach on the field, rallying his editors for another day of stories. Starting on the day after the attacks, Raines was on the telephone with Jill Abramson. He predicted that this would prove to be an intelligence failure and ordered the Washington bureau to dig into the activities of the FBI and the CIA in the months leading to the attack. Never take your eye off that, Raines told her.

Three weeks after the planes flew into the World Trade Center and the Pentagon, *The Washington Post* reported that FBI investigators found a five-page leaflet of Muslim prayers and last-minute instructions—bring "knives, your will, IDs, your passport"—in the luggage of Mohamed Atta, one of the hijackers. It was deflating enough that the *Times* had been beaten on a major development in the investigation of the attack,*

---

* Atta's luggage was never loaded onto the plane, which was why the FBI was able to retrieve it.

but this story, which dominated the coverage that day, was written by Bob Woodward. It had been twenty-nine years since Woodward and Carl Bernstein broke the story about Watergate, and the sting of that humiliation was still painful at the *Times*, even for employees like Raines who were not there in 1972. It had informed his view of complacency in the newsroom, and now, less than a month after he had taken over as executive editor, it had happened again. He was livid when he arrived at the office.

We are not going to get beaten again on this story, Raines declared at the morning meeting of editors.

Raines called Abramson in Washington to remind her how Max Frankel, when he held her position, had been embarrassed by the *Post* on Watergate. I'll be damned to see that happen again, he said. Abramson was shaken; in her entire career, she had rarely been spoken to so sharply by a boss. Arthur Sulzberger, Jr., would not have to wait long to learn whether the newspaper was now being run by Raines the editorial page editor—the one who had assured the publisher he had matured into a less abrasive leader—or Raines the Washington editor, with all his flaws and brilliance.

Raines had been away from the news operation for nine years, but he knew from his years running the Washington bureau how to propel a newsroom in a way few editors did—with gusts of inspiration, bravado, and, at times, intimidation. He would tell his new team of editors how his years as an editor in Washington taught him to slam his foot on the gas pedal every Monday morning, to rouse reporters who would otherwise spend their mornings drinking coffee, reading the newspapers, and chatting with deskmates. Raines the editor had a gut sense of where a big story was heading, and he was always pushing his staff to leap ahead of the news.

The terrorist attack on New York and Washington provided a stage for the kind of journalism Raines had wanted to bring to the *Times*. There could never be too many articles, sidebars, photographs, and charts; never too many reporters, editors, photographers, and designers; never too many pages to showcase all this work. He commissioned sweeping stories that became known as "All Known Thought"—the broad, amorphous description signaling the ambition of the assignment. Photographs that had been limited to three columns, or half the width of a page, under Joseph Lelyveld were routinely stretched out to five columns. There were so many dispatches and photographs from New York, Washington, and around the world that Raines asked Al Siegal if they could create a daily section to display all the coverage in one place. The special daily section that emerged from that conversation, A Nation Challenged, first appeared one week after the towers collapsed.

One of the biggest journalistic challenges in those early days was chronicling a massive loss of life when there was no accounting of who had perished in the incineration of the two 110-story skyscrapers. Janny Scott, a metropolitan reporter, was assigned to write about the injured and the dead. It seemed an impossible task, until she went over to NYU Medical Center's Tisch Hospital looking for survivors to interview and spotted the pieces of paper that had appeared overnight—taped to walls and bulletin boards, pleading for information about missing family members—most with a snippet of biographic information, a photograph, and a telephone number to call. She and other reporters began collecting the information from the leaflets and returned to the newsroom. If we can't establish that anybody is dead, why don't we write about them individually and call them "the missing" rather than "the dead"? Scott suggested.

A metropolitan desk editor, Christine Kay, proposed writing essays that captured intimate and distinctive qualities of those who had been victims of the attack. In its ambition and informality, it was quite unlike anything the *Times*, or probably any newspaper, had attempted before. The fliers were divided among a half dozen reporters. The first profiles appeared on September 15, under the headline "Among the Missing." The next day, the standing feature was renamed Portraits of Grief: a page—sometimes two—of short essays that would anchor the section and come to define the *Times*'s coverage of the tragedy.

The six-foot, four-inch security guard who played basketball, whom his friends called "Big Man"; the firefighter from Engine Company 207 in downtown Brooklyn with a spirit-lifting sense of humor; the associate at a brokerage firm who would get up from the Thanksgiving table, saying that she was going to "see a friend," then head off to feed the homeless in a soup kitchen.

"In a story producing great journalism, none has been more exceptional than the *New York Times*'s Portraits of Grief, the mini-profiles of the lives of those who perished on Sept. 11," Albert R. Hunt wrote in *The Wall Street Journal.* By January, when the project was scaled back and the special section ended, 1,800 intimate thumbnail sketches had been written by over one hundred reporters; the project would ultimately account for the lives of 2,400 men, women, and children.

But those early days offered misleading lessons for the new executive editor. His reporters and editors had jumped into action on September 11—tireless, resourceful, collegial, dashing from early in the morning to late at night on this once-in-a-lifetime story. No one refused an assignment, or complained about how they were edited, or questioned why they didn't get a byline and where their story had been placed in the newspaper.

It's like watching a Maserati run, Raines remarked late one afternoon, standing off to the side of the newsroom.

But that would last only so long. By nature, reporters challenge authority and question motivation and judgment. A. M. Rosenthal had dominated his newsroom and discouraged dissent with a style that led to fear and submission. Rosenthal's son, Andrew, who was now Raines's third-in-command, liked to say that was one way Raines reminded him of his father. But this was not the *Times* that Raines found when Rosenthal hired him in 1978. The newsroom was changing as this new decade began; the staff, particularly its younger members, were no longer reflexively deferential to institutions like the *Times* or to editors who once seemed infallible. Within weeks, Raines encountered the first waves of resistance that would swell over his tenure.

And this was a traumatized newsroom. The reporters and editors were not only covering a harrowing event; they were living it. They could smell the acrid scent rising across lower Manhattan from the wreckage of the World Trade Center for months; it was the odor of destruction and death. They paused at the leaflets with pictures of missing relatives on walls around Washington Square Park; and the bouquets of flowers piled in front of firehouses, where so many of the firefighters who'd raced down to lower Manhattan minutes after the sounding of the first alarm had been stationed. Many knew people who had perished. They would be reminded by the momentary roar of an F-16 jet fighter flying overhead of the ever-present fear of another terrorist attack. They left work to deserted streets and subways filled with riders glancing nervously around them.

Three weeks after the attacks in lower Manhattan, envelopes laced with anthrax began arriving at workplaces across the country, including the *National Enquirer,* the New York headquarters of NBC News and ABC News, and the offices of Tom Daschle of South Dakota, the Senate majority leader. It set off a spasm of fear across the country; five people would die from inhaling anthrax spores. Shortly after the first death, on October 12, Judith Miller was going through her mail at her third-floor desk in New York while talking on the telephone to Jeff Gerth in Washington. She opened a letter and white powder spilled out. "It looked like baby powder," she wrote in a first-person account for the *Times.* "A cloud of hospital white, sweet-smelling powder rose from the letter—dusting my face, sweater and hands. The heavier particles dropped to the floor, falling on my pants and shoes." The area was evacuated, and thirty-two people, including Miller, were tested for anthrax exposure. The powder turned out to be harmless. Newsrooms are always tense places, particularly in the midst of a fast-moving, competitive story, but this was different. A sense of acute anxiety and sorrow settled over the *Times,* and it lasted for weeks.

Raines was by every appearance oblivious to the emotional strain of living at the edge of a battlefield. He had come in promising systemic change to a newspaper trapped by its legacy and success, and he intended to power through his agenda. If anything, Raines was emboldened by the praise of the coverage to demand even more from his staff. The Page One meetings grew longer and longer, the instructions to editors and story ideas more detailed. His two lieutenants, Boyd and Andrew Rosenthal, would follow up to make sure the stories were done the way he wanted them done—and would make it clear when Raines was unhappy with how they had turned out. "A truly miserable day," Glenn Kramon, the business editor, wrote in his journal a few days after the September 11 attack. "Never have I, or many I work with, seen so much second-guessing and micromanaging."

Raines made no secret of his unhappiness with parts of the newspaper. The business and culture sections are on autopilot, he would declare at meetings of editors—larded with uninteresting stories and losing readers to rivals like *The Wall Street Journal*.*

At one point, with Raines, Boyd, and Rosenthal criticizing their work, two of Kramon's reporters came into his office and broke down in tears. There was little Kramon could offer them; he was in fear of losing his own job. "I can't remember a boss who so disdained me," he wrote in his journal. But most of Raines's impatience was focused on the report out of Washington. The *Post* story on Atta had reinforced his misgivings about Abramson. Raines was annoyed that Lelyveld had filled such a critical position when he knew he would be retiring, and he had tried to nudge her out soon after he was appointed. Raines took Abramson to dinner at Baldoria, an Italian restaurant in Midtown, and told her he wanted her to move to New York and become business editor. Abramson refused the offer on the spot.

You would not have wanted to be the business editor, Abramson said. You wanted to be Washington bureau chief, and that is what I want to be. I'm a political journalist. I love Washington, and my kids are in high school. I'm not moving to New York. He backed down. The conversation would set the tone for their dealings for the next two years.

Raines wanted to replace Abramson with Patrick Tyler, the Moscow bureau chief. He had served as the *Times*'s Beijing bureau chief, which meant he had learned to speak Chinese and Russian after he turned forty, taking a year off in each case to immerse himself in the languages—no small accomplishment, as he liked to point out when talking about himself. He had covered national security and defense while he was at the *Post*, and had moved in the same Georgetown circles as Ben Bradlee. Tyler fit Raines's image of a Washington bureau chief: the newspaper's ambassador to the capital, with his elegant dress and self-assured bearing, his flair for writing. He was a raconteur and a bit of a rogue, charming over cigars and dinner, a man around Washington, telling stories about his years as a foreign correspondent—of, for instance, sleeping in

---

* For all their early troubles, Raines would come to view Kramon, a Pulitzer Prize–winning editor, as a success story who turned around and, at Raines's prodding, improved his section—particularly with its coverage of the collapse of Enron.

the desert to skirt the Chinese secret police so he could file stories away from the watchful eyes of government monitors. He tooled around town on a scooter.

Tyler had been in Moscow for eighteen months when Raines took over. He and Raines met in New York for coffee in August, a few weeks before Raines began. The incoming executive editor told Tyler he wanted him to be his Washington bureau chief but warned that it would take time to ease out Abramson. His return to Washington was hastened by the World Trade Center attacks; Roger Cohen, the acting foreign editor, called Tyler and told him that given the lack of national security expertise in the Washington bureau, Raines and the rest of the masthead wanted him to fly to the U.S. capital. Tyler left that day, flying first to London, and from there, on to Bermuda, gambling that he could hop a boat to New York or Baltimore. He was marooned in the Atlantic waiting for the airspace over the United States to open, finally arriving in Washington that Saturday and checking into the Jefferson hotel.

Looking to fortify the bureau during a national crisis, Raines also brought Michael Gordon, the newspaper's chief military correspondent, in from London and Judith Miller from New York to help cover the aftermath of the terrorist attack. Raines thought Gordon—and Tyler—were the two best national security correspondents at the newspaper. Raines had forced Miller out of Washington when he took over the bureau, but earlier that year, well before the attacks, she had been part of a team of *Times* reporters who wrote a three-part series on a terrorist network assembled by a little-known Saudi businessman named Osama bin Laden and the threat it posed to the United States. The series was called "Holy Warriors"—a feat of reporting that was ahead of what anyone else had written on this subject—and it was part of a package of coverage that would win a Pulitzer Prize in 2002.

Raines told Abramson he wanted Miller to make up for the shortcomings in the Washington bureau.

Miller has sources in the Bush White House who are not talking to your reporters, he told her. I want her to have carte blanche to do whatever she needs. Abramson responded that she welcomed Miller and assured him, as Raines recalled the conversation in his office in New York, that she knew how to handle her. Abramson was unhappy that Raines was sending outsiders into her bureau, but she understood the stakes—the vastness and complexity of the story, the fierceness of the competition with *The Washington Post*. Abramson was aware of Miller's history with the bureau and how unpopular she was with the staff, and of Raines's decision to send her to New York, but she also knew that Miller was a tenacious and well-connected reporter. And Miller was empowered by the newspaper's top editors: Boyd ordered her to "do whatever it takes" to keep the *Times* competitive in Washington; to "run amok," as she wrote in her memoir. Before long, Boyd and Andrew Rosenthal were calling the bureau every day with detailed directions on the stories they wanted, often telling Abramson and her deputies to assign particular reporters to write them. There had always been tension between New York and Washington—this was hardly the first time that editors in New York decreed who should write a story or how much space it should get—but there was a new insistence to this intervention, and it reflected Raines's dissatisfaction with the energy and initiative at the Washington bureau.

How are things up there with the Taliban? John Broder, who was Abramson's deputy, asked Rosenthal on the phone.

What? Rosenthal said.

That's what we call you: the Taliban, Broder said. Because you just hand down these edicts.

The management from New York seemed like a vote of no confidence in Abramson and her sixty-person bureau—and, to an extent, that is precisely what it was. On one conference call with editors, Raines ordered Washington to produce a story on civil liberty restrictions being advocated by the White House in the wake of the September 11 attacks. Abramson pushed back.

We've done that story, she said. I don't think you want to be doing the same story again.

Raines called her back once the conference call was over. I don't ever want you to speak up against me in front of anybody else, he told her. When she argued back, Raines cut her off. You don't understand. I am officially reprimanding you.

Boyd went to Washington in mid-October to try to manage the rising tensions in the bureau and "reassure them how valuable they were," as he later described his trip to *The New Yorker*. He was unprepared for the hostile reception from colleagues gathered around a conference table over sandwiches. Why was New York telling Washington what to write?

We decide, Boyd finally responded, pushing his sandwich off to the side as he dismissed the challenges to his authority.

Afterward, he and Abramson strolled over to a bench at Lafayette Park, across from the White House. I'm having a really hard time, she told Boyd. She felt ill-treated by Raines—it was disrespectful how he would cut her off during the conference calls. She was considering leaving the *Times.* Boyd told her that she needed to learn how to work with the new executive editor. We are new and it's going to be bumpy, he said.

Boyd returned to New York unsettled by what he had heard from Abramson about the distress in the bureau. "Each word felt like a punch in the gut," he later wrote.

The turmoil swept across the organization. Raines wanted reporters to leap at a moment's notice. They should be grateful to have such assignments, he thought, and this was a moment of triumph and testing for the *Times.* He paid little attention to the logistical hassles of flying across war zones, how an editor might be calling a reporter late into the evening with a get-on-a-plane assignment, or whether a correspondent's son or daughter was starring in the school play that Saturday night. The burden of implementing Raines's commands often fell on Roger Cohen, who had just taken over the foreign desk and was struggling to balance Raines's demands with the concerns and practical anxieties of his staff. He would leave a meeting with Raines, return to the foreign desk, and call a reporter in the field with an order to get on a plane. In one case, he reached Mark Landler, the Hong Kong bureau chief, at ten o'clock at night, a few days before Christmas 2001. Landler was in Myanmar with his wife and parents, touring and gathering material for stories. Cohen told Landler to get to Afghanistan, a trip of nearly two thousand miles by air. I need you to do this, Cohen said.

Landler balked. He did not have his computer with him, and Myanmar was a tropical climate; he did not have the winter wear he would need for the weather in Afghanistan. It was a tense conversation. Cohen relented and agreed to let Landler return to Hong Kong before making the trip.

Six months after the attacks, in the third week of March 2002, Raines addressed eighty editors gathered for a retreat at a conference center in White Plains, twenty-five miles from Manhattan. It was a triumphant speech, brimming with the flourishes and boasts that were becoming familiar to his staff. These were, he proclaimed, "days of legend at *The New York Times.*" They had produced newspapers "that can stand with any ever published from Forty-third Street." He reminded his editors how he had talked about "raising the competitive metabolism of our report" and recounted the accomplishments of the past six months: A Nation Challenged, the coverage of the Olympics in Salt Lake City and the collapse of the scandal-ridden Enron Corporation. "I do hereby declare that, as far as I'm concerned, our competitive metabolism has been raised," he said.

"In the process, I believe we created the kind of bond among ourselves that Shakespeare invoked in Prince Hal's speech from *Henry V:* we few, we happy few, we band of sisters and brothers," he said, with a slight tweak on Shakespeare's words.

But by now, his band was hardly happy. It was always difficult to manage an organization like the *Times,* where reporters were expected to be on call at all times—to pick up their families and move across the globe, to accept the indignity of a two-week reporting trip resulting in a story buried deep in the newspaper. But there were more families with two working parents now, with children whose mother and father would not move during a school year—even for the *Times,* even if ordered to do so by the executive editor. William Schmidt, a former national correspondent and deputy national editor, was the assistant managing editor for administration, the person who dealt with employee grievances, discipline, budgets, expense accounts, and the correspondent with a drinking or drug problem. He had been tapped for the job by Lelyveld, a position that he described, with wryness, as a combination of concierge and consigliere for the executive editor. He would resolve disputes over where people sat, and it would sometimes fall to him to fire someone. It was a job few people wanted. Schmidt knew the newsroom; he understood the unease of being a reporter in the field, untethered from New York. He was capable of dropping a hammer, but he was so empathetic and of such good cheer that he had, it seemed, no enemies. Schmidt agreed with Raines that national correspondents had become too sedentary. But there was a way to handle that without producing so much anguish.

Think of yourself as a tugboat, Schmidt would say to Raines. If you want to get the ship to dock, you bump it a little bit, and you bump it a little bit more, and you move it along.

But Schmidt had seen warning signs back when Raines and Boyd went to Atlanta for that contentious meeting with southern correspondents. Now, editors and reporters he had known for years were coming to him anxious about their jobs, unsure about what the new regime wanted. At one masthead meeting, Raines wanted to know what his editors were hearing around the newsroom. Morale is suffering, Schmidt said. Yes, you have to make the changes you want to make, but this is happening too quickly.

Raines would listen, but he always returned to his track. To some of his editors he sounded like a character out of the Old Testament, handing down his commandments, comfortable in his certitude. He struck others as a bully. He called Martin Nisenholtz, who was running New York Times Digital, to his office one evening, angry over a space that had been set aside on the home page for an advertisement. No one had checked with him.

I never want this to happen again; this is not acceptable, Raines told him. Nisenholtz was staggered by the encounter. A few hours later, he found himself seated next to Raines at a dinner at Sulzberger's home. Raines, taking note of how flustered Nisenholtz had appeared during their earlier encounter, leaned over to him and said, as Nisenholtz recalled the conversation: Well, Martin, maybe you're just too fragile a flower to work at *The New York Times.*

Max Frankel had warned Raines to watch his temperament when he was the Washington editor in the 1980s, and Sulzberger had said the same to him when he was the editorial page editor in the 1990s. Raines heeded the advice in both cases, or at least tried to, his eye firmly on his ambition to lead the newspaper one day. But now, in the glory of this moment, he seemed resistant to criticism, self-assured, and convinced of the urgency of his mission and the superiority of his vision. He felt a sense of absolute calm, and that "everything I'd done in my life since I was twenty-one years old had prepared me for this moment," he told Charlie Rose when he went on television to discuss the paper's coverage of September 11. The Pulitzer Prizes announced that spring were a validation of everything he had talked about, both to Raines himself and even to some of his critics. The paper's coverage of these events, he told the newsroom, "will be studied and taught as long as journalism is studied and practiced."

One morning, Raines joined a small group of copy editors for coffee in the cafeteria to talk about his job. One asked how he felt about his reputation as an autocrat.

I've got more arrows in me than Custer's horse, Raines responded. Do I feel them? Yes. Is it going to stop me from doing what I think needs to be done? No.

The relationship between Arthur Ochs "Punch" Sulzberger (left) and Abe Rosenthal was competitive, cooperative, and mutually dependent. They were partners and, in their own transactional way, friends. *Photo by Dirck Halstead, Halstead Photographic Archive © Briscoe Center for American History, University of Texas at Austin*

Iphigene Ochs Sulzberger was the wife, mother, grandmother, and great grandmother of *Times* publishers. She conveyed her displeasure with stories she found prurient, and her occasional suggestions on what to cover were typically granted. "Very few things are pleasanter than obliging your mother!" Abe Rosenthal wrote to Punch Sulzberger. *Photo: Eddie Hausner/The New York Times/Redux*

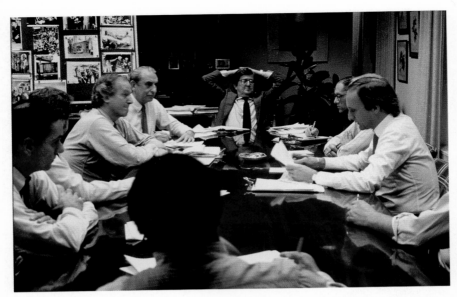

Abe Rosenthal (center), shown here leading a Page One meeting in 1983, was an intimidating and intemperate executive editor, dismissive of anyone whom he thought mediocre or suspected of bringing a left-leaning mindset to stories. But even his detractors noticed the paper lost its edge when he was away from the newsroom. *Photo: The New York Times Company Archives*

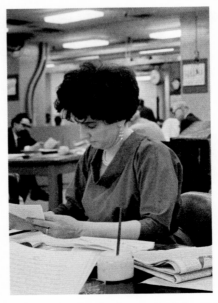

Betsy Wade was the lead plaintiff in the discrimination suit filed by the Women's Caucus of *The New York Times* against management. The women won—and Wade's career was sidelined. We are not in the habit of promoting people who sue us, an executive told her one day. *Photo: The New York Times/Redux*

Susan Dryfoos, the daughter of Orvil Dryfoos and granddaughter of Iphigene Ochs Sulzberger, was the founder and director of Times History Productions. Here, she is interviewing Abe Rosenthal for the documentary film *Abe*. Photo: *The New York Times Company Archives*

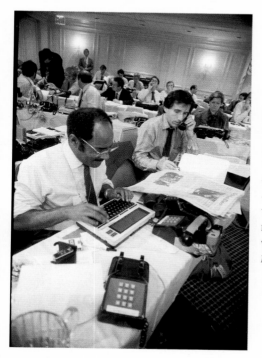

Gerald Boyd (left) and Bernard Weinraub (right) covered the Reagan White House. Weinraub spoke at Boyd's funeral about the burden of being a Black managing editor in a white newsroom—"to carry the weight of his race and represent his race every single moment he walked into the paper." *Photo: Paul Hosefros/The New York Times/Redux*

"All the News That's Fit to Print"

The New York Times

Late Edition

Weather: Partly cloudy and cold today, chance of snow; chance of snow tonight. Partly cloudy tomorrow. Temperatures today 27-30, tonight 13-19, yesterday 14-23. Details, page C19.

VOL.CXXXV... No. 46,669   Copyright © 1986 The New York Times   NEW YORK, WEDNESDAY, JANUARY 29, 1986   60 cents beyond 75 miles from New York City, except on Long Island   30 CENTS

THE SHUTTLE EXPLODES

6 IN CREW AND HIGH-SCHOOL TEACHER ARE KILLED 74 SECONDS AFTER LIFTOFF

11:39:13 A.M.

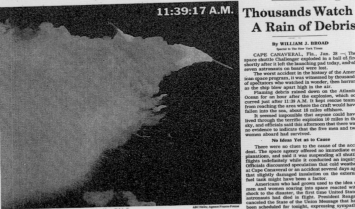
11:39:17 A.M.

ABC News/Agence France-Presse

Thousands Watch A Rain of Debris

By WILLIAM J. BROAD
Special to The New York Times

CAPE CANAVERAL, Fla., Jan. 28 — The space shuttle Challenger exploded in a ball of fire shortly after it left the launching pad today, and all seven astronauts on board were lost.

The worst accident in the history of the American space program, it was witnessed by thousands of spectators who watched in wonder, then horror, as the ship blew apart high in the air.

Flaming debris rained down on the Atlantic Ocean for an hour after the explosion, which occurred just after 11:39 A.M. It kept rescue teams from reaching the area where the craft would have fallen into the sea, about 18 miles offshore.

It seemed impossible that anyone could have lived through the terrific explosion 10 miles in the sky, and officials said this afternoon that there was no evidence to indicate that the five men and two women aboard had survived.

No Ideas Yet as to Cause

There were no clues to the cause of the accident. The space agency offered no immediate explanations, and said it was suspending all shuttle flights indefinitely while it conducted an inquiry. Officials discounted speculation that cold weather at Cape Canaveral or an accident several days ago that slightly damaged insulation on the external fuel tank might have been a factor.

Americans who had grown used to the idea of men and women soaring into space reacted with shock to the disaster, the first time United States astronauts had died in flight. President Reagan canceled the State of the Union Message that had been scheduled for tonight, expressing sympathy for the families of the crew but vowing that the nation's exploration of space would continue.

Killed in the explosion were the mission commander, Francis R. (Dick) Scobee; the pilot, Comdr. Michael J. Smith of the Navy; Dr. Judith A. Resnik; Dr. Ronald E. McNair; Lieut. Col. Ellison S. Onizuka of the Air Force; Gregory B. Jarvis, and Christa McAuliffe.

Mrs. McAuliffe, a high-school teacher from Concord, N.H., was to have been the first ordinary citizen in space.

After a Minute, Fire and Smoke

The Challenger lifted off flawlessly this morning, after three days of delays, for what was to have been the 25th mission of the reusable shuttle fleet that was intended to make space travel commonplace. The ship rose for about a minute on a column of smoke and fire from its five engines.

Suddenly, without warning, it erupted in a ball of flame.

The shuttle was about 10 miles above the earth, in the critical seconds when the two solid-fuel rocket boosters are firing as well as the shuttle's main engines. There was some discrepancy about the exact time of the blast: The National Aeronautics and Space Administration said they lost radio contact with the craft 5 seconds into the flight, plus or minus five seconds.

Two large white streamers raced away from the blast, followed by a rain of debris that etched white contrails in the cloudless sky and then slowly

Continued on Page A5, Column 4

Reagan Lauds 'Heroes'

President Reagan, shaken by the explosion of the space shuttle, postponed his State of the Union Message. "We mourn seven heroes," he said in a talk broadcast from the White House after the disaster. "There will be more shuttle flights and more shuttle crews and, yes, more volunteers, more civilians, more teachers in space."

He also sought to console the nation's pupils, many of whom saw telecasts of the loss of the teacher who was to have been sent into space. Article and transcript, page A9.

From the Beginning to the End

The last flight of the shuttle Challenger lasted about 74 seconds. Here is the transcript, as recorded by The New York Times, of its final moments, before and after liftoff.

PUBLIC AFFAIRS OFFICER: Coming up on the 90-second point in our countdown. Ninety seconds and counting. The SI-L Mission ready to go. . . .

T minus 10, 9, 8, 7, 6, we have main engine start, 4, 3, 2, 1. And liftoff. Liftoff of the 25th space shuttle mission and it has cleared the tower. . . .

MISSION CONTROL CENTER: Watch your roll, Challenger.

PUBLIC AFFAIRS OFFICER: Roll program confirmed. Challenger now heading down range. [Pause.] Engines beginning throttling down now at 94 percent. Normal throttle for most of flight one 104 percent. Will throttle down to 65 percent shortly. Engines at 65 percent. Three engines running normally. Three good cells, three good APU's. [Pause.] Velocity 2,257 feet per second, altitude 4.3 nautical miles, down range distance 3 nautical miles. [Pause.]

Engines throttling up, three engines now at 104 percent.

MISSION CONTROL: Challenger, go with throttle up.

FRANCIS R. SCOBEE, CHALLENGER COMMANDER: Roger, go with throttle up.

PUBLIC AFFAIRS OFFICER: One minute 15 seconds, velocity 2,900 feet per second, altitude 9 nautical miles, down range distance 7 nautical miles. [Long pause.]

Flight controllers here looking very carefully at the situation. [Pause.]

Obviously a major malfunction. We have no downlink [communications from Challenger]. [Long pause.]

We have a report from the flight dynamics officer that the vehicle has exploded.

How Could It Happen? Fuel Tank Leak Feared

By MALCOLM W. BROWNE

Debris from the explosion of the shuttle Challenger was scattered so widely over the Atlantic Ocean that investigators may never recover enough of it to pin down the cause of the disaster. But suspicions quickly focused on the craft's huge external fuel tank, a potential bomb that carried more than 385,000 gallons of liquid hydrogen and more than 140,000 gallons of liquid oxygen at liftoff.

The most logical explanation is that a large leak must have occurred either in the tank itself or in the pipeline and pumping system that carried liquid hydrogen to the orbiter's three main engines.

Barbara Schwartz, a spokesman for the Johnson Space Center, acknowledged that pure liquid or gaseous hydrogen cannot burn; only if the pure hydrogen carried in the rear section of the shuttle's tank were allowed to come into contact with air, or with the liquid oxygen in the tank's nose section, could it have burned or exploded.

Potential Dangers of Hydrogen Gas

But what might have started the leak, and what could have ignited the explosion that followed?

Parallel questions, never fully answered, were raised after the fire that destroyed the German airship Hindenburg as it was landing at Lakehurst, N.J., on May 6, 1937. The shuttle Challenger, like the Hindenburg, had been releasing hydrogen gas into the air shortly before the disaster, and some of the gas might have remained aboard the craft, mixed with air and ready to detonate if exposed to the smallest spark.

Neither NASA nor Martin Marietta Aerospace, the manufacturer of the external fuel tank, would comment yesterday on possible causes of the disaster.

But the geometry of the shuttle's external fuel tank, as described by official manuals from NASA and the Rockwell International Corporation, a major shuttle contractor, suggest one potential danger point in particular: the "interstank," or midsection of the structure, which separates the liquid oxygen tank from the liquid hydrogen tank. The bulk of the hydrogen fuel is closest to the liquid oxygen at this point, and a rupture or leak in the plumbing or walls of the intertank could have flooded the two fluids together to create a gigantic bomb.

Suggestions that the unseasonably cold weather at

Continued on Page A4, Column 1

After the Shock, a Need to Share Grief and Loss

By SARA RIMER

The nation came together yesterday in a moment of disaster and loss. Wherever Americans were when they heard the news — at work, at school or at home — they shared their grief over the death of the seven astronauts, among them one who had captured their imaginations, Christa McAuliffe, the teacher from Concord, N.H., who was to have been the first ordinary citizen to go into space.

Shortly before noon, when the first word of the explosion came, daily events seemed to stop as people awaited the details and asked the same questions: "What happened? Are there any survivors?"

In offices, restaurants and stores, people gathered in front of television sets, mesmerized by the terrible scene of the shuttle exploding, a scene that would be replayed throughout the day and night. Children who had learned

one another, friends telephoned classrooms across the country.

It seemed to be one of those moments, enlarged and frozen, that people would remember and recount for the rest of their lives — what they were when they heard that the space shuttle Challenger had exploded. The need to reach out, to speak of disbelief and pain, was everywhere. Family members telephoned

'I Felt Very Close to Her'

Florine Israel, a legal secretary at the New York Civil Liberties Union, echoed the sentiments of many when she spoke of Mrs. McAuliffe not as an astronaut but as a friend. "I felt very close to her," she said. "You felt ordinary people. She was a mother, a working woman. I felt like I was a part of it."

The image of the shuttle exploding flashed across 100 television sets in the electronics department of Macy's, in midtown Manhattan, where a crowd of workers from nearby offices and facto-

Continued on Page A3, Column 1

Francis R. Scobee
Commander

Michael J. Smith
Pilot

Judith A. Resnik
Electrical Engineer

Ellison S. Onizuka
Engineer

Ronald E. McNair
Physicist

Gregory B. Jarvis
Electrical Engineer

Christa McAuliffe
Teacher

"We put out a good paper today," Abe Rosenthal wrote to Punch Sulzberger the morning after the space shuttle *Challenger* exploded in midair in January 1986. "Newspapering at its best," Sulzberger responded. Rosenthal would be ousted by the end of the year. *Photo: From The New York Times. © 1986 The New York Times Company. All rights reserved. Used under license.*

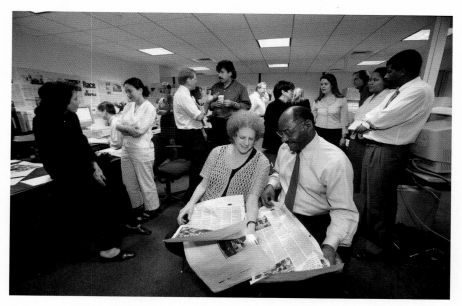

Soma Golden Behr and Gerald Boyd were pioneers in a newsroom that was historically dominated by white men. Golden Behr was the first woman national editor; Boyd was the first Black journalist to appear on the newspaper's masthead of senior editors. *Photo: Marilynn K. Yee/The New York Times/Redux*

Max Frankel (above) urged Punch Sulzberger in 1976 not to appoint Abe Rosenthal executive editor—he wanted the job himself. But Sulzberger was intent on making Frankel his editorial page editor, a job that ultimately positioned him to succeed Rosenthal in 1986. *Photo: The New York Times Photo Archives/Redux*

Punch Sulzberger's attempt to anoint his son, Arthur Jr., as publisher did not go smoothly, at least initially. He encountered resistance from the board of directors—and members of his own family—concerned that Arthur was not ready for the job. *Photo: Burk Uzzle/The New York Times/Redux*

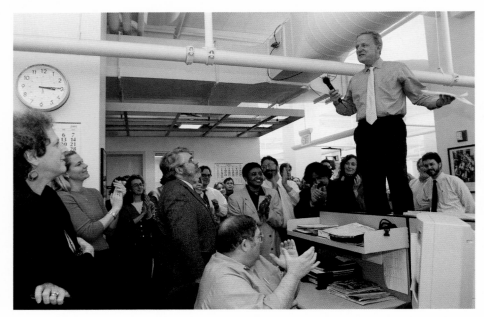

Joe Lelyveld (on desk, announcing the *Times* had won two Pulitzers in 1991) steered the newspaper through a time of changing journalism standards, driven by the Monica Lewinsky scandal. The *Times* was at first slow to jump on a story that delved into a public official's private life and that would lead to Clinton's impeachment. "We were asleep, I have to admit it," Lelyveld told a private Sulzberger family gathering. *Photo: Ruth Fremson/ The New York Times/Redux*

There had never been anyone at the *Times* like Martin Nisenholtz, the first head of New York Times Digital. His attempt to innovate and grow the new digital operation put him at odds with Joe Lelyveld, who was wary that it would undermine the print newspaper. *Photo: Rick Maiman/Polaris*

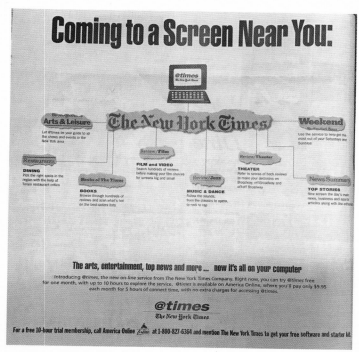

The *Times*'s first venture into the electronic world was in June 1994. It was a collaboration with AOL called @times, a product one editor described as "the Tiffany name on a Timex watch." This is an advertisement the *Times* published announcing the new service to its readers. *Photo: From The New York Times. © 1994 The New York Times Company. All rights reserved. Used under license.*

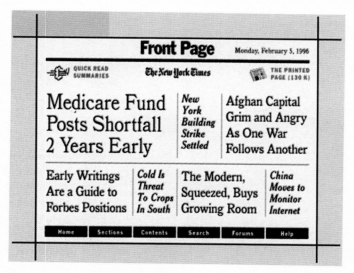

The early *Times* website was primitive, and so slow that readers would often have to wait fifteen seconds for a story to download. *Photo: From The New York Times. © 1996 The New York Times Company. All rights reserved. Used under license.*

Joe Lelyveld urged Arthur Sulzberger, Jr., to pick Bill Keller as his successor as executive editor, but Sulzberger wanted Howell Raines. (Left to right: Lelyveld, Raines, Keller, Sulzberger.) *Photo: Fred R. Conrad/The New York Times/Redux*

Sulzberger (facing the camera) was drawn by Howell Raines's flair, spark, and promise of change. The publisher was withdrawn and despondent for months after he was forced to fire him. *Photo: Fred R. Conrad/The New York Times/Redux*

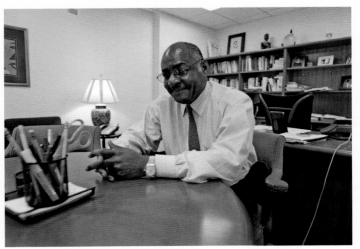

Gerald Boyd, shown here in his office after he became managing editor, had hoped to become the paper's executive editor; instead, he was forced out in the wake of the Jayson Blair scandal. *Photo: Nicole Bengiveno/The New York Times/Redux*

CHAPTER 23

At Swords' Point

Jill Abramson and Howell Raines were journalists of accomplishment and talent, competitive and simmering with ambition. They were lavish in their attention to favored reporters, who produced stories that drew acclaim, and paid little attention to those they considered mediocre or disloyal. Raines and Abramson were calculating and ruthless when they needed to be and capable of the rawest candor—characteristics that would help lift them to the top of the newsroom.

For two years, they were at swords' point in a clash fueled more by their egos and idiosyncrasies than by differences in philosophy or ideology. It was not just another turf skirmish at a newspaper, between a bureau chief in Washington and an executive editor in New York. Their rivalry unfolded during a challenging time for the nation and for the *Times*, as attention shifted from the September 11 attacks to the run-up to a war on Iraq. The *Times* was struggling to balance the demand for skeptical examination of the government's case for war against the concerns of a nation awash in fear and patriotic furor. Abramson was not the only editor Raines would battle in the months and years ahead, but the differences between Raines and Abramson, deeply personal and disruptive to a newsroom trying to chronicle this unsettled era, would frustrate and undermine Raines throughout his tenure as executive editor—and position Abramson as a formidable force in the newspaper for years after he left.

For all their shared characteristics, these two editors could hardly have been more different. Abramson was raised on the Upper West Side, a graduate of Harvard University, a product of New York's Jewish intellectual elite. She grew up reading the *Times*, in an apartment on Central Park West where two copies of the newspaper were delivered each day. Abramson was forty-three years old when she was hired from *The Wall Street Journal* to join the Washington bureau, a relatively late age to step onto the stage that is the *Times*.

Abramson had worked for a political consultant in South Carolina, at one point assigned to the campaign of Bill Clinton when he was running for governor of Arkansas. She had written two books, including *Strange Justice: The Selling of Clarence Thomas*, an account on Anita Hill and the Supreme Court confirmation hearings, which she wrote with her friend Jane Mayer while still at the *Journal*. It was a finalist for the National Book Award in 1994. She worked as a reporter at *The American Lawyer* and as the editor in chief of *Legal Times*, both publications owned by Steven Brill. She spent ten years at the *Journal*, hired in 1987 as a reporter and appointed six years later as a deputy bureau chief writing about the influence of money on politics, which had established her as a respected investigative reporter in Washington. Abramson ended up at the *Times* after she ran into Maureen Dowd at a book party. Dowd had told Michael Oreskes, the head of the Washington bureau, that he needed to hire some women for the bureau, and Oreskes invited her to suggest some candidates. Dowd asked Abramson if she knew any talented women who might want to be reporters in the Washington bureau of the *Times*.

What about me? Abramson said.

It never occurred to me that you would want to leave the *Journal*, Dowd said.

Don't be so sure, Abramson responded. By the week's end, Oreskes had asked her to lunch, and she was soon hired.

Abramson was more the sophisticated reporter than the stylish writer, which was not uncommon for someone drawn to the investigative side of the news business. She had a formidable memory; seemed to read every major newspaper, website, and blog; catalogued every interview with a news figure she heard on the Sunday morning talk shows; and had an ability to spot patterns in what might otherwise seem to be random events. When Joseph Lelyveld told her, the morning after the still-unsettled 2000 presidential election, that she would be the next head of the Washington bureau—We don't know who the president is going to be, but we know who the next Washington bureau chief is going to be, he said—she immediately appreciated the historical significance of her promotion as the first female to run the Washington bureau of the *Times*.

By contrast, Howell Raines grew up a Methodist in Birmingham and attended Birmingham-Southern College and the University of Alabama. He was wary of Ivy League elitism. He was thirty-four years old when he began writing at the *Times* in 1978. From his earliest days there, he had wanted to be a star reporter, a columnist, the Washington bureau chief, and eventually the executive editor. Raines had won a Pulitzer, and he had been a foreign correspondent, albeit for a relatively short time. He was one of the most accomplished writers at the paper, and his elegant and vivid stories may have fed Abramson's insecurities as much as her Ivy League credentials and intellectual bearing may have fed his.

Raines had firm ideas about how the bureau that was once under his command should operate: it should set the pace for coverage of the nation's capital, it should be an outpost of big personalities, endless energy, and a steady flow of stories that would dominate the front page and drive the morning conversation of its audience of readers. He thought Abramson was too slow and deliberative. "She was a great disappointment for me," he said years later. She made him impatient. She was drawn to the long-form, investigative stories that took time to report and present, such as the two-thousand-word front-page story she wrote with a colleague about a scheme by the Democratic National Committee that used state political parties to evade federal campaign laws to help Bill Clinton's reelection campaigns. Raines would remark on her languid voice, which could stretch out words to twice their normal length, when he complained about her to colleagues. He found it irritating. Raines wanted someone in Washington who would defer to him—who would be, if not sycophantic, then at least in accordance with his philosophy of how the bureau should operate. He wanted a bureau chief who was swaggering and adventurous, someone built in the model of the man who he held out as a model of engaged, propulsive leadership: Bear Bryant, the college football coach. He decided that the bureau under Abramson was trailing the *Post*, the *Journal*, and the networks in Washington. It was a harsh verdict, arrived at by a new top editor looking for justification to replace Abramson with his own candidate.

The choice of a Washington bureau chief is the prerogative of an executive editor. And it was a prerogative that—to his anger, frustration, and ultimate amazement—he could never exercise. For all his mastery of the *Times* bureaucracy, Abramson proved to be the more tenacious infighter. She parried each job he offered to move her out of Washington—investigative editor, book review editor, business editor—with an avowed determination to remain in D.C. until her children had graduated from high school. Raines could have forced her out, perhaps, but she was the first woman bureau chief and had come from the *Journal* with a strong reputation. And she had the backing of the publisher. Abramson would never be particularly close to Arthur Sulzberger, Jr., but she took care in tending her ties to him.

The simmering conflict between the executive editor and the Washington bureau chief was destabilizing for Abramson, Raines, and the Washington bureau. Roger Cohen, the foreign editor, called Richard Berke, her deputy, one morning in the late spring of 2002 and found him sitting in a chair at his dentist's office, a short walk from the office.

How are you doing, Rick? he asked.

I'm going to have dental work and I realize this is the most relaxed I've felt all week, Berke joked darkly.

The idea that Raines thought Abramson incapable of running the bureau was not idle media chatter about the latest intrigue at *The New York Times.* No one denied it. Newsrooms are filled with people who are curious, perceptive, inquisitive, and gossipy. There was no mystery about what was taking place. It was dark theater, and a source of distraction for a bureau at the center of covering one of the biggest stories in a generation. When Raines came to Washington for a bureau lunch in the spring of 2002, he talked warmly about Berke, who he had recruited to come to the *Times* as a political reporter.

I've known Rick for years and years, he told the correspondents around the table. I can trust Rick.

Berke felt uncomfortable; the executive editor was singling him out and, intentionally or not, undermining Abramson, who finally rose from her seat and left the room. Raines noticed; he thought it rude and unprofessional.

That spring, Raines had written a long, exacting, and encouraging evaluation of Abramson, saying she needed to take a firmer hand in national security stories and stretch herself to improve her editing and managing skills. He praised her performance: "You led the way through some of the most difficult days any team of journalists ever experienced." But Raines reiterated his understanding of their agreement that her time in Washington was limited. "As we've discussed, we will under no circumstances ask you to leave before [her son] Will is out of high school. After that, we'll arrive at a mutually agreeable schedule, which can be adjusted as we see fit." The evaluation was laying down an explicit marker that would go into her personnel file. His lack of faith undercut Abramson in the bureau. Reporters in Washington are adept at forming alliances with the editors who wield power as they maneuver to draw the better stories and assignments. But with Abramson in one office and the heir apparent in his own office right next to hers—a conference room had been converted to make way for Tyler—the bureau was mired in uncertainty, its reporters struggling with the often toxic crosscurrents between Abramson and Tyler.

Tyler, the bureau-chief-in-waiting, was a bit of a self-promoter (though certainly a talented one), showing little sensitivity to what was happening to Abramson. He was understandably frustrated at the roadblocks he encountered upon making his way to Washington to help cover the aftermath of September 11. On that visit, he did not last through Christmas. He returned to Moscow, impatient with Raines's pace in clearing the way for his appointment, frustrated at Abramson's intransigence. But Raines lured him back that spring by appointing him the paper's chief correspondent, with a renewed promise that he would become bureau chief the following year. Tyler settled in quickly, talking to Raines almost every morning, gossiping about what was going on in the bureau, in the Middle East, and in the White House. He would share his views of what he would do if he were in charge, as well as his criticisms of Abramson and the bureau. Even with Tyler back in Washington, with a prestigious title and his own office, Raines felt thwarted by Abramson. She wasn't pushing Tyler's stories at the Page One meetings; he was being sidelined by other talent in the bureau. Tyler would write news analyses that he had pitched directly to Raines and file them to the Washington desk. Berke would read them and walk into Abramson's office, rolling his eyes.

Are we too dumb to understand his ideas? Abramson would ask sardonically. Berke would ship Tyler's stories to New York, unedited. Eventually, Raines summoned Abramson to New York to discuss his unhappiness with her performance. They met at a restaurant in the Bryant Park Hotel overlooking the expanse of green next to the New York Public Library. There were only two people at the table, and there are inconsistencies in their recounting of their discussion, but it is clear this was a tense confrontation between two headstrong and wary editors, and Pat Tyler was a central topic of conversation.

Abramson resented Tyler's presence, his maverick and disruptive ways, how he was hovering, waiting for her to leave. She considered him a spy for Raines, a view she shared with her colleagues. It was making it impossible for her to do her job, she told Raines. The executive editor was upset with the bureau's performance, with how Abramson was managing a key reporter. He presented specific directions on how she should do her job, a "task list of how to get it done to suit me," which he recorded in a journal he kept at the time. Taking care of Pat Tyler was high on that list of requirements.

I brought a premier investigative and combat correspondent back from Russia to be a power reporter in Washington, Raines told her, as he described the conversation. Manage this person and get him in the newspaper.

By Abramson's account, Raines grew increasingly upset and banged his hand on the table, the slap of his flesh echoing through the dining room. Raines said that never happened. But in any case, the conversation crashed to a halt. The two sat in silence until Raines got the check. He accompanied her as she caught a cab on Sixth Avenue back to her sister's apartment, where she was staying. "I had always sort of been the pet of very difficult male bosses," she said years later, able to win them over with her intelligence and easy banter about politics, the news business, and office gossip. None of this was working with Raines. Frustrated, she asked Gail Collins, who had succeeded Raines at the editorial page, to lunch. Abramson had watched Collins become one of the most powerful women at the *Times*, and Raines was her mentor.

I just need to know—why does Howell hate me? Abramson asked. I was always the good girl in class. I was always the one the authority figures liked.

Collins had a pretty good notion of what it was that Raines did not like about Abramson—he didn't think Abramson was very good at her job—but she was not about to tell her that. I have no idea, she said. Abramson found her opaque and dismissive and decided she had taken a risk asking her for guidance. She turned to another powerful woman at the paper—Soma Golden Behr, an assistant managing editor. When Golden Behr visited the bureau, Abramson pulled her aside to ask why she was not backing her up when Raines belittled her at editors' meetings.

Cone of silence? Abramson said, a phrase she often used to suggest that she was bringing someone into her confidence. The two had settled on a bench at a park just outside the Washington bureau. Raines is undercutting the senior women editors at the paper, Abramson said.

What good is it to have a woman on the masthead? she asked Golden Behr. You're doing nothing for us.

Golden Behr was the newspaper's first woman national editor, but that had never been particularly significant to her, and she was put off by how Abramson presented her appeal. She was skeptical that Abramson's differences with Raines amounted to anything more than the usual struggle between a powerful executive editor in New York and a Washington bureau chief.

I didn't know I wasn't helping, Golden Behr finally responded. I don't think that is my job.

Abramson's discontent became known around Washington. In July 2002, Leonard Downie, Jr., the executive editor of the *Post*, invited Abramson to his house to recruit her to the *Post*. "This is a very important time for the country and its capital," he wrote her in a follow-up note the next day. "Our work is more challenging and rewarding than ever. I hope that, after thinking it all over this summer, you will come and join us. It would be mutually rewarding. You would be at home here."

Shortly after that, Donald Graham, the chairman of the *Post*, invited Abramson to his home, where he grilled salmon and opened a bottle of white wine and made the same appeal. She was tempted but she could never bring herself to leave. As fine as it was, the *Post* was not the *Times*, and if she stayed, she might have an opportunity to run the top newspaper in the country.

* * *

Abramson was not the only senior editor at odds with Raines. Jonathan Landman was the head of the metropolitan desk and had, over the course of his years at the *Times*, gone from being an admirer of Raines, when they worked together as editors in Washington, to becoming one of his biggest detractors. Landman was thirty-nine years old, lanky, and jittery with energy and ideas when he arrived in Washington as a deputy editor in 1991. Raines was running the bureau, and he tended to his A-team. That left Landman with the other reporters. They were less flashy, but they were good, and they welcomed an editor to talk to— someone who would steer assignments their way, advocate for them at the front page meetings. Landman enjoyed working with Raines in those days. He had come from the metropolitan desk, where he had been openly disdainful of the stories he read out of Washington—an opinion which, very much in character, he would convey to Joseph Lelyveld.

Nobody cares about these stories, Landman told Lelyveld, referring to incremental coverage about the daily intrigues and machinations in Washington.

I'd respect your opinion more on these things if you knew something about Washington coverage, Lelyveld responded. So he sent him to Washington.

Landman brought a dash of tabloid sensibility to the *Times*; he had worked at the *Daily News* and the *Chicago Sun-Times*, as well as *Newsday* on Long Island. He was aggressive and competitive, but also contemplative and measured. He was, from his earliest days as a *Times* editor, provocative—the contrarian always ready to argue the unpopular side, and sometimes just for the sake of the argument. He was filled with notions about different ways to approach a story, and opinions about what the *Times* was doing wrong. In Washington one day, he called Lelyveld at his desk in New York because the late-afternoon list of front-page stories for the next day's newspaper did not include an article that he had advocated for from the Washington bureau. Worse, it was made up entirely of stories from the foreign desk. This was at a time when *New York Newsday* was making a run for *Times* subscribers in New York.

God, it looks like the front page was designed by the marketing department of *New York Newsday,* Landman told him.

Lelyveld bristled, affronted that a junior editor in Washington had called him directly to complain about his news judgment. But a short while later, a revised front-page listing that included a Washington story was faxed down to Washington.

A few years later, at an editors' retreat in Westchester County, Landman, who was now running the Week in Review, rose and said that the *Times* had become boring. Lelyveld, now the executive editor, discarded the remarks he had prepared for the retreat, instead addressing this goading from an editor.

If it's boring, it's not just boring because we make bad decisions, Lelyveld said. It's boring because you don't give us interesting stories. But even as Lelyveld spoke, he appreciated that, in reacting to Landman's provocation, he had stumbled onto a better speech for editors looking to him for guidance. You don't realize how much authority you have, he told the editors. You can do all sorts of things that are exciting. You don't need our stamp of approval on everything you think of.

It was a trade-off. Defying authority was fundamental to Landman's nature, and this was seen, depending on the editor he was defying, as stimulating and refreshing or obnoxious and disruptive. His defiance of the people above him made him popular with the reporters below him. Lelyveld found it annoying, but he liked the way Landman pushed his colleagues into unexplored corners. And he found he often agreed with Landman, even if he might not want to admit it. "He let me be an asshole," Landman said with admiration years later about Lelyveld. "He rewarded me for being an asshole."

The odd chemistry that existed between Lelyveld and Landman failed to materialize with Raines when he became the executive editor. Now that Landman was the metropolitan editor, a position to which Lelyveld had appointed him, Raines seemed different—no longer the person he remembered from their time in Washington. Traits Landman hadn't liked but could overlook—the glimmers of grandiosity and self-importance, a belief in his own superiority—seemed to have worsened. Landman enjoyed the independence he had at the metropolitan desk under Lelyveld, and he resented Raines telling editors what to cover and, not incidentally, whom to hire. Landman would scoff when Raines talked about himself as a change agent. Change to what? he asked. It was a cliché.

There was an important difference between Raines's struggles with Abramson and those he had with Landman. Raines thought Landman had excelled running the coverage of September 11, and he admired the Metropolitan section. "Jon Landman—our brilliant metro editor" was how he described him in a television appearance in the summer of 2002. (Raines made a point of letting Landman know that he had praised him during his television appearance, just in case Landman had not seen it.) Still, the defiance of authority that had pleased Lelyveld struck Raines as the rebellious petulance of an adolescent, and he confronted him about it, at another retreat of editors in Westchester in early 2002. Raines had finished describing the assertive role he intended to play in shaping the news report when Landman rose to object.

That was not the way it should be done, Landman said. Ideas should come from reporters in the field, not editors dreaming up story ideas in their offices. Raines was disturbed by how Landman was challenging him in front of other editors. After the session, he and Landman walked off and sat down in a lounge. Their alliance in Washington seemed long ago.

You've been one of the greatest disappointments I've had since I took this job, Raines told him, as Landman recollected their conversation. Raines rejected Landman's concerns about meddling from his superior editors.

You're basically saying that I've worked all these years to be executive editor, and now I'm not supposed to be editing the paper, Raines said. But I reserve the right to manage the news report, and there are areas that I want to target.

Landman was not standing down. When Ken Auletta of *The New Yorker* did a profile of Raines in 2002, the executive editor invited him in for the morning discussions with editors and the front page meetings and granted him long interviews in his office. Landman talked with Auletta about his concerns about Raines, coloring a profile that Raines had hoped would be a tribute to his editorship. "There is nothing wrong with the executive editor having story ideas," Landman told Auletta. "The problem is when these story ideas become commands and overwhelm everything else. . . . There's a feeling of a one-way windstorm." The *New Yorker* story related how Landman pushed an article for the front page about a state-sponsored study in New Jersey that found that Black drivers were more likely to speed than other drivers. The results suggested that racial profiling—troopers stopping people because of their color—was not as clear-cut a case of discrimination as it might have seemed. Raines, according to the *New Yorker* account, told Boyd he was concerned about the study's methodology. The story was held for six days before finally being published—not on the front page but on the first page of the Metropolitan section. When asked by Auletta if he thought Raines was being politically correct in holding the story, Landman responded: "You'll have to draw your own conclusions."

Even in a newsroom that was becoming more assertive, this kind of public criticism of an executive editor was extraordinary enough that Sulzberger remarked on it to Raines.

What are you going to do about Landman? he asked.

I'm going to ignore it, Raines said.

That would prove to be a mistake. Landman—like Abramson—was running one of the biggest desks at the newspaper. Like Abramson, he was influential and admired by many of his reporters. And, again like Abramson, he was known and respected outside the newsroom, including by reporters who were beginning to notice that something seemed wrong at Howell Raines's *Times*.

CHAPTER 24

House on Fire

On the morning of August 15, 2002, Patrick Tyler, the paper's chief correspondent and a close friend of Howell Raines, opened up *The Wall Street Journal* to an op-ed column by Brent Scowcroft, the national security adviser under Presidents Gerald Ford and George H. W. Bush. The column was a rebuttal to months of belligerent talk from President George W. Bush and Vice President Dick Cheney as they tried to rally the American public behind an invasion of Iraq. "Don't Attack Saddam," read the headline. "It is beyond dispute that Saddam Hussein is a menace," Scowcroft wrote, but the Bush Administration had yet to make the case that military action was justified. "There is scant evidence to tie Saddam to terrorist organizations, and even less to the Sept. 11 attacks," he wrote. An invasion, he warned, could provoke Iraq to retaliate with chemical or biological weapons, setting off a war between Israel and its Arab neighbors.

Scowcroft was a pillar of the Republican Party foreign-policy establishment, a member of George H. W. Bush's inner circle. He and the elder Bush had collaborated on a book in which they defended their decision in 1990 not to remove Saddam Hussein after the first Gulf War, so his op-ed read like guidance from father to son. As such, it carried more weight than the concerns that had been voiced by such Republicans as House majority leader Dick Armey and Chuck Hagel, a maverick senator from Nebraska. Tyler sent an email to Raines saying it was urgent that the *Times* jump on the story. The Republicans are cutting loose on this, he said.

Raines agreed. He had told Tyler to call him directly whenever he had a suggestion for what the Washington bureau should be covering, and this was the kind of story he wanted. Tyler and Todd Purdum, the State Department reporter, were assigned to write about Republicans breaking from their president on Iraq. Scowcroft's dissent would not be enough to carry an article of the ambition Raines wanted. Henry Kissinger had written an essay for *The Washington Post* that week that had questioned the need for military action, but, characteristically for the former secretary of state, it was elliptical and nuanced. Tyler and Purdum included Kissinger's concerns in their story. Purdum wrote in caveats, in an attempt to account for the conditionality of Kissinger's view. The headline on the front-page story read, "Top Republicans Break with Bush on Iraq Strategy." The story completed, Purdum headed to Santa Barbara for vacation and told his colleagues to be careful in doing follow-up stories not to lump Scowcroft and Kissinger together without accounting for Kissinger's more complex positions. The following day, a White House reporter, Elisabeth Bumiller, who traveled with President Bush to his ranch in Crawford, Texas, filed a story that failed to make that distinction. In reporting on Bush's response to his party's dissenting voices on Iraq, she identified Kissinger as an opponent.

While Kissinger's views may have been exaggerated in Bumiller's telling, the initial *Times* account was a fairly conventional newspaper story exploring what turned out to be well-grounded reservations among some Republicans about the rush to war. But the attacks from conservatives came immediately, and they were directed as much at Raines as they were at the paper. "There's nothing subtle about the opposition of the New York Times to President Bush's plan for military action to depose Saddam Hussein in Iraq," said the conservative *Weekly Standard*. The essay, under the headline "When It Raines It Pours," was a brushback pitch aimed at the *Times* from proponents of removing Saddam. It had been barely a year since Raines had stepped away from writing editorials, but his views of military intervention—as represented, for instance, by his Robert S. McNamara editorial—were still fresh in the minds of conservatives already resentful of the *Times*'s influence and ideology. "Not since William Randolph Hearst famously cabled his correspondent in Cuba, 'You furnish the pictures and I'll furnish the war,' has a newspaper so blatantly devoted its front pages to editorializing

about a coming American war as has Howell Raines's New York Times,"
wrote Charles Krauthammer, the conservative columnist for *The Washington Post.**

The *Wall Street Journal* editorial page found the Tyler-Purdum story
implausible. "The Times's theme is that the Scowcroft article means the
Republican party, or at least some major faction of it, is in revolt against
the Bush foreign policy," their editorial read. "This is not news; it's a wish
in the eye of the remnants of the old anti-Vietnam left."

The *Times* that summer had published several articles that spotlighted
the risks of invading Iraq; there were stories on the threat of a spike in oil
costs, the risks of a surge of refugees, and the costs of a war without a
clear end. When David Sanger, a White House reporter, arrived in Crawford, Texas, to cover Bush on vacation at the end of August, Condoleezza
Rice, the national security adviser, met him for coffee and scolded him
about his newspaper's reporting.

You guys are coming up with every conceivable reason for us not
being allowed to do this, she told him. And what are you going to do if
Saddam is allowed to get a nuclear bomb? Rice's admonition to Sanger
was a sign of the escalating effort by the White House to shape the
Times's coverage during this critical period. By the end of the summer,
the White House had launched a full-fledged campaign to convince the
American public, Congress, international allies, and the United Nations
of the need to disarm Saddam Hussein. Cheney delivered a warning
about the Iraqi dictator in a speech in late August to the 103rd National
Convention of the Veterans of Foreign Wars in Nashville. "Simply stated,
there is no doubt that Saddam Hussein now has weapons of mass destruction; there is no doubt that he is amassing them to use against our
friends, against our allies, and against us," he told an audience of combat veterans.

Cheney plucked quotes from the Kissinger essay in the *Post* to make
his case that Iraq was indeed a threat—something that was not lost on
anyone at the *Times*. Raines went back and studied the Kissinger op-ed

---

* Raines always admired the "muscular" way Krauthammer wrote his attack on the
Times—and, years later, would say he was "not offended at being compared to William
Randolph Hearst."

and the story by Purdum and Tyler and concluded the two reporters got tangled up in Kissingerian duplicity, as he later put it, and that there needed to be some clarification—all the more so because the attacks from conservatives had piqued the interest of the publisher.

Don't we need to comment on this? Arthur Sulzberger, Jr., asked Raines.

Raines told the publisher that he was preparing an editors' note. The first story by Tyler and Purdum, the note said, "should have made a clearer distinction between his [Kissinger's] views and those of Mr. Scowcroft and other Republicans with more categorical objections to a military attack." The note was less equivocal about the story the following day by Bumiller. "The second article listed Mr. Kissinger incorrectly among Republicans who were warning outright against a war," it said.

The criticism was being heard inside the newsroom, and the *Times* coverage was about to change—ultimately leading to one of the frankest public admissions of failed journalism in the paper's history. On Sunday, September 8, 2002, four days after the publication of the editors' note, all but one of the five articles on the front page addressed the threat of Iraq. There was an interview with Colin Powell, the secretary of state, defending Bush's policy of pre-emption against regimes that threaten the United States. There was a lengthy story by Tyler recounting how the United States failed to appreciate the danger posed by Osama bin Laden, suggesting that the attacks of September 11 could have been anticipated. There was a Times/CBS News poll that found Americans were increasingly doubtful that the government had done enough to protect the nation from terrorism, and were convinced, despite misgivings, that war with Iraq was inevitable. And leading the newspaper was a story that Raines had ordered up, laying out everything the *Times* knew about Saddam and his effort to build an arsenal of chemical, biological, and nuclear weapons. Andrew Rosenthal, the third-in-command in the newsroom, gave the assignment to Washington. There was never any question who would write it: Judith Miller and Michael Gordon, two of the reporters Raines had dispatched to the bureau after the attacks of September 11.

The story reported that over the previous fourteen months, Iraq had sought to buy specially designed aluminum tubes to be used as components of centrifuges needed to produce enriched uranium. It conveyed concern from anonymous administration officials "that Washington dare not wait until analysts have found hard evidence that Mr. Hussein has acquired a nuclear weapon. The first sign of a 'smoking gun,' they argue, may be a mushroom cloud."

The publication of the story about the aluminum tubes, which was based on information provided anonymously by senior administration officials, was then used by the White House to justify an invasion of Iraq, "as if it were somehow independent confirmation of their case," Peter Baker wrote in *Days of Fire*, his account of the Bush-Cheney years. Cheney, Rice, and other White House officials orchestrated a series of appearances on the Sunday morning talk shows the day it appeared. "There's a story in *The New York Times* this morning," Cheney said on *Meet the Press*. "It's now public that, in fact, he has been seeking to acquire, and we have been able to intercept and prevent him from acquiring through this particular channel, the kinds of tubes that are necessary to build a centrifuge." Rice echoed language in the *Times* story when she appeared on *Late Edition with Wolf Blitzer* on CNN. "We don't want the smoking gun to be a mushroom cloud," she said. A few days later, President Bush spoke of the aluminum tubes before the United Nations General Assembly in New York. "Iraq has made several attempts to buy high-strength aluminum tubes used to enrich uranium for a nuclear weapon," he said to a skeptical audience. "Should Iraq acquire fissile material, it would be able to build a nuclear weapon within a year."

This story would not only provide ammunition for a White House looking for evidence of the danger Saddam posed to the world; it would come to represent a broader failure by the *Times* that would shadow the newspaper for the next fifteen years. The aluminum tubes story was one of a number of reports that would appear in the *Times* in the coming months about Iraq's weapons capabilities. The newspaper, after being criticized by conservatives for standing in the way of the invasion of Iraq, would stand accused of being complicit in leading the nation into a costly, deadly, and arguably pointless war. This criticism was an exaggeration of the newspaper's role and influence, without doubt, but it was not without merit.

It was also an early sign of what would become a breakdown of the

Times newsroom, straining under the pressure from Raines to produce exclusive stories. And it would establish Judith Miller—not entirely fairly (other reporters and editors shared some of the blame)—as the prime villain in what many critics came to see as ideologically driven reporting that bolstered the Bush Administration's case for war. This was a clear example of how the *Times* could shape a national debate, because of its reputation as authoritative and independent and the assumption that editors would never publish anything without carefully checking it first. That was the reputation Cheney and Rice played to their advantage when they invoked the *Times* after the tube story was published. For years, as some of the Iraq coverage dissolved under examination, Howell Raines, Jill Abramson, and Andrew Rosenthal would trade blame over who was responsible for this institutional failure.

There was, in fact, disagreement among nuclear experts in the administration about whether the tubes could be used to produce nuclear material, but that was barely noted in the 3,400 words of the story. Miller and Gordon would address the dissent in the sixth paragraph of a story that appeared five days later, but that story made it clear that this skepticism among some intelligence experts was a minority view. (Gordon later contributed to two stories, published in January 2003, that reported that the International Atomic Energy Agency had challenged the White House claims about the tubes; both stories ran deep inside the newspaper.) In the weeks ahead, other news organizations faced with the challenge of reporting on confidential intelligence from an administration intent on going to war were more skeptical. The Knight-Ridder News Service found "a growing number of military officers, intelligence professionals and diplomats in [Bush's] own government privately have deep misgivings about the administration's double-time march toward war." The story quoted officials who said the administration was exaggerating the evidence of links between Saddam Hussein and al-Qaeda and noted the belief of many experts that Iraq had purchased the tubes to make conventional military weapons. The tubes story would ultimately be largely discredited by the *Times* itself, after a team of reporters, returning to this chapter in American history years later, concluded that administration officials seized on the direst intelligence assessments while ignoring the doubts of other experts.

The focus of the newsroom after Raines became editor—the deployment of its correspondents and photographers, the choice of stories to cover, the front page—reflected a world reordered by the threat of terror and the prospect of an invasion of Iraq. This was new terrain for the newsroom leaders. Raines had served less than two years overseas, in London, and Boyd had never worked as a foreign correspondent. Abramson had no foreign reporting experience. The newsroom was covering an international crisis of great complexity fueled by historical rivalries and grievances going back centuries. The attacks on New York and Washington had been followed by United States–led airstrikes against Taliban terrorist camps and military installations in Afghanistan, where bin Laden had fled for shelter, leading to a protracted war during which bin Laden escaped. Bush, in his first State of the Union speech, warned of the threat to world peace by an "axis of evil"—Iran, Iraq, and North Korea. The United States was stunned and disoriented, threatened within its borders.

Reporters and editors felt the same tug of patriotism as other Americans, aware that there was now an expectation—stated or not—that the interests of newspaper and country should align in a time of shared peril. Roger Cohen, the foreign editor, who had spent twenty-one years overseas for the *Times*, Reuters, and *The Wall Street Journal* and covered wars in Bosnia and Lebanon, was overwhelmed by the death toll in his new hometown. We are a newspaper in a wounded city, with nearly 2,800 dead, and every New Yorker is angry, he thought.

That sentiment extended to the publisher. Arthur Sulzberger, Jr., the Vietnam War protester, the son of a marine, was concerned that the *Times* might appear unpatriotic during this period. Sulzberger's ambivalence could be seen in the editorials, which on important matters typically reflect the views of the publisher. They were cautionary and conflicted. "The debate over Iraq has exhausted everybody," read one. "Many people now think an American invasion is inevitable; many more are desperate just to get whatever happens over. There's nothing less satisfying than calling for still more discussion. But that's right where this page is." The kind of skepticism the newspaper should have brought to evaluating suspect intelligence information was hard to find after the summer of 2002. Cohen noticed that meetings of editors began with the

assumption that *we are going to war,* without resolving a more fundamental question: *did the evidence show that going to war was justified?*

There was much on Raines's mind as he steered the coverage from
that summer through the start of hostilities in March 2003: the pressure from the White House, the criticism from conservative corners,
his legacy as a liberal editorial writer, the concern from the publisher
that the newspaper could be perceived as disloyal, and the memories of
Watergate and *The Washington Post.* To some extent, his editorship during this time reflected the calculations of a politically astute journalist
navigating external and internal pressure, deciding what stories
should be assigned and where they should be played. But the motivations of people in powerful positions managing institutions through a
storm are rarely that simple. Raines had covered civil rights in the
South and defied President Bill Clinton when he was the editor of the
editorial page; he was no stranger to pressure, and his ego thrived on
criticism. He expected the *Times* to come under attack when it waded
into contentious subjects, and to be subject to manipulation and attempts to shape its coverage, and he would argue that the best response
was to dig in. He liked to recount the story of when Ari Fleischer, the
White House press secretary, asked the *Times* not to publish complete
transcripts of videotaped remarks bin Laden had made from his hideaway after the September 11 attacks. The White House was concerned
he was sending coded messages to sleeper cells preparing to unleash
new waves of terror against U.S. targets. Raines said any such request
would have to be made from the president to the publisher, and that the
newspaper's policy was to share the information that it learned with its
readers.

Raines was less driven by ideology than competitiveness. He wanted
stories that commanded public attention, that were exciting to write and
to read. Every ambitious reporter at the *Times* knew this was how he
measured success, and that included Judith Miller. And the single biggest
unanswered question in the summer of 2002, the most obvious target
for a story, was the one that had been assigned to Miller and Gordon
about weapons of mass destruction.

* * *

Miller had a wealth of knowledge about Iraq and the Middle East, a command of the region's history and conflicts, and a network of sources and contacts. Her passion for the Middle East stretched back to 1972, when she was sent to study in Jerusalem while she obtained a master's degree at the Woodrow Wilson School of Public and International Affairs at Princeton. "I became fascinated with the Israeli and the Palestinian dispute, and spent the rest of the summer traveling for the first time to Egypt, Jordan and Lebanon," she said in an email response to questions from Franklin Foer at *New York* magazine in 2004. "By the end of the summer, I was hooked." She reported from the region for NPR and for *The Progressive.* Knowing her background, A. M. Rosenthal sent her to Cairo in 1983 and gave her free rein to cover the region.

Her career seemed to stall in 1988, when Raines pushed her off the Washington desk and she went to New York to become a deputy editor on the media desk. But Frankel and Lelyveld sent her back to help cover the first Gulf War in 1990. "With a view to bringing all the energy and expertise we have to bear on our coverage of the Gulf crisis, I've asked Judy Miller to return to writing," Lelyveld wrote in announcing her new assignment. Miller was a bulldozer of a reporter: driven and unyielding in her dealings with sources and editors. She convinced Lelyveld to allow her to go to Beirut in 1991—a dangerous assignment in a country just coming out of a civil war. She wrote high-impact stories bristling with sensitive intelligence information.

In August 1996, she and Jeff Gerth had written the first investigative story on Osama bin Laden that appeared in *The New York Times.* It detailed the suspicions of intelligence officers that this "scion of a wealthy Saudi family" was financing terrorist activities around the world, including the 1993 bombing of the World Trade Center. Bin Laden was such an unknown figure that his name did not appear until the fourth paragraph; the headline referred only to a "Persian Gulf Businessman."

As a reporter, Miller was consumed with the story—"a house on fire," in the words of Raines. Her editors (or at least some of them) would welcome the "we've got to get this in the newspaper tonight" telephone calls she would make after she picked up a bit of information at a cocktail party or an embassy reception. But she could be exhausting and overbearing with her certitude and condescension to other reporters and her editors. She was territorial and had a reputation for swooping in and filching stories from other reporters, so much so that her behavior stood out even at the *Times*, which was hardly a collegial place. Some of this resentment reflected the different standards by which men and women in the newsroom were judged; there were plenty of male reporters known for undercutting colleagues. Yet Miller, struggling throughout her career to break into a male-dominated environment, was seen as a reporter who took the fight to a new level and was unapologetic for how she came across. "I have strong elbows," she said. Maureen Dowd, a White House reporter in the 1990s, was sitting in the assigned *Times* seat in the White House for a national security briefing when she noticed Miller standing at the side of the room, visibly agitated. Halfway through the briefing, Miller walked over to where Dowd was seated.

I think I should be sitting in the *Times* seat, she whispered. Dowd—taken aback, if amused by the forwardness of the request—rose and yielded her position.

Alison Smale, an editor running the foreign desk at night, grew accustomed to hearing from Miller late in the evening with a story that needed to be published. Judy, it would be really hard to get the story into the paper now, but why don't you sit down and send me what you think the first three or four paragraphs would be, Smale would say. And when Miller would do that, Smale would tell her how interesting it seemed, but it needed more checking, and promise to leave it for the editors in the morning. She admired Miller's doggedness.

In July 2001, Miller went to her editor, Stephen Engelberg, who would collaborate with her on a book on biological warfare published in 2002, to alert him to a sensitive conversation her intelligence sources had picked up between two al-Qaeda operatives. One of the operatives expressed regret that the United States never retaliated for the suicide attack on the USS *Cole*, a guided missile destroyer that was bombed while it was refueling in the port of Aden in Yemen in 2000. The other responded by saying, Don't worry, we're going to do something so big they're going to have to retaliate.

We have to do a story, Miller said.

Okay, that's interesting, Judy, Engelberg said. What's the second paragraph? Who are they? There was not enough to write, he told her. That conversation was one of the first things that came to Engelberg's mind in the days after September 11. I wonder what would have happened if we had written this? he thought.

From the start of her career, Miller moved in the social circles of the people she covered, and over the years, she had been warned about crossing lines. This was an issue going back to her earliest days in Washington, when she was living with Representative Les Aspin, Jr., of Wisconsin, who headed the House Armed Services Committee. There were often rumors surrounding her dating life. Some of them were the kind of unsubstantiated gossip that often attached to strong, independent women reporters while similar behavior by male reporters was overlooked. But she would write in her memoirs about being part of an era of changing morals and standards. "A child of the 1960s, I had what was then regarded as a traditionally 'male' attitude toward sex: I enjoyed fairly casual encounters that neither my partners nor I assumed would lead to a long-term commitment," she wrote. That meant there was enough truth to the rumors to worry Bill Kovach, who ran the Washington bureau.

We're working very hard to protect Judy's reputation and she's not making it easy, Kovach said to a young Howell Raines in the early 1980s.

Miller brought expertise to her coverage of Iraq, but she also brought strong views on the threat that Saddam Hussein posed to the world. Reporters in mainstream journalism are usually diligent about not expressing their opinions, but here again Miller was different from her colleagues. She was as knowledgeable about the subjects she covered as many public officials, and she had come to share their views about the dangers of Saddam Hussein. She had written a biography of Saddam; she viewed him as a mortal threat. "I feared there was nothing he wouldn't do if he had access to such weapons," Miller told a Style reporter from *The Washington Post* over the course of a three-hour interview after she left the *Times*. "I was genuinely fearful of what he might do to American forces, to American installations in the Middle East." Her eyes brimmed with tears. "But I will make no apologies for my continuous commitment, my desire to pursue stories about threats to our country." Tyler, one of the correspondents with whom she would clash over the years, alluded to her strong opinions in a note to Raines after learning that Gordon and Miller had been assigned to write the tubes story. "I don't see anything wrong with it; I think Gordon will keep it level, but Judy is in a war whoop mode."

The previous December, Miller wrote about an Iraqi engineer who claimed to have direct knowledge of twenty secret weapons sites in Iraq. "An Iraqi defector who described himself as a civil engineer said he personally worked on renovations of secret facilities for biological, chemical and nuclear weapons in underground wells, private villas and under the Saddam Hussein Hospital in Baghdad as recently as a year ago," the story said. Knight-Ridder would later report that American officials took the defector back to the sites and found no evidence to back up the claims. The defector story would be cited in *The New Yorker* in 2004 when it described how Ahmed Chalabi, an Iraqi dissident, planted unsubstantiated stories in American newspapers as part of his effort to draw the United States into Iraq. The article, as well as the tubes story, would be listed in a later accounting the *Times* published addressing the failings of its coverage.

Miller's lines of command were never clear, which would make it easier in the years to come for editors to distance themselves from her work. She often reported to Raines and Boyd while she traveled Iraq; she would, as she recounted in her memoir, call them on her satellite phone with updates. (This was unusual; reporters do not normally report directly to the top editors of a newspaper, since it can undercut the authority of the editors below them.) Her stories would go through the investigations editor, the foreign desk, or the Washington desk, depending on the subject. For long patches, she did not even have a supervising editor. Engelberg, the investigations editor, whose responsibilities included editing Miller, left in the spring of 2002, after months of quarrels with Raines, to become the managing editor of *The Oregonian*. Douglas Frantz would replace him that fall, but, frustrated in his dealings with Boyd and Raines, he would leave in March 2003 for the *Los Angeles Times*, weakening the newspaper's investigative coverage. Miller had a desk in Washington and a desk in New York. She kept her home in New York; in Washington, she stayed at the Ritz-Carlton, an easy walk to the bureau. She spent so many nights there that she became a hotel VIP; they embroidered her initials in her pillowcases.

If she did not like what an editor on the foreign desk told her, she would go to the Washington desk or the investigations desk or someone higher in the newsroom. She would remind people how Raines and Boyd had sent her down to Washington, and that, combined with the knowledge of her history with Sulzberger—how they had shared a weekend house with other reporters when they were both in the Washington bureau twenty years earlier—gave her an aura of invincibility. In one case, Miller filed a report saying that Iraq had turned to Turkey to purchase large quantities of atropine—a medicine used to treat nerve gas exposure—as well as syringes to administer it. Atropine would permit Iraq to use sarin gas on the battlefield without endangering their troops. Frantz had been the Istanbul bureau chief, and he told Miller he was doubtful Turkey had the capacity to manufacture large quantities of the substance. She went to Boyd, who called Frantz to his office. Miller is a Pulitzer Prize winner, Boyd told him. Your job is to get her stories into the paper, not to block them.

She was not easy to manage. She would agree to a round of editing changes during the day and then call back late at night and restore them with another editor. Some of her own colleagues would refuse to work with her, concerned about getting tarnished by disputes about the balance or accuracy of her stories. When Sulzberger came down to Washington to meet with reporters for lunch, Richard Berke, Abramson's deputy, pulled him aside. I have six reporters who don't want their name on a story with her, Berke said.

But when it came to Miller, that was a price that some editors thought was worth paying. Raines was not the first one who valued her and looked the other way at her excesses. "I think you are a person of enormous ability, talent and creativity and that you have a magnificent mind," Abe Rosenthal wrote her as he was stepping down as executive editor. "I'm happy about a number of decisions in my professional life but few have, I think, meant more to the paper than recognizing what was inside the head of Judith Miller." He signed the letter, "Love, Abe."* Lelyveld was always aware of the risks—the "danger to our reputation" posed by her relationships with her sources; the stories that would prove

---

* Rosenthal was responding to a letter from Miller: "You took the chance on me as a foreign correspondent; you sent me to Cairo; you transferred me to Paris."

to be wrong. He thought she lacked judgment. But Lelyveld admired how energetic she was, how excited she would get about the story. He appreciated how she picked up information at cocktail parties and dinners, and how she was always ready to jump on a plane. Andrew Rosenthal would stand by her when reporters from *The Washington Post* called researching a story about her exploits. And he defended her within the newsroom. Rosenthal was in a crowded elevator in the *Times* building one day when a colleague started complaining about Miller.

You know what? Rosenthal responded. On my top-ten list of all-time assholes at *The New York Times*, I'm not positive that Judy Miller gets on it.

There was a reason she would become the face of the *Times*'s coverage, and the focus of blame by her colleagues in Washington. Miller took the lead on the coverage. She fought to go to Iraq and wrote many of the stories that would come to symbolize the newspaper's failures. "I took America to war in Iraq. It was all me," Miller wrote sarcastically years later in an essay in *The Wall Street Journal.* But it was Michael Gordon who came up with the first tip on the tubes story (from, he would later say, intelligence sources, not from the White House). Other reporters, at the *Times, The Washington Post,* and *The New Yorker,* also wrote stories that were too reliant on American sources or Iraqi dissidents and that would not stand the test of time after troops swept through Iraq in what turned out to be a fruitless search for the weapons. A front-page story by Tyler in October 2001 claiming that Mohamed Atta, one of the organizers of the September 11 attacks, had met with an Iraqi intelligence official in Prague five months before the planes crashed into the World Trade Center and the Pentagon, was filled with caveats, and other newspapers that day contained much of the same information. But Tyler's report, which turned out to be wrong, had the platform of the *Times,* which made it that much more credible and concerning.

The *Times* was an editors' newspaper, and any shortfalls in coverage reflected not only the errors of its reporters but failures across its ranks of editors: the executive editor, the managing editor, the investigations editor, the foreign editor, and the Washington bureau chief. Raines would later say that he was not her editor. So would Abramson. So would Rosenthal. So would Cohen. But Raines and Boyd enabled her, valued her kind of journalism, made it clear they wanted her prominent in the coverage. They put Miller's stories on the front page, which elevated her status and made editors less willing to challenge her reporting. Many of the stories had been edited—and recommended for the front page—by Abramson's Washington bureau. Sulzberger never knew who to hold accountable. "At the end of the day, you've got a Washington bureau chief, you've got the national editor, international editor," Sulzberger said. "You've got a managing editor. You've got an executive editor. It's a shared responsibility at some point, isn't it?"

Miller would later say that she reported what credible sources had told her. "W.M.D.—I got it totally wrong," she said in a *Times* story in 2005, referring to weapons of mass destruction. "The analysts, the experts and the journalists who covered them—we were all wrong. If your sources are wrong, you are wrong. I did the best job that I could."

But other newspapers did not get the story wrong, or at least not as wrong as the *Times* had.

CHAPTER 25

Raw Talent

J ayson Blair walked into the offices of *The New York Times* in the summer of 1998, a twenty-two-year-old journalism student at the University of Maryland, College Park, who been recruited as a summer intern. He was promoted to a full-time reporter in January 2001. His rise from intern to a staff writer was at once quick and turbulent. Blair was the kind of eager-to-please reporter who would never push back—"Why is this a story?"—when asked to head out to a Sunday afternoon news conference or to do legwork for a writer in the office. He was the kind of reporter who made a weekend desk grateful: eager to leap when called by his editors—assuming his editors were able to find him, which they sometimes could not. His productivity was reflected in the rush of headlines that began appearing over this new byline.

BROOKLYN MAN CHARGED WITH SETTING WIFE ON FIRE

I KILLED AND 3 HURT IN GUNFIRE AT 3 BARS

6 ARE KILLED AND ONE IS HURT BY CARBON MONOXIDE IN HOUSE

NEW HOTEL, FIRST SINCE 1980S, IS PLANNED AT KENNEDY AIRPORT

His byline would appear over 750 stories in just under five years. Does he ever sleep? Jerry Gray, a metropolitan editor, would ask his colleagues. And Blair was not only prolific. His stories, while not extraordinary, soon began to display more flair than might be expected from a reporter in his twenties—the kind of work that catches the eye of an editor. "Older men remember it as one of the first places where they could find the titles that really meant something to them," Blair, at the age of twenty-four, wrote about the closing of an iconic gay bookstore in Chelsea in 2001. "Young men and women talk about how the books on those shelves answered their questions and helped them shape their identities." A young Black man in a newsroom that even now was overwhelmingly white, Blair was short—five-foot-two—and disheveled, his shirt tails hanging over his pants. He was engaging if ingratiating, a newsroom gossip with a loud laugh and a bright smile who would leave the message "gone fishing" on his computer screen when he slipped out for a cigarette in the third-floor stairwell (and would return reeking of tobacco smoke).

As 2003 began, Blair was showing glimmers of finally becoming the frontline reporter that he thought he should be, of seeming to overcome stretches marked by confrontations with editors, stories strewn with errors of fact, and binges on alcohol and cocaine—a habit that was overlooked (or excused) by colleagues. He would be seen at Robert Emmett's Bar and Restaurant on Eighth Avenue disappearing for a quick trip to the bathroom and emerging with a spring to his step. The previous fall, he had received a *Times* Publisher's Award for his "first-class work" while reporting for the website about the late-night arrest of two suspects in a sniper case that had left ten people dead and terrorized the Washington, D.C., area for three weeks. Blair "helped to maintain *New York Times* excellence in this new medium, where there is a deadline every minute, not just one a night," the citation read. Publisher's Awards conveyed recognition from the highest level of the newspaper and came with a $500 bonus. Blair was also given a $5,000 merit raise, bringing his annual salary to $81,000—more than respectable for a reporter with his experience. Editors were ready to give him a tryout for a full-time posting on the national desk.

And Howell Raines was delighted with his work. While Raines was the editorial page editor, with an eye out for talent in the newsroom he hoped to run one day, he had noticed this intern's byline. Now, after fourteen months as executive editor, he saw Blair as the kind of reporter who could help reinvigorate the newsroom: hungry, industrious, on the hunt for stories that would set the *Times* apart. "My feeling was, here was a guy who had been working hard and getting into the paper on significant stories," Raines would say.

Blair was at his apartment in Brooklyn on April 29, 2003, when Jim Roberts, the national editor, reached him on his cellphone and asked him to come into the office. Blair knew why. A *Washington Post* reporter had called the day before to question Blair about what appeared to be an act of plagiarism under his byline in a story about the family of a missing soldier, written with a Los Fresnos, Texas, dateline. A reporter from the *San Antonio Express-News*, who had known Blair from when they worked together as interns at the *Times* as part of a minority recruitment program, had complained that Blair had lifted descriptions and quotations from an article she had written earlier that month. Blair knew what Roberts and other editors at the *Times* did not know and would soon discover: He had not been in Texas. He had indeed copied the details from the *Express-News* that made his story so vivid and compelling.

And this was also not the first time he had resorted to fabrication and plagiarism or claimed to be someplace he was not. Roberts, when he called Blair, thought he was reaching his reporter in Fairfax, Virginia, where he had been assigned to cover a trial. In truth, Blair had been ensconced in his apartment for most of the previous four months, notwithstanding the datelines on his dispatches that invited readers to think he was moving across the country. As he walked in off Forty-third Street and through the door into the *Times* building to meet with Roberts and other editors, notebooks in hand, Blair was fairly sure how this would end for him. But he did not anticipate that his name would become synonymous with a national plagiarism scandal that would tarnish *The New York Times* for a decade and would pitch the newsroom into one of the most wrenching transformations in its history.

Blair's career had blossomed despite concerns that might have derailed another reporter of his age and experience. The story of his success was often presented through the prism of race, as a Southern white liberal executive editor and the paper's first Black managing editor blindly advancing the career of a promising Black reporter. Conservatives would seize on Blair as an affirmative action morality tale; liberals would insist that race had nothing to do with what happened. Raines would never deny that race was a factor in his handling of Blair, or the possibility, as he put it in reprising a canard, that "Jayson flew through on my watch because I was a southerner, a guilt-ridden southerner." But it was not that simple. It was also a reflection of the premium Raines was putting on high-octane journalism, which resulted in editors looking over their shoulders in this tense newsroom and suspending (as had happened with Judith Miller) the skepticism that they had been trained to apply to a story that seemed too good. Blair was a product of this moment.

* * *

Jayson Blair was born in Columbia, Maryland, and—apart from a few years living in Houston and Atlanta, as his father moved around different government jobs before becoming the inspector general for the Smithsonian Institution in Washington—had grown up in a single-family home in Centreville, a middle-class Virginia suburb outside of Washington. He took an early interest in journalism and would write letters of criticism to the student newspaper at Centreville High School filled with criticism of the stories he was reading there, until the newspaper's faculty adviser suggested that instead of carping, he join the staff, which he did. Upon graduating, he enrolled at Liberty University, the Baptist college founded by Jerry Falwell, and considered becoming a minister. That adventure lasted one semester, after which Blair transferred to the University of Maryland and joined the college newspaper. He interned at *The Washington Post* and *The Boston Globe*, and then he was spotted by Joan Motyka, a recruiter from the *Times* looking for summer interns. She was immediately impressed with this "very ambitious and self-confident" young reporter.

Blair's poise, swagger, and savvy were evident from his response to a question on his internship application: "Pretend your most recent editor was omniscient. What prediction would he or she make about your career track in journalism?" That editor would describe him "as a hardworking reporter, who is willing to go anywhere for her at any time," Blair began. From there, he ventured down a more interesting road, displaying both candor and self-awareness, or so it must have seemed to anyone reviewing his application. "She would probably say that people who work with me are easily turned off, because I don't play well with others in the sandbox of life," he wrote. "I'm a bit of a loner when it comes to work, and surprising to some, a bit of an introvert. . . . As much as my hard work will help me succeed, it will make me a lot of enemies outside and, unfortunately, inside the business." That answer might have been calculating and manipulative, but it helped get him the intern job on the metropolitan desk working under Jerry Gray, the political editor. Gray took a liking to him and decided, as he later said, that Blair had "the most raw talent that I've seen in a younger reporter." But even then there were concerns; his sloppiness in dress and copy, the trail of disorder that followed him through the newsroom. He would show up to the office wearing stained pants. There were holes in his shoes. Gray offered to take him shopping for shirts and ties.

I'm a fifty-year-old male, and I don't expect you to dress like a fifty-year-old male, Gray told him. But there's a decorum here. Nobody is going to send you to city hall if you look like a bum.

Gray, who was also Black, was trying to help this young reporter adjust to the idiosyncratic and white-dominated culture of the *Times*. There are some of the most eccentric people in the world in this newsroom, Gray told him. But let me tell you—they have earned their weirdness. On an impulse, Gray invited him along to a dinner with the governor of New York, George Pataki, and his top aide, Zenia Mucha, at a Greek seafood restaurant in Manhattan. He was struck by how comfortable Blair was at this table—the confidence he displayed in engaging the governor, a moderate Republican who had defeated a once-popular incumbent, Mario Cuomo. Gray's early written evaluations of Blair reflected his high estimation of this young man. "Despite my apprehensions, Metro did not kill Jayson, or his smile," he wrote. "Jayson arrived with a grace, demeanor and drive that won over everybody he encountered."

Blair returned as an intern in the summer of 1999 in a "blaze of productivity," as a confidential report on his employment history later described it, writing 130 stories in five months, during which time he was promoted to intermediate reporter, a provisional job. He was a model of promise, hustle, and spirit through the first half of 2000. But more warning signs began to emerge that summer. Blair made seven reporting errors in the space of nine weeks. He was brash enough to complain about his supervisor to Nancy Sharkey, an editor in charge of recruiting, and asked to be assigned a new editor—a request she gently deferred. Jonathan Landman, the metropolitan editor, got wind of the conversation. "I REALLY hope you were unsympathetic," he wrote her. "The last thing we need is Jayson thinking this is about his compatibility with editors. Jayson still doesn't know what he's doing. He makes a million mistakes. He needs to be very closely watched, pushed, pulled, etc. He may not like it. Too bad."

Blair was one of four intermediate reporters up for a promotion to full-time reporter at the end of 2000. He learned that Landman was holding up the promotions and emailed Sharkey at one o'clock in the morning to urge her to see that his colleagues be promoted, even if he was left behind. Sharkey wondered, as later recounted in an internal report, whether Blair had possibly hacked into the computer system and spied on email traffic; she had "a suspicion that his seemingly intimate knowledge of upcoming personnel moves and other bits of newsroom gossip might have come from something other than just keeping his ear to the ground; was he hacking into computer files late at night to read emails or personnel evaluations?"* Nonetheless, Blair was formally hired as 2001 began, at the recommendation of a recruiting committee headed by Gerald Boyd, who was then a deputy managing editor. Landman thought Blair was not ready, and that his race was a "decisive factor" in a premature promotion, but did not attempt to block it. "It was clear that Gerald felt pressure to promote Jayson and that he thought it was the right thing to do," Landman told a committee of outside journalists who the publisher, Arthur Sulzberger, Jr., would later recruit to investigate Blair's career at the *Times*. "The racial dimension of this issue and Gerald's obvious strong feelings made it especially sensitive; in that sense, it is fair to say that I backed off a bit more than I would have if race had not been a factor."

Blair's promotion did little to steady his behavior. After September 11, he falsely told his supervisors that a cousin had perished in the attack on the Pentagon. When Bill Schmidt, the associate managing editor for ad-

---

* Blair would later say, in an email exchange in May 2020, that he had not hacked into the private computers of either Sharkey or Landman and had gleaned the information about the promotions around the office. "It was never a state secret," he said. "Or, if it was, it was not a very well kept one."

ministration, wanted to include Blair on a list of staff members who had lost relatives in the attacks, Blair first said yes but emailed back five minutes later. "I am sort of changing my mind. i would rather people not know. not sure why."

Blair was unraveling. He covered a fundraiser at Madison Square Garden for victims of the terrorist attack and produced a story that was riddled with errors. He listed the cost of tickets as $1,000; they were $10,000. He misquoted Bill Clinton. He reported that Bono and The Edge, from the band U2, had performed; in fact, they had been scheduled to appear but did not. Blair also was not there. He had turned up that night at a party at the Upper West Side home of Alison Smale. She was surprised to see him because he had told her that he had to cover the concert, on assignment from the metropolitan desk. Oh, no concert? she asked. He told her the *Times* was not given the credentials needed for entrance. She thought that odd and said so but then let it pass; he did not work for her desk. Blair had a few drinks and went back to the office to watch coverage of the fundraiser on television and wrote his story there, taking breaks to slip into a third-floor stairway that led from the newsroom to the street to do lines of cocaine.

On the same day that he was supposed to cover the fundraiser, Blair sent an email to an editor listing "my grievances of the week" and demanding that "you've got to at least pretend to treat me with respect. . . . I am on your team—insomuch as it does not run afoul of what I need to do for myself." The note included a line for the editor to sign to acknowledge that she agreed to the demands. She did not sign it. Landman told Blair he was out of line, only to have Blair sound off to him. Blair was advised to apologize to Landman, which he did, unhappily. "I held my nose and sent him this message, incorporating some of those notions on my own fault," he told Sharkey. "I am still a tad steamed on the way things were handled and not thrilled at the fact that I have to eat a ton of shit on this one." He ended it by saying, "it's all going in the book."

Blair had been drinking and taking drugs since college, struggling with waves of self-doubt, anxiety, and manic behavior. He kept a bottle of gin next to his bed at a New York University dormitory during his first summer as an intern. It all got worse, as he told it, after September 11. He would end up at the bar at Emmett's five nights a week and sometimes not make it back to his Brooklyn apartment. He would check into a hotel, drinking and consuming cocaine late into the night, and show up at the office after picking up a change of clothes at the Gap. In the first week of January 2002, Blair asked to have breakfast with Susan Edgerley, the deputy metropolitan editor. They arranged to meet at Teresa's, a Polish restaurant in Brooklyn Heights. Blair rolled in after another late night of alcohol and cocaine. Edgerley was not surprised to see him in bad shape; it confirmed what she had suspected accounted for his erratic behavior. By the end of their breakfast, Blair had confided about his use of cocaine and alcohol. She paid the check, took him back to the office, and sent him to the employee assistance program, which, following office protocol, enrolled him in an inpatient rehabilitation center. When he emerged, Blair would continue outpatient treatment three days a week, four hours a day, for more than a year. He would later say he did not return to using drugs, but the professional problems resumed.

In mid-February, Landman sent Blair another negative evaluation, telling him that while he had "the basic tools to be a success in the world of journalism," his self-destructive behavior was endangering his career. Landman forwarded the evaluation to Boyd and Schmidt, with a cover note: "There's big trouble I want you both to be aware of." Schmidt's role as personnel manager meant he had no shortage of problems on his plate. But this involved a young, talented Black reporter at a newspaper with a weak record on promoting minority employees. Boyd stepped in. I will talk to him, he told Schmidt.

"I said, 'you have enormous promise and potential but your career is in your hands,'" Boyd later recounted of his conversation with Blair. "I don't know what you're doing, drugs or what, and I don't care. The issue is your performance and unless you change, you are blowing a big opportunity."

On March 28, shortly after that conversation, Blair did not show up at work, and he made another mistake in a story. Landman sent a note to Schmidt and Sharkey. "Bill, Nancy: We have to stop Jayson from writing for the *Times*. Right now. cheers, jl."* Blair's editors prepared a detailed

---

* This note from Landman would come to symbolize, fairly or not, the failure by the *Times* to catch Blair early on. Blair said he never knew of it until he read about it after he resigned from the newspaper.

list of steps necessary for him to salvage his career, including no more corrections. It would have effectively put Blair on probation. But Boyd blocked that, contending that it could open the newspaper to a legal challenge on discrimination. "At the very least, Gerald said, it would [be] patronizing in the extreme," the internal report said. "We did not need to tell him how to conduct himself professionally."

* * *

It was Boyd who suggested recruiting Blair to work on the sniper-attack story in Washington in October 2002. The *Times* was struggling, as Raines kept reminding his editors every morning when *The Washington Post* or *The Baltimore Sun* would beat them on a story. Boyd had gathered Andrew Rosenthal and Jim Roberts, from the national desk, in his office to discuss expanding the team of reporters on the story. Boyd had a list of names scribbled on a piece of paper, including Jayson Blair. He thought Blair would be a good addition; he had grown up in the Washington area and had covered the police while in New York. Boyd knew about Blair's struggles with accuracy, his battles with editors, and his time in rehabilitation. He did not mention them to Roberts, who, as national editor, barely knew this reporter from the metropolitan desk. "My failure to disclose Blair's history was a huge oversight," Boyd wrote years later. It would set Blair on a perilous path in his career. And it would link the fortunes of these two men, raising questions about whether Boyd had been complicit in Blair's rise.

Boyd would occasionally offer career advice to reporters and editors, but he did not consider himself much of a mentor to anyone; it was complicated enough trying to manage his own career as a Black man in the *Times* newsroom. "I didn't feel I should take people under my wing and move them up the ladder," he would later tell a committee investigating what happened with Blair at the *Times*. "I incurred some criticism from journalists of color who felt I was not looking out for them. My view was that it was competitive and a matter of merit." Blair tried to befriend him, seeking him out in the stairway to share cigarettes. In the end, though, he never viewed Boyd as an ally. "As the first black managing editor of the paper, Gerald had always seemed to me to take a special interest in not promoting the careers of minorities over others in the newsroom in order to protect his standing," Blair later said. When Blair read speculation that Boyd had been his mentor, he wondered if people—white people—were mixing up Gerald Boyd and Jerry Gray, who he did view as a mentor.

Yet as much as Boyd kept his distance from Blair, he helped Blair's career at crucial moments, drawn—like so many other editors—to the talent, energy, potential, and sheer ambition Blair displayed from his earliest days. It seems unlikely that Blair would have gotten as far as he did, considering his history, without Boyd's support, as tentative as it might have been. Raines also knew about Blair's problems with substance abuse. But the newsroom had always been a place with people who drank too much or who were caught using recreational drugs and were given second chances. Raines had noted "a vibrancy and a returning vitality" in Blair after he returned from rehabilitation, as he put it in private testimony to an outside panel investigating the case.

Blair appeared to live up to the faith shown in him when he began working on the sniper story. He won the Publisher's Award after racing into the night to follow a tip about the impending arrests from a police officer, calling in notes from a pay phone at a highway rest stop in Maryland where the two men had been captured. Later that month, he broke a story that the U.S. attorney, acting at the direction of the White House, had halted the interview of one of the suspects by local law enforcement officials as he was on the verge of a confession. It set off a scramble among his competitors—and some bad-mouthing of this new face in town who'd managed to land a scoop six days after arriving, based on five unnamed sources.

Blair's article was correct in reporting that federal and state prosecutors were in a territorial battle over who would get the case; he was chasing a report that appeared in *Newsweek*. But *The Washington Post* challenged Blair's reporting that the suspect, John Allen Muhammad, was on the verge of "explaining the roots of his anger" when the interview was shut down. The *Post* quoted the Maryland U.S. Attorney, Thomas M. DiBiagio, denying he had forced the end to the investigation. "The allegations in the New York Times article today are false," he said.

Blair defended his exclusive when the *Washington City Paper*, a weekly, called about the spat between the *Times* and *The Washington Post*. "The

Post got beat in their own back yard, and I can understand why they would have sore feelings," he told the newspaper, breaking from *Times* etiquette with his chest-thumping criticism of a competitor. But the concerns could be heard inside the *Times* as well. Reporters and editors in Washington had questioned its accuracy with editors in New York. Still, Raines sent Blair a note of praise. "That is great shoe-leather reporting and especially impressive because you were dropped into the middle of a very big running story being covered by scores of other reporters," he wrote. Raines sent copies to fifteen other senior editors. The recipients include Landman, who had been Blair's supervisor, and Jill Abramson, the Washington bureau chief who Raines complained had not been aggressive enough in chasing this story.

Raines was aware of the complaints about Blair from his colleagues but dismissed them as carping by jealous competitors. Jayson's really getting it for us, isn't he? Raines said to Jim Roberts.

Roberts had heard one warning about Blair. Watch out for that guy, Landman told him. I really don't trust him. Roberts waved it off as the product of Landman's differences with Raines. He was trying to run a complicated, competitive story under intense scrutiny from Raines, Boyd, and Rosenthal. Every day he felt the same pressure: run, run, run, go, go, go, get the story. Boyd had called him one day—a Sunday—when he was at home washing his car. Why aren't you in the office? Boyd asked him. Don't you know there's a war going on? Roberts headed for the office.

Blair was a gift. He was breaking stories—energetic and ready to jump. That was Jayson Blair: seductive; adept at making his editors feel confident and invested in his success.

CHAPTER 26

A Room Filled with Gas

He was unwavering: he had never seen the story he was accused of plagiarizing from the *San Antonio Express-News.* He had gone, as he said, to Texas for the national desk and interviewed the family of an American soldier who was missing in action and later turned out to have been killed in Iraq. But Jayson Blair knew—even as he answered questions from Jim Roberts, who had called him to the office on this day in late April 2003 to ask about the complaint by the *San Antonio Express-News* reporter—that he was building a wall that could not hold back the flow of the facts and his own troubled journalistic history. He thought about the questions about his sniper coverage, the growing resentment in the newsroom toward Howell Raines over this past year, the overlay of race and affirmative action on his career. But most of all, Blair thought about how the allegations against him were true. "I could see in my head the way the thread was going to go," he said years later.

Roberts told Blair to assemble a chronology of his travels and reporting, and to turn over his reporting notebooks from the trip. How did you get to Texas? Where did the interview take place? What did the house look like? Blair responded with details and description: the white stucco house with the roses in bloom and a red roof and a red Jeep in the driveway. He could convincingly answer Roberts's questions because he had found his way into the newspaper's computerized photo archive and examined unpublished images of the home. Blair left Roberts to meet with Bill Schmidt, the associate managing editor for administration, along with his representative from the Newspaper Guild of New York, which steps in when a guild member faces the threat of dismissal or discipline.

For the next four hours, Schmidt asked questions informed by his years as a national and foreign correspondent: What airline did he fly? How did he book his ticket? When did it land? Where did he rent a car and spend the night? Blair left with a promise to return the next day to continue the session. The facts of his story fell apart when Schmidt conducted a cursory check of airline schedules and the hours at the car rental office, which had been open when Blair said he was unable to rent a car because it was closed. He went to find Boyd.

There's no point in going any further, Schmidt said. We have to fire him. Blair quit before the paper had a chance to act, with a brief typed letter of resignation the next morning. He told colleagues he was thinking about hanging himself with a belt and was placed on suicide watch at Silver Hill Hospital, a psychiatric facility in New Canaan, Connecticut. Within two weeks, he would be shopping a book proposal.

On May 2, 2003, the *Times* published a story on Blair's resignation along with an editors' note acknowledging that he had lifted passages and information from an article that appeared on April 18 in the *San Antonio Express-News*. "The *Times* has been unable to determine what original reporting Mr. Blair did to produce it," the note said. "The *Times* regrets this breach of journalistic standards and plans an apology to the soldier's family as well as a review of other work by Mr. Blair." By now, Blair's editors had realized that he had not even been in Texas. "The *Times* apologizes to its readers for a grave breach of its journalistic standards," the news story quoted Raines as saying. "We will also apologize to the family of the soldier, who has since been reported dead, for heightening their pain in a time of mourning."

The *Times* had made mistakes over the years; its flawed reporting on Iraq's purported efforts to stockpile weapons of mass destruction would contribute to one of the most grievous United States foreign-policy adventures in its history. But as would become clear over the coming days, Blair had committed a systematic deception that revealed fundamental weaknesses in the newsroom. Blair claimed he was in places he was not, that he spoke with people he had never met. He stole the reporting and writing of other newspapers in a frenzy of falsification and deception. He had not been caught until now, because the *Times* was built on a contract of trust between reporter and editor. Years later, someone would ask Schmidt, who spent two years dealing with Blair's disciplinary problems, how this could happen at a place like the *Times*. He would describe it as, in part, a failure of imagination: he had never imagined the possibility of a reporter inventing a trip or fabricating a story. Schmidt had overseen the writing of the *Times* ethics manual, and as he observed, "There was no clause in it saying you're not going to make shit up."

The night before Blair resigned, Arthur Sulzberger had taken Jonathan Landman, the metropolitan editor, to dinner at Gallaghers Steakhouse, a restaurant on West Fifty-second Street in the theater district—tablecloths, wood ceiling beams, a selection of marbled steaks on display—to tell the metropolitan editor that he wanted him to go overseas as a reporter.

You're not exercising leadership: I want to send you to London, Sulzberger said as soon as Landman ordered a steak and a glass of red wine. Landman was startled. The metropolitan desk had been at the forefront of the paper's coverage of the September 11 attacks. And he had not been a reporter since he covered Suffolk County for *Newsday* seventeen years earlier. He had little desire to be a correspondent. Landman was perplexed by the offer, and though suspicious of Sulzberger's motivations (this is Raines trying to get me out of the newsroom, he thought), he told the publisher he would discuss it with his wife.

Sulzberger was indeed acting at the bidding of the executive editor. Raines's strategy for managing one of his most public critics—of ignoring him, as he had told Sulzberger after Landman was quoted in a *New Yorker* story criticizing the executive editor—had not worked. Raines had come to view Landman as a poisonous presence, a leader of the newsroom opposition against him, who he suspected was a source of damaging stories about him to other publications. "Jon's disenchantment and anger have been so consistent and openly apparent that it is undermining morale and managerial discipline in a way that cannot be ignored indefinitely," Raines wrote Sulzberger. "We now have an attitudinal situation that is toxic, if not cancerous." Raines laid out the arguments the publisher should press on Landman to convince him to go to London: this was one of the most prestigious beats at the paper, and in time it would help groom "one of our best desk editors."

The next morning, Raines emailed the publisher.

"I'm curious as to how your dinner went?"

"No surprise he's not a happy puppy," Sulzberger wrote back. "He [chafes] at what he sees as your management and decision-making style, which he views as very top-down."

But that dinner was the beginning and the end of any negotiation about moving Landman out of New York. With the resignation of Jayson Blair, Raines was facing the biggest crisis of his editorship.

* * *

Howell Raines was eighty-five miles west of *Times* headquarters, enjoying a delayed honeymoon at his weekend house. He had married Krystyna Anna Stachowiak on March 8, 2003, at the Trinity Episcopal Church in Mount Pocono, Pennsylvania. They celebrated their marriage the next day in Manhattan at the Bryant Park Hotel with a reception that drew three hundred guests, the kind of New York media society that merited a story in the *New York Observer:* Tom Brokaw, Dan Rather, Mayor Michael Bloomberg, Governor George Pataki, and Senator Charles Schumer, along with a delegation from the *Times* led by Arthur Sulzberger, Jr. The nation was on the brink of war (the invasion of Iraq would come less than two weeks later), so the couple delayed their honeymoon until the last week of April. The first signs of spring were in the air as they finally drove the two hours from Manhattan to the house in Henryville, Pennsylvania, just past the Delaware Water Gap. It was a steep-roofed gray house, and Raines had an office in the second-floor bedroom, with a stand-up desk that commanded views over the horizon. There was a screened-in porch off the dining room that looked across a green rolling meadow to an orchard of old apple trees, with the Kittatinny Mountains just visible way in the distance. That was where he was, sitting on the porch, a hot mug of coffee in one hand, when Gerald Boyd called. He was in the Page One meeting room, talking over a speakerphone. There was a problem. Raines cut short his honeymoon.

When Raines walked into the newsroom on Friday morning, Schmidt handed him a folder of memos, evaluations, and email correspondence from Blair's personnel file. Raines took it to his office and read the file with the eye of a *Times* manager. A pattern of bad performance, documented for the files but ignored, he thought. He did not see it as his failure, but he suspected that others in the newsroom would not share his view. He would say he had not known the history of discipline, mistakes, erratic behavior, fights with editors—or if he had a notion of Blair's problems, he never grasped how serious they were. He had not noticed, he said, the caboose of corrections affixed to Blair's story on the Madison Square Garden fundraiser. He could not understand why Al Siegal, who oversaw the paper's standards, had not alerted him.* But he was the executive editor, and he should have been keeping an eye on the corrections column. In particular, he should have noticed a correction of such magnitude that it became the subject of discussion and concern.

Raines paused when he turned the page to Landman's note urging the paper to stop Blair from writing. Raines would later say he had never seen it before that morning, and found it suspicious that Landman had not personally alerted him to the problem.

Raines walked into Boyd's office. How did this not reach me? Raines asked. Why didn't I see the Landman memo?

But how he'd missed it didn't matter. This note was extraordinarily damaging, presenting the newspaper's top editors as negligent if not complicit in Blair's behavior. And if Raines did not know the troubled history of Blair's employment at the *Times*, he arguably should have. Raines knew Blair had struggled with alcohol and cocaine. And Blair's reporting on the sniper had been challenged by prosecutors and other reporters, including members of his own Washington bureau.

Boyd told Raines he had appointed a team of editors to investigate the failure. Raines rejected the idea. We can't have the people who handled the bad copy investigating the handling of the bad copy, he said. For a moment, Raines considered a dramatic gesture to deal with this crisis: another editors' note, this one putting the blame on the paper's personnel procedures, followed by a purge of editors who had played a role in Blair's career—Schmidt, for not showing him that memo, and perhaps Boyd, who, in Raines's estimation, had known that Blair was not professionally trustworthy. But he ultimately decided that could paralyze his

---

* Siegal, in an email exchange years later, said he could no longer recall why he never brought the Blair correction to Raines.

editorship and that the best way to respond to this crisis was with a story examining what happened with Jayson Blair, published in the pages of the *Times*, written by a team of reporters. An article of that ambition, Raines thought, would address the concerns about the *Times* among its readers and, more important for his own survival, address the anger in the newsroom.

Boyd pushed back, arguing that the investigation should be handled by senior newsroom editors. But Raines rejected Boyd's counsel. It's my editorship that's riding on this, he said. I have to go with my gut.

He informed Sulzberger of the plan and assured the publisher that he and Boyd would have no involvement in the story. Siegal would oversee the project. It would be edited by Glenn Kramon, the business editor, and Lorne Manly, a media editor. The team would include an investigative reporter, David Barstow; a former Times Company lawyer whom Raines had convinced to cover legal affairs for the newspaper, Adam Liptak; a media reporter, Jacques Steinberg; one of the paper's most graceful writers, Dan Barry; and a business and legal reporter, Jonathan D. Glater, who was recruited after Siegal realized the team was all white. Siegal would later say that adding someone who was "young and Black and a lawyer was a no-brainer."

Raines initially wanted a story published by that Sunday and met with Kramon that Friday. At the meeting, Kramon wrote in his journal, "Howell instructed me to search for 'everything we've told our readers we now believe is not true. . . . We've published some bad journalism.'" But Kramon and his reporters decided they needed to explore the failure in editing that allowed Blair to escape detection for so long. That would mean an examination of the actions of Raines, Boyd, and the editors below them. When the story was not ready for Sunday, and then not Monday or Tuesday or Wednesday, Raines bristled with impatience. He did not understand why Barstow and Barry had not come to interview him and brought his concerns to Kramon. "He told me he knew investigative journalism (he really doesn't), and we were going about it the wrong way," Kramon wrote in his journal. Boyd appeared unannounced in the team's workspace on the fourth floor one day. He wandered around the desks, making awkward conversation. Years later, Boyd said he had gone there to share more details about his decision to send Blair to cover the sniper story. But the reporters made it clear that Boyd, a subject of the story, was unwelcome.

During the week that the story was being prepared, Raines's relatively low profile created a vacuum that was filled by an institutional fury over this latest injury visited on the *Times* reputation. It's like the room filled up with gas, William Safire, the op-ed columnist, said to Raines one afternoon. Raines took in the rage with disdain. "When I saw that panic was sweeping the newsroom, it filled me with a feeling of disgust and contempt," Raines would say years later. "You are journalists. You live in an evidence-based, fact-based world. And now you're behaving like the Pied Piper is coming through Hamelin."

Barry and Barstow put off their interview with Raines until the end of the week. It was a difficult session for all involved. Like Raines, Barstow was an alumnus of the *St. Petersburg Times*. Raines, when he was editorial page editor, had invited Barstow to join him for lunch in a private dining room. Barstow, who would win four Pulitzer Prizes over the course of his career at the *Times*, admired Raines's reporting and writing; the Robert McNamara editorial—"the ceaseless whispers of those poor boys in the infantry, dying in the tall grass"—had taken his breath away. But Barstow had spent the week examining Blair's sniper coverage, and he could not understand how Raines had ignored those red flags. It defied credibility that someone with Blair's lack of experience could jump into a story on unfamiliar terrain and find five sources willing to talk about a highly sensitive investigation in less than a week. Barstow had always found Blair to be obvious in his obsequiousness, and could not understand how Raines had not detected that from their first meeting. Raines was jaunty as the interview began, but as the hours dragged on, with these two serious and unsmiling reporters volleying questions, he began to slump in his chair. It was impossible to see how he had any other choice, but Raines wondered if he made a mistake recusing himself from editing the story. He was frustrated they were not focusing on what he thought was the real story here—this obvious personnel-management failure. As they rose, Barry, who had won a Pulitzer for investigative reporting as part of a team at *The Providence Journal* in 1994 and now felt like a member of the internal-affairs division at a local police department, looked at Raines. Thank you for giving us your time, he said.

Barry and Barstow returned to the fourth floor. They were incredulous at Raines's claim that he was unaware of Blair's disciplinary history and his view of this as an administrative breakdown. They had shared one of the team's major findings with Raines: there was evidence of plagiarism or fabrication in thirty-six of the seventy-three stories Blair had written since joining the national staff. Please keep this to yourself, Barstow said, wanting to protect a key part of their reporting until it was published.

Raines went on the *PBS NewsHour* that Friday night and, in an interview with Terence Smith, disclosed what was going to be published on Sunday. (Raines later said he did not recall Barstow's request.) "They tell me, in the course of interviewing me today, two of our reporters told me that they had already found thirty-six instances of fabrication," Raines said to Smith, himself a former *Times* reporter. "As I say, we're committed to fully disclosing every circumstance of this."

Raines was shad fishing with John McPhee, a *New Yorker* writer, on the Upper Delaware River the Sunday the article appeared. It was a foggy morning, and he stopped at a convenience store to pick up the *Times*. He slipped it into his gear bag, clambered into the boat, pulled it out, and began to read. "Correcting the Record: Times Reporter Who Resigned Leaves Long Trail of Deception." The two-column headline ran over the top of the left side of the page. The story had five bylines. It ran for 7,445 words, filling four inside pages, and included a separate accounting of every episode of fabrication or questionable reporting the team had documented.

"The widespread fabrication and plagiarism represent a profound betrayal of trust and a low point in the 152-year history of the newspaper," the story said in its first paragraph. The memo from Landman ("We have to stop Jayson from writing for the Times") was highlighted in the eighth paragraph, though the story did not say who had seen it. The first quotation in the story, near the top, was from Sulzberger: "It's a huge black eye. It's an abrogation of the trust between the newspaper and its readers."

The *Times*'s decision to devote so much space to self-criticism drew praise from some quarters. "I've just read the piece for Sunday's paper about Jayson Blair, and, while it is shocking, it is also, to me, deeply moving," David Remnick, the editor of the *New Yorker,* wrote Raines. "You must be heartsick and exhausted. But you did an extraordinary and admirable thing this week, you and yours. Thank you for it." The view was not universally shared. Arthur Gelb thought it an "apocalyptic four-page saga of self-incrimination, and its unrelenting insistence on beating up on itself—including Howell's own defensive cries of mea culpa—licensed a release of pent-up resentment harbored by many on the newsroom staff." Sulzberger initially thought it a testament to the integrity of the *Times*—this is devastating, he thought, approvingly, as he read it—though he would come to think that it may have gone too far. Jayson Blair, who would read it after he left the psychiatric hospital, thought the story handed Raines's enemies ammunition they could use to bring him down.

Over time, the Blair episode would change the culture of the *Times* for the better: the newsroom would impose new systems to assure accuracy and fairness and, in a concession that ran counter to its institutional nature, invite its readers and critics to flag mistakes and errors of tone and judgment in its pages. It would appoint an ombudsman to independently review the paper's performance. But if Blair changed the culture of the *Times* for the better, he changed its reputation for the worse. The *Times* became the butt of jokes on late-night comedy talk shows. The name Jayson Blair became a symbol, a shorthand that was invoked by anyone who felt wronged by, or just disagreed with, a story in the *Times*. This was, like the paper's coverage of Iraq, a threat to the currency that made the newspaper such a force in American life: its credibility and reliability. Sulzberger could not ignore that. His family could not ignore that. The board of directors and the company's executives who were in charge of protecting its reputation and its value could not ignore that.

CHAPTER 27

Losing the Newsroom

Howell Raines sent a memo to the newsroom the day after the Jayson Blair story was published.

"Dear friends and colleagues: Now that we have seen our team's report on Jayson Blair's fabrications and how they got into our pages, I want to outline for you the steps we are going to take starting today to protect The Times from another such painful occurrence," it said. "I have not written or spoken directly to you in the last week because I wanted our reporting and editing team to have the time and freedom to do this valuable work." Raines would appoint a commission, led by Al Siegal, who had overseen the preparation of the newspaper's front-page story on Blair, to make recommendations on how the *Times* should address these failures in management.

Raines had hoped that the story would allow the *Times* to move on and let him return to running the newsroom. But the intensity and sweep of the article, written with the authority of an indictment, had further antagonized journalists in this usually proud newsroom. "I've never heard such hostility," Kramon wrote in his journal that week. "It makes me think that Howell and Gerald will not survive it. They seem to have no base of support in the newsroom. People truly resent them for arrogance, favoritism, intimidation and overworking the staff." Raines's first instinct was to arrange a series of meetings with small groups of reporters and editors to discuss the findings in the story; he was wary that a large assembly of the newsroom could veer out of control. He remembered what happened when Max Frankel met with his staff after publishing the name of a rape victim in the William Kennedy Smith case. Raines liked to bounce ideas off William Safire, the former Nixon speech writer and public-relations consultant who Punch Sulzberger had hired in 1973 to write a column for the Op-Ed page. Safire warned him against holding a town hall meeting. All you'll do is provide a megaphone to anyone with a petty discontent, he said.

But it would prove impossible to avoid. Raines invited David Barstow to his office to ask about the mood of the staff. You are losing the newsroom, Barstow told him. This business of small meetings isn't working. This is one of those big moments when you have to assemble everyone in the newsroom.

Raines went to Arthur Sulzberger, Jr., and offered to resign; Sulzberger declined the offer. It's not your fault, it's just your turn, he said. But Sulzberger was rattled. He knew he had taken a gamble on Raines. He would later say he had no idea of how the atmosphere in the newsroom had curdled, though there had been no shortage of evidence of the discontent. "Perhaps not since Abe Rosenthal's last, autocratic years had the din of newsroom complaint been as loud," Ken Auletta had written in *The New Yorker* nine months after Raines took over. Sulzberger wanted a town hall meeting, with Raines, Boyd, and the publisher sitting on a stage, hearing the concerns and questions of the staff.

The town hall took place at the Loews Astor Plaza, a 1,440-seat theater in Times Square, and drew six hundred reporters and editors. Reporters from other news organizations were barred from attending. Even Jacques Steinberg, the media reporter covering the story for the *Times*, was kept out, in what Elizabeth Kolbert, a former *Times* correspondent, described in an essay for *The New Yorker* as "a somewhat convoluted effort at high-mindedness." Because the theater was across Forty-fourth Street, Raines, Boyd, and Sulzberger were forced to navigate a thicket of reporters and television crews—an unseemly entrance to an event that turned into a two-hour, slow-rolling disaster.

The three men sat at the front. The publisher was holding a crumpled brown paper bag from which he pulled out a stuffed toy moose. The moose was a prop for a management exercise Sulzberger had learned from the newspaper's corporate consultants; its presence was meant to remind people not to ignore the unsettling subject that needed to be addressed. "Never in my career at the *Times* have I seen the moose put to better use than we did in the Sunday paper with our painful but thorough look at Jayson Blair and ourselves," Sulzberger said. Few reporters or editors had the slightest idea what he meant, as was evident by the deadened reaction in the room, and Raines picked up the conversation.

"I'm here to listen to your anger, wherever it's directed; to tell you that I know that our institution has been damaged, that I accept my responsibility for that and I intend to fix it," Raines said. He saw no evidence of Blair gaining preferential treatment because he was Black. The *Times* was struggling to transform a newsroom that remained predominantly white, and Raines saw that mission as part of his charge. He was a son of the South who had lived through the civil rights struggles of the 1960s. "Does that mean I personally favored Jayson? Not consciously. But you have a right to ask if I, as a white man from Alabama with those convictions, gave him one chance too many by not stopping his appointment to the sniper team. When I look into my heart for the truth of that, the answer is yes."

Boyd felt compelled to declare that he had done nothing to facilitate Blair's rise. He resented what he saw as the facile story line that presented him as the Black mentor for a younger Black reporter. "I can tell each and every one of you, that is absolute drivel," he said. "There is no truth in it. Did I smile at Jayson when I walked in sometimes? Did I pat him on the back sometimes and say, hang in there? Yes. I do that with every reporter who I come in contact with as much as I can." Raines and Boyd were appearing together in a show of unity, but by now their relationship—which was never a real alliance—was crumbling under the pressure of a scandal. Raines listened to Boyd with disbelief. He had concluded, no matter what Boyd said, that Boyd was Blair's counselor and promoter. Is there anything involving you and Jayson that you need to tell me? Raines had asked when Boyd challenged his decision to appoint a team of reporters to write about Blair. Boyd was indignant. Of course not, he said. I hardly know Jayson.

Before the session, Raines and his wife, Krystyna, had had lunch at the Millennium Broadway on Times Square, where she'd given him a bit of advice: whatever you do, don't tell them to go fuck themselves. Raines thought that if he was contrite and deferential, he would survive the day. He realized as the questioning began how much he had misread the moment. "Have you considered resigning?" demanded Alex Berenson, a business reporter. Sulzberger interrupted to say he would not accept Raines's resignation and offered a defense of Raines's performance. But he would become less certain of that position as he witnessed the churn of resentment in the auditorium.

"You guys have lost the confidence of vast portions of the newsroom," said Joe Sexton, a deputy metropolitan editor. ". . . These are some immensely talented and devoted and crucial people who absolutely do not feel a sense of trust and reassurance that judgments are properly being made. These are people who feel that they have been less led than they have been bullied, often against their own considered and better judgement." Sexton did not understand why the masthead had not been alarmed when Robert Horan, Jr., the commonwealth attorney in Fairfax County, Virginia, had dismissed as "dead wrong" a story by Blair reporting that "all the evidence" pointed to Lee Boyd Malvo, the teenage accomplice, as the triggerman. "Forget the fucking paper trail," Sexton said. "It's right there."

For a moment, Raines discarded the admonition from his wife. "We don't have to worry about the paper trail, no matter what kind of profanity we put in front of it; the reconstructive record is clear," he said. "I want to listen to you with courtesy. I have to tell you in honesty you've stated that in a demagogic and inaccurate way." Raines had seen David Carr, a business reporter at the time, at the side of the stage, clapping enthusiastically as Sexton spoke. It fed his anger; he had pushed for Carr to be hired. He simmered as old friends like R. W. Apple, whom he'd asked to fly up from Washington, and Andrew Rosenthal, his number-three person in the newsroom, sat silently, not speaking up for him. I wish you had gotten up and defended me, Raines told Rosenthal afterward. Raines had to battle his contempt as this "dancing mania" swept through the theater. He had spent years covering politics, and he could see his power draining away.

That was brutal, Sulzberger said to Raines as they walked off the stage. We have work to do. Sulzberger called Landman when he got back to the *Times* building and reminded him of their discussion over dinner at Gallaghers Steakhouse.

Well, Sulzberger said, I guess London is off the table.

Sulzberger still believed Raines could lead the newsroom out of this crisis. But that meant making peace with Jill Abramson and Landman. Sulzberger asked Abramson to come up from Washington to meet with

Raines in his private office. The three sat around a table, Abramson scooping up handfuls of M&M's from a jar. Sulzberger told Abramson to tell Raines what she needed from him to make their relationship work. Abramson glanced at Raines. He looked defeated.

I'm done with this Pat Tyler crap, she said, as she recalled the conversation—referring to how she was being undercut by Raines's elevation of Tyler as the putative future Washington bureau chief. What I need to hear from you is that you want me to be your Washington bureau chief. Raines assured her that he did.

The meeting with Landman did not go well. Raines accused Landman of undermining him. Landman pushed back, noting they had worked well together in Washington, and said he was initially enthusiastic when Raines was named executive editor. But, Landman said, his view of Raines had soured over these past twenty months.

If I did undermine you, I was proud to do it, Landman said.

Raines was keeping a journal of these weeks. It showed him realizing the depth of his challenge, but there is little evidence of remorse or an eagerness to change. "Moved too fast," he wrote. "Underestimated envy and threat to status quo."

* * *

It was six-thirty in the morning, eight days after the town hall meeting, when Sulzberger woke up and sent a note to Raines and Boyd. "As I've mentioned to both of you, there will be highs and lows in our journey through this thicket," he said. "After a reasonably sleepless night, I am at a low." Sulzberger was still hoping Raines would survive. And perhaps he would have were it not for Rick Bragg. A complaint from a reader that arrived after the publication of the Blair investigation alerted editors that Bragg had relied almost entirely on the reporting of a freelancer in writing a lively story the previous June about oyster fishermen in Apalachicola, Florida, facing economic ruin. Correspondents at the *Times* often augmented their work with the reporting of freelancers who were paid for their services; it was a longtime practice that permitted them to turn stories around more quickly. But in this case, nearly all the research had been done by a freelancer; Bragg made a quick trip there so he could claim a dateline.

Bragg and Raines had both worked at the *St. Petersburg Times.* They'd had dinners together, and Bragg was a guest at Raines's wedding. Bragg was one of Raines's favorite correspondents: a storyteller with a lush writing style. He was a roving national correspondent, and Raines pressed other desks to use him on big stories. The foreign desk, reluctantly and at Raines's orders, sent him to Pakistan after the attacks of September 11. The sports desk, again at Raines's instruction, sent him to Salt Lake City to cover the Winter Olympics. He wrote the kinds of stories that Raines wanted on the front page. The Bragg revelation led to a new lashing of the newspaper. Once again, as with Patrick Tyler, the staff was in turmoil because of a reporter who enjoyed favored treatment because of his friendship with Raines. Once again, as with Judith Miller, the newspaper was embarrassed because of the actions of a reporter whose career had been promoted by its executive editor. Sulzberger's sleepless night came after he learned Bragg had spoken to *New York* magazine for a story Sulzberger believed would be "focused on 'Howell's Favorites,' in particular, Rick and Pat." Sulzberger did not attempt to hide his exasperation. "I'm baffled as to why he would do such a thing, but that's the least of our problems," he wrote. "I may be overreacting, but I fear that if we don't handle the next few days with speed and wisdom we could be in a very unhappy place." He drafted a conciliatory statement that Raines could give to *New York* and directed the paper's communications director to find out what Bragg had told the magazine's reporter. And he said he wanted Jill Abramson brought into the discussions. "We could really use her on our side right now," he wrote. "We'll be working toward that, and a lot depends on her believing Tyler isn't anymore going to be considered a protected person."

The story Sulzberger feared never appeared, or at least not in the form that he'd envisioned. The next day, Bragg was suspended, and the *Times* appended an editors' note to his story, acknowledging how much of the work had been done by a freelancer. When *The Washington Post* called to ask about his suspension, Bragg was dismissive. "My job was to ride the airplane and sleep in the hotel," he told the *Post.* "Those things are common at the paper. Most national correspondents will tell you they rely on stringers and researchers and interns and clerks and news assistants."

That claim was, at the least, an exaggeration of how much correspondents drew on the work of stringers, and his claims set off a wave of indignation. "I for one am not going to sit by and let those statements go unchecked," Jennifer Steinhauer, the city hall bureau chief and a former clerk who had done legwork for correspondents, wrote in a posting for Romenesko, a website devoted to media news. "I have never, in the time I have been here, heard of a case of another reporter at this paper relying on extensive stringer work for feature stories, major works of enterprise or even daily localized coverage in the manner in which the editors' note on Mr. Bragg's article addressed." Adam Clymer, the longtime national correspondent, pleaded with his colleagues to end their quarrels. "The time has come to stop feeding this destructive monster of reporting. The Times that we are honored to work for will be damaged if we continue to fight with each other in public," he wrote in a memo that was, not surprisingly, leaked.

Raines could not protect Bragg any longer, and Bragg resigned from the paper. Raines and Boyd felt compelled to rebuke Bragg as he left the paper, though not by name. "In the last couple of days, we have all been seeing our great corps of correspondents, especially those on the national staff, depicted unfairly in various news accounts involving the use of stringers and freelancers," they wrote the newsroom. "We don't recognize ourselves or you in that picture."

* * *

Sulzberger was losing faith in Raines and shared his frustration with Steve Rattner, his deskmate from Washington. This isn't going to work, he said. Howell just doesn't get it. Raines went to Sulzberger and said he wanted to make Landman an associate managing editor. People will view that as rearranging the deck chairs on the Titanic, Sulzberger responded. Sulzberger was facing pressure from his family, the board of directors, and company executives to remove Raines. The display of rancor at the town hall meeting convinced Michael Golden, who was Sulzberger's cousin and the vice chairman of the New York Times Company, that Raines would never be able to steer the newsroom out of this predicament. "We crossed Howell off," he said later.

This was not just a crisis at the *Times* but a crisis in American journalism. Old *Times* hands like David Halberstam were registering their alarm over what was transpiring at the newspaper with Sulzberger. "I write as someone who still feels himself, thirty-six years after I left the paper, to be a devoted member of the Times family," Halberstam wrote. "It's probably the worst internal crisis in my memory, made especially serious because the toughest media judges of all—the members of the staff—seem so alienated." The newspaper was being pilloried. "The Blair crisis is an unfortunate gift to those ideologically-driven critics who have unfairly attacked the paper for its war coverage and other issues," Al Hunt wrote in *The Wall Street Journal*. "It's not just the Times, however, that will suffer; these stories hurt the whole business." *The Weekly Standard* compiled a rough calculation of errors by Blair, compared to those of other *Times* correspondents. In an article headlined, "Correctamundo," the magazine said Blair had a 6.9 percent error rate. "That's not so great. But it's not nearly so bad as the factual strikeout average posted, to take one random example, by *Times* Washington-bureau stalwart Adam Clymer over the exact same period: 400 bylines with 36 corrections (9.0 percent). Or how's about *Times* associate editor R.W. 'Johnny' Apple Jr., whose 327 bylines with 46 corrections (14.1 percent spoiled copy) would seem to label him—the numbers don't lie—less than half as reliable a newsman as the hapless youngster Howell Raines is now banishing to Purdah."*

Bill and Hillary Clinton offered Sulzberger their sympathies and urged him to stay strong. "Both of you called me last night, each at a time when I very much needed to hear what you had to say," Sulzberger wrote the Clintons the next day. Raines drew encouragement from another *Times* executive editor. You're behaving very well, A. M. Rosenthal told Raines as he recounted their telephone conversation in his journal. I'd like to put my foot in that staff's butt. Do not resign, do you hear me? Do not resign.

Raines was coming down on the elevator with Boyd after a meeting with the publisher, this one to discuss Bragg.

Where do you think we are? Boyd said, as Raines described the conversation.

---

* This is a very imprecise measure, because corrections can range from a major misstatement of fact to a misspelled name, a typographical error, or a mistake in a picture caption.

Can I tell you what I really think without scaring you? Raines responded. One more bad story and we're done.

But Boyd was already despondent, his dream of someday editing the *Times* slipping away. He began rising at four in the morning, while it was still dark, and heading to the kitchen of his brownstone to brew a pot of coffee and boot up his computer so he could read the latest stories about the breakdown at the *Times*. It was, he would later write, "a form of self-torture, but I was so obsessed that I could not break it." He took Andrew Rosenthal to lunch at the Millennium on Times Square. I wake up every morning and all I can think about is, how can I save my job today? he said. He called Soma Golden Behr at home one evening at ten-thirty. He was convinced that it was only a matter of days until he was fired. Soma, can't you do something? he asked. She didn't know what to say.

Boyd's fears were well-founded. Sulzberger blamed him for many of Raines's problems. The job of the managing editor was to manage, he thought, and that included managing personnel problems before they get to the executive editor. He had started avoiding Boyd in the newsroom, seeking out Raines or Andrew Rosenthal to discuss any concerns. Shortly after the *Times* story about Blair was published, he called Boyd to his office. You have not served Howell well, he told him.

The publisher said the same thing to Raines. One thing we've learned from this already is you need a new managing editor.

In the last days of May, Sulzberger assembled his top editors for lunch in the executive dining room. This would prove to be his final effort to salvage Raines's job. They gathered at a table—Boyd, Raines, Rosenthal, Golden Behr, Al Siegal, Michael Oreskes—as waiters circled, serving lunch. Sulzberger asked them to tell Raines what he needed to do to win back their confidence.

You are a control freak who hates details, said Oreskes. (Raines was not insulted; he considered that a clever observation.) But the session soon degenerated into something of a spectacle: senior editors criticizing the executive editor in front of his subordinates and the publisher. Golden Behr asked why he couldn't just ask his editors to become ambassadors to the newsroom.

The reason is, Soma, I don't trust you, Raines responded. You contribute to the discord rather than fixing it. Raines rose to his feet.

I don't have to listen to this, he said, and headed out the door.

Yes, you do, Sulzberger said, following him out and pulling him back to the table.

Sulzberger would remember that as the moment he gave up on Raines. Later that day, he telephoned Joseph Lelyveld and invited him to dinner. If Howell has to leave, would you be willing to come back as an interim editor to give me time to find a successor? Sulzberger asked. Lelyveld told him he would.

* * *

The skies had not yet begun to darken over the Hudson River when Sulzberger called Raines and asked him to come up to his suite of offices. Raines rode the elevator eleven floors and followed the long hall to Sulzberger's office. It was late on a Wednesday, June 4, 2003, and the executive quarters were mostly empty. The publisher waved him into his office and then walked him down a hallway to his sitting room, in which stood a grandfather clock given to Adolph Ochs by the people of Chattanooga. This was once the publisher's private apartment, with its own elevator, built by Ochs and used by Sulzberger's grandfather, Arthur Hays Sulzberger. Raines thought of the stories of how Sulzberger had used it for assignations with Madeleine Carroll, the British actress with whom he had a long-term affair. He wondered if Arthur Sulzberger knew about that.

This is not going to be easy, Sulzberger said. This has been going on for six weeks, and it's not getting better. We've got to make a change.

Sulzberger reached out and put his hand on Raines's arm. What the *Times* needs now is a leader who can calm the newsroom. That is not your strength, he said. You are an activist. This is not the time for a change agent. Raines did not resist. "I had run enough people off the paper to know that going on about whys and what-ifs is tedious and undignified," he wrote later. Raines told the publisher he was scheduled to have dinner that night with a small group of reporters and editors. Just cancel it, Sulzberger said.

Raines and Krystyna had martinis in the garden of their townhouse when he got home. He felt no anger or resentment or even regrets on how he had handled the crisis—that would come later. Sulzberger telephoned that evening to tell him that Lelyveld would be replacing him as interim editor and asked that he come in the next day to bid farewell to the staff.

Boyd was crushed when Sulzberger called him to his office after Raines had left.

I have never in my life failed at anything, he told Sulzberger. I'm scared.

Boyd asked him if there was any position he might take at the paper, including returning to a job as a reporter, as Sulzberger described the conversation. Sulzberger assured him he would have a future in journalism. But it would not be at the *Times.* He was not going to fire Raines—an editor he admired to the end—and leave in place an editor he blamed in part for Raines's collapse.

At ten-thirty the next morning, Raines and Boyd gathered the staff by the national desk to announce their departures. Gail Collins watched from the side of the room, crying. "There is so much to say, but it really just boils down to this: This is a day that breaks my heart, and I think it breaks the hearts of a lot of people in this room," Sulzberger said. He looked stricken. Raines, clutching a hand-held microphone, and wearing a double-breasted suit with a polka-dot handkerchief poking out of his breast pocket, was crestfallen as he gave a final salute. "And remember, when a big story breaks out, go like hell," he said. Boyd, crushed, embittered, alienated from the man who had brought him so close to the pinnacle of journalism, was not as measured. "Now some of you have heard a lot about our senior newsroom failures, which have been painfully obvious in the last few weeks," Boyd said. "But let me just say one thing to you, as one who sat in on masthead meetings and counseled Howell privately. We passionately and repeatedly tried to bring these issues up." Raines listened at this final rupture in their relationship. Lacking in grace, he thought. He picked up his straw hat, paused to shake hands with his now former colleagues who were lined up to say farewell, and walked out of the building. Raines had backed his Toyota truck into the parking bays on Forty-fourth Street. He assumed reporters would be waiting at his home in Greenwich Village, so he and Krystyna drove straight to Pennsylvania. He spent the rest of the afternoon fishing.

The editorial board weighed in the next day. "The forced introspection The Times has been going through since the Jayson Blair story surfaced will, in the long run, be healthy. A string of rather spectacular successes might have made us too cocky, too sure that the future would simply bring more of the same. Now, we are re-examining some of our internal rules and structures. The recent weeks have not been particularly enjoyable for those of us on the inside, but even in the moments of greatest internal stress the reporters and editors have done their jobs."

The end for Howell Raines unfolded with stunning force over just five weeks, the result of a storm of discontent that became an irrefutable case for his ouster and a refutation of the rapid transformation of the newsroom culture he had promised Sulzberger. Jayson Blair and Judith Miller. The editors and reporters he had demoted, forced to move, belittled at meetings, marginalized, or shunned. The stories that stepped too far and rebounded on the *Times*, shadowing the newsroom with questions about its integrity, accuracy, and mission. When Raines learned the extent of Blair's abuses, he'd thought he had the political capital with Sulzberger to survive, given the seven Pulitzer Prizes, their shared vision and pact to transform the newspaper. Raines had been one of the most perceptive reporters to have walked into the newsroom, the shrewd editor who could see where a story was heading. But he'd missed this one: he did not see the kindling piling up around his feet. He did not understand how much he had alienated the newsroom and how that mattered in a way that would not have been true when he joined the newspaper, when A. M. Rosenthal was the executive editor. He did not anticipate how distressed Sulzberger would become with a newsroom in revolt. Raines would say Sulzberger got rolled by the staff in a way his father never would have, but really, the times were different, and Arthur Sulzberger was a different publisher than his father.

Raines had been intent on shaking things up and pitching things forward. "It's slowly dawning [that] we may never come off this level of performance," Francis X. Clines, his friend in the Washington bureau, wrote him soon after he took over. " '*Why should we*' I already hear you asking. In traveling, I hear everyone's gratitude for the paper in this time, and I tell them that's what we do."

Raines's style and sensibility presaged the digital age with its pace, its voice, its challenge to civility and business as usual. He was right about where the *Times* needed to go. But he was the wrong person to take it there.

PART V

TRANSITIONS

2003–2011

CHAPTER 28

The Cure for What Ailed Us

"So. As I was saying."

A soft patter of applause and laughter trickled across the *New York Times* newsroom. The editors, reporters, and photographers were gathered to hear Joseph Lelyveld on his first day as interim executive editor, looking, with his crooked half smile and crinkled eyes, just a little bit older than the last time he had stood before them, in 2001. With those five words, Lelyveld erased twenty-one months of turmoil and anxiety, or at least that was how it felt to the people gathered to hear him.

It was a personal vindication, really, though he would never put it like that; Lelyveld had watched as Howell Raines, who had walked out of the building for the last time as executive editor the day before, built his editorship as a repudiation of Lelyveld's stewardship. There were people who thought Raines should never have had to leave; that he had given the paper a spark it had not had since the A. M. Rosenthal era. But for at least some in the audience, Lelyveld's return made it seem like the end of a bad dream. Awkward, shy, grouchy, arch, a little intimidating—yes, Lelyveld was all those things. But he had a connection with this staff that Raines, marching in from the editorial page with a mission, had never been able to achieve. "The cure for what has ailed us is called journalism," Lelyveld told the newsroom. "The only way to communicate is to speak up in an atmosphere where outspokenness is sometimes rewarded and never penalized. Wherever you are, whatever you do, take it on faith: you now work in that atmosphere."

Lelyveld was the obvious person for Arthur Sulzberger, Jr., to turn to at this moment, even if he had disregarded Lelyveld's advice on the biggest personnel decision he had made since he became publisher. Sulzberger was chagrined about that, but not too embarrassed to ask Lelyveld to help him now. On his first day back, Lelyveld took his old seat at the table in the Page One conference room and glanced over the list of stories for the next day's newspaper about the turmoil at the *Times*. Enough navelgazing, he thought.

We are devoting too much space to the resignation, Lelyveld proclaimed, and at that moment, everyone in the conference room knew that the era of Howell Raines was over.

Lelyveld's first task was to calm the newsroom, but just as important, he was guiding Sulzberger through the process of choosing a third executive editor. They had agreed on the same short list of candidates, including two former *Times* editors who were now working at other newspapers: Dean Baquet, the managing editor at the *Los Angeles Times*, and Martin Baron, who had been named in July 2001 as executive editor of *The Boston Globe*, which was owned by the *Times*. But there was never really any doubt in Sulzberger's mind, or in Lelyveld's, who would succeed Raines. Lelyveld had wanted Keller to become executive editor when he had retired—a judgment that had been, in his view, affirmed by Raines's performance in the job.

You should know: it's Bill's to lose, Lelyveld told Baquet after he and Sulzberger flew to Los Angeles to meet him at Shutters on the Beach in Santa Monica and discuss the prospect of Baquet returning to New York. (Still, Lelyveld told Baquet, if he was offered the job, he should take it.)

Bill Keller had moved into Abe Rosenthal's old office on the tenth floor, looking over West Forty-third Street, just off the *Times* library, and had settled into a life of writing columns and stories for the Sunday magazine. My happy exile, he called it. After losing his bid to become executive editor, he'd initially told Sulzberger he wanted to be the next editorial page editor. He wrote a three-page pitch with a critical assessment of the page under Howell Raines. "We have good writers, and at times the editorials have soared. It is, as you say, well beyond the days of being 'solid,' " Keller wrote the publisher. "But it is still, too often for my taste, too smug, too predictable, and—too often—boring." Sulzberger turned him down in a response that was two sentences in its entirety, polite but perfunctory. "Thank you for this very thoughtful analysis," he wrote. "It offers up exactly the sort of insights I was seeking to learn about you." And that was that. It was Raines's idea that Sulzberger give him the column, parking him far from the third floor, to write 1,500 words every other Saturday—roughly twice the length of an ordinary column. Keller was happy with that. He would be able to return to work on a long-overdue book on the Soviet Union, which had taken on a new urgency after the publisher, Simon & Schuster, informed him he would have to return his $250,000 advance if he did not deliver the manuscript. And now Sulzberger was telling him that, while there would be a search for Raines's successor as executive editor, he was at the top of the list. I'm not going to drag you along needlessly, Sulzberger promised. After they talked, Keller realized two things: He was indeed the front-runner this time, and he was going to have to begin repaying that book advance.

Keller was about to take command of a newspaper that was different from the one he had hoped to run two years earlier. Its confidence and public image had been battered by Judith Miller, Jayson Blair, and the public spectacle of a newsroom in turmoil. Keller was less flashy, more reserved, and more attuned to the concerns of his reporters and editors than his predecessor. That made him particularly suited for the task he now faced: to move the *Times* beyond this moment and help it find its footing again.

* * *

It was Bastille Day of 2003, just over a month since Raines stepped down, when Keller walked into the newsroom with Sulzberger. He stood in shirtsleeves in front of a microphone, a whisper of a smile on his face. Sulzberger stayed to the side, his head tilted as he applauded. Raines had helped set the stage for this moment the previous Friday with an hour-long public television interview with Charlie Rose. The news of Keller's imminent selection was not a secret, and Raines used his conversation with Rose to recount his struggle to change a newsroom that had "settled into a kind of lethargic culture of complacency." That caught Sulz-

berger's attention. "There's no complacency here," the publisher said as
he introduced Raines's successor. "Never has been, never will be."*

Keller looked across a room of reporters, editors, and photographers
exhausted by the pace since September 11, the internal turmoil of these
past months, and the anxiety that always arises with a change in management. As he spoke, American troops were still in Iraq, but it was becoming clearer by the day that the weapons of mass destruction that the
White House warned of—and that the *Times* had written about credu-
lously on its front page—were not to be found. "Friends, it's time to move
on," he said. "A little introspection is a tonic, but too much of it is poison.
I want you to know, also, that I have no time for grudges. I don't believe
in purges, in guilt by association, in witch hunts. The only loyalty that
counts is your loyalty to this paper."

Keller was not about looking back, and the front-page examination by
reporters of Jayson Blair's years at the *Times* helped him move the newsroom past this episode. The Blair committee, headed by Al Siegal, had
prepared its own accounting of what happened, along with recommendations to make sure it did not happen again. The harder edges of the
Siegal report would be sanded down before it was made public at the end
of the month. "That's because Al had some second thoughts about the
vividly self-critical language and how it would play in public," Jonathan
Landman wrote his colleagues on the committee that prepared the report, referring to Siegal. "He wants to tone a bit of it down." But the disclosures were nonetheless bracing, and the recommendations ambitious.
Chief among them was the appointment of an independent ombudsman, or public editor, to monitor the *Times*'s journalism—a position that
existed in about three dozen other U.S. newspapers. Keller thought it was
a bad idea. Pretty much anyone who had been the executive editor of the
Times thought an ombudsman was a bad idea. "I thought that was my
job," Joe Lelyveld would say later. There were corrections to fix factual
errors, and editors' notes to deal with more nuanced questions of fair-

---

* Raines responded to Sulzberger's response about complacency nearly a year later in
a long essay in the May 2004 issue of *The Atlantic*. "I can guarantee that no one in that
newsroom, including Arthur himself, believed what he said. It was a ritual incantation
meant to confirm the faith of everyone present in the *Times*'s defining myth of effortless
superiority."

ness and tone, all produced in-house rather than delegating an outsider to critique the *Times* on its own pages. But Keller recognized the reality of this post-Blair moment; this was the primary recommendation of the Siegal committee and had the support of the publisher. On his first day as executive editor, he announced the creation of a public editor position. The ombudsman, he said, would "have license to write about issues of our coverage, and to have those independent, uncensored commentaries published in our pages, whenever he or she feels that is warranted."

If Max Frankel had been the not-Abe, Bill Keller would be the not-Howell. "The Blair fiasco—according to the outside participants—was made possible in part by a climate of isolation, intimidation, favoritism, and unrelenting pressure, and we are determined to correct that," Keller wrote the newsroom. He asked Jill Abramson to become one of his two managing editors,* offering her the job over beers and hamburgers while sitting at a bar off Eighth Avenue. The symbolism of tapping one of Raines's biggest antagonists, convincing her to come to New York and putting her in line to run the newspaper, was lost on no one. As the newsroom's third-in-command, Andrew Rosenthal had carried out many of Raines's edicts and had become nearly as polarizing. But it had been just over three years since Sulzberger had forced out Abe Rosenthal as a columnist. He was not about to push out his son.

Don't even think about leaving, Sulzberger told him. We will figure this out.

Rosenthal wanted to remain in the newsroom. That was out of the question, as far as Keller was concerned, and he took Rosenthal to lunch at Orso, a favorite *Times* hangout on West Forty-sixth Street, to tell him he was coming off the masthead.

You've really been busting your ass at this job and you really need a break, Keller said, as Rosenthal recalled the conversation. The two men were at a standstill; Rosenthal had no desire to leave the masthead, with the loss in status and, presumably, salary that would entail. Gail Collins, the editorial page editor, who was looking for someone with foreign policy experience to become her deputy on the editorial page, stepped in and, with Sulzberger's approval, invited Rosenthal to fill the job. It was a

---

* The other was John Geddes, a deputy managing editor.

lifeline; in less than four years, Rosenthal would rise to replace Collins as editorial page editor when she went back to writing a column.

Andrew Rosenthal and Arthur Sulzberger, Jr., would never create the kind of alliance that their fathers had forged in the 1970s. The relationship between these two men—who carried the burdens and scrutiny of being the sons of Abe Rosenthal and Punch Sulzberger—was one of wariness and distance. And with Rosenthal running the editorial page, their quarrels became more frequent and intense, disagreeing, to name two examples, over U.S. policy in Afghanistan and abolishing term limits for the mayor of New York City. "At the end of the day I couldn't disguise the fact that I thought he was a moron," Rosenthal said years later of Sulzberger. Rosenthal would be dismissed by Sulzberger in 2016, as abruptly as he had fired Abe Rosenthal as a columnist in 1999. Rosenthal's replacement would be James Bennet, the editor of *The Atlantic*, who had worked as a reporter for Rosenthal in the Washington bureau.

Raines's departure spelled the end for Patrick Tyler's ambitions of becoming the Washington bureau chief. Keller would eventually push Tyler off the paper entirely. Abramson wanted him out, and Tyler was a polarizing figure in the bureau. Keller never liked him. "The man's a cancer," he wrote Abramson, as he shared a note Tyler had written to Sulzberger listing his complaints about Abramson. A month later, Tyler asked Sulzberger if his situation at the *Times* was irreparable. "My opinion, since you asked, is that it is irreparable," Sulzberger responded. Keller announced Tyler's departure—"it pains me," he told his staff, though of course it did no such thing—at the end of 2004.

The Siegal commission had spared Keller from dealing with the aftermath of Blair and freed the new executive editor—and the newspaper—to move beyond those years. "I'm the foremost beneficiary of this work," Keller told committee members soon after his appointment was announced. "Without the labor and thought you all have donated over the past couple of months, I'd be starting my tenure as executive editor looking backward, doing damage assessment."

* * *

Daniel Okrent did not hesitate when Arthur Sulzberger offered him the job of public editor. He was fifty-five years old, had taken an early retirement with a generous severance from *Time* magazine two years earlier, and was starting work on a book about Prohibition.

You passed the test: You're not a thief and you haven't murdered anyone, Sulzberger said as Okrent came into his office. Okrent would come to realize that this was the publisher's odd sense of humor. Sulzberger went on with a more pointed inquiry: Why would anyone want this job? he said. A perfectly reasonable question, Okrent thought. But this was the *Times*, and he would be the first person to hold the position. He would not have done this at any other newspaper, and he would not have been interested in becoming the second public editor of *The New York Times*.

Okrent would serve an eighteen-month term. He was promised free range on what to write, and his column would appear as often as he wished (once in the job, he settled on every other week) in the Week in Review section. He would be edited for grammar but not for content or *Times* style.*

Okrent had been raised in Detroit and was now settled in the East Coast book-and-magazine firmament. He had been an editor at Alfred A. Knopf and at Harcourt Brace Jovanovich; the managing editor of *Life* and editor of *Time*'s new media operations; the founder of *New England Monthly*; and a columnist for *Esquire*. For all his experience in the literary world, he had spent little time working in a newsroom, apart from a year as a stringer for the *Times*, when he was nineteen years old and living in Ann Arbor, and a brief stint as a copyboy at the *Detroit Free Press*. There, he would watch the weekend news editor study the front page of the *Times* before deciding what would go on the front page of the *Free Press*. Okrent conveyed self-assurance more than arrogance; tempered by an edge of unease and slight insecurity, traits that were about to be tested in his new assignment. He was cosmopolitan; a man of many interests (Okrent was best known as the inventor of Rotisserie League Baseball, a fantasy baseball game) and firm opinions, freely expressed. "Dan doesn't talk, Dan lectures," John Huey, the editorial director of *Time*, told the *Times* about his old colleague. He was a stylish and lucid writer; Keller, who would quarrel with Okrent before very long, came to think that

---

* That was why Okrent never used honorifics in his column, as dictated by the *Times* stylebook.

Okrent was more drawn to turning out a well-crafted turn of phrase than toiling in the fields of press criticism.

From the beginning, Okrent assumed he would not be welcomed at a newspaper "arrogantly convinced of its primacy, historically dismissive of both critics and competitors," as he later wrote. But the institutional resistance to an outside proctor was fiercer than he might ever have imagined; he was directly challenging the *Times*'s view of its own superiority. Arthur Gelb, who was now the director of the *Times* college scholarship program, had a desk in the same small upper-floor suite of offices where Okrent worked. For the eighteen months that Okrent was there, Gelb would not even say hello as they squeezed through the narrow passageway between the desks in the hall outside their office. These old-timers just don't know how to deal with me, Okrent thought. One day, he found himself sharing a table at the monthly meeting of the Century Association, a private New York social club, with Abe Rosenthal, who related with distress the news that his old employer had appointed a retired journalist as an ombudsman.

I'm that person, Okrent said.

Rosenthal fixed his gaze on him. Please be kind to the paper, he said, as Okrent described the moment.

It was not long before Okrent was counting off the remaining days of his tenure as though he were drawing lines on the cement wall of a prison cell, and his first thought when he dropped his weary body into a subway seat at night was the ice-cold martini waiting for him at home. Each morning brought a deluge of complaints, attacks, and defiance from reporters, editors, readers, and media critics. "I have great admiration for you, and have found you a personable and honorable man," Joe Sexton, an editor on the metropolitan desk, wrote him. "But I think I have come to conclude that I am going to invoke my right not to respond directly to you or your inquiries. It's a decision I like to think is based on something approaching principle for me, and not one of convenience or insecurity. I think the creation of the public editor's job was a profound mistake for the paper." Reporters dreaded his calls. They think you're internal affairs, David Carr, the media columnist and an old friend, once told him. Okrent knew how to draw attention with his punchy writing and provocative observations. "Is The New York Times a Liberal Newspaper?" he wrote as the headline for one of his columns. He answered the question in his first paragraph: "Of course it is." It was a fair point: This was a New York City newspaper, so it focused on topics that seemed worthy of examination to its readership (and its reporters and editors), such as same-sex marriage or a provocative museum exhibition. But critics seized on that headline as proof that the newspaper was biased against conservatives. It took Okrent a few days to recognize that his exercise in showy headline writing had empowered the newspaper's enemies. Okrent was becoming, in this insular world of journalism, something of a celebrity—even the subject of a front-page story in *The Wall Street Journal.*

PAPER TRIAL: NEW YORK TIMES FINDS ITS WATCHDOG HAS A STRONG BITE

"PUBLIC EDITOR" DANIEL OKRENT, RECRUITED AFTER SCANDAL, DRAWS IRE OF REPORTERS

TOP ACHIEVEMENT: "SURVIVING"

Al Siegal, who championed the creation of the public editor's position—and who thought, after interviewing him, that Okrent was an ideal candidate for the post—liked what he was seeing. He made that clear after Okrent shared with him a note from an aggrieved reader who had turned to Okrent after getting a brush-off from a senior editor. This is why I invented you, Siegal told the public editor.

CHAPTER 29

The Second Choice

For months after he fired Howell Raines, Arthur Sulzberger, Jr., was glum and withdrawn. The *Times* had become the subject of mockery under his watch, and he had never built the foundation of support and confidence that had carried Punch Sulzberger through difficult stretches. And this was also a personal loss. Raines and Sulzberger had been friends since their time in the Washington bureau. Mourning takes a year, doesn't it? he told Raines over a lunch a few months after the departure.

Sulzberger had had the kind of relationship with Raines that he would not develop with an executive editor for another eleven years. He was approaching the halfway point of what would be twenty-five years as publisher. During his annual performance evaluation with the organization's governing executive committee, a little more than six months after Raines's departure, Sulzberger shared his misgivings, while suggesting he alone was not to blame for the newspaper's difficulties. "The summer of 2003 was full of lessons for all of us," Sulzberger said. "One, and just one, was that I depend on all of you to help me know what I don't know. Whether I should have been or not, I was unaware of the depth of anger and frustration the *Times* newsroom felt toward Howell. I've been called to account for that, which is fair. But I also wish I had received more directly the concerns from senior newsroom leaders than I feel I did." He was acutely conscious of how his missteps reflected on his family, and of his responsibility to keep the Sulzbergers united behind the *Times.* Other family newspapers had been torn apart by internal feuding or the lure of a wealthy outside buyer: the Chandlers in Los Angeles, the Binghams in

Kentucky, the Taylors in Boston. "There's more than a career at stake here for me," he wrote the executive committee. "I'm at the intersection of business and family. It's where I wanted to be so don't take this as a complaint."

Sulzberger confided his distress to Bill Keller at the end of 2003. "This year took a lot out of me, and while I feel those days receding, it will take a while yet to fully recover my emotional sense of balance," he wrote. But Keller, too, was a problem. He had not passed the six-month mark and Sulzberger was reminded why he had not chosen him the first time. Keller made him uncomfortable. He found Keller distant and aloof, and he missed the flair that Raines brought to the job and to their relationship. Keller was quiet and reserved, in a way that Raines was not, and Sulzberger would wonder if his new executive editor was thinking, *This wouldn't have happened if you had put me in charge in the first place.*

Keller was a bright and highly acclaimed correspondent and editor, the son of a wealthy business executive, and he could come across as haughty. He had his friends—Jill Abramson among them—and glided comfortably through literary and social circles in Manhattan and the Hamptons, where he and his wife, Emma, had a home. But he was a man who was comfortable with silence, who would send an email to someone sitting at the next desk, who could seem austere in character. Emma, who read his deficits well, reviewed a stack of anonymous employee evaluations of her husband and summarized what she read in a succinct "they want you to" note: Reply to their telephone calls and emails, be more outgoing, and walk around the newsroom. And Keller had never showed much patience for the rituals of career advancement at the *Times*, in particular the cultivation of superiors, and that would include Sulzberger.

Sulzberger was concerned enough about their relationship that he broached the subject with Keller in the note he sent him at the end of 2003. He praised Keller for how he "embraced the job in all its myriad aspects," as demonstrated by a newspaper that "shows a liveliness and range that matches your own eclectic mind." But the quality of the news report did not outweigh the publisher's concern about the man who was running it. "So what worries me?" Sulzberger wrote. "Well, quite frankly, our relationship. In the beginning it seemed to me to be somewhat tender, perhaps not surprisingly. What's bothered me is that over the last few months it has continued that way."*

"I may be overreacting to your sense of humor or your style with everyone," he said. "That's what I don't know. Is this just Bill Keller or does it belie a discomfort working together?"

Keller was uncomfortable with Sulzberger as well: he was the second choice, and he knew it, and he walked in every day feeling he had to prove himself to the publisher. Keller was taking over at a difficult time. The *Times* was suffering "a crisis of morale and credibility," as Keller put it in an interview the day he stepped down eight years later. It was confronting another financial downturn. Advertising revenues rise and fall with the economy, but there was concern that this wasn't just another turn of the wheel—that advertisers of all sorts, following classified advertisers, were fleeing for the more cost-efficient world of the Internet.

* * *

The answer to Sulzberger's question about the personality of the new executive—"Is this just Bill Keller?"—would become clear in the years to come.

It was Bill Keller, and it had always been Bill Keller. He grew up in an affluent San Francisco suburb, the eldest of three sons of Adelaide and George M. Keller. His father was a leader in the oil industry who would become the chief executive officer of Chevron Oil. Raised in San Mateo, attending local Catholic schools, going to Mass most Sundays (he would give that up with time), Bill Keller was different from his father and two brothers. He was a reader and a writer, with little interest in engineering. Keller delivered the *San Mateo County Times* on a bicycle and worked for the high school newspaper. George Keller, with his view of the world as a series of mathematical problems waiting to be solved, never understood Keller's romance with the written word. Keller's mother was a frustrated writer—Adelaide Keller did not like being viewed as a housewife—and

---

* To explain his concern, Sulzberger reminded Keller of how he had asked him and Gail Collins to stay behind at the end of a lunch with corporate executives. Oh, I thought we'd been dismissed, Keller responded. That, Sulzberger wrote, made him think "you don't see me as a partner in this great enterprise but rather as some overlord who must be acknowledged."

encouraged her son to write. Keller's parents were Republicans, but their son, coming of age in the political and cultural tumult that churned through the nation in the 1960s—and particularly the Bay Area—was not. He marched in demonstrations against the war in Vietnam and knocked on doors for Eugene McCarthy, the liberal senator from Minnesota who ran against Hubert Humphrey for the Democratic nomination for president in 1968. He would later drift from activism—not out of deference to his parents but because he found he was more comfortable as an observer.

As a freshman at Pomona College, he majored at first in chemistry. That lasted a semester; by his second year he had switched to English literature. And when he became a junior, he and his friend Harry Stein, who would also go into a career in journalism, founded the *Spectator*, a renegade alternative to the official Pomona campus newspaper, the *Collegian*, where Keller had worked for his first two years in college. The *Spectator* was very much in the defiant spirit of the era, an early glimpse of the Keller irreverence that would come to bother Sulzberger. One *Spectator* cover contained a single word, drawn in ornate type barely visible in the swirls and psychedelia that were in the fashion of the posters advertising concerts at the Fillmore West, the rock concert hall in San Francisco. "Fuck," it said. School administrators rushed to retrieve all the copies they could find.

The *Spectator* of October 2, 1969, contained an essay by Keller entitled, "All the News That's Shit to Print," in which the writer, who was twenty years old, explained the mission of this countercultural newspaper. "I would like to introduce the *Spectator* in terms of what we're trying to avoid: the tedium of straight journalism and the myopia of narrow journalism." Keller enjoyed the tweak of the *Times*'s motto in the headline, even though he did not actually read the paper. The *Times* was not easy to get in those days on the West Coast, and Keller's taste in newspaper writers at the time ran more to Hunter S. Thompson than James B. Reston.

After graduation, Keller took a job as an intern at *The Oregonian*, which soon hired him as a full-time staff reporter and eventually sent him to the Washington bureau; and that was the end of his years in the West. He arrived at the *Times* in 1984, after working for *Congressional*

Quarterly and the *Dallas Times Herald,* having been hired by Abe Rosenthal. Keller was surprised when, just two years after he arrived, Bill Kovach, the Washington editor, sat on the edge of his desk and asked if he would like to go to Moscow. That set him off on the foreign tour that would take him to the Soviet Union—where he won a Pulitzer—to South Africa, before Joe Lelyveld brought him back to New York and put him on the foreign desk.

* * *

In January 2004, a few weeks after Sulzberger raised his concerns with Keller about their relationship, the newspaper's senior managers and editors assembled at the Tarrytown House Estate in Westchester County for two days of self-examination, panels, and speeches. Keller set the tone for the meeting. "I worry that the combined effect of last summer's blow to our self-esteem and the persistent troubles of the newspaper economy have shaken our confidence," he said. "Throughout our long history, some of our bravest and most successful ventures have begun in periods of economic distress—because we believed deeply in ourselves and our mission. . . . We need that confidence back and we are entitled to it." The attacks of September 11 had jolted the country into a short recession. The *Times* was showing signs of financial distress. Earnings had dropped from a high of nearly $450 million in 2001 to $292.5 million at the end of 2004. The stock price had slipped from $53 a share in June 2002 to $47 a share when Keller spoke at the start of 2004; it would hit $38 by September. The newspaper's economic health was a recurring topic for the Mohonk group, a committee of senior editors and corporate vice presidents assembled by Sulzberger to thrash out the kind of business-editorial intramural squabbles that he did not want to referee.* In the seven months between Howell Raines's dismissal and Keller's speech in Tarrytown, Mohonk became a window into the anxiety at the highest levels of the paper. "Deep concerns, candidly expressed, off the record," read the heading on item three of the Mohonk minutes of January 20, 2004. "It's impossible to overstate the urgency of the present

---

* Mohonk, as it was called, was named for the Mohonk Mountain House resort near Sulzberger's home in New Paltz where it first met.

moment," the notes of the session reported. "Over the years we have successfully preached that our business success, our brand's power, flows directly from the quality of our news product. We've made that case. Last year that was thrown into question, not just by the Jayson Blair episode but also by reader perceptions of bias on various reporting fronts."

None of this should be much of a surprise after these past six months, Al Siegal said at another Mohonk Committee meeting. "When Letterman and Leno are still saying 'I read it in the NYT but it might be true anyway,' that has to have an effect." The subtext was that the scandals of the newsroom were fueling the financial decline at the *Times*. The tensions between the newsroom and the business side played out again before a larger audience at that January retreat in Tarrytown. "Over the years the business side has become quite adept at self-funding: when we've had something new we wanted to do, we've found the money for it internally or made trade-offs," said Liam Carlos, the chief financial officer. Keller bristled at the suggestion that the newsroom had not carried its weight in cutting costs and that it was not appreciative of what the business division had done.

"Do you really believe we don't do that in the newsroom all the time?" he fired back. "We created a Baghdad bureau by closing the Bangkok bureau. . . . We have a long history of self-funding, in the face of this impression that the newsroom always has its hand out for more."

A few weeks later, Adam Moss, a young magazine editor recruited by Lelyveld, and whom Keller had appointed as the newspaper's first assistant managing editor for features, announced he was leaving to run *New York* magazine. Moss had been the founding editor of *7 Days*, a magazine that covered New York politics, art, and culture, when Lelyveld hired him as the "agent of his mischief-making side," as Moss liked to put it. He would edit the *Times Magazine*, and eventually oversee the newspaper's culture and style pages. He was not cut in the mold of the classic *Times* editor; he was boyish, stylish, and gay, if discreetly at the time.

Moss, fresh out of Oberlin College in 1979, had smoked marijuana before coming in for his interview with Sydney Gruson, who hired him as a copyboy. In his return run at the paper as a Lelyveld recruit, he had been scolded for running a pictorial display in the *Magazine*'s style pages that portrayed a Japanese form of consensual sexual bondage.

He thought the photos of models tied up were provocative and legitimately newsworthy, a window into a subculture in Japan. The resulting furor led to an editors' note. "The starkness of some of the pictures, in the absence of a compelling news context, conflicts with the desired tone of the *Times*; they should not have been published," the note said. Sulzberger summoned Moss to his office. You shouldn't have published those pictures, he said. But keep at it. Moss understood the message; Sulzberger liked that he was pushing the newspaper into unfamiliar corners.

Masthead editors, generally speaking, did not leave the paper for the competition, and Scott Heekin-Canedy, a senior vice president, confided to his colleagues at one Mohonk session that he worried that Moss's exit could be perceived by outsiders as a lack of confidence in the future of the *Times*. Moss knew how to edit a high-quality magazine, and how to appeal to upscale advertisers and a new generation of readers. He also knew what reporters and editors were paid at the *Times*, which would make it easier for him to poach talent.

"Now Adam's out to eat our lunch," read one entry in the Mohonk minutes.

All of this weighed on Sulzberger. Usually a bundle of swagger and exaggerated self-confidence, his distress and worry showed on his face. Sulzberger did not like open displays of conflict, particularly between the business and news sides of the organization. Normally, the president and chief executive officer of the Times Company—Janet Robinson moved into the job in late 2004—was responsible for revenues and growth, while the executive editor oversaw the newspaper. Now Sulzberger, who was the publisher and also the chairman of the company, found himself squarely at the center, trying to mediate disputes between these two camps. At one meeting in Tarrytown in which editors and business executives participated, Jonathan Landman, whom Keller had appointed as an assistant managing editor, questioned a proposal that the business side inform editors when the *Times* was facing a financial downturn. Landman thought it was a bad idea. "We don't want department heads pulling their punches because they've heard about some terrible thing on the business side." Sulzberger did not see how the *Times* could manage business downturns if his editors and corporate executives were not collaborating. "Doesn't that amount to infantilizing your department heads?" Sulzberger retorted.

* * *

Sulzberger was invested in Keller succeeding, and Keller admired his commitment to the *Times.* And as the newspaper approached the one-year anniversary of Raines's departure, it appeared that the passage of time—and the daily demands of running a newspaper—were easing the strains that had undercut their relationship. But that was about to get knocked off the tracks.

Sulzberger was at his weekend home in New Paltz when he saw a 20,900-word essay Raines had written for the May 2004 issue of *The Atlantic,* promoted as "a no-holds-barred assessment of what he sees as a great newspaper in crisis." He felt violated. It was filled with details of private conversations and critical observations about the publisher and his top editors. Raines recounted how he told Sulzberger, as they talked about why he should be executive editor, that the newspaper under Lelyveld, with Keller as his managing editor, was boring. He described the *Times* as "not nearly as good as it could be and ought to be," and said that his mission was "getting the *Times* off its glide path toward irrelevance." Raines recounted the conversation when Sulzberger offered him the job. "Since I thought the paper was becoming duller, slower, and more uneven in quality with every passing day, I suggested that the transition happen sooner. Arthur laughed and said I had no idea how hard it had been to get Joe to fix a retirement date at all."

Raines's history with the Sulzberger family made his assessment of Arthur Sulzberger that much more stinging. "I had not realized how rattled he was, and frankly I don't think I worked hard enough to stiffen his spine for the survival battle we could have won." Arthur Ochs Sulzberger, Sr., would have not buckled the way his son had, Raines wrote. "Punch in his prime would never have thrown over one of his executive editors under the pressure of employees who didn't like the editor personally or who disagreed with a legitimate strategy for reinvigorating the *Times*'s journalism."

Sulzberger sent a note to Lelyveld after reading the Raines story. "I very much regret that I've been seen as an accomplice in some dastardly plot by Howell," he said. "I think the world of your leadership of our newsroom—or would not have asked for you to return. It was your newsroom that gave us the journalism of 9/11. We both know that." Lelyveld was not placated. "The paper was not broken; it was not getting worse every day; on the contrary, it had probably never been better," he responded. "But you bought that platform because it seemed to promise a new burst of vigor, even though at various levels, you had plenty of reason for skepticism."

"I know you liked me and supported me and were proud of the paper we produced," Lelyveld said. "I'll always be grateful for that. You then chose a guy who had a psychic need to despise most things we did and anyone who got too close to me. In his view, I wasn't good enough for the *Times:* he was too good."

Lelyveld and Sulzberger were on firm ground in pushing back on Raines's depiction of the newsroom he inherited. The lack of spark that Raines noted is common in the waning days of any editorship. But even during his final years, Lelyveld's *Times* was admired: the coverage of the attacks of September 11, which drew Raines praise and Pulitzers, was produced by a team that had been assembled by Lelyveld. Keller, too, was shaken by what he read. He kept imagining Raines with a glass of bourbon and Sulzberger with a martini, cackling upstairs about what a failure he and Lelyveld had been. Sulzberger assured him this was not the case.

Ninety percent of this is bullshit, Sulzberger said. I want you to know that I am cutting off any relationship I had with Howell.

But Raines's piece would put a chill over the relationship between the publisher and Keller that would last for much of the next eight years.

* * *

Judith Miller had returned to Iraq in the spring of 2003, the final weeks of Raines's tenure, as a journalistic embed observing the U.S. military team MET Alpha (for Mobile Exploitation Team) while it searched for the weapons of mass destruction she and Michael Gordon had written about in the lead-up to the war.* Nothing was found. While in Iraq, she had run up against Patrick Tyler, who Raines had made the Baghdad bureau chief during the war. Turf battles were nothing new at the *Times*, but few matched the tenor of the one that erupted after Tyler learned Miller was working on a story about Ahmed Chalabi, the Iraqi dissident. "i will not work in a situation where I have a major correspondent of the paper working outside the bureau assiduously trying to cover the major political figure in iraq today," he wrote her in a seemingly dashed-off email. "if I am not in charge of the political story in iraq. i will not take this assignment. i don't give a damn about coordination and you demonstrated right off the bat that you did not either. we have been in communication for two weeks about your stray clothes, medical supplies and hair coloring sticks and yet you withheld that you were negotiating with chalabi."

Miller had had a similar face-off a little more than a week earlier with Tyler's predecessor, John Burns, on the eve of his departure. Again, it was over Chalabi. "I am deeply chagrined at your reporting and filing on Chalabi after I had told you on Monday night that we were planning a major piece on him—and without so much as telling me what you were doing," Burns wrote her. In a demonstration of how much she was disliked by many of her colleagues—viewed as untrustworthy, protected by Raines and Boyd, and producing stories that were discrediting the newspaper—copies of the Burns-Miller emails, including one in which she described Chalabi as the source for some of her front-page stories in the *Times*, showed up in *The Washington Post* after being circulated around the Washington bureau.

When Lelyveld stepped in as acting executive editor that June, he took Abramson, the future managing editor, to dinner at Ouest, an upscale restaurant on the Upper West Side. He was distressed about the newspaper's coverage of Iraq and the spectacle of the feuding in Washington.

I'm only going to be here a fairly short time, but I need you to do some-

---

* Roger Cohen, the foreign editor, agreed under duress to let Miller return to Baghdad to accompany troops on inspection missions but sent instructions on what she could do—and what she could not do—that read almost like a court order. He sent a copy of the same note up the ladder.

thing for me, he said. You can't have Judy Miller do anything embarrassing on my watch.

Lelyveld was not the only one concerned. Later that summer, Abramson went with Sulzberger to a conference of the Asian American Journalists Association in San Diego. The publisher invited Abramson to join him for a stroll outside the convention hotel.

Do you think we have a Judy Miller problem here? Sulzberger asked.

Abramson returned to New York, where she and Keller discussed what to do about Miller. Keller did not think the newsroom could endure another round of self-criticism so soon after Jayson Blair. Abramson agreed.* But Keller gave Miller specific instructions on what she could cover in her job. Do not write about Iraq or WMD, he said.

Keller and Abramson had hoped that pushing Miller off the stage of national security would allow them to move forward. But with the beginning of 2004, it was clear the criticism was not abating. Jack Shafer, the media columnist at *Slate*, repeatedly questioned why the *Times* would not correct the flaws in Miller's reporting. In February 2004, Michael Massing, a former executive editor of the *Columbia Journalism Review*, published a 7,900-word essay in *The New York Review of Books* entitled "Now They Tell Us." He noted how newspapers were finally documenting the failures of intelligence by the Bush Administration that led the nation into war. "Watching and reading all this, one is tempted to ask, where were you all before the war?" Massing wrote. "Why didn't we learn more about these deceptions and concealments in the months when the administration was pressing its case for regime change—when, in short, it might have made a difference?" Miller, he wrote, had relied too heavily on Ahmed Chalabi and other sources eager to draw the United States into the conflict, and ignored credible arguments of rebuttal that had been published by other news organizations. Miller told Massing she had reported what she had learned from credible sources. "The fact that the United States so far hasn't found WMD in Iraq is deeply disturbing," she told him. "It raises real questions

---

* It was a decision that both Keller and Abramson would later come to describe as a mistake. "In retrospect," Abramson said in an interview in 2018, describing her counsel to Keller not to immediately confront the questions about Miller, "I served him badly."

about how good our intelligence was. To beat up on the messenger is to miss the point."

From his first days as the public editor, Daniel Okrent had thought the questions being raised by Massing and other critics about Judith Miller and the paper's Iraq coverage needed to be addressed by Keller and Abramson. Okrent did not believe he should embark on this new assignment by looking backward at the history of flawed *Times* coverage. Otherwise, he would say, why shouldn't he also examine the *Times*'s meager coverage of the Holocaust, or Walter Duranty's credulous stories about the Soviet Union that won him a Pulitzer Prize in 1932? But Okrent soon realized the questions about the *Times*'s coverage of Iraq were not going away; it was a major lapse, he told Abramson over lunch, and it would be a dereliction to have this job and not address these criticisms. He stopped by Keller's office to inform him he was devoting the next three weeks to reviewing the newspaper's Iraq coverage.

Keller decided that the newsroom needed to publicly address the criticisms of Judith Miller and the Iraq stories before Okrent published his findings. He turned to Abramson and asked her to review the coverage to determine if the *Times* needed to write a corrective story or an editors' note. Many of the stories leading up to the war were written while Miller had a desk in the Washington bureau, across the room from Abramson, who was the bureau chief. But Keller never saw any conflict in putting Abramson in charge of the investigation. He had heard her talk about the campaign by Raines and Patrick Tyler to unseat her. He had not a moment's doubt about her account of how Raines had commandeered the coverage of Iraq and promoted Miller's stories; he believed her when she said she barely touched the coverage. Keller had grown close to his managing editor, and that would be reflected in years of warm employee evaluations. And Abramson understood the culture of the Washington bureau and the culture of the *Times*, the thrill of the front page, the pressure to break exclusive stories, the competitiveness that fueled the newsroom and motivated Miller, in Keller's view. Keller could not think of anyone else he would have trusted to unravel this. "Jill didn't decide to lead the paper with those WMD stories," he would say later.

For three days, Abramson printed out dozens of stories—from the *Times* and also, for comparison, *The Washington Post*, and separated them in piles around the floors of her office and her apartment. She divided the stories by subject and filed them in manila folders, scrawling her critiques on the front of each one. "The tubes," she wrote, circling the words, on the folder containing the September 2003 story about the aluminum tubes, and noted the byline: Gordon and Miller. "Terrible story," she wrote. "Too much of story based on unverified info from defectors." The sentence in that story about the warning from anonymous "hard-liners"—"The first sign of a 'smoking gun,' they argue, may be a mushroom cloud"—should never have appeared in print. "Any editor should have cut out this hyperbole," she wrote. Then there was a story on April 21, 2003, when Miller was traveling with the military intelligence unit hunting for evidence of weapons of mass destruction. Miller reported that an unidentified scientist informed the team that Iraq had destroyed chemical weapons and biological warfare equipment days before the war began. The scientist had buried some of the material; Miller, after saying she had been barred from identifying or interviewing the scientist, described how she was allowed to watch him from a distance. "Clad in nondescript clothes and a baseball cap, he pointed to several spots in the sand where he said chemical precursors and other weapons materials were buried." Andrew Rosenthal had edited that story and added some of the details about the restrictions put on Miller to make her account more transparent. "We got mocked for those caveats when that was actually good journalism," he would say later. Mocked, indeed; Abramson ridiculed the story as one of the most embarrassing examples of the paper's flawed coverage. *"Eureka we've found it,"* she wrote. "Completely unacceptable. No independent confirmation. Should not have been published."

The newspaper needed to acknowledge its mistakes with an editors' note, Abramson said as she presented her findings. Keller would draft it, and he and Abramson called in Miller to inform her of the decision. Miller spent hours in Keller's office trying to dissuade the paper's senior editors, warning of the repercussions if they went ahead with such a repudiation of the newspaper's reporting.

If you run this, you had better prepare a second editors' note to correct the errors, omissions, and unsupported innuendo in this version,

Miller said, as she later recounted the conversation. And you'll have to explain why I'll be denouncing my own paper on CNN.

Keller was not swayed; shoulders hunched as he leaned over his computer, he kept writing and rewriting the note that he was determined to publish before Okrent's column. The note appeared on May 26, 2004, ten months after Keller took over as executive editor, and it was striking. This was not like the editors' notes that addressed the articles about Wen Ho Lee, or the one that detailed the fabrications and plagiarism by Jayson Blair. This was an acknowledgment of a systematic failure in the coverage of a major story in what was one of the most rigorously edited newspapers in the world. "From the Editors: The Times and Iraq," tucked inside the newspaper on page A10, tipped a hat to the newspaper's stories about the failures of American intelligence, as it set the stage for self-examination.

"We have studied the allegations of official gullibility and hype. It is past time we turned the same light on ourselves." The coverage "was not as rigorous as it should have been," presenting readers with information that was "insufficiently qualified or allowed to stand unchallenged" and relied on "informants, defectors and exiles bent on 'regime change' in Iraq." It singled out Chalabi.

"Administration officials now acknowledge that they sometimes fell for misinformation from these exile sources. So did many news organizations—in particular, this one," the newspaper told its readers. "Looking back, we wish we had been more aggressive in re-examining the claims as new evidence emerged—or failed to emerge." There was no mention of Judith Miller or Patrick Tyler—or, for that matter, Howell Raines, Gerald Boyd, Andrew Rosenthal, or Jill Abramson. But Keller made clear who he thought was at fault. "Editors at several levels who should have been challenging reporters and pressing for more skepticism were perhaps too intent on rushing scoops into the papers." The note was equivocal on some points and defensive about others; it ended by pledging to "continue aggressive reporting aimed at setting the record straight." Yet, for all that, it was an exercise in self-criticism—portraying the *Times* as a newspaper that had allowed itself to be duped. "It is still possible that chemical or biological weapons will be unearthed in Iraq, but in this case it looks as if we, along with the administration, were taken in," it said.

Raines responded on the website of the Poynter Institute. "Somewhat to my surprise, I was not contacted by anyone at the *Times* prior to today's commentary," he wrote. "Had I been I would have repeated my concern that editors' notes do not give readers the facts, analysis and context they need about disputed stories. I found this editors' note as vague and incomplete as some that have preceded it." He disputed the central finding in an interview with the media columnist for the *Los Angeles Times* and said the blame for Miller lay with Abramson, as the Washington bureau chief. "My feeling is that no editor did this kind of reckless rushing while I was executive editor," he said. "I can tell you positively that in 25 years on the Times and in 21 months as executive editor, I never put anything into the paper before I thought it was ready."

When Okrent went to Washington to begin working on his Iraq column, so many of Miller's colleagues were eager to talk that he felt, as he put it years later, like a psychiatrist stacked up with hourly patients. He was struck by the animus. But Okrent found Miller a sympathetic figure when they spoke later that week at a café on Broadway and Eighty-fifth Street; her eyes moistened with tears as she talked about meeting with Iraqi families who were fearful of Saddam. And in the end, he decided, this was an editors' newspaper, and the editors were responsible for what appeared on its pages. "The failure was not individual, but institutional," Okrent wrote in his column, published four days after the editors' note. Raines had asserted that standard editorial safeguards had not been bypassed in the interest of scoops. "But my own reporting (I have spoken to nearly two dozen current and former Times staff members whose work touched on W.M.D. [weapons of mass destruction] coverage) has convinced me that a dysfunctional system enabled some reporters operating out of Washington and Baghdad to work outside the lines of customary bureau management," he wrote. "In some instances, reporters who raised substantive questions about certain stories were not heeded. Worse, some with substantial knowledge of the subject at hand seem not to have been given the chance to express reservations."

Keller and Abramson decided that, even after the editors' note and Okrent's column, questions about the government's campaign to take the nation to war, and the media's credulous coverage (in some quarters) of claims by the White House, remained unresolved. They assigned three reporters—David Barstow, William J. Broad, and Jeff Gerth—to explore the mistakes made by the government and the media, including the *Times*. Their story would take nearly six months to complete and would appear under the headline "How White House Embraced Suspect Iraq Arms Intelligence." Miller would not be part of this project. Keller called her in to tell her she would no longer be writing about national security. People are now suspicious of your reporting, Keller told her. "I came close to rage in his office that day," Miller later wrote. She threatened to leave the *Times*. "It was, without a doubt, the ugliest meeting I have ever had with any senior editors at this paper," she wrote in her notebook.

Years later, Sulzberger would say that the Jayson Blair episode did more damage to the *Times* and its reputation than anything else that took place while he was publisher. "It went to the very core of what we stand for." But it's hard to separate Blair and Miller. They overlapped and amplified each other; they harmed the newspaper in different ways and with different audiences. Blair might have been a fluke, a man struggling with mental illness and addiction; as Bill Schmidt would say, how do you guard against someone making stuff up? But Iraq was a more conventional failure of reporting and editing, albeit on a much grander scale, with bigger stakes and more colorful characters: a credulous reporter, encouraged by editors hungry for flash and exclusivity, who repeatedly promoted her work on the front page.

The damage from these two reporters was cumulative. By the time it was over, it was clear, if there was ever doubt, that the *Times* was a newspaper run by talented but often imperfect men and women who were coming under unaccustomed scrutiny in this new era. The newspaper was now shadowed by skepticism and at times scorn, in a way that emboldened even loyal readers who were unhappy with a story. "For a newspaper who has been working steadfastly to repair their reputation for false stories, I was surprised to see the Sunday Style's 11 July 2004 cover piece," Monica Lewinsky wrote Sulzberger about a Sunday Styles story that said she had fled from a Manhattan restaurant upon learning Chelsea Clinton was having a drink upstairs. "Aside from the spelling of my name, the only morsel of truth was that we all did dine at the same restaurant the same evening." The chastening of the *Times* emboldened the conservative establishment that had already been trying to dislodge the newspaper from its perch of influence. But it also shook its readers on the left. Abramson saw this when she went to Boston to attend the 2004 Democratic convention and sat down for an interview with Samantha Bee, a correspondent for *The Daily Show with Jon Stewart*. This was the year the Democratic Party nominated John Kerry to run for president against George W. Bush, and it was the convention that would be remembered for the keynote speech delivered by a young state senator and candidate for the U.S. Senate from Illinois, Barack Obama. But that was not what Abramson found herself talking about as she settled in for her moment on Comedy Central.

How does it feel to be the managing editor of the paper that makes things up? Bee asked.

CHAPTER 30

In the National Interest

ight days before Election Day in 2004, the *Times* reported that 380 tons of powerful explosives had disappeared from Al Qa'qaa, an Iraqi depot thirty miles outside of Baghdad that had been intermittently under American military control. The *Times* account came under attack from the White House and conservatives, challenging its accuracy—and its timing, since it was published in the final days of a presidential campaign. John Kerry, the Democrat seeking to unseat President George W. Bush, seized on the report to assail Bush's management of the war in Iraq. Bill Keller had expected the story would draw fire. But fifteen months into his editorship, he had not realized how intense the condemnation would become. "What we did not anticipate was the extent to which the explosives story would generate a firestorm of hostility towards the *New York Times*," Keller told the newspaper's board of directors at its private year-end meeting in December.

He and his managing editor, Jill Abramson, who had also been invited to speak to the board, had been barraged with emails and telephone messages. Conservatives were pushing an "alternative version of events," as Keller put it: that the munitions had actually disappeared before the war. Even in the face of more reporting by the *Times* and other news organizations substantiating the story, "the Internet jungle drums continued to beat out their version." The "smear of our journalism," Keller said, continued well beyond the election. "This whole episode was sobering and depressing," he told the board. "When the *Times* publishes a story of this magnitude, why are so many people prepared to believe not only that it is untrue, but that it is motivated by a political agenda?" Abramson offered one answer to that question. "The Jayson Blair scandal was a deep stain," she told the board. "Our apologies for overly credulous pre-war stories was the right thing to do but it confirmed criticisms of our thoroughness and sourcing." It was broader than that. The polarization that shaped and distorted the country's politics was now entangling its media. The Internet was creating an information free-for-all, with platforms for bloggers to attack the reporting of mainstream newspapers and seize on high-profile targets, including reporters. *The New York Times* was under a political and public microscope, and a response that had once been sufficient no longer worked. "The idea that we should let our journalism speak for itself is alluring—and much of the time it is absolutely right," Keller told his staff. "But it's just impractical to think that if we ignore our critics all the time they will go away. Unanswered criticism does not go away in the age of the Internet."

It had been a difficult year. The *Times* was buffeted by challenges to its credibility and stature, while under the command of a reserved executive editor and a publisher who were weakened by the upheaval in the newsroom. It was being assailed by the right for exposing national security practices, and by the left for failing to hold to account an administration that had taken the nation to war on false pretenses. And in the midst of preparing the munitions story, Keller, under pressure from the White House and after a rancorous internal debate involving reporters and editors, had decided against printing yet another sensitive national security story—this one disclosing a potentially illegal domestic surveillance operation by the National Security Agency tracking millions of telephone calls and emails by American citizens.

* * *

In the fall of 2004, as the *Times* was preparing to publish the Al Qa'qaa story, two Washington reporters—James Risen, who covered the CIA, and Eric Lichtblau, who covered the Justice Department—flew to New York to press editors to publish their account of how Bush had authorized the National Security Agency to spy on Americans without seeking approval from the Foreign Intelligence Surveillance Court. It was a tense meeting, as Risen and Lichtblau urged Keller, Abramson, and Phil Taubman, the Washington bureau chief, to print their findings. Keller was skeptical. Jane Harman, the ranking Democrat on the House Intelligence Committee, who had been briefed on the surveillance program, had spoken to Taubman and urged the *Times* not to disclose the operation, warning it could endanger national security. And Keller and Abramson were not convinced that Risen and Lichtblau had demonstrated that the surveillance program was illegal—a hurdle they said the reporters needed to clear if the *Times* was going to print a story that the White House warned could undermine national security. That was, in the view of Risen and Lichtblau, an unrealistic bar—one that would preclude the publication of most investigative stories.

In the course of their discussions, Risen said his source had threatened to take the story to another publication if the *Times* did not move before Election Day. Keller stiffened; he said he thought a threat like that spoke to a political motivation of the Risen source, and he would not let the *Times* be used by a partisan seeking to influence the outcome of the election.

That surely was one reason why Keller killed the story at the time. But sources often have their own agendas in trying to push a story; editors routinely take that into account in deciding whether an article should be printed. In this case, the government was also warning Keller that the *Times* was putting the nation at risk if it disclosed this surveillance operation. The argument would seem flimsier in the year to come, but it carried some weight in the fall of 2004. Keller, too, had memories of living in New York City on September 11, how that morning—his first day as a columnist—he and Emma retrieved their children from school and brought them to the safety of their Upper West Side apartment. Now Bush and his aides were invoking the threat of terrorist attacks on the stage of the presidential campaign. "Three years after 9/11, we, as a country, were still under the influence of that trauma, and we, as a newspaper, were not immune," Keller told the paper's public editor, Margaret Sullivan, when she revisited the episode in 2013.

The relationship between an editor and a reporter is an exercise in power, leverage, and manipulation. Editors decide whether the story will run, how much space it will get, and whether it will be put on the front page. Reporters have control of the facts and the sources, and the ability, for example, to warn editors that a competing newspaper is about to publish a similar story. This relationship can be particularly fraught when it comes to investigative reporters, who are wary by nature, be it with sources or editors. Those dynamics infected the negotiations over the surveillance story. Keller was, by his account, suspicious of Risen; he had been one of the reporters involved in the Wen Ho Lee coverage, and Keller would later talk about him as a top-notch reporter who nonetheless could seem "an advocate of his sources beyond just the advocate of the information."

The meeting in New York marked the beginning of thirteen months of debate at the newspaper about the conflicting demands of exposing government malfeasance and safeguarding national security, and occasional discussions with a White House anxious to block the story's publication. Lichtblau and Risen renewed their reporting after Election Day, seeking to address the concerns Keller and Abramson had raised about the legality of the program. The White House turned to Taubman, the Washington bureau chief, as it sought to convince the newspaper not to publish a story. He had written extensively on national security over the years, and his opinions carried weight with Keller; they had worked together in the Moscow bureau. Taubman knew Michael V. Hayden, the director of the National Security Agency, and Condoleezza Rice, who was Bush's national security advisor and later secretary of state. Hayden clashed from the beginning with Risen and preferred to deal with Taubman, who, Hayden wrote later, "had spent a lifetime balancing the needs of transparency and security, so from our point of view, we could hardly have had a better interlocutor." Hayden took the extraordinary step of inviting the Washington bureau chief to the NSA headquarters in Fort Meade, Maryland, for a top-secret briefing on the surveillance operation.

I'm going to read you into the program today, Hayden told Taubman as he opened the door to this secret world. Taubman had spent enough time covering espionage to recognize the provenance of that kind of jargon and presumed (correctly) this could only have happened with the personal approval of the president himself.

Do you realize you've gone where no one in your profession has gone before? Hayden told Taubman as he rose to leave.

Yeah, and I expect to get bumped off in the parking lot, Taubman responded.

Hayden's willingness to lift the curtain on the operational details of a top-secret surveillance program convinced Taubman it must be critical to the nation's security, an assessment that Keller came to share. Risen and Lichtblau thought Taubman was naïve, a credulous mark for an agency that was expert at manipulating people. His willingness to accept Hayden's invitation deepened the wedge between him and his reporters—particularly as he declined, in keeping with the ground rules of his briefing, to share much of what he had learned with them. "When I returned to the bureau, I recall that Eric and you, not surprisingly, were eager to hear about the meeting," Taubman wrote Risen in an email. "I described my visit in general, but said I had agreed not to tell anyone about the technical details I had learned, but would employ my knowledge by telling you if I saw anything in your draft story that I thought was incorrect." Before long, Risen and Lichtblau would close the door when they discussed the story with their editor, Rebecca Corbett, whose office was next to Taubman's, because they didn't want him to overhear what they were talking about. By the end of 2004, Risen, angry and discouraged, took a leave of absence to write a book about George Tenet and the CIA. When he returned to the bureau the following May, Risen had made a crucial decision: his book would include the account of the secret surveillance program that the *Times* had refused to publish.

Risen's decision to reveal the surveillance program in his book stunned his editors and ultimately pushed them to act. Taubman called Risen to his office, enraged that Risen would take a story he had researched on the newspaper's time—and one that had been rejected by the newspaper—for use in a book.

If you publish it, that is an act of insubordination, Taubman told him. Abramson warned Keller that the newspaper and its editors would look hapless if they were beat on a major story by one of their own reporters. She thought that the story had benefited from the additional reporting and was ready to be published. In the first week of December 2005, as the *Times* moved toward running the story, the administration played its strongest card. Sulzberger, Keller, and Taubman were asked to come to the White House to meet with the president and his national security advisers in the Oval Office. Sulzberger, as a reporter in the Washington bureau, had covered George H. W. Bush when he was a candidate for vice president in 1980, and he had met his son George W. Bush in the course of the campaign. But Bush showed no signs of remembering the publisher as he settled into the wingback chair next to him. Sulzberger began with a joke about the dynastic paths the two men had followed to power. I know what it's like to sit in your father's office, he said. Bush stared through him. The meeting was somber. Bush said publishing this story would imperil American intelligence gathering and invite a deadly attack on an American city. If there's another 9/11 and we're called before Congress, the president said, you should be sitting right behind us. As the *Times* delegation walked out on to the White House driveway, Sulzberger, Keller, and Taubman paused to assess what had just happened. I didn't hear anything that would change my mind, Keller said.

The exposé that Keller had refused to publish before the presidential election of 2004 finally appeared on December 16, 2005. "Bush Lets U.S. Spy on Callers Without Courts," read the headline on the top left corner of the front page. Keller would say the extra year of reporting gave him the assurance that the program was of dubious legality, and that the White House's warnings about national security no longer carried the force they once had.

You have to concede that the administration's credibility on matters of national security had eroded somewhat between 2004 and 2005, Keller told Hayden in one of their negotiating sessions.

But for all that, the story also ended up on the front page of the *Times* because Risen made clear he would be publishing it in a book. Perhaps the *Times* would eventually have been convinced on the merits that the story deserved publication, but Risen had forced its hand. There was no substantial new reporting, and Keller continued to have his apprehensions about Risen. This was a matter of optics, and how it would look for the paper and its editors if this compelling story appeared in a book because they had blocked it from being published in the *Times*.

The day after the story ran, the Senate, its members distressed to learn that this program had been secretly churning along even while the White House sought legislative authorization for expanded surveillance, refused to renew the Patriot Act. "I went to bed undecided," Senator Charles Schumer of New York said on the Senate floor. "But today's revelation that the government has listened in on thousands of phone conversations is shocking and has greatly influenced my vote."

The *Times* was again attacked by the Bush White House and conservatives for publishing a story that could undermine national security. And it was assailed by the left for being too accommodating and making a decision that might have assisted Bush's reelection to the White House. The final version of the story recounted how the *Times* had initially agreed to a White House request not to publish the article, on the grounds that it could jeopardize ongoing terrorism investigations. Is he insane? Risen had asked his editor when he heard Keller wanted to include the behind-the-scenes detail to delay publication. But Keller insisted. "Whatever its path to publication, Mr. Sulzberger and Mr. Keller deserve credit for its eventual appearance in the face of strong White House pressure to kill it," wrote Byron Calame, who was now the newspaper's public editor. "And the basic accuracy of the account of the eavesdropping stands unchallenged—a testament to the talent in the trenches. But the explanation of the timing and editing of the front-page article by James Risen and Eric Lichtblau caused major concern for scores of *Times* readers." He called the newspaper's explanation for delaying the story "woefully inadequate."

No matter how it got there—under duress, out of fear of embarrassment, by its merits, or just through the passage of time—the *Times* had published an article it had declined to publish a year earlier. A corner had been turned. But the accumulated damage of these past few years—Raines, Boyd, Blair, Miller, and now the surveillance story—drew harsh assessments of a publisher who still suffered a reputation of being too young, too brash—of not being his father. "You get a bad king every once in a while," Gay Talese, an admirer of Punch Sulzberger and author of *The Kingdom and the Power,* told Ken Auletta for a critical profile of the publisher in *The New Yorker.* (Talese blanched when he saw his quote in the *New Yorker* story and sent a note of apology to Sulzberger.) Arianna Huffington, the publisher of *The Huffington Post,* said Sulzberger should be ousted. Some of the publisher's peers rushed in with support. "So you're criticized by Arianna—God!—and Gay Talese, who hasn't been at the *Times* in 40 years," wrote Donald Graham, the chairman of

The Washington Post. "And a lot of anonymous cowards. This is just a tempest in a teapot."

The surveillance story would be awarded a Pulitzer Prize. The *Times* celebrates these moments with a ceremony in the newsroom, where the honorees are invited to speak. When it was his turn, Risen lumbered over to the microphone and looked across the audience of colleagues celebrating this high moment of his career. He thought about a year in which he felt that the *Times* was as much his enemy as the Bush White House, when he was so worried about getting fired for putting the surveillance story into his book that his blood pressure spiked and he could not sleep. Risen considered talking about all that but decided that this was not the time. Instead, he glanced over at Keller and Sulzberger.

Well, thanks, he said. You guys know what happened, how tough this was.

The *Times* had seemed to lose its way those first years after the September 11 attacks—unsteady after its mistakes in Iraq and the surge of patriotism that gripped the nation. But as the shock of the attacks faded, the paper showed signs of regaining its confidence, of becoming less deferential to governmental claims of "national security." The world no longer felt like quite as dangerous a place; the feared second wave of terrorism had not landed on American shores. And the government's credibility had been undercut by the failure to find the weapons of mass destruction.

CHAPTER 31

Hand on the Wheel

Bill Keller thought he had sidelined Judith Miller when he directed her not to work on national security stories. But at the beginning of 2005, she became ensnared in a standoff with the government, under subpoena from a special grand jury investigating the leak by White House officials to reporters of the name of a covert CIA agent, a potential violation of the Intelligence Identities Protection Act of 1982. With the elevation of her case by the publisher, Arthur Sulzberger, Miller would become a high-profile symbol of a First Amendment struggle involving the *Times* and the government's national security apparatus.

The episode involved a secret CIA operative, Valerie Plame, whose husband, Joe Wilson IV, a retired career diplomat, went to Niger at the request of the CIA to investigate whether Saddam Hussein tried to purchase yellowcake, a yellow powder generated in the processing of uranium ore, which can be used to produce enriched uranium. Wilson concluded he had not. He wrote an op-ed essay for the *Times* saying the Bush White House was distorting evidence to rally the nation to war. Eight days after the op-ed appeared, Robert Novak, a syndicated columnist, identified Wilson's wife as a CIA operative, citing two anonymous senior administration officials. The Justice Department opened an inquiry into what appeared a possible act of retaliation against Wilson—the public release of Plame's name potentially put her life in danger—and, in December 2003, named a special prosecutor, Patrick J. Fitzgerald, to investigate the case.

Fitzgerald subpoenaed Miller and Matthew Cooper of *Time* magazine—reporters who he suspected had been recipients of leaks from I. Lewis Libby, known as Scooter, the chief of staff for Vice President Dick Cheney—to appear before the grand jury. Cooper had named Plame in a dispatch for *Time*. Miller had never written a story identifying Plame but had met with Libby during the period that Fitzgerald was investigating. Miller and Cooper both refused to testify, saying that as reporters, they were legally shielded from divulging the names of confidential sources.

A protracted court battle culminated on June 27, 2005, when the United States Supreme Court declined to hear an appeal from Miller and Cooper of a lower court ruling ordering them to cooperate. Cooper avoided jail when his sources, he said, signed a waiver freeing him from any confidentiality agreement and permitting him to testify. But lawyers for Miller and Libby were unable to come to terms on a similar dispensation, and Miller said she would not testify. "If journalists cannot be trusted to guarantee confidentiality, then journalists cannot function and there cannot be a free press," she said at her sentencing. Judge Thomas F. Hogan of federal district court sent Miller to a federal detention center in Alexandria, Virginia, and ordered her to remain there until she testified, or at least until late October, when the term of the grand jury expired. She would spend eighty-five days in jail.

Sulzberger rallied the paper behind Miller, though the facts of her case would turn out not to be nearly as clear-cut as the publisher had presumed. He distributed "Free Judy, Free Matt, Free Press" buttons. The editorial page ran fourteen editorials advocating her cause, invoking the Boston Tea Party, Rosa Parks, and M. A. Farber, a *Times* journalist who spent forty days in jail in 1978 for refusing to release confidential notes. "We stand with Ms. Miller and thank her for taking on that fight for the rest of us," one editorial said. Two days after the Supreme Court ruling on their case, Sulzberger poked his head in on a quarterly lunch of senior editors and business executives, members of the Mohonk Committee, to say he was heading to Washington to attend a hearing where, Sulzberger told his colleagues, "the judge will tell her this is her final opportunity to comply" before being imprisoned. Sulzberger wanted to stand by an embattled colleague.

It is tempting to look at the Miller case as Arthur Sulzberger's own Pentagon Papers, a replay of the confrontation with the United States

"All the News
That's Fit to Print"

The New York Times

Late Edition
New York: Today, sunny, a few afternoon clouds. High 77. Tonight, slightly
more humid. Low 65. Tomorrow, sun
then clouds. High 81. Yesterday, high
81, low 63. Weather map, Page C19.

VOL. CL ... No. 51,874   Copyright © 2001 The New York Times   NEW YORK, WEDNESDAY, SEPTEMBER 12, 2001   [?] beyond the greater New York metropolitan area.   75 CENTS

U.S. ATTACKED

HIJACKED JETS DESTROY TWIN TOWERS AND HIT PENTAGON IN DAY OF TERROR

A CREEPING HORROR

**Buildings Burn and Fall
as Onlookers Search
for Elusive Safety**

By N. R. KLEINFIELD

It kept getting worse.

The horror arrived in episodic bursts of chilling disbelief, signified first by trembling floors, sharp eruptions, cracked windows. There was the actual unfathomable realization of a gaping, flaming hole in first one of the tall towers, and then the same thing all over again in its twin. There was the merciless sight of bodies helplessly tumbling out, some of them in flames.

Finally, the mighty towers themselves were reduced to nothing. Dense plumes of smoke raced through the downtown avenues, coursing between the buildings, shaped like tornadoes on their sides.

Every sound was cause for alarm. A plane appeared overhead. Was another one coming? No, it was a fighter jet. But was it friend or enemy? People scrambled for their lives, but they didn't know where to go. Should they go north, south, east, west? Stay outside, go indoors? People hid beneath cars and each other. Some contemplated jumping into the river.

For those trying to flee the very epicenter of the collapsing World Trade Center towers, the most horrid thought of all finally dawned on them: nowhere was safe.

For several panic-stricken hours yesterday morning, people in Lower Manhattan witnessed the inexpressible, the incomprehensible, the unthinkable. "I don't know what the gates of hell look like, but it's got to be like this," said John Maloney, a security director for an Internet firm in the trade center. "I'm a combat veteran, Vietnam, and I never saw anything like this."

The first warnings were small ones. Blocks away, Jim Farmer, a film composer, was having breakfast at a small restaurant on West Broadway. He heard the sound of a jet. An odd sound — too loud, it seemed, to be

Continued on Page A7

A Somber Bush
Says Terrorism
Cannot Prevail

By ELISABETH BUMILLER
with DAVID E. SANGER

WASHINGTON, Sept. 11 — President Bush vowed tonight to retaliate against those responsible for today's attacks on New York and Washington, declaring that he would "make no distinction between the terrorists who committed these acts and those who harbor them." "These acts of mass murder were intended to frighten our nation into chaos and retreat, but they have failed," the president said in his first speech to the nation from the Oval Office. "Our country is strong. Terrorist acts can shake the foundation of our biggest buildings, but they cannot touch the foundation of America."

His brief speech this evening came after a day of trauma that seems destined to define his presidency. Seeking to at once calm the nation and declare his determination to exact retribution, he told a country numbed by repeated scenes of carnage that "these acts shattered steel, but they cannot dent the steel of American resolve."

Mr. Bush spoke only hours after returning from a zigzag course across the country, as his Secret Service and military security teams moved him from Florida, where he woke up this morning expecting to press for his education bill, to command posts in Louisiana and Nebraska before it was determined the attacks had probably ended and he could safely return to the capital.

It was a day of the catastrophic

Continued on Page A4

Kelly Guenther for The New York Times
SECOND PLANE United Airlines Flight 175
nearing the trade center's south tower.

Steve Ludlum

Justin Lane for The New York Times

AMERICAN TARGETS A ball of fire exploded outward after the second of two jetliners slammed into the World Trade Center; less than two hours later, both of the 110-story towers were gone. Hijackers crashed a third airliner into the Pentagon, setting off a huge explosion and fire.

Paul Hosefros/The New York Times

Ruth Fremson/The New York Times

President Vows to Exact
Punishment for 'Evil'

By SERGE SCHMEMANN

Hijackers rammed jetliners into each of New York's World Trade Center towers yesterday, toppling both in a hellish storm of ash, glass, smoke and leaping victims, while a third jetliner crashed into the Pentagon in Virginia. There was no official count, but President Bush said thousands had perished, and in the immediate aftermath the calamity was already being ranked the worst and most audacious terror attack in American history.

The attacks seemed carefully coordinated. The hijacked planes were all en route to California, and therefore gorged with fuel, and their departures were spaced within an hour and 40 minutes. The first, American Airlines Flight 11, a Boeing 767 out of Boston for Los Angeles, crashed into the north tower at 8:48 a.m. Eighteen minutes later, United Airlines Flight 175, also headed from Boston to Los Angeles, plowed into the south tower.

Then an American Airlines Boeing 757, Flight 77, left Washington's Dulles International Airport bound for Los Angeles, but instead hit the western part of the Pentagon, the military headquarters where 24,000 people work, at 9:40 a.m. Finally, United Airlines Flight 93, a Boeing 757 flying from Newark to San Francisco, crashed near Pittsburgh, raising the possibility that its hijackers had failed in whatever their mission was.

There were indications that the hijackers on at least two of the planes were armed with knives. Attorney General John Ashcroft told reporters in the evening that the suspects on Flight 11 were armed that way. And Barbara Olson, a television commentator who was traveling on American Flight 77, managed to reach her husband, Solicitor General Theodore Olson, by cell phone and to tell him that the hijackers were armed with knives and a box cutter.

In all, 266 people perished in the four planes and several score more were known dead elsewhere. Numerous firefighters, police officers and other rescue workers who responded to the initial disaster in Lower Manhattan were killed or injured when the buildings collapsed. Hundreds were treated for cuts, broken bones, burns and smoke inhalation.

But the real carnage was concealed for now by the twisted, smoking, ash-choked carcasses of the twin towers, in which thousands of people used to work on a weekday. The collapse of the towers caused another World Trade Center building to fall 10 hours later, and several

Continued on Page A14

Awaiting the Aftershocks

*Washington and Nation Plunge Into Fight
With Enemy Hard to Identify and Punish*

By R. W. APPLE Jr.

WASHINGTON, Sept. 11 — Today's devastating and astonishingly well-coordinated attacks on the World Trade Center towers in New York and on the Pentagon outside of Washington plunged the

News Analysis

nation into a warlike struggle against an enemy that will be hard to identify with certainty and hard to punish with precision.

The whole nation — to a degree the whole world — shook as hijacked airliners plunged into buildings that symbolize the financial and military might of the United States. The sense of security and self-confidence that Americans take as their birthright suffered a grievous blow, from which recovery will be slow. The aftershocks will be nearly as bad, as hundreds and possibly thousands of people discover that friends or relatives died awful, fiery death.

Scenes of chaos and destruction evocative of the nightmare world of Hieronymus Bosch, with smoke and debris blotting out the sun, were carried by television into homes and workplaces across the nation. Echoing Franklin D. Roosevelt's description of the attack on Pearl Harbor as an event "which will live in infamy," Gov. George E. Pataki of New York, a Republican, spoke of "an incredible outrage" and Senator Charles E. Schumer of New York, a Democrat, spoke of "a dastardly attack."

But mere words were inadequate vessels to contain the sense of shock and horror that people felt.

As Washington struggled to regain

a sense of equilibrium, with warplanes and heavily armed helicopters crossing overhead, past and present national security officials earnestly debated the possibility of a Congressional declaration of war — but against precisely whom, and in what exact circumstances? Warships were maneuvering to protect New York and Washington. The North American Air Defense Command, which had seemed to many a relic of the cold war, adopted a pos-

Continued on Page A24

MORE ON THE ATTACKS

RESCUERS BECOME VICTIMS Firefighters who rushed to the Trade Center were killed. **PAGE A7**

OFFICIALS SUSPECT BIN LADEN Eavesdropping intercepts after the attacks were cited. **PAGE A23**

TERRORISTS EXPLOITED WEAKNESS Investigators had criticized precautions against hijacking. **PAGE A17**

CASUALTIES IN WASHINGTON An unknown number of people were killed at the Pentagon. **PAGE A5**

SEARCH FOR SURVIVORS Some people trapped in the rubble were rescued. **PAGE A1**

0 35461 38 5 37301

Gail Collins became editorial page editor after Howell Raines. She was the first woman to hold the job and ran the opinion side during an ideologically fraught time, as the *Times* struggled to decide whether to back President George W. Bush's call to invade Iraq. *Photo: Samantha Paltrow-Krulwich/Our Times/Redux*

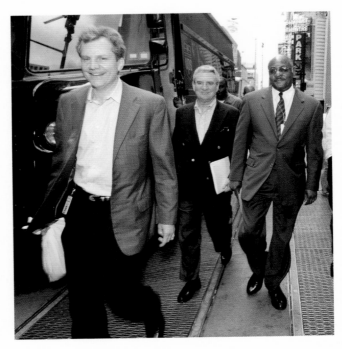

The decision to hold a town hall about Jayson Blair outside the *Times* headquarters forced Sulzberger, Raines, and Boyd (left to right) to navigate a line of reporters and photographers waiting on the street. *Photo: AP Photo/Mary Altaffer*

Raines, Sulzberger, and Boyd were not prepared for the outrage at the newsroom meeting about Jayson Blair. We have work to do, Sulzberger said to Raines as they left the stage. *Photo: Ruby Washington/ The New York Times/Redux*

Jayson Blair walked into the news-room as a summer intern in 1998. He left five years later, identified with a plagiarism scandal that would tarnish the *Times* and pitch the newspaper into one of the most wrenching transformations of its history. *Photo: The New York Times/Redux*

Arthur Sulzberger dis-regarded Joe Lelyveld's advice not to pick Howell Raines as exec-utive editor, but that did not stop him from turning to Lelyveld to step in as interim exec-utive editor after he fired Raines. *Photo: James Estrin/The New York Times/ Redux*

Arthur Sulzberger dismissed Howell Raines and Gerald Boyd after the Jayson Blair episode, but spared Andrew Rosenthal. Don't even think about leaving, the publisher told Rosenthal, the number three person in the newsroom. Rosenthal would go on to become the editorial page editor. © *Rafael Fuchs*

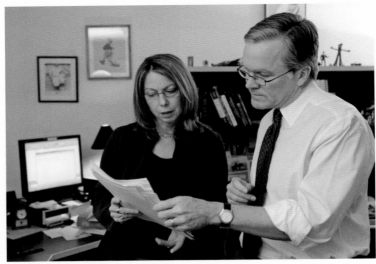

Bill Keller, the new executive editor, convinced Jill Abramson to do what she would not do under Howell Raines: come to New York as his managing editor. *Photo: Ozier Muhammad/The New York Times/Redux*

Dan Okrent was the paper's first public editor, a job that he found so stressful that he began counting down the remaining time of his tenure as if he were a prisoner marking off his days on the concrete wall of a prison cell. *Photo: Barton Silverman/The New York Times/Redux*

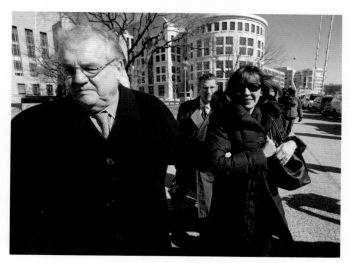

The *Times* stood by reporter Judith Miller, pictured outside the U.S. District Courthouse in Washington, D.C., with her lawyer, Robert S. Bennett, when she was jailed in 2005 for refusing to cooperate in a White House leak investigation. But Bill Keller and Arthur Sulzberger, Jr., never pressed Miller on why she was being investigated, and ultimately forced her off the newspaper. *Michael Temchine/The New York Times/Redux*

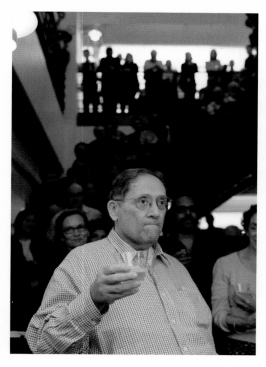

For nearly thirty years, starting in 1977 and through his retirement in 2006, Allan M. Siegal was the embodiment and the enforcer of *Times* standards on journalistic fairness, grammar, and style. Any proposed use of a vulgarity or profanity, sexual reference, graphic description of violence—and any mention of *The New York Times* itself in the news columns—needed to be approved by the news desk, which he controlled. *Photo: Fred R. Conrad/The New York Times/Redux*

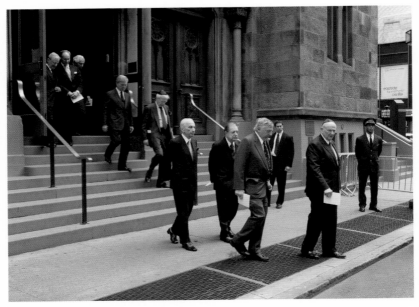

Abe Rosenthal's reputation after his years running the *Times* newsroom was reflected in the lineup of honorary pallbearers at his funeral. From left: Joseph Lelyveld, Warren Hoge, Seymour Topping, James F. Hoge, Jr., Bernard Kalb, Gay Talese, James L. Greenfield, William F. Buckley, Jr., and former mayor Ed Koch.
Photo: James Estrin/The New York Times/Redux

At the suggestion of Arthur Sulzberger, Jr., Jill Abramson chose Dean Baquet (left) as managing editor when she took over from Bill Keller. Abramson came to conclude it had been a mistake to pick a rival for executive editor to be her managing editor. *Photo: Fred R. Conrad/The New York Times/Redux*

Abramson with Mark Thompson (left), the *Times*'s chief executive, in the newsroom as Sulzberger (center) celebrates the paper's four Pulitzers. Susan Chira is seated at the terminal. *Photo: Ruth Fremson/The New York Times/Redux*

Dean Baquet would prove to be a bridge between the *Times* of a passing generation, its standing and dominance undermined by declining influence, circulation, and revenues, and the new *Times* that was slowly being invented around him. *Photo: Earl Wilson/The New York Times/Redux*

Five of the six executive editors who had served under Arthur Sulzberger, Jr., turned up for his retirement party in June 2018 at The Modern in New York. From left to right: Jill Abramson, Joe Lelyveld, Dean Baquet, Howell Raines, and Max Frankel. The sixth, Bill Keller, was out of the country. *Photo: Rebecca Smeyne for The New York Times/Redux*

Arthur Gregg Sulzberger (shown here with his father) became publisher on January 1, 2018, the sixth member of the Ochs-Sulzberger family to serve, in the words of the official announcement, as "the main steward of the editorial independence and excellence of *Times* journalism" since Adolph Ochs purchased the newspaper in 1896. *Photo: Damon Winter/The New York Times/Redux*

government that defined his father's legacy as a publisher. Certainly, many of his editors suspected this was what motivated him. And for Sulzberger it was, at the very least, a welcome respite from the two difficult preceding years—a battle that could lift his spirits, burnish his standing as a publisher, and remind the public of the *Times*'s mission. But Miller presented a murkier case than the one that confronted his father in 1971. There was no attempt to disclose wrongdoing by a government official, or to bring to light a questionable policy or corrupt practice by the White House or the Pentagon. As would become clear with time, this was a campaign by a political aide to punish a critic, Joe Wilson.

The decision by Sulzberger and Keller to rally behind Miller was reflexive, in keeping with the history of news organizations backing reporters confronted by prosecutors. But this meant that Miller had her hand on the wheel, as Sulzberger acknowledged at the time; it was her decision to go to jail or not to go to jail, to testify or not to testify, to negotiate or not to negotiate with prosecutors and with Libby. And Miller was not just any reporter. She had a complicated history at the newspaper and was by now defined for the public largely by her coverage of Iraq. Sulzberger and Keller embraced the cause of a *Times* journalist in legal jeopardy, but never pressed her on what information she might have that would have drawn the interest of law enforcement. Michael Golden, Sulzberger's cousin, who was the vice chairman of the New York Times Company and publisher of the *International Herald Tribune*, counseled Sulzberger that he was moving too hastily in backing Miller. Philip Taubman warned Sulzberger and Keller against allowing this to become a First Amendment battle, with its imperfect protagonist, and with reason to think that a face-saving deal could be negotiated. Abramson had been wary of Miller since their days in Washington. By litigating the case, she argued, the *Times* was inviting an adverse judicial outcome that would make it *more* difficult for reporters to protect their sources.

When Miller was jailed, Keller encouraged his staff to write letters of support to inmate number 45570083, and even to pay her a visit. Abramson took a trip to the detention center while she was in Washington one day, though as she would later say, not for the best of reasons. She thought Miller had damaged the newspaper's reputation and took some dark delight in seeing her behind bars. Abramson talked about how much weight Miller had lost and the streak of gray in her hair—a reminder that inmates are not afforded the luxury of coloring their hair. She could not resist remarking on that detail when she left the visitor room to rejoin her friend, Jane Mayer, the *New Yorker* writer, who had accompanied her for the outing.

She ain't going to be there long, Abramson said.

On September 29, Miller walked out, ready to testify before the grand jury. Keller, Taubman, and Sulzberger were in the parking lot to greet her. As the van left the prison grounds, Sulzberger chased alongside it, pounding on the windows and shouting, "Judy! Judy!" until a marshal, reaching for a gun, ordered him to step back from the vehicle. He's my boss, Miller responded, as she later described the scene. They took her to the Ritz-Carlton Georgetown for a massage, a manicure, and a steak dinner. She returned to work on October 3, to a tepid reception from a newsroom that was mystified about what had led her to testify. Miller said she'd received a personal assurance from Libby that he was not being coerced to give her permission to reveal his identity as a source, though that of course invited the question about why she could not have negotiated such an arrangement without this long ordeal. "I'm sure I did many things that were not completely perfect in the eyes of either First Amendment absolutists or those who wrote every day saying, 'Testify, testify, you're covering up for these people,'" she said to her colleagues. "The pressures were enormous. I did the only thing I could do. I followed my conscience, and I tried to follow the principles that I laid out at the beginning."

Miller was eager to get to work. "This is my clan, this is my tribe," she told the *Times* reporter assigned to write a story about her return. "I belong here."

Abramson did not believe Miller's explanation for her change of heart. Judy went to jail until she decided she did not want to go to jail, Abramson would say. Her decision to testify signaled to prosecutors that a reporter, threatened with jail time, could back down. M. A. Farber never bowed to the prosecutors and was eventually released. "We looked like idiots," Abramson would say years later.

If there was any prospect of Miller returning to her job—and in truth, by the end of her eighty-five days, there probably was not—it ended with a 6,100-word front-page self-examination by the *Times*, written by three reporters and published October 16, 2005, under the headline "The Miller Case: A Notebook, a Cause, a Jail Cell and a Deal." That, along with a personal account Miller wrote, published the same day, reinforced the doubts that already ran deep about her. Her recollections seemed muddled: A notebook had the name "Valerie Flame" scribbled on it, but she said she could not recall who told her the name and thought it had not come from Libby. She had to return to the grand jury because she forgot that she had talked to Libby three times, not two, as she originally testified. When Taubman asked her if she was one of the beneficiaries of the White House leak campaign, she had responded no—a technically defensible response that Keller found misleading. She had agreed to identify Libby as "a former Hill staffer," which, given his long career and prominence in the White House, was imprecise at best and misleading at worst—and not in keeping with customary journalistic standards in describing unnamed sources. Miller said she had gone to Abramson and suggested the *Times* write a story about what the White House was up to after she was tipped off about Plame and was turned down. Abramson denied that conversation ever happened.

The *Times* story on Miller portrayed the editors as unaware of the details of her interactions with Libby. "I wish it had been a clear-cut whistle-blower case," Keller said in the story. "I wish it had been a reporter who came with less public baggage." When Abramson was asked what she regretted about her paper's handling of the matter, she replied: "The entire thing." As a work of self-examination, the story drew praise from some notable quarters, including Dean Baquet, the former national editor who was now the editor of the *Los Angeles Times*. "It takes courage to publish a story like you ran on Sunday," Baquet wrote Sulzberger. "No matter what you think you could have done differently in retrospect, keep in mind that all of your actions were guided by journalistic principle, not commercial interests."

Keller's position had become untenable; even knowing what he knew about Miller, he had not pushed her for details about her encounters with the White House. To his great frustration, he found himself embroiled in another controversy that was hurting the newspaper's reputation, just as it was trying to recover from the fallout of the Iraq coverage and Jayson Blair. The *Times* needed to distance itself from Miller, and without causing further embarrassment to the paper, its executive editor, and its publisher. Keller had left for a tour of foreign bureaus in Southeast Asia by the time the story appeared—a trip he made against the advice of his wife, Emma, who, with characteristic directness, told her husband that this was no time to leave the country. With the furor growing, and between dinners with bureau chiefs and meetings with foreign dignitaries, he hammered out a memorandum to the newsroom expressing remorse. He did not know that "Judy had been one of the reporters on the receiving end of the anti-Wilson whisper campaign," and he should have wondered why he was hearing this from a special prosecutor a year after it happened. "I wish that when I learned Judy Miller had been subpoenaed as a witness in the leak investigation, I had sat her down for a thorough debriefing, and followed up with some reporting of my own." That, he said, might have changed the fervency of the paper's support for its reporter. "If I had known the details of Judy's entanglement with Libby, I'd have been more careful in how the paper articulated its defense, and perhaps more willing than I had been to support efforts aimed at exploring compromises," he wrote.*

Sulzberger backed Keller. "Bill spoke for the newsroom but I concur with his position," he said when *The Wall Street Journal* emailed for comment. "In that regard, some of Bill's 'culpas' were my 'culpas' too." To the outside world—and to Miller—it looked as if the newspaper was turning against her—an impression that was reinforced when the columnist Maureen Dowd offered a scathing view of her colleague's career at the paper. "Sorely in need of a tight editorial leash, she was kept on no leash at all, and that has hurt this paper and its trust with readers," Dowd wrote in an op-ed column that appeared on October 22, 2005. "She more than earned her sobriquet 'Miss Run Amok.'"

"I admire Arthur Sulzberger Jr. and Bill Keller for aggressively backing reporters in the cross hairs of a prosecutor," Dowd continued. "But before turning Judy's case into a First Amendment battle, they should

---

* Keller was assailed by Miller for using the word "entanglement," which appeared to suggest that she had some kind of romantic relationship with Libby. Keller had not, by his later account, thought that; in fact, the wording came from Abramson, who he had asked to put together a draft memo he could work from.

have nailed her to a chair and extracted the entire story of her escapade."

John Geddes, the managing editor for news operations, had sent Miller a joke a day while she was in prison to lift her spirits. Now it fell to him to tell her that her twenty-eight years at the *Times* were over. Keller was still overseas. Abramson did not want to do it, given their strained relationship. Geddes invited her for a drink at a Times Square hotel. He was, in size and appearance, a bear of a man. Geddes was soft-spoken with an easy laugh, but calculating and clinical when it came time to deliver bad news—he had experience in laying people off. He told Miller she should consider taking one of the buyouts the *Times* was offering to reduce the size of the company workforce by five hundred people. Miller was stunned and felt abandoned, particularly by Sulzberger. She had tended to her ties with the publisher since their days in the Washington bureau, when they'd shared a summer house with other reporters in Bethany Beach in Delaware. She had sent Sulzberger a handwritten note after Raines's essay appeared in *The Atlantic:* "I'm sure the piece is hurtful—& I didn't want that to pass without letting you know how much I still believe in what you were trying to do. And what eventually you *will* do. Your old friends know you, Arthur. XOXO-Judy." Miller called Steven Rattner, a friend from the Washington bureau and a Bethany Beach housemate, who remained close to Sulzberger after leaving the *Times.* I don't understand this, she said. The *Times* had just defended her during her eighty-five days in jail, and now it wanted to fire her?

Rattner called the publisher and found his mind was set. Steve, there's no way she can work for the *Times* anymore, Sulzberger said.

Miller and the *Times* announced her retirement on November 9, 2005. Keller and Sulzberger marked her departure with short statements. Miller wanted to write an op-ed column about her departure but was permitted instead to write a letter explaining her decision, which would be published on the Letters to the Editor page. "I have chosen to resign because over the last few months, I have become the news, something a New York Times reporter never wants to be," she wrote. "Even before I went to jail, I had become a lightning rod for public fury over the intelligence failures that helped lead our country to war." A few days before the *Times* announced her retirement, Miller sat down at Balthazar, a restaurant in Soho, with a Style reporter for *The Washington Post*, who presented her with what was probably the most discussed question in journalism circles about what had happened: Was this just a stunt to rescue a reputation battered by her coverage of Iraq? "Anybody who thinks that I would have gone to jail as a career move doesn't know jail, doesn't know me," she said.

In many ways, it was remarkable that Miller lasted at the paper as long as she had. Her survival was testimony to her talent and tenacity, but also to how much even the most scrupulous editors were willing to overlook—from the instances of dubious coverage to her disruptive presence in the newsroom—in the interest of an attention-grabbing story and a Pulitzer Prize. As much as the Times thought of itself as operating in a stratum above its competitors, it was motivated by the same impulses, some noble, some not, that had always defined journalism. Miller had helped win the newspaper a Pulitzer Prize and assembled an impressive canon of investigative stories, but her mistakes and excesses splashed off on the careers of three executive editors, and would help to permanently associate the newspaper with some of the most flawed coverage in its history.

CHAPTER 32

A Painful Legacy

Gerald Boyd never told his former colleagues at the *Times* he was dying. He had collapsed while watching his son run practice drills at a winter baseball clinic in February 2006 and was diagnosed with stage-four lung cancer. A family friend, Dana Canedy, a *Times* editor who Boyd had hired as a reporter, visited his home for dinner and recoiled when Boyd appeared in the doorway and walked haltingly to the table, weak and frail. She'd had no idea he was sick. Canedy asked Boyd's wife, Robin Stone, to allow her to discreetly inform the *Times* of Boyd's approaching death, so the newspaper could prepare an obituary commensurate with the career of this fifty-six-year-old man who had been its first Black managing editor. Arthur Sulzberger, Jr., upon being told of Boyd's prognosis, wanted to visit him at his home in Harlem, but Boyd would not see him. Fuck Arthur, he said. His departure in June 2003 had been humiliating and, in his view and those of many of his friends, unfair: another gesture of disrespect by the *Times* toward its Black employees.

Boyd had never understood why Sulzberger had ousted him, and he dwelled on that question for the remaining years of his life. Canedy visited from time to time and found a man who was broken, listless, and defeated. Carolyn Lee, a *Times* editor who had been pushed out by Raines, had gone to Boyd's house unannounced a few weeks after he left the paper, worried that he had ignored her emails.

You can't stop living because of this, Lee told him when he finally came to the door. You are a strong journalist who's had a wonderful career, and, yes, this is a setback, but it's something you can overcome. Boyd had always been a proud man, and he was one of those *Times* journalists who in no small part defined themselves by the words that often followed their name: "of *The New York Times.*" My life is not my own, Boyd would say when a friend called him at his desk and asked him to dinner. It was the newspaper he had wanted to work at from the moment he read *The Kingdom and the Power* in college, and he had dreamed that he might run it one day. Four months after he left, Boyd stopped himself midsentence while answering questions at an editors' convention. "But we also at the *Times*—I have to stop saying 'we,' folks, I'm trying," he said.

Still, he was different in one important way from others at the *Times* who calculated their self-worth by where they worked. Boyd had become a symbol, from the day that Max Frankel, as executive editor, tapped him to become an editor in Washington and told him he would be the newspaper's Jackie Robinson. That made the ignominy of his dismissal much greater. So he stayed away from the newsroom and ignored most of the telephone calls, emails, and notes from colleagues inquiring about his well-being. He did not want to be an object of pity. When he was diagnosed with lung cancer, he became even more the recluse; he did not want anyone to know he was sick, which made the news of his death, on November 23, 2006, a shock—a reminder of how much he had shunned the *Times.* Joe Lelyveld first heard about Boyd's funeral when he was heading to the dentist, after Soma Golden Behr, who had been promoted to the masthead the same day as Boyd, called to ask if he was going. Lelyveld caught a taxi to the church and arrived to find a procession of limousines lining up for the ride to the cemetery. Lelyveld jumped out of his taxi and trotted back and forth alongside the procession, but no one opened a door; this was the private friends-and-family ceremony, and he was not supposed to be there. Lelyveld felt like a "ridiculous figure" as he watched the motorcade drive off without him to Woodlawn Cemetery in the Bronx, where Boyd would be buried on a hillside, his casket sprinkled with flowers by his family and the few people he still considered friends in those final years of his life.

There were two services to mark Boyd's death: the private funeral at the Memorial Baptist Church on 115th Street in Harlem, and a public celebration the next day to accommodate colleagues from the *Times,* as well as other news organizations like *The Washington Post,* twenty blocks north at the Schomburg Center for Research in Black Culture. The second service, the public celebration, was videotaped and lasted for two and a half hours. Much of it was a warm, affectionate tribute to the competitive and perpetually tense man who grew up in poverty in St. Louis to become a symbol of Black success at the most powerful newspaper in the country. It had been a gratifying rise for a man whose mother died when he was three and whose father, a heavy drinker, abandoned the family and moved to New York when he was eleven, leaving him and his older brother to be raised by their grandmother. Boyd was eulogized as an exacting supervisor, and even here, no one tried to disguise the fact that some people did not like him. His brother, Gary, poked fun at his self-importance. "Oh man, he was a very important person," he said. "And he's been telling me that for the last few years." In the newsroom, Gerald Boyd was known as Mr. Gruff; it was not quite an accurate description, Al Siegal, the assistant managing editor, said in his remarks, though sometimes it seemed one that Boyd welcomed.

The tragedy of Gerald Boyd was that he was unsuited for the job he was desperate to have, the appointment that Howell Raines was eager to make, and that was an undercurrent of the day. But his memorial was not only about Boyd's career. It was also an exhumation of how the *Times* had treated Boyd, and how so much of his career had been defined by that one episode involving a rogue reporter, and not by the Pulitzers he helped the *Times* win for the coverage of the first World Trade Center attack, or for the "How Race Is Lived in America" project. "I am here tonight to reclaim a friend," George Curry declared as he walked before the thick floor-to-ceiling curtains that served as a somber backdrop for this event. He had met Boyd thirty years earlier when they were both reporters at the *St. Louis Post-Dispatch.* They'd founded the Greater St. Louis Association of Black Journalists together in 1976.

"I am here to restore his good name," Curry said to the audience of Boyd friends and colleagues. "I am here to set the record straight. . . . Gerald had an extremely successful career. And we as his friends should not allow those in our field to sully his reputation now that he can no longer speak for himself." Boyd was never Blair's direct supervisor, Curry noted. "Gerald certainly did not fabricate any of his stories, but you would never know that from some of the coverage of his death—including that in *The New York Times*," said Curry. "Gerald Boyd was a victim of Jayson Blair, not his protector."

Seventeen people would speak at Schomburg. One of them was Bernard Weinraub, a former *Times* reporter who had been Boyd's partner covering the White House under Ronald Reagan, and the best man at his second wedding. He was the sixth speaker and the first white one. Weinraub had left the *Times* to become a playwright and was living in Los Angeles. Robin Stone, who Boyd had married ten years earlier when she was a deputy editor on the Living section, called the night before Thanksgiving to tell him that Boyd was close to death.* Weinraub jumped on an overnight plane and, upon arrival, took a taxi from John F. Kennedy International Airport to Boyd's home; he arrived moments after Boyd died. Stone asked Weinraub to join the private church service and for a meal of mourners at Sylvia's, a restaurant in Harlem, after Boyd's burial. And Stone invited Weinraub to speak the next day at the public memorial. Weinraub had been angered to read in the *Times* obituary what Frankel had said to Boyd when he promoted him, and it lit up the eulogy he scribbled on a piece of yellow paper on the taxi ride up to the service. "Well, that's one hell of a burden: being Jackie Robinson," Weinraub said. "Gerald's job was not only to publish a good newspaper but to carry the weight of his race and represent his race every single moment he walked into the paper. That is a brutal weight to carry." He was and had always been, Weinraub said, "a Black man at a white paper."

It was telling that most of the white attendees were clustered in one part of the auditorium, separated from the Black attendees. All the living executive editors were there, including Raines, who sat almost unnoticed toward the back of the hall. He had written Boyd suggesting the two get a drink a year after they left. Boyd might have agreed, but he had just read the *Atlantic* magazine story, which as far as Boyd was concerned made clear that Raines had always harbored doubts about his abilities and considered him culpable for Blair. Boyd never responded. "I was tired of being betrayed, tired of the *Times*, and tired of him," Boyd wrote. It was an excruciating two hours for the delegation of current and past *Times* management. Sulzberger would years later remember the memo-

---

* Robin Stone was Boyd's third wife.

rial as an evening of attacks on him for destroying Boyd; he returned home, he said, and broke down in tears. In fact, the publisher's name was hardly mentioned, but the scorn directed at the *Times* was of course scorn directed at the man whose family owned the newspaper and who decided that he could not fire Raines without terminating Boyd as well. It was only at this service that most of Boyd's former colleagues began to grasp the profound sadness of his story and to confront the inescapable possibility that his purge from the *Times* had somehow contributed to this sad day of remembrance. "Working at the *Times*, which was everything to Gerald, was abruptly and brutally severed," Weinraub said in his eulogy. "And Gerald was lost. He felt incorrectly that he had lost his dignity. And he felt correctly that he was treated without dignity."

The service was neither calming nor cathartic. Frankel was stunned by the level of hostility and anger in the room. As the tribute ended, Lelyveld walked over to Boyd's widow, Robin Stone, to share his discomfort.

Not everything here needed to be said, he said, as she recounted the moment.

This is not your event, Joe, Stone said, turning away to thank other attendees as they departed the hall.

Frankel had promoted Boyd to address the racial inequities in the newsroom, and Boyd's memorial twenty years later was a reminder that there was much work to be done. Sulzberger had pressed his editors to hire and recruit Blacks and Latinos in the newsroom. But two months before Boyd's death, Sulzberger had tried to remove Bob Herbert, whom he had appointed as the newspaper's first Black columnist soon after he became publisher in 1993. Sulzberger had rarely hesitated in removing a columnist whose work he had come to not like, as had been shown with A. M. Rosenthal, and he did not like the Bob Herbert column. He had tapped Herbert to write about New York City and urban issues; he was unhappy that Herbert was devoting so much of his space to national and international issues. Herbert learned of this when he ran into Sulzberger in the elevator one Tuesday morning in September and the publisher greeted him by saying, almost offhandedly, that he wanted Herbert to retire. Herbert was sixty-one years old and had been a columnist for thirteen years. The abruptness of their encounter stunned him, and he registered his distress with Sulzberger several days later.

"I was so shocked and so shaken that I found it difficult to respond to you on the spot," Herbert wrote. "It was surely one of the most painful and puzzling conversations I've ever had." He had thought he would be at the *Times* for the rest of his life.

Herbert's column on the morning that he wrote his letter to Sulzberger was "The Kafka Strategy," and it argued that senior officials in the Bush Administration could face charges of war crimes for their treatment of suspected terrorists. By Sulzberger's count—as recorded in written talking points he prepared before responding to Herbert—thirty-nine of the sixty-six columns he had written in 2006 were on Bush foreign policy, on issues like Guantanamo and wiretapping. Only thirteen were on subjects that were supposed to be his bailiwick: New York City, poverty, injustice, and race.

Sulzberger waited a few days before responding to Herbert; when he did, he assured Herbert he had considered his arguments. "In the end, however, my position hasn't changed. For several years now, I've felt that your column has run its course." Sulzberger was by now comfortable with firing people. "Some of my worst moments have come with telling great journalists that it was time to leave the Op-Ed Page and move on," he wrote Herbert. "I look back on those conversations with pain, but not regret." The *Times* would give him a severance package of $280,000; three weeks of pay for each year he was at the paper.

Herbert refused the offer. He wrote Sulzberger objecting to "the unfairness of this sudden assault on a long and distinguished career in journalism" and threatening "any and all legal remedies," which could mean an embarrassing racial discrimination battle. "The last thing that I want is a protracted confrontation over my unfair treatment at the *Times*, which would inevitably be played out in the court of public opinion and most likely resolved in a court of law," he wrote. "But I will not shrink from that path if it is the only way to prevent you from unfairly—and illegally—destroying a career that I have built over the course of my adult life." Sulzberger backed down; Herbert would stay on for another five years.* The spectacle of the *Times* trying to fire the paper's first Black columnist—at a time when it was still struggling under

---

* Herbert would retire to become a fellow at Demos, a national progressive think tank.

the shadow of Jayson Blair and Gerald Boyd—would invite more critical attention on the issue of race and the *Times*.

A year before Boyd died, Roger Wilkins, a former *Times* editorial writer and member of the commission that investigated Jayson Blair's time at the newspaper, wrote Sulzberger to share the despair he had heard over lunch from a young Black *Times* reporter about the pace of minority hiring and promotion in this post-Blair era. "The racial situation at the paper has deteriorated just as Black reporters had feared it would in the wake of the Blair disaster and the lingering bad tastes of Howell's 'white-southern racial guilt' and Gerald's 'mean ineptitude,'" Wilkins wrote (without saying who he was quoting). "Sorry to be the bearer of bad news, but I wouldn't bother writing you if I didn't respect you as a publisher and also your instincts on these issues." Sulzberger assured him that he shared his concern. "There is no question that we are stalled here," he replied. "The good news is we have a lot in the works. People feel a new sense of urgency—one that I am helping to stoke." But now Boyd's death was a reckoning, a reminder of how much the paper had fallen short on racial diversity in the decades since Punch Sulzberger had gone before his editors to deplore the overwhelmingly white newsroom. On the day that Boyd was buried, there were still no Blacks or Latinos at the highest ranks of the newsroom. It would be another five years before that would change.

CHAPTER 33

Mother Times

A. M. Rosenthal looked at Barnaby Feder across his desk. Feder was a thirty-year-old reporter with a law degree who worked at the *World Business Weekly*, and who was about to become a technology reporter for the *Times*. I am not hiring you for a job, Rosenthal told him. I am hiring you for a career.

This was the fall of 1980, and Feder would spend the next twenty-seven years and six months at the *Times*. By 2008, he was aware of the difficulties facing the nation's economy, the newspaper industry, and his own newspaper; he had written stories about companies downsizing and laying off workers. Still, he felt secure in his job, and he was not concerned when John Geddes, one of the managing editors, called him up to a private office on the fourteenth floor, well away from the newsroom. Feder found Geddes waiting with a pile of legal documents on his desk. Feder was being bought out. His career at the newspaper was over.

Rosenthal's meaning—I am not hiring you for a job; I am hiring you for a career—was clear to Feder on the day he joined the *Times*, as it was to almost every job applicant who crossed that threshold and heard similar words from an executive editor. A newsroom job at the *Times* was as close to a lifetime appointment as existed in journalism. Reporters who proved undistinguished, whose work was scattered with factual errors, who drank too much or didn't show up or were guilty of sexual indiscretions, were rarely pushed out. They were shuffled to an overnight shift in the police shack, perhaps, or one of the weekend regional sections, where there were fewer responsibilities and expectations. If they left, which some did, it was because they wanted to do something else. Jayson

Blair's actions were so egregious that he could not stay. But there was a long line of reporters with offenses that would cost them their jobs almost anywhere else, who would come to work at the *Times* every day until they died. It was part of *Times* lore. "God is our personnel manager," Punch Sulzberger would say ruefully over his years as publisher.

This was Mother Times, as the editors came to talk about their place of work: one of the most brutal newspaper cultures in the country, but one that nonetheless had the compassion that came from being a family business, that wrapped its arms around a reporter burdened by a health crisis or a dying spouse. And Mother Times was not only there during a moment of personal crisis or when it came time to deal with a miscreant. When Bill Schmidt was a London correspondent, he told Punch Sulzberger over dinner that the kitchen in the *Times* apartment where he lived was showing its age—dowdy and dank. Get it painted, Sulzberger responded. And send me the bill.

All of which made the clouds that settled over the newsroom in 2008 so disorienting. The *Times*'s financial challenges—the upheavals in the newspaper publishing industry, the advances of digital publications—had accelerated over Bill Keller's tenure. On Valentine's Day, Keller had gathered photographers, researchers, and news clerks in the Times Center, a 378-seat first-floor auditorium with red cushioned seats and a glass wall overlooking the outdoor courtyard. It was a showpiece of the new $850 million headquarters on Eighth Avenue, which the paper had moved into two months earlier. The executive editor spent the first ten and a half minutes praising his reporters and editors and celebrating the successes of his first five years in charge. "We—all of us—-have taken a badly wounded, publicly humiliated newsroom and restored it, largely by dint of great journalism, to a position of international esteem," he said.

But Keller was there to prepare members of his staff for the kinds of cuts they had never experienced before. The *Times* had largely been spared the economic turmoil that was upending newsrooms like the *Los Angeles Times*. Over these past four years, the *New York Times* had laid off employees in the business offices, but reporters and editors in the newsroom paid little attention to that. There had been a scattering of buyouts, in which employees were typically paid a year's salary severance to retire; those were voluntary and mainly picked off older reporters who were nearing the end of their careers. But, as Keller told his audience, it seemed almost certain this Valentine's Day that this was the first throes of a recession. He did not know how bad it would get; six months later, the nation plunged into its worst economic downturn since the 1930s.

"You don't have to edit the newspaper—you just have to read it—to know this year will test our courage and confidence severely," Keller told his employees that day. There were 1,332 people in the newsroom as the year began; 254 more than ten years earlier. By the end of the year, Keller announced, that force would be reduced by 100 bodies. Some of that would be done by attrition, and some with another round of the voluntary buyouts that had nibbled at the corners of the newsroom over the years. But that would almost certainly not be enough. For the first time in the history of the *Times*, there would be layoffs in the newsroom. Even then, after he uttered those words and the thick packets of legal documents outlining the terms of the buyouts were mailed to the homes of the newsroom staff, few reporters who had made their lives at the *Times*—reporters like Barnaby Feder—thought they would have to leave.

The Great Recession was beginning, and it would undermine the foundation of a newspaper industry already struggling after years of declines in advertising and circulation. Newspapers were not only chronicling the wave of economic despair sweeping the nation; they were among its victims. "The newspaper industry exited a harrowing 2008 and entered 2009 in something perilously close to free fall," the Pew Research Center wrote in its annual report on the state of the news media for 2008. "Perhaps some parachutes will deploy, and maybe some tree limbs will cushion the descent, but for a third consecutive year the bottom is not in sight." This was the sixth annual report issued by the foundation on the state of the news industry. "It's also the bleakest," the authors said. Newspaper advertising revenues had posted a two-year, 23 percent decline over 2007 and 2008, and 5,900 full-time newspaper jobs were cut in 2008 alone, the report found. Daily newspaper circulation had dropped 13.5 percent since 2001; Sunday circulation declined 17.3 percent. By the time general economic conditions began to improve—advertising revenue would fall another 26 percent in 2009—this economic crisis would destroy or hollow out some of the great newspapers of the day. Denver's *Rocky Mountain News* shut down, while the *Seattle Post-Intelligencer* closed its print edition and began publishing only online. The Tribune Company filed for bankruptcy. Newspapers like the *Los Angeles Times,* the *Miami Herald,* the *Chicago Tribune* and *The Boston Globe* closed foreign and national bureaus, reduced the number of pages they set aside for news, and laid off reporters and editors.

Revenue from classified ads for real estate, already fleeing to websites like Craigslist, was pummeled by an economy staggered by the subprime mortgage crisis. But even more concerning was the realization that this was becoming a fundamental threat to what had been the economic model for the newspaper industry for more than a century: the revenue streams of advertising and circulation. The Internet was drawing away readers who could find for free what they would otherwise have to pay for in the print newspaper, and this was siphoning off advertisers. (The *Times* was charging readers to read the paper's op-ed columnists online, but even that modest attempt at monetizing the website would soon be abandoned.) It was not a matter of waiting for the recovery; this would become a race against the clock of declining advertising revenue and circulation to find a new business model.

The 2008 recession would shake the self-confidence of the organization and its reporters and editors. For all its importance and self-regard, the *Times* was not immune to economic forces that were reshaping the economy.

* * *

In some ways, the *Times* was better prepared than its competitors for the downturn. The sheer size of its newsroom permitted it to make cuts with less obvious damage to quality. And though its weekday circulation was dropping (by 2008, it had fallen nearly 10 percent over two years and would dip below one million for the first time since 1984 by 2009), it was sustained by an intensely loyal base of readers. The floor, company executives believed, was eight hundred thousand paid subscribers—those who were not deterred by ever-escalating subscription rates.

It also had the support of a family that, for the most part, was not driven by a bottom line or a stock price. Still, as much as editors and reporters appreciated the Sulzbergers—"I believe in the monarchy," Max

Frankel would say—there were doubts about the business acumen of what was still something of a family shop. A series of dubious decisions, easy to overlook during better times, had left the newspaper in a precarious position as the economy had turned against it. In 1993, the *Times*, under Punch Sulzberger, acquired *The Boston Globe* for $1.1 billion. It was a huge miscalculation that underlined how much Punch Sulzberger and others in his generation did not see what was becoming so visible to their younger associates: that the Internet would transform the newspaper business. "Colossally bad timing," as Michael Golden, the vice chairman of the company, later observed. The *Times* had reported a $600 million loss in the last quarter of 2006, which it blamed largely on the poor performance of the *Globe.* In 2004, the *Times* sold its old headquarters on West Forty-third Street to Tishman Speyer Properties, the New York commercial real estate giant, for $175 million. Three years later, after renovations, Tishman turned around and sold it to an Israeli diamond billionaire for three times as much. As the decade came to a close, the *Times* was saddled with $1.1 billion in debt, driven in part by an ill-considered decision to buy back $2.7 billion of its own stock from 1998 to 2004.

Wall Street was losing faith in the company's management. By December 4, 2007, Times Company stock had plummeted to $16.39 a share, less than a third of the $53 price of June 2002.* Shareholders were rebelling. A group of activists demanded the company abandon the two-tier stock structure that gave the Sulzberger family absolute control of the company and instead put the *Times* under the stewardship of a professional class of shareholders with an unsentimental focus on the bottom line. "It is time for the company's board to combine Class A and Class B common stock into a single class of common stock that would provide equal rights, voting power and representation for all shareholders," the leader of the activist rebellion, Hassan Elmasry—the managing director of Morgan Stanley Investment Management, who owned a 7.6 percent stake in the Times Company—declared in a statement as the battle intensified. It unnerved Arthur Sulzberger, who sent a note to Keller after

---

* That $16.39 price did not look quite so bad in another fourteen months; *Times* stock sold for $3.44 on February 20, 2009.

reading a *Times* account about the "difficult" annual shareholder meeting. "I need to get this off my chest so here goes," the publisher began, as he described the story as unsophisticated and "among the weakest of the articles written by major news organizations on our annual meeting."

"There are two critical drivers of the situation we find ourselves in," Sulzberger wrote. "The first is the transformation our industry is undergoing and the effect that is having on the stock price. . . . The second is that shareholder activism is giving different groups the ability to make names for themselves under the guise of corporate governance without much in the way of accountability." His unhappiness might well have derived from his realization that the story was accurate.

The stockholders' campaign against the paper's family stock-ownership structure would fail, and Elmasry would sell his shares, but the episode suggested that the Times Company was now seen as vulnerable by its shareholders and circling competitors. In the summer of 2007, Rupert Murdoch moved to take control of Dow Jones & Company and *The Wall Street Journal* from the Bancroft family and position it as a threat to the *Times*, in its backyard and at this moment of weakness. Murdoch telegraphed his aspirations at the Web 2.0 Summit in San Francisco in October 2007 when he was asked if he was aiming to "kill" the *Times*. "That would be nice," Murdoch responded. The *Journal* under Murdoch would put a new emphasis on general-interest stories, along with coverage of New York City, culture, lifestyle, and the arts.

Keller had been struggling with the feeling, as he put it in a note to Dean Baquet at the end of 2005, that "our business is slowly sliding off a cliff." He had followed the decline in circulation and advertising, and the wave of staff reductions in the business department. He had watched the *Times*, in service of reducing newsprint expenditures, halt the printing of daily stock tables and prepare to reduce the width of its pages by one and a half inches, to twelve inches. Keller started to leave foreign and national correspondents in place for more than three years rather than rotating them to new assignments, as had been the practice, to save on the relocation costs. He thought back to his days as a correspondent when he'd covered a trip to the United States by Mikhail Gorbachev. The tour ended in San Francisco, where R. W. Apple, the paper's high-living chief Washington correspondent, took him and a table of reporters to dinner at Stars, the restaurant that helped define California cuisine in the 1980s, charging it to his expense account. Apple and Keller had flown there first class from Washington. Those days were over.

He devoted a section of one of his "Throw stuff at Bill" sessions, as he called his regular meetings with reporters and editors, to the question of "will *The New York Times* make it?" He walked onstage to the sounds of the "Not Dead Yet" song-and-dance skit from Monty Python's *Spamalot*. Keller had little doubt that the newspaper would survive this. But it was stressful, and he struggled to hide his anger when Times Company executives demanded to know why he could not make deeper cuts in the newsroom. That contributed to new tensions with Sulzberger. The publisher described their relationship as "confrontational and lacking in trust" at the start of 2008. "I was very pleased to read in your assessment that you, too, were unhappy with where we find ourselves," Sulzberger wrote him. "Both of us agree that the current level of pain and dysfunction can't go untreated, especially given the economic and competitive challenges ahead."

"So now let me move to our relationship," he wrote. "In truth, I find it painful—more so than I have had with any previous editor of this paper. I am glad to read that you are worried about it as well."

As the Valentine's Day meeting with the newsroom approached, Keller made one more effort to head off cuts with Sulzberger, who wanted him to reduce the newsroom budget by about $10 million, or 3 percent. Keller warned that it would weaken the paper's ability to compete with Murdoch's reinvigorated *Journal*, undercut the ongoing transition from print-only to the Web, and set back efforts to hire more women and minorities. "We are not here to plead that the newsroom or editorial page be spared cuts," Keller said. "We won't pretend we like the plan. We're skeptical that this will strengthen us as a company. But we are realists."

The Newspaper Guild called it the Saint Valentine's Day Massacre. There were not enough volunteers for buyouts, which meant that between fifteen and twenty people would be forced to leave. Keller had anticipated this and instructed department heads to prepare a confidential survey of staff productivity, with lists of expendable newsroom employees. The reports tabulated the number of bylines for each reporter, how many of their stories appeared on the front page, and how many were what the study described as high-impact stories. The column-inches of copy written by each reporter were tabulated. Keller and his editors went through the lists when deciding who to lay off. The paper would lose experience and institutional memory. But Keller realized there were benefits to this exercise. There would be some staff reductions, but it would also free up money for new hires who would bring energy and new perspectives to their reporting. It was a chance to rid the paper of people who were not as productive as they once were, or who were on beats that no longer seemed important or interesting.

The reporters facing dismissal were called at home and instructed to report to an office upstairs from the newsroom. At Geddes's suggestion, boxes of tissues were perched on the desk, next to the stack of severance documents. No one was subjected to the indignity of being escorted out of the building. Feder's name appeared in bold in one of the staff performance reports, identifying him as a target. Later, when he thought about the fact that he was being laid off, he was neither surprised nor embarrassed. He was a fine reporter, but he was not a star. His stories rarely ended up on the front page. Feder understood that this was not the same newspaper it had been in 1980, when Rosenthal hired him for a career, and he tried to share that insight at his farewell gathering. The news business has changed, he told his colleagues. Always have a fallback plan. Feder would leave the newspaper and enter the ministry.

For weeks, reporters and editors would gather in a corner of the room to raise a cup of sparkling wine in honor of departing colleagues. There would be speeches followed by applause, the sharp retort of the claps echoing across the cavernous newsroom. Keller would try to go to each one, standing in the outer circle of the gathering. The claps reminded him of the sound of a firing squad. It was a moment of realization about what was happening at the *Times*. It was becoming a business.

* * *

And it wasn't enough. In September the *Times* announced that it was ending the stand-alone Metro Section, folding it into other sections of the main newspaper. The paper slashed dividends to shareholders by 74 percent—a financially punishing cutback for members of the Sulzberger family, many of whom were dependent on the dividends for a large portion of their incomes. It began selling advertisements at the bottom of the front page. "I know that the idea of strip ads on section fronts is a hard one for the newsroom to swallow," Sulzberger wrote Joe Sexton, an editor who had objected to the decision. "It's a hard one for me to swallow. . . . Why do this at all? Well compared to what. In a world of increasingly narrow choices, adding this revenue beats the hell out of finding the offsetting costs to cut without it." Keller had fought Sulzberger when he wanted to put those advertisements on the front page of the other sections.

It's like putting up a billboard in a national park, he said. This time, Keller barely said a word. The *Times*, in a humbling moment, was forced to borrow $250 million from Carlos Slim, a Mexican billionaire, at an interest rate of 14 percent. The *New York Post* lampooned the transaction by printing a mocking sketch of Sulzberger, a sombrero perched on his head. A rumor swept through the building one day that the paper would not be able to meet the payroll that week; it was unfounded but not far-fetched. Employees had already agreed to a temporary 5 percent pay cut to forestall any more layoffs.

It was difficult to imagine how things could get worse, though an essay by Michael Hirschorn in *The Atlantic* suggested that they most certainly could. "Specifically, what if *The New York Times* goes out of business—like, this May?" he wrote at the start of 2009. "It's certainly plausible. . . . As of December, its stock had fallen so far that the entire company could theoretically be had for about $1 billion. The former *Times* executive editor Abe Rosenthal often said he couldn't imagine a world without *The Times*. Perhaps we should start."

The worry began to wear on Sulzberger. It was visible in the slump in his shoulders, his blank stares into the distance, the unfinished sentences. He had never been good at hiding his emotions, and that mattered now: these were the clues reporters were watching for when they encountered him in the elevator or the cafeteria. Michael Golden was also worried about the future of the company. But he would remind himself to pep up as he walked out of the subway every morning, and he shared that advice with Sulzberger. You can't walk around like the world's coming to an end, the publisher's cousin told him. If you look worried, everyone in this place is going to panic.

Over the next two years, another 150 jobs would be eliminated through layoffs and buyouts The revenues that had carried the paper since the days of Adolph Ochs were not going to be enough to pay for what the *Times* had become, with its 1,200-person newsroom, website, book review, Sunday magazine, bank of op-ed columnists, two benches of arts critics, the bureaus around the nation and the world, and the new headquarters on Eighth Avenue. If the *Times* wanted to continue being that *Times*, it needed to figure out a new way to pay the bills.

CHAPTER 34

Paying the Bills

t was six hours before deadline—a lull in the workday, when reporters and editors are typically returning from lunch and beginning to focus on stories that need to be filed by the evening. But in one corner of the newsroom, a few weeks before the first day of spring in 2008, editors and reporters at the metropolitan desk had just finished work on an investigative story about the governor of New York, Eliot Spitzer. They looked up at the television sets hanging overhead, tuned to CNN. On the screen was an image of the home page of *The New York Times.*

Moments before, at 1:58 P.M., the newspaper had posted an exclusive report that Spitzer, the Democratic governor of New York, had been caught in a federal investigation of a high-priced prostitution ring catering to blue-chip clients. William K. Rashbaum, who covered courts and corruption, had been tipped off to the investigation the previous Thursday. This led to a tense weekend as a team of reporters and editors raced to nail the story down, wary that the *Daily News* or the *New York Post* would get wind of it. Working off wisps of information in a court filing—Room 871 at a hotel in Washington, D.C.; the date of a rendezvous with a prostitute—the reporters tried to determine the name of the man identified in the court papers as Client Nine, and who Rashbaum was told was a wealthy New York political figure of some renown. They assembled a list of figures who fit that description: Rudolph Giuliani, Bill Clinton (who lived in Chappaqua), Michael Bloomberg, Bernard Kerik, and Eliot Spitzer. A reporter in the Washington bureau surveyed District of Columbia hotels searching for a Room 871 and determined the assignation had likely taken place at the Mayflower Hotel.

Back in New York, other reporters cross-referenced travel records from the governor's office with dates in the court filing; Spitzer had been in Washington without his wife, Silda, when the encounter with the prostitute took place. A reporter went to Fifth Avenue and staked out the lobby of Spitzer's building to look for signs of circling-of-the-wagons activity by his staff. By Saturday night, it was becoming clear that the *Times* might publish a story implicating the governor of New York in a prostitution ring, and Jill Abramson, who had taken a break from overseeing the story to go to dinner, realized she had better alert the publisher. She left the table to call him.

Shit, Arthur Sulzberger said, as their conversation came to a close. I'm having lunch with Silda on Wednesday.

A story of this magnitude would normally be held for the next day's front page and posted online when the first print papers rolled off the presses that night. But Spitzer had apparently spotted the reporter in his lobby when he came back from a jog and guessed what was unfolding. He called a news conference to disclose the investigation himself. There was a bit of a scramble in the newsroom as Spitzer was driven from his apartment to the governor's office. Abramson was standing next to Rashbaum and over Carolyn Ryan, the metropolitan political editor, who was editing the story on her computer one final time. Hit it, Abramson said, and with that, the story was on the home page. The affirmation of that decision came with stunning speed, as the image of the *Times* home page—"Spitzer Is Linked to Prostitution Ring" read the headline—flickered across television screens around the newsroom. It was a lesson. There was no such thing as a deadline anymore; no incentive to wait and risk losing an exclusive story. There should be no more talk about the website scooping the print edition, or discussion of holding an exclusive story from the Web until after it had appeared in print. The website was becoming as effective a platform for distributing news as the front page of the *Times*. "More people visited our site on Monday than in [a] single day in the website's history," the editors of the website informed the staff. The story set off a journalistic squall, and Spitzer would resign within a week.

If this was a sign of where the newspaper was heading, or needed to go, it was also a reminder of how slow the change had been. This was a

lesson that had been learned before and since forgotten. The story disclosing the domestic surveillance operation by the National Security
Agency was published on the Web the night before it appeared in print
three years earlier, that time out of concern that the Bush Administration might seek an injunction to prevent it from being printed. But the
print and digital newsrooms were now parallel and competitive worlds,
with ambitious people who had different philosophies of how journalism
should be presented and how to appeal to a younger generation of readers. The newspaper had come a long way since 1996, when Bernard
Gwertzman complained about being stranded in Antarctica as he ran
the digital newsroom two blocks from the main office. But even now, Bill
Keller, the executive editor, felt, in his own words, like Julius Caesar visiting the Gauls when he walked over to the digital newsroom.

In many ways, the divisions had grown more intractable as the website became more successful and its editors, producers, and writers more
confident, assertive, and independent. They wanted to be associated with
the prestige of the *Times*, but they didn't want to lose the freedom that
came from operating in their own sphere or be forced to compromise the
pace and energy of the *Times* website—a dynamic twenty-four-hour operation not tethered to the constraints of a clock, and certainly not the
New York time zone. They were wary of editors and reporters who, sensing that the center of power at the *Times* was shifting, wanted to move in
and take command, slowing the pace of transformation and imposing
their own print-centric vision on the digital operation. Many of the digital staffers were paid less, and they knew it. The suspicions went both
ways: many print reporters believed standards that assured excellence at
the *Times*—a commitment to accuracy over speed, a measured if slightly
understated voice in writing, a go-slow approach to experimenting with
anything new—were threatened by this new type of journalist. The demands of the Web meant print reporters were working harder, rewriting
stories to reflect updated information, and being told they did not have
that extra five minutes for another call. Keller would hear complaints
when he visited the bureaus: his correspondents would talk about the
cascading demands on their time and the mistakes that were beginning
to creep in because of the emphasis on speed.

But the melding of these newsrooms wasn't only a journalistic imperative. It was a business one as well. The website was brimming with energy and urgency, as the Spitzer story had demonstrated, and it was brimming with readers: a growing digital audience, a largely untapped source of revenue that could be the salvation for a newspaper at a time when advertisers were leaving and were unlikely to return.

* * *

The *Times* website was a glimmer of good news in the swirl of plummeting revenues, declining readership, and layoffs that engulfed the newspaper as it struggled through the 2008 recession and the reordering of the industry. The site showed the potential of digital journalism as a business—reassuring, at a time when the newspaper's own publisher was predicting the eventual end of the print edition. More immediately, it held the promise of replacing some of the millions of dollars in revenue lost as advertisers and readers fled the print paper. But it would be a challenge. The Internet was powered by readers—millions of them—clicking from website to website, jumping into online debates and discussions, unencumbered by paywalls. They were not paying to read the *Times* online, the way they would pay to buy a copy of the print newspaper.

Since his first days as the head of what would become known as New York Times Digital, Martin Nisenholtz had opposed charging for the website, and at that he represented the consensus of his division and the online world. The *Times* website would succeed, in this view, by drawing huge numbers of readers from this expanding new universe, which in turn would bring advertisers. By 2008, it was registering over forty-five million unique visitors a month. It was a significant readership base but also a fragile one. Nisenholtz thought charging for access would chase readers away to other sites that were free.

But online advertising was turning out not to be as lucrative as print advertising; a deflating realization that there was no equivalent on a screen for the full-page marquee print ad that went for thousands of dollars. Janet Robinson, the chief executive of the Times Company, told Abramson that if the *Times* were forced to rely on digital advertising alone, it would have to make drastic cuts across the company, including in the newsroom. The *Times* was already preparing to sell and lease back part of its new building, eliminate one hundred more jobs on the business side, and cut newsroom salaries by 5 percent. This was on top of the $250 million loan from Carlos Slim and the selling of display advertisements at the bottom of its front page. None of that was enough.

The *Times* had tried to impose a domestic paywall on its website once before, with a limited pay plan known as TimesSelect, in September 2005, less than ten years after nytimes.com was launched with a champagne toast in front of a computer terminal.* It had not gone well. At the time, *The Wall Street Journal* was the only major United States publication charging readers to access its website; the *Los Angeles Times* had earlier abandoned its own pay plan. "Best of luck with TimesSelect," Michael Kinsley, the founding editor of the online magazine *Slate*, wrote Sulzberger. "As you may recall, we tried the same experiment at Slate, with limited success (aka total failure). Would you like an official Slate umbrella? (A $19.95 value, which we offered as a premium for a $20 subscription.) I believe there's a closet somewhere at Microsoft with about 12,000 of them." But Sulzberger was growing dubious about the advertising potential of the Web and approved the idea. "I understand your feelings about TimesSelect but we made a business decision that we deem critical to our financial future," Sulzberger wrote a reader who complained about the charge. "It would do us little good to keep our columns open to all at the risk of going out of business." TimesSelect was a confection, jury-rigged to accommodate the different concerns of newsroom and digital editors, circulation and advertising executives, the company's chief executive, and the publisher. Readers would pay to read columnists—popular writers like Maureen Dowd, Thomas Friedman, and Bob Herbert—and have access to one hundred free articles a month from the newspaper's archives. The rest of the website would be free. Print subscribers paid $481 a year for seven-day-a-week home delivery in the New York metropolitan area in 2005. TimesSelect would cost $49.95 a year. The columnists grew to loathe TimesSelect, as their readership dropped by as much as 82 percent within the first year. Friedman had encouraged Sulzberger

---

* Overseas readers of the *Times* were charged thirty-five dollars a month to read the newspaper online when the site first was launched in 1996; the company dropped the pay plan on Bastille Day of 1998.

to try the limited paywall, but he changed his mind as he encountered online readers outside the country, where the print newspaper was not available, who told him they would not pay to read a column that had been free. "There was no question in my mind," he said years later as he discussed how TimesSelect had driven readers away from columnists. "People would say, 'I'm not going to pay for the paywall.' I have a lot of overseas readers. That's where I have a lot of strength. And I knew I was losing them." Friedman began handing out codes providing free access to TimesSelect, and before long, he and the other columnists pleaded with the publisher to abandon the experiment. At first, Sulzberger stood fast. We just have to give this a shot, Sulzberger told Friedman. That shot lasted for two years; engineers began uninstalling the TimesSelect software on September 19, 2007, after the company decided that removing the wall would increase traffic to the site, resulting in enough new advertising to make up any lost in subscription revenue.

TimesSelect was an imperfect solution to a real problem. The paying audience was older than the readership of the free website, with a median age of fifty-six years old, compared with the website's forty-seven years old. That was an unnerving realization for a newspaper worrying about its future. But it would eventually draw 227,000 paid subscribers and produce revenues of $10 million a year. And though that was a modest gain at a considerable cost, the *Times* drew a lesson from this experiment: that under the right circumstances, its devoted customers would pay to read the *Times* online.

* * *

David S. Perpich was a thirty-one-year-old senior associate at Booz & Company, a management-consulting firm, his first job after graduating Harvard Business School. He was also a Sulzberger: grandson of Punch Sulzberger and nephew of Arthur Sulzberger, Jr. Bright and earnest, he was a member of the fifth generation of this newspaper dynasty, and one of three cousins who would one day find themselves in contention to be the next publisher. The other cousins, A. G. Sulzberger and Sam Dolnick, had embarked on careers as reporters out of college. By contrast, Perpich had become a vice president and founder at Scratch Music Group, a disc jockey school and booking service for cruise lines and music festivals, indulging his own interest in hip-hop. But he was drawn to the *Times*, and on the advice of Arthur Sulzberger and Michael Golden, he decided to go to business school to prepare himself for a career in publishing.

Dolnick and A. G. Sulzberger were interested in the journalism side of newspapers, but Perpich was drawn to the business side, and in particular the challenge news organizations faced in financing their operations in a digital world. That was what he'd studied at Harvard, and at Booz his portfolio included advising media companies on how to increase online revenues. There were few better examples of a media company struggling with this challenge than the *Times*. So Perpich perked up when he came across a post in *Eat Sleep Publish*, a journalism and publishing blog, extolling the paywall that had been developed by the *Financial Times* of London. The *Financial Times* model offered an alternative to TimesSelect, or the rigid paywall on the website of *The Wall Street Journal*, whose specialized audience included customers able to write off their subscriptions on their expense accounts. This was a wall, but it was a porous one that treated the newspaper's most loyal readers differently from those who might have wandered there from a link. It allowed readers to view a set number of stories each month before they had to start paying.

At the end of 2008, Perpich sent a note to Michael Golden. *"I truly believe this is the model of the future and I think the Times could pull off some version of this,"* Perpich wrote him. "I truly believe the *Times* will never unlock its real value if it doesn't charge subscribers given that online advertising will never replace the full value lost in print. That said, going to a fully paid model will never work on the web. I believe this is the right compromise—a subscription model built for the dynamics of the web." Arthur Sulzberger had also concluded that the business model that had carried his family's newspaper for more than a century was faltering; the only remaining question was the speed of the decline. In the first weeks of 2009, Sulzberger stopped by Nisenholtz's corner office on the seventeenth floor, a floor above his own, with expansive windows looking south toward downtown Manhattan and west over to the Hudson River. The publisher was somber as he talked to Nisenholtz about the crossroads the newspaper had reached.

I understand your emotional attachment to the free model, Sulzberger told Nisenholtz. But let's fast-forward twenty years. We are dependent on digital, we are free, and we have a situation like we're facing here. We'd have to fire one-quarter of our people.

That February, Sulzberger assembled fifteen of his top editors and business executives to ask if the *Times* should try again to charge the growing audience that was reading the *Times* for free online. That set off one of the most critical debates in the paper's history. Its outcome would, more than anything else, define Sulzberger's legacy and determine whether the *Times* would survive the greatest challenge to its existence.

At first, the battle lines were familiar. Nisenholtz warned, as he had when Sulzberger was considering TimesSelect, that a paywall would gut the business model that he had championed since he arrived at the *Times*: creating a huge audience of nonpaying readers that would bring in digital advertisers to fill in the loss in revenues created by the exodus of print advertisers. Nisenholtz, making his case in the Eagle Room, reminded his colleagues of the drop in traffic experienced by columnists caught behind the TimesSelect paywall and invoked the lesson of the London *Times*, which had suffered a huge drop in traffic after creating its own paywall.

We have built the largest newspaper website in the world with the largest advertising base in the world, Nisenholtz said. It is scary to think what will happen if we put it behind a paywall. We need to be really careful about potentially destroying what we have built over these past thirteen years.

Jonathan Landman, who had crossed over from print to become a deputy managing editor overseeing the newsroom's Web operations, warned that a paywall would ultimately chase away younger readers who surfed an Internet where almost everything was free and whom the *Times* would need to prosper in the decades to come.

But Nisenholtz and Landman stood nearly alone in resisting what now seemed inevitable. The recession of 2008, the layoffs in the newsroom, and the continued decline of the paper's economic fortunes—ad revenues in 2008 had dropped 14.2 percent over the year before—had rattled the paper's editors and managers, demonstrating that the *Times*'s survival could not be taken for granted. It now seemed that much of the print advertising revenue that had disappeared was not going to return:

the days of newspaper sections thick with classified advertisements were behind them. At meeting after meeting, Bill Keller argued that the time had come to adopt a paywall. Keller was ready to retire as executive editor, though that was not well-known in the newsroom, and he viewed this as his final mission. Keller liked to talk about himself as the "house optimistic," but he did not see how the *Times* could survive without charging its digital audience. It was a disservice to *Times* journalists—as well as its loyal readers—to give away such a high-quality product. "Good journalism isn't cheap," Keller said years later. *Times* print readers were willing to pay for this product: the continued escalation of yearly subscriptions had proved that. Indeed, the *Times*'s own marketing studies found an intensity of reader devotion verging on addiction—so much so that company executives began likening the newspaper to tobacco. Keller argued that digital readers would ultimately make the same calculation.

The deliberations would last six months. A parade of consultants appeared before the committee, reviewing internal and external studies of different types of paywalls, with extrapolations of how they might work at the *Times*. But the focus kept returning to the metered pay model that had been established at *Financial Times*. Its elegance—the way it enticed its most steadfast readers to pay without scaring off the occasional visitor who might one day subscribe—was comforting. And it seemed vastly superior to the alternative of a hard paywall that required a credit card to read more than a few paragraphs of a story, a pay plan Nisenholtz warned would "destroy the website." Keller embraced it; so did Andy Rosenthal and Jill Abramson and Janet Robinson.

Sulzberger listened to the discussion as it moved around the table, without sharing his own views. But in truth, almost from the beginning, when he visited Nisenholtz in his office, he knew what he wanted to do. Sulzberger was aware of the risks—he appreciated the warnings from Nisenholtz and Landman—but he had always been drawn to risks, to trying new things that might or might not work. He did not see how the *Times* could survive unless it charged its online audience. "The digital people said, 'No, we shouldn't have a pay wall,' but in the end, it became clear that we had no business model without it," Sulzberger said years later.

After months of debate that had divided the digital newsroom from the print one, a discussion that could literally decide the fate of the *Times*, the end was almost anticlimactic. No one was surprised—and more important, no one was upset—when Sulzberger, in September 2009, after going around the table one last time, said he wanted the paper to follow the road laid out by the *Financial Times*. Even Nisenholtz accepted the outcome. He would prefer that the website be free, but he realized, after watching Sulzberger, that that was not going to happen—and perhaps, given the changes in the economic climate, should not happen. The metered paywall was less drastic than the uncompromising paywall that had been on the table at the beginning of the discussion.

The most consequential decision of Sulzberger's twenty-five years as publisher was announced to the newsroom on January 20, 2010, in a statement from the publisher and Janet Robinson. It was a gamble, and it would take almost eighteen months before it was launched. Sulzberger said if it did not work, the *Times* could roll it back, as it had with TimesSelect, and try something else. But that was not entirely true. Print circulation had dropped 7.2 percent in fall 2009 compared to one year earlier; it was not going to come back. The *Times* was running out of options.

CHAPTER 35

A Digital Divide

Bill Keller had first proposed merging the digital and print newsrooms in May 2005, in a ten-page report to Arthur Sulzberger, Janet Robinson, and Martin Nisenholtz. "They should serve one master," Keller wrote. "And I think they would be happy to do so." He acknowledged the hurdles. The two newsrooms were separated—financially, administratively, physically, and culturally. Print editors considered the website an afterthought. But the gulf between the digital and print newsrooms was paralyzing. The *Times* was preparing to move into its new building in 2007, and this would be, in Keller's view, a chance to finally force these two newsrooms to work as one. The merger seemed at once daunting and inevitable. "You're doing precisely and exactly the right thing," Andrew Rosenthal, the deputy editor of the editorial page, wrote Keller. "Fight hard. This is St. Crispin's Day." Keller and Nisenholtz announced the change after it was approved by the publisher. "By integrating the newsrooms we plan to diminish and eventually eliminate the difference between newspaper journalists and Web journalists," they wrote, adding: "Our readers are moving, and so are we." Keller appointed Jonathan Landman as a deputy managing editor overseeing the transition.

Yet, five years later, with the paywall debate resolved as 2009 came to a close, and the digital and print newsrooms working out of the same new building, the merger was stalled. The digital newsroom had become a fiefdom. It was like the Washington bureau: sovereign and overseen by editors resistant to meddling from superiors who did not really understand this new world. It was a struggle for control, but it was also a philosophical dispute about how much the *Times* needed to change. Keller and Jill Abramson were the senior editors of the *Times*. But in many ways, Jim Roberts and Fiona Spruill—the two editors running the website—were just as powerful as their counterparts running the print newspaper. Abramson took to referring to them as the "shadow executive editor and managing editor." They decided what stories should go on the home page and how long they should stay there. They would often assign stories to their own staff writers, to make sure the Web had something to post first thing in the morning or to cover an event that the print editors considered beneath their standards. Abramson and Keller would talk about how the home page on a computer screen was becoming as much the face of the newspaper as the front page. (This would change as digital readers migrated from computer screens to mobile devices.) The front page had been the dog and the home page its tail, as Keller put it to Abramson; but now, the tail had begun to wag the dog.

* * *

Jim Roberts was a late convert to the Web. He had arrived at the *Times* at the end of 1986, hired from the *Dallas Times Herald* as a copy editor for the national desk. He had been an editor on the sports desk, the metropolitan desk, the political desk, the national desk, and the continuous news desk. He had been the national editor and the political editor. He had overseen the coverage of the 2000 presidential election and edited Jayson Blair during his final months at the newspaper. He was known as a newshound: aggressive and at times argumentative, passionate about colorful, breaking stories. His annual evaluations, while generally positive, described him as a bit of a control freak. He lumbered across the newsroom in cowboy boots, a picture of journalistic swagger, a first-to-arrive, last-to-leave editor who had a hint of a drawl from growing up in Virginia.

Landman had turned to him to run the digital news operation, drawn by his skill at driving the coverage of a breaking news stories, but Roberts's print background meant he was not an obvious choice. Competitive and territorial, he had been seen in the digital newsroom as the embodiment of the disdain and condescension they felt from their print colleagues. He once refused to allow a link in a story on the website that would send readers to the sites of competing organizations. It was understandable, but only in an old-school kind of way. Before making a final decision, Landman told Roberts to go to Landman's deputy, Richard Meislin, to reassure him that he was committed to the digital world.

All those concerns were put to rest soon after Roberts settled into his new job. Many print reporters and editors saw the website as little more than a new platform on which to distribute stories. Not Roberts. He and Spruill took chances. He would press correspondents to file articles on the Web throughout the day that were fresh and timely, often to the irritation of the writers. He hired a reporter to file early to the website on overnight developments—usually overseas, given the time difference with New York—and keep writing during the day, often to the irritation of the foreign desk. He and Spruill asked readers to send in their own photographs—from a Grateful Dead reunion tour (Roberts was a fan of the group), from the 2009 inauguration of Barack Obama—and published them on the site, often to the irritation of the photo desk.

He championed the hiring of Nate Silver, the founder of the FiveThirtyEight polling site, who brought a new emphasis on polls that challenged the paper's traditional interpretation of this kind of data, often to the irritation of the paper's in-house polling unit and some of the political writers. Silver was a jarring new presence; he had his own brand, with a dedicated audience of readers. His hiring foreshadowed how the Internet would shift the dynamics of mainstream journalism and elevate high-profile journalists over the institutions where they worked. Silver was given a desk a floor below the newsroom, away from his writing colleagues. Silver never went through the round of introductory meetings and dinners with the Washington bureau and political staff that he'd assumed would happen. From the beginning, he noticed the chill when he walked into a conference room where a meeting on political coverage was going on. It was a struggle to learn how to adjust to the stuffier style of writing found in the *Times;* he was steeped in the breezy conversational tone of the Web, which made it easier to walk readers through arcane discussions of statistical and polling science. But that was the kind of writing the *Times* needed to master if it was to become conversant on the Web. Silver would become a flashpoint, and Roberts his biggest defender. Roberts recruited Keller early on as a supporter, who saw in Silver a way to signal his own openness to change. "If you want yet another sign that this is the place Web innovators want to be you can look at the news today that Nate Silver, a wizard with numbers, is joining The Times," Keller announced to his staff.

* * *

In the spring of 2010, Keller told Abramson he wanted her to take a leave from the print newsroom to spend six months in the digital newsroom. Keller was thinking about the future. He thought Sulzberger should appoint Abramson as his successor when he stepped down. But Abramson was a product of the print world; she had only visited the digital offices two times while she was managing editor—and Keller anticipated how critical digital experience would be to the publisher when it came time to choose the next executive editor. But his decision to dispatch Abramson to the digital newsroom was only partially to burnish her résumé. Keller was frustrated at how the two newsrooms were still moving in different orbits, how his call to merge them continued to languish. "The website is still too much of an afterthought," he told the newsroom as he described Abramson's assignment. "In the priorities of senior editors—including me to be completely honest—web journalism remains secondary to the traditional business of deploying reporters and picking stories for the front page of the print edition." He knew the obstacles and tried to smooth the way. "It is not a takeover of digital by print. On the contrary, we aim to raise the stature of Web journalism and increase its influence in this partnership." But the agenda was clear. Keller wanted the print desks to have control and responsibility over what appeared online. He wanted his editors to wake up every morning thinking about what they would offer for the front page the next day, and what should be on the Web page that morning. He wanted the same editors who decided what went on the front page to determine what should be promoted on the home page.

Combining the newsrooms meant dismantling the digital newsroom, and that meant removing Roberts and Spruill. Keller had promoted Roberts to associate managing editor. But he began to see Roberts, whom he referred to as the "digital czar," as an obstacle, and he wanted Abramson to deal with that. Abramson's six-month immersion offered one more stage for the tensions that simmered between these two operations. Roberts and Spruill thought Abramson was never serious about learning about the Web. Spruill felt she had spent years fending off bad ideas from the newsroom, and she came to consider Abramson's mission a hostile takeover. Before long, Roberts and Spruill were barely trying to hide their contempt when Abramson showed up on her assignment. Abramson would complain how difficult it was to get information from Roberts and Spruill, who were both her subordinates, how they kept the doors to their offices shut. "They were impossible," she said years later. She would go to the website news meetings and notice Roberts and Spruill retreating to their phones, tapping out messages, in what she took as an expression of disrespect.

I'm the managing editor, she said to a colleague after one meeting. How dare they.

Lisa Tozzi, who had joined the website as a politics producer for the 2000 presidential election, warned Abramson that senior members of the website staff would leave the *Times* if the digital unit was disbanded and they were forced to move to the print-news desks. But Tozzi felt Abramson had made up her mind. She was a hard person to disagree with, Tozzi would say.

Abramson concluded her assignment with a damning, if not surprising, report. "There are still many Web-focused colleagues who feel they work for a separate news organization run by Jim and Fiona," she wrote. "Many work on 'web only' stories and features ordered up by Jim and Fiona; some of these are good, some not, but they don't seem bolted firmly onto the main journalistic priorities set by the desk heads." Digital employees "still feel largely divorced from the main newsroom and cut off from the editors who are making the crucial calls about our news report, including the desk heads and, especially, the top of the masthead, especially the Executive Editor and the two Managing Editors."

To deal with this, Abramson said the producers in charge of graphics, videos, and blogs should be reassigned to the print news departments and report to editors who ran the desks. Those print editors should decide how to promote stories, videos, graphics, and photographs on all the *Times*'s digital platforms. The daily meeting of editors should begin at ten o'clock in the morning—thirty minutes earlier than usual—so the editors could start the day focusing on what should go on the website. New assignments would be found for Roberts and Spruill.

Roberts and Landman got wind of her recommendations and tried to block them. "I could hardly bear to see the team that Fiona and I built and nurtured over the past 4–5 years broken up in that fashion, unless there were significant benefits, which I don't see," Roberts wrote Abramson. Landman complained directly to Keller. "It will do more harm than good," he said. "It feels more to me like conquest, or absorption, than integration. In every case the underlying idea is that print people know best. There is no evidence in this document of looking for alternative points of view. This document is the work of somebody who has made up her mind."

There were fewer complaints from the print newsroom. The concerns and suspicions had not gone away, but foreign correspondents had come to appreciate the reach of the website; readers could not buy the morning *Times* on the streets of Paris or Bangkok. And the economic collapse had left reporters and editors worried about their jobs. The retirements and buyouts over the previous two years had created a younger newsroom, less shackled by ritual and adherence to tradition. Blogs, and the more casual writing that could be found on the website, as epitomized by Nate Silver, were not alien to the younger writers. It had taken five years, but the merger of the print and digital newsrooms happened in 2010. Keller would always consider that the greatest success of his years as executive editor—and would wonder if he and Abramson would get the credit they deserved.

* * *

The *Times* paywall was unveiled to the public on March 28, 2011. "It's an important step that we hope you will see as an investment in The *Times*, one that will strengthen our ability to provide high-quality journalism to readers around the world and on any platform," Sulzberger said in a note to readers. "The change will primarily affect those who are heavy consumers of the content on our website and on mobile applications."

The first twenty articles per month would be free. The charge for those who wanted access to more stories ranged from fifteen dollars a month to thirty-five dollars a month. In the media industry, the reception was skeptical. "By my back-of-the-envelope math, the paywall won't even cover its own development costs for a good two years, and beyond that will never generate enough money to really make a difference to NYTCo revenues," Felix Salmon, the financial journalist, wrote in *Wired*.

"For the time being, though, I just can't see how this move makes any kind of financial sense for the NYT," he wrote. "The upside is limited; the downside is that it ceases to be the paper of record for the world. Who would take that bet?" There was apprehension at the top levels of the *Times* as well—but those concerns were swept away on the first day that digital subscribers were allowed to register. A group of editors and engineers gathered around a computer, champagne at the ready, and watched the numbers click up: ten thousand people on that first day. When he wrote his column, Salmon bet a colleague that the *Times* would not reach three hundred thousand paid subscribers within two years. He reconsidered that prediction as the *Times* reported a surge in new subscriptions. "There seems little doubt that, barring something enormous and unexpected, I'm going to lose my bet; the only question is by how much," Salmon wrote. McKinsey & Company, the management consultants that the *Times* retained to help develop the pay model, had put the ceiling for digital subscribers at 650,000. By the end of 2011, 390,000 people had already signed up for the *Times* and the *International Herald Tribune*, according to the company's annual report. There would always be advertisers, but the early success of the paywall showed the possibility of a new business model, of a newspaper reliant first and foremost on loyal readers willing to pay, and less subject to the whims of an economic cycle.

PART VI

CHANGE

2011–2016

CHAPTER 36

A Tiger on the News

On June 2, 2011, Arthur Sulzberger announced the first change in the newsroom's management in eight years. Bill Keller would step down as executive editor in September. Keller had shared his retirement plans with Jill Abramson over a boozy dinner in the West Village in the summer of 2010, but at her urging (and also the urging of his wife, Emma) delayed his departure until the paywall was established and its success assured. That moment had arrived. Keller was only sixty-two years old, but he had been at the *Times* since Abe Rosenthal hired him as a general assignment reporter for the Washington bureau in 1984; he was restless and wanted to return to writing a column.

In the fourteen years since she had arrived at the *Times* from *The Wall Street Journal*, Abramson had gone from reporter to Washington editor to Washington bureau chief before being named managing editor. And now, at the age of fifty-seven, she was Keller's choice to become the next executive editor, a recommendation he made to Sulzberger as he prepared to step down. But there was a distance between Abramson and Sulzberger, born of an accumulation of slights and uncomfortable interactions over the years. Sulzberger's impressions of Abramson were colored by her battles with Howell Raines, when she was the Washington bureau chief. Abramson's career soared as Raines's collapsed, but it was the kind of confrontational behavior, by both parties, that Sulzberger disliked. Sulzberger would talk about how Abramson grimaced at executive lunches when the topic turned to matters of business, and it rankled him. There was a personal element as well: Sulzberger once told Keller he could not stand her voice, which he described as fingernails on a chalkboard. Abramson sensed this; she thought he had not liked her from the first time she introduced herself at a party celebrating the appointment of Michael Oreskes as Washington bureau chief in 1997, when she was still at *The Wall Street Journal.*

I know who you are, Sulzberger said, with what she took as dismissiveness.

Abramson found Sulzberger irritating, with his social ineptness, strained attempts at humor and camaraderie, and his punctilious attention to seating charts at dinners. He was unreadable and opaque, and that frustrated her. Abramson appreciated him as a publisher who, as a rule, did not meddle with the news coverage, but she felt he had never shown much interest in her, or much enthusiasm about her career. She had flown to Washington to testify at the perjury trial of Scooter Libby in 2007; defense attorneys were hoping Abramson would discredit Judith Miller, one of the main witnesses against Libby, by disputing Miller's account of a conversation she claimed to have had with Abramson about orchestrated White House leaks. Abramson was only on the stand for four minutes—she testified that she did not recall the details of the conversation in question—but she knew how much attention her testimony would draw, and she'd spent hours preparing with a lawyer. When she ran into the publisher back in New York, he not only failed to inquire about her experience in court but made a flippant joke about it. She was livid and followed him back into his office.

You know, Arthur, it was not fun to go to Washington to testify in the Libby trial, and I never heard boo from you about it, she said. I was doing this for the company. Arthur, I am your managing editor.

You sure are, Sulzberger responded, though he looked slightly mystified. When Abramson arrived at her desk the next day, a handwritten note was perched on her computer terminal. "I feel bad that I wasn't more attuned to what you were going through," he wrote her. "But I feel good that we have a strong enough relationship so that you felt comfortable raising this with me." Abramson tried to prod him into talking about her career when they were alone together at lunch, about two years after she testified at the Libby trial. In all the time that I've been in this job, you have never given me any sense of whether I'm doing okay, if there is anything you want me to improve on, Abramson said. Sulzberger looked uncomfortable. Oh, Jill—you know you're my go-to girl, he responded.

Sulzberger had given her reason to worry about the executive editor job when he took her to Le Bernardin, one of New York's most elegant restaurants, to interview her for the position. He started talking about her temperament the moment they sat down. Everyone knows there's a good Jill and a bad Jill, Sulzberger said. I don't know which Jill I am going to get.

Abramson froze; they had not even begun to eat. She talked about her credentials and experience and love of journalism and the *Times*, why he should choose her; and when they were done, she excused herself, saying she had to attend to an errand. She wandered the streets convinced she would never get the job. Abramson wrote Sulzberger a memorandum entitled "WHY ME," making the case for her appointment. "To be utterly frank, tensions between you and Bill have created a bit of awkwardness in our relationship to this point," she said. "It is my sincere desire to clear away any remnants of that distance." She acknowledged the concerns Sulzberger may have heard from the newsroom. "Yes, I can be intense," she said. "But I don't smother." The next executive editor "must be a tiger on the news," as she put it. "I am built for these big news times."

Abramson did not fit the classic model of a *Times* executive editor. She had not worked overseas. She had not won a Pulitzer. She had not spent most of her career at the *Times*. And Sulzberger had been told there were risks in putting Abramson in a job like this. Susan Chira, the foreign editor, who had known Sulzberger from their days working together on the metropolitan desk, had gone to his office to urge him not to appoint her. Chira had been one of the first reporters to stand up and criticize the Raines newsroom at the town hall meeting after Jayson Blair left the newspaper in 2003. "This could not have happened in a culture in which people felt freer to contest what people at the top felt," she said at the time. And now Chira described Abramson to the publisher as volatile, sporadically cruel, intolerant of dissent, and prone to making decisions through a lens of what was best for her. Keller, in one of his evaluations of Abramson, which would have landed on Sulzberger's desk, praised her as an editor who noticed when a rival newspaper had beaten the *Times* "before the desk heads whose job it is to be on top of the story." But he quoted what Abramson had said in describing herself in a self-evaluation: "I can be abrupt and judgmental and even self-righteous. I can be too critical and impatient. I interrupt." Keller said there was some truth to that.

Sulzberger was also considering Dean Baquet, who was now the Washington bureau chief, and Martin Baron, who was running *The Boston Globe* and would later be the executive editor of *The Washington Post*, both of whom had impressive résumés. But he would ultimately overlook the warnings and pick Abramson. She had held two of the top positions in the *Times* newsroom—the Washington bureau chief and the paper's managing editor—and had come to the *Times* as an award-winning writer at *The Wall Street Journal*. Keller strongly endorsed her as his successor. For all their differences, Sulzberger thought she had "gumption and guts," as he put it. And Sulzberger was still intent on blazing his own path as publisher by showing how he was different from his father. He knew about the newspaper's problematic history with women, the lawsuit that charged the newspaper with discriminating against women in hiring, promotion, and pay. He had appointed the first woman to run the editorial page, Gail Collins, and the company's first woman chief executive, Janet Robinson, but he was eager to make further amends. He had misgivings, but he was ready to put them aside.

I've made my decision, Sulzberger told Abramson, calling her on her cellphone. I'd love you to be the next executive editor.

It would be the honor of my life, Abramson responded.

On the day Sulzberger announced the appointment to the newsroom, Max Frankel and Joseph Lelyveld came to the *Times* headquarters to witness the transition. "You are, in truth, as ready for this position as anyone can be," the publisher said. "Jill, this is your time and I deeply look forward to the years ahead and our working together as friends and partners."

On September 6, 2011, Abramson took over a newspaper that seemed to have picked the lock of how to charge online readers. It was approaching four hundred thousand paid subscriptions, well past all projections. But advertising revenues were plummeting, and more layoffs would be needed. Even with its adoption of a paywall, viewed as groundbreaking in the industry, the *Times* trailed its competitors in reinventing itself for a world where information was presented on mobile devices and computer screens rather than sheets of newsprint. Expectations for the job of executive editor were changing. The rules that set the barriers between the newsroom and the business side, that established the primacy of the newsroom, that judged executive editors first and foremost by the journalism of the newsroom, were being reconsidered.

The *Times* has long been a stage for struggles among highly qualified, often brilliant people scrambling for position, prestige, and power. The depth of talent at the paper is so great—and the sheer momentum of the *Times* is so great—that the paper survives. Progress might be slowed, mistakes might be made, talented people cast aside and ordinary ones advanced, but the stories of the players are rarely as important as the story of the organization itself. The battles that would be played out among the highest-level actors at the paper over the next two years of Abramson's editorship would prove more critical to the paper's survival. They took place at a pivot between a print and digital age, where the old ways were being discarded, the paper's business model was collapsing, and the *Times* was struggling to complete a troubled transition to a modern-day news organization. Abramson, with her commanding knowledge of Washington and government, her sharp news sense, and her years of experience as an investigative reporter and editor, would have been an obvious choice at another time in the paper's history. But as would soon become clear—to her and ultimately to Sulzberger—she was not the right person for this moment; she was not the executive editor the *Times* needed to lead it through the wrenching years ahead.

* * *

Betsy Wade was the first woman to edit news copy in the paper's history, so she took note when Abramson was appointed executive editor. Wade was eighty-two years old and had retired in 2001, ending a forty-five-year career that was distinguished by, among other things, being the lead plaintiff in the 1974 class-action lawsuit that accused the *Times* of discriminating against women. She became the lead copy editor on the foreign desk, but that was as far as she would rise in the editing ranks.

Wade always saw Abramson's appointment as the final victory of *Elizabeth Boylan et al. v. The New York Times*, as her case was known. Abramson had been in the same class as Wade's son at the Ethical Culture Fieldston School in New York, so Abramson's appointment, Wade liked to say, answered the question people would ask her back in the 1970s: What would it take before a woman would run the *Times* newsroom? "Now we know exactly what it takes," Wade said in the last years of her life. "One generation."

Abramson was aware of the burden she carried as the newspaper's first woman executive editor. She had been the paper's first woman Washington bureau chief and the first woman managing editor. "The ascension of Jill Abramson to the editor's chair of the New York Times will make the history books," the *Los Angeles Times* wrote. Abramson had become a symbol, much the way Gerald Boyd had been when he became the highest-ranking Black editor in the newspaper's history. "Women who have struggled to reach the top in journalism saw her as a model for better days," Wade would later write.

Her appointment was a cause of celebration, but being "the first," carrying that torch for her gender, meant scrutiny and expectations. It all fed the insecurity, the imposter syndrome doubts of do-I-really-deserve-to-be-here that plague even the most accomplished journalists who reach the top ranks of the *Times*. When, a week before she took over, an editor, Glenn Kramon, asked how she was holding up, Abramson confided that she was "extremely nervous," as he recounted in his journal. Still, Abramson embraced the attention that came with her prominence. She arrived on her first day at work shadowed by a correspondent from *The New Yorker*. She had given the writer, Ken Auletta, access as she crossed this threshold—much the way Howell Raines had, with the same writer, when he became executive editor. She would, she later said, prepare for each session with Auletta by taking a Xanax. But she need not have worried. "Abramson made a point of doing something that Raines was unlikely to have done: walking over and calling out, 'Good morning, Metro desk!'" Auletta wrote of her first day. "Then she offered congratulations for a front-page story on the admissions policies of New York private schools." This was part of a flood of adulatory attention: she was named one of the ten most powerful women in media of 2011 in *Forbes*.

Abramson quickly made clear this would not be a continuation of a Keller administration. Within her first weeks, she had installed a new managing editor, two new assistant managing editors, and new editors to run the national desk, the foreign desk, and the Washington bureau. Her first appointments signaled how she would be taking chances and breaking with tradition, with an emphasis on youth in a newspaper that typically rewarded seniority. The new Washington bureau chief was David Leonhardt, a columnist who Abramson described as "one of our finest writers and most elegant thinkers" and who had won a Pulitzer Prize for commentary, but who was thirty-eight years old and, apart from serving as editor-in-chief of the *Yale Daily News* while in college, had not been an editor before. Sam Sifton, who was forty-five, the restaurant critic, and former editor of the dining section, would become national editor.*

Sulzberger suggested she consider Dean Baquet to be managing editor. Suggestion or not—Sulzberger always told his executive editors that they chose their own managing editors—it did not leave her much choice, unless she wanted to begin her tenure by refusing a request from the publisher. Abramson asked Baquet to be her managing editor over dinner the following weekend in New Orleans, where they were attending a journalism convention. She knew Baquet, and she liked him. They shared an interest in investigative reporting, and she had helped convince him to leave the *Los Angeles Times* and return to *The New York Times*. She went to Baquet's mother's funeral—a gesture that Baquet never forgot. But as a matter of politics, it was questionable. Baquet had been one of her rivals for the job. Sulzberger considered it a bold move, but Abramson would come to decide she had made a mistake. She also appointed Susan Chira as an assistant managing editor, at Baquet's suggestion. She would learn later, from Janet Elder, a deputy managing editor, how Chira had urged Sulzberger not to promote her to the top of the newsroom. "Team of executioners," she would come to call her team of editors, a dark homage to *Team of Rivals*, Doris Kearns Goodwin's biographical portrait of Lincoln and his cabinet, published in 2005.

---

* Neither would hold those positions for long, but both Sifton and Leonhardt would continue in long, successful careers as editors.

* * *

Abramson arrived at the *Times* building early one morning in December 2011 and took the elevator to the cafeteria on the fourteenth floor, with its floor-to-ceiling windows offering vistas of sun-speckled streets and office towers to the south and the Hudson River to the west. She had just settled in for coffee with a reporter when Sulzberger rounded the corner, gesturing for her attention.

I need to see you, he said.

Sulzberger looked worried. He pulled her into a stairway and announced he had just fired Janet Robinson, the chief executive officer of the Times Company. He had called Robinson into his office to tell her that her career at the *Times* was over; it was an abrupt and unexpected dismissal that would stun the company and Wall Street.

Robinson was sixty-one years old, a former schoolteacher who had worked for the *Times* for twenty-eight years. She was hired as an account executive in the company's magazine division, and her career had taken off: senior vice president for advertising at the Times Company, president and general manager of the *Times* newspaper, the chief executive of the company. Robinson was a force behind the creation of the national edition and the paywall, both of which would prove critical to the paper's financial success. She had been a tough and intimidating executive, and she held her own in a male-dominated environment. But the publisher always thought Martin Nisenholtz—the senior vice president for digital, the person that Sulzberger years later would call the smartest hire he ever made—had retired in 2011 because he was weary of battling Robinson. And Sulzberger was under pressure from the family and stockholders to improve the company's financial outlook. The stock price had lost almost 80 percent of its value since Robinson became chief executive in 2004.

More than anything, her twenty-eight years of experience had become as much of a burden as an asset for a company that was talking about reinvention. Robinson was a product of the old order, comfortable with the way things had once been done. She and Bill Keller, when he was executive editor, operated in their own universes; they were cordial at best, and certainly not ready to engage in the kind of symbiotic relationship that would be needed for the retooling Sulzberger had in mind. Early in his tenure, Keller proposed to the publisher that he and Martin Baron, the executive editor of *The Boston Globe*, which was owned by the *Times*, be given seats on the company's governing executive committee. Sulzberger ran the idea by Robinson, who shot it down instantly, angered that Keller thought the committee needed help to understand the news department. "Frankly, I would put my experience and knowledge on a higher perch than Bill evidently does and so would MANY MANY MANY others in the newspaper and magazine worlds," Robinson told the publisher. (Sulzberger went back to Keller to say he would gain nothing from sitting in on meetings. "The truth is, the vast majority of the stuff would bore you to tears," he said.)

Robinson's ouster was unsettling for Abramson, who had been in her job for just three months. Robinson had been an ally during her fights with Howell Raines. She had urged Sulzberger to appoint Abramson as executive editor. And she struck Abramson as collegial and appropriately deferential to the newsroom. "Janet Robinson has been an unwavering friend," Abramson said at the newsroom ceremony where Sulzberger introduced her as his new executive editor. "During a rough patch in Washington, Janet called me and said, 'You will leave over my dead body.' Because of Janet I stand here today."

It was another seven months before the *Times* settled on a successor: Mark Thompson, the former director general of the BBC—a public-broadcast media executive who had never worked in newspapers (save for when he was an editor at his college magazine, *The Isis*, as an Oxford undergraduate). At the BBC, Thompson oversaw a quasi-government agency with over twenty-three thousand employees—more than four times the workforce at the private-sector corporation he would now run—spread across fifty radio stations, eight television stations, and a website. He had spent most of his life in England. Thompson could hardly have been more different from his predecessors, which he realized from the start.

Are you sure this is the right moment in the *Times* history to appoint an English civil servant to run it? Thompson asked rhetorically at his final interview with Sulzberger and the board of directors.

Thompson was fifty-five years old, a burly and boisterous character with a light beard who burst with enthusiasm when he talked about change and disruption; in short, precisely the kind of character who had always intrigued Sulzberger. His Britishness added to the mystique, particularly for an American publisher who quoted Winston Churchill and had set aside a room close to his office to display Churchill memorabilia. (Churchill's American grandfather, Leonard Jerome, had been an early investor in *The New-York Times*.) Thompson had been a transformative figure at the BBC, prodding an old-line media company into the digital age, aspiring to elevate this British institution into a global media powerhouse. And that was what Sulzberger wanted him to do for the *Times*. Sulzberger and Michael Golden had assured Thompson that the company intended to radically change to accommodate the rise of digital media and the collapse of print advertising.

A large part of that transformation would be redefining the relationship between the chief executive and the executive editor. Thompson was more aggressive than Robinson in formulating new ways the newspaper could make money and expand its audience. His vision presumed the active participation of reporters and editors in moneymaking ventures, some of which strayed far beyond what would have been countenanced in the era of an Abe Rosenthal or a Max Frankel. He imagined *Times*-sponsored conferences, cruises, podcasts, and radio shows that featured reporters, editors, and columnists who would promote their work and promote the *Times*. He assured Abramson that he was respectful of tradition and her authority, but he expected the newsroom and its executive editor to be a full partner in developing new ways to display and market the news in a digital era. And, he said, audience development could not be left to the business department alone: the newsroom needed to understand and respond to what readers wanted.

There had always been an uneasy relationship at the *Times* between the company's chief executive and the executive editor—a reflection of the different values and priorities in the two silos of the newspaper. The story of Abe Rosenthal ordering an advertising executive out of the newsroom showed that the *Times* was a caste society. People who worked in the corporate offices would hesitantly ask Michael Golden if they could join the crowd assembled in the newsroom to hear the Pulitzer announcements each spring. "I hope to convince you that many of your colleagues on the business-side do indeed understand the sacrosanct nature of a free and independent press," Russell Lewis, a Robinson predecessor, wrote Howell Raines in 1993. "For many of us, it is an important reason why we've chosen to work here at the Times." The two sides were not equal in stature or authority, and Thompson was intent on changing that.

Thompson's relationship with Abramson was destined to be difficult, and it was immediately complicated by the circumstances of Thompson's arrival in New York. Shortly after he stepped down from the BBC, reports on rival television stations revealed that his network had killed a report on *Newsnight*, a current-affairs program, examining allegations that Jimmy Savile, a legendary BBC host who had since died, had sexually abused scores of teenagers over the course of his career. Thompson was running the BBC when the report was killed. He denied knowing about the decision until after it was made.

Thompson's appointment seemed in jeopardy, and Sulzberger was once again facing questions about his judgment. Thompson's "integrity and decision-making are bound to affect the Times and its journalism—profoundly," Margaret Sullivan, the newspaper's public editor, wrote in a column. "It's worth considering now whether he is the right person for the job, given this turn of events." Abramson assigned Matt Purdy, the investigations editor who had written about the problems of the Wen Ho Lee investigation, to fly to London and look into Thompson's dealings. It all made for an uncomfortable juxtaposition: the celebration of Thompson as he prepared to take a new job alongside an investigation into potential impropriety at his last one. Thompson tried to move ahead, sending out a note at the end of his first week about his ambition and plans, and announcing he would be hosting town hall meetings with the staff. A few weeks later, he put off those town halls because an official inquiry by the BBC would not be completed until early 2013. "I know that there's been considerable—and quite understandable—interest in this topic inside as well as outside the *Times*," he wrote. In the end, the BBC report and the *Times* stories found no evidence to contradict Thompson's account that he was not involved in killing the investigative report. Abramson's decision to pursue the story was in keeping with how the *Times* reported on problems in its house. By all indications, neither Sulzberger nor Thompson ever registered a complaint with Abramson or tried to stop it (though it is hard to see how they could have, had they wanted to). Still, it was an uncomfortable start to a relationship.

Abramson invited Thompson to join her on a trip to Silicon Valley, which turned into days of driving and talking. The newspaper was still moving through difficult waters: revenues were dropping, and more newsroom cuts seemed inevitable. When she returned to New York, she spoke warmly of Thompson and expressed confidence that he would help the newspaper survive this latest downturn.

"Mark impresses me as a great mind who can help us cross to safety," she told her staff just before Christmas in 2012. "Though the BBC has a different business model, Mark built lucrative, successful new ventures there, including its brilliant website. He is also a first-class journalist." The *Times* would need to change the way it operated, and she wanted to assure the newsroom that she was on board with that. "Lines between our journalism and business decisions are not being blurred," she said. "The newsroom and the business side must be partners in many more things right now, from *IHT*"—the *International Herald Tribune*—"to the build-out of DealBook, including last week's successful conference, to the redesign of our website. Strengthening that partnership is important to our future."

But despite what she had said to her staff, Abramson was wary of Thompson and his talk about partnerships between the newsroom and the business side. She was offended by all the strategizing about audience development, conferences, cruises, even a *New York Times* wine club. If I wanted to do this, I would have gone to Harvard Business School, she thought.

CHAPTER 37

No Switzerland

"I have no doubts at all you are the right person to be our Executive Editor," Arthur Sulzberger, Jr., wrote Jill Abramson in January 2013. "I applaud your focus and your commitment to this institution. The *Times* is absolutely in your blood—and that shows." Sulzberger's annual evaluation of Abramson glowed with praise for how she handled budget cuts, shepherded the *Times* into a digital world, and oversaw the complications of reporting on the BBC scandal that had threatened the appointment of Mark Thompson as the new *Times* chief executive.

Journalistically, 2012 had been a strong year under Abramson. The newspaper would win four Pulitzer Prizes for its coverage that year, three of them for the kind of enterprise journalism Abramson had championed throughout her career: in-depth investigations of government and corporate malfeasance. There were stories on corruption at the highest ranks of the Chinese government, the use of bribery by Walmart to gain market dominance in Mexico, and an examination of how Apple had outsourced tens of thousands of jobs from the United States by moving the manufacture of millions of iPhones and iPads to cheaper and less regulated factories in China. The fourth Pulitzer was for "Snow Fall: The Avalanche at Tunnel Creek," a digital presentation that incorporated video and graphics with evocative writing to tell the story of a deadly avalanche. It drew praise across the industry as a model of how a legacy print newspaper could embrace the storytelling tools of a digital age.

But by the start of 2013, Abramson had come to loathe being the executive editor of the *Times*. "I hated that job from the first day," she said years later. She was deadened by the meetings on budget cuts, personnel issues, and business and digital strategy that filled her schedule in fifteen-minute increments, while her managing editor, Dean Baquet was free, as she saw it, to spend his time talking to reporters about stories. She saw Thompson as a threat to the integrity of the newsroom and to her own authority. When they traveled around Silicon Valley, Thompson said he intended to restructure the company, and that she would not like it very much. Her fears were confirmed when Sulzberger called her to his office. There, as Thompson watched, the publisher announced that Tom Bodkin, a deputy managing editor for design who reported to the executive editor, would henceforth report to Thompson as well.

Thompson had always described himself as a journalist, because of his work at the BBC. And there he was, standing next to Abramson and Sulzberger when the paper learned it had won those Pulitzers, the moment memorialized in a photograph showing Sulzberger holding up four fingers. Thompson's ambitions were clear, as far as Abramson was concerned. He thinks he can do my job, she thought.

Abramson was confronting an avalanche of destabilizing forces: drastic changes in the way newspapers work, demands that pulled her away from what she saw as her strengths, and a new chief executive, empowered by the publisher, who was hands-on in the newsroom in a way no executive editor had experienced before. The decision of what news was fit to print was no longer the sole province of the executive editor. Her unhappiness was etched across her face as she walked, head down, through the newsroom. Feeling isolated and embattled, Abramson became polarizing—a leader whom many reporters, editors, corporate executives, as well as the publisher, were wary to cross. "I accept the criticism that I can seem aloof and even scary," she said in a meeting with reporters and editors one year after she began as executive editor. "I sure don't mean to be."

Abramson would later argue that being an aggressive woman in a newsroom with a troubled history of accepting women in its highest ranks accounted for many of the complaints about her management. Years later, speaking at the Stanford Graduate School of Business, she said her style had been shaped, in part, by trying to survive in a man's world, by being forced to speak over men who were louder, and often dismissive of her abilities. Many people, inside and outside the newsroom, would come to her defense, saying she was being judged by a different standard because she was a woman.

That explained much of her difficulties. But these were not new issues; they were the same concerns that Susan Chira, the first woman foreign editor, had voiced to Sulzberger before he picked her. Gail Collins, the newspaper's first woman editorial page editor, had been unsympathetic when Abramson, then the Washington bureau chief, came to her distressed about how she was being treated by Howell Raines. Soma Golden Behr, the first woman national editor, had been similarly unmoved when Abramson took her to a park bench in Washington and complained about the sexism she was encountering from editors in New York; in Golden Behr's experience, Washington bureau chiefs were always upset about how they were being treated by editors in New York.

Some of the same criticisms of Abramson had showed up over the years in evaluations written about her from editors and reporters. "When 'Bad Jill' comes to work—when she's in a foul mood—it poisons the well for everybody," one of her employees wrote in an anonymous review that was shared with Abramson in 2006. Susan Edgerley, an editor in charge of compiling the performance reviews, had raised these concerns with her at the time. When Abramson became executive editor, she appointed Edgerley as her special assistant with the charge, as described in the official announcement, of making sure "I can live up to my promise to get around the newsroom more." Edgerley suggested that Abramson bring in a management coach. There's no shame in that, Edgerley said. Abramson initially rejected the idea, though she later asked to work with one.

In truth, she was not stylistically all that different from some of her most prominent predecessors, Abe Rosenthal and Howell Raines. But this was a time of a cultural transition in many workplaces, and that included the *Times*. The era of the imperious executive editor was ending, and it's doubtful that a Rosenthal or Raines would have been tolerated by this embattled and more experienced publisher, by the increasingly defiant newsroom that awaited Abramson when she arrived at work each morning, or by Thompson, who was becoming such a powerful and demanding force at the organization. Her years as Washington bureau chief had been unhappy as well, but this was different: in Washington, she was managing a bureau that produced some of the most sensitive stories in the newspaper, while dealing with an executive editor who did not want her there and took steps that undercut her authority and confidence. Her troubles as executive editor of the *Times* were as much of her own making.

*   *   *

All twenty-four seats around the bowed twenty-five-foot-long table that swept the length of the Page One conference room were filled. The reporters, editors, producers, photographers, clerks, and secretaries who had not been able to grab a chair stood pressed up against the walls, and those who could not squeeze their way in peered through glass windows or the open doorways. On this day in February 2013, at three o'clock in the afternoon, the turnout was for Jim Roberts, now an assistant managing editor, who was leaving the *Times* after twenty-six years. Roberts had taken a buyout at the age of fifty-seven, a departure that, with pointed symbolism about the changing media world, he announced to his followers on Twitter.

By now, the newsroom was inured to the rituals of colleagues leaving—either bought out or forced out: the speeches, the plastic cups filled with sparkling wine, the applause. This latest round of budget reductions did not seem as traumatic as the earlier waves. Abramson had been asked to cut about thirty positions in the newsroom, as opposed to the one hundred that had been slashed in 2008 by Keller, John Geddes, and herself. But these cuts would prove particularly unsettling to some of her staff, in no small part because Abramson used them to reshape her team of senior editors.

She wanted to clear a masthead clogged with older men, to make way for women and younger editors; to replace "Bill's guys," as she thought of her predecessor's cabinet, with her own team. It would allow her to push out people she did not trust—like Roberts, who'd battled her when he ran the digital newsroom, and Jon Landman, now the culture editor, who she was certain did not like her, respect her, or want to work for her. "Jon Landman should not have life tenure at culture where there is a young editor, Sia Michel, who would be a great successor," Abramson had told Sulzberger in her memo applying for the job.* It was a generational housecleaning: the editors who would leave in 2013 were still productive and admired, but they were not, in her view, the future. Like many managers confronted with shrinking budgets and a demand to cut costs, Abramson looked first to editors who made the most money—often over $250,000 a year, not including stock incentives and bonuses. It meant that fewer people would have to go; better to lose one high-paid editor than two reporters who, combined, made the same salary, in her view. It also meant that the people leaving had cut a large swath through the newsroom—this in contrast to the previous newsroom reductions, where the farewells tended to be for accomplished if unremarkable colleagues approaching the twilights of their careers. "We pretty much savaged the masthead," she said later. And gone meant gone. "In the past, we've had the luxury of giving employees who were department heads and other newsroom leaders different assignments, sometimes with less responsibility, but often at the same salary," Abramson explained to the newsroom after it was all done. "We can't afford to do this any longer."

Abramson was, in many cases, pushing on an open door. Landman was sixty years old and ready to leave; the buyout was generous, there was nothing else he wanted to do at the *Times*, and he knew there was not much of a future for him in an Abramson newsroom. Another fixture, Bill Schmidt, had reached the traditional retirement age and was also ready to step down. John Geddes, the managing editor for operations, had not turned sixty-five, but it was a lucrative buyout, and he could see how Abramson was turning to a new cast of players. Abramson never believed the losses hurt the newspaper. "The newsroom has gone through a big transition," she told her staff when it was over. "A group of our most senior editors have left the company. They were the heart and soul of the newsroom for a long time, cherished colleagues. But think about it. This leadership change has not been all that traumatic for the newsroom. Others have stepped up. That's how all of you operate." Still, it was disruptive and unsettling, even for a newspaper that was accustomed to disruption.

---

* Michel would be named editor of Arts and Leisure; Danielle Mattoon, the travel editor, was named culture editor to replace Landman. Michel would be named culture editor in 2023.

Over the coming months, there was a flurry of additional departures, reporters and editors who were well-known among *Times* readers: Richard Berke, David Pogue, Brian Stelter, Matt Bai, Joe Sexton, and Nate Silver. Some moved for bigger opportunities, like Silver, who had been courted by ESPN, the cable television sports network, and Sexton, who went to ProPublica and brought a bottle of Jameson Irish whiskey to Abramson so they could drink a toast as he told her he was leaving. But some left to get away from the *Times*. In either case, the message was clear: the *Times* could no longer assume its employees would want to spend their lives there, riding out the ups and downs of a career, a shift that had started before Abramson took over but accelerated over her tenure.

Abramson was holding one of the most prestigious jobs in American journalism, at a newspaper that was becoming a model of reinvention in a transforming industry. But she felt—and showed—little joy in her position. Her desk, visible through a glass wall, was at times empty; she would travel for events like South by Southwest or the Kentucky Derby, or to tour the foreign bureaus. These are the duties and benefits of being the executive editor. Yet the frequency of her absences was noticed by her deputies and, eventually, the publisher. Abramson had not come into the office the first day after Hurricane Sandy devastated New York in October 2012—flooding streets, paralyzing transit lines, shutting down hospitals, and knocking out power for millions of New Yorkers for days. She lived in Tribeca, one of the hardest-hit neighborhoods, and stayed at home to deal with the loss of electricity and water. Abramson later said that she remained in touch with the office through that day, and noted that Keller oversaw the coverage of Hurricane Katrina, the storm that devastated New Orleans, from his rental house in Southampton. Both Baquet and John Geddes told her that her absence was noticed, and she needed to come to work. She went to the newsroom the next day.

Abramson was feeling increasingly alienated—from Sulzberger, from Mark Thompson, and before long, from Baquet. She had considered Baquet a friend and a like-minded colleague. When Abramson, as a reporter, was assigned to write about the investigative findings of Ken Starr, the independent counsel on Bill Clinton and Monica Lewinsky, Baquet, the national editor, suggested she read the report as if it were a romance novel and frame her story as the tale of the Bill-and-Monica romance. "She called him the Big Guy and smuggled presents and notes to him in the Oval Office," Abramson wrote in the first sentence of the story. "He told her that she made him feel young and that he loved her energy and smile." It would always be one of her favorite stories. They had both spent formative years of their careers working at other major newspapers. And they both worked under the glare of being path breakers at the *Times*. But she could never forget that he had been a candidate for her job. She had worked under Baquet, and now she was expected to supervise the man who had edited the *Los Angeles Times.*

Baquet had reservations when he accepted Abramson's offer to become managing editor. He did not want to be the second-in-command after running his own newspaper. He was two years younger than Abramson, which meant he was unlikely to ever become executive editor if she served until she was sixty-five years old. And he knew what it was like to work with Abramson from his dealings with her when she was managing editor. He disapproved of the way she would talk over reporters and editors, conveying what he thought was both superiority and insecurity. Baquet wanted to be liked by his reporters. He had grown up working in a family restaurant, so he knew about hospitality and courtesy and how to amiably defuse conflicts and accommodate demands. Baquet was generally easygoing, but he had a temper that rose like a fast-moving storm, and Abramson—and other editors who worked under him—would experience that firsthand.

The relationship started off well. They marked their new collaboration by taking a two-week trip to war-torn Afghanistan and Pakistan, a reconnaissance by two editors who missed the daily excitement of reporting. It was a chance to observe a war zone and spend time with the correspondents in the field. They met with an Afghan warlord, a member of Parliament who clutched prayer beads as they spoke, and Karl Eikenberry, the outgoing U.S. ambassador to Afghanistan. They toured eastern Afghanistan on a Black Hawk helicopter and paid a visit to Abbottabad, the site of the hideaway compound in Pakistan where U.S. commandos killed Osama bin Laden. They saw Dexter Filkins, a reporter and war correspondent who had left the *Times* for *The New Yorker,* for coffee at the hotel and tried, without success, to convince him to return to the paper. It was a morning-to-night chance to build their new partnership.

When they returned, Baquet found he had more authority than he expected. A large part of that, he came to realize, was because Abramson had been drawn into the whirlwind of meetings on business strategy, and he wondered whether she resented him for that. Her absences, including when she went upstairs for those meetings, were an opening; he seized it and he became a very powerful second-in-command. If Baquet was happy with the arrangement, Abramson was not. She missed Keller. He had deferred to her and respected her; he had his areas of expertise and she had hers. They had soldiered through some difficult years—the layoffs, fighting with the White House and their own reporters on national security stories, getting rid of Judith Miller—and they remained friends. They were known as Bill and Jill. Keller had described their collaboration, in his 2009 evaluation of her, as nearly "perfect."

By the end of their first year, Abramson determined that Baquet did not want that kind of relationship with his executive editor. She felt he was not consulting her on stories and strode around the newsroom in an "I'm in charge" kind of way. She would notice the reporters and editors gathered around Baquet discussing stories when she walked past his office and she felt, she said years later, excluded. Abramson confronted Baquet, walking into his office and closing the door behind her. You're taking the newsroom away from me, she said, as he recounted the conversation.

Baquet told her she should feel free to join any discussion going on in his office. But the truth was, he did not want her there. Her presence, in his view, froze conversation and dissent. He would go through the motions of telling her what was going on, but he did not consider her a partner, and their discussions would often end in acrimony.

You don't want to listen when anyone disagrees with you, he said to her at one point, as Abramson described their conversation.

There are always tensions between an executive editor and a managing editor; as a rule, they remain private. But the breakdown between Abramson and Baquet was hard to hide. When Abramson returned from a trip to China, she called Chira and Baquet into her office to complain about the stories they had put on the front page in her absence.

Everything in this paper is dull, she said. That story is boring. Boring, boring, boring.

Baquet offered a perfunctory response. Jill, I disagree, he said. But he ultimately left the office and smashed his fist into a wall, in a display of anger that was witnessed by people in the newsroom. He decided he did not want to stay at the *Times* working under Abramson and began talks with a headhunter.

Politico learned of Abramson's fight with Baquet and, in April 2013, published a story that described her as a polarizing and struggling leader. "Just a year and a half into her tenure as executive editor, Abramson is already on the verge of losing the support of the newsroom," it read. Among those who read the story was Bill Keller. The description of Abramson in this story seemed so different from what he had seen when she was his second-in-command. In May 2007, when Abramson was managing editor, she was struck by a refrigerated food delivery truck as she was crossing the street on the southwest corner of Seventh Avenue and Forty-fourth Street, wearing her gym clothes, on the way to the Harvard Club for a morning workout. Her left femur was shattered, and her right foot was crushed. She was in critical condition and was taken to the trauma center at Bellevue Hospital, where she stayed for three and a half weeks, confined to a wheelchair. She was out of work for two months. It would take her nearly two years before she could walk normally again; her friends would later talk about her dealing with post-traumatic stress and bouts of anxiety and depression. Keller thought of that now when he read the *Politico* story about her as executive editor. He wondered if the experience of nearly dying had changed her, made her more impatient and less trusting.

Baquet called Abramson the night the *Politico* story was published to offer her his support. Sulzberger stopped by her office to give her reassurance, using the stock line he offered in moments like this, the one he gave to Howell Raines in the difficult weeks after Jayson Blair left the newspaper. It's not your fault, it's just your turn, he said. A group of women editors sent flowers. But Abramson felt violated. If she had put her fist through a wall, she thought, she would have been vilified. Baquet was treated as a hero. It was obvious to her that people she worked with every day, her own editors, were leaking damaging information and were not to be trusted. She was estranged from Mark Thompson, and relations with Sulzberger were as tense as ever. When Joe Hagan, a reporter from *New York* magazine, called and asked if he could interview her for a story he was preparing on Thompson and the newsroom, she declined with a laugh. "Do you want to cause me to kill myself?" she asked.

And the publisher was worried. The turmoil and unhappiness were becoming hard to ignore. He had learned a lesson from Howell Raines—"I had been through this process"—and had ever since tried to keep an eye on the mood of reporters and editors. Sulzberger took Baquet to lunch and quizzed him about what he was hearing about Abramson. Baquet, as he described the conversation, did not answer the question, or at least did not answer in any detail. But Sulzberger left convinced that for the second time in a decade, he had a problem with his executive editor.

Abramson was carrying what she felt was a lonely battle to protect the journalistic standards of the *Times* newsroom against the ambitions of the business leaders of the company. She was wary of any incursion of a corporate culture into the newsroom.

I don't do PowerPoint, she declared at a presentation by David Perpich, the vice president of product management and a grandson of Punch Sulzberger. After that, Perpich and his colleagues began to print out the PowerPoint presentations they offered at meetings she attended. She stiffened when anyone, particularly someone from the newsroom, used words like "content" or "alignment" or "brand." Sulzberger took note of this in an exchange of memos with her. "As I respond and give you my thoughts, I will do all I can to avoid 'corporate-speak,' " he wrote. Clifford J. Levy, who was twice awarded a Pulitzer Prize for his work as a reporter before moving to digital, used the word "iterate" when he and his team updated her on their work developing NYT Now, an app that was intended to provide a curated list of stories aimed at younger readers. If you use one more business term like that, I am going to kick you out of my office, Abramson said. They could not tell if she was joking. (She later said she was not serious.)

She wandered out of her office one day and came across Tony Brancato, who introduced himself and told the executive editor he had just been hired as the executive director of Web products.

What does that mean? she asked.

Well, product management sits at the intersection of the news side, the business side, and technology, trying to figure out how to create a user experience, Brancato responded. She stared at him. Brancato became flustered as he struggled to explain a job that straddled the business and news worlds, a position that would not have existed ten years earlier.

Jill, he finally said. I am Switzerland.

There is no Switzerland, Abramson responded and walked away.

Abramson did not want the *Times* to become a news organization where the worth of stories was measured by traffic and clicks, or where reporters and editors were expected to come up with revenue-producing ideas. She believed in the wall between the newsroom and the business side, in guarding the sanctity of the newsroom, because that had been her life and career in newspapers. From her perspective, she was protecting the institution, but from the perspective of people who were now trying to reimagine the *Times*, and this included the three Sulzberger cousins who were in line to be the next publisher, she was a member of the old guard rallying behind the Gray Lady, trying to stop the change that was essential for the *Times* to expand beyond its aging, shrinking base.

Thompson assured Abramson he had no desire to tell the newsroom how to operate. She never believed him. And in truth, he arrived in New York with the grandest of ambitions.

When I got here, the newspaper was in the operating room and I felt like a surgeon up to my elbows in blood, Thompson said when Jim Rutenberg, the media columnist for the *Times*, stopped by his office one day. He found a newspaper with a "magnificent newsroom and a great brand," but wedded to a fading product. He saw his charge as nothing short of "saving *The New York Times*," as he would later put it. He wanted reporters and editors to produce morning and afternoon newsletters, podcasts, videos, and a dynamic website and mobile app that kept on top of the news all day. Abramson warned that placing this additional burden on the reporters and editors would diminish the quality of the finished newspaper.

You just have to figure out how to do it, Thompson responded.

He would say he was astonished at what he saw as her indifference to the imperative of the newsroom playing a leading role in what needed to be done. He complained that Abramson would come late and leave early from the meetings with his managers, often spending the time texting messages on her phone. From Abramson's perspective, Thompson displayed "a command-and-control ferocity" in pushing his ideas, and she would talk about him "gaslighting" her at meetings. It came to a head at a small lunch of Sulzberger and his top aides in the publisher's dining room, where Thompson laid out what he expected from the executive editor. The newspaper's future depended on developing paid digital products, and the newsroom—Abramson—would have to be involved in developing them.

The future is going to be digital—and you guys have to lead it, Thompson said to Abramson, as he recalled the conversation. You've got to come forward. You've got to step into this conversation.

If that's what you want, you have the wrong executive editor, Abramson responded.

A stunned silence fell over the table. Andrew Rosenthal, the editorial page editor, thought he had just witnessed Abramson resign as the executive editor. Thompson, discussing the confrontation, later said that he was not simply demanding that Abramson lead the newsroom in the creation of revenue-producing digital products; he wanted Abramson to oversee a digital transformation in how it collected and presented information. Abramson did not hear it that way (nor, for that matter, did Andrew Rosenthal). But Sulzberger, watching the exchange unfold in front of him, was shaken and took her response as evidence of Abramson's unwillingness to "think and act more experimentally."

As 2013 came to a close, Abramson pulled Thompson aside. Earlier that week, Janet Elder, whose responsibilities included being the newsroom's liaison to the business side, had complained to Abramson that Thompson bullied her in a dispute over lines of authority involving a lower-level manager. Abramson recounted the conversation to Thompson and made clear she had no doubt it was true. You bully me, too, Abramson said. She reminded him of how he "dressed me down in front of two colleagues" for fostering "a culture of secrecy in the newsroom," as she described their exchange in a memo she wrote later that day for her files. Thompson said he did not believe his behavior with the two women was bullying, but he said he was aware he could be "emphatic" and promised to tone it down. Their conversation left her with a feeling of dread.

"All feels very fraught," she wrote in a note to herself after leaving Thompson's office. "Have not discussed with anyone else."

CHAPTER 38

The Pivot

"This is going to be a tough assessment," Arthur Sulzberger, Jr., wrote Jill Abramson in January 2014. It was twelve months after he had praised Abramson in her annual evaluation and eight months after the *Times* won four Pulitzer Prizes. But these five pages seemed to be laying the groundwork for her dismissal. Sulzberger walked the evaluation to her office and stayed there while she read it. It began by acknowledging that she was managing the newspaper through turbulent times and praised her news judgment and determination. "You have one of the best guts for news in the business," he told her. But with that, Sulzberger turned to the "real problems that have arisen in the last year that are tied to you—both to your personality and your management style.

"You are viewed as so unpredictable that people are scared of you," he wrote. "Over and over again I have heard some version of: 'We don't know which Jill we will get. Will it be the judgmental, lecturing Jill who will humiliate me in public or will it be the listening and processing Jill who will engage and support?'" People were afraid of presenting ideas to her that she might not like, he wrote. She delivered sweeping pronouncements to subordinates as she walked by their desks, without giving them a moment to respond. She fostered an atmosphere of fear and anxiety. "An enormous amount of time is being spent on both the news and business sides trying to anticipate you. Is Jill having a good day; is Jill having a bad day?" Sulzberger wrote. Reporters and editors thought she promoted favored associates before they were ready, and "that you shame your colleagues through biting public comments." He was distressed by the breakdown in her relationship with Dean Baquet, her managing editor. "Everyone in the newsroom is fixated on how you and Dean are doing," he wrote. "They are fearful that Dean is feeling isolated or minimized."

"In journalism you often go with your gut and that works," he wrote. "In management, you often go with your gut and it is not working."

Abramson looked at him after she finished reading the evaluation.

Arthur—do you want somebody else in the job?

He assured her he did not. But, he said, I want you to take these issues seriously.

Abramson was furious. Her employee evaluations since she arrived at the *Times* had always been favorable. She was certain that, as much as she disliked the job and as obvious as that may have become to some of her colleagues, she had overseen a newspaper producing some of the best journalism in the country. Sulzberger was not talking about the quality of the newspaper under her watch; this was a critique of her style. She read Sulzberger's complaints about her moods as diminishing her as a woman. "It basically said I had my period," she said years later. Still, Abramson did not believe her job was in danger; she did not think that Sulzberger would fire another executive editor after Howell Raines—and certainly not the newspaper's first woman executive editor. But it could hardly have been more ominous.

Sulzberger's evaluation reflected what he was hearing from the newsroom and from senior editors and reporters, but also from two members of his family who were now working as editors and being groomed as his potential successor: His son, Arthur Gregg Sulzberger, an editor on the metropolitan desk who would later be known as A.G., and his cousin's son, Sam Dolnick, who was on the sports desk, had first-hand knowledge of an increasingly unhappy newsroom. She had rebuked A. G. Sulzberger—and moments later, reprimanded his supervisor, Wendell Jamieson, the metropolitan editor—because they had included a sensitive investigative story about the Brooklyn district attorney, Charles J. Hynes, on their list of stories they wanted editors to consider for the next day's front page. Sulzberger had been the editor on the story. Hynes was up for reelection and this was just one week before a Democratic primary for his office, a window when newspapers traditionally refrained from running damaging stories about a candidate, for fear of unduly influencing a race in its closing hours.* The story had been sitting around for weeks, waiting for senior editors to review it, which often happened with complicated and sensitive stories. Abramson put it on the front page, but, in what Jamieson later described as a searing exchange after the front page meeting, said she had felt cornered into making a journalistically unsound decision that could embarrass the newspaper. Jamieson went to Sulzberger to complain about his encounter.

* * *

Arthur Gregg Sulzberger was twenty-eight years old, a reporter at *The Oregonian* in Portland, when Abramson, who was managing editor at the time, recruited him to join the metropolitan desk in 2009. His father, Arthur Sulzberger, Jr., was fifty-seven years old, and his thoughts were turning to succession. He had asked Abramson to take the lead in bringing Arthur Gregg Sulzberger and Sam Dolnick, who was a correspondent for the Associated Press in New Delhi, to the paper and to watch over their newsroom careers.† She read Arthur Gregg's clips, liked what she saw, and called him in Portland. Arthur Gregg demurred at first; he told Abramson he was not ready to join a newspaper bursting with such talent or to endure the scrutiny he knew he would get as the publisher's son. Abramson assured him not to worry. She read stories by journalists across the country who wanted to work at the *Times* every day. You are ready for this, Abramson told him.

Arthur Gregg Sulzberger had grown up in a newspaper family, but he and his father were more likely to go camping or rock climbing in New Paltz in upstate New York than to talk about the *Times.* His father rarely brought the office home with him. But Arthur Gregg had followed the troubles swirling around the newspaper and his father, the collapse of the advertising model, the economic downturn, the layoffs, and the crises of Howell Raines, Jayson Blair, and Judith Miller. He never heard his father complain about the harsh accounts of his tenure as publisher

---

* The story was an investigation into how Hynes had used a rogue Brooklyn homicide detective to help win convictions in a series of murder cases.

† She would be less involved in preparing a third cousin in contention to be publisher, David Perpich, since he worked on the business side.

over these years, but Arthur Gregg thought they were unfair. He was a reserved, cerebral young man, with a dry sense of humor, and it gave him pause as he considered his future. Growing up in New York City, attending the Ethical Culture Fieldston School (where Abramson went to school), he had been uncomfortable with how he was defined by his last name, and how people assumed he would do what his father and grandfather had done before him. He was thinking about a career outside of journalism—going to law school, perhaps, or working on a political campaign.

Tracy Breton, an investigative reporter from *The Providence Journal* who taught journalism at Brown University, where Sulzberger studied political science, steered him to newspapers. He had enrolled in her feature-writing class, and she turned back one of his first articles with a sharp critique: it lacked the clarity and precision of newspaper writing. He liked that. He had come to find academic writing tiresome, in how it relied on complicated language to convey simple thoughts—the opposite of newspaper writing. Suddenly, a career in journalism seemed appealing. When he graduated in 2003, he applied, at her urging, for an internship at the *Journal.* He was assigned to cover Narragansett, a community of under fifteen thousand people, thirty miles from the newspaper's headquarters in Providence, and he approached the task with fervor. In 2006, after two years, he headed for *The Oregonian* in Portland, where he worked for the managing editor, Steve Engelberg, who had left the *Times* under Howell Raines. He soon settled into writing long investigative stories. Both Arthur Gregg's father and his grandfather had taken note of his ambivalence about working at the *Times.* Punch Sulzberger had pulled him aside at a family gathering to remind him of the importance of the Sulzbergers to the *Times,* and of the *Times* to the Sulzbergers. When Arthur Gregg headed for Oregon, his father called Engelberg and asked him to keep an eye on his son, though there was probably no need for that. It was a fast rise; he was a better writer and reporter than either his father or his grandfather.

Arthur Gregg arrived in New York in 2009, only to be told he needed to change his byline. "Arthur Gregg Sulzberger" took up twenty-one characters (twenty-three with spaces), and that would not fit over a news column at the *Times.* It was fifteen minutes before deadline, and his first story, co-bylined with Sewell Chan, was going on the front page. He settled on A. G. Sulzberger.* He was known as Arthur and Arthur Gregg among his family and friends, but henceforth became "A.G." at the *Times*. He began writing for a *Times* blog called City Room, which, if innovative by *Times* standards, was hardly adventurous compared with what was being pioneered by its competitors. City Room was a churning chronicle of the day, a chatty blend of breaking news updates and offbeat stories from around the city. The frothy assignments often went to A. G. Sulzberger. This may have not been the best match of story to reporter, but he made two decisions as the boss's son: he would try not to refuse an assignment, and he would try not to argue with an editor. Inevitably, he became a target of *Gawker*, a website focusing on media and celebrities, which took to describing him as "heir to the *New York Times* throne." There probably was no way to avoid the razzing, as his father could have told him from his own experience with *Spy* magazine, but some of the assignments—"the goofiest fucking assignments," he would say years later—put a target on his back. "*New York Times* crown prince A 'to the' G Sulzberger has triumphed in his most demeaning test thus far: writing an entire story about bathroom breaks," *Gawker* wrote. "You don't have to take this, AG! Put those editors in their place!" (The headline read, "What Haughty Peon Dared Force Young Sulzberger to Investigate Urine?") He was relieved when, after a year, he was assigned to cover federal courts in Brooklyn, before being sent to the Midwest to reopen the paper's Kansas City bureau in Missouri, about sixty miles from where his mother, Gail Gregg, had grown up and where his grandmother still lived.

He would be a reporter for just two years; his family had bigger plans for him. Abramson joined him in Iowa for the 2012 presidential caucuses and told him it was time to come back to New York. She suggested he work on the business side—an idea that was being advanced by Michael Golden, who was overseeing the succession process—but he turned that down. Instead, he joined the metropolitan desk as an editor, and that was where he was when Abramson turned to him to help respond to

---

* "Despite Outcry, Gandhi's Meager Belongings Sell for $1.8 million," a story about the outcry over the auction of items that represented the life of Mahatma Gandhi, was written by A. G. Sulzberger and Sewell Chan.

Mark Thompson's directive that she develop ideas to bolster the newspaper's digital reach. She had created a committee to compile a list of new digital products, such as apps or additional newsletters, that she could suggest to Thompson. She wanted A.G. to run it.

It will make us look like we're cooperating, Janet Elder, a deputy managing editor who suggested A. G. Sulzberger for the job, told the executive editor, and Abramson did not disagree. The committee as envisioned by Abramson would be limited in scope and ambition. It would be "a new ideas task force, which will function as the newsroom's version of a skunk-works team, a creative team that will think up and propose new ways to expand our news offerings digitally," she said in announcing the A. G. Sulzberger assignment. She sent the publisher's son a "big ideas memo" to seed the deliberations. It suggested a "*Times* for Kids," which would be a paid app with bigger type, more videos and pictures, and "no upsetting or controversial material"; and a "digital magazine experience" that would be called *Need to Read*—a compilation of some of the paper's popular narrative stories. "It would be designed for people to enjoy reading at night or on a 90-minute plane ride," she wrote Sulzberger.

The ideas from Abramson struck A. G. Sulzberger as unoriginal and pedestrian—"it was a window into how small this place was thinking," he said years later—but he did not feel he had the credentials to push back; Sulzberger considered himself a print reporter, someone who thought first about how to write a story that would end up on the front page. He told Abramson he wanted to approach this assignment as if it were an ambitious journalism project. He recruited seven people to join him on the committee. In his notes for a meeting with Abramson, he described it as "a full assault, old school, NYT deep dive on our own paper and our own industry."

Sulzberger camped out in the fourteenth-floor cafeteria and, over coffee, presented editors, reporters, Web producers, videographers, and photographers with questions: How do you think the *Times* is doing in digital? What ideas do you have? Why haven't those ideas been put into practice? Which publications do you think are doing a good job on digital? Before long, A. G. Sulzberger began to understand why members of the digital staff were leaving for *BuzzFeed, The Guardian* and *The Huffing-*

ton Post. They had what they thought were good ideas that were being ignored by the senior editors in the newsroom. Their digital ambitions had been undermined by the exodus of digitally experienced editors—Jim Roberts, Jonathan Landman, and Fiona Spruill among them. They felt like second-class citizens. Their competitors were abandoning the imperatives of a print newspaper and were willing to try new ideas even if they failed. It was as if the *Times* was playing on an entirely different field, A. G. Sulzberger would say, watching lethargically as their competitors bounded ahead.

The committee needed to reconsider its mission; the future of the *Times*, Sulzberger told its members, would not be determined by a new application targeted at niche readers. He wanted the committee to consider fundamental changes—in how the *Times* collected and presented the news, in how it engaged and expanded its audience—in order to establish itself as a player in a field that included competitors like *BuzzFeed* and *The Huffington Post.* He went to Abramson to ask her approval, and she embraced the idea. It would be months before Abramson appreciated the ramifications of putting A. G. Sulzberger—frustrated with the newspaper's pace in embracing digital journalism, quietly ambitious, skeptical of the way things had been done, and twenty-five years her junior—in charge of an empowered committee that would investigate the paper's success and failures, which meant by extension the success and failures of its executive editor.

Sulzberger would come to call this the pivot. And this was a pivot for what had come to be called the Innovation Committee. But it would also prove to be the pivot in the newspaper's transformation to the Web. And it would be a pivot for A. G. Sulzberger. He would become a next-generation symbol of this emphatic moment of change at the *Times.* A. G. Sulzberger had kept a low profile, but these months would elevate his standing. He was different from his father in many ways. He did not eat meat and was so thin that he was almost spectral in his bearing. With his dark, deep-set eyes and full head of hair (he would begin buzzing his head to a close crop when he began balding in his thirties) he looked more like his grandfather than his father. He had an ease that recalled Punch Sulzberger, and a confidence and self-assurance that his father had lacked at his age. His affect was deferential and low-key; his performance as a reporter had surprised some of his editors at the *Times*, versed as they were in the legend of Punch Sulzberger and the automobile race in Le Mans. "To keep you in the loop, Arthur will be one of our nominees this quarter for pub's award," Richard Berke, the national editor, wrote a senior editor in nominating A. G. Sulzberger for a Publisher's Award for his work as Kansas City bureau chief. "I know this is tricky, but in our view he [is] clearly very deserving."*

The Innovation Report, as it was known, was shared with a small group of editors and executives—only on paper, to guard against leaks—on March 24, 2014. It was nearly one hundred pages long and written in language that was neither bureaucratic nor polemic, largely free of findings of fault that might lead to an argument. We are not, A. G. Sulzberger would say, talking about doing away with Page One. But it contained an unmistakable message: the newspaper was falling behind its competitors. "The *New York Times* needs to accelerate its transition from a newspaper that also produces a rich and impressive digital report to a digital publication that also produces a rich and impressive newspaper," the report declared. "Our leaders know this and we have taken steps in these directions. But it has become increasingly clear that we are not moving with enough urgency. This may be the single most important long-term challenge facing the newsroom and its leaders."

"To those charged with worrying about the newsroom's future," the report said, "it's clear we're just a fraction of the way there. And compared to many of our competitors, we're falling behind."

Sulzberger's committee declared that the standards that had guided the *Times* for a century made less sense at a time when "the business side" no longer referred simply to the people who sold advertisements. It now included data analysts, product managers, and programmers who measured audience, developed new digital presentations of stories that had once been told only with words and pictures, and made sure the *Times* app worked when a reader clicked on a headline. Yet those employees felt discouraged from talking to anyone in the newsroom. "The wall dividing the newsroom and business side has served the Times well for decades, allowing one side to focus on readers and the other to focus on

---

* Sulzberger declined the Publisher's Award; he thought it would look odd.

advertisers," the report declared. "But the growth in our subscriptions and steady decline in advertising—as well as the changing nature of our digital operation—now require us to work together." The first step "should be a deliberate push to abandon our current metaphors of choice—'The Wall' and 'Church and State'—which project an enduring need for division," the report said. In this new world, "[i]ncreased collaboration, done right, does not present any threat to our values of journalistic independence."

The report cited the work of Janine Gibson, the editor of *The Guardian's* American website, which it held up as an example of a legacy media company having made the transition into a digital world, and understood how readers were finding stories through Twitter and Facebook. "The hardest part for me has been the realization that you don't automatically get an audience," she told the committee. But at the *Times*, the Sulzberger committee found, editors and reporters spent their days writing and editing stories, moving on to the next story and the next day without considering how to draw readers to their work.

A. G. Sulzberger did not want the report lost in the dust of a damaging battle with an executive editor who saw this as an attack on her leadership. How will Jill take this? he asked Adam Bryant, a former editor on the national desk who he had recruited to work on the committee. They combed through the document, softening criticism of shortcomings in the newsroom. The report was strewn with praise for Abramson's performance. The news report was extraordinary, it said. "Both Mark Thompson and Jill Abramson have established themselves as willing and eager to push the company in new, sometimes uncomfortable directions," the report said.

Abramson read the report on a plane back from China, where she and Joseph Kahn—the foreign editor, who would go on to become executive editor in 2022—had unsuccessfully sought to convince Chinese authorities to stop blocking the *Times* website there. She paused at the passages detailing the frustration of business colleagues with her newsroom. The subtext of the committee's call to reconsider the business-newsroom divide was not lost on her; defending the sanctity of that division had been a defining feature of her career. She read the report as a commentary on her performance. And it was written by the publisher's son. It had not even been three months since Arthur Sulzberger had written that searing evaluation of her performance.

I am fucked, she thought.

Abramson said nothing for weeks. A. G. Sulzberger and members of his committee grew agitated—worried their work would be buried. And when she finally met with them in the Page One room on the third floor, she was terse. She offered perfunctory thanks, but she objected to what she called the report's deference to the business side and said it failed to give her appropriate credit for her success in combining the digital and print newsrooms. This session only heightened the anxiety among members of the committee. A. G. Sulzberger assembled the group after she left. Change in an institution like this is really hard, and we're going to go through periods like this, he said. I'm really sorry you saw that.

Andrew Rosenthal, the editorial page editor, would come to talk about this period of Abramson's tenure as suicide by cop, a reference to someone with a death wish who charges at a police officer. It is a good way to understand the events that unfurled in those early months of 2014. Even as the Innovation Report was in its final stages, Abramson was in a dispute with Sulzberger about her salary. Janet Elder had prepared a survey of executive salaries in the newsroom to investigate if there were disparities between men and women, and found that there were.

You are exhibit A, Elder told Abramson. Elder scribbled down her findings in a note. When he left, in 2011, Keller was being paid $559,000 a year, which, adjusted for inflation, by Elder's calculation would be $587,216 in 2014. As of March 1, 2014, Abramson was making $503,880. Elder advised Abramson to seek an immediate raise of $90,698, to bring her closer to Keller, and to demand an additional raise of $89,186 at the start of the next year.

Abramson, by her account, had not thought to raise the question of her compensation when the publisher offered her the job, assuming it was not a matter for negotiation. Now, she went to Arthur Sulzberger who, never comfortable with confrontation or numbers, sent her to Michael Golden. The base salary figures were correct, but there were mitigating factors, Golden told her. She could not compare what she was being paid at the beginning of her time as executive editor to what Keller was being paid after eight years in the job. Keller had been at the *Times* longer; he started as a reporter in the Washington bureau in 1984, at a salary of $46,932. Abramson had started thirteen years later, in 1997, at a salary of $121,999. In addition, it was no longer a matter of just an annual salary. Compensation for executives had become, over the years, an increasingly complex package that also included performance bonuses and deferred and long-term compensation calculated on the company performance and stock price.

Nonetheless, the baseline salary disparity between herself and Keller was jarring. This was probably not resolvable; there was little trust at this point between Abramson and the rest of the paper's management.

Abramson brought her case to Mark Thompson, arguing that her responsibilities had expanded since her appointment, and she was being paid less than other senior *Times* executives. She wrote a letter to Sulzberger and Thompson proposing a compensation package of up to $1,350,417 a year over the next three years, including performance bonuses and retention and cash incentives. That compared with $1,081,034 in salary and performance bonuses she received in 2014, by her calculation. "I need an answer on my compensation soon," she wrote Thompson. "I've been frank with Arthur about talking about opportunities outside the *Times*. Before I close certain doors I need to know that my future is, quite literally, secure." Finally, Abramson hired an attorney. Sulzberger was offended that she was coming at the newspaper so aggressively at a time when she knew he had doubts about her capacity to handle the job. She is relentless, he thought.

Abramson was battling the publisher, the publisher's son, the newspaper's chief executive, her managing editor, and much of the masthead. Her idea of enlisting A. G. Sulzberger to defuse Thompson's assignment had backfired, and she was now convinced that Thompson was behind what she saw as an Innovation Report that was written from the perspective of the business side of the company. (By both men's account, A. G. Sulzberger was the primary writer of this report and spoke infrequently to Thompson during its preparation.) But her survival depended on navigating the Innovation Report, on convincing Arthur Sulzberger and Thompson that she was embracing its recommendations. And she saw an opportunity in Janine Gibson, the *Guardian* editor whose work steering her newspaper into digital had been praised in the Innovation Report.

Gibson was scheduled to finish her U.S. assignment and return to London, but Abramson heard Gibson did not want to leave the States. She had worked with Gibson before. The *Times* and *The Guardian* had cooperated in publishing leaked documents from the National Security Agency that they had obtained from Edward Snowden, the former NSA contractor who had lifted a trove of highly classified materials. When Thompson and Sulzberger pressed her about how she was going to implement the Innovation Report, Abramson said she was thinking about hiring Gibson as managing editor for digital.

Both applauded the idea. Within days, Abramson brought Gibson into the *Times* building for a series of meetings with the editors. It was presented as a round of interviews for a high-level job, but in truth, by the time Gibson arrived, Abramson had all but offered her the position of managing editor for digital. She did not share her plans with Baquet. Gibson joined Baquet for lunch in a private *Times* dining room. It was a cordial conversation, and Baquet asked Gibson what job Abramson had discussed with her. Managing editor for digital operations, Gibson responded. Baquet just nodded. After lunch, he took the elevator down to the third floor and walked into Abramson's office, where she was sitting with Janet Elder.

This is bullshit, he said. You get to have two managing editors. You get to do whatever you want to do. What you don't get to do is not tell me about it. He walked angrily out of the office.

Elder looked over at Abramson. He is going to leave, she said.

It was the last time that Abramson and Baquet would see each other as colleagues in the newsroom. Baquet was on jury duty the next day and surrendered his phone when he walked into the courtroom. When he retrieved it, he saw a string of unanswered calls and texts from Sulzberger and Abramson. He ignored the ones from Abramson but he called the publisher. Sulzberger asked him to come up to his apartment, where they ordered in Chinese food. He said Abramson realized she had made a mistake in the way she had tried to hire Gibson. She had told him she wanted to stay through the next election; after that, Sulzberger said, you will be the next executive editor. But Baquet said he would not stay. He had rehearsed what he intended to tell the publisher before he arrived; he did not want a reprise of the dramatic departure he made at the *Los Angeles Times*

I will do this in a way that does not hurt the paper, Baquet said. I think you should bring Janine on. I will make that work. But I can't stay. I don't trust [Abramson] and she clearly doesn't trust me.

As far as Sulzberger was concerned, Baquet was giving him a choice: Abramson or Baquet. The publisher told Thompson he was ready to replace Abramson with Baquet; Thompson cautioned Sulzberger to consider the "reputational damage" the newspaper would suffer if he did this. You are about to fire the first woman editor of *The New York Times*, he said. It had been barely three years since he had fired Janet Robinson as the paper's chief executive. But Sulzberger was determined. Yes, he would be firing the newspaper's first woman executive editor, but he would be replacing her with a Black man. For Sulzberger, firing Howell Raines had been excruciating. This was not difficult. He thought Abramson's performance had worsened in the four months since he gave her the negative evaluation. He had even come to suspect that Abramson had only put A. G. Sulzberger in charge of the Innovation Report to sideline him. ("In the end, it was the exact opposite," he said years later.) More than anything, he was not going to lose Baquet—easygoing, engaging, charming Baquet, a man with whom he could go outside and enjoy a cigar, and whose departure, he knew, could stir up yet another uprising in the newsroom.

The next day, Baquet retrieved his telephone after jury duty to find another message from Sulzberger. That evening, the publisher came to Baquet's apartment in Greenwich Village.

I've decided to fire Jill and make you the executive editor, he told him.

Since Baquet was on jury duty, Sulzberger asked him not to tell anyone until the following week. Sulzberger called Abramson later that evening and asked her to come up to his office the next morning.

Abramson had coffee that morning with Gibson, again to try to convince her to join the *Times*. When she arrived at work, she took the elevator up to Sulzberger's office. He had a folder on his desk, and a press release saying she had chosen to leave.

We are doing this for you, Sulzberger said, explaining the wording of the press release. Abramson would not agree to that; she wanted the announcement to say what had happened. You are firing me, and that is what it is, she said.

The meeting lasted ten minutes. When she got downstairs, she called Gibson. Stay at *The Guardian*, she said.

Abramson's departure would be made public the following week. The day before Baquet was to be appointed, Sulzberger called Abramson at her desk to tell her there was no need for her to come in to the office for the announcement. Abramson gathered some papers, including her emails to Thompson over salary—she thought those could come in handy—and walked out the door. Her *Times* email account was shut down by the next morning, and her assistant would pack up her office the following day. Her tenure as executive editor of *The New York Times* had lasted just over thirty-two months.

Sulzberger's voice was tremulous as he announced the change to a stunned newsroom, and his explanation of why was elliptical. There was no disagreement about moving the newspaper down a digital road. She had done "an outstanding job" in preserving and elevating the newspaper's excellence. "Rather, I chose to appoint a new leader for our newsroom because I believe that new leadership will improve some aspects of the management of our newsroom. You will understand that there is nothing more I am going to say about this, but I want to assure all of you that there is nothing more at issue here." Baquet stood at Sulzberger's side as he spoke; it was the first time he had been in the newsroom since he had walked out of Abramson's office the week before. The *Times* noted the moment with a story on the bottom left corner of the next day's front page, with a picture of Baquet: "Times Ousts Its Executive Editor, Elevating Second in Command."

The vagueness of Sulzberger's explanation left a door open for Abramson. After she left, she arranged for the information about her salary dispute to be delivered to Ken Auletta, who presented her case within days in *The New Yorker*. Her departure became the story of a big organization firing a strong, underpaid woman who had defied management, and the paper struggled to respond. "I am writing to you because I am concerned about the misinformation that has been widely circulating in the media since I announced Jill Abramson's departure yesterday," Sulzberger said in a note to employees. "It is simply not true that Jill's compensation was significantly less than her predecessors." Taking into account deferred compensation based on performance and other salary enhancements, he wrote, "Her pay is comparable to that of earlier executive editors. In fact, in 2013, her last full year in the role, her total compensation package was more than 10 percent higher than that of her predecessor, Bill Keller, in his last full year as executive editor, which was 2010. It was also higher than his total compensation in any previous year."

"Compensation played no part whatsoever in my decision that Jill could not remain as executive editor," he said. But this was a public-relations battle, and Abramson—savvy, connected, and determined—was winning. Women rallied to her side. Sulzberger and the *Times* were under attack. "Abramson, the first woman to lead the masthead of the nation's most prominent newspaper, was ousted amid stories of her 'brusque' leadership style and, horrors, her gall in pursuing equal pay to her male predecessor," Kathleen Parker wrote in *The Washington Post*. Abramson's daughter posted a photograph on Instagram of her mother wearing boxing gloves, a tattoo of a New York City subway token visible on her right bicep. (What wasn't visible was the tattoo on her back: a Gothic capital *T*, from the *New York Times* logo.) The New York tabloids loved it. "What did he think, he could take a shit on me and I'm going to do nothing?" Abramson said years later of Arthur Sulzberger. "I mean, come on, what planet does he live on?"

Sulzberger and his son were rock climbing in New Paltz that Saturday when he got a call on his cellphone about another round of critical stories on how the *Times* had fired Abramson. Sulzberger rappelled down, returned to his home, and got on the phone with Michael Golden, who had driven to New York from his home in Chatham to join Mark Thompson at the office to decide how the *Times* should deal with its latest public relations crisis. "We were losing the narrative," Thompson said years later. The result was an extraordinary statement from Sulzberger, released Saturday evening, directly assailing a former senior employee. "During her tenure, I heard repeatedly from her newsroom colleagues, women and men, about a series of issues, including arbitrary decision-making, a failure to consult and bring colleagues with her, inadequate communication and the public mistreatment of colleagues," Sulzberger said.

The battle would now fade. With her dismissal and the clear sentiment expressed by the publisher, there was less incentive for members of the newsroom to rally to her side, particularly as she sought to cast her departure as a case of a male-dominated organization casting out a strong woman manager. The *Times* "is being caricatured as a bastion of sexism, which isn't true, and hasn't been my experience there," Carolyn Ryan, an editor who Abramson had made Washington bureau chief, said on *Meet the Press* the day after Sulzberger issued his Saturday evening statement.

In what would turn out to be her final days as executive editor, Abramson had agreed to the public release of an abbreviated version of the Innovation Report, summarizing its main points, though without its most disquieting findings. It included a memorandum from Abramson and Baquet endorsing its recommendations. "The Innovation report being presented today represents another milestone in our newsroom's digital transformation," they wrote. "Their study was rigorous. Their conclusions are urgent. The masthead embraces the committee's key recommendations." Abramson did not believe that. But what could she do? The report had the support of the publisher and the man who could be the future publisher. It was meticulous, almost lawyer-like, in making its case. She had to look like she endorsed it.

The full text of the Innovation Report was leaked to *BuzzFeed* two days after Abramson left and—initially, at least—presented a damaging image of an organization in crisis. "Exclusive: New York Times Internal Report Painted Dire Digital Picture," read the headline in *BuzzFeed*. The unabbreviated report included proprietary information and unvarnished warnings about the newspaper's performance that were never intended for public consumption, and A. G. Sulzberger worried that the newsroom would recoil at the bluntness of the language and the sweep of its recommendations. But there was little backlash. This was a roadmap for an organization that was in trouble, and it was embraced by reporters and editors who were ready to try things that might once have seemed unthinkable. It was applauded by the industry. "The leaked New York Times innovation report is one of the key documents of this media age," said the headline in the *Nieman Lab*, an online publication from the Nieman Foundation for Journalism, an institution at Harvard University. "I've spoken with multiple digital-savvy Times staffers in recent days who described the report with words like 'transformative' and 'incredibly important' and 'a big, big moment for the future of the Times,'" wrote Joshua Benton, the director of the *Nieman Lab*. "One admitted crying while reading it because it surfaced so many issues about Times culture that digital types have been struggling to overcome for years."

CHAPTER 39

Diplomat

Dean Baquet ignored the pain in his lower back. He was standing in the newsroom next to Arthur Sulzberger, Jr., as the publisher announced that Jill Abramson had been dismissed and Baquet was the new executive editor. He had been in discomfort for weeks; he assumed he had pulled a muscle during a morning exercise routine. Baquet's first month as executive editor was hectic—a mass killing in an oceanside college town in California; a Sunni militant uprising in Iraq; a contentious swap by the Obama White House of five Taliban detainees for a U.S. prisoner of war from the Afghanistan conflict; not to mention the death at age ninety of Arthur Gelb, whose passing merited a front-page obituary—so he would not get around to consulting a doctor until the middle of June 2014. It took one visit and a scan to diagnose cancer: a potentially lethal tumor on his left kidney.

Baquet was scheduled to have his first meeting as executive editor with the board of directors, but that would have to wait. He went home, packed a bag, and headed to Lenox Hill Hospital for emergency surgery. The hospital admitted Baquet under an assumed name; the new executive editor of the *Times* fell under the category of "celebrity patient" in Manhattan, and the *Daily News* and the *New York Post* would be calling if they learned he was there, all the more so given the attention paid to the messy change in leadership at the *Times* newsroom. Baquet had thought the operation would involve scraping the tumor off his left kidney, but he was told the night before that the surgeons intended to remove the entire organ. The procedure took place on a Saturday, and he sent an understated note to the newsroom the following Monday. "As some of you may have noticed, I've been out of the office for the past few days," he wrote. "On Thursday, doctors found a malignant tumor on my kidney that they felt required immediate attention. I had minimally invasive, completely successful surgery on Saturday and my doctors have given me an excellent prognosis." He would be out of the office for about a week.

Sulzberger liked to say there was always a plan B, but there was no plan B for this. Baquet's appointment had been sudden. He had not picked a managing editor; there was no second-in-command to step in while he was recovering or to replace him should that prove necessary. The toll of the ordeal on Baquet was apparent as he returned to work; he was gaunt and would leave for home every day in the early afternoon. This would not have been an easy transition for a new executive editor in the best of health. Baquet had to calm a newsroom shaken by Abramson's departure and the findings of the Innovation Committee's report. He needed to appoint his team of editors; the urgency of that task was reinforced by the cancer diagnosis. (It would take him until September to appoint four deputy executive editors to replace the managing editor, a position Baquet said he was eliminating.)* Financially, this was shaping up as another bad year. Digital subscriptions were on the rise, and almost two years earlier, the *Times* reported that for the first time, the combined revenue from digital and print subscriptions exceeded advertising revenue. But it was not enough: there would have to be more newsroom cuts, though Sulzberger told Baquet that could wait until things settled down.

Baquet was a figure of historical note: the newspaper's first Black executive editor—a milestone at a paper whose leadership had been so white for so long. And after all this uncertainty, his appointment signaled stability and a new direction for the newsroom. Baquet was confident and disarming, with an engaging manner that earned him trust from the people above him and loyalty from people below him. He was also reserved and slightly opaque; he would struggle to control his episodic flashes of temper, which he considered a weakness. Baquet had stopped drinking after a brother died from alcoholism, and that set him apart from most of his colleagues in the newspaper business. Baquet was

---

* Baquet reinstated the managing editor job in September 2016 and named Joe Kahn, the international editor, to the position.

a diplomat and a survivor; politically agile and accommodating to Arthur Sulzberger in a way that Abramson had not been. He would take A. G. Sulzberger, Sam Dolnick, and David Perpich to long dinners and share the journalistic and personnel deliberations that were informing his management of the newsroom—the kind of real-time tutorials that any future publisher would value and remember. The cousins would talk about how different he was from his predecessor, and before long they proposed that Baquet join the committee helping to select the next publisher.

More than anything, though, Baquet was different because he embraced the idea of collaboration with the business side of the newspaper. He understood how important that was to the publisher; and in any case, he thought, *The New York Times* was in a perilous financial position as he took over. Over the following years, the newspaper would go through a storm of change and experimentation as it tried to distinguish what it did in the name of habit and tradition from the essential values that defined the *Times*. It was as if a dam had broken. This was the challenge that had frustrated other legacy companies attempting to retool for a changing world: determining what to keep and what to discard. And it was particularly daunting at the *Times*, which was reinventing itself under the scrutiny of exacting readers—and a newsroom on guard for any sign that it was abandoning the standards that set the newspaper apart. But the change was happening.

The Innovation Report was a major force behind the transformation. So was the fact that the three Sulzberger cousins—one of them likely to be the future publisher—were in top management jobs, engaged in this day-to-day effort to discover the possibilities of this digital world. But the rapid onslaught of change also arrived because the newspaper had a new executive editor. Baquet would prove to be a bridge between the *Times* of a passing generation—its standing and dominance undermined by declining influence, circulation, and revenues—and the new *Times* that was slowly being invented around him. His experience in journalism—the Pulitzer Prizes, a history that included resisting the owners' demands for more layoffs when he ran the *Los Angeles Times*—gave him the standing to break established rules and traditions. Baquet never saw this as a threat to the *Times* or its standards; he would talk about himself as "one of the old dinosaurs," the kind of self-effacement that would give comfort to some of his older colleagues as he nudged them down a new road. "A chunk of the newsroom would be more willing to follow me than anybody else," he said years later, and that was almost certainly correct.

*   *   *

Baquet had the kind of novelistic biography that had piqued the interest of generations of *Times* editors and publishers. He grew up in the back of Eddie's, a Creole restaurant in a Black working-class neighborhood in New Orleans. Eddie was Edward Baquet, Sr., Baquet's father, who had left a job as a mail carrier and opened a restaurant with his wife, Myrtle. Baquet lived behind the restaurant with his four brothers. He mopped the floors in the morning before heading off to an all-Black elementary school, and later St. Augustine High School, a private Catholic all-boys and all-Black high school. The first time Baquet boarded an airplane—and the second time he ever left Louisiana—was to fly to New York to study literature at Columbia University.

It was a disorienting and alienating experience. Baquet would take his seat and notice how almost every other face in the class was white. Back in New Orleans, the only white people in his life had been the priests at St. Augustine. New York was a rough and polarized city in 1974, and his circle of friends were drawn from the small outpost of Black students who attended Columbia. He missed New Orleans, and he missed his old classmates who had followed a more traditional path after high school, enrolling at historically Black colleges like Xavier University of Louisiana. Baquet applied for a summer internship at the New Orleans *States-Item*, which would later merge with *The Times-Picayune*. He did not expect to like it as much as he did; the pace and the energy were intoxicating. He would return to New York for a semester, but he gave up on Columbia, dropping out to make a life in newspapers.

Young, competitive, aggressive, Baquet was writing two or three stories a day at his first newspaper job. He arrived at five in the morning for a shift that was scheduled to end at noon, but he would often stay late into the evening. The job opened new vistas of New Orleans he had never experienced growing up. Baquet got lost when he was dispatched to the wealthy Uptown district to cover a fire, so he knocked on doors collecting eyewitness accounts, which allowed him to re-create—in colorful detail, as if he were there—the story of the fire that he had missed. He was soon recruited to work with a team of reporters investigating corruption in Jackson Parish. Baquet left New Orleans for the *Chicago Tribune* in 1984, to become an investigative reporter and editor. Within four years, he and two colleagues had been awarded the Pulitzer Prize for Investigative Reporting for their account of self-dealing and malfeasance by the Chicago City Council.

His reporting caught the eye of Dave Jones, a senior editor in New York, who called Baquet in April 1989—he was at home, preparing for the celebration that night for the Pulitzer he had won—and asked him to come to New York to talk to editors about joining the *Times*. Baquet went to New York but, after spending a day with the *Times* editors, concluded that they had neither the interest nor the aptitude for the kind of investigative reporting that he had been doing since he was a young reporter in New Orleans. It took Joseph Lelyveld, who was then the managing editor, to persuade him to join the paper. Lelyveld flew to Chicago and invited Baquet to lunch. The *Times* was weak on investigative reporting, and it needed correspondents with his skills.

We don't do this kind of reporting very well, Lelyveld told him. Baquet was taken by his candor; he liked Lelyveld from the start. He and his wife, Dylan Landis, who he had met when they were both reporters at *The Times-Picayune*, left Chicago and came to New York in April 1990. He joined the metropolitan desk as an investigative reporter and before long was reporting directly to Lelyveld—an unusual arrangement that signaled his elevated status in the newsroom. He could investigate whatever struck his fancy: corruption and favoritism in the purchase of voting machines at the New York City Board of Elections; influence peddling in a $290 million water-meter installation program. After four years, Lelyveld, now the executive editor, asked him to become an editor on the metropolitan desk and, shortly after that, promoted him to be the national editor.

That was the job Baquet was holding when the *Los Angeles Times* asked him to become its managing editor in 2000. He had been in New York for ten years. Given his history with *The New York Times*—but more than that, his personal history with Lelyveld—it was an uncomfortable departure, and from his perspective, it strained their relationship for years. Lelyveld was unprepared for Baquet to leave. A year earlier, he had convinced Baquet to turn down an offer to run the *Miami Herald,* and Baquet, in sharing his decision with Lelyveld, talked warmly about the man he considered his mentor. "You're also a hard editor to leave," Baquet wrote Lelyveld. "You're a good friend and I can't imagine I'm gonna find anyone in the business anytime soon who means as much to me personally or professionally." When the *Los Angeles Times* tried to recruit Baquet, Lelyveld invited him to spend a weekend at his home in Maine. This time, Lelyveld's entreaties did not work.

I'm leaving, Joe, Baquet said, when Lelyveld, driving back to New York, called from a pay phone to press him for a decision. Baquet told him he would stick around for a few weeks to help with the transition. But he could feel the chill on the other side of the phone.

This is business, not personal, Lelyveld responded, as Baquet recounted the conversation. You need to leave now.

There were many reasons why Lelyveld was distressed. This was a professional relationship that benefited both parties; Baquet had come to the *Times* and risen quickly in no small part because of the personal interest taken by Lelyveld. He was a finalist for the Pulitzer Prize in 1994 for stories he co-wrote on fraud and mismanagement at Empire Blue Cross Blue Shield in New York. He had established a reputation as an editor who had both strong journalistic instincts and an ability to manage a difficult staff. His success reflected on Lelyveld. So did his departure. And the fact that Baquet was a thriving Black editor at a newspaper that was still overwhelmingly white made Lelyveld even more invested in his success, not least because of his doubts about Gerald Boyd.

From Baquet's perspective, he was forty-three years old and was being recruited for a job that would put him in line to run one of the nation's great papers. That might have happened at some point in New York, but in 2000, there was a line in front of him, and near the front, in his view, was Boyd, who was six years older and already on the masthead. Lelyveld was sixty-three years old, and his days as executive editor, and as a mentor, would soon end. Baquet would stay in Los Angeles for more than six years, through the retirement of Lelyveld, the arrival and de-

parture of Howell Raines and Gerald Boyd as executive editor and managing editor, and the appointment of a new executive editor and
managing editor—Bill Keller and Jill Abramson. The *Los Angeles Times*
would be awarded thirteen Pulitzer Prizes while Baquet was there.

But by October 2006, Baquet, who had been promoted to executive
editor in July 2005, was in open conflict with his own management.
He had refused a directive from the Tribune Company of Chicago, the
owner of the *Los Angeles Times,* to make more cuts of the newsroom staff,
which stood at about 940. It was a show of defiance against Chicago by
Baquet and the publisher, Jeffrey M. Johnson. For leaders at *The New York
Times*—remorseful about letting Baquet leave, still struggling with the
dearth of senior Black editors in management—it was an opening. Sulzberger sent a note to Baquet. "Bold move my friend," read the subject
line. The message contained three words: "Courage you got." Baquet's
future at the Los Angeles newspaper was imperiled, and he was grateful
for Sulzberger's support. "I know this may seem like an impetuous move
by an angry editor," Baquet wrote the publisher. "But as you know it has
been building for months. Jeff and I have never been able to get a real
discussion or debate about the impact of three years of layoffs and losses
through attrition. I'm not afraid of cuts. Hell I've done more layoffs than
any editor in America. But we aren't so financially ailing that we can
justify this kind of cutting." Baquet was fired six weeks later.

There was immediate speculation that he was maneuvering to return
to *The New York Times,* including in a story in the *Los Angeles Times.* In
truth, over the previous two years, the *Times* had been quietly campaign-
ing to convince Baquet to return.

We want you back, Jill Abramson told Baquet as she and Maureen
Dowd took him to the Polo Lounge at the Beverly Hills Hotel. Abramson's
role in convincing Baquet to return to New York was so striking that
Keller highlighted it as one of her most significant accomplishments in
her 2006 annual evaluation, parenthetically (and presciently) observing that Abramson was helping to hire someone who could one day become a rival. "Your enthusiastic recruiting of Dean is a little like Howell
asking me to stay on as managing editor—which, to my lasting good
fortune he did not do," he wrote. "You know—and you know the media

obsessives will make much of this—that if he returns he becomes instantly perceived as a rival." As for Baquet, Keller told him he would ultimately end up on the masthead if he came—and in this he was conveying a message from Sulzberger.

One position seemed likely to draw him back to *The New York Times:* Washington bureau chief, the job that was held by Philip Taubman. Abramson had been unhappy with Taubman from the moment Keller chose him to take over the Washington bureau. She thought he was too soft on George W. Bush and too close to Condoleezza Rice. Her doubts were reinforced by what she saw as his overly solicitous engagement with the White House during the debate over publishing the surveillance story. This would not be easy: Taubman had been the Moscow bureau chief when Keller was there, and he had given his second-in-command so much freedom that Keller won a Pulitzer Prize for his coverage of the Soviet Union in 1989. But Keller had come to share Abramson's concerns about his old friend. The change was not made gracefully. Taubman was home sick with the flu when a reporter called from the *Los Angeles Times,* asking his reaction to the decision by *The New York Times* to name Dean Baquet as the next Washington bureau chief. Taubman had had no idea.

* * *

Alexandra MacCallum was not sure how the new executive editor knew her. She was a product manager for Cooking, a mobile app that offered a visually appealing catalog of recipes drawn from the food pages. The app was in its infancy, but its potential—as a source of revenue and as a model of how to expand the market of new subscribers—was clear. Growing up in New York City, she had wanted to be a journalist and was one of the first three hires at *The Huffington Post* in 2005. She had started there as a senior news editor, but after leaving to study law at the University of California at Berkeley, she decided she had a stronger aptitude for business. She later returned as *The Huffington Post*'s corporate counsel.

The *Times* hired MacCallum in March 2013 to work on strategy and business development and, six months later, moved her to a senior role developing the Cooking app. She did not even know how to cook. Her job was to build the app and develop a business plan that would meet a goal of 160,000 new paid subscribers by the end of 2014—a benchmark set by an outside consulting firm guiding the newspaper through this transition. Audience development was still a new concept at the *Times*, but it was not new at places like *The Huffington Post*, and it was not new to her.

MacCallum was fascinated by the challenge of drawing an audience of readers for Cooking and, once they were there, converting them into paid subscribers. She would grow animated talking about how engineers in New York could tap into the operating system on an iPhone to determine when, say, temperatures hit ninety degrees where a mobile phone with the Cooking app was online—and then push out a recommendation for a seasonally appropriate warm-weather recipe to its owner. That is how you use technology and content to engage readers, she would say. And before long, the success of the strategy became clear: in June 2015, Cooking reported that four million readers had visited the site and app, marking the third month of double-digit growth.

Baquet did not know how to build an audience, or create a digital report, or what it meant to write a story to be read on a mobile device instead of on newsprint. Most of his top editors were from his generation, with similarly limited digital literacy. That is what led him to ask MacCallum to help create an audience-development team to work in the newsroom alongside reporters and editors, who were wary of a new initiative they saw as commercial promotion rather than journalism. MacCallum responded with an eight-page analysis, written in language that could be understood by someone unfamiliar with a digital workplace. The *Times* needed to capture readers drifting from the home page to places like Facebook and *The Huffington Post*, to write headlines geared for Google searches, to make mobile devices its top priority, since that was where readers were heading. Reporters and editors should be involved in building its audience—their audience. "It is essential that we move into this new world, and that we do so with the full weight of the organization behind the initiatives," she wrote. "We cannot continue to age with our readers, as has happened over the last ten years."

Her time at Cooking had shown how challenging this could be. "Here is an example from a recent Cooking article about how to make ice cream," MacCallum wrote. "The original headline on the story was 'A

Frozen Canvas, A Spectrum of Flavors.' The headline is poetic, Timesean and lovely but it should not exist in the digital world." That headline would not get caught in the net of a Google search for ice cream recipes or clicked on by a curious reader scrolling through a mobile device. "It took strong push back from a digitally-savvy backfielder, over the persistent objections of a copy editor, to change the headline to 'The Only Ice Cream Recipe You'll Ever Need.' "

After reading her report, Baquet appointed MacCallum as an assistant managing editor in charge of audience development. She would have a desk in the newsroom, and her name would be listed on the masthead, which was a departure from *Times* tradition: MacCallum was not a former foreign correspondent or an accomplished editor; she was just thirty-three years old.

In a second promotion that also suggested the changing tides, Baquet appointed Steve Duenes, who had come to the *Times* in 1999 as a graphics editor, to the masthead as an assistant editor in September 2014, fourteen months after Jill Abramson had made him an associate managing editor for visualization. His quick rise was a measure of how a newspaper that had been so focused on print was changing the way it told stories in a digital world. The graphics desk was no longer a "service department," as Duenes had long called it, expected to fulfill sometimes unimaginative requests from reporters and editors for charts to supplement a print story. "Basically, anyone could come into the graphics department and produce some request," Duenes said years later. " 'Here are my eight numbers; where's the chart?' " Graphics had, under him, evolved into a freestanding news desk that pioneered the use of maps, videos, photography, and charts to create a visual form of storytelling. These were part of the coverage of election nights, sporting events like the Olympics, and big breaking stories like wildfires in the Western states. Duenes was the editor who oversaw the presentation of the digital story "Snow Fall: The Avalanche at Tunnel Creek."

As 2015 began, half the *Times* audience was reading the newspaper's journalism digitally. But there were still pockets of resistance to digital innovations across the newsroom—an impulse to do things the way they had always been done. Ian Fisher, a foreign correspondent who in 2008 become an editor for the digital foreign report, would plead with colleagues to file updates for the website, or to insert links in their stories that would take readers to competing news sites. For a while, he brought daily reports from Chartbeat, an analytics company that tracked the digital audience of stories, to the Page One meeting, where he would share the latest readership numbers—a way to measure what stories were of interest to readers. His presentations were met with silence. The *Times* had always based its news judgments on what its editors determined was important, not on what might be popular. No one was quite sure what to do with this data.

Baquet, like Abramson, was steeped in an era of deadlines and newsstands, of defining journalistic success with Pulitzer Prizes for long-form investigations. But now, taking over, Baquet shifted quickly. He read the publisher and the moment. He was a student of *Times* politics and history, so he knew how Abe Rosenthal had accommodated Punch Sulzberger during the economic downturn of the late 1970s by creating the new sections to draw readers and advertisers. Before long, he began to sound almost like Mark Thompson, the company's chief executive, as he questioned the line between the newsroom and the rest of the company. The "business side," Baquet would say to colleagues, invoking what had once been a phrase of disparagement for some in the newsroom, no longer meant the advertising department, where the potential for conflict—a movie-studio head buying full-page advertisements in an attempt to influence coverage—was quite real. It now encompassed the developers who designed the *Times* app, devised visual ways of telling stories, and helped produce podcasts. And it included audience-development analysts like MacCallum.

"I see this whole group of talented, creative people as something like Switzerland," Baquet said at the time, with language that recalled Abramson's encounter with the newly hired executive director of Web products. Baquet was going to convince the newsroom that considering what its audience wanted to read did not violate the *Times*'s ideals—"that building audience was vital to our future: that if we weren't read, we weren't going to change the world," as he said years later. Like Bernard Gwertzman, the former foreign editor who oversaw the first Web newsroom, Baquet was comfortable being an ambassador from another era. He, too, said yes to almost any idea brought to him by this younger, more digitally oriented cohort, even if he did not completely understand what they were talking about.

Clifford Levy, an editor and former foreign correspondent who was nearly eleven years younger than Baquet, suggested blocking access to the *Times* website on desktop computers in the newsroom for one week to force editors and reporters to read the newspaper on their mobile devices, the way many readers did. Great idea—let's do it, Baquet said. He asked David Leonhardt, who, after stepping down as Washington bureau chief under Abramson, now ran The Upshot—a digital desk experimenting with new forms of storytelling in its coverage of policy and politics—to prepare a primer for the newsroom on writing for a mobile device. "Readers are hungry for more non-articles," Leonhardt wrote. "Please don't mishear: The article is not going away. Readers love news articles and narrative. But they clearly want more journalism that doesn't consist mostly of blocks of text." Innovations that had been dismissed as gimmicks when they'd appeared in *BuzzFeed* would be pressed into the *Times* arsenal: conversational daily newsletters, a less stilted voice in stories and in headlines, and, before long, Five Takeaways on major news events, more accessible than the traditional news analysis. Reporters and editors were encouraged to engage on Facebook and Twitter.

This is all journalism, Baquet would say. Before long, editors were arriving to work to find reports from the audience-development team, with data detailing which stories were popular and how readers found them (linking through Facebook, Google, Twitter), presented in a jargon that was new for many of the more traditional editors in the newsroom. "Big day out of National yesterday," read the audience analytics report sent to editors on April 2, 2015. "The drought story was the most read on the site, 40% of its traffic came in from Facebook. Our lede-all on Arkansas/Indiana and the piece on AK Governor Asa Hutchinson's son were each in the top ten most read yesterday too. Google was the top referrer for both as a result of great SEO heds"—search engine optimization headlines, which were crafted with words that would be picked up by search engines.

"The Jeremy Egner piece on the young female stars from Game of Thrones was the second most read item on the site yesterday with 400K readers," the note continued. "Nearly 80% came in from Facebook.

Great photos of the two actresses that helped bring the story to life and increase sharing. And that sharing remains high this morning too."

Reporters and lower-level editors were soon given access to data on the traffic to stories—the same metrics Fisher had tried to share at front page meetings a few years before. This kind of information might tempt them to gravitate to stories that would draw the most clicks, but it could also guide editors in writing headlines that would interest readers. The data reports helped determine the optimal times to post a story. And they would shape decisions on what not to cover: incremental news developments with information the audience could find elsewhere.

"Widening access to data is not about chasing clicks or keeping score on which article gets best read, or about deciding what to cover," Baquet and Andrew Rosenthal told the staff. "There will be no traffic goals for desks or writers. But we're flying blind in many parts of the organization about how readers are finding, reading, sharing, reacting to and following up on our journalism."

Whatever benefits this strategy brought to a newsroom in the midst of a reinvention, it was strewn with risks. Reporters crave readers, and the numbers were seductive. They influenced basic news judgment, including deliberations on what stories should be chased and promoted. An early sign of this came in March 2015, in the coverage of a presidential campaign that would come down to a contest between Hillary Clinton and Donald Trump. A front-page story reported that Clinton, while she was secretary of state under Barack Obama, had used her private email account to conduct government business. "Her expansive use of the private account was alarming to current and former National Archives and Records Administration officials and government watchdogs, who called it a serious breach," the story said.

Four months later, the FBI opened an investigation into her handling of classified information. In those early days, the political and legal implications of this story were vague; and in July 2016, James Comey, the director of the FBI, announced the agency had found no "clear evidence that Secretary Clinton or her colleagues intended to violate laws governing the handling of classified information," while adding "there is evidence that they were extremely careless in their handling of very sensitive, highly classified information." But whatever the merits of the story, it was apparent from the first audience-traffic reports delivered to editors that readers were flocking to this coverage. "Our political audience continues to stay highly interested in the Clinton emails story," read the report distributed to editors on March 6, 2015. "Yesterday's story had 250K visits. 34% has come from the apps, further evidence of this story really catching on with our core audience. The original scoop is now up to 1.2 million visits."

* * *

The first front page meeting at *The New York Times* took place in 1946: a gathering of editors that began at four-thirty in the afternoon in the office of Turner Catledge, an assistant managing editor, to debate which stories merited a spot on the front of the next day's newspaper. In those early days, there was not even a table, much less enough chairs for everyone to sit. Over the next seventy years, the front page meeting turned into an intimidating ritual that became central to the daily rhythm of the newspaper—a combative exercise in ego, intellect, manipulation, and power. Reporters and editors measured their accomplishments by how often their stories were selected for the front page.

By 2015, the front page meeting was becoming a relic. Weekday print circulation was 603,700 in 2015, down from 648,900 the year before. Sunday print circulation was stronger, as had historically been the case, but the trend lines were clear: 1,127,200 in 2015, compared to 1,185,400 the year before. By contrast, paid digital circulation had jumped to 1,094,000 in 2015, up from 910,000 the year before. Readers were getting news on their mobile phones, iPads, and computers. The front page was becoming a distraction that squandered expertise, energy, and time, and a new generation of editors wanted to change that. "The editing, approval and production of much of our enterprise remains tethered to print," Cliff Levy wrote Baquet. "The needs of print in particular dominate the 4 P.M. meeting, making it difficult for the newsroom's leadership to plot digital strategy for nights and mornings."

On May 5, 2015, Baquet announced that Page One would no longer be discussed at the Page One meeting. Those decisions on what would appear on the front page of the *Times*—once the primary expression of the newspaper's authority in setting the agenda for its readers every morning—would be left to a select group of editors, who would gather earlier in the day. The *Times* needed to "move more decisively away from the grip of print deadlines," Baquet said. Editors should shift their attention to "coverage regardless of where it appears, as well as to plan our digital report for the following morning." The following Friday, twenty editors assembled in a conference room around the corner from the bank of elevators on the third floor of the new *Times* building on Eighth Avenue. Marc Lacey, the weekend editor, flicked on his iPhone to capture the scene. "This is for a documentary on the former Page One meeting," Lacey said. Baquet seemed neither nostalgic nor sentimental as he oversaw this last meeting from his place at the center of the table. The quality of the digital report *and* the print report had improved, he said. "And," he continued, "we are also gaining more readers, which is what we care about."

It had been one year since Baquet had taken over, and now, his cancer in remission, he felt empowered to push through changes that once would have triggered resistance. He embraced collaborations that might have made his predecessors recoil: conferences with corporate sponsorships featuring reporters and columnists; links in the *Times* that would send readers to Amazon to buy a book recommended by the Book Review, or a refrigerator approved by Wirecutter, the newspaper's product-review website; appointing a senior editor to propose reporting projects that would be attractive to readers *and advertisers*. When Mark Thompson asked Baquet to join a committee of the company's senior business executives who were drafting a business strategy report called "Our Path Forward," Baquet accepted on the spot. Every Friday afternoon for six months of 2015, Baquet sat with the paper's chief financial officer, chief advertising officer, executive vice president for digital products, and general counsel, as well as Andrew Rosenthal from the editorial page, to consider issues that would once have been kept far from editors and reporters. Was it more important to sell advertising or subscriptions? Did it matter whether their audience found *Times* news on Facebook, the newspaper's app, or its website? Should the *Times* reconsider its basic mission, to make it a destination not only for news but also for advice on where to go for a weekend getaway or fix a balky Wi-Fi connection?

These discussions were not taking place in a vacuum. In 2015, the *Times* digital circulation had reached one million paid subscribers. "If, half a decade ago, you'd been able to put money down in Vegas on the New York Times' chances of reaching 1 million digital subscribers by 2015, what kind of odds could you have gotten?" Ken Doctor, a news industry analyst, wrote in the *Nieman Lab*. "Longer than longshot." The committee, now joined by the three Sulzberger cousins, reflected that new reality in its final report. "Our Path Forward" called for reimagining the business model that had guided the *Times* throughout its history. Paying subscribers should be the primary source of revenue. Advertising still mattered—a larger digital audience would also mean more digital advertising—but nothing was more important than expanding its base of subscribers. That meant investment in the news report to offer "content and products worth paying for" and to "always put our readers at the center of everything we do."

Three weeks after the release of "Our Path Forward," Arthur Sulzberger walked into the Times Center on the ground floor of the *Times* headquarters. It was the beginning of November, and he was there for his annual "State of the Times" address. This was one of his favorite events of the year: two sessions, an attentive audience in the morning and the afternoon, a chance for a man who tended to stay on the sidelines to talk about the past twelve months at the newspaper. He would spend weeks preparing for these meetings and review the points he wanted to make with editors, business executives, and friends. As the years went on, what once had been a rote recitation of scripted remarks had turned into an elaborate presentation, commensurate with the sophistication of the newspaper: videos, charts, photographs, and a display of the major headlines of the year.

On this day, Sulzberger had something else he wanted to say. He squinted into the lights, looking up at the ascending rows of seats. There were many faces he did not recognize. It had been thirty-seven years since Sulzberger joined the Washington bureau as a reporter. He was sixty-four years old. He realized that he was looking at the generation who would lead the newspaper through the transformations envisioned in "Our Path Forward," but also, inevitably, the one after that and the one after that—as this 164-year-old newspaper sought to keep up with the world.

Sulzberger was there to say he would not be part of this journey. He waited almost until the end of his presentation to make the announcement. "I've been in my role as publisher for more than twenty years, and I've hit my mid-sixties," he said. "So it should come as no surprise that the task of choosing my successor has begun."

* * *

Sulzberger would face one more challenge as publisher before he stepped down. On November 8, 2016, Donald Trump was elected the forty-fifth president of the United States. The *Times*, through its stories, analyses, and polling, had prepared readers for an early night and an easy victory for Hillary Clinton. She won the popular vote, but Trump captured the Electoral College. On election night, the *Times* published an interactive feature on its website with a thermometer needle that offered a minute-by-minute forecast of the likely outcome. The needle was a high-profile example of the kind of data-driven visual journalism that was distinguishing the *Times*'s campaign coverage and that drew the attention of millions of readers. Early in the evening, the *Times* estimated that Clinton had an eighty-five percent chance of winning; by ten o'clock, the needle had swung to the other side of the dial and assigned Trump a ninety-five percent chance of victory.

The needle, with its prediction of a Clinton victory, had misled reporters and editors in the closing days of the election, as well as on election night, much as it had misled the public. When the first results from Florida signaled that the vote would not turn out as expected, a hush fell over the newsroom. Reporters and editors began scrapping stories and headlines that had been weeks in the planning. Alex Burns, a national political correspondent, moved into a private office off the newsroom to assemble from scratch a profile of the new president-elect—a story that would have typically been written and edited days in advance. (A profile of Clinton was, by contrast, ready to publish.) A front-page headline had been drafted for this moment—"MADAME PRESIDENT," it would have said, marking the election of the first woman to the White House. But as the hour grew late, Baquet, in disbelief at what he was watching and at the order he was about to give, directed his editors, including Carolyn Ryan, the political editor who had run the coverage, to prepare a front-page headline declaring Trump the next president of the United States.* Ryan enlisted Michael Barbaro and Matt Flegenheimer, two political reporters, to cobble together the account of the Trump victory. Amid the scramble of the evening, their final election-result story mistakenly appeared under the bylines of Patrick Healy and Jonathan Martin, the reporters who had prepared the Clinton victory story that had been written in advance.

For all the expertise and the resources it had invested in covering the race, the *Times* had largely missed the voter discontent rising across wide swaths of the country, which had fueled Trump's victory. At that, it was hardly alone: most news organizations had missed it as well, and Trump himself was stunned by his victory. But the backlash against the paper was fast and harsh. The needle became a symbol of the misleading projections offered by the nation's major pollsters and newspapers. And the *Times* was blamed by Democrats for contributing to Clinton's loss with its focus on her use of the private email account as secretary of state—the story it had broken the year before. Throughout her campaign, Clinton would have to grapple with questions about her email practices as secretary of state. The *Times* returned to the subject repeatedly, and Trump seized on the issue as he accused his rival of trying to conceal damaging information from the public.

Comey, after clearing Clinton in July 2016 of criminal wrongdoing in her handling of the emails, reopened the investigation two weeks before Election Day, citing newly uncovered information.† The *Times* published three stories on his decision, spread across the top of its front page. And

---

* The final headline on the election night story: "TRUMP TRIUMPHS: Outsider Mogul Captures the Presidency, Stunning Clinton in Battleground States."

† Comey told Congress he was reopening the investigation after new Clinton emails were found on the laptop computer of Representative Anthony Weiner, the husband of a top Clinton aide.

then, nine days later, Comey shut down the investigation again, saying he had found no evidence of criminal wrongdoing by Clinton. His actions—and the coverage of them—rocked Clinton's campaign and almost certainly contributed to her loss. Baquet would contend that an FBI investigation of a potential national security breach by a major-party presidential candidate demanded that kind of attention in the *Times*, but by Election Day, the tone and intensity of the coverage had begun to seem disproportionate to any actual offenses. This was one factor among many why she lost a close election, but it would feed the anger and bewilderment of Democrats distressed by Trump's victory.

The governing executive committee of the Times Company gathered in the boardroom on the sixteenth floor one week after Election Day to consider what a Trump presidency might mean for a newspaper in the throes of transition. The editors and executives, coffee cups and water bottles in hand, had been unprepared, as had much of the nation, for the outcome. There was reason for concern. The *Times* was under attack by the president-elect; the weekend before, he had mocked the newspaper on Twitter for its "very poor and highly inaccurate coverage of the 'Trump phenomena.'" Readers had threatened to cancel their subscriptions to protest the coverage of the campaign and, in particular, its stories about Clinton. It had been twelve months since the "Our Path Forward" report urged the *Times* to adopt a subscriber-first revenue model—the urgency of that goal having been reinforced earlier that month when the *Times* had reported an 18.5 percent drop in print advertising revenue. Arthur Sulzberger and Baquet posted an extraordinary "To Our Readers" note on the website. "After such an erratic and unpredictable election there are inevitable questions: Did Donald Trump's sheer unconventionality lead us and other news outlets to underestimate his support among American voters?," they wrote. "What forces and strains in America drove this divisive election and outcome?"

The attendance at the executive committee signaled the importance of the moment: the executive editor, the publisher, the future publisher, the editorial page editor, and Mark Thompson, the chief executive, calling in from Los Angeles, where he was on a business trip. Thompson began by asking Baquet to describe the mood in the newsroom. "There has been since then a lot of soul-searching," Baquet responded. "Everyone thinks the press in general . . . could have done a better job in taking the pulse around the country. We all agree we could have done that better." James Bennet, the head of the editorial page, described the challenges the opinion pages faced finding conservative voices to round out its stable of mostly liberal opinion writers. "A lot of people are coming to work wanting to cry on our pages and call for revolution on our pages," Bennet said. "That's not going to get us anywhere. Working out how we have a constructive impact on this administration is a really interesting challenge that we are debating among ourselves."

The business executives at the table expressed a different sentiment. It had been a harrowing week, but the threat of mass cancellations by readers had sputtered. Instead, the interest and anxiety that accompanied Trump's election had produced a surge of subscriptions.

"Let me start with the good news," said Meredith Kopit Levien, the executive vice president and chief revenue officer. "What we have seen is the number of cancellations have dropped off significantly. Unbelievable performance." The paper had added 41,000 new digital subscribers since Election Day: the largest weekly subscription increase since the introduction of the paywall. The number itself wasn't huge, but it was encouraging: A Trump presidency might actually be a boon for a newspaper that was reliant on subscribers. Indeed, by the end of that year, the *Times* would have 1.8 million digital subscribers—up from 1.1 million digital subscribers the year before. The *Times* had always sought to give the readers what the newspaper thought they *needed* to read; now it was beginning to also consider what its audience *wanted* to read.

Thompson, his voice echoing across the table from a speaker on the ceiling, suggested that this was a roadmap for the transition, a path to building a base of loyal subscribers that could assure the paper's long-term prosperity. "What people are going to be hungry for is great journalism so they can figure out what's actually happening in the country," he said. Baquet told the executive committee that the *Times* was going to hire more investigative reporters and editors in Washington so it could aggressively cover this new administration, he said. It would serve a readership hungry for this news, keeping with the *Times*'s longstanding mission and his own appetite for investigative reporting. But Baquet had a word of caution: the *Times* would need to respond to this extraordinary news story—and the demands of its impassioned readers—without turning into "the organ of the opposition party."

Striking that balance—protecting the newspaper's reputation as an evenhanded news source while catering to a concerned and politically activated audience and an increasingly outspoken staff—would prove to be one of the most difficult challenges of Baquet's coming years as executive editor.

The election of Donald Trump in 2016 brought another blizzard of changes to *The New York Times,* a period of reinvention, public criticism, and internal dissension. Over the next five years, the *Times* would complete its transformation to become a primarily digital newspaper. And it would shift to a new business model with startling speed: paid subscribers, rather than advertisers, would become its main source of revenue—enacting the central recommendation of the "Our Path Forward" report and allowing the *Times* to survive the industry collapse that diminished some of the best newspapers in the nation.

The Trump presidency was a major force behind the business transformation; his election riveted a divided nation, drawing millions of new subscribers and a surge in revenues. But Trump was also a challenge to journalism, and particularly the *Times.* His presidency forced the paper to reexamine the promise that Adolph Ochs had made to his readers when he purchased the newspaper in 1896: to "give the news impartially, without fear or favor, regardless of party, sect, or interests involved." Some of those new readers and subscribers, as well as some of the reporters and editors, wanted the *Times* to step away from what they saw as an archaic tradition of detachment and embrace a more adversarial form of journalism that seemed demanded by these polarized times. These debates over the newspaper's role and obligations rolled through the *Times* over the years of the Trump presidency and into the Biden presidency, and will help shape the *Times,* and journalism, for years to come. The final account of these struggles, and how they are ultimately resolved, must be left to future histories.

This was the backdrop for Dean Baquet's remaining years as executive editor. From the first days after Trump was elected, when he gathered reporters in his office on the third floor and met with the executive committee on the sixteenth floor, Baquet had pledged not to let the *Times* become the voice of the anti-Trump movement and talked about the need for the *Times* to be an objective voice in covering the world. It was a challenge. The success of the subscription-first business model was shifting economic power from advertisers to subscribers, many of whom expected this historically liberal newspaper to join the battle against Trump. The separation between the business department and the newsroom had once allowed an executive editor to largely discount the complaints of a big advertiser—a department store or auto manufacturer—unhappy with a story. It was more difficult to disregard paying subscribers. Now, to succeed as a business in this new environment, the newspaper needed the loyalty that came with making an emotional connection with that audience. Readers had the power to command attention by canceling subscriptions or using social media platforms to organize protests against coverage, the work of individual reporters, and even single headlines they considered timid or biased.

Because of the tools that the *Times* embraced to analyze readership, its editors now knew which stories their audiences most wanted to read and which headlines drew the most attention. This became a factor, if one of many, in determining which stories should be written, and which should be promoted on mobile devices and the website. The newspaper's readership was more liberal than the nation at large, as captured in an internal poll of *Times* readers conducted for the newspaper and shared with editors and business executives in 2019. Eighty-four percent of paid subscribers described themselves as "liberal," the report said, including forty-eight percent who said they were "very liberal." Sixty-five percent of subscribers said they liked the fact that the *Times* favored liberal values. "Some readers subscribe to NYT because they project their opposition to the administration on us," the editors were told. "A majority of readers believe that NYT favors liberal values and viewpoints. Most subscribers are OK with this. However, non-subscribers are more likely to say they would prefer that we did not favor liberal values and viewpoints."

The pressure was coming from within the newspaper as well. A new generation of journalists had moved into the newsroom: younger, less restrained in expressing their ideology, and, like many readers, impatient with the way the *Times* was responding to Trump, as well as the political and cultural debates about race, gender identity, and economic class that had accompanied his rise to power. They were not as reflexively loyal as some of their older colleagues to the ideal of the *Times* as the unbiased chronicler of the world. Some chafed at the standards that governed the newsroom: that its employees should be observers who refrain from bringing a point of view to their stories; that the paper's news columns should strive for balance and fairness, even if that risked creating a false equivalence between two points of view when one seemed clearly wrong. Many looked down on what they viewed as stenographic journalism, seeing their role as flagging falsehoods and calling out, in language and headlines, hypocrisy and racism. Some reporters turned to social media platforms like Twitter to express their personal opinions or criticize public figures, particularly Trump—and even, at times, some of their own colleagues and the newspaper itself.

Baquet was sixty years old when Trump was elected. He had always preferred conciliation and consensus to confrontation in running a newsroom. That had become difficult in this environment, as he sought to balance his adherence to tradition and established journalistic standards with the complications of covering a president who routinely lied, and whom many readers, and colleagues in the newsroom, saw as a threat to democracy.* Baquet would resist pressure to, for example, use words like "racist" or "liar" in writing about the president. "My view is that we are always better off telling and laying out comments rather than characterizing them," he said. Baquet assembled *Times* journalists for a town hall in August 2019 to thrash out these issues, where he was confronted by some members of a newsroom who had grown impatient with how the *Times* was covering this president.

"Could you explain your decision not to more regularly use the word

---

* There were a number of ways this new president was forcing the *Times* to change. When the president used profanity, words like "fuck" or "shit," the *Times* occasionally quoted him verbatim, a departure from standards that were once, with the very rarest of exceptions, inviolable.

racist in reference to the president's actions?" one staffer demanded of the executive editor. (The meeting was private, but a recording of it was provided to *Slate*, which published a transcript.)

"I'm actually almost practiced at this one now," Baquet responded. "Look, my own view is that the best way to capture a remark, like the kinds of remarks the president makes, is to use them, to lay it out in perspective. That is much more powerful than the use of a word." But practiced or not, Baquet was aggravated by the question. "I think that a bizarre sort of litmus test has been created," Baquet finally said. "If you don't use the word racist, you're not quite capturing what the president said." It was a striking moment: the first Black executive editor in the newspaper's history being challenged by his staff on how his newspaper was covering issues of race.

Two days later, the *Times Magazine* published the first installment of The 1619 Project, a work sweeping in its ambition and scope, which set out to reconsider the nation's history by "placing the consequences of slavery and the contribution of black Americans at the very center of our national narrative," beginning with the arrival in 1619 of the first enslaved African people. The project would be awarded a Pulitzer Prize, and was held up by the paper's editors as an example of the *Times* grappling with issues of race and equity that it had so often neglected. But even as it won praise in some quarters, it was also assailed by some scholars as a distortion of the nation's history, evidence of the newspaper pandering to the political views of its readership.

Abe Rosenthal had always boasted that he had kept the paper straight; his credo would now be invoked against the *Times* by critics who saw the newspaper catering to the sensibilities and opinions of its readership. It was a matter of concern for A. G. Sulzberger. In the same month that Baquet held a town hall with the newsroom, Sulzberger gathered his top editors and business executives in a session "to discuss the newsroom's perspective on perceptions that The New York Times is biased." In preparation for the meeting, Sulzberger asked the newspaper's conservative columnists to critique the paper's coverage; they responded with examples of stories, headlines, and word choices that suggested bias. "There are occasions reading the Times one can get the feeling that ideas that only gender-studies professors and critical-race theorists believed ten years ago are just banal conventional wisdom, while pretty typical conservative perspectives are dangerous, fringe, alt-right," Ross Douthat, the columnist, wrote. Another columnist, Bret Stephens, surveyed the online report of July 18, 2019, and pointed out a description on the home page of how Trump reacted after the House rejected a resolution to impeach him for statements that the members of the chamber had earlier condemned as racist. "The president brushed off the vote as a victory, and hours later, at a rally in North Carolina, he showed no signs of toning down his vicious language," it read.

"What purpose does the word 'vicious' serve, other than as anti-Trump editorializing by the news editors?" Stephens wrote Sulzberger, his analysis shared with the attendees at the conference.

* * *

The strains of this period were particularly visible on the opinion pages. In the months after Trump's election, with the support of the outgoing and incoming publishers, James Bennet, the editorial page editor, had recruited conservatives who could write about Trump's appeal and the ideological shifts that led to his election. Bennet hired Stephens, a deputy editorial page editor at *The Wall Street Journal,* and Bari Weiss, an editor and writer at the *Journal* and *Tablet* magazine. In his first column, Stephens questioned the science behind global warming; he was hardly the first conservative to do that, even on these pages, but his argument drew a surge of indignation from readers as well as some members of the newsroom. Weiss would, during a television appearance on MSNBC, question whether the sexual assault allegations against Brett Kavanaugh were grounds for rejecting his nomination to the Supreme Court, again stirring a wave of protest.

In June 2020, the opinion pages published an essay by Senator Tom Cotton, a conservative Republican from Arkansas, entitled "Send In the Troops," calling for the military to be deployed to stop the looting and violence that broke out at some demonstrations after the murder of George Floyd, a Black man killed by a white police officer arresting him in Minneapolis. A. G. Sulzberger initially stood by publication of the Cotton column. "I believe in the principle of openness to a range of opinions, even those we may disagree with, and this piece was published in that spirit," he wrote to employees. But one thousand people in the newsroom signed a petition decrying its publication. Bennet defended the publication of the piece. "Times Opinion owes it to our readers to show them counter-arguments, particularly those made by people in a position to set policy," he wrote on Twitter. But he also said he had not read the essay before it was published, and the paper issued a statement saying an internal review found that "a rushed editorial process led to the publication of an Op-Ed that did not meet our standards." Sulzberger dismissed Bennet the following weekend, pointing to "a significant breakdown in our editing processes"; he would later appoint Katie Kingsbury, who had served as Bennet's deputy, as his replacement.

Bennet later said he was following the direction of the publisher in trying to highlight conservative points of view on the page. "When push came to shove at the end, he set me on fire and threw me in the garbage and used my reverence for the institution against me," he later told *Semafor,* a news website. Weiss would leave the *Times* following a backlash after she wrote on Twitter that "the civil war inside The New York Times between the (mostly young) wokes [and] the (mostly 40+) liberals is the same one raging inside other publications and companies across the country." Her resignation letter to Sulzberger spoke of "bullying by colleagues" and an "illiberal environment."

* * *

For all the public turmoil, there would not, over these years, be a breakdown in the newsroom on the scale of Jayson Blair and Judith Miller. There would be more layoffs, but they were more scattered and strategic than past newsroom-wide reductions—among them, eliminating the copy desk to ease a path to a faster-paced, digital-first newsroom. (In a journalistic environment where seconds now counted, polishing the copy was no longer the priority it had once been.) Arthur Gregg Sulzberger became the next publisher of *The New York Times* on January 1, 2018: the sixth member of the Ochs-Sulzberger family to serve, in the words of the official announcement, as "the main steward of the editorial independence and excellence of *Times* journalism." This time, the selection was not imposed by an outgoing publisher on a recalcitrant board of directors, as Punch Sulzberger had done when he sought to anoint

Arthur, Jr., but recommended by a committee of company executives, company directors, and family trustees. Arthur Sulzberger, Jr., would recuse himself; the family was another generation bigger, and there were three Sulzbergers in open contention for the job, including his son. Baquet retired on June 14, 2022, after becoming the first executive editor to stay in that post past his sixty-fifth birthday—in Baquet's case, by nine months—since Turner Catledge stepped down in 1968 at the age of sixty-seven. He was replaced by his managing editor, Joe Kahn—again, an orderly succession.

And the most important question overshadowing the paper, whether it would survive as a powerful and profitable newspaper in a post-print age, would appear to have been answered. In August 2020, the *Times* announced that it reached a record 6.5 million digital subscriptions, well on its way to what had once seemed an ambitious goal of ten million digital subscribers by 2025. Digital revenues had outpaced print revenues for the first time in its history.* "It's clearly a watershed moment," Mark Thompson, the company's chief executive, said in announcing the second-quarter numbers. It was validation of the decision to charge digital readers, as it had always charged print readers. The Trump presidency was a big reason for the surge of subscribers and its financial success, but he was as much an accelerant as the cause. The *Times*'s digital circulation kept growing after Trump's defeat in 2020; readers who had been lured by the coverage of his presidency were now drawn by the coverage of the Covid pandemic and the Russian invasion of Ukraine.

In the end, a newspaper mired in tradition and habit, confident in its superiority, and historically aloof to criticism, recast itself for a world with new expectations and new readers. The *Times* took a legacy print newspaper and created a brand—and its executives used words like "brand" to discuss its aspirations—that straddled video, podcasts, computer screens, mobile phones, magazines and, of course, printed newspapers. That outcome was twenty-seven years in the making, from the

---

* The paper collected $185.5 million from digital circulation and advertisements in the second quarter of the year, $10 million more than it got from what had been the economic engine of the *Times*, the print edition.

time when Richard Meislin, the editor in charge of graphics, wrote his "What is the Internet?" memorandum, asking and answering that question, for the paper's senior editors. The *Times* was a different newspaper than it had been under A. M. Rosenthal. Indeed, it was no longer just a *news*paper. It was a destination, by its own description: a place where readers went for news and opinion, recipes, consumer advice, and an online crossword puzzle and word games. The *Times* was signing up new subscribers in markets across the country and around the globe.

There was still a robust print newspaper, but it was siloed into a separate and smaller operation in the newsroom. Daily print circulation had declined from a high of 1.2 million in 1993 to 374,000 in 2020. The front page was a measure of success for reporters and editors, but so was Stela, an internal website that tracked page-view numbers for every story. And yet, as much as it had changed, this *Times* was in many ways the *Times* that Arthur Sulzberger, Jr., had picked up and read when he joined the newspaper as a young correspondent in Washington in 1978: in the ambitions of its news report, its network of foreign and national correspondents, its photographers and artists, the critics on the culture pages and the essayists on the opinion pages. It had won thirteen Pulitzer Prizes since Trump's election in 2016, including one for the investigation of sexual misconduct by Harvey Weinstein. The revelations in that coverage upended the nation's politics and culture and was one of the forces that helped to create the #MeToo movement.

On the afternoon of December 18, 2017, Arthur Sulzberger, Jr., attended his final State of the Times session as publisher. Afterward, his audience—young and old, print and digital journalists—filed out of the auditorium for a reception. Waiters carrying trays of glasses of red wine and plates of chocolate cake circulated through the room as A. G. Sulzberger raised a glass to honor his father. "The only publisher of his generation who was handed a great news organization and left it even better than he found it," Arthur Gregg said. His father seemed moved by this moment, but his response was characteristically flip. "I've been told I should not give a speech. So I will not. All I will say is that it was a blessing for me, and thank you for everything you do. And the bar is open."

These past fifty years are prologue to the next chapters of journalism and economic disruption that will confront A. G. Sulzberger as he settles in for what he can only hope will be his own quarter-century as the publisher of *The New York Times*. The newspaper Sulzberger has inherited has again and again managed to change for the times; to transform itself without seeming to lose the values that have been embedded in the newsroom since Ochs first bought it. That was often the product of trial and error. And it was testimony to the leadership of the Sulzberger family. But the *Times* is also what it is today because of the men and women, in the newsroom and on the business side, who, decades ago, saw how the ground was beginning to shift and set out to transform an American newspaper that was resistant to change. This is a success story, of a legacy organization that reinvented itself in the midst of a storm of societal, technological, political, and journalistic upheaval and emerged as an institution that could thrive in a new era—this at a time when it is arguably needed more than ever.

ACKNOWLEDGMENTS

This book would not have been possible without the cooperation of hundreds of people who have worked at *The New York Times*. Over seven years, they sat down for interviews and opened their files to share all kinds of documents—memos, emails, letters, minutes of meetings, confidential reports, personnel files, and personal diaries—in service of this history. This project began in 2016, when I asked Arthur Ochs Sulzberger, Jr., the publisher, if he would cooperate with a book examining the modern-day history of his family's newspaper. Several weeks later, he called me to his office to say he would sit down for as many interviews as I needed—but made clear that he was speaking for himself and not the newspaper, and he would not direct anyone to cooperate. His son, A. G. Sulzberger, who took over as publisher in 2018, was also generous with his time as he recounted his early years at the *Times* and, notably, for the purposes of this history, his work on The Innovation Report.

The Times opens with the appointment of A. M. Rosenthal as executive editor in December 1976 and ends with the election of Donald Trump as president in 2016. There were seven executive editors over the course of this history, and six survive today: Max Frankel, Joseph Lelyveld, Howell Raines, Bill Keller, Jill Abramson, and Dean Baquet. They could not have been more gracious and generous over the course of this project, inviting me into their homes for interviews and meals, retrieving boxes of personal papers from closets, basements, attics, and summer homes. Their cooperation was essential in telling this story. There was an added benefit in working with journalists of such accomplishment: again and again, I paused and took note when they offered what we in the newsroom call "thoughts": ways to present and frame complicated events, overarching themes, observations, and insights. I thank them for that.

David Dunlap, who spent forty-two years at the paper and now serves as its not-so-unofficial historian, was invaluable from the earliest days of this project, opening his files, making suggestions large and small, his dedication to the *Times* evident in the scrupulousness he brought in making sure the smallest details were right. He was one of three former *Times* journalists who brought an outsider-insider eye to reading the manuscript. Todd Purdum shared the judgment, authority, and informed eye of someone who spent much of his professional life at the *Times*. Dan Okrent, the paper's first public editor, was rigorous and generous with his time and insights in helping me shape the book.

Gillian Blake, the publisher and editor-in-chief at Crown, was a source of inspiration, ideas, encouragement, insight, and wisdom. She was endlessly patient and supportive: it was never a question of "When are you going to give me a chapter?" but always "How do we make this better?" You can't ask for more from an editor. Amy Li, an associate editor, was tireless and meticulous, always keeping me on track and improving the book at every turn. I was lucky to work with both of them. Tim Duggan was the editor who originally signed me to write the book; he moved on to another house, but I am grateful for his enthusiasm and support.

I wish every author could have an agent like Kathy Robbins. I have worked with her for thirty years, since I wrote *Out for Good* with Dudley Clendinen, and she has always been there for me, as much a friend as an agent. Throughout the long process of creating *The Times,* Kathy was persistent and focused in helping me bring this book to reality. She was a critical part of this process: from the multiple rewrites of the book proposal to reviewing the manuscript right up through the final stages of editing. She is a treasure. I am also grateful to her associate, David Halpern, for his support and guidance over the years.

* * *

This book was inspired by *The Kingdom and the Power,* the history of the *Times* that Gay Talese wrote in 1969. I visited Gay at his townhouse in New York shortly after I began this project.

I've been waiting fifteen years for someone to do this book, he said, by my recollection, before inviting me in to share how he would approach a book like this—and then off to dinner we went. Gay opened his files and address book, putting me in touch with retired editors and reporters at the *Times* who otherwise might have been lost to history. He was a model of class and collegiality. Alex Jones, who with his late wife, Susan Tifft, wrote *The Trust: The Private and Powerful Family Behind The New York Times*, the 1999 account about the Sulzbergers and the *Times*, was incredibly generous in sharing his work and insights. He let me spend hours plowing through boxes of documents at his home in Charleston, South Carolina. He could not have been more encouraging and supportive.

The *Times* is filled with people devoted to honoring the paper's history, and eager to recount their roles during critical parts of its history. The late Betsy Wade invited me to her home and discussed her early years at the *Times* and her leading role in the women's discrimination suit. Martin Nisenholtz described the early debates about digital at the *Times* and across the industry, and his own successes—and frustrations—in helping the newspaper through the transition. Paul Delaney welcomed me to his apartment in Washington and shared boxes of documents that tracked the paper's troubled history in hiring and promoting Black journalists. Glenn Kramon opened up his personal journals, which brought a particularly difficult period at the newspaper to life. Kevin McKenna was crucial in sketching out the earliest days of the digital awakening; he kept meticulous records, his own archive of a critical time in the paper's evolution. Susan Dryfoos, the founder of Times History Productions, guided me through her trove of videos, interviews, transcripts, and documents, forever reaching into her memory—or for a shelf or box—when she thought of something else I should examine. Sam Zucker, the paper's records manager, steered me through the newspaper's collections of papers and oral histories, pulling out file after file stored at the *Times* building. Jeff Roth spent hours digging through archives finding photographs to illustrate the book. Eileen Murphy was a constant source of support.

I have been lucky to work over the years with journalists of the highest caliber, many of whom shared their own experience and wisdom to bear and helped me understand difficult passages of the paper's history. Dick Stevenson, an editor in the Washington bureau, and Peter Baker, the White House reporter and author, are both outstanding journalists and were invaluable in bringing this book to fruition. Among current and former colleagues at the *Times*, I am grateful for the advice and counsel of Jim Rutenberg, Patrick Healy, Julie Bloom, Andrew Rosenthal, Anna Quindlen, James Bennet, Jerry Gray, Frank Bruni, Gail Collins, David Barstow, Liza Tozzi, Eric Nagourney (yes, we are related), Carmel McCoubrey, Rick Berke, Tom Kulaga, Alan Flippen, David Leonhardt, Matt Purdy, Jim Roberts, Jonathan Martin, and Alex Burns. Richard Meislin, who died before this book was completed, was an essential source of memos, memories, and perspective. Janet Elder also did not live to see this project completed, but she encouraged me to do it. The late Adam Clymer was a source of support throughout my years at the *Times* and during my early years working on this book.

Maureen Dowd told me many years ago, on a hotel elevator in Boston, that I would one day work at the *Times;* she was good to her word and has been a loyal friend and colleague. At the paper, my thanks as well to Elisabeth Bumiller, Jennifer Medina, Michael Cooper, Sam Sifton, Alison Mitchell, Carolyn Ryan, Marc Lacey, Maggie Haberman, and Sam Dolnick. I benefited from the support and ideas of friends and colleagues in and outside of journalism: Nick Goldberg and Amy Wilentz were there from the earliest discussion of this project, offering ideas and needed criticism. I am grateful to Maralee Schwartz, Dan Balz, Jeff Zeleny, Ian Lovett, Elizabeth Kolbert, Andrew Fine, and Jim Courtovich, who put me up in Washington and in South Carolina. Alice Mayhew, the late editor at Simon & Schuster, pushed and encouraged me to do this for a decade.

The exhaustive *Times* papers are stored at the Archives and Manuscript division of the New York Public Library, and my thanks to everyone there—particularly Kyle Triplett and Tal Nadan and Thomas Lannon—who helped me find my way around this incredible resource. My thanks to the staff at the Rare Book & Manuscript Library at Columbia University, the repository of papers from Max Frankel and Harrison Salisbury, as well as at the Newseum, where I examined the Gerald Boyd papers. In the mid-1980s, the *Times* stopped requiring editors and executives to turn their papers over to the archives; thankfully, journalists (at least in those days) tended to be packrats. Jeff Gerth has what is effectively a *Times* archive in his basement in Washington; he spent countless hours retrieving documents for me, and even more hours explaining what was there and what it meant. Joe Lelyveld and Bill Keller handed over boxes crammed with documents for me and told me to have at it. Jill Abramson spent a day walking me through binders filled with memos, letters, clippings, and documents that marked her years at the *Times*. Howell Raines shared stacks of papers from his years as editor as he welcomed me to his home in Pennsylvania. A complete list of people who provided their papers is contained in the notes section of this book and I mention a few more of them here: Bernard Gwertzman, Fiona Spruill, Jerry Gray, Patrick Tyler, David Perpich, Anne Cronin, Jim Newton, the family of Arthur Gelb, Rob Larson, Dan Okrent, Cliff Levy, Tom Kulaga, Bernie Weinraub, and Jayson Blair.

I have also drawn on the memoirs written over the decades by some of the players in these pages, among them: Arthur Gelb, Harrison Salisbury, James Reston, Turner Catledge, Seymour Topping, Iphigene Sulzberger (with Susan Dryfoos), Dan Okrent, Gerald Boyd, Craig Whitney, Bernard Gwertzman, Martin Tolchin, Margaret Sullivan, Judith Miller, and Jayson Blair. Four former executive editors—Frankel, Lelyveld, Raines, and Abramson—also wrote about their careers, and their accounts were invaluable.

I am lucky to have friends who love journalism and indulged my long absences from their world: Andrew Kirtzman, Claire Brinberg, Justin Blake, Wendy Schmalz, Michael Wilde, JoAnne Wasserman, Stu Marques, Tony Tommasini, Ben McCommon, Mark Halperin, Karen Avrich, Tim Naftali, Kevin McCoy, Ruth McCoy, Michael Janofsky, Joan Harrison, Dee Dee Myers, Bob Shrum, and Marylouise Oates. Thanks to Neil Bauman and Theresa Mazich, who invited me to join a *Times*-sponsored cruise they were organizing whose panelists included Arthur Sulzberger, Jr., providing an opportunity for me to interview him on the high seas.

In addition to Gillian Blake and Amy Li, I am grateful to all the people at Crown for the care and diligence they brought to ushering this complicated book to publication: Evan Camfield, Mark Maguire, Mimi Lipson, Simon Sullivan, Patricia Clark, and Sally Franklin.

I am extremely grateful to my friend Kyle Froman for the author photograph that appears on the jacket of this book. Hilary McClellen was a superb fact checker; if any mistakes nevertheless crept into these final pages, they are the fault of the author. Jefferson Farber was a fast and accurate transcriber. Research was provided by Amanda Millner-Fairbanks and Ian Lovett.

My parents, Herb and Ruth Nagourney, were passionate *Times* readers; the newspaper was delivered to our home every day. I wish they were here today to read this book. (My father was publisher at Quadrangle Books when it was a *Times* company. I was reminded of this when I stumbled across letters he had written forty years ago to Abe Rosenthal encouraging him to write his memoirs. I drew on Rosenthal's notes for his never-published memoirs, which he put in his archives, so I suppose in a way this came full circle.) My thanks to my sister, Beth, my brothers Eric and Sam, and to my stepmother, Ann Bramson. They are all much more than relatives; they are treasured friends.

Ben Kushner has been at my side since we met in college. He spent days with me combing through Jones-Tifft files in the early days of researching this book, and over these past three years has read chapter after chapter, offering encouragement and support. I never forget how lucky I am for our decades together.

The New York Public Library, Archives and Manuscripts Division, was the repository for the following documents from the New York Times Company archives, as marked in endnotes: Frankel papers, NYPL; Gelb papers, NYPL; Gruson papers, NYPL; Topping papers, NYPL; Autograph file; NYTC general files. There are two collections of Rosenthal papers: "Rosenthal papers, NYT" refers to his official company archives; "Rosenthal papers, personal" refers to his personal collection. The oral history project conducted by Susan Dryfoos is marked NYTHPOHC (New York Times History Project/Oral History Collection) and is at the New York Public Library. This book also draws on the New York Times archives files of John B. Oakes, Orvil Dryfoos, Adolph S. Ochs, Anna Quindlen, James Reston, William Safire, Iphigene Ochs Sulzberger, the Foreign Desk, the Metropolitan Desk and the National Desk.

The Columbia University Libraries, Archival Collection was the repository for the following papers: Frankel papers, Columbia; Salisbury papers; Topping, Columbia. The Newseum in Washington, D.C. (since closed), was the repository for the Gerald Boyd papers.

Documents cited here were also drawn from the personal papers of Jill Abramson, Rick Berke, Jayson Blair, Anne Cronin, Paul Delaney, John Geddes, the family of Arthur Gelb, Jeff Gerth, Jerry Gray, Bernard Gwertzman, Alex Jones and Susan Tifft, Bill Keller, Tom Kulaga, Rob Larson, Joseph Lelyveld, Cliff Levy, Kevin McKenna, Richard Meislin, Jim Newton, Martin Nisenholtz, Dan Okrent, David Perpich, Howell Raines, Jim Roberts, Fiona Spruill, A. G. Sulzberger, Gay Talese, Patrick Tyler, Bernie Weinraub, and Carey Winfrey.

In the notes below, AOS refers to Punch Sulzberger; AOSJR is Arthur Sulzberger Jr.; and AGS is Arthur Gregg Sulzberger.

Preface

viii　**his total compensation:** "Notice of 2018 Annual Meeting and Proxy Statement," New York Times Company, April 19, 2018.

viii　**Sulzberger arrived early for the reception:** This account is from the author, who was in attendance.

ix　**with a daily circulation of:** Alliance for Audited Media, formerly known as the Audit Bureau of Circulations.

x　**We *tell* them what they:** Janofsky interview with author, August 1, 2021.

x　**far fewer print subscribers:** Print subscriptions: Alliance for Audited Media, formerly known as the Audit Bureau of Circulations. Digital subscriptions: Annual Report, The New York Times Company, 2018.

xiv　**"One never truly":** This account of the farewell remarks by Arthur Sulzberger is from the author, who was in attendance.

1　*A Man of His Times*

4　**You have to understand:** David Shribman interview with author, January 27, 2019.

4　**"I'm a very good editor":** Rosenthal interview with Dryfoos, February 26, 1986, NYTHPOHC.

4　**"A disaster":** AOS interview with Gruson, March 29, 1983, NYTHPOHC.

4　**sent Reston back to Washington:** "He never did give it the commitment that he would have had to give it if he really, I suppose in retrospect, wanted it to work out," AOS to Sydney Gruson, June 22, 1983, NYTHPOHC.

5　**"I will become executive editor":** Memo, December 17, 1976, Rosenthal papers, NYT.

5　**"I am quite unhappy":** Rosenthal to Topping, Gelb, Jones, Greenfield, December 6, 1976, Rosenthal papers, NYT.

5　WELCOME TO THE KINGDOM AND POWER: Bradlee to Rosenthal, undated (December 1976), Rosenthal papers, NYT.

5　**"Titles, schmitles!":** Frankel to Rosenthal, December 17, 1976 and Rosenthal to Frankel, December 24, 1976, Max Frankel papers, Columbia.

6　**Are you happy here:** Rosenthal interview with Dryfoos, March 9, 1987, NYTHPOHC.

6　**"This is the candor department?":** Rosenthal interview with Gruson, April 21, 1983, NYTHPOHC.

7　**could not hold his liquor:** Rosenthal interview with Gruson, April 21, 1983, NYTHPOHC.

7　**From his earliest days . . . Rosenthal had been distressed:** Rosenthal interview with Dryfoos, March 9, 1987, NYTHPOHC.

7　**"radical or militant element":** Rosenthal to Reston, September 4, 1968, Rosenthal papers, NYT.

8　**"essential not only to American journalism":** Rosenthal to AOS, September 4, 1969, Rosenthal papers, NYT.

8 **"The turmoil in the country is so widespread":** Rosenthal to staff, October 7, 1969, Delaney papers.

8 **"the role of a policeman":** Rosenthal to staff, October 7, 1969, Delaney papers.

8 **"written by a thousand SDS kids":** Rosenthal to Curtis, August 6, 1975, Rosenthal papers, NYT.

8 **"passed a hand over his face":** A. M. Rosenthal, "Combat and Compassion at Columbia," *The New York Times*, May 1, 1968.

9 **"haughty and blind to the end":** Steven Roberts, "The University that Refused to learn," *The Village Voice*, May 9, 1968.

9 **"used extremely bad judgment":** Rosenthal memo to file, May 22, 1968, and Roberts note to Rosenthal, undated: Rosenthal papers, NYT.

9 **"Not to be Nixonian":** Rosenthal interview with Gruson, June 7, 1983, NYTHPOHC.

9 **"To call a Communist":** Rosenthal to Semple, September 15, 1977, Rosenthal papers, NYT.

9 **"editorialized in the extreme and terribly naïve":** Rosenthal to Gelb, Levitas, April 24, 1973, Jones-Tifft papers.

9 **a story on a crime bill:** Warren Weaver, Jr., "Senate Approves Stiff Crime Bill for Washington," *The New York Times*, July 24, 1970.

9 **"a distinct tendency":** Rosenthal to Frankel, July 24, 1970, Rosenthal papers, NYT. The letter was not sent, but note on top says Rosenthal spoke with Frankel about it by telephone on this date.

10 **I probably turned:** Kovach interview with author, January 4, 2017.

10 **pact not to drink:** Kovach interview with author, January 4, 2017.

10 **how he wanted to be remembered:** Rosenthal interview with Dryfoos, February 28, 1986, NYTHPOHC.

10 **"goddamn difficult thing":** Rosenthal interview with Gruson, August 30, 1983, NYTHPOHC.

10 **You must dress:** Talese email to author, March 26, 2019, elaborating on account in Harrison E. Salisbury, "Mr. New York Times," *Esquire*, January 1980.

10 **five feet, nine-and-a-half inches:** Harrison E. Salisbury, "Mr. New York Times."

10 **came to wear suspenders:** Lord interview with author, November 11, 2016.

11 **ferrying his briefcase:** Adam Moss interview with author, October 8, 2017, and November 28, 2019.

11 **Brooklyn Botanic Garden:** Rosenthal letter to Botanic Gardens, September 2, 1975, Rosenthal papers, NYT.

11 **carting bricks and dirt:** Meislin email to author, February 20, 2019.

11 **"holy-shit newspaper man":** Quindlen interview with author, October 4, 2017.

11 **"Attributing information":** Rosenthal memo to staff, December 3, 1974, Rosenthal papers, NYT.

11 **"rules against anonymous attacks":** Rosenthal to Roberts, December 17, 1970, Jones-Tifft papers.

11 **"stick our fingers":** Rosenthal to staff, October 7, 1969, Paul Delaney papers.

12 **"like the plague":** Rosenthal to Betsy Wade and Bob Crandall, December 27, 1977, Rosenthal papers, NYT.

12 **Rosenthal took her to lunch:** Quindlen interview with author, October 14, 2017.

12 **"Why do you want to be President?":** Rosenthal interview with Dryfoos, March 11, 1986, NYTHPOHC.

12   **"I found the paper dull"**: Rosenthal to senior editors, June 4, 1975, Rosenthal papers, NYT.

12   **"Our Paris bureau"**: Rosenthal to Semple, November 12, 1980, Rosenthal papers, NYT. Note never sent; discussed with Craig Whitney instead.

13   **"I hated getting phone calls"**: Frankel interview with author, October 4, 2017.

2   *Do This for Me*

14   **"You paid your salary"**: AOS to Rosenthal, July 10, 1973, Rosenthal papers, NYT.

14   **best male traveling companion**: Rosenthal interview with Dryfoos, March 9, 1987, NYTHPOHC.

14   **After the late-afternoon**: Hoge interview with author, November 21, 1978.

14   **bottle of wine**: Greenfield interview with author, June 4, 2017.

15   **"to relax the reader"**: Gelb to Rosenthal, May 24, 1976 Rosenthal papers, NYT.

15   **a barrier that few managed to penetrate**: See Gruson interview with Dryfoos, March 27, 1994, NYTHPOHC.

15   **'If you don't do this, I quit'**: AOS interview with Gruson, June 22, 1983, NYTHPOHC.

16   **He was punctual**: Arthur Gelb, *City Room* (New York: Putnam, 2003), 205.

16   **"I would not voluntarily go"**: AOS to Gelb, November 2, 1981, Gelb papers, NYPL.

16   **shop for antiques**: Greenfield interview with author, June 3, 2017.

16   **"have to be a pig pen"**: AOS to Peter Millones, June 16, 1980, Topping papers, NYPL.

16   **"can't even keep his shirt tucked in"**: AOS interview with Gruson, May 12, 1983, NYTHPOHC.

17   **Mayo Clinic**: Robert D. McFadden, "A. M. Rosenthal, Editor of The Times, Dies at 84," *The New York Times*, May 11, 2006.

17   **he would begin to cry**: Arthur Gelb eulogy for Rosenthal, May 15, 2006, Central Synagogue, Rosenthal papers, personal.

17   **Café des Artistes**: Rosenthal diaries, April 12, 1984 entry, Rosenthal papers, personal.

17   **Trump apologized**: Trump to Rosenthal, December 2, 1983, Autograph papers, NYT.

17   **before signing it "Donald"**: Trump to Rosenthal and Shirley Lord, July 15, 1999, Rosenthal papers, personal.

18   **Weather Channel**: "Cable Network for Weather," *The New York Times*, July 31, 1981.

18   **"PLEASE, PLEASE"**: AOS to Rosenthal, July 24, 1981, Gelb papers, NYPL.

18   **"I'm left very cold"**: AOS to Rosenthal, July 12, 1976, Rosenthal papers, NYT, and Rosenthal reply to AOS July 13, 1976, Rosenthal papers, NYT.

18   **settled a paternity suit**: Susan E. Tiff and Alex S. Jones, *The Trust: The Private and Powerful Family Behind The New York Times* (Boston: Little, Brown and Company, 1999) 297–99.

19   **"I'd just break my ass"**: Topping interview with author, April 9, 2017.

19   **"As it is such a well-known place"**: AOS to Rosenthal, March 4, 1986, Rosenthal papers, NYT.

19   **"Don't quote me"**: Iphigene Sulzberger to AOS, September 30, 1983, Rosenthal papers, NYT.

19   **"Very few things are pleasanter"**: Rosenthal to AOS, October 3, 1983, Rosenthal papers, NYT.

19   **spelling the word "employee"**: AOS to Rosenthal, November 10, 1975, Rosenthal papers, NYT.

20 **"I like to cook"**: AOS to Rosenthal, February 29, 1984, Rosenthal papers, NYT.

20 **"We have country club memberships"**: AOS to Rosenthal, December 1, 1975, Rosenthal papers, NYT.

20 **"Now that we have put the comics"**: AOS to Rosenthal, August 5, 1985, Rosenthal papers, NYT.

20 **"the highest possible compliment"**: March 1, 1984, Rosenthal papers, NYT.

20 **"any kind of a problem"**: AOS to Rosenthal, May 24, 1978, Rosenthal papers, NYT.

20 **"We can't really decide"**: Rosenthal to AOS, July 15, 1978, Rosenthal papers, NYT.

20 **a friend, Armand Hammer:** Rick Jacobs email interview with author, December 8, 2016. Jacobs was a longtime assist to Hammer.

21 **"a mishmosh of weak denials"**: Rosenthal confidential journal entry, December 3, 1982, Rosenthal papers, personal.

21 **"not the first time"** : Rosenthal confidential journal entry, December 3, 1981, Rosenthal papers, personal.

21 **the Hammer letter was printed:** Armand Hammer, "A Response from Armand Hammer," *The New York Times Magazine*, December 20, 1981.

21 **"He's got a bunch of bullshit"** . . . **"has moods"**: AOS interview with Gruson, May 12, 1983, NYTHPOHC.

21 **how much bitterness:** Gruson interview with Dryfoos, March 27, 1994 (date of transcription; date of interview not noted), NYTHPOHC.

21 **"Punch liked the results"**: Gruson to Dryfoos, March 27, 1994 (date of transcription; date of interview not noted), NYTHPOHC.

21 **Rosenthal was what he was, Sulzberger would say:** AOS to Gruson, May 12, 1983, NYTHPOHC.

21 **"There is one item"**: AOS memo to *Times* managers and supervisors, August 27, 1976, Rosenthal papers, NYT.

21 **cover story in *Businessweek*:** "Behind the Profit Squeeze at the New York Times," *Businessweek*, August 30, 1976.

22 **"Unless drastic changes are made"**: Chris Welles, "The Bad News in Store for The New York Times," *New York*, April 12, 1976.

22 **"open the window and jump"**: Arthur Gelb, *City Room*, 607.

22 **"The conclusion is inescapable"**: Mattson, memo for his files, January 6, 1976, Rosenthal papers, NYT.

22 **"liked it more than they read it"**: Rosenthal interview with Dryfoos, February 28, 1986, NYTHPOHC.

22 **noticed the success of *New York*:** Lord interview with author, November 11, 2016, and Greenfield interview with author, June 4, 2017.

22 **Clay Felker is on to something here:** Greenfield interview with author, June 4, 2017.

23 **Get your ass out of here!:** Arthur Gelb, *City Room*, 363.

23 **"it is essential"**: AOS to Rosenthal, June 28, 1974, Jones-Tifft papers.

23 **five music critics:** Rosenthal interview with Dryfoos, February 28, 1986, NYTHPOHC.

23 **"This is the News Department's"**: Rosenthal to AOS, Mattson, June 29, 1976, Rosenthal papers, NYT.

24 **the kind of ridicule:** Richard Pollak, "Abe Rosenthal Presents The **New** New York Times; Supereditor Ignores New York's Demise in Mad Scramble to Print Soufflé Recipes," *Penthouse*, September 1977.

24 **the average daily circulation:** "The Kingdom and the Cabbage," *Time*, August, 15, 1977.

24   **"I've been an editor"**: Rosenthal to Henry A. Grunwald, August 12, 1977, Rosenthal papers, NYT.

24   **seven or eight news organizations:** AOS to editors, May 13, 1977, Topping papers, NYPL.

24   **were doing stories on the "new *New York Times*"**: One example: William H. Jones and Laird Anderson, "The Old 'Gray Lady' Gets a Face-Lifting," *The Washington Post*, July 25, 1977.

24   **"half a page on asparagus"**: Rosenthal interview with Dryfoos, February 28, 1986, NYTHPOHC.

24   **"I just wonder"**: AOS interview with Gruson, March 15, 1985, NYTHPOHC.

3   The Tenth Floor

25   **"I am not an editorial writer"; "Harsh about others"**: Frankel memo to AOS, February 18, 1976, Jones-Tifft papers.

25   **Sulzberger was pushing out John Oakes:** AOS to Gruson, June 22, 1983, NYTHPOHC.

25   **There were too many mornings:** AOS to Gruson, May 3, 1983, NYTHPOHC.

26   **opinion that appeared in *The Washington Post*:** Frankel interview with author, October 4, 2017.

26   **"I don't think either Punch or I"**: Gruson interview with Wicker, May 3, 1983, NYTHPOHC.

27   **"I never fully accepted"**: Max Frankel, *The Times of My Life and My Life with The Times* (New York: Random House, 1999) 382.

27   **working the "lobster shift"**: Max Frankel, *The Times of My Life and My Life with The Times* (New York: Random House, 1999), 130–31.

28   **"just a dumb accident"**: Frankel interview with author, October 4, 2017.

28   **Berger was probably the most admired:** "Meyer Berger, 60, of Times is Dead," *The New York Times*, February 9, 1959.

28   **twenty-five-dollar raise:** Max Frankel, *The Times of My Life*, 133.

28   **"I have run out of any way"**: Wicker to Frankel, undated but appears to be 1968, when Wicker urged Turner Catledge to nominate Frankel story on LBJ death for a Pulitzer Prize. Frankel papers, Columbia.

28   **"Twice, entirely on her own"**: Text of Frankel remarks at Tobi Frankel service, undated: Salisbury papers.

28   **Frankel's resignation letter:** Frankel to AOS, September 3, 1964, Frankel papers, Columbia.

29   **Frankel had second thoughts:** Frankel interview with author, October 3, 2017.

29   **Carol Sulzberger . . . answered the telephone:** Max Frankel, *The Times of My Life*, 304.

29   **I just don't want to stay:** Frankel interview with author, October 4, 2017.

29   **years of tension:** Gay Talese, *The Kingdom and the Power* (New York: Random House, 1966), 494–504.

29   **"I am horrified to discover"**: Frankel letter, February 1, 1973, Frankel papers, Columbia.

30   **"taking a beating on the Watergate case"**: Rosenthal to Jones, September 20, 1972, Rosenthal papers, NYT.

30   **one of those arrested, James W. McCord, Jr.:** Bob Woodward and Carl Bernstein, "GOP Security Aide Among Five Arrested in Bugging Affair," *The Washington Post*, June 19, 1972.

31 **"not a kid's game":** Rosenthal interview with Dryfoos, March 9, 1987, NYTHPOHC.

31 **He had decided he would leave:** Rosenthal interview with Dryfoos, March 9, 1987, NYTHPOHC.

31 **"If we had surrendered":** Rosenthal to Hohenberg, September 11, 1979, Jones-Tifft papers.

31 **"the most fruitful":** Rosenthal to Sheehan, June 29, 1971, Rosenthal papers, NYT.

31 **"No jokes this time":** Rosenthal to Bradlee, May 10, 1973, Rosenthal papers, NYT.

31 **"out to cut my throat":** Rosenthal to Salisbury, per Salisbury typed notes of session, August 9, 1979, Salisbury papers.

32 **I should have fired you:** Frankel interview with author, September 21, 2016.

32 **thirty-five thousand words:** *Times Talk*, May-June 1973.

32 **"one foot out the door.":** Frankel interview with author, April 10, 2017; he used the same turn of phrase in defending his performance in an interview with Charlie Rose, April 14, 1995.

32 **We got beat because:** Frankel interview, *Charlie Rose*, April 14, 1994.

32 **"Not even my most cynical":** Max Frankel, *The Times of My Life*, 345.

33 **"We got beaten":** Raines interview with author, August 14, 2017, afternoon session.

33 **the phrase "investigative reporter":** AOS to Rosenthal, September 13, 1978, author's papers.

33 **lacked an investigative mentality:** Dave Jones interview with author, November 19, 2018; confirmed in January 3, 2019 email exchange with Gene Roberts and author.

33 **"sort of a bloodbath":** AOS to Gruson, June, 22, 1983, NYTHPOHC.

33 **directed his board:** Boffey interview with author, June 9, 2017.

33 **"Maxed and Jacked":** Golden Behr interview with author, November 20, 2016.

34 **"According to the information":** O'Connor to Frankel, October 5, 1983, Frankel papers, Columbia.

4 Dead Ends

35 **a job she lost:** Wade interview with author, June 20, 2016.

35 **first woman to edit news copy:** Wade interview with author June 20, 2016, and David W. Dunlap, "Look Back: 1986: 'Ms.' Joins The Times's Vocabulary," *The New York Times*, April 6, 2017.

35 **"as archaic as McSorley's":** Betsy Wade to Mary Marshall Clark, Washington Press Club women in journalism oral history project, Columbia University Center for Oral History, October 12, 1992.

35 **At the end of his shift:** Wade interviews with author, June 20, 2016 and November 19, 2017.

36 **sharpen a fistful of pencils:** Betsy Wade to Mary Marshall Clark, women in journalism project, October 12, 1992.

36 **a bad speller, if self-aware:** Siegal email interview with author, January 15, 2020.

36 **When Abe Rosenthal was writing a speech:** Wade interview with author June 20, 2016.

37 **"I have taken pride":** Wade to Rosenthal, January 13, 1973, Iphigene Sulzberger papers.

37 **founded the previous February:** Nan Robertson, *The Girls in the Balcony* (New York: Fawcett Columbine, 1992), 142.

37   **"The voices of women":** Women's Caucus to AOS, May 31, 1972, Rosenthal papers, NYT.

38   **over warnings from her husband:** Shanahan to Mary Marshall Clark, June 6, 1993, women in journalism oral history project, Columbia.

38   **"I had always assumed":** Nan Robertson, *The Girls in the Balcony*, 179.

38   **Shanahan wanted to bring her grievance:** Shanahan to Mary Marshall Clark, June 6, 1993, women in journalism oral history project, Columbia University Center for Oral History.

39   **on average $98.67:** Nan Robertson, *The Girls in the Balcony*, 181.

39   **settlement was announced:** Nan Robertson, *The Girls in the Balcony*, 206.

39   **"Money amount is smallest":** Elliott M. Sanger, Jr., to M. E. Ryan, October 3 1978, Rosenthal papers, NYT.

39   **"completely vindicates The *Times*"** . . . **"Such stringent requirements":** "The Times Settles Sex-Bias Suit Filed by Female Workers in U.S. Court," *The New York Times*, November 21, 1978.

39   **"'What do you think about this person'":** Salisbury typed notes of his interview with Rosenthal, August 9, 1979, Salisbury papers.

40   **"Absolutely nothing":** AOS to Rosenthal, November 21, 1978, Rosenthal papers, NYT.

40   **"If you want to die":** Wade to Mary Marshall Clark, May 21, 1994, women in journalism project, Columbia University Center for Oral History.

40   **she sent Rosenthal:** Wade to Rosenthal, June 29, 1972, Rosenthal papers, NYT.

40   **He would refer to Wade:** Siegal to Dryfoos, NYTHPOHC, February 28, 1987.

40   **We are not in the habit:** Wade interview with author, June 20, 2017.

40   **journalistic backwater:** Wade interview with author, June 20, 2016.

40   **"Those of us":** Gail Collins, *No Stopping Us Now: The Adventures of Older Women in American History* (Boston: Little, Brown and Company, 2019), 296.

40   **"dead end for all of us":** Wade interview with author June 20, 2016.

41   **My whole career:** Quindlen interview with author, October 4, 2017.

41   **"I am utterly confident":** Salisbury typed notes of his interview with Rosenthal, August 9, 1979, Salisbury papers.

42   **The Caucus, in its initial 1972 count:** Women of the news staff to AOS et al., undated (approximately May 31, 1972), Rosenthal papers, NYT.

42   **Rosenthal would sympathize:** Rosenthal letter to Stacie L. Jacob, October 14, 1971, Jones papers.

42   **"The people who run NOW":** Rosenthal to AOS et al., June 20, 1974, Rosenthal papers, NYT.

42   **So, this is the last one:** Quindlen interview with author, October 4, 2017.

43   **"I should like to proclaim":** AOS to Frankel, undated, Frankel papers, Columbia.

43   **"If you insist upon reading":** AOS to Rosenthal, August 3, 1977, Rosenthal papers, NYT.

43   **"I don't think that the time has come":** Rosenthal to AOS and Frankel, June 18, 1974, Frankel papers, Columbia.

44   **"It isn't possible":** Steinem to Rosenthal, November 23, 1973, Rosenthal papers, NYT.

44   **"Miss, If She Chooses":** David W. Dunlap, "Look Back: 1986: 'Ms.' Joins The Times's Vocabulary," *The New York Times*, April 6, 2017.

44   **"At the end of the year":** AOS to Frankel and Rosenthal, December 19, 1974, Frankel papers, NYPL.

5 *Winners and Sinners*

46 **"We do not use this expression":** Siegal to Nancy Newhouse, June 14, 1982. Rosenthal papers, NYT. The story: Ann Crittenden, "Pro-Abortion Group Sets a Major Political Drive," *The New York Times,* June 14, 1982.

46 **"Please pay attention":** Siegal to Lelyveld, September 25, 1979, Topping papers, NYPL.

47 **"This is Allan Siegal":** Siegal interview with Dryfoos, February 28, 1987, NYTHPOHC.

47 **"Is Rosenthal's Time":** Joe Mandese, "Is Rosenthal's Time Up at the Times?" *Adweek,* August 15, 1983.

47 **"This is an extra task for you":** Rosenthal to Siegal, December 3, 1979, Rosenthal papers, NYT.

48 **"In the long run":** Siegal to Rosenthal, Topping, July 24, 1980, Rosenthal papers, NYT.

48 **"particular kind of hell":** Siegal interview with Dryfoos, February 17, 1987, NYTHPOHC.

48 **she called it a phobia:** Siegal interview with Dryfoos, February 17, 1987, NYTHPOHC.

49 **"Abjectly humiliating":** Siegal interview with Dryfoos, February 17, 1987.

49 **I'll fix him:** Siegal interview with Dryfoos, February 17, 1987, NYTHPOHC.

49 **column written by Francis X. Clines:** Siegal interview with Dryfoos, February 19, 1987, NYTHPOHC; Clines, in an email on November 1, 2016, said he did not know of the incident. "But I was on Abe's shit list a number of times when he was offended."

49 **Well, that was last night:** Siegal interview with Dryfoos, February 19, 1987, NYTHPOHC.

49 *Washington Journalism Review:* Gerald Lanson and Mitchell Stephens, "The Man and His Times," *Washington Journalism Review,* July/August 1983.

49 **"Abe was able to convince himself":** Siegal interview with Dryfoos, February 17, 1987, NYTHPOHC.

50 **"twist the paper":** Siegal interview with Dryfoos, February 17, 1987, NYTHPOHC.

50 **"that in the guise":** Siegal interview with Dryfoos, February 17, 1987, NYTHPOHC.

50 **Rosenthal met her on a trip:** Warren Hoge interview with author, November 21, 2018, and Hoge email to author, March 23, 2019.

50 **Rosenthal spent a week there:** Christian interview with author, March 25, 2019.

50 **"the Sandinista bandwagon":** Shirley Christian, "Covering the Sandinistas," *Washington Journalism Review,* March 1982.

50 **"I've never rejected a liberal":** Rosenthal interview with Dryfoos, November 15, 1984, NYTHPOHC.

50 **see her name in *The Village Voice*:** Christian interview with author, March 25, 2019.

51 **in defense of Jerzy Kosinski:** John Corry, "17 Years of Ideological Attack on a Cultural Target," *The New York Times,* November 7, 1982.

51 **"Like many powerful editors":** Charles Kaiser, "Friends at the Top of the Times," *Newsweek,* November 22, 1982.

51 **should have been awarded:** Rosenthal interview with Dryfoos, March 9, 1987, NYTHPOHC.

51 **"We avoided writing":** Rosenthal to Corry, April 20, 1983, Rosenthal papers, NYT.

51 **"They have tried to destroy you":** Talese to Rosenthal, December 8, 1982, Rosenthal papers, personal.

51 **Guilty as charged:** Siegal interview with Dryfoos, February 28, 1987, NYTHPOHC.

51 **Lelyveld grew disillusioned:** Lelyveld interview with author, October 1, 2017.

51 **It's ironic:** Frankel interview with author, October 4, 2017.

51 **morale in the newsroom:** Raines interview with author, August 14, 2017, afternoon session.

52 **"If no one does speak to them"**: Leonard Harris to Rosenthal, April 20, 1983, Rosenthal papers, NYT.

52 **Rosenthal asked Nicholas Gage**: Gage to Rosenthal, May 15, 1985, Rosenthal papers, personal.

52 **"I've been probably"**: Rosenthal interview with Gruson, August 30, 1983, NYTHPOHC.

52 **"Retreat from Radicalism"**: Dinesh D'Souza, "Retreat from Radicalism: The Times It Is A-Changin'," *Policy Review*, Fall 1984.

52 **"a tribute to"**: Roy Cohn to Rosenthal, October 29, 1984, Rosenthal papers, NYT.

52 **"I expect the Left"**: Rosenthal to Roy Cohn, November 5, 1984.

52 **forced himself to go on a diet**: Frankel interview with author, September 21, 2016.

53 **Do you think Africa can feed itself**: Darnton interview with author, June 29, 2022.

53 **"dying and going to heaven"**: Siegal interview with Dryfoos, February 19, 1987, NYTHPOHC.

53 **"I hated the man"**: Siegal interview with Dryfoos, February 19, 1987, NYTHPOHC.

53 **The article, . . . by Cliff Jahr**: Cliff Jahr, "The All-Gay Cruise: Prejudice and Price," *The New York Times*, April 6, 1975.

54 **"We will respect your wish"**: Frankel to AOS, undated, Frankel papers, Columbia.

54 **a chill on gay coverage**: David W. Dunlap, "How The Times Gave 'Gay' Its Own Voice (Again)," *The New York Times*, June 19, 2017.

54 **banned the use of the word "gay"**: Susan E. Tifft and Alex S. Jones, The Trust: The Private and Powerful Family Behind The New York Times (Boston: Little, Brown and Company, 1999), 570; David Dunlap, "How the Times Gave 'Gay' Its Own Voice (Again)," The New York Times, June 19, 2017.

54 **"lack of reportage"**: Voeller to Rosenthal, June 15, 1975, Rosenthal papers, NYT.

54 **"As a newspaper"**: Rosenthal to Schanberg, October 13, 1977, Topping papers, NYPL.

55 **"They're really not outraged"**: Randy Shilts interview by Terry Gross for WUHY Philadelphia, May 3, 1982; transcript provided to Rosenthal by Daniel Miller, associate producer of *Fresh Air*, May 11, 1982; Rosenthal papers, NYT.

55 **"The coverage of the gay"**: Apuzzo et al. to AOS, May 20, 1983.

55 **"While it may be too much to ask"**: Mel Rosen to Rosenthal, May 6, 1983, Rosenthal papers, NYT.

55 **"I really have no explanation"**: Rosenthal to Rosen, May 11, 1983, Rosenthal papers, NYT.

55 **The *Times* did not run**: Robert Pear, "Health Chief Calls AIDS Battle 'No. 1 Priority,'" *The New York Times*, May 25, 1983.

56 **"We did it very deliberately"**: Frankel interview with author, September 21, 2016.

56 **Two of Rosenthal's clerks**: Kaiser interview with author, April 3, 2018, Meislin interview with author, August 8, 2017.

56 **Rosenthal's colleagues**: Frankel interview with author, April 10, 2017.

56 **"The homosexual clique"**: Abe Rosenthal journal, undated, Rosenthal papers, personal.

57 **I am worried about**: Siegal interview with Dryfoos, February 28, 1987, NYTHPOHC.

6 *Upward and Onward*

58 **"Oh my God!"**: From videotape of day, Susan Dryfoos, producer and director, *Abe*, New York Times History Productions, 1987.

58 **the worst tragedy:** William J. Broad, "The Shuttle Explodes," *The New York Times*, January 29, 1986.

59 **This was all clear to him:** Rosenthal interview with Dryfoos, March 9, 1987, NYTHPOHC.

59 **"There are one or two things":** From videotape of day, Susan Dryfoos, producer and director, *Abe*.

59 **Rosenthal declared that every story:** Rosenthal interview with Dryfoos, March 9, 1987, NYTHPOHC.

59 **we try to keep a certain continuity:** Siegal interview with Dryfoos, February 28, 1987, NYTHPOHC.

60 **"We put out a good paper today":** Rosenthal to AOS, January 29, 1986, Rosenthal papers, NYT.

60 **"This morning's *New York Times*":** AOS to Rosenthal, January 29, 1986, Rosenthal papers, NYT.

60 **the time had come to remove:** Notes of Salisbury-AOS conversation, February 12, 1986, Salisbury papers.

61 **"Abe is under no illusions":** Robert Kuttner, "The Royal Succession," *Washington Journalism Review*, January 1985.

61 **There are rumors out there:** Siegal interview with Dryfoos, February 28, 1987, NYTHPOHC.

61 **He did not want to see:** Rosenthal to AOS, September 15, 1983.

61 **Doesn't the publisher have anything to do with this:** Lelyveld interview with author, April 16, 2017.

61 **Can we go to dinner now?:** Lelyveld interview with author, April 16, 2017.

61 **"He had just conquered":** Jane Perlez, "Mortimer Zuckerman: A Developer Who Thrives on High-Stakes Dealing," *The New York Times*, August 5, 1985.

62 **Zuckerman wrote Rosenthal:** Zuckerman to Rosenthal, August 5, 1985, Rosenthal papers, NYT.

62 **"Under the heading":** Rosenthal to staff, February 7, 1983, Rosenthal papers, NYT.

62 **Rosenthal's editors did not share:** Rosenthal to Herbert Schmertz, vice president of public affairs, Mobil Oil, January 20, 1986, Rosenthal papers, NYT.

62 **"I have received virtually no cooperation":** Rosenthal to editors, August 22, 1983, Rosenthal papers, NYT.

63 **"Through opinionated phrases":** Editors' Note, *The New York Times*, August 7, 1986.

63 **Perlez was shocked:** Perlez interview with author, June 5, 2019.

63 **"Gosh Abe":** Manning to Rosenthal, August 13, 1985, Rosenthal papers, NYT.

63 **"genuine rudeness to Perlez" . . . "Who's Zuckerman?":** Eleanor Randolph, "Criticism Dogs The New York Times Editor Over Power, Politics and Personality," *The Washington Post*, January 8, 1986.

63 **"The quote was accurate":** Rosenthal to Zuckerman, January 16, 1986, Rosenthal papers, personal.

63 **"And with all the good will":** Siegal interview with Dryfoos, February 28, 1987, NYTHPOHC.

64 **"Fear and Favor":** Pete Hamill, "Fear and Favor at 'The New York Times': Pete Hamill on the Zapping of Sydney Schanberg and Other Atrocities," *The Village Voice*, October 1, 1985.

64 **"Our newspapers":** Sydney H. Schanberg, "Cajun Flies and Westway," *The New York Times*, July 27, 1985.

65   **would raise his concerns:** Frankel interview with author, October 4, 2017.

65   THE ONLY THING EYE ASK: Rosenthal cable to Schanberg, undated (approximately April 1975), Rosenthal papers, NYT.

65   **"terribly dissatisfied":** Rosenthal to Topping, undated memo, Rosenthal papers, NYT.

65   **"This is what obviously got under Punch's skin":** Salisbury account of visit with Schanberg, September 27, 1985, Salisbury papers.

65   **among them Carol Bellamy:** Bellamy to AOS, September 11, 1985, Autograph file, NYPL.

65   **"Mr. Schanberg was not fired":** Gruson to Mr. and Mrs. Robert Wilson, November 19, 1985, Gruson papers, NYPL.

65   **"took a great step forward":** Trump to Rosenthal, August 26, 1985, Autograph file, NYPL.

66   **"I realize that part of it":** Rosenthal to Greeley, October 10, 1985, Rosenthal papers, personal.

66   **"Perhaps the most important thing":** Rosenthal to Marten, October 4, 1985, Rosenthal papers, NYT.

66   **Don't respond to this:** Frankel interview with author, September 21, 2016. See also *The Times of My Life*, 414–15.

66   **Sydney Gruson visited London:** Lelyveld interview with author, April 16, 2017.

66   **"The situation, I believe":** Sydney Gruson, Reflections from a Sick Bed, November 28, 1985, Jones-Tifft papers.

67   **"Ben, to the best of his recollection":** Kaiser to Rosenthal, October 22, 1985, Rosenthal papers, personal.

68   **Rosenthal never thought Arthur, Jr.:** Greenfield, Lord, and Talese interviews with author, 2017–19.

68   **Don't ever come:** AOSJR interview with author, February 21, 2017.

68   **Arthur Sulzberger . . . heard of their concerns:** AOSJR interview with author, February 21, 2017.

68   **The publisher summoned both of them:** Lord interview with author, November 11, 2016, and Greenfield interview with author, June 4, 2017. AOSJR does not remember this, "but it could have happened."

68   **"a blessing":** AOSJR interview with author, April 17, 2017.

69   **"I hate to raise":** AOS to Rosenthal, May 16, 1986, Rosenthal papers, NYT.

69   **"He didn't have a nervous breakdown":** Susan E. Tiff and Alex S. Jones, *The Trust: The Private and Powerful Family Behind The New York Times* (Boston: Little, Brown and Company, 1999) 592.

69   **Rosenthal seemed haunted:** Kovach interview with author, January 19, 2017.

69   **It's turning into a Greek tragedy:** Salisbury notes from lunch with Gruson, August 21, 1985, Salisbury papers.

69   **"one of our very best reporters":** Rosenthal to AOSJR, June 3, 1986, Rosenthal papers, NYT.

69   **"I think we did":** Rosenthal to AOS, June 18, 1986, Rosenthal papers, NYT.

69   **"Until now, 'Ms.'":** Rosenthal memo to staff, June 19, 1986, Rosenthal papers, NYT.

70   **"When, oh when":** Judith Hope to Siegal, March 26, 1985, Rosenthal papers, NYT.

70   **"the issue of Ms.":** Whitney to Rosenthal, September 5, 1985, Rosenthal papers, NYT.

70   **Paula Kassell, a feminist:** David W. Dunlap, " 'Ms.' Joins The Times's Vocabulary," *The New York Times*, April 6, 2017.

70   **If I had known it would have:** Quindlen interview with author, October 4, 2017.

71 **"I was taken aback"**: Betsy Wade, "On Rosenthal's Watch," Women's Media Center, May 17, 2006.
71 **but Rosenthal refused:** Lord interview with author, November 11, 2016.
71 **"You've had a great run"**: Salisbury to Rosenthal, October 11, 1986, Salisbury papers.
71 **"I knew that his duty"**: Rosenthal diaries: July 25, 1992, Rosenthal papers, private.
72 ***"EXEC ED: How it happened"***: Frankel notes on his appointment, 1986, Frankel papers, Columbia.
72 **make a great newspaper:** Frankel interview with author, September 21, 2016.
72 **happy place again:** Frankel interview with author, April 10, 2017.
72 **"I want to tell you now"**: Rosenthal to Andrew and Nancy, September 13 1985, Rosenthal papers, personal.
73 **"It will be upward"**: "A. M. Rosenthal Leaving Executive Editor's Post at the Times, and Max Frankel Is His Successor," *The New York Times*, October 12, 1986.
73 **"Was I difficult to work for?"**: Rosenthal interview with Dryfoos, March 9, 1987, NYTHPOHC.

7 *Changing Course*

77 **"It's Friday evening"**: Frankel to Rosenthal, October 10, 1986, Rosenthal papers, NYT.
77 **"I had no plan"**: Max Frankel, *The Times of My Life and My Life with The Times* (New York: Random House, 1999), 428–29.
78 **I've wrecked that person:** Frankel interview with author, September 21, 2016.
78 **He accepted an invitation:** Oreskes email to author, May 1, 2019.
78 **He considered Rosenthal's huge office:** Frankel interview with author, April 10, 2017.
78 **"We need more and still more articles"**: Frankel to Gelb, February 3, 1987, Frankel papers, Columbia.
79 **an opportunity for Frankel to vent:** Frankel email to author, January 10, 2018.
79 **"AMR and MF do not mix"**: Frankel letter, undated, Frankel papers, Columbia. Frankel guesses the letter was written in the late 1960s.
80 **"I really don't think"**: Rosenthal to Frankel, January 23, 1973, Jones-Tifft papers.
80 **"I know that Max Frankel"**: Rosenthal to Daniel, November 9, 1967, Jones-Tifft papers.
80 **you know how seriously:** Raines interview with author, October 6, 2017, morning session.
80 **"He didn't like my politics"**: Frankel interview with author, April 10, 2017.
80 **"A stylistic device"**: Rosenthal to Frankel, January 24, 1977, Rosenthal papers, NYT.
81 **"In the context"**: Frankel to Rosenthal, February 21, 1977, Frankel papers, NYPL.
81 **editorial assailing Israel:** "Israel's Illusion," *The New York Times*, June 9, 1981.
81 **"harsh and denunciatory"**: Memo in Rosenthal files; undated, written in third person, describing his conversation with Sulzberger. Rosenthal papers, personal.
81 **Frankel would later express regret:** Max Frankel, *The Times of My Life*, 394.
81 **"So, Tobi"**: Rosenthal to Tobi Frankel, October 20, 1975, Rosenthal papers, NYT.
81 **Tobi would . . . berate him:** Max Frankel, *The Times of My Life*, 241.
81 **"If you were interested"**: Frankel to Rosenthal, December 10, 1980, Jones-Tifft papers.
82 **"it came as second nature"**: Max Frankel, *The Times of My Life*, 228–29.
82 **"It's a revolution"**: Frankel interview with Dryfoos, December 5, 1986, NYTHPOHC.
82 **"I was flabbergasted"**: Siegal interview with Dryfoos, undated, NYTHPOHC.

83 That's a holy-shit job: Soma Golden Behr interview with author, November 20, 2016.

83 He's a solid journalist: Frankel interview with author, September 21, 2016.

83 "the *Times* has always been in my blood": Andrew Rosenthal to AOS, September 26, 1986, Frankel papers, NYPL.

83 "It is something that": AOS to Andrew Rosenthal, October 7, 1986, Frankel papers, NYPL.

83 I need Gelb to teach me: Frankel interview with author, September 21, 2016.

84 "From this moment on": Frankel memo to staff, October 11, 1986, Frankel papers, NYPL.

84 "A sense of relief and hope": Millones to Frankel, October 9, 1986, Frankel papers, Columbia.

84 "good fun" would be welcome: Frankel to staff, October 11, 1986, Frankel papers, NYPL.

84 "my first 3 months": Frankel notes, "First Meeting with Dept. Heads," undated, Frankel papers, Columbia.

84 He would complain to Tom Bodkin: Bodkin interview with author, May 29, 2019.

84 "we are drowning the reader in ink": Frankel to editors, July 21, 1987, Frankel papers, Columbia.

84 The publisher's wife: Frankel interview with author, September 21, 2016.

85 "I always like to make things": Frankel interview with author, November 15, 2017.

85 "high bureaucratic mentality": Robert Sam Anson, "The Best of Times, the Worst of Times," *Esquire*, March 1993. Talese in the same interview said Frankel was "neither a hell of a journalist nor a man of vaunting imagination."

85 Since he had no time: Frankel interview with author, September 21, 2016.

85 "I probably was more authoritarian": Frankel interview with author, November 15, 2016.

85 Screw it, Phil: Golden Behr interview with author, November 20, 2016.

85 going to your own execution: Taubman interview with author, October 28, 2016.

85 "There was a brutality": Taubman interview with author, October 28, 2016.

86 "You have been a loyal": Frankel to Roberts, February 16, 1989, Frankel papers, Columbia.

86 This guy plays hardball: Raines interview with author, October 6, 2017, afternoon session.

8   Two Hundred Miles

87 "When the opposition": Rosenthal to Kovach, September 23, 1980, Jones-Tifft papers.

87 "Have someone get hold of": Hedrick Smith to Rosenthal, July 12, 1978, Rosenthal papers, NYT.

88 "consistently beaten": Gelb to Rosenthal, April 23, 1986 Rosenthal papers, NYT.

88 "We are No. 3": Salisbury to Frankel: December 7, 1986, Frankel papers, Columbia.

88 biggest crisis: Bernard Weinraub, "Iran Payment Found Diverted to Contras; Reagan Security Adviser and Aide Are Out," *The New York Times*, November 26, 1986.

88 "It is ironic": Salisbury to Frankel, December 14, 1986, Frankel papers, Columbia.

88 "Those 200 miles": AOS interview with Gruson, June 22, 1983, NYTHPOHC.

89 complained that Smith: Clymer interview with author, December 23, 2016.

89 "I didn't quite fit": Kovach interview with author, December 29, 2017.

89 **"I have been forced to conclude":** Kovach to Rosenthal, July 16, 1981, Gelb papers, NYPL.

89 **"In short, we've become":** Kovach to editors and reporters, February 19, 1982.

89 **"the brooding Bill":** Frankel to Kovach, March 31, 1989, Frankel papers, Columbia.

90 **"nothing but the wrecking":** Frankel interview with Dryfoos, December 5, 1986, NYTHPOHC.

90 **"I had just had no respect":** Kovach interview with author, January 19, 2017.

90 **He had logged 3,200 bylines:** Craig R. Whitney website, craigrwhitney.com/craig -whitney.html.

90 **he asked for a raise:** Whitney interview with author, November 21, 2017.

90 **"This is for your eyes only":** Whitney to Frankel, November 19, 1986, Frankel papers, Columbia.

91 **"I thought your statement":** Raines to Frankel, October 13, 1986, Frankel papers, Columbia.

91 **Frankel left little doubt:** Frankel interview with Dryfoos, December 5, 1986, NYTHPOHC.

92 **The one thing you can take off the table:** Raines interview with author, October 6, 2017, morning session.

92 **This guy has just won an election:** Raines interview with author, October 6, 2017, morning session.

92 **a job for which she was probably not qualified:** Judith Miller, *The Story: A Reporter's Journey* (New York: Simon & Schuster Paperbacks, 2015), 41.

92 **twice at demonstrations:** Judith Miller, *The Story*, 50–51.

93 **There's no news in Paris:** Judith Miller, *The Story*, 81.

93 **Why not Judy?:** Whitney interview with author, November 21, 2018, AOSJR interview with author, August 10, 2018.

93 **"She's competitive":** Frankel to Dryfoos, December 5, 1986, NYTHPOHC.

93 **Frankel wanted to put a women in that post:** Frankel interview with author, June 20, 2018.

93 **"Miller is a great gunslinger":** Salisbury to Frankel, December 7, 1986, Frankel papers, Columbia.

93 **put an end:** Frankel to Gelb, December 3, 1986, Gelb papers, NYPL.

94 **"Great report!":** Gelb to Whitney, March 17, 1987, Gelb papers, NYPL.

94 **Within the week:** Eleanor Randolph, "Questions Too Pointed, N.Y. Times Editor Says;" *The Washington Post*, June 20, 1987.

94 **"the low point":** Anthony Lewis, Abroad at Home: "After the Fall," *The New York Times*, May 12, 1987.

95 **"This is what 'too far' looks like":** Ellen Goodman, "Privacy Invaders Stoop to New Low," *Chicago Tribune* June 7, 1987.

95 **"do you know what she says?":** Mike Royko, "Turnabout Fair Play for The Times," *Chicago Tribune*, Jun 16, 1987,

95 **"Now, let's get to it":** A. M. Rosenthal, "On My Mind: Sex, Money and the Press," *The New York Times*, June 7, 1987.

95 **Whitney was flabbergasted:** Whitney interview with author, November 21, 2017 and Whitney email to author, May 20, 2019.

95 **He had consulted:** Craig Whitney, *Unraveling Time* (Self-published, Tiny Diver Press, 2016), 161.

95 **"In this valid pursuit":** Frankel to staff, June 19, 1987, Frankel papers, Columbia.

95   **"bathe a while in their moods":** Frankel to Whitney, July 2, 1987, Frankel papers, Columbia.

96   **"A Correction":** Fox Butterfield, "A Correction: Times Was in Error on North's Secret-Fund Testimony," *The New York Times*, July 13, 1987.

97   **When he saw the story the next day:** Lelyveld interview with author, April 16, 2017.

97   **Butterfield was stunned:** Butterfield interview with author, June 3, 2019.

97   **"They felt we were":** Frankel to Dryfoos, Single-subject interview on front page correction, July 1987, NYTHPOHC.

97   **"I was not as principled":** Lelyveld interview with author, April 16, 2017.

97   **"If that causes morale problems":** Elizabeth Kastor, "N.Y. Times Corrects Fund Story," *The Washington Post*, July 14, 1987.

97   **"My view of this bureau":** Whitney to Gelb and John Lee, November 16, 1987 Gelb papers, NYPL.

97   **he had Frankel's support:** Whitney interview with author, November 21, 2018.

98   **"how deeply troubling":** Washington bureau reporters to Frankel, January 14, 1988, Frankel papers, NYPL.

98   **"Max, by imposing the transfer":** Molotsky to Frankel, January 14, 1987, Frankel papers, NYPL.

98   **"I told Irv by phone":** Frankel note to self, January 15, 1987, Frankel papers, NYPL.

98   **Molotsky ended up staying:** Molotsky email to author, May 23, 2019.

98   ***The Washington Post* learned:** Eleanor Randolph, "Shuffle at Times Bureau Protested," *The Washington Post*, January 16, 1988.

98   **"we're talking here":** Frankel to Gelb, January 19, 1988, Gelb papers, NYPL.

98   **a monologue of explanations:** Whitney speech to bureau, January 18, 1988, Frankel Papers, NYPL.

98   **"the biggest mistake":** Craig Whitney, *Unraveling Time*, 161.

98   **"I realize, Craig":** Gelb annual evaluation of Whitney, February 11, 1988, Gelb papers, NYPL.

99   **Why did I take this job?:** Whitney interview with author, November 21, 2018.

99   **"The longer I walk around":** Raines to Frankel, December 9, 1986, Frankel papers, Columbia.

99   **In truth, he was still disappointed:** Raines interview with author, May 24, 2018, afternoon session.

99   **I hate these kinds of conversations:** Raines interview with author, May 24, 2018, afternoon session.

99   **Are you and Susan:** Raines interview with author, October 6, 2017, morning session.

100 **"I had made such a mess":** Frankel interview with author, September 21, 2016.

9   *The Shoe at Home*

101 **"it is important for us to acknowledge":** AOS remarks to Equal Employment Opportunity Meeting, April 8, 1969, Rosenthal papers, NYT.

101 **"Call Max Frankel":** Delaney interview with author, June 27, 2019.

102 **sent letters to fifty newspapers:** Delaney interview with author, June 7, 2017.

102 **Frankel never mentioned race:** Delaney interview with author, June 27, 2019.

102 **"Mr. Delaney is a Negro":** Richard Mooney to Reston, et al., July 11, 1969, Rosenthal papers, NYT.

102 **That became clear to Delaney:** Delaney interview with author, June 27, 2019.

102 **when he arrived, Black reporters:** Delaney interview with author, June 27, 2019.

103 **A white high school graduate:** Statement from the New York Times Minority Caucus, October 1980, NYTC general files.

103 **"I believe that the door":** Affidavit of Paul Delaney in *Benilda Rosario et al. v. The New York Times Company,* May 15, 1979, Delaney papers.

103 **"The employment practices of this newspaper":** Robert Friedman, "Malign Neglect at the 'Times,'" *The Village Voice,* May 21, 1979.

103 **"This year has been":** Stockton to Rosenthal, April 8, 1983, NYTC general files.

103 **An internal newsroom survey:** Report by Human Resources Planning & Development, October 30, 1983, NYTC general files.

104 ***Times*-sponsored receptions:** Jerry Gray interview with author, July 8, 2017.

104 **"I have no illusions":** Rosenthal to AOS, August 21, 1984, Delaney papers.

104 **"failure on of the part of management":** M. L. Stein, "'Abe' Meets the Press," *Editor & Publisher,* April 25, 1987.

104 **We're looking:** Delaney interview with author, June 27, 2018.

105 **"We have a sprinkling":** Millones to Frankel, January 9, 1987, Frankel papers, Columbia.

105 **Of thirty-five top editors:** George Freeman to Katharine Darrow, August 19, 1987 NYTC general files.

105 **"He was not good enough":** Frankel interview with Dryfoos, December 5, 1986, NYTHPOHC.

105 **"My impression is":** George Freeman to Katharine Darrow, August 19, 1987, NYTC general files.

106 **"already hired and matched":** Hoge to Frankel, August 16, 1989, Delaney papers.

106 **his editors would often resist:** Delaney interview with author, June 27, 2018.

106 **Carolyn Lee . . . would listen to editors:** Carolyn Lee interview with author, June 22, 2018

106 **"There was a natural shortage":** Frankel interview with author, April 10, 2017.

107 **"People, suddenly interested":** Frankel interview with author, April 10, 2017.

107 **"The problem, as I see it":** Driscoll to Rosenthal, September 4, 1986, Rosenthal papers, NYT.

107 **"What you really are saying":** Rosenthal to Driscoll, September 19, 1986, Rosenthal papers, NYT.

107 **the results had been . . . "uneven":** Frankel to Sulzberger, August 18, 1988, Frankel papers, Columbia.

107 **"We really need to get busy now":** Frankel to Delaney, June 2, 1987, Delaney Papers.

108 **"We have certainly taken those risks":** Frankel to Delaney, October 25, 1988, Frankel papers, Columbia.

10 *Palm Beach*

109 **could not remember ever being as scared:** Golden Behr interview with Mary Marshall Clark, March 24, 1987, NYTHPOHC, and Golden Behr interview with author, November 20, 2016.

109 **"Jesus! I mean":** Golden Behr interview with Mary Marshall Clark, March 24, 1987, NYTHPOHC.

109   **"I'm a word salad":** Golden Behr interview with author, November 20, 2016.

110   **"doesn't have the great writers":** Golden Behr interview with Mary Marshall Clark, March 24, 1987, NYTHPOHC.

110   **"reawakened the national desk":** Golden Behr employee evaluation by Gelb, January 29, 1988, Gelb papers, NYPL.

110   **Golden Behr never doubted:** Golden Behr interview with author, November 20, 2016.

110   **Max, it's okay:** Golden Behr interview with author, November 20, 2016.

110   **"There's kind of a feeling":** Golden Behr interview with Mary Marshall Clark, March 24, 1987, NYTHPOHC.

111   **"an integral part":** Roberto Suro, "Kennedy's Nephew Is Identified as Rape Suspect," *The New York Times*, April 5, 1991.

111   **Young Smith is being dragged through the mud:** Frankel interview with author, June 20, 2018.

111   **Butterfield knew the Kennedy family:** Butterfield interview with author, July 14, 2018.

112   **We are depriving the readers:** Frankel interview with author, September 21, 2016.

112   **Why are we asking for trouble?:** Lelyveld interview with author, April 16, 2017.

112   **The lid's off:** Frankel interview with author, June 20, 2018.

112   **Butterfield only learned:** Butterfield interview with author, July 14, 2018.

112   **The story appeared:** Fox Butterfield with Mary B. W. Tabor, "Woman in Florida Rape Inquiry Fought Adversity and Sought Acceptance," *New York Times*, April 17, 1991.

113   **"The Times has withheld":** "On Names in Rape Cases," *The New York Times*, April 17, 1991.

114   **There's a revolution:** Golden Behr interview with author, November 20, 2016.

114   **Her "female sensibility":** Max Frankel, *The Times of My Life and My Life with The Times* (New York; Random House, 1999), 458.

114   **I'm confused about what the standards are:** Purdum interview with author, July 3, 2018.

115   **"This is the most troubling time":** Transcript of WQXR meeting on William Kennedy Smith, April 19, 1991, Kulaga papers.

115   **"I read of a woman":** Transcript of WQXR meeting.

115   **"loose girl":** Golden Behr interview with author, November 20, 2016.

115   **"we can trust readers":** William Glaberson, "Media Memo: Times Article Naming Rape Accuser Ignites Debate on Journalistic Values," *The New York Times*, April 26, 1991.

115   **"The people with the weird minds":** Howard Kurtz, "Furor at N.Y. Times Over Rape Policy," *The Washington Post*, April 20, 1991. Golden Behr, in interview with author on November 20, 2016, said the remark was made by an editor in the business section.

115   **"The right thing":** William Glaberson, "Media Memo: Times Article Naming Rape Accuser Ignites Debate on Journalistic Values," *The New York Times*, April 26, 1991.

115   **"A Mistake":** Anna Quindlen, "Public & Private: A Mistake," *The New York Times*, April 21, 1991.

116   **"I don't have any problem":** Frankel interview with author, June 20, 2018.

116   **Quindlen worried:** Quindlen interview with author, October 4, 2017.

116   **he thought it was a mistake:** Frankel notes on meeting with Punch and AOSJR, May 1, 1991, Frankel papers, Columbia.

116   **and he wanted his columnists:** AOSJR interview with author, December 27, 2018.

116   **"If you are covering local teas":** Roxanne Roberts, "The Newspaper Editors, at a Loss for Words," *The Washington Post*, April 4, 1990.

117   **"their outrage":** Petition to Max Frankel, April 19, 1991, Frankel papers, Columbia.

117 **"You are a great":** Rather to Frankel, May 8, 1991, Frankel papers, Columbia.

117 **"the one who has always":** William Glaberson, "Media Memo: Times Article Naming Rape Accuser Ignites Debate on Journalistic Values," *The New York Times,* April 26, 1991.

117 **too much attention:** Frankel notes on meeting with Punch and AOSJR, May 1, 1991, Frankel papers, Columbia.

117 **"I didn't realize":** Frankel interview with author, June 20, 2018.

11 *Not Punch*

118 **"always a man of some distance":** AOSJR interview with author, February 21, 2017.

118 **You can listen:** Heiskell interview with author, February 20, 2017.

119 **"I had a front-page story":** AOSJR interview with author, February 17, 2017.

119 **Karen was closer to her mother:** Karen Sulzberger email interview with author, May 30, 2022.

119 **Topping always assumed:** Topping interview with author, April 9. 2017.

120 **"Being a small town paper":** AOSJR to Topping, undated (but sometime between 1974 and 1976), Topping papers, NYPL.

120 **"As for their style":** AOSJR to Topping, October 15, 1974, Topping papers, NYPL.

120 **"could not be more delighted":** Topping to AOSJR, November 24, 1975, Topping papers, NYPL.

120 **"Perhaps, if the desire":** AOSJR to Topping, January 7, 1976, Topping papers, NYPL.

120 **Punch Sulzberger's short reporting career:** "Arthur O. Sulzberger, Publisher Who Transformed The Times for New Era, Dies at 86," *The New York Times,* September 29, 2012, Clyde Haberman.

120 **He was well aware:** AOSJR interview with author, February 21, 2017.

120 **"literally on the phone":** AOSJR interview with author, February 21, 2017.

121 **"highlight of my experience":** AOSJR to Topping, June 24, 1977, Topping papers, NYPL.

121 **"To say the least":** Topping to AOSJR, June 13, 1977, Topping papers, NYPL.

121 **"my greatest moment":** AOSJR interview with author, February 21, 2017.

121 **"Top, I would very much appreciate":** AOS to Topping, June 1, 1978, Topping papers, NYPL.

121 **"Punch says he has already":** Topping to Rosenthal, June 2, 1978, Topping papers, NYPL.

121 **His first print byline:** AOSJR wrote stories during the strike for the news service; this would have been his first byline in print. AOSJR to author, email, February 25, 1017.

121 **a strike by the pressmen:** Damon Stetson, "The Times and News Resume Publication," *The New York Times,* November 6, 1978.

122 ***"Your son is a class act":*** Bush to AOS, November 8, 1980, Autograph papers, NYT.

123 **"bore his son-ship":** Raines interview with author, October 6, 2017, morning session.

123 **"Everybody pretended":** Rattner interview with author, September 13, 2019.

123 **I don't want to tell you:** Kovach interview with author, January 19, 2017.

123 **"light—very light":** Kovach interview with author, January 19. 2017.

124 **The younger Sulzberger had been waiting:** AOSJR interview with author, February 24, 2017; Susan E. Tifft and Alex S. Jones, *The Trust: The Private and Powerful Family Behind The New York Times* (Boston: Little, Brown and Company, 1999), 635–37.

124 **It's not going to work:** AOSJR interview with author, February 24, 2017.

124   **"hippie-dippy":** AOSJR interview with author, February 21, 2017.

125   **Can I just tell:** Haberman interview with author, July 4, 2017.

125   **One of your biggest dangers:** Gruson interview with Dryfoos, March 27, 1994 (transcription date), NYTHPOHC.

125   **Why are those little packages of peanuts:** Raines interview with author, May 24, 2018, afternoon session.

125   **found him cold and unapproachable:** Heiskell interview with author, February 20, 2017.

125   **Carol Sulzberger . . . urged her husband:** Gruson interview with Susan Dryfoos, March 27, 1994 (transcription date), NYTHPOHC.

125   **"see if you can just":** Warren Hoge interview with author, November 21, 2018.

126   **"That whole crowd":** Hoge interview with author, December 31, 2018.

126   **"Perhaps the idea is goofy":** AOSJR to Frankel, January 19, 1989, Jones papers.

126   **"He needs to be assured that our use of color":** AOSJR to Frankel, Primis, March 27, 1990 AOSJR papers.

127   **Is it really necessary to do this?:** Lelyveld interview with author, April 16, 2017.

127   **"devoid of zingers":** AOS to Frankel, May 1, 1991, Frankel papers, Columbia.

128   **"individual success in a team environment":** AOSJR interview, *Charlie Rose*, December 11, 2001.

128   **What's to talk about?:** Frankel interview with author, September 16, 2016.

128   **Punch Sulzberger was a marine:** Frankel interview with author, September 21, 2016.

128   **"a ritual which struck":** Max Frankel, *The Times of My Life and My Life with The Times* (New York: Random House, 1999), 491.

129   **"Just for your records":** AOSJR to Cullman, March 8, 2005, AOSJR papers.

129   **Trump also addressed:** Trump to AOSJR, March 2004, AOSJR papers.

129   **"A man deserves":** Susan E. Tifft and Alex S. Jones, "Scion of the Times," *The New Yorker*, July 26, 1999.

129   **never made a decision before:** Lelyveld interview with author, April 16, 2017.

129   **"I'll say this about Arthur":** Susan E. Tifft with Alex S. Jones, "Scion of the Times," *The New Yorker*, July 26, 1999.

130   **"Keep pushing":** Edwin Diamond, "Old Times, New Times," *New York*, September 30, 1991.

130   **Punch Sulzberger was concerned:** Carolyn Lee interview with author, June 22, 2018.

130   **"more and more ethnic":** AOS letter to Frankel, August 26, 1992, Frankel papers, Columbia.

130   **"My father was anti-gay":** AOSJR interview with author, February 21, 2017.

130   **"Paris Has Burned":** Jesse Green, "Paris Has Burned," *The New York Times*, April 18, 1993.

130   **"I get a very definitive":** AOS to AOSJR, April 19, 1993, Frankel papers, Columbia.

12   *The Next Horizon*

132   **"We hit it off immediately":** Howell Raines, *The One That Got Away* (New York: Scribner, 2006), 33.

132   **"looking over the next horizon":** AOSJR interview with author, August 8, 2017.

132   **might be the executive editor:** Raines interview with author, May 24, 2018, afternoon session.

132 **It is not my first choice:** Raines interview with author, October 7, 2017, morning session.

133 **This will give you the chance:** Raines interview with author, October 6, 2017, afternoon session; AOSJR email exchange with author, August 30, 2019.

133 **The new publisher wanted Raines to learn:** AOSJR interview with author, September 4, 2019.

133 **And he would join Sulzberger's inner group:** Raines interview with author, October 6, 2017, afternoon session.

134 **everyone has a timeline:** AOSJR interview with author, August 8, 2017.

134 **Any applicant who changed:** Carmel McCoubrey email interview with author, July 9, 2020.

134 **Let's be more aggressive:** AOSJR interview with author, August 8, 2017.

134 **"He wanted editorials with greater muzzle velocity":** Howell Raines, *The One That Got Away,* 29.

135 **They were his first bylines:** Howell Raines, "War Eagle IV, A Proud Symbol, Rides High (Like Auburn Spirit)," (one of three), *Birmingham Post-Herald,* November 27, 1964.

135 **Raines drew the assignment:** Raines email to author, March 19, 2019.

135 **"Every so often":** Anthony Lewis, "The Right to Have a Coke," *The New York Times Book Review,* October 23, 1977.

135 **Two of the leading:** Raines interview with to author, August 14, 2017, afternoon session.

135 **He had read both Raines's novel:** Raines said Rosenthal told him that in their interview; Raines interview with author, August 14, 2017, afternoon session.

135 **clarity and strength of the writing:** Ken Auletta, "The Howell Doctrine," *The New Yorker,* June 10, 2002.

135 **"I want this guy on the paper":** Ken Auletta, "The Howell Doctrine."

136 **a Japanese imperial court:** Raines interview with author, August 14, 2017, afternoon session.

136 **People say I am a maniac:** Raines interview with author, August 14, 2017, afternoon session.

136 **"The habit I was forming":** Raines interview with author, August 14, 2017, afternoon session.

138 **"the best of anyone covering":** Jones to Rosenthal, November 17, 1980, Rosenthal papers, NYT.

138 **Raines swept his desk clean:** Raines interview with author, July 15, 2017.

138 **"Howell because he has a gut instinct":** Kovach to Rosenthal, December 30, 1982, Rosenthal papers, NYT.

139 **Raines struck Keller as a classic Timesman:** Keller interview with author, January 5, 2018.

139 **"I would really be quite surprised":** Rosenthal to AOS, February 5, 1985, Rosenthal papers, NYPL.

139 **"pick up the heartbeat":** Kovach interview with author, December 29, 2017.

139 **No, Les:** Raines interview with author, September 29, 2018, morning session.

140 **This ends today:** Raines interview with author, May 23, 2018, afternoon session.

141 **"You drive the report with the top talent":** Raines interview with author, October 6, 2017, afternoon session.

141 **Just because all the members:** Maureen Dowd, *Are Men Necessary? When Sexes Collide* (New York: Putnam, 2005), 285.

141   "It's hard to believe": Gelb evaluation of Raines, February 22, 1989, Gelb papers, NYPL.

142   "sending thunderbolts": Jack Rosenthal interview with author, December 27, 2016.

142   We're going to write one-sided: Boffey interview with author, June 9, 2017.

142   "I've always identified": Howell Raines, "Speaking in the Voice of The Times," *Inside The New York Times,* home-delivery subscriber newsletter, vol. 2, no. 2, Summer 1998, Jones papers.

142   "to promise rashly": Max Frankel, *The Times of My Life and My Life with The Times* (New York: Random House, 1999), 392.

142   "Congress is in a mood": "Stopping the Yellowstone Mine," *The New York Times,* March 27, 1995.

143   Dole denounced Raines on the Senate floor: Howard Kurtz, "Talking Tough at The Times; Howell Raines's Editorials Don't Finesse with Politesse," *The Washington Post,* May 10, 1993.

143   *The New York Observer* found: Eric Konigsberg, "Times Pulpit: More Taste, Less Filling," *The New York Observer,* July 19–26, 1993.

143   wrote in a "white heat": Raines interview with author, October 11, 2019, afternoon session.

143   "His regret cannot be huge enough": "Mr. McNamara's War," *The New York Times,* April 12, 1995.

143   "The Howell Raines Question": Peter J. Boyer, "The Howell Raines Question," *The New Yorker,* August 22, 1994.

144   "I find the current page": Frankel to AOSJR, "Some Valedictory Thoughts," July 15, 1994.

144   "It was too much Howell's page": Lelyveld interview with author, September 15, 2016.

144   "very happy" with the page: Eric Konigsberg, "Times Pulpit."

144   his "biggest disagreement": AOSJR interview with author, April 17, 2017.

144   His face in repose: Boffey interview with author, June 9, 2017.

144   I wish you were easier: Raines interview with author, October 6, 2017, afternoon session.

13   *A Timex Watch*

145   "What is the Internet?": Meislin to Frankel, Lelyveld, Siegal, September 21, 1993, Meislin papers.

146   "The New York Times is a newspaper": Rosenthal interview with Gruson, August 30, 1983, NYTHPOHC.

146   "I must apologize": Frankel to AOSJR, April 7, 1993, Frankel papers, NYPL.

146   "It is my contention that newspapers": Text of AOS speech of May 25, 1994, to Midwest Research Institute's Fiftieth Annual Dinner, courtesy of Julius A. Karash, who covered it for *The Kansas City Star.*

147   "Hell, if someone would be kind enough": Benjamin Weiser, "All the News That's Fit to Transmit," *The Washington Post,* April 2, 1995.

147   "If we don't pursue": AOSJR Town Hall address, February 1 and February 2, 1994, Jones papers.

148   Meislin had learned: Meislin interview with author, September 20, 2016.

148 **"an extension of what we give readers":** William Glaberson, "New York Times to Begin On-Line Computer Service," *The New York Times,* December 17, 1993.

149 **"Make no mistake about it":** Meislin to Frankel, Lelyveld, December 27, 1993, Meislin papers.

149 **"being careless by leaving":** Frankel to AOSJR, December, 29, 1993, Frankel papers, Columbia.

149 **"It's functional, but humiliating":** Meislin to Frankel, Lelyveld, May 23, 1994, Meislin papers.

149 **"Not only was there no hoopla":** Jon Katz, "The Times Enters the Nineties; Doesn't Like It Much," *New York,* June 27–July 4, 1994.

150 **"The *Times* must not be afraid of this new world":** AOSJR to Senior Management Conference, November 14, 1994, Lelyveld papers.

14 *Marching Around My Head*

153 **We have to decide about Joe Lelyveld:** Max Frankel interview, *Charlie Rose,* April 14, 1994.

153 **thought he looked beaten down:** Jack Rosenthal interview with author, December 27, 2016.

153 **"Do I feel overworked and overburdened":** Ken Auletta, "Opening Up the Times," *The New Yorker,* June 28, 1993.

154 **"I think of the page-one meeting":** Ken Auletta, "Opening Up the Times"; Susan E. Tifft and Alex S. Jones, *The Trust: The Private and Powerful Family Behind The New York Times* (Boston: Little, Brown 1999) 645–48.

154 **"*Esquire* offers an article":** Frankel to staff, February 10, 1993, Frankel papers, Columbia.

154 **"snippy little piece on you":** Graham to Frankel, undated (approximately March 1993, per dated Frankel response), Frankel papers, Columbia.

155 **"From a very personal perspective":** AOSJR-Frankel, 1991 (otherwise undated), Frankel papers, Columbia.

155 **"I feel very awkward":** AOSJR remarks at Frankel-Lelyveld turnover, April 17, 1994, video by Susan Dryfoos.

156 **I'm not going to do this:** Lelyveld interview with author, October 1, 2017.

156 **overstuffed Victorian couch:** Lelyveld interview with author, October 1, 2017.

156 **"for which I'd applied":** Joseph Lelyveld, *Omaha Blues: A Memory Loop* (New York, Farrar, Straus and Giroux, 2005), 168.

156 **Lelyveld wanted to be a foreign correspondent:** Lelyveld interview with author, October 1, 2017.

156 **would comb through:** McFadden email interview with author, October 17, 2019.

157 **"This is the end":** Joseph Lelyveld, "Former Nazi Camp Guard Is Now a Housewife in Queens," *The New York Times,* July 14, 1964.

158 **"My wife, sir":** Joseph Lelyveld, *Omaha Blues,* 181.

158 **If I get a story:** Joseph Lelyveld, *Omaha Blues,* 182.

158 **"In the past six days":** Lelyveld to Rosenthal, August 12, 1971, Jones papers.

158 **"He just thought there was something wacky":** Lelyveld interview with author, October 1, 2017.

159 **Do whatever the fuck you want to do:** Lelyveld interview with author, April 16, 2017.

159   "He replaced my father": Lelyveld interview with author, October 1, 2017.

159   "It was hard to know what to say": Joseph Lelyveld, *Omaha Blues*, 172.

159   "Suddenly I imagined": Joseph Lelyveld, *Omaha Blues*, 212.

160   "For reasons I'm not sure": AOSJR letter to Lelyveld, April 22, 1996, Lelyveld papers.

160   Just tell me how you want the cuffs: Clines email interview with author, December 11, 2019.

160   I would rather have: Purdum interview with author, July 3, 2018.

161   Why didn't you ask me: Lelyveld interview with author, September 15, 2016.

161   "What all this kibitzing": Lelyveld to Andrews, Boffey et al., December 15, 1989, Lelyveld papers.

161   "unsubstantiated gossip": Max Frankel, *The Times of My Life and My Life with The Times* (New York: Random House, 1999), 497.

161   left the office in dismay: Dowd email interview with author, December 12, 2019.

161   "stealthy disagreement": Frankel email interview with author, December 10, 2019.

162   "I am now satisfied": Frankel to AOS and AOSJR, March 3, 1988, Frankel papers, Columbia.

162   Are you leaving me with no choice?: Frankel interview with author June 20, 2018.

162   Sulzberger had his own candidate in mind: AOSJR interview with author, April 2, 2018.

162   "You've got to be more outgoing": Joseph Lelyveld, *Omaha Blues*, 76.

162   "excessively self-involved": Lelyveld to Rosenthal, February 4, 1975, Rosenthal papers, NYT.

162   "I spent much of the morning": Lelyveld to Rosenthal, April 5, 1976 Jones papers.

162   "a little tight": AOSJR interview with author, February 24, 2017.

162   Sulzberger invited Lelyveld to join him: Lelyveld interview with author, September 15, 2016; AOSJR interview with author, April 17, 2017.

163   "It became literally": Lelyveld to AOSJR, April 29, 1998, Lelyveld papers.

163   I need a brother: Lelyveld interview with author, April 16, 2017.

163   As Lelyveld arrived: Lelyveld interview with author, September 15, 2016. Sulzberger did not recall the offer being made in the woods by his home.

163   What was that all about?: Lelyveld interview with author, September 15, 2016.

15   *"Our Jackie Robinson"*

165   Reagan had called him "Gerry": Gerald M. Boyd, *My Times in Black and White: Race and Power at the New York Times* (Chicago: Lawrence Hill Books, 2010), 113–14.

165   You have the job: Gerald M. Boyd, *My Times in Black and White*, 118.

165   "bust my butt": Boyd to Rosenthal, November 12, 1983, Rosenthal papers, NYT.

165   "We will bust our butts": Rosenthal to Boyd, November 18, 1983, Rosenthal papers, NYT.

165   "a euphemism": Gerald M. Boyd, *My Times in Black and White*, 124.

166   "not ready to be editors": Frankel interview with Dryfoos, December 5, 1986, NYTHPOHC.

166   told him he did not need overseas experience: Gerald M. Boyd, *My Times in Black and White*, 159.

166   "A special assignment": Frankel memo to staff, December 8, 1988, Frankel papers, Columbia.

168 **our Jackie Robinson:** Frankel interview with author, April 10, 2017.

169 **"did not know the A Train from the Q":** Gerald M. Boyd, *My Times in Black and White*, 179.

169 **"In this highly charged":** Gerald M. Boyd, *My Times in Black and White*, 170.

169 **smoking cigarette after cigarette:** Oreskes interview with author, November 14, 2018.

170 **Boyd arrived to a stack:** Gerald M. Boyd, *My Times in Black and White*, 210.

171 **"Will you just stay over there":** Lelyveld interview with author, September 15, 2016.

171 **"My old mentor":** Lelyveld memo to staff, April 7, 1994, Frankel papers, Columbia.

171 **"He said that Roberts's contract":** Gerald M. Boyd, *My Times in Black and White*, 202–3.

172 **"I knew better than that":** Lelyveld interview with author, September 15, 2016.

172 **Boyd did not applaud:** Geddes interview with author, August 17, 2017.

172 **I'd rather stick pencils in my eyes:** Keller interview with author, July 30, 2016.

173 **never thought he should be managing editor:** Baquet interview with author, November 11, 2018.

173 **Boyd felt betrayed:** Robin Stone interview with author, June 23, 2018.

173 **"The name felt like a dagger thrust into my gut":** Gerald M. Boyd, *My Times in Black and White*, 225.

173 **I need you:** Lelyveld interview with author, April 16, 2017.

173 **"There are those who spend":** Boyd to Lelyveld, April 6, 1998, Lelyveld papers.

174 **"I can only repeat":** Lelyveld to AOSJR, December 20, 1994, Lelyveld papers.

174 **"It became such a preoccupation":** Lelyveld interview with author, September 16, 2016.

16 *Newspaper Dot Com*

173 **Luciani had come to think:** Luciani email interview with author, November 7, 2019.

174 **"A book to get":** McKenna to author email, June 9, 2021.

174 **had one pressing question:** McKenna interview with author, August 10, 2017. AGS, in an email exchange on October 27, 2019, does not remember the exchange.

175 **which would account for $300 million:** Dickson L. Louie with Professor Jeffrey F. Rayport, "The New York Times Electronic Media Company," case study, Harvard Business School, Harvard University, Case 897-051, March 1997.

176 **Well, of course:** McKenna interview with author, August 10, 2017.

176 **"We must generate":** Gang of Four to Lelyveld, Lewis, Raines, AOSJR, February 7, 1995, McKenna papers.

177 **Why can't we:** Bernard Gwertzman, *My Memoirs: Fifty Years of Journalism, from Print to the Internet* (Xlibris US, 2016), 220–21, 225.

177 **"kids with no journalistic background":** Lelyveld interview with author, November 18, 2016.

177 **"I am looking forward":** Gwertzman to Lelyveld, April 7, 1995 Lelyveld papers.

177 **"Many of us will sleep better":** Lelyveld to staff, April 17, 1995, McKenna papers.

177 **"a lucky throw":** Lelyveld interview with author, November 18, 2016.

177 **He would tell people:** Gwertzman interview with author, November 6, 2016.

178 **hired by Seymour Topping:** Bernard Gwertzman, *My Memoirs: Fifty Years of Journalism*, 100.

178 **"the best foreign affairs reporter":** Reston to Topping, October 12, 1982, Topping papers, NYPL.

178 **elephant forging through the jungle:** Raines interview with author, October 7, 2017, morning session.

179 **"It won't be my call":** Lelyveld to Gwertzman, January 30, 1989.

179 **"the greatest run":** Lelyveld memo to staff, April 17, 1995, McKenna papers.

179 **The first edition of the *Times*:** Carolyn Lee to Max Frankel, May 28, 1991, Frankel papers, NYPL.

180 **He was an early pioneer:** "The Times Appoints a President for New Digital Ventures Unit," *The New York Times*, June 23, 1995.

180 **Why do you want to do this:** AOSJR interview with author, April 17, 2017.

181 **"one of the smartest":** AOSJR interview with author, April 2, 2018.

181 **"I replied, probably too bluntly":** Nisenholtz address to Senior Management Conference, Palm Beach, Florida, June 24, 1999, Nisenholtz Papers.

181 **The *New York Times* website went live:** David W. Dunlap, "In Gamble, Newspaper Push into On-Line Publishing," *The New York Times*, January 22, 2016.

182 **asked everyone to sign it:** Nisenholtz email interview with author, November 15, 2019.

182 **The arrival:** Peter H. Lewis, "The New York Times Introduces a Web Site," *The New York Times*, January 22, 1996.

182 **registering every second:** Martin Nisenholtz, "Venturing Boldly into Cyberspace, The Times Launches its Web Site," *Times Talk*, January/February 1996.

182 **By March 1997:** Dickson L. Louie with Professor Jeffrey F. Rayport, "The New York Times Electronic Media Company."

183 **The *Times*'s online operation required:** Dickson L. Louie with Professor Jeffrey F. Rayport, "The New York Times Electronic Media Company."

183 **an online-only section:** Lisa Napoli interview with author, October 14, 2016.

184 **fee of thirty-five-dollars:** Kimberly Patch, "Salvation or Mirage? The New York Times Paywall," case study, The Journalism School, Case Consortium @ Columbia, Columbia University, CSJ-14-0054.0, 2014.

184 **"didn't embarrass us":** Lelyveld interview with author, April 16, 2017.

185 **"my God, the world is changing":** Napoli interview with author, October 14, 2016.

185 **"calm the waters":** AOSJR interview with author, April 17, 2017.

185 **Antarctica:** Gwertzman interview with author, November 6, 2016.

185 **He read the online version:** Lelyveld interview with author, September 15, 2016.

185 **the hourly broadcasts:** Lelyveld interview with author, November 18, 2016.

185 **"I never really believed":** Lelyveld interview with author, September 15, 2016.

17 No Cigar

186 **"We were asleep":** Lelyveld remarks to Sulzberger family assembly, April 16, 1999, transcript from Susan Dryfoos, New York Times History Productions.

187 **The paper tucked:** "Clinton Denounces New Report of Affair," *New York Times*, January 24, 1992.

187 **deserved no more attention:** Frankel interview with author, November 14, 2016.

187 **"I'm quite ashamed":** Howard Kurtz, "Reports on Clinton Pose Quandary for Journalists," *The Washington Post*, January 30, 1992.

188 **"Our modest handling":** Frankel to Goulden, January 4, 1994, AOSJR papers.

188 **"We worked extremely hard":** Lelyveld remarks to Sulzberger family assembly, April 16, 1999, transcript from Susan Dryfoos.

188 **zone of privacy:** Lelyveld interview, *Charlie Rose*, May 23, 2000.

188 **"Actually, I might have given it less":** Richard Zoglin, "The Last Great Newspaper," *Time*, September 29, 1997.

188 **"sneaking pleasure":** Lelyveld interview with author, September 15, 2016.

189 **seriousness of purpose:** Lelyveld interview with author, September 15, 2016.

189 **had teased Lelyveld:** Keller remarks at his marriage to Emma Gilbey, April 10, 1999, Keller papers.

189 **"That is not why most of us":** Lelyveld remarks to Sulzberger family assembly, April 16, 1999, transcript from Susan Dryfoos.

189 **This high ground became harder:** Susan Schmidt, Peter Baker and Toni Locy, "Clinton Accused of Urging Aide to Lie," *Washington Post*, January 21, 1998.

190 **The dispute grew heated:** Gerth memo to author, June 3, 2019; Keller email interview with author, December 7, 2019.

190 **I guess we do have to print this:** Lelyveld remarks to Sulzberger family assembly, April 16, 1999, transcript from Susan Dryfoos.

190 **the most challenging decision:** Lelyveld interview, *Charlie Rose*, May 30, 2000.

191 **Purdum was on the way:** Purdum email interview with author, December 6, 2019; Todd Purdum, "Impeachment for Breakfast, Lunch, and Dinner," *The Atlantic*, October 4, 2019.

191 **"If we had published that story":** Lelyveld remarks to Sulzberger family assembly, April 16, 1999, transcript from Susan Dryfoos.

192 **he asked Martin Baron:** Lelyveld interview with author, September 15, 2016.

192 **"closely held (and not left around on desktops)":** Lelyveld to Masthead, Baquet and Oreskes; February 17, 1998, Lelyveld papers.

192 **"Major portions of our January 22":** Baron to Lelyveld, Keller; February 15, 2018, Lelyveld papers.

193 **Lelyveld wandered the rows of desks:** The scene in the newsroom described here, including the Lelyveld-Keller-Oreskes conversation, from Susan Dryfoos videotape, September 11, 1998, Susan Dryfoos Collection.

195 **"Journalistically, this has been":** AOSJR to Lelyveld, October 13, 1998, Lelyveld papers.

195 **Abe Rosenthal had the Pentagon Papers:** Lelyveld interview with author, September 15, 2016.

195 **"China Stole Nuclear Secrets":** James Risen and Jeff Gerth, "China Stole Nuclear Secrets for Bombs, U.S. Aides Say," *The New York Times*, March 6, 1999.

196 **"Mr. Lee has been the prime":** James Risen, "U.S. Fires Scientist Suspected of Giving China Bomb Data," *The New York Times*, March 9, 1999.

196 **"We are now informed":** William Safire, "The Deadliest Download," *The New York Times*, April 29, 1999.

196 **disconnected the telephone:** James Brooke, "This Man Is the Talk of Los Alamos," *The New York Times*, March 10, 1999.

197 **"Keeping him locked up":** Matthew Purdy with James Sterngold, "The Prosecution Unravels: The Case of Wen Ho Lee," *The New York Times*, February 5, 2001.

197 **"They have embarrassed":** Transcript of remarks by Federal District Judge James A. Parker, *The New York Times*, September 14, 2000.

198   **We've got this in balance:** Lelyveld interview with author, November 15, 2018 AOSJR does not recall the conversation.

198   **The FBI screwed up:** Gerth interview with author, June 27, 2019.

198   **Risen left the meeting in anger:** Abramson email interview with author, May 18, 2022, Gerth interview with author, June 27, 2019. Risen does not recall walking out.

198   **We have done what you asked:** Engelberg interview with author, November 12, 2018; Keller email interview with author, February 23, 2020.

198   **Raines was more stunned:** Raines interview with author, September 28, 2018, afternoon session.

199   **"I thought your editors' note":** Graham to Lelyveld, undated, Lelyveld papers.

199   **This is the way they treat reporters?:** Risen interview with author, June 28, 2019.

200   **"didn't bother to point out":** Wen Ho Lee with Helen Zia, *My Country Versus Me: The First-Hand Account by the Los Alamos Scientist Who Was Falsely Accused of Being a Spy* (New York: Hyperion, 2001), 91.

18   *Please Read This Column*

201   **We will only discuss:** Quindlen interview with author, October 4, 2017.

201   **"At the end of the month":** C. L. Sulzberger, "Memories I—Faded Dreams," *The New York Times*, December 11, 1977.

201   **Punch Sulzberger, his cousin, removed him from the page:** AOSJR interview with author, April 17, 2017; Susan E. Tifft and Alex S. Jones *The Trust: The Private and Powerful Family Behind The New York Times* (Boston: Little, Brown and Company,1999), 527–530.

201   **He was featured prominently:** Carl Bernstein, "The CIA and the Media: How Americas Most Powerful News Media Worked Hand in Glove with the Central Intelligence Agency and Why the Church Committee Covered It Up," *Rolling Stone*, October 20, 1977.

202   **Quindlen surmised:** Quindlen interview with author, October 4, 2017, and AOSJR interview with author, January 20, 2020.

202   **Threw his arms around her and the two jumped up and down:** Quindlen interview with author, January 29, 2020.

202   **"I joked once before":** AOSJR to Frank Rich, October 19, 1992, Frankel papers, Columbia.

203   **Spoke to friends of winning a second Pulitzer prize:** Greenfield interview with author, June 4, 2017.

204   **"As you cultivate":** William Safire, "Abe Rosenthal: Conquering a New World," Times Talk, December 1986, Rosenthal Papers, NYT.

204   **"He was one of the worst:"** Gay Talese interview with author, September 20, 2016.

204   **Among his critics:** Jonathan Alter, "Abe Speaks his Mind," *Newsweek*, March 9, 1987.

204   **Although I don't believe:** M.L. Stein, "'Abe' Meets the Press," *Editor & Publisher*, April 25, 1987.

204   **and the attendees included:** Lord Interview with author, November 11, 2016, and Andy Rosenthal email interview with author, January 14, 2020.

205   **I'm-writing-as-bad-as-I-can Rosenthal:** AOSJR interview with author, April 17, 2017.

205   **a stunning assemblage:** Collins interview with author, November 25, 2019.

205   **Raines spent Rosenthal's final hours:** Raines interview with author, August 14, 2017, afternoon session.

206 **white-faced, trembling:** Shirley Lord interview with author, November 11, 2016.

206 **He later vowed to Arthur Gelb:** Arthur Gelb, *City Room* (New York: Putnam, 2003), 633. He made the same pledge to Shirley Lord; Lord interview with author, November 11, 2016.

206 **"The decision of one man":** Rosenthal to M. J. Akbar, December 2, 1999, Rosenthal papers, personal.

206 **"except a mumble that it was time":** Rosenthal to Kollek, February 29, 2000, Rosenthal papers, personal.

207 **"There is only one person":** Talese to Rosenthal, November 7, 1999, Rosenthal papers, personal.

207 **"I hope that the Times":** Rosenthal to AOSJR, January 7, 2000.

207 **"the *Daily News* simply was not":** Rosenthal to Jonathan Friendly, March 29, 1982, Rosenthal papers, NYT.

207 **Shirley Lord always thought:** Lord interview with author, November 11, 2016.

19 *Renegades*

209 **This is the best party:** Tozzi interview with author, December 31, 2017.

210 **Tozzi would break away and command:** Jim Roberts interview with author, April 4, 2017.

210 **Here I am:** Tozzi interview with author, December 31, 2017.

210 **This is Joe Lelyveld:** Rinehart interview with author, February 12, 2020. Lelyveld does not recall the exchange.

210 **I feel like I'm sitting:** Rinehart interview with author, February 12, 2020. Stanley has no memory of the meeting, "but it certainly sounds like me."

210 **Rinehart was crestfallen:** Rinehart interview with author, February 12, 2020.

211 **Meislin thought they cherished:** Meislin interview with author, August 8, 2017.

212 **You guys are our answer:** Robert Larson interview with author, November 11, 2016, and Nisenholtz email interview with author, January 21, 2020.

212 **"We were hiring":** Gwertzman interview of Naka Nathaniel and Meredith Artley, March 2, 2015, Gwertzman papers.

213 **had been warned by senior officials:** Johnston email interview with author, February 12, 2020.

213 **"Coverage of the investigation":** Kevin Sack, "Report of a Hero-Turned-Suspect Rivets Attention in Atlanta," *The New York Times*, July 31, 1996.

213 **Baquet returned to his desk:** Baquet interview with author, December 27, 2018.

214 **after Diana, it became clear:** Gwertzman interview with author, November 6, 2016.

214 **We are not going to be static:** Spruill interview with author, April 4, 2017.

214 **Relations with the newspaper:** Gwertzman to McKenna, January 26, 1998, McKenna papers.

215 **"This needs to be presented":** Lelyveld and Keller to AOSJR, Robertson and Raines, undated, Jerry Gray papers.

215 **"Your lives are about to change":** Keller memo to staff, January 21, 2000, McKenna papers.

215 **"comfortable with the Internet":** Keller memo to newsroom, August 17, 1999, Gray papers.

215 **He set a large jar:** Gray interview with author, April 16, 2017.

216   **talking about fine-tuning:** Lelyveld address to editors retreat, September 1998, McKenna papers.

217   **"a menace":** Lelyveld interview with author, November 18, 2016.

217   **"The Internet is a sexy topic":** AOSJR to Lelyveld, December 16, 1999, Lelyveld papers.

217   **"That would take my approval":** Lelyveld to AOSJR, August 4, 1999, Lelyveld papers.

218   **"For the record":** AOSJR to Lelyveld, undated response to Lelyveld letter of August 4, 1999, Lelyveld papers.

218   **he was impatient with a newsroom:** AOSJR interview with author, January 27, 2020.

218   **"I'm not so sure, Mr. Publisher":** Nisenholtz remarks at *Times* off-site meeting, May 8, 1996, Nisenholtz papers.

218   **"Kicking our ass":** Nisenholtz interview with author, November 25, 2016.

218   **"stupid traditional":** Nisenholtz interview with author, November 25, 2016.

219   **felt like an oddity:** Nisenholtz interview with author, August 12, 2017.

219   **"I didn't really understand":** Lelyveld interview with author, April 16, 2017.

220   **"we've been fighting this battle":** Nisenholtz speech to *Times* senior management conference, Palm Beach, June 24, 1999, Nisenholtz papers.

220   **"It gives us an ability":** AOSJR remarks to senior management conference, Palm Beach, June 24, 1999, Jones papers.

220   **"Nobody asked me":** Lelyveld to Cynthia Augustine, August 20, 1999, Lelyveld papers.

221   **"We are faced with an unhappy":** Augustine to Lelyveld, August 21, 1999, Lelyveld Papers.

221   **To deal with the resentments:** AOSJR memo to staff, August 19, 1999, McKenna papers.

221   **"hold the envy":** Lelyveld remarks to newsroom retreat, September 16, 1999, Lelyveld papers.

221   **"If anything, I thought":** Meislin to Nisenholtz, September 18, 1999, Meislin papers.

222   **the quiet of the room:** Nisenholtz interview with author, August 12, 2017.

222   **"We all accepted":** Lelyveld to AOSJR, October 19, 2000, Lelyveld papers.

20   *Tête d'Armée*

225   **twice ordered the presses to stop:** Allison Fass, "Stop the Presses," *Times Talk*, November 2000.

226   **"We treated it":** Lelyveld interview with author, April 16, 2017.

226   **"If ever there was an occasion":** AOSJR to Lelyveld, December 13, 2000, Lelyveld papers.

227   **Raines liked the fight:** Raines interview with author, May 23, 2018, morning session.

227   **He had studied how A. M. Rosenthal:** Howell Raines, "My Times," *The Atlantic*, May 2004.

227   **he let Raines know:** Raines interview with author, May 23, 2018, morning session.

227   **Wow, he's really good:** Taubman interview with author, October 27, 2016.

228   **Raines . . . would host dinners:** Taubman interview with author, October 28, 2016.

228   **Raines stuck to white wine:** Howell Raines, "My Times."

228   **"National report—stale":** Raines talking points on interview with AOSJR (undated) Raines papers.

229   **go in as a change agent:** Raines interview with author, October 6, 2017, afternoon session.

229 **It's a French term:** Raines interview with author, September 19, 2018, afternoon session.

230 **Bill Keller would say:** Keller interview with author, July 30, 2016.

230 **What about Gerald:** Keller interview with author, July 30, 2016.

231 **"At the heart of it":** Janet Battaile to AOSJR, October 29, 1992,

231 **"competent mover of copy":** Raines interview with author, October 11, 2019, afternoon session.

231 **Sulzberger remembers seeing the letter from Battaile:** AOSJR interview with author, April 2, 2018.

231 **You are going to bring in a guy:** Rattner interview with author, September 13, 2019.

232 **to Janet Robinson:** Robinson email interview with author, February 29, 2020.

232 **"really wasn't a contest":** Gerald M. Boyd, *My Times in Black and White: Race and Power at the New York Times* (Chicago: Lawrence Hill Books, 2010), 249.

232 **It's time for something new:** Baquet email interview with author, March 9, 2020.

232 **Sulzberger asked Phil Taubman:** Taubman interview with author, October 28, 2016.

232 **"I thought the paper":** Howell Raines, "My Times," *The Atlantic*, May 2004.

232 **"our esteemed fire-breathing":** AOSJR memo to staff, May 21, 2001, Raines papers.

232 **Raines was a gamble:** AOSJR interview with author, August 8, 2017.

232 **"I felt from the start":** AOSJR to Lelyveld May 17, 2001, Lelyveld papers.

233 **"I do not expect to see":** Lelyveld to AOSJR, May 17, 2001, Lelyveld papers.

233 **I'd like you to be:** Raines interview with author, May 23, 2018, morning session, and Howell Raines, "My Times," *The Atlantic*, May 2004.

233 **That guy you said you wouldn't pick:** Keller interview with author, January 15, 2018.

233 **Only two people thought:** Okrent email interview with author, July 25, 2021.

234 **Just because we're going through:** Raines interview with author, October 11, 2019, morning session. Lelyveld does not recall the conversation.

234 **But Frankel thought that Boyd:** Frankel interviews with author, June 20, 2018, and April 10, 2017. Raines does not recall the warning being so stark.

235 **White editors of unproven:** Raines email interview with author, March 22, 2022.

235 **"I could not believe":** Gerald M. Boyd, *My Times in Black and White*, 273.

236 **"We both wanted the paper":** Gerald M. Boyd, *My Times in Black and White*, 252–53.

236 **Why is Gail Collins:** Quindlen interview with author, January 29, 2020.

236 **writing unsigned editorials:** Collins interview with author, November 25, 2019.

236 **made sense to everyone:** Collins interview with author, November 25, 2019.

236 **"If God really wanted":** Gail Collins, "Public Interests: Campaign Finance 101," *The New York Times*, March 2, 2001.

237 **"It taught me never":** Collins interview with author, November 25, 2019.

21 *A Terrible Beauty*

238 **"cusp of sixty":** Raines interview with author, October 6, 2017, afternoon session.

238 **"In my first communication":** Raines memo to staff, September 5, 2001, Raines papers.

239 **do you have a sense:** Abramson interview with author, December 17, 2017.

239 **"did not take more forceful steps":** Richard L. Berke and David E. Sanger, "Bush's Aides Seek to Focus Efforts on the Economy," *The New York Times*, September 9, 2001.

239 **he called Berke at home:** Berke interview with author, March 13, 2020.

240   **The bridges into Manhattan:** McFadden email interview with author, March 13, 2020.

241   **had gone to vote:** Judith Miller, *The Story: A Reporter's Journey* (New York: Simon & Schuster Paperbacks, 2015), 147.

241   **The World Trade Center blew up!:** Smale interview with author, November 18, 2018.

241   **Thank God you're here:** Cohen interview with author, October 12, 2018.

241   **What if a cop:** Cronin interview with author, June 12, 2020.

241   **Who's there:** Melena Z. Ryzik, "A Rude Awakening," *Ahead of the Times*, September 19, 2001.

242   **I've got to go kill:** Cronin interview with author, June 12, 2020; Geddes interview with author, June 18, 2020.

242   **As his taxi:** Landman interview with author, April 13, 2020.

243   **grabbed her cellphone:** Katherine E. Finkelstein, "A 36-Hour Report from Ground Zero," *Ahead of the Times*, September 19, 2001.

243   **"Glass, woman's shoe":** Sarah Slobin, "No Air, No Light, but Ash Everywhere," *Ahead of the Times*, September 19, 2001.

243   **Manhattan is closed:** Lew Serviss, "But They Need Me!" *Ahead of the Times*, September 19, 2001.

243   **was blocked:** "How We Lived the News," *Ahead of the Times*, special edition, September 19, 2001.

244   **"grim sense of duty":** Schmemann interview with author, March 11, 2020.

244   **"While we have no reason":** Marc Kramer to staff, September 11, 2011, Kulaga papers.

244   **no one paused:** Edgerley email interview with author, March 19, 2020.

244   **Cronin first thought:** Cronin interview with author, June 12, 2020.

244   **Boyd called home:** Gerald M. Boyd, *My Times in Black and White: Race and Power at the New York Times* (Chicago: Lawrence Hill Books, 2010), 260–61.

244   **his daughter, Rachel:** Landman interview with author, April 13, 2020.

244   **was jolted awake:** Abramson email interview with author, April 3, 2018.

245   **The publisher and his wife:** Raines interview with author, March 12, 2020.

245   **Better luck with the next guy:** Sexton interview with author, November 17, 2018.

246   **This is a historically violent:** Raines interview with author, March 12, 2020.

246   **Wilson, a photo editor:** Wilson interview with author, October 24, 2018.

246   **did not like Siegal's idea:** Winfield interview with author, April 20, 2020. Siegal does not recall suggesting the original headline.

248   **never thought about how:** Abramson email interview with author, April 3, 2018.

248   **"In some ways":** Nisenholtz to NYT board of directors, February 21, 2002, Nisenholtz papers.

249   **a dead-end assignment:** Barron interview with author, March 9, 2020.

249   **peak of my career:** Raines interview with author, March 12, 2020.

249   **"Thank you one and all":** Ken Auletta, "The Howell Doctrine," *The New Yorker*, June 10, 2002.

250   **"Just wanted to say":** Hamill to Raines, December 18, 2001, Raines papers.

250   **"amazing & wonderful letters":** AOSJR to Raines, undated (probably late November 2001), Raines papers.

250   **"The old guys":** Russell Baker to AOSJR, October 26, 2001, Raines papers.

250   **"I can't let the year end":** Lelyveld to Raines and Boyd, December 31, 2001, Raines papers.

22   Custer's Horse

251   **Let's do this:** Andrew Rosenthal interview with author, November 19, 2018.

251   **Never take your eye off that:** Abramson interview with author, December 17, 2017.

251   **Three weeks after the planes:** Bob Woodward, "In Hijacker's Bags, a Call to Planning, Prayer and Death," *Washington Post*, September 28, 2001.

252   **We are not going to get beaten:** Cohen interview with author, October 12, 2018.

252   **had rarely been spoken to so sharply:** Abramson email interview with author, April 3, 2018.

253   **Raines asked Al Siegal:** Raines email interview with author, April 1, 2010; Ken Auletta, "The Howell Doctrine," *The New Yorker*, June 10, 2002.

253   **If we can't establish:** Janny Scott interview with author, March 30, 2020.

254   **"In a story producing":** Albert R. Hunt, "Some Blessings in a Bad Year," *The Wall Street Journal*, December 27, 2001.

254   **By January, when the project:** Mark Singer, "The Grief Desk," *The New Yorker*, January 14, 2002.

254   **It's like watching a Maserati:** Raines interview with author, March 12, 2020.

254   **reminded him of his father:** Andrew Rosenthal interview with author, May 14, 2018.

255   **"It looked like baby powder":** Judith Miller, "Fear Hits Newsroom In a Cloud of Powder," *The New York Times*, October 14, 2001.

255   **"A truly miserable day":** Kramon journal, September 14, 2001, Kramon papers.

256   **You would not have wanted to:** Abramson interview with author, March 31, 2018.

256   **"I can't remember a boss":** Kramon journal, October 24, 2001, Kramon papers.

257   **called Tyler and told him:** Cohen interview with author, April 7, 2020.

257   **Tyler left that day:** Tyler interview with author, April 3, 2020.

257   **best national security correspondents:** Raines interview, *Charlie Rose*, July 11, 2003.

257   **carte blanche:** Abramson interview with author, March 31, 2018.

257   **she knew how to handle her:** Raines interview with author, May 23, 2018, afternoon session.

258   **"do whatever it takes":** Judith Miller, *The Story: A Reporter's Journey* (New York: Simon & Schuster Paperbacks, 2015), 148.

258   **How are things up there with the Taliban?:** Andrew Rosenthal interview with author, November 19, 2018; John Broder email interview with author, April 2, 2020.

258   **"I am officially reprimanding you":** Abramson interview with author, December 17, 2017. Raines does not recall the conversation.

258   **"reassure them how valuable they were":** Ken Auletta, "The Howell Doctrine," *The New Yorker*, June 10, 2002.

259   **I'm having a really hard time:** Abramson interview with author, December 17, 2017.

259   **"Each word felt":** Gerald M. Boyd, *My Times in Black and White: Race and Power at the New York Times* (Chicago: Lawrence Hill Books, 2010), 281.

259   **he reached Mark Landler:** Landler interview with author, April 10, 2020.

261   **Think of yourself as a tugboat:** Schmidt interview with author, May 14, 2019.

261   **Morale is suffering:** Schmidt interview with author, May 14, 2019.

261   **I never want:** Nisenholtz interview with author, August 12, 2017.

261   **too fragile a flower:** Nisenholtz interview with author, August 12, 2017. Raines does not recall the exchange.

261   **"everything I'd done in my life":** Raines interview, *Charlie Rose*, August 6, 2002.

262   **"will be studied and taught"**: Felicity Barringer, "Pulitzers Focus on Sept. 11, and The Times Wins 7," *The New York Times*, April 9, 2002.

262   **"I've got more arrows"**: Raines interview with author, October 7, 2017, afternoon session.

23   *At Swords' Point*

264   **Dowd had told Michael Oreskes**: Dowd email interview with author, April 1, 2021.

264   **We don't know who**: Abramson interview with author, May 20, 2018.

265   **"a great disappointment"**: Raines interview with author, May 23, 2018, afternoon session.

266   **I'm going to have dental work**: Berke interview with author, April 18, 2020.

266   **I can trust Rick**: Berke interview with author, April 18, 2020.

267   **"we will under no circumstances"**: Raines to Abramson, March 11, 2002, Abramson papers.

267   **He returned to Moscow**: Tyler interview with author, April 3, 2020.

268   **Berke would ship Tyler's stories**: Berke interview with author, April 18, 2020; Abramson interview with author, April 27, 2020.

268   **presented specific directions**: Raines journal entry of January 27, 2003; Raines interview with author, September 18, 2018, afternoon session.

268   **I brought a premier**: Raines interview with author, May 23, 2018, afternoon session.

268   **"been the pet"**: Abramson interview with author, April 30, 2020.

268   **she asked Gail Collins**: Collins interview with author, November 25, 2019; Abramson interview with author, April 30, 2020.

269   **why does Howell hate me?**: Collins interview with author, November 25, 2019.

269   **What good is it**: Abramson interview with author, March 31, 2018.

269   **I didn't know I wasn't helping**: Golden Behr interview with author, March 29, 2018.

269   **"a very important time"**: Downie to Abramson, July 12, 2002, Abramson papers.

270   **Where he grilled salmon**: Abramson interview with author, January 7, 2018.

270   **I'd respect your opinion more**: Lelyveld interview with author, September 15, 2016.

271   **looks like the front page**: Landman interview with author, May 16, 2018.

271   **If it's boring**: Lelyveld interview with author, September 15, 2016.

271   **"He let me be"**: Landman interview with author, May 16, 2018.

272   **"our brilliant metro editor"**: Raines interview, *Charlie Rose*, August 6, 2002.

272   **Raines made a point**: Raines interview with author, May 24, 2018, morning session.

272   **one of the greatest disappointments**: Landman interview with author, September 14, 2016.

272   **You're basically saying**: Raines interview with author, May 23, 2018, afternoon session.

273   **"draw your own conclusions"**: Ken Auletta, "The Howell Doctrine," *The New Yorker*, June 10, 2002.

273   **do about Landman?**: Raines interview with author, October 7, 2017, morning session.

24   *House on Fire*

274   **"Don't Attack Saddam"**: Brent Scowcroft, "Don't Attack Saddam," *The Wall Street Journal*, August 15, 2002.

274 **The Republicans are cutting loose:** Tyler interview with author, April 26, 2020.

275 **The headline on the front-page:** Todd S. Purdum and Patrick E. Tyler, "Top Republicans Break with Bush on Iraq Strategy," *The New York Times*, August 16, 2002.

275 **failed to make that distinction:** Elisabeth Bumiller, "President Notes Dissent on Iraq, Vowing to Listen," *The New York Times*, August 17, 2002.

275 **"When It":** "When It Raines, It Pours," *The Weekly Standard*, August 16, 2002.

275 **"Not since William Randolph Hearst":** Charles Krauthammer, "Kidnapped by the Times," *The Washington Post*, August 18, 2002.

276 **"The Times's Theme":** "This Is Opposition?" *The Wall Street Journal*, August 19, 2002.

276 **You guys are coming up:** Sanger interview with author, May 3, 2020.

277 **tangled up in Kissingerian:** Raines interview with author, October 11, 2019, morning session.

277 **Don't we need to comment:** Raines interview with author October 11, 2019, afternoon session.

277 **"should have made a clearer distinction":** Editors' Note, *The New York Times*, September 4, 2002.

278 **"that Washington dare not wait":** Michael R. Gordon and Judith Miller, "U.S. Says Hussein Intensifies Quest for A-Bomb Parts," *The New York Times*, September 8, 2002.

278 **"somehow independent confirmation" . . . "It's now public":** Peter Baker, *Days of Fire: Bush and Cheney in the White House* (New York: Doubleday, 2013), 217.

278 **"Iraq has made several attempts":** "Text: Bush's Speech to U.N. on Iraq," *The New York Times*, September 12, 2002.

279 **Miller and Gordon would address:** Judith Miller and Michael R. Gordon, "White House Lists Iraq Steps to Build Banned Weapons," *The New York Times*, September 13, 2002.

279 **Gordon later contributed:** Michael Gordon, "Agency Challenges Evidence Against Iraq Cited by Bush," *The New York Times*, January 10, 2003; and Michael Gordon and James Risen, "Findings of U.N. Group Undercut U.S. Assertion," *The New York Times*, January 28, 2003.

279 **"a growing number":** Warren P. Strobel, "Some in Bush Administration Have Misgivings about Iraq Policy," Knight-Ridder News Service, October 7, 2002.

280 **We are a newspaper:** Cohen interview with author, October 12, 2018.

280 **"The debate over Iraq":** "Power and Leadership: The Real Meaning of Iraq," *The New York Times*, February 23, 2003.

281 **we are going to war:** Cohen interview with author, October 12, 2018.

282 **"I became fascinated with":** Franklin Foer, "The Source of the Trouble," *New York*, May 28, 2004.

282 **"With a view":** Lelyveld to staff, April 23, 1985, Frankel papers, Columbia.

282 **She persuaded Lelyveld:** Lelyveld to Gwertzman, April 22, 1991, Frankel papers, NYPL.

282 **she and Jeff Gerth had written:** Jeff Gerth and Judith Miller, "Funds for Terrorists Traced to Persian Gulf Businessmen," *The New York Times*, August 14, 1996.

282 **"house on fire":** Raines interview with author, May 23, 2018, afternoon session.

283 **"I have strong elbows":** Don Van Natta, Jr., Adam Liptak, and Clifford J. Levy, "The Miller Case: A Notebook, a Cause, a Jail Cell and a Deal," *The New York Times*, October 16, 2005.

283 **I think I should be sitting:** Maureen Dowd, "Woman of Mass Destruction," *The New York Times*, October 22, 2005.

283 **grew accustomed to hearing from Miller:** Smale interview with author, November 18, 2018.

283 **"that's interesting, Judy":** Engelberg interview with author, November 12, 2018.

284 **"A child of the 1960s":** Judith Miller, *The Story*, 59.

284 **We're working very hard:** Raines interview with author, October 6, 2017, morning session; Kovach interview with author, December 29, 2017.

284 **"I feared there was nothing":** Lynne Duke, "The Reporter's Last Take: In an Era of Anonymous Sources, Judy Miller Is a Cautionary Tale of the Times," *The Washington Post*, November 10, 2005.

285 **"I don't see anything wrong with it":** Tyler to Raines, August 19, 2002, Tyler papers.

285 **"An Iraqi defector":** Judith Miller, "Iraqi Tells of Renovations at Sites for Chemical and Nuclear Arms," *The New York Times*, December 20, 2001.

285 **The defector story:** Jane Mayer, "The Manipulator," *The New Yorker*, May 31, 2004.

285 **embroidered her initials:** Judith Miller, *The Story*, 148.

286 **Miller is a Pulitzer Prize winner:** Frantz interview with author, November 30, 2018.

286 **I have six reporters:** Berke interview with author, April 29, 2018.

286 **"I think you are a person":** Rosenthal to Miller, November 6, 1986, Rosenthal papers, NYT.

287 **He appreciated how:** Lelyveld interview with author, April 16, 2017.

287 **On my top-ten:** Andrew Rosenthal interview with author, November 19, 2018.

287 **"I took America":** Judith Miller, "The Iraq War and Stubborn Myths," *The Wall Street Journal*, April 3, 2015.

287 **Michael Gordon who came up:** Gordon e-mail interview with author, January 9, 2023.

288 **"At the end of the day":** AOSJR interview with author, April 18, 2019.

288 **"I got it totally wrong":** Don Van Natta, Jr., et al.

25 Raw Talent

289 **Does he ever sleep?:** Gray interview with author, July 8, 2017.

289 **"Older men remember it":** Jayson Blair, "Bookstore on Gay Life Is a Victim of Tolerance," *The New York Times*, March 19, 2001.

290 **received a *Times* Publisher's Award . . . $5,000 merit raise:** Report to Times lawyers on Jayson Blair; Schmidt, Sharkey and Rule to Freeman, McCraw and Kraft, May 5, 2003, author's papers.

290 **noticed this intern's byline:** Transcript of Raines testimony to the Siegal Committee, July 11, 2003, Raines papers.

290 **"My feeling was":** Dan Barry, David Barstow, et al., "Times Reporter Who Resigned Leaves Long Trail of Deception," *The New York Times*, May 11, 2003.

291 **Blair knew why:** Blair interview with author, June 30, 2018.

291 **A reporter from the *San Antonio Express-News*:** Seth Mnookin, *Hard News: The Scandals at The New York Times and Their Meaning for American Media* (New York: Random House, 2004), 103–4.

292 **"Jayson flew through":** Raines interview with author, September 18, 2018, morning session.

292 **"very ambitious and self-confident":** Report to Times lawyers on Jayson Blair; Schmidt et al.

292 **"She would probably say"**: Report to Times lawyers on Jayson Blair; Schmidt et al.

293 **"the most raw talent"**: Gray interview with author, July 8, 2017.

293 **He would show up to the office**: Gray interview with author, July 8, 2017.

293 **"Despite my apprehensions"**: Gray evaluation of Jayson Blair, August 12, 1998, author's papers.

293 **"blaze of productivity"**: Report to Times lawyers on Jayson Blair; Schmidt et al.

294 **"The last thing we need"**: Landman to Sharkey, September 21, 2000, author's papers.

294 **"a suspicion that his seemingly intimate"**: Report to *Times* lawyers on Jayson Blair; Schmidt, Sharkey, and Rule to Freeman, McCraw, and Kraft, May 5, 2003. Private Papers.

294 **"It was clear that Gerald"**: Landman interview with outside members of the Siegal committee (Louis D. Boccardi, Joann Byrd, Roger Wilkins), "The Jayson Blair Case," Report of the Committee on Safeguarding the Integrity of Journalism, July 28, 2003.

295 **Blair first said yes**: Report to *Times* lawyers on Jayson Blair; Schmidt, Sharkey and Rule to Freeman, McCraw and Kraft, May 5, 2003. Private Papers.

295 **Oh, no concert?**: Smale interview with author, November 18, 2018; Blair interview with author, June 25, 2020.

295 **lines of cocaine**: Blair interview with author, June 25, 2020.

295 **"I am on your team"**: Blair to Pinder, October 20, 2001, author's papers.

295 **"I held my nose"**: Blair to Sharkey, October 30, 2001, author's papers.

296 **It all got worse**: Blair interview with author, June 30, 2018.

296 **By the end of their breakfast**: Edgerley interview with author, June 21, 2018.

296 **I will talk to him**: Schmidt interview with author, May 14, 2019, morning session.

296 **"I said, 'you have enormous promise' "**: Boyd interview with outside members of Siegal committee (Boccardi et al.), "The Jayson Blair Case," July 28, 2003.

296 **"We have to stop Jayson"**: Landman to Sharkey, Schmidt, April 1, 2002, author's papers.

297 **Boyd had a list**: Roberts email interview with author, June 12, 2022.

297 **"My failure to disclose Blair's history"**: Gerald M. Boyd, *My Times in Black and White: Race and Power at the New York Times* (Chicago: Lawrence Hill Books, 2010), 329.

297 **"I didn't feel"**: Boyd interview with outside members of Siegal committee (Boccardi et al.), "The Jayson Blair Case," July 28, 2003.

297 **"As the first black managing editor"**: Jayson Blair, *Burning Down My Masters' House* (Beverly Hills: New Millennium Press, 2004), 12.

298 **"vibrancy and a returning vitality"**: Transcript of Raines's testimony to outside members of the Siegal committee, July 12, 2003, Raines papers.

298 **calling in notes**: Blair interview with author, May 30, 2020.

298 **"The allegations in the New York Times"**: Susan Schmidt and Katherine Shaver, "Muhammad Interrogation in Dispute," *The Washington Post*, October 31, 2002.

298 **"The *Post* got beat"**: Erik Wemple, "Sniping Coverage," *City Paper*, November 8, 2002.

299 **"That is great shoe-leather"**: Raines to Blair, November 1, 2002, Jeff Gerth papers.

299 **Jayson's really getting it for us**: Roberts interview with author, June 21, 2018, and Raines interview with author, September 28, 2018, afternoon session.

299 **Watch out for that guy**: Roberts interview with author, June 21, 2018.

299 **Why aren't you in the office?**: Roberts email interview with author, June 12, 2022.

299 **energetic and ready to jump**: Nick Fox interview with author, May 29, 2019.

299 **making his editors feel confident**: Roberts interview with author, June 21, 2018.

26   A Room Filled with Gas

300   **he was building a wall:** Blair interview with author, September 30, 2018.

300   **"I could see in my head":** Blair interview with author, September 30, 2018.

300   **Blair responded with details:** Dan Barry, David Barstow, et al. "Times Reporter Who Resigned Leaves Long Trail of Deception," *The New York Times*, May 11, 2003.

301   **We have to fire him:** Schmidt interview with author, May 14, 2019.

301   **thinking about hanging himself:** Jayson Blair, *Burning Down My Masters' House* (Beverly Hills: New Millennium Press, 2004), 23.

301   **"The Times apologizes":** Jacques Steinberg, "Times Reporter Resigns After Questions on Article," *The New York Times*, May 2, 2003.

302   **"There was no clause in it":** Schmidt interview with author, May 14, 2019, morning session.

302   **I want to send you to London:** Landman interview with author, September 14, 2016.

302   **Raines trying to get me out of the newsroom:** Landman interview with author, September 14, 2016.

302   **"Jon's disenchantment":** Raines to AOSJR, April 30, 2003, AOSJR papers.

303   **"No surprise he's not":** AOSJR to Raines, May 1, 2003, AOSJR papers.

303   **They celebrated their marriage:** David Margolick, "The Times's Restoration Drama," *Vanity Fair*, August 2003.

303   **sitting on the porch:** Raines interview with author, September 28, 2018, morning session.

304   **never seen it before that morning:** Raines interview with author, September 28, 2018, morning session.

304   **Raines considered a dramatic gesture:** Raines interview with author, September 28, 2018, morning session.

305   **"young and Black and a lawyer":** Seth Mnookin, *Hard News: The Scandals at The New York Times and Their Meaning for American Media* (New York: Random House, 2004), 146.

305   **It's my editorship:** Gerald M. Boyd, *My Times in Black and White: Race and Power at the New York Times* (Chicago: Lawrence Hill Books, 2010), 318.

305   **"Howell instructed me":** Glenn Kramon journal, May 2, 2003, Kramon papers.

305   **Boyd appeared unannounced:** Seth Mnookin, *Hard News*, 163.

305   **Years later, Boyd said:** Gerald M. Boyd, *My Times in Black and White*, 331.

305   **He wandered around:** Barry interview with author, July 10, 2020.

306   **It's like the room:** Raines interview with author, September 28, 2018, morning session.

306   **"When I saw that panic":** Raines interview with author, September 28, 2018, morning session.

306   **internal-affairs division:** Barry interview with author, July 10, 2020.

307   **Please keep this to yourself:** Barstow interview with author, July 18, 2020.

307   **"They tell me":** Raines interview with Terence Smith, *PBS NewsHour*, May 9, 2003.

308   **"You must be heartsick":** Remnick to Raines, May 10, 2003, Raines papers.

308   **"apocalyptic four-page saga":** Arthur Gelb, *City Room* (New York: Putnam, 2003), 636.

308   **may have gone too far:** AOSJR interview with author, April 17, 2017.

308   **handed Raines's enemies ammunition:** Blair interview with author, September 30, 2018.

27   *Losing the Newsroom*

309   **"Dear friends and colleagues":** Raines to newsroom, May 12, 2003, Gerth papers.
309   **"I've never heard such hostility":** Kramon journal, May 13, 2003, Kramon papers.
310   **All you'll do:** Raines interview with author, September 28, 2018, morning session.
310   **You are losing the newsroom:** Barstow interview with author, July 18, 2020.
310   **"Perhaps not since":** Ken Auletta, "The Howell Doctrine," *The New Yorker,* June 10, 2002.
310   **"a somewhat convoluted effort":** Elizabeth Kolbert, "Tumult in the Newsroom," *The New Yorker,* June 30, 2003.
310   **"Never in my career at the *Times*":** Transcript, town hall meeting with AOSJR, Raines, and Boyd, May 14, 2003, Keller papers.
311   **"Does that mean I personally":** Transcript, town hall meeting.
311   **Is there anything involving:** Gerald M. Boyd, *My Times in Black and White: Race and Power at the New York Times* (Chicago: Lawrence Hill Books, 2010), 324.
311   **whatever you do:** Raines interview with author, September 28, 2018, afternoon session.
312   **"You guys have lost":** Transcript, town hall meeting.
312   **It fed his anger:** Raines interview with author, October 11, 2019, morning session.
312   **"dancing mania":** Raines interview with author, September 29, 2018, morning session.
312   **That was brutal:** AOSJR interview with author, August 8, 2017; Raines interview with author, September 28, 2018, morning session.
312   **I guess London:** Landman interview with author, September 14, 2016.
313   **I'm done with this Pat Tyler:** Abramson interview with author, December 17, 2017.
313   **I was proud to do it:** Landman interview with author, September 14, 2016. Raines does not recall this remark.
313   **"Moved too fast":** Raines journal, May 23, 2003, Raines papers.
313   **"As I've mentioned to both of you":** AOSJR to Raines and Boyd, May 22, 2003, author's papers.
314   **reluctantly and at Raines's orders:** Cohen interview with author, October 12, 2018.
314   **"My job was to ride the airplane":** Howard Kurtz, "Suspended N.Y. Times Reporter Says He'll Quit," *The Washington Post,* May 27, 2003.
315   **"I for one am not":** Steinhauer letter to Jim Romenesko, May 23, 2003, and Steinbrenner email interview with author, August 9, 2020.
315   **"The time has come":** Adam Clymer to newsroom, May 30, 2003, Geddes papers.
315   **"In the last couple of days":** Raines and Boyd to newsroom, May 29, 2003, Geddes papers.
315   **This isn't going to work:** Rattner interview with author, September 13, 2019.
315   **People will view that:** Raines interview with author, September 28, 2018, afternoon session.
315   **"We crossed Howell off":** Golden interview with author, December 22, 2017.
316   **"I write as someone":** Halberstam to AOSJR, May 20, 2003, AOSJR papers.
316   **"The Blair crisis":** Albert R. Hunt, "The New York Times Scandal: About Values, More Than Race," *The Wall Street Journal,* May 15, 2003.
316   **"That's not so great":** "Correctamundo," *The Weekly Standard,* May 12, 2003.
316   **"Both of you called":** AOSJR to Bill and Hillary Clinton, May 20, 2003, AOSJR papers.

316   **You're behaving very well:** Raines journal, May 21, 2003, Raines papers.

316   **Where do you think we are?:** Raines interview with author, September 28, 2018, afternoon session.

317   **He began rising:** Gerald M. Boyd, *My Times in Black and White*, 7.

317   **I wake up every morning:** Andrew Rosenthal interview with author, November 19, 2018.

317   **Soma, can't you do something?:** Golden Behr interview with author, November 20, 2016.

317   **Sulzberger blamed him for many:** AOSJR interview with author, August 8, 2017.

317   **You have not served:** Gerald M. Boyd, *My Times in Black and White*, 337.

317   **One thing we've learned from this:** AOSJR interview with author, September 28, 2018.

317   **You are a control freak:** Oreskes interview with author, November 14, 2018.

317   **I don't trust you:** Raines interview with author, September 28, 2018, afternoon session.

318   **a long-term affair:** Susan E. Tifft and Alex S. Jones, *The Trust: The Private and Powerful Family Behind The New York Times* (Boston: Little, Brown and Company, 1999), 191–92.

318   **"I had run enough people":** Howell Raines, *The One That Got Away: A Memoir* (New York: Scribner, 2006) 19.

318   **Just cancel it:** Raines interview with author September 28, 2018, afternoon session.

319   **I have never in my life:** Gerald M. Boyd, *My Times in Black and White*, 13.

319   **Boyd asked him if:** AOSJR interview with author, August 8, 2017.

319   **"There is so much to say":** Jacques Steinberg, "Executive Editor of The Times and Top Deputy Step Down," *The New York Times*, June 5, 2003.

319   **"And remember, when a big story":** Raines farewell remarks to newsroom, "Talk of the Times," undated, Jeff Gerth papers.

319   **"passionately and repeatedly tried":** Boyd farewell remarks to newsroom, "Talk of the Times," undated, Jeff Gerth papers.

319   **Lacking in grace:** Raines interview with author, September 18, 2018, afternoon session.

319   **"The forced introspection":** Editorial, "Leadership at the Times," *The New York Times*, June 6, 2003.

320   **Sulzberger got rolled by the staff:** Raines interview with author, September 28, 2018, morning session.

320   **"It's slowly dawning":** Clines to Raines, undated, Raines papers.

28   *The Cure for What Ailed Us*

323   **"The cure for what has ailed us":** Lelyveld address to newsroom, June 6, 2003, *Talk of the Times*, Gerth papers.

324   **Enough navel-gazing:** Lelyveld interview with author, November 18, 2016.

324   **We are devoting too much space:** Kramon journal, June 5, 2003, Kramon papers.

324   **it's Bill's to lose:** Baquet interview with author, November 11, 2018. Lelyveld does not recall the exchange.

324   **My happy exile:** Keller interview with author, July 30, 2016.

324   **"We have good writers":** Keller to AOSJR, June 4, 2001, Keller papers.

325 **"Thank you for this very thoughtful analysis":** AOSJR to Keller, June 4, 2001, Keller papers.

325 **I'm not going to drag you along:** AOSJR interview with author, November 21, 2017.

325 **"settled into a kind of":** Raines interview, *Charlie Rose*, July 11, 2003.

326 **"There's no complacency here":** Transcript of AOSJR remarks, *Ahead of the Times*, August 2003.

326 **"Friends, it's time to move on":** Remarks of Bill Keller, July 14, 2003, Keller papers.

326 **"That's because Al":** Landman memo to the Siegal Committee, July 2003, Gerth papers.

326 **"I thought that was my job":** Lelyveld interview with author, November 18, 2016.

327 **Keller recognized the reality:** Keller interview with author, May 21, 2018.

327 **"have license to write":** Keller to newsroom, July 30, 2003, Gerth papers.

327 **"The Blair fiasco":** Keller to newsroom, July 30, 2003, Gerth papers.

327 **Don't even think about leaving:** Rosenthal interview with author, May 14, 2018; AOSJR email interview with author, November 22, 2020.

327 **You've really been busting:** Rosenthal interview with author, November 18, 2016.

328 **"At the end of the day":** Rosenthal interview with author, November 19, 2018.

328 **"The man's a cancer":** Keller memo to Abramson, June 14, 2004, author's papers.

328 **"My opinion, since you asked":** AOSJR to Tyler, July 17, 2004, AOSJR papers.

328 **"I'm the foremost beneficiary":** Keller to Siegal Committee, July 28, 2003, Keller Papers.

329 **You passed the test:** Okrent interview with author, March 28, 2018.

329 **experience in the literary world:** Jacques Steinberg, "The Times Chooses Veteran of Magazines and Publishing as Its First Public Editor," *The New York Times*, October 27, 2003.

329 **came to think that Okrent:** Keller interview with author, January 5, 2018.

330 **"arrogantly convinced of its primacy":** Daniel Okrent, *Public Editor #1: The Collected Columns* (New York: Public Affairs, 2006), 10.

330 **These old-timers; found himself sharing a table:** Okrent to author, March 28, 2018.

330 **Please be kind:** Okrent interview with author, March 28, 2018.

330 **"I have great admiration":** Sexton to Okrent, March 11, 2004, Okrent papers.

330 **They think you're internal affairs:** Okrent interview with author, March 28, 2018.

330 **"Is The New York Times":** Daniel Okrent, "Is The New York Times a Liberal Newspaper?" *The New York Times*, July 25, 2004.

331 **Okrent was becoming:** James Bandler, "New York Times Finds Its Watchdog Has a Strong Bite," *The Wall Street Journal*, July 12, 2004.

331 **This is why:** Okrent interview with author, March 28, 2018.

29 *The Second Choice*

332 **Mourning takes a year:** Raines interview with author, October 6, 2017, afternoon session; AOSJR interview with author, April 2, 2018.

332 **"The summer of 2003":** AOSJR response to his performance evaluations from colleagues, early 2004, AOSJR papers.

333 **"This year took a lot out of me":** AOSJR to Keller, December 15, 2003, Keller papers.

333 **This wouldn't have happened:** AOSJR interview with author, April 2, 2018.

333 **"So what worries me?":** AOSJR to Keller, December 15, 2003, Keller papers.

334 **"crisis of morale":** Scott Raab, "Exclusive Q&A: Bill Keller on Leaving the *Times*, Fox & More," *Esquire*, June 2, 2011.

335 **"I would like to introduce":** Bill Keller, "All the News That's Shit to Print," *Claremont Spectator*, October 2, 1969.

335 **Keller's taste in newspaper writers:** Keller interview with author, July 20, 2016.

336 **"I worry that":** Keller remarks at off-site meeting, Tarrytown retreat, January 22, 2004, Keller papers.

336 **to $292.5 million at the end of 2004:** Annual Report, The New York Times Company, 2004.

336 **"Deep concerns, candidly expressed, off the record":** Minutes, Mohonk Committee meeting, January 20, 2004, author's papers.

337 **"When Letterman and Leno":** Minutes, Mohonk Committee meeting, November 21, 2003, author's papers.

337 **"Over the years the business side":** Transcript of off-site meeting, Tarrytown retreat, January 23, 2004, author's papers.

337 **"agent of his mischief-making":** Moss interview with author, October 8, 2017.

337 **had smoked marijuana:** Moss interview with author, October 8, 2017.

338 **"The starkness":** Editors' note, *The New York Times*, June 26, 1994.

338 **You shouldn't have published:** Moss interview with author, October 8, 2017; AOSJR email interview with author, November 22, 2020.

338 **confided to his colleagues:** Minutes, Mohonk Committee meeting, February 11, 2004, author's papers.

338 **worried that Moss's exit:** Minutes, Mohonk Committee meeting, February 11, 2004, author's papers.

338 **"Now Adam's out to eat":** Minutes, Mohonk Committee meeting, March 10, 2004, author's papers.

338 **"We don't want department heads":** Transcript of off-site meeting, January 23, 2004, author's papers.

339 **"Since I thought the paper":** Howell Raines, "My Times," *The Atlantic*, May 2004.

340 **"I very much regret":** AOSJR to Lelyveld, March 28, 2004, author's papers.

340 **"I know you liked me":** Lelyveld to AOSJR, March 28, 2004, author's papers.

340 **He kept imagining Raines:** Keller interview with author, August 26, 2016.

340 **Ninety percent of this:** AOSJR interview with author, November 21, 2017.

341 **"i will not work":** Tyler to Miller, May 6, 2003, Tyler papers.

341 **"I am deeply chagrined":** Howard Kurtz, "Intra-Times Battle Over Iraqi Weapons," *The Washington Post*, May 26, 2003.

342 **You can't have Judy Miller:** Abramson interview with author, December 17, 2017; Lelyveld interview with author, November 15, 2018.

342 **Do you think we have a Judy Miller problem?:** Abramson interview with author, December 17, 2017.

342 **"Do not write":** Abramson interview with author, April 1, 2018.

342 **"Watching and reading all this":** Michael Massing, "Now They Tell Us," *The New York Review of Books*, February 26, 2004.

342 **"The fact that the United States so far":** Massing, "Now They Tell Us."

343 **the *Times*'s meager coverage of the Holocaust:** Okrent interview with author, March 28, 2018.

343 **it was a major lapse:** Abramson interview with author, March 31, 2018.

343 **"Jill didn't decide":** Keller interview with author, April 19, 2019.

344 **"The tubes":** Abramson review of Iraq coverage, Keller papers.

344 **"Clad in nondescript clothes":** Judith Miller, "Illicit Arms Kept Till Eve of War, an Iraqi Scientist Is Said to Assert," *The New York Times*, April 21, 2003.

344 **"We got mocked":** Rosenthal interview with author, November 19, 2018.

344 ***"Eureka we've found it":*** Abramson notes to Keller on Miller and Iraq coverage, undated, Keller papers.

344 **If you run this:** Judith Miller, *The Story: A Reporter's Journey* (New York: Simon & Schuster Paperbacks, 2015), 207.

345 **"We have studied":** "From the Editors: The Times and Iraq," *The New York Times*, May 26, 2004.

346 **"Somewhat to my surprise":** Raines email to the Poynter Institute, May 26, 2004, poynter.org/reporting-editing/2004/raines-i-never-rushed-to-get-wmd-scoops-into -the-times/.

346 **"My feeling is that no editor":** Josh Getlin, "Former Editor Rejects Thrust of N.Y. Times Note," *Los Angeles Times*, May 27, 2004.

346 **But Okrent found Miller:** Okrent interview with author, March 28, 2018.

346 **"The failure was not":** Daniel Okrent, "Weapons of Mass Destruction? Or Mass Distraction?" *The New York Times*, May 30, 2004.

346 **"It was, without a doubt":** Judith Miller, *The Story*, 237–38.

347 **"It went to the very core":** AOSJR interview with author, April 18, 2019.

347 **"For a newspaper":** Monica Lewinsky to AOSJR, July 22, 2004, AOSJR papers.

348 **How does it feel:** Jill Abramson, *Merchants of Truth: The Business of News and the Fight for Facts* (New York: Simon & Schuster, 2019), 79.

30 *In the National Interest*

349 **"What we did not anticipate":** Keller and Abramson remarks to the board of directors, December 2004, Keller papers.

350 **"The idea that we should":** Keller remarks to staff, November 29, 2005, Keller papers.

350 **flew to New York:** Lichtblau interview with author, June 26, 2019.

351 **he thought a threat like that:** Keller interview with author, January 5, 2018.

351 **"Three years after":** Margaret Sullivan, "Lessons in a Surveillance Drama Redux," *The New York Times*, November 9, 2013.

352 **"an advocate of his sources":** Keller interview with author, March 27, 2018.

352 **preferred to deal with Taubman:** Michael V. Hayden, *Playing to the Edge: American Intelligence in the Age of Terror* (New York: Penguin Books, 2016), 94.

352 **I'm going to read you:** Taubman interview with author, March 17, 2019.

352 **Do you realize:** Michael V. Hayden, *Playing to the Edge*, 98.

353 **"When I returned to the bureau":** James Risen, "My Life as a New York Times Reporter in the Shadow of the War on Terror," *The Intercept*, January 3, 2018.

353 **If you publish it:** Taubman interview with author, March 17, 2019; Risen interview with author, June 28, 2019.

353 **Abramson warned Keller:** Abramson interview with author, March 31, 2018.

354 **I know what it's like:** Peter Baker, *Days of Fire: Bush and Cheney in the White House* (New York: Doubleday, 2013), 434.

354 **You have to concede:** Keller interview with author, July 5, 2017.

354   **"I went to bed undecided":** Sheryl Gay Stolberg and Eric Lichtblau, "Senators Thwart Bush Bid to Renew Law on Terrorism," *The New York Times*, December 17, 2005.

355   **Is he insane?:** Risen interview with author, June 28, 2019.

355   **"woefully inadequate":** Byron Calame, "Behind the Eavesdropping Story, a Loud Silence," *The New York Times*, January 1, 2006.

355   **Talese blanched:** Talese interview with author, May 15, 2016.

355   **"So you're criticized":** Graham to AOSJR, December 12, 2005, AOSJR papers.

356   **He thought about a year:** Risen interview with author, June 28, 2019.

356   **You guys know what happened:** James Risen, "My Life as a New York Times Reporter."

31   *Hand on the Wheel*

358   **"If journalists cannot":** Miller remarks on sentencing, July 6, 2005, Levy papers.

358   **The editorial page ran:** Ken Auletta, "The Inheritance," *The New Yorker*, December 19, 2005.

358   **Sulzberger poked his head:** Minutes, Mohonk Committee meeting, June 29, 2005, author's papers.

359   **Taubman warned Sulzberger and Keller:** Taubman interview with author, October 28, 2016.

360   **She ain't going to be there:** Abramson interview with author, April 1, 2018.

360   **"Judy! Judy!":** Judith Miller, *The Story: A Reporter's Journey* (New York: Simon & Schuster Paperbacks, 2015), 279.

360   **a massage, a manicure:** Don Van Natta, Jr., Adam Liptak, and Clifford J. Levy, "The Miller Case: A Notebook, a Cause, a Jail Cell and a Deal," *The New York Times*, October 16, 2005.

360   **"I'm sure I did many things":** Katharine Q. Seelye, "Freed Reporter Says She Upheld Principles," *The New York Times*, October 4, 2005.

360   **"We looked like idiots":** Abramson interview with author, April 1, 2018.

361   **She had agreed to identify:** Judith Miller, "My Four Hours Testifying in the Federal Grand Jury Room," *The New York Times*, October 16, 2005.

361   **"I wish it had been a clear-cut":** Don van Natta, Jr., Adam Liptak, and Clifford J. Levy, "The Miller Case: A Notebook, a Cause, a Jail Cell and a Deal," *New York Times*, Oct 16, 2005.

361   **"It takes courage":** Baquet to AOSJR, October 17, 2005, AOSJR papers.

362   **this was no time:** Emma Keller interview with author, October 3, 2017.

362   **"If I had known":** Keller memo to the newsroom, October 21, 2005, Levy papers.

362   **"Bill spoke for the newsroom":** Joe Hagan, "Support Wanes for Reporter in CIA Leak," *The Wall Street Journal*, October 24, 2005.

362   **"Sorely in need of":** Maureen Dowd, "Woman of Mass Destruction," *The New York Times*, October 22, 2005.

363   **Geddes invited her for a drink:** Geddes interview with author, October 5, 2017. Judith Miller has no recollection of this event.

363   **she should consider taking:** Geddes interview with author, October 5, 2017.

363   **"I'm sure the piece":** Miller to AOSJR, undated, AOSJR papers.

363   **Steve, there's no way:** Rattner interview with author, September 13, 2019.

363   **"I have chosen to resign":** Judith Miller, "Judith Miller's Farewell," *The New York Times*, November 10, 2005.

364 **"Anybody who thinks"**: Lynne Duke, "In an Era of Anonymous Sources, Judy Miller Is a Cautionary Tale of the Times," *The Washington Post*, November 10, 2005.

32 *A Painful Legacy*

365 **Canedy asked Boyd's wife:** Canedy interview with author, November 13, 2018.
365 **Boyd had never understood:** Gerald M. Boyd, *My Times in Black and White: Race and Power at the New York Times* (Chicago: Lawrence Hill Books, 2010), 372.
365 **You can't stop living:** Carolyn Lee interview with author, June 22, 2018.
366 **My life is not my own:** Remarks of Jacki Moffi, memorial service for Gerald Boyd, November 30, 2006.
366 **"But we also at the *Times*"**: Remarks of Gerald M. Boyd, Associated Press Managing Editors Convention, posted October 20, 2003 by the Poynter Institute, Boyd papers.
366 **Lelyveld felt like a "ridiculous figure":** Lelyveld interview with author, April 16, 2017.
367 **The second service:** Remarks delivered by Gary Boyd, Al Siegal, and George Curry at the public Boyd memorial service are taken from a videotape of the event, courtesy of Al Siegal.
368 **Weinraub jumped on an overnight plane:** Weinraub interview with author January 31, 2017.
368 **Stone asked Weinraub to join:** Stone interview with author, June 23, 2018.
368 **Weinraub had been angered:** Weinraub interview with author, January 31, 2017.
368 **"I was tired of being":** Gerald M. Boyd, *My Times in Black and White*, 369.
368 **Sulzberger would years later remember:** AOSJR interview with author, August 8, 2017.
369 **"Working at the *Times*, which was everything to Gerald":** Weinraub remarks at Boyd memorial service, November 30, 2006, Weinraub Papers.
369 **Frankel was stunned:** Frankel interview with author, April 10, 2017.
369 **This is not your event:** Stone interview with author, June 23, 2018. Lelyveld does not recall the exchange.
370 **"I was so shocked and so shaken":** Bob Herbert to AOSJR, September 18, 2006, AOSJR papers.
370 **By Sulzberger's count:** Talking points for meeting with Herbert, September 20, 2006, AOSJR papers.
370 **"In the end":** AOSJR to Herbert, September 20, 2006, AOSJR papers.
370 **"the unfairness of this sudden assault":** Herbert to AOSJR, January 22, 2007, AOSJR Papers.
371 **"The racial situation":** Wilkins to AOSJR, February 6, 2005, AOSJR papers.
371 **"There is no question":** AOSJR to Wilkins, February 11, 2005, AOSJR papers.

33 *Mother Times*

372 **I am hiring you for a career:** Feder interview with author, January 20, 2021.
373 **"God is our personnel manager":** Susan E. Tifft and Alex S. Jones, *The Trust: The Private and Powerful Family Behind The New York Times* (Boston: Little, Brown and Company, 1999), 471.
373 **Get it painted:** Schmidt interview with author, January 24, 2021.
373 **"have taken a badly wounded':** Keller to newsroom, February 14, 2008, Keller papers.

374   **"You don't have to edit"**: Keller to newsroom, February 14, 2008, Keller papers.

374   **There were 1,332**: Schmidt to Keller, February 14, 2008, Keller papers.

374   **"The newspaper industry exited"**: Pew Research Center, "The State of the News Media," 2009.

374   **Daily newspaper circulation had dropped**: Pew Research Center, "The State of the News Media," 2009.

375   **its weekday circulation was**: Richard Pérez-Peña, "U.S. Newspaper Circulation Falls 10%," *The New York Times*, October 26, 2009.

375   **"I believe in the monarchy"**: Frankel interview with author, November 15, 2016.

376   **"Colossally bad timing"**: Golden interview with author, March 9, 2017.

376   **an Israeli diamond billionaire**: Ryan Chittum, "Israeli Diamond Billionaire Buys Historic New York Times Building," *The Wall Street Journal*, May 1, 2007.

376   **driven in part by**: Richard Pérez-Peña, "Resilient Strategy for Times Despite Toll of a Recession," *New York Times*, February 8, 2009.

376   **"It is time"**: Gregory Zuckerman and Chris Reiter, "New York Times Faces Share-Class Challenge," *The Wall Street Journal*, April 19, 2006.

377   **a *Times* account**: Landon Thomas, Jr., "A Difficult Annual Times Meeting for the Sulzbergers," *The New York Times*, April 24, 2007.

377   **"I need to get this off my chest"**: AOSJR to Keller, April 27, 2007, AOSJR papers.

377   **"That would be nice"**: Bobbie Johnson, "Murdoch Outlines Drastic Plans for WSJ," *The Guardian*, October 18, 2007.

377   **"our business is slowly sliding off a cliff"**: Keller to Baquet, November 16, 2005, Keller papers.

378   **took him and a table**: Keller interview with author, August 26, 2016.

378   **"let me move to our relationship"**: AOSJR to Keller, January 15, 2008, author's papers.

378   **"We are not here"**: Keller presentation to AOSJR, February 5, 2008, Keller papers.

378   **Saint Valentine's Day Massacre**: memo to guild members, Newspaper Guild of New York, New York Times Unit, February 15, 2008, Keller papers.

379   **boxes of tissues**: Schmidt interview with author, May 14, 2019.

379   **The claps reminded him**: Keller interview with author, August 16, 2016.

380   **"I know that the idea of strip ads"**: AOSJR to Sexton, August 15, 2006, AOSJR papers.

380   **It's like putting up a billboard**: Keller interview with author, August 26, 2016.

380   **A rumor swept through the building**: Jill Abramson, *Merchants of Truth: The Business of News and the Fight for Facts* (New York: Simon & Schuster, 2019), 182.

380   **"what if *The New York Times*"**: Michael Hirschorn, "End Times," *The Atlantic*, January/February 2009.

380   **You can't walk around**: Golden interview with author, May 2, 2019.

34   *Paying the Bills*

382   **Moments before**: Sexton interview with author, November 17, 2018.

382   **had been tipped off**: Rashbaum interview with author, March 13, 2021.

383   **realized she had better alert the publisher**: Abramson interview with author, January 7, 2018.

383   **Hit it**: Abramson interview with author, May 20, 2018.

383   **"More people visited"**: Jonathan Landman and Vivian Schiller to newsroom, March 14, 2008, AHOT.

384   **The story disclosing:** Abramson interview with author, March 31, 2018.

384   **like Julius Caesar visiting the Gauls:** Keller interview with author, August 26, 2016.

384   **Keller would hear complaints:** Keller interview with author, March 27, 2018.

385   **over forty-five million unique visitors a month:** "Comscore Media Metrix Releases Top 50 Web Rankings for February," Comscore Inc., comscore.com/Insights/Press-Releases/2008/03/Top-50-US-Web-Sites, March 19, 2008.

385   **drastic cuts across the company:** Abramson interview with author, May 20, 2018, Robinson email to author, April 28, 2022.

386   **"Best of luck":** Kinsley to AOSJR, September 27, 2005, AOSJR papers.

386   **"I understand your feelings":** AOSJR to Waddell Robey, October 21, 2005, AOSJR papers.

386   **as much as 82 percent:** "TimesSelect: A Year in Review," October 23, 2006, New York Times Company.

387   **"no question in my mind":** Friedman interview with author, September 19, 2018.

387   **began handing out codes:** Friedman interview with author, September 19, 2017.

387   **We just have to give this a shot:** AOSJR interview with author, August 10, 2018.

387   **The paying audience:** "TimesSelect: A Year in Review," October 23, 2006, New York Times Company.

388   **"I truly believe":** Perpich to Golden, November 26, 2008, Perpich papers.

388   **"I understand your emotional attachment":** Nisenholtz interview with author, November 25, 2016.

389   **assembled fifteen of his top editors:** "Salvage or Mirage? The *New York Times* Paywall," The Journalism School Case Study @ Columbia, 2012, CSJ-4-0054.0

389   **We have built:** Nisenholtz interview with author, January 30, 2023.

389   **Landman . . . warned that a paywall:** Landman interview with author, May 16, 2018.

390   **Keller liked to talk:** Keller address to conference of advertisers, March 16, 2006, Keller papers.

390   **"Good journalism isn't cheap":** Keller interview with author, August 26, 2016.

390   **verging on addiction:** Alan Flippen interview with author, July 8, 2016.

390   **"destroy the website":** Nisenholtz interview with author, August 12, 2017.

390   **"The digital people said":** AOSJR interview with author, August 10, 2018.

391   **The most consequential decision:** Sulzberger and Robinson to newsroom, January 20, 2010, AHOT.

391   **Sulzberger said if it did not work:** AOSJR interview with author, August 10, 2018.

35   *A Digital Divide*

392   **"They should serve one master":** Keller to AOSJR, Robins, Nisenholtz, "NYT Newsroom Integration: A Proposal," May 23, 2005, Meislin papers.

392   **"You're doing precisely":** Andrew Rosenthal to Keller, May 25, 2005, Keller papers.

392   **"By integrating the newsrooms":** Keller and Nisenholtz to newsroom, August 2, 2005, Levy papers.

393   **"shadow executive editor":** Abramson interview with author, May 20, 2018.

393   **The front page had been the dog:** Keller interview with author, March 27, 2018.

394   **he noticed the chill:** Silver interview with author, May 31, 2019.

394   **"If you want yet":** Keller remarks to the newsroom, June 3, 2010, Keller papers.

395   **she had only visited:** Abramson interview with author, May 20, 2018.

395 **"The website is still too much":** Remarks of Keller to staff, October 5, 2010, Keller papers.

395 **He wanted his editors to:** Keller interview with author, August 16, 2016.

395 **referred to as the "digital czar":** Keller interview with author, March 27, 2018.

396 **never serious about learning:** Roberts, Spruill interview with author, April 4, 2017.

396 **"They were impossible":** Abramson interview with author, May 20, 2018.

396 **Tozzi felt Abramson:** Tozzi interview with author, December 31, 2017.

396 **"There are still many":** Abramson report to Keller, October 6, 2010, Keller papers.

397 **"I could hardly bear to see":** Roberts to Abramson, October 7, 2010, Roberts papers.

397 **"It will do more harm":** Landman to Keller, October 6, 2010, author's papers.

397 **Keller would always consider:** Keller email exchange with author, November 16, 2022.

398 **"By my back-of-the-envelope":** Felix Salmon, "The New York Times Paywall Is . . . . Weird," *Wired*, March 17, 2011.

398 **"There seems little doubt":** Felix Salmon, "The New York Times Paywall Is Working," *Columbia Journalism Review*, July 26, 2011.

398 **ceiling for digital subscribers at 650,000:** Perpich email interview with author, February 26, 2021.

36   *A Tiger on the News*

401 **she was Keller's choice:** Keller interview with author, March 27, 2018.

401 **he could not stand her voice:** Keller interview with author, July 6, 2017.

402 **I know who you are:** Abramson interview with author, May 20, 2018.

402 **attention to seating charts:** Abramson interview with author, April 1, 2018.

402 **it was not fun to go to Washington:** Abramson interview with author, December 17, 2017.

402 **"I feel bad":** AOSJR to Abramson, undated, Abramson papers.

403 **Oh, Jill:** Abramson interview with author, December 17, 2017.

403 **Everyone knows there's a good Jill:** Abramson interview with author, December 17, 2017; AOSJR interview with author, August 5, 2018.

403 **"WHY ME":** Abramson to AOSJR, undated, Abramson papers.

403 **"This could not have":** Transcript, town hall meeting with AOSJR, Raines, and Boyd, May 14, 2003, Keller papers.

403 **Through a lens of what was best:** Chira email interview with author, February 23, 2023.

404 **"I can be abrupt":** Keller to Abramson, December 23, 2004, Abramson papers.

404 **"gumption and guts":** AOSJR interview with author, August 5, 2018.

404 **I've made my decision:** Abramson interview with author, June 8, 2018, afternoon session.

404 **"You are, in truth":** Transcript of Abramson appointment ceremony, *Ahead of the Times*, June 2, 2011.

406 **"Now we know exactly":** Wade interview with author, June 20, 2016.

406 **"The ascension of Jill Abramson":** James Rainey, "On the Media: The Task Ahead for the New York Times' Jill Abramson," *Los Angeles Times*, June 4, 2011.

406 **"Women who have struggled":** Betsy Wade, "Jill Abramson Was Haunted by NYT's Family Ghosts," *Women's eNews*, May 19, 2014.

406 **"extremely nervous":** Kramon journal, August 30, 2011, Kramon papers.

406 **by taking a Xanax:** Abramson email interview with author, April 15, 2021.

406 **"Abramson made a point":** Ken Auletta, "Changing Times," *The New Yorker*, October 24, 2011.

407 **"one of our finest writers":** Abramson memo to staff, July 22, 2011, AHOT archives.

407 **She went to Baquet's mother's funeral:** Baquet interview with author, December 27, 2018.

407 **Sulzberger considered it:** AOSJR interview with author, August 5, 2018.

407 **"Team of executioners":** Abramson interview with author, June 8, 2018, afternoon session.

408 **She had just settled in for coffee:** Abramson interview with author, April 1, 2018.

409 **"Frankly, I would put":** Robinson to AOSJR, November 12, 2004, AOSJR papers.

409 **"The truth is":** AOSJR to Keller, November 15, 2014, AOSJR papers.

409 **"Janet Robinson has been an unwavering friend":** Abramson remarks to the newsroom, June 2, 2011, AHOT.

409 **Are you sure this is the right moment:** Thompson interview with author, January 9, 2018.

410 **People who worked in the corporate offices:** Golden interview with author, May 2, 2019.

410 **"I hope to convince you":** Lewis to Raines, January 27, 1993, Jones papers.

411 **Thompson's "integrity and decision-making":** Margaret Sullivan, "Times Must Aggressively Cover Mark Thompson's Role in BBC's Troubles," *The New York Times*, October 23, 2012.

411 **"I know that there's been":** Thompson to staff, "On the Record," November 30, 2012, AHOT.

412 **Abramson invited Thompson:** Thompson interview with author, May 29, 2019.

412 **"Lines between our journalism":** "These Are Tough Times," transcript of Abramson remarks to newsroom, December 20, 2012, AHOT.

412 **I would have gone to Harvard Business School:** Abramson interview with author, April 1, 2018.

37 *No Switzerland*

413 **"I have no doubts":** AOSJR to Abramson, January 7, 2013, Abramson papers.

413 **"I hated that job":** Abramson interview with author, April 1, 2018.

414 **He thinks he can do my job:** Abramson interview with author, April 1, 2018.

414 **"I accept the criticism":** Abramson remarks to newsroom, "Saving All That We Do," September 30, 2013, AHOT.

414 **she said her style had been shaped:** Abramson remarks to the Stanford Graduate School of Business, May 21, 2015.

415 **"When 'Bad Jill'":** Employee evaluation of Abramson, undated, Abramson papers.

415 **had raised these concerns with her:** Edgerley interview with author, June 21, 2018.

415 **"I can live up to my promise":** Abramson memo to newsroom, "Three Special Missions," September 13, 2011, AHOT.

415 **There's no shame in that:** Edgerley interview with author, June 21, 2018.

415 **she later asked to work with one:** Abramson email to author, August 19, 2022.

416 **to replace "Bill's guys":** Abramson interview with author, June 8, 2018, afternoon session.

416   **did not like her:** Abramson interview with author, June 8, 2018, afternoon session.

416   **"Jon Landman should not":** Abramson to AOSJR, "Why Me," undated, Abramson papers.

417   **"We pretty much savaged":** Abramson interview with author, June 8, 2018, afternoon session.

417   **"In the past":** Abramson remarks to the newsroom, "These Are Tough Times," December 20, 2012, AHOT.

417   **pushing on an open door:** Landman interview with author, September 14, 2016.

417   **"The newsroom has gone through a big transition":** Transcript of Grill Jill session, October 1, 2013, AHOT.

418   **brought a bottle of Jameson:** Sexton interview with author, November 17, 2018.

418   **Both Baquet and John Geddes:** Baquet interview with author, December 27, 2018, and Abramson email to author, August 20, 2022. She does not recall a note from Baquet.

418   **suggested she read the report:** Abramson interview with author, May 20, 2018.

419   **Baquet had reservations:** Baquet interview with author, December 27, 2018.

419   **He disapproved of the way:** Baquet interview with author, December 27, 2018.

419   **They toured eastern Afghanistan:** Jill Abramson and Dean Baquet, "Jill and Dean in bin Laden Country," July 7, 2011, AHOT.

419   **They saw Dexter Filkins:** Filkins email interview with author, May 7, 2021.

420   **She missed Keller:** Abramson interview with author, May 20, 2018.

420   **nearly "perfect":** Keller to Abramson, February 12, 2009, Abramson papers.

420   **She felt he was not consulting:** Abramson interview with author, June 8, 2018, afternoon session.

420   **She would notice the reporters and editors:** Abramson interview with author, May 20, 2018.

420   **"You're taking the newsroom":** Baquet interview with author, December 27, 2018.

420   **You don't want to listen:** Abramson interview with author, June 8, 2018, afternoon session.

421   **decided he did not want to stay:** Baquet interview with author, December 2, 2018.

421   **"Just a year and a half":** Dylan Byers, "Turbulence at the Times," *Politico*, April 23, 2013.

421   **post-traumatic stress:** Ken Auletta, "Changing Times," *The New Yorker*, October 24, 2011.

421   **He wondered if the experience:** Keller interview with author, July 5, 2017.

421   **If she had put her fist through a wall:** Abramson interview with author, June 8, 2018, afternoon session.

422   **"Do you want to cause me":** Joe Hagan, "The Suit in the Newsroom," *New York*, August 23, 2013.

422   **"I had been through this process":** AOSJR interview with author, December 27, 2018.

422   **Sulzberger left convinced:** AOSJR interview with author, December 27, 2018.

422   **I don't do PowerPoint:** Perpich interview with author, January 30, 2020.

422   **"As I respond and give you my thoughts":** AOSJR to Abramson, January 7, 2018, Abramson papers.

422   **If you use one more business term:** Levy interview with author, May 15, 2018.

423   **I am Switzerland:** Brancato interview with author, April 28, 2021.

423   **She never believed him:** Abramson email, August 20, 2022.

423   **When I got here:** Thompson email interview with author, December 21, 2021.

423 **"saving *The New York Times*"**: Thompson interview with author, May 18, 2021.

423 **You just have to figure out:** Thompson interview with author, May 18, 2021.

423 **"a command-and-control"**: Jill Abramson, *Merchants of Truth: The Business of News and the Fight for Facts* (New York: Simon & Schuster, 2019), 213.

424 **"gaslighting" her at meetings:** Abramson interview with author, March 31, 2018.

424 **thought he had just witnessed:** Rosenthal interview with author, May 14, 2018.

424 **that Abramson lead the newsroom:** Thompson email to author, August 23, 2022.

424 **"think and act more experimentally":** AOSJR email to author, August 24, 2022.

424 **You bully me, too:** Abramson interview with author, May 20, 2018.

424 **aware he could be "emphatic":** Thompson interview with author, May 18, 2021.

424 **"All feels very fraught":** Abramson notes from Thompson meeting, December 22, 2018, Abramson papers.

38 *The Pivot*

425 **"This is going to be a tough assessment":** AOSJR to Abramson, January 15, 2014, Abramson papers.

426 **do you want somebody else:** Jill Abramson, *Merchants of Truth: The Business of News and the Fight for Facts* (New York: Simon & Schuster, 2019), 216; AOSJR email interview with author, June 9, 2021.

426 **"It basically said":** Abramson interview with author, January 7, 2018.

426 **Abramson did not believe:** Jill Abramson, *Merchants of Truth*, 217.

426 **She had rebuked A. G. Sulzberger:** Jamieson interview with author, July 18, 2021; AGS interview with author, April 22, 2019.

427 **a searing exchange:** Jamieson interview with author, July 18, 2021.

427 **You are ready for this:** AGS interview with author, January 2, 2019.

428 **Punch Sulzberger had pulled him aside:** AGS interview with author, January 2, 2019.

428 **asked him to keep an eye on his son:** Engelberg interview with author, November 12, 2018.

428 **would not fit:** Patrick LaForge interview with author, June 27, 2021.

429 **he made two decisions:** AGS interview with author, January 2, 2019.

429 **"the goofiest":** AGS interview with author, January 2, 2019.

429 **"*New York Times* crown prince":** Hamilton Nolan, "What Haughty Peon Dared Force Young Sulzberger to Investigate Urine?" *Gawker,* March 22, 2010.

430 **It will make us look:** Abramson interview with author, June 8, 2018. Janet Elder died in December 2017.

430 **"a new ideas task force":** Abramson to newsroom, July 12, 2013, AHOT archives.

430 **"big ideas memo":** Abramson to AGS, July 18, 2013, AGS papers.

430 **"it was a window":** AGS interview with author, April 22, 2019.

430 **"a full assault":** AGS notes for meeting with Abramson, December 4, 2013, AGS papers.

432 **"To keep you in the loop":** Berke to William Schmidt, September 22, 2011, Berke papers.

432 **"The *New York Times* needs to accelerate its transition":** AGS et al., "Innovation," March 24, 2014.

433 **How will Jill take this?:** Bryant interview with author, June 7, 2021.

433 **"Both Mark Thompson and Jill Abramson"**: AGS et al., "Innovation," March 24, 2014.

434 **I am fucked:** Abramson interview with author, June 8, 2018, morning session.

434 **Change in an institution like this:** AGS interview with author, April 22, 2019.

434 **suicide by cop:** Andrew Rosenthal interview with author, May 14, 2018.

434 **You are exhibit A:** Abramson interview with author, June 8, 2018.

434 **Elder scribbled down her findings:** Elder to Abramson, undated, Abramson papers.

435 **a compensation package:** Abramson to Sulzberger, Thompson; undated, Abramson papers.

435 **"I need an answer":** Abramson to Thompson, undated, Abramson papers.

435 **She is relentless:** AOSJR interview with author, August 10, 2018.

436 **Gibson joined Baquet for lunch:** Gibson interview with author, April 19, 2021; Baquet interview with author, December 27, 2018.

436 **This is bullshit:** Abramson interview with author, June 8, 2018; Baquet interview with author, December 27, 2018.

436 **He is going to leave:** Abramson interview with author, June 8, 2018.

437 **I will do this in a way:** Baquet interviews with author, December 27, 2018, and September 28, 2021.

437 **Thompson cautioned Sulzberger to consider:** Thompson interview with author, May 29, 2019.

437 **"In the end, it was the exact opposite":** AOSJR interview with author, April 18, 2019.

437 **I've decided to fire Jill:** Baquet interview with author, December 27, 2018.

438 **You are firing me:** Abramson interview with author, June 8, 2018, morning session.

438 **Stay at The *Guardian*:** Gibson interview with author, April 19, 2021.

438 **"Rather, I chose to appoint a new leader":** AOSJR remarks to the newsroom, May 14, 2014, AHOT.

438 **she arranged for the information:** Abramson interview with author, June 8, 2018, afternoon session.

438 **who presented her case:** Ken Auletta, "Why Jill Abramson Was Fired," *The New Yorker*, May 14, 2014; and Auletta, "Jill Abramson and the Times: What Went Wrong?" *The New Yorker*, May 15, 2014.

439 **"It is simply not true":** AOSJR to newsroom, May 15, 2014, AHOT.

439 **"Abramson, the first woman to lead":** Kathleen Parker, "Hillary Clinton and Jill Abramson Could Affect 2016," *The Washington Post*, May 16, 2014.

439 **"What did he think":** Abramson interview with author, June 8, 2018, afternoon session.

439 **Michael Golden, who had driven to New York:** Golden interview with author, March 9, 2017.

439 **"We were losing":** Thompson email to author, March 15, 2022.

439 **"During her tenure":** Statement of Arthur Sulzberger, Jr., May 17, 2014, New York Times Company.

440 **"is being caricatured":** Ryan on *Meet the Press*, May 18, 2014.

440 **"The Innovation report being presented today":** Abramson and Baquet to newsroom, May 8, 2014, AHOT.

440 **what could she do?:** Abramson interview with author, June 8, 2018, morning session.

440 **"The leaked":** Joshua Benton, "The Leaked New York Times Innovation Report Is One of the Key Documents of This Media Age," *Nieman Lab*, May 15, 2014.

39 *Diplomat*

442 **Baquet was scheduled:** Baquet interview with author, November 23, 2021

442 **"As some of you may have noticed":** Baquet memo to staff, June 16, 2014, AHOT.

443 **but there was no plan B:** AOSJR interview with author, January 27, 2020.

443 **Sulzberger told Baquet that could wait:** Baquet interview with author, September 28, 2021.

444 **The cousins would talk about how different he was:** Dolnick interview with author, February 6, 2019.

444 **a perilous financial position:** Baquet interview with author, April 22, 2019.

445 **"one of the old dinosaurs" and "A chunk of the newsroom":** Baquet interview with author, November 23, 2021.

445 **The first time Baquet boarded an airplane:** Baquet interview with author, November 11, 2018.

446 **so he knocked on doors:** Baquet interview with Max Linsky, June 23, 2020, *Longform* (podcast).

446 **who called Baquet in April 1989:** Baquet interview with author, November 11, 2018; Jones places the call a few year earlier.

446 **We don't do this kind of reporting:** Baquet interview with author, November 11, 2018.

447 **"You're also a hard editor to leave":** Baquet to Lelyveld, November 8, 1999, Lelyveld papers.

447 **This is business:** Baquet interview with author, November 11, 2018. Lelyveld does not recall the exchange.

448 **"Bold move my friend":** AOSJR to Baquet, September 15, 2006, AOSJR papers.

448 **"I know this may seem":** Baquet to AOSJR, September 19, 2006, AOSJR papers.

448 **We want you back:** Abramson interview with author, May 20, 2018.

448 **"Your enthusiastic recruiting":** Keller to Abramson, December 21, 2006, Abramson papers.

449 **Taubman was home sick:** Taubman interview with author, October 28, 2016.

449 **did not even know how to cook:** MacCallum interview with author, October 25, 2021.

450 **goal of 160,000 new paid subscribers:** MacCallum interview with author, October 25, 2021.

450 **four million readers:** Sam Sifton and Ben French to newsroom, June 1, 2015, AHOT.

450 **"Here is an example":** MacCallum to Baquet and Andrew Rosenthal, June 2014, MacCallum papers.

451 **"Basically, anyone could come":** Duenes interview with author, October 3, 2019.

451 **half the *Times* audience:** MacCallum to Baquet and Andrew Rosenthal, undated memo, MacCallum papers.

452 **he brought daily reports from Chartbeat:** Fisher interview with author, October 12, 2021.

452 **"I see this whole group":** Margaret Sullivan, "An Unusual Hire, for Uncommon Times," August 23, 2014, *The New York Times.*

452 **"that building audience":** Baquet interview with author, November 23, 2021.

453 **Great idea—let's do it:** Levy interview with author, May 15, 2018.

453 **"Readers are hungry":** Dean Baquet (David Leonhardt) to newsroom, July 10, 2015, AHOT.

453 **This is all journalism:** Perpich interview with author, January 3, 2020.

453   **"Big day out of National":** Audience-development team memo to editors, April 2, 2015, author's papers.

454   **"Widening access to data":** Baquet and Rosenthal to newsroom, May 1, 2015, AHOT.

454   **"Her expansive use":** Michael S. Schmidt, "Hillary Clinton Used Personal Email Account at State Dept., Possibly Breaking Rules," *The New York Times*, March 2, 2015.

454   no **"clear evidence":** "Statement by FBI Director James B. Comey on the Investigation of Secretary Hillary Clinton's Use of a Personal E-Mail System," F.B.I. News/Press Release, July 5, 2016, fbi.gov/news/press-releases/statement-by-fbi-director-james-b-comey-on-the-investigation-of-secretary-hillary-clinton2019s-use-of-a-personal-e-mail-system.

455   **"Our political audience":** Audience-development team memo to editors, March 6, 2015, author's papers.

455   **The first front page meeting:** Turner Catledge, *My Life and The Times* (New York: Harper & Row) 1971, 178.

455   **an intimidating ritual:** David W. Dunlap, "What Does a Page 1 Room Look Like When Page 1 Isn't on the Agenda?" *The New York Times*, August 17, 2017.

455   **"The editing, approval":** Levy to Baquet, Chira, November 13, 2014, Levy papers.

456   **The *Times* needed to "move more decisively away":** Baquet memo to newsroom, May 5, 2015, AHOT.

456   **attractive to readers *and advertisers*:** Baquet and Andrew Rosenthal to newsroom, September 24, 2015, on appointment of Trish Hall as senior editor, AHOT.

457   **"If, half a decade ago":** Ken Doctor, "Newsonomics: 10 Numbers on The New York Times' 1 Million Digital-Subscriber Milestone," *Nieman Lab*, August 6, 2015.

457   **"content and products worth paying for":** "Our Path Forward," October 7, 2015.

458   **"I've been in my role":** Ravi Somaiya, "New York Times Co. to Name Deputy Publisher Within Two Years," *The New York Times*, November 2, 2015.

458   **moved into a private office:** Burns interview with author, November 29, 2022.

459   **Baquet, in disbelief:** Baquet interview with author, November 23, 2021.

460   **Baquet would contend:** Baquet interview with author, November 23, 2021.

460   **"After such an erratic and unpredictable election":** Sulzberger and Baquet, "To Our Readers, from the Publisher and Executive Editor," *The New York Times*, November 13, 2016.

460   **"There has been since":** This account of the executive committee meeting is from the author, who was in attendance.

460   **"a lot of soul-searching":** Baquet remarks to executive committee, from the author, who was in attendance.

461   **"wanting to cry on our pages":** Bennet remarks to executive committee, from the author, who was in attendance.

461   **41,000 new digital subscribers:** Eileen Murphy email interview with author, December 20, 2022.

Epilogue

464   **Eighty-four percent of paid subscribers:** NYT Audience Insights, Opinion Research Findings, September 2018, from preparatory materials for senior staff meeting of August 1, 2019: "Pre-Reading for Aug. 1 Offsite," author's papers.

464 **"Some readers subscribe to NYT"**: Introduction to preparatory materials for senior staff meeting of August 1, 2019: "Pre-Reading for Aug. 1 Offsite," author's papers.

465 **"My view is"**: Lizzie O'Leary, "'I Know People Want a Richer, More Thoughtful Explanation,'" *The Atlantic*, August 7, 2019.

465 **"Could you explain your decision"**: Transcript of Dean Baquet Town Hall meeting with *New York Times* employees, *Slate*, August 15, 2019.

466 **"to discuss the newsroom's perspective"**: Introduction to preparatory materials for senior staff meeting of August 1, 2019: "Pre-Reading for Aug. 1 Offsite," author's papers.

466 **"There are occasions"**: Ross Douthat to AGS, undated, from preparatory materials for senior staff meeting of August 1, 2019: "Pre-Reading for Aug. 1 Offsite," author's papers.

467 **"What purpose does the word 'vicious'"**: Bret Stephens to AGS, from preparatory materials for senior staff meeting of August 1, 2019: "Pre-Reading for Aug. 1 Offsite," author's papers.

467 **published an essay:** Tom Cotton, "Send in the Troops," *The New York Times*, June 3, 2020.

467 **"I believe in the principle"**: AGS to staff, June 4, 2020.

468 **"Times Opinion owes it"**: Marc Tracy, "Senator's 'Send In the Troops' Op-Ed in The Times Draws Online Ire," *New York Times*, June 3, 2020.

468 **"rushed editorial process"**: Marcy Tracy, Rachel Abrams and Edmund Lee, "New York Times Says Senator's Op-Ed Did Not Meet Standards," *New York Times*, June 4, 2020.

468 **"significant breakdown in our editing"**: AGS to staff, June 7, 2020, author's papers.

468 **"When push came to shove"**: Ben Smith, "Inside the Identity Crisis at *The New York Times*," *Semafor*, October 28, 2022.

468 **"bullying by colleagues"**: Weiss to AGS, undated, bariweiss.com/resignation-letter.

468 **"It's clearly a watershed"**: Mark Thompson remarks, second-quarter 2020 earnings conference call, "The New York Times Company," transcript from *The Motley Fool*, August 5, 2020.

470 **"What is the Internet"**: Meislin to Frankel, Lelyveld, Siegal, September 21, 1993, Meislin papers.

ADAM NAGOURNEY covers national politics for *The New York Times*. Since joining the newspaper in 1996, he has served as Los Angeles bureau chief, West Coast cultural affairs reporter, chief national political correspondent, and chief New York political reporter. He is the co-author of *Out for Good*, a history of the modern gay rights movement.